A Resource Guide for Elementary School Teaching
Planning for Competence

FIFTH EDITION

RICHARD D. KELLOUGH
PATRICIA L. ROBERTS

California State University, Sacramento

Merrill
Prentice Hall

Upper Saddle River, New Jersey
Columbus, Ohio

Library of Congress Cataloging in Publication Data

Kellough, Richard D. (Richard Dean)
    A resource guide for elementary school teaching : planning for competence / Richard D. Kellough,
      Patricia L. Roberts. 5th ed. Upper Saddle River, N.J.: Merrill, 2002.
      p.   cm.
    Includes bibliographical references and index.
    ISBN 0-13-027844-0
    1. Elementary school teaching. 2. Competency based education.   I. Roberts, Patricia
LB1555.K39   2002
372.1102 21   12-230195

Vice President and Publisher: Jeffery W. Johnston
Acquisitions Editor: Debra A. Stollenwerk
Editorial Assistant: Penny S. Burleson
Assistant Editor: Daniel J. Parker
Production Editor: Kimberly J. Lundy
Production Coordinator: Carlisle Publishers Services
Design Coordinator: Diane C. Lorenzo
Cover Designer: Linda Fares
Cover Art: Super Stock
Production Manager: Pamela D. Bennett
Director of Marketing: Kevin Flanagan
Marketing Manager: Krista Groshong
Marketing Services Manager: Barbara Koontz

This book was set in New Century Schoolbook by Carlisle Communications, Ltd. It was printed and bound by
Courier Kendallville, Inc. The cover was printed by The Lehigh Press, Inc.

Photo Credits: CEM/Merrill, p. 31; Scott Cunningham/Merrill, p. 59, 187, 298; Anthony
Magnaca/Merrill, p. 91, 324, 353; Barbara Schwartz/Merrill, p. 239, 396; URS Architectural Design,
photographed by Gary Quesada, p. 3; Anne Vega/Merrill, p. 267; Tom Watson, p. 139.

Prentice-Hall International (UK) Limited, *London*
Prentice-Hall of Australia Pty. Limited, *Sydney*
Prentice-Hall Canada, Inc., *Toronto*
Prentice-Hall Hispanoamericana, S.A., *Mexico*
Prentice-Hall of India Private Limited, *New Delhi*
Prentice-Hall of Japan, Inc., *Tokyo*
Prentice-Hall Singapore Pte. Ltd.
Editora Prentice-Hall de Brasil, Ltda., *Rio de Janeiro*

10 9 8 7 6 5 4 3 2 1
ISBN 0-13-027844-0

Preface

Welcome to the fifth edition of *A Resource Guide for Elementary School Teaching: Planning for Competence.* The purpose of this resource guide is to provide a practical and concise guide for college or university students who are preparing to become competent elementary schoolteachers. Others who may find it useful are experienced teachers who desire to continue developing their teaching skills and curriculum specialists and school administrators who desire a current, practical, and concise text of methods, guidelines, and resources for teaching in elementary school.

NEW TO THIS EDITION

Because of all the activity in education today, the research and preparation for this fifth edition was unusually demanding. Major changes for this fifth edition are described below:

- Chapter 1 is, we believe, a better organized and more focused overview of elementary school teaching today.
- **A new chapter** has been added, Chapter 2, devoted to elementary school children, their development and their diversity, and specific ways of working with them in the classroom, topics that were part of Chapter 1 of the previous edition.
- Although we strive to keep this book a comprehensive guide of methods and resources for teaching elementary school, we are also sensitive to the book's size and cost to its users. This edition has fewer chapters and, in general, is more condensed than the previous edition. This was accomplished by (a) eliminating material that was dated or worn or that could be moved to the Companion Website, (b) condensing or relocating material that was covered in more than one chapter (for example, cooperative learning was previously addressed in both Chapters 6 and 9; it now is addressed principally in Chapter 8), (c) reorga-

nizing the content of Part II into two rather than three chapters, (d) eliminating what was formerly Chapter 7 and moving its major content to Chapter 6, and (e) eliminating Chapter 12 of the previous edition, which described the various subjects of the elementary school curriculum, material better left to the special methods courses of your program of teacher preparation. There are now 12 chapters rather than the 14 chapters of the previous edition.

- Despite the blue ribbon commissions, authors, and politicians who vilify what they perceive as the failures of public school education, thousands of committed teachers, administrators, parents, and community representatives struggle daily, year after year, to provide children with a quality education. So that readers can learn about or visit exemplary schools and programs, many are recognized and identified by name throughout this text.
- Found throughout the text, sometimes at the front of a chapter, are instructional scenarios and classroom vignettes that serve as additional springboards for thinking and class discussion.
- To reflect the concerted efforts throughout the nation to help students at all grade levels to connect academic learning, personal growth, and a sense of civic responsibility, this edition of the resource guide identifies many sample projects and resources for service learning, especially in Chapters 1 and 8.

Other changes made for this edition are mentioned in the paragraphs that follow.

OUR BELIEFS: HOW AND WHERE THEY ARE REFLECTED IN THIS RESOURCE GUIDE

In the preparation of this book, we saw our task *not* as making the teaching job easier for you—effective teaching is never easy—but as improving your teaching effectiveness and providing relevant guidelines and current resources. You may choose from these resources and build upon what works best for you. Nobody can tell you what will work with your students; you will know them best. We do share what we believe to be the best of practice, the most useful of recent research findings, and the richest of experiences. The highlighted statements present our beliefs and explain how they are embraced in this resource guide.

The best learning occurs when the learner actively participates in the process, which includes having ownership in both the process and the product of the learning. Consequently, this resource guide is designed to engage you in "hands-on" and "minds-on" learning about effective teaching. For example, rather than simply finding a chapter devoted to an exposition of the important topic of cooperative learning, in each chapter you will become involved in cooperative and collaborative learning. In essence, via the exercises found in every chapter, you will practice cooperative learning, talk about it, practice it some more, and finally, through the process of doing it, learn a great deal about it. This resource guide *involves* you in it.

The best strategies for learning about teaching are those that model the strategies used in exemplary teaching of children. As you will learn, integrated learning is the cornerstone of effective teaching for the 21st century, and that is a premise upon which this resource guide continues to be designed.

To be most effective, any teacher, regardless of grade level and subject, must use an eclectic style in teaching. Rather than focusing your attention on particular models of teaching, we emphasize the importance of an eclectic model—that is, one in which you select and integrate the best from various instructional approaches. For example, there are times when you will want to use a direct, expository approach, perhaps by lecturing; there are many more times when you will want to use an indirect, social-interactive, or student-centered approach, perhaps through project-based learning. This resource guide provides guidelines that will help you both decide which approach to use at a particular time and develop your skill in using specific approaches.

Learning should be active, pleasant, fun, meaningful, and productive. Our desire is, as it always has been, to present this book in an enthusiastic, positive, and cognitive-humanistic way, in part by providing rich experiences in cooperative and collaborative learning. How this is done is perhaps best exemplified by the active learning exercises found throughout the book. Some exercises have been rewritten, ones that were worn and dated have been deleted, others have been moved to the Companion Website, and some new ones have been added to ensure that you become an active participant in learning the methods and procedures that are most appropriate in facilitating the learning of the active, responsive children present in today's elementary schools.

Teaching skills can be learned. In medicine, certain knowledge and skills must be learned and developed before the student physician is licensed to practice with patients. In law, certain knowledge and skills must be learned and developed before the law student is licensed to practice in a courtroom. So it is in teacher preparation: Knowledge and skills must be learned and developed before the teacher candidate is licensed to practice the art and science of teaching children. We would never consider allowing just any person to treat our child's illness or to defend us in a legal case; the professional education of teachers is no less important! Receiving professional education in how to teach children is absolutely necessary, and certain aspects of that education must precede any interaction with children if teachers are to become truly accomplished professionals.

ORGANIZATION OF THIS BOOK: AN OVERVIEW

Competent elementary school teaching is a kaleidoscopic, multifaceted, eclectic process. When preparing and writing a resource guide for use in teacher preparation, by necessity one must separate that kaleidoscopic process into separate topics, which is not always possible to do in a way that makes the most sense to everyone using the book. We believe that *there are developmental compo-*

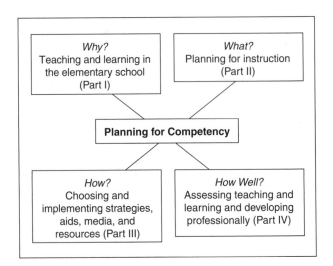

nents involved in *becoming a competent teacher.* This book is organized around four developmental components: *why, what, how,* and *how well.* Each of the four parts of this resource guide clearly reflects one of these four components. Each part is introduced with the objectives of that part and reflective thoughts relevant to topics addressed in its chapters. The visual map on p. iv illustrates how these four developmental elements are divided.

Part I: Orientation to Elementary School Teaching and Learning

To better reflect the *why* component—the reality and challenge of elementary school teaching today— Part I underwent substantial reorganization and updates for this edition. It now includes four rather than three chapters. Chapter 1 presents an important overview of that reality and the challenge of teaching grades elementary school today. Chapter 2 presents a detailed explanation and explicit guidelines for meeting that challenge. In preparing Chapter 2 we considered the developments in cognitive learning theory that enhance and celebrate the differences in students and their styles of learning. *Regardless of gender, social or physical abilities, and ethnic or cultural characteristics, all students must have equal opportunity to participate and learn in the classroom.* This belief is reflected throughout this resource guide. Chapter 3 reflects the expectations, responsibilities, and classroom behaviors that are characteristic of competent elementary school teachers. Whereas Chapter 2 is about children, Chapter 3 is about teachers and Chapter 4, is about the learning environment, specifically the classroom. Because a teacher must have the students' attention to effectively implement any instructional plan, guidelines for establishing and maintaining a supportive environment for learning are presented in Chapter 4.

Part II: Planning for Instruction

Effective teaching is performance-based and criterion-referenced. This resource guide continues to be constructed in this manner. Because we also believe that teaching, indeed living, must allow for serendipity, encourage the intuitive, and foster the most creative aspects of one's thinking, we cannot always be specific about what students will learn as a result of our instruction, and hence the occasional ambiguity must be expected. To reflect the planning, or *what,* component, Part II includes two chapters.

Chapter 5, on the rationale for planning and selecting the content of the curriculum, contains information about standards that have been developed for subject areas of the elementary school curriculum. The section on preparing and using instructional objectives emphasizes the relationship of objectives to planning and assessment.

Chapter 6 presents instructional planning as a three-level and seven-step process, and introduces the topics of unit planning and lesson planning. Also, to bridge the primary topic of this chapter with the strategies introduced in Part II, Chapter 6 provides the theoretical considerations for the selection of instructional strategies.

Part III: Strategies, Aids, Media, and Resources for Effective Instruction

Although it is very difficult to predict what the children of today will really need to know to be productive citizens in the middle of this century, we do believe they will always need to know how to learn, how to read, how to communicate effectively, and how to think productively. We believe that young people need skills in how to gain knowledge and how to process information, and they need learning experiences that foster effective communication and productive, cooperative behaviors. We hope all children will feel good about themselves, about others, and about their teachers, schools, and communities. This resource guide continues to emphasize the importance of helping students to develop these skills, feelings, and attitudes.

The appropriate teaching methods for reaching these goals are those that incorporate thoughtful planning, acceptance of the uniqueness of each individual, honesty, trust, sharing, risking, collaboration, communication, and cooperation. Furthermore, we believe children best learn these skills and values from teachers who model the same. This resource guide continues to be faithful to that hope and to that end.

For this edition, the *how* component, Part III, has been reduced from six to four chapters. Chapter 7 is about the use of questioning, with enhanced emphasis on the encouragement and use of children's questions. The resource guide contains three micro peer teaching exercises; the first of these is in Chapter 7. Chapter 8 emphasizes various ways of grouping children for instruction, using assignments, ensuring equity in the classroom, using project-centered teaching, and writing across the curriculum.

For this edition, several sections in this chapter were enhanced, including but not limited to those of cooperative learning, equality in the classroom, and learning from assignments and homework.

Chapter 9 provides guidelines and resources for the use of teacher talk, demonstrations, teaching of thinking, use of inquiry, and educational games. Also in Chapter 9 is the second micro peer teaching exercise.

Chapter 10 reflects the practical use of instructional aids, media, and resources, including current information about the placement and use of computers in schools, the online classroom, and technological resources.

Part IV: Assessment and Professional Development

Part IV focuses your attention on the fourth component of competent teaching—*how well* the students and teacher are doing.

Chapter 11 is about assessing what students know or think they know before, during, and after the instruction. In addition to the use of portfolios, scoring rubrics, checklists, performance assessment, and student self-assessment, the chapter provides practical guidelines for parent-teacher collaboration and for marking and grading.

Chapter 12, traditionally considered an important chapter by student users, emphasizes how well the teacher is doing—the assessment of teaching effectiveness and guidelines for ongoing professional development. It also contains the third and most sophisticated of the three micro peer teaching exercises, which, in essence, is a performance assessment-type final examination for the course or program for which this book is being used. Also in Chapter 12 are other items that have been popular with student users, such as emergency teaching kits (a new one for this fifth edition) and guidelines for student teaching, finding a teaching position, and continued professional development.

FEATURES OF THE TEXT

To achieve professional competency, you need guided learning, guided practice, productive feedback, encouragement, and positive reinforcement. To reach this goal, this resource guide is organized as follows.

- The four parts serve as advance organizers—that is, they establish a mind-set.

- **Exercises for active learning** are found within every chapter. The exercises are designed to (a) require you to assess and reflect continually on your progress in understanding and in skill development for teaching, and (b) involve you in collaborative and cooperative learning. Some exercises necessitate a visit to a school to have a dialogue with children and staff. Review the exercises early so you can plan your visits and work schedule. In fact, because certain exercises build upon previous ones or suggest that you obtain help from teachers in the field, you are advised to review all exercises at the beginning of your study of this resource guide. Because it is unlikely that more than 50 exercises could be (or should be) completed in one course, you, your classmates, and your instructor will have to select the exercises to be done. Pages of the resource guide are perforated for easy removal of the exercises to be available for future reference.
- Useful **Websites** for teachers and students are abundant and given in relevant locations throughout the book, such as Figures 1.5, 1.7, 2.2, 5.1 and 8.7.
- **Three micro peer teaching exercises** found in Chapters 7, 9, and 12 encourage authentic assessment rather than a paper-and-pencil testing of your teaching skills development.
- **Questions for class discussion** at the end of each chapter extend your competencies.
- **Suggested readings** at the conclusion of each chapter offer additional sources, both classic and current, that can deepen and broaden your understanding of particular topics.
- An updated **glossary, name index,** and **subject index** are found at the end of the book.

ANCILLARIES

The following ancillaries are available to instructors who adopt this text. To request any of the following ancillaries, contact your Prentice Hall representative or visit our website at **http://www.merrilleducation.com**. (If you do not know how to contact your local sales representative, please call faculty services at 1-800-526-0485 for assistance.)

- The **Instructor's Manual** provides professors with a variety of useful resources, such as chapter overviews, teaching strategies, and ideas for classroom activities, discussions, and assessment.
- The **Companion Website** contains additional information for students and instructors to use in an online environment. For more information

on what the Companion Website provides, please see the "Discover the Companion Website Accompanying This Book" section following the preface.

ACKNOWLEDGMENTS

We would never have been able to complete this edition had it not been for the valued help of numerous people—former and current students and teachers in our classes who have shared their experiences with us; administrators and colleagues who have debated with us about important issues in education; and authors and publishers who have graciously granted permission to reprint materials. To each we offer our warmest thanks.

Although we take full responsibility for any errors or omissions in this resource guide, we are deeply appreciative to others for their cogent reviews and important contributions in the development of this edition. We express our special appreciation to the following individuals: Linda Current,

California State University at Sacramento; Robert W. Burke, Ball State University; Margaret M. Ferrara, Central Connecticut State University; Gae R. Johnson, Northern Arizona University; Josefina R. Saavedra, University of South Florida; and Elizabeth A. Simons, George Mason University.

In addition, we want to express our deepest admiration and appreciation to the highly competent professionals at Merrill/Prentice Hall, with whom we proudly have shared a professional relationship for many years. We especially thank Debbie Stollenwerk for her confidence in our ability, her positive attitude, and her healthy sense of humor which she willingly shares with us when we need it the most.

We are indeed indebted and grateful to all the people in our lives, now and in the past, who have interacted with us and reinforced what we have known since the days we began our careers as teachers: Teaching is the most rewarding profession of all.

R. D. K.
P. L. R.

Discover the Companion Website Accompanying This Book

The Prentice Hall Companion Website: A Virtual Learning Environment

Technology is a constantly growing and changing aspect of our field that is creating a need for content and resources. To address this emerging need, Prentice Hall has developed an online learning environment for students and professors alike—Companion Websites—to support our textbooks.

In creating a Companion Website, our goal is to build on and enhance what the textbook already offers. For this reason, the content for each user-friendly website is organized by chapter and provides the professor and student with a variety of meaningful resources.

For the Professor—

Every Companion Website integrates **Syllabus Manager™,** an online syllabus creation and management utility.

- **Syllabus Manager™** provides you, the instructor, with an easy, step-by-step process to create and revise syllabi, with direct links into Companion Website and other online content without having to learn HTML.
- Students may log on to your syllabus during any study session. All they need to know is the web address for the Companion Website and the password you've assigned to your syllabus.
- After you have created a syllabus using **Syllabus Manager™,** students may enter the syllabus for their course section from any point in the Companion Website.
- Clicking on a date, the student is shown the list of activities for the assignment. The activities for each assignment are linked directly to actual content, saving time for students.
- Adding assignments consists of clicking on the desired due date, then filling in the details of the assignment—name of the assignment, instructions, and whether or not it is a one-time or repeating assignment.

- In addition, links to other activities can be created easily. If the activity is online, a URL can be entered in the space provided, and it will be linked automatically in the final syllabus.
- Your completed syllabus is hosted on our servers, allowing convenient updates from any computer on the Internet. Changes you make to your syllabus are immediately available to your students at their next logon.

Common Companion Website features for students include:

For the Student—

- **Chapter Objectives**—outline key concepts from the text
- **Interactive Self-Quizzes**—complete with hints and automatic grading that provide immediate feedback for students
- After students submit their answers for the interactive self-quizzes, the Companion Website **Results Reporter** computes a percentage grade, provides a graphic representation of how many questions were answered correctly and incorrectly, and gives a question-by-question analysis of the quiz. Students are given the option to send their quiz to up to four e-mail addresses (professor, teaching assistant, study partner, etc.).
- **Web Destinations**—links to www sites that relate to chapter content
- **Message Board**—serves as a virtual bulletin board to post—or respond to—questions or comments to/from a national audience
- **Chat**—real-time chat with anyone who is using the text anywhere in the country—ideal for discussion and study groups, class projects, etc.

To take advantage of the many available resources, please visit the Companion Website for *A Resource Guide for Elementary School Teaching: Planning for Competence, Fifth Edition* at

www.prenhall.com/kellough

Brief Contents

Contents

NOTE: Every effort has been made to provide accurate and current Internet information in this book. However, the Internet and information posted on it are constantly changing, so it is inevitable that some of the Internet addresses listed in this textbook will change.

Orientation to Elementary School Teaching and Learning

Part I assists you with your needs concerning:

- Characteristics of elementary school children, how the children learn, think, and develop intellectually
- Decision-making phases of instruction
- Developing an effective classroom management system
- Establishing and maintaining a safe and supportive classroom learning environment
- Knowledge of expectations, responsibilities, and facilitating behaviors of a competent elementary school classroom teacher
- Preparing for and beginning the school year
- Recognizing characteristics of child abuse and realizing your obligation when child abuse is suspected
- Responsive practices for helping all elementary school children succeed in school
- Styles of learning and teaching
- The role of telecommunications, the teacher, the principal, and home, school, and community partnerships in the learning of children
- Today's elementary schools, key trends and practices, problems, and issues

REFLECTIVE THOUGHTS

Although as a classroom teacher you cannot solve all the ailments of society, you do have an opportunity and responsibility to make all children feel welcome, respected, and wanted while they are in your classroom. History is brimming with examples of how a relatively few but positive moments with a truly caring and knowledgeable teacher can drastically change for the better the life of a person who until then had a history of mostly negative experiences.

During one school year you will make thousands of decisions, many of which can and will affect the lives of children for years to come. You may see this as an awesome responsibility, which it is.

Being detached and consistent is not the same as being fair and professional. As a teacher of children you are a professional who deals in matters of human relations and who must use professional intuition and judgment.

As a teacher for the twenty-first century, you must be knowledgeable and skilled in using teaching strategies that recognize, celebrate, and build upon the cultural, ethnic, and linguistic diversity of the classroom, the community, and the nation.

When teaching a group of children of mixed learning abilities, mixed modality strengths, mixed language proficiency, and mixed cultural backgrounds, the integration of learning modalities is a must.

As an elementary schoolteacher you must use every opportunity to help children become effective communicators by teaching them to think reflectively, to listen attentively, to speak clearly, to write accurately, and to read with comprehension.

Today's movement to transform schools into caring and responsive learning environments has as its sole purpose that of helping all children to make the transitions necessary to succeed in school and in life.

To become an accomplished classroom teacher your task is twofold: (a) develop your awareness of and skills in using the fundamental teaching behaviors, and (b) develop your repertoire and skills in selecting and using appropriate instructional strategies.

What Do I Need to Know About Today's Elementary Schools?

Greetings to you and welcome to the exciting and protean world of elementary school teaching. Whether you are in your early twenties and starting your first career, or older and in the process of beginning a new career, this book is for you—it is written for any person interested in and starting the journey toward becoming a professional teacher of children in kindergarten through grade six.

If you are now in a program of teacher preparation, then it is possible that near the completion of the program you will be offered your first teaching contract. When that happens, you will be excited—eager to sign the contract and to begin your new career. But after the initial excitement, you will have time to reflect. Many questions will then begin to surface. You undoubtedly will ask: What grade(s) will I have? What preparations will I need to make? Will I be a member of a teaching team?

Whatever elementary grade you are being hired to teach, you will want to know: What will the students be like? What will their parents or guardians be like? If it is a multiple-school district, to which school will I be assigned? Will it be a traditional school or will it be a *magnet school,* that is, a school that focuses on a particular academic or philosophical area. For example: Burling Magnet School (Pennsauken, NJ) is a K–5 school that focuses on the performing arts; Capitol Hill Magnet School (St. Paul, MN) provides a program for gifted and talented children in grades 1–8; at Chollas Elementary School (San Diego, CA), the focus is on mathematics and science; at High Peaks Core Knowledge Elementary School (Boulder, CO), the focus is on the Core Knowledge curriculum;[1] at Irwin Avenue Elementary School (Charlotte, NC), the focus is on the philosophy of open education;[2] O'Connor Elementary School (Victoria, TX) is a year-round magnet school with a focus on individualized learning; and, at Zuni Elementary School (Albuquerque, NM), the focus is on computers and communication.

It could be a *charter school,* "an autonomous educational entity operating under a charter, or contract, that has been negotiated between the organizers, who create and operate the school, and a sponsor, who oversees the provisions of the charter".[3] Or a *full-service community school,* a school that serves as a center for education and various health, social, and cultural services all under one roof.[4] Or an *International Baccalaureate school* with a curriculum approved by the International Baccalaureate Organization (IBO), a nonprofit worldwide educational foundation based in Switzerland.[5] Or a *Comer School,* a school based on James Comer's School Development Program that is designed specifically as a way to improve the educational experiences of poor minority children.[6] Or a *for-profit school,* a public school that is operated by a private company. Or it may be some combination, such as a magnet-open education-charter school. A school might be a church-affiliated school or a private school. And these are only some of the possibilities. Although in different ways and with various terminologies, the historical practice of providing different routes for children with different needs and different vocational and academic aspirations continues.

How can I prepare for students I have never met? What are the school and district policies that I need to learn? What support services will I have? What standardized tests are given, when will they be given, and how shall I prepare students for them? What reading, mathematics, social studies, and science programs will I be using? Where and how do I obtain classroom supplies? What are my extracurricular responsibilities? Is there a school dress code for the children? How shall I contact parents? How often will I be evaluated and by whom? Will there be an orientation for new teachers? How do I get answers to all of my questions?

To guide you through this initial experience and to help answer some of the questions you might have now and in the future, the following information about schools, students, teachers, administrators, and parents and guardians offers a basic glimpse into today's world of elementary school teaching. This ebullient, active, polymorphous world is so complex that few authors can say everything that needs to be said to every teacher. But we must begin somewhere and this chapter is it.

CHAPTER OBJECTIVES

Upon completion of this first chapter you should be able to

1. Describe essential characteristics of exemplary elementary school education.
2. Describe similarities and differences between schools that have some combination of grades K–6.
3. Describe current trends, problems, and issues in American public elementary school education.
4. Demonstrate knowledge of an elementary schoolteacher's daily schedule.
5. Identify and describe responsive educational practices for helping all elementary school children succeed.
6. Describe the significance of home, school, and community connections to a child's education, and of efforts being made by elementary school educators to enhance the connections among the home, school, and local and global communities.

THE ELEMENTARY SCHOOL: GETTING TO KNOW IT

The elementary school usually enrolls children between the ages of 5 and 11 (see Figure 1.1); converting these ages to what traditionally have been known as grades (see the section, The Graded School, that follows), we get grades kindergarten through six (K–6).

Figure 1.1
Age by state for beginning compulsory school attendance
[*Source: Digest of Educational Statistics 1996* (Washington, DC: National Center for Education Statistics, 1996), downloaded from the Internet (http://nces.ed.gov/pubs/d96/D96T149.html) 22 January 1999.]

AGE 5	AGE 6	AGE 7	AGE 8
Arkansas	Arizona	Alabama	Pennsylvania
Delaware	California	Alaska	Washington
Kansas	Florida	Colorado	
Maryland	Hawaii	Connecticut	
New Mexico	Iowa	District of Columbia	
North Dakota	Kentucky	Georgia	
Oklahoma	Massachusetts	Idaho	
South Carolina	Michigan	Illinois	
Virginia	Mississippi	Indiana	
	New Hampshire	Louisiana	
	New Jersey	Maine	
	New York	Minnesota	
	Ohio	Missouri	
	Rhode Island	Montana	
	South Dakota	Nebraska	
	Texas	Nevada	
	Utah	North Carolina	
	West Virginia	Oregon	
	Wisconsin	Tennessee	
		Vermont	
		Wyoming	

Primary and Elemiddle Schools

In some places, the elementary school is a *primary school,* with grades K–3 or K–4, followed by a middle school, and then a high school with its grades 9–12. In other places, the elementary school grade ranges are K–8. Because it houses children of both elementary and middle school age, a K–8 school is sometimes referred to as an *elemiddle school.* The K–8 elementary schools ordinarily are followed by a 4-year high school. The K–6 elementary schools are usually followed by a 3-year junior high school, or a middle school, followed by a 3-year senior high school. However, a K–6 elementary school with a 2-year middle school and a 4-year high school is not uncommon.

Grade Six and Its Location

While sixth grade is housed in some school districts at an elementary school, in other districts it is located at a middle school. In some large districts, both situations can be found. In districts where both options are available, and when space allows, parents or guardians may be given the option of sending their sixth-grade child to either the elementary school or the middle school.

Whereas any combination of grades 5–9 may be included in a middle school, the trend and the most common configuration is grades 6–8. Sixth graders are increasingly becoming a part of middle schools, while ninth graders are continuing to be excluded. The trend of including sixth graders and excluding ninth graders is a reflection of the recommendation of the National Middle School Association.[7] The trend continues. For example, in California the number of middle schools that include sixth graders has more than doubled since 1987. Grades six through eight are now the most common grade span inclusion of middle schools in that state.[8]

When you receive your state teaching credentials, you may or may not be certified to teach at the middle school level. While in some states the elementary school credential limits the holder's teaching to grades K–6, in others it certifies a person to teach in any grade, K–8.

Middle School versus Junior High School

At this point you should note that there are two sometimes quite different types of schools, both of which may be called middle schools. One is the

Table 1.1
Summary of differences between junior high schools and middle schools

Characteristic	Junior High School	Middle School
Most common grade-span organization	Grades 7–8 or 7–9	Grades 6–8
Scheduling	Traditional	Flexible, usually block
Subject organization	Departmentalized	Integrated and thematic; interdisciplinary, usually with language arts, math, science, and social studies
Guidance/counseling	Separate advising by full-time counselors on individual or as needed basis	Adviser-advisee—home base or homeroom
Exploratory curriculum	Electives by individual choice	Common "wheel" of experiences for all students
Teachers	Subject-centered; grades 7–12 certification	Interdisciplinary teams; student-centered; grades K–8 or 6–8 certification
Instruction	Traditional; lecture; skills and repetition	Thematic units; discovery techniques; "learning how to learn" (study skills)
Athletics	Interscholastic sports, emphasizing competition	Intramural programs, emphasizing participation

traditional junior high school with perhaps a few minor changes, such as changing its name to *middle school*. The second is the exemplary middle school, which is, as shown in Table 1.1, quite different from the traditional junior high school. To understand the significance of what has become known as the **middle school concept,** certain background information may prove helpful.

Used historically from about 1880, the term *junior high school* most commonly refers to schools having grades 7–8 or grades 7–9, in which a program is designed to approximate the type of education commonly found in traditional high schools. Thus, a junior high school might be considered a "not-quite-yet-but-trying-to-be" high school. Students graduating from a junior high school often would then move on to a *senior high school.*

The term *middle school* gained favor as a result of the movement away from the concept of "junior" high school. Reasons for the reorganization away from the concept of junior high school and the adoption of a middle school education include: (a) to provide a program specifically designed for children of the 10–14 age group, (b) to set up a more effective transition between the elementary school and the high school, and (c) to move ninth graders to the high school or, as has happened in some school districts in recent years, to a location designed solely for ninth graders, known as a *ninth-grade center.*[9]

The term *middle level education* identifies school organizations based on a philosophy that incorporates curricula and instructional prac-

tices specifically designed to meet the needs of students ages 10 through 15. This philosophy is referred to as the *middle school concept.* The notion that greater and more specific attention should be given to the special needs of young adolescents became known as the *middle school movement.* Basic to the movement that began in the 1960s is the belief that middle school teachers need specialized training to work most effectively with young adolescents. At least 33 states now provide a middle school teaching credential to candidates who have successfully completed a program specifically designed to prepare teachers for that level.

The Self-Contained Classroom

The most common classroom arrangement of teacher and students for elementary school organization is the self-contained classroom. A self-contained classroom is one in which one teacher is assigned to a group of children of approximately the same age or of mixed ages in an ungraded school (see section that follows) for an academic year. Having primary responsibility for implementing the program of instruction for those children, that teacher is the teacher of record for those children for an entire school year, even though other teachers of special subjects, such as music, art, physical education, or computers, may work with the children part of the time.

The Graded School

Schools in colonial America and those of the early national period did not use the age-grouping system we call *grades*. Children of varying ages were assigned to a single teacher, who tutored them individually or who taught them in small mixed age groups. It was not until the middle of the 19th century that the practice of grouping children according to age (i.e., age grading) became widespread. This practice was developed in Germany in the 8-year *Volkschule*. It appealed to American educators as an efficient way of managing the teaching of a large number of children.

Following the Civil War, there was rapid acceptance of the practice of grouping children who were of a similar age and keeping those groups intact from one year to the next as children progressed through school. Schools were therefore *graded* by age, and communities and states used the term *graded* in curriculum documents and school regulations and names. Continuing today the expression "grade school" is commonly used in ordinary parlance in speaking of the elementary school.

Arguments in favor of the graded school concept are that

- Children's social development, to some extent, relates to age, and therefore, age groups tend to be natural social groups.
- It allows teachers to specialize their teaching skills in the age of the children with whom they work best.
- It equalizes educational opportunity by exposing all children to the same curriculum.
- It is an efficient way to accommodate the large number of children who are required to attend school.
- It is possible to require set standards of achievement for the various grades.
- It reduces variability within instructional groups by keeping the age of children within the groups constant.
- Textbooks, instructional materials, and achievement tests can be constructed on the basis of age-grade norms.

Arguments against the graded school concept are that

- It encourages a rigid and undifferentiated curriculum.
- It encourages an authoritarian classroom atmosphere which is antagonistic to what is now known about how children best learn.
- It encourages mechanical teaching, analogous to assembly-line production in industry.
- It encourages traditional recitation-response teaching practices, ignoring what has been learned in recent years about learning.
- It is too lock-step, encouraging teachers to disregard individual differences in children and in their individual developmental patterns.
- It sets unrealistic standards for children and is especially unfair to underachievers.
- The competitive and comparative system of determining grades (marks of achievement) and promotion are educationally dysfunctional and psychologically unsound.

Although in the United States most elementary schools are graded, some are not. While the practice of using ungraded classrooms is not new there has in recent years been renewed interest in it. At *ungraded* (or *nongraded*) *schools* (known also as continuous promotion or continuous progress grouping, family grouping, heterogeneous grouping, mixed-age or multiage grouping, open education, and vertical grouping), such as Jo Mackey Magnet School (Las Vegas, NV), children are grouped and regrouped, not according to ages or grade levels, but for different purposes, such as interests, abilities, and outcomes.[10]

Orientation Meetings for Teachers

As a beginning teacher, you will be expected to participate in an orientation meeting for teachers. Some school districts start the academic year with a districtwide orientation, and others schedule on-site orientations at each school. Many school districts do both, with perhaps a districtwide meeting in the morning followed by on-site meetings in the afternoon. Of course, the scheduling and planning of orientation meetings will vary district by district and school by school. The objectives for all orientation meetings, however, should be similar. As a new teacher, you will be encouraged by district personnel to do the following:

1. Become familiar with the district's (or school's) written statement of its unique beliefs and goals—its *statement of mission* (or philosophy or vision)—and what that statement means to the people affiliated with the district or school. See sample statements shown in Figure 1.2. [*Note:* Although the terms *mission statement, philosophy statement,* and *vision statement* are often used interchangeably, and while in our opinion the first two are synonymous, the vision statement is or should be a statement of intention that goes beyond the immediate mission of the school and gives future direction to the school's stated mission.]

Figure 1.2
Sample elementary
school mission
statements reprinted
by permission.

- The mission of Julian Harris Elementary School (Decatur, AL; grades K–5; available online http://www.ptc.dcs.edu/schools/elem/jh/jh.html, January 2, 2000) is to develop lifelong learners who will be productive members of society. The nurturing staff will set high expectations for all students and will provide a risk-free learning environment that embraces a child-centered, developmentally appropriate curriculum.
- At Sierra Oaks Elementary School (Sacramento, CA; grades K–6; 1999–2000 Parent Handbook) we believe that the education of children is a responsibility mutually shared by parents and the school. Our goal is for each student to develop to his/her full potential academically, socially, emotionally, and physically. We believe that all students should know, value, and act on positive character traits such as respect, responsibility, honesty, and courage to contribute to the development of a humane and democratic society. Therefore, we as schools, parents, and communities pledge to work together to develop and demonstrate these character traits in each of our daily lives. We believe all students can and should develop respect for themselves and others in order to assume responsibility for a full and productive life as a member of this society of free people.
- Whittier School (Chicago, IL; grades K–6; available online http://www..cps.k12.il.us/Mission.html; January 2, 2000) is a community of learners who desire healthy bodies, emotional strength, confidence, ambition, and integrity. We hope always to respect and appreciate the work of others, experience the rich heritage of diverse cultures as well as our own, be participating citizens in a democracy, and to know, respect, and protect the Earth and share the vision of global interdependence. Whittier School strives to be a community of children, parents, and teachers committed to individual dignity, cooperation, and excellence.
- The staff of Woodland Hills Elementary School (Lawton, OK; grades K–6; available online http://www.woodsmen.com; October 5, 1999) holds high expectations for student success and is dedicated to providing an education setting in which all students can learn and develop to their full intellectual, social, physical, and emotional potential. The staff seeks to instill in students an appreciation of their American heritage, a positive attitude, and the responsibility for lifelong learning skills through cooperation and support of parents and the community.

2. Become familiar with the policies of the school and district. Such policies are many and often cover a wide range of topics. There are policies for visitors to the campus; procedures relating to injuries of students at school; violence at school; natural disasters, such as earthquakes or severe storms; students who need to take prescribed medications; the discovery of nonprescription drugs, other controlled substances, and weapons; playground use; parking on campus; school dress/uniform; classroom behavior; school programs, off-campus field trips, and parties in the classroom; grading, promotion, and retention; absentee and tardy forms; bathroom privileges; students who are sent to the office; and sponsorship of student activities. And these examples are just the beginning!

3. Become familiar with the myriad forms that teachers must complete. There are forms for injuries at school, textbook loans, key loans, attendance, academic deficiencies, student activities, field trips, supplies requisitions, AV and media equipment use, and student misbehavior, to name just a few.

4. Become familiar with the approved curriculum that defines what teachers are to teach and what students are to learn. This means that you must become familiar with the curriculum documents and standards, resource units, teacher's manuals, student textbooks, media and software programs, and supplementary materials—all of which should reflect the school's stated mission and approved curriculum.

5. Meet other teachers and establish the beginning of new collegial friendships and professional relationships. Many school districts sponsor *beginning teacher induction programs* that provide special assistance to new teachers (discussed in Chapter 12).

6. Become familiar with the school or district plan for monitoring, assessing, and supervising implementation of the curriculum.

7. Study available resource materials and equipment, and learn the procedures for reserving them for use on certain dates.

8. Become familiar with the school library/resource center, its personnel, and its procedures.

9. Meet district and school personnel, and become familiar with the many services that support you in your classroom.

10. Become knowledgeable about the standardized proficiency assessment tests that will be administered to your students during the school year—the procedure, your responsibility, and dates for their administration.

11. Prepare your classroom for instruction.

As a candidate in a program for teacher preparation, you may be expected to participate in an orientation meeting at your university. The meeting may be held at the beginning of the program, just before the beginning of your field experience, or at both times. Perhaps this meeting will be part of one of your university courses. You will receive the name of your assigned school and district, the school's location, the date when you should report, the name of your cooperating teacher(s),[11] the grade level(s), the subject(s), and perhaps the name of your university supervisor. You will probably be encouraged to follow many of the suggestions listed above and to meet other teacher candidates.

After you have arrived at your assigned school and the introductions have been made, you can begin to become familiar with the school campus and the school organization. Walk around the campus, perhaps with a copy of the school map, and learn the location of your classroom, discover the playground area assigned for your class, and locate the nearest restrooms for girls, boys, and faculty. Become familiar with such areas as the teachers' workroom and the faculty lunchroom. Determine where students eat their lunches and their snacks. Is there a multipurpose room—a room used for lunch as well as for educational activities? Where is the nurse's room? the nearest first-aid and emergency equipment? How do you notify maintenance personnel quickly and efficiently? Where are the written procedures for fire drills and other emergencies? Where is information about the warning system? Is there a plan posted in a conspicuous place for all to see? Where are the various administrative offices? Where is the library? the media center? the office of the media specialist? the resources room? Where are textbooks stored? How are they checked out and distributed? Where is the attendance office? Are there offices for resource specialists?

At an orientation session, you may meet the grade-level chairperson, department chairperson, or the teaching team leader. How can you discover where those persons are to be found at various times during the school day? Where are teaching supplies kept, and how do you obtain them? Have you located your faculty mailbox and the place to check in and out when you arrive and leave school? What procedures do you follow if you are going to be absent or late? Do you have the necessary phone numbers, pager numbers, and e-mail addresses?

And, not least in importance, if you drive to school, where do you park? Otherwise, what is the best local transportation for getting to and from school?

After becoming familiar with the school site and obtaining answers to your more urgent questions, you will want to focus your attention on schedules, long-term school schedules, and daily teaching schedules.

School Schedules

School schedules vary from state to state, from district to district, and from school to school. Many school years begin in late August or early September and continue through late May or mid-June. Other schools operate on a year-round schedule with the school year beginning in August and ending in June or July.[12] In a school with year-round education (YRE), a teacher might teach for 3 consecutive months followed by a month off, then for another 3 months on and then a month off, and so on, throughout the year, or might teach in a 45/15 program, which means a year-long schedule of 9 weeks (45 days) of school followed by 3 weeks (15 days) off.

Regardless of whether it is a traditional 9-month calendar or a year-round schedule, in most places in the United States the school year is still approximately 180 days out of a 365-day calendar year. Some schools, however, such as the Brooks Global Studies Extended-Year Magnet Elementary School (Greensboro, NC) have extended their school year to a longer time such as 210 days and are called *extended-year schools*.

Not to be confused with the extended-year school is the *extended-day school*. Fremont Magnet Elementary School (Bakersfield, CA), for example, provides for its 1,000 students a regular (mandatory) school program from 8:00 a.m. until 2:10 p.m. each day (Monday through Friday) followed by an optional magnet program until 5:00 p.m.

Still other schools are on a shorter than 5-day week, such as 4 days.[13] Most schools that are on a 4-day week are small rural schools, often including grades K–12 and where children spend several hours each day riding the school bus. Schools on a 4-day week usually go longer each day, such as from 8 a.m. until 4 p.m., with Monday or Friday off.

After being assigned to a school and becoming familiar with the campus, you should turn your attention to all of the available school schedules for playground duty, lunch, bus duty, the library, special programs, and special days. The school day usually begins at about 8:00 a.m. and lasts until about 3:00 p.m. In schools that are crowded, beginning and ending times may be staggered, and some students and teachers may start as early as 7:30 a.m. and leave at 2:30 p.m. Others may begin at 9:00 a.m. and continue until 4:00 p.m. District and state laws vary, but they generally require that teachers be in the classroom no less than 15 minutes prior to the start of school and remain in the classroom no less than 15 minutes after dismissal of the children.

Subjects of the Curriculum

The time spent daily on each subject taught will vary with grade level and may be dictated by adopted program, state law, or district policy; but for each grade the curriculum plans should include lessons for multiple subjects: English/reading/language arts (known also as *literacy*), mathematics, science, history/social sciences/geography—the four subject areas of the **core curriculum**—and art, music, physical education, health, and sometimes foreign language. In some schools and in some grades, not all of these subjects are taught every day, nor are they necessarily all taught in one classroom of children by just one teacher.

While studies demonstrate that the early study of a second language provides cognitive benefits, gains in academic achievement, and positive attitudes toward diversity, study of a second or foreign language, unfortunately, is not a part of the curriculum for very many elementary schools.[14] There are some elementary schools, however, such as Sunset Elementary School (Miami, FL) where foreign language study is a significant component of the core curriculum.[15]

The choice of language offered by elementary schools varies, of course, depending to some extent on the community, the availability of teachers, and whether the program can be sustained for several years.[16] Generally, elementary school foreign language programs fall within a spectrum of types. At one end are *total immersion* programs, where all of the classroom instruction is in the target foreign language. At the other end of the spectrum are *foreign language experience (FLEX)* programs, where classes may meet only a few times a week and the goal is to introduce children to one or more foreign languages and cultures rather than to develop proficiency in the use of a target foreign language. Somewhere in the middle on the spectrum are what are known as *foreign language in the elementary school (FLES)* programs, which focus mostly on cultural awareness and developing listening and speaking skills in a target foreign language.

FLES programs follow the natural sequence of language learning: understanding, speaking, reading, and writing. For young children a typical FLES lesson would include physical activities such as songs, rhymes, games, and playacting with puppets.[17]

In addition to the specialized skills of the subjects mentioned above, students learn other, more general, skills as components of the elementary school curriculum. These include critical thinking skills, socialization skills, and organizational and study skills.

Teaching Teams

Traditionally, elementary schoolteachers have taught their groups of children in their self-contained classrooms for most of the school day, while fairly isolated from other teachers and school activities—not unlike the parallel play of preschool children, that is, playing side-by-side but not really together. In some schools, that is still the case. Increasingly, however, elementary schoolteachers are finding themselves members of a collaborative **teaching team** in which several teachers work together to reflect, plan, and implement a curriculum for a common cohort of students. The teaching team may comprise only a few teachers, for example, all second-grade teachers of a particular elementary school, or the teachers who teach the same cohort of sixth-grade children in English/reading/language arts and in history/social studies/geography at the same or another school. They may meet periodically to plan a curriculum and learning activities around a common theme.

Sometimes teaching teams comprise one teacher each from the four areas of the core curriculum. In addition to teachers of the core subjects, specialty-area teachers may be part of the team, including teachers of foreign language, physical education, the arts, and even special education teachers and at-risk specialty personnel or school counselors. Because the core and specialty subjects cross disciplines of study, these teams are commonly called *interdisciplinary teaching teams,* or simply **interdisciplinary teams.**

Looping

In some schools, a teacher or a team of teachers remain with the same cohort of children for two or more years, a practice known as **looping** (also referred to as *multiyear grouping, multiyear instruction, multiyear placement, persistent teams,* and *teacher-student progression*). While the practice of looping is not new, in recent years there has been renewed interest in it because of the positive findings from recent research studies. Positive findings indicate that the benefits of looping include improved student-teacher relationships, more efficient instruction, better learning, improved attendance, fewer referrals to special education programs, and improved student behavior.[18] Perhaps the positive findings can be summarized as being the result of an effective teacher (or teaching team) getting to know a group of children well and being able to remain with that group longer than one school year, rather than starting all over again in a year with an entirely different group of children. Figures 1.3 presents sample teacher schedules.

Inside your own busy classroom, you will be learning the names of your students, making decisions, following your detailed instructional plans, and keeping one eye on the clock for a day or two—a behavior that helps you observe the schedule for recess, lunch, coordination with other teachers, and dismissal at the end of the school day.

Figure 1.3a
A kindergarten class schedule*
[*Source:* Courtesy of Lynne Baker and Connie Thomas, kindergarten teachers, Sierra Oaks School, San Juan Unified School District, Carmichael, California]

---

*This is the a.m. schedule shared by the two teachers; the schedule is repeated in the afternoon when a second group of children arrive at 12:05 and are dismissed at 3:25.

9:10–9:25	Opening
	Attendance
	Weather
	Calendar
	Message
9:25–10:25	Language Arts
10:25–10:40	Snack/Recess
10:40–10:50	Music and Movement
10:50–11:50	Math
11:50–12:15	Free Choice Learning Centers
12:15–12:30	Review, Story, Dismissal

Figure 1.3b
A first-grade class schedule
(*Source:* Courtesy of Teri Schuddeboom, first-grade teacher, Hemlock Elementary School, Vacaville Unified School District, Vacaville, California)

8:25–8:55	Community circle
	Attendance
	Flag salute
	Patriotic song
	Community song
	Calendar process
	Weather graph
	Lost tooth chart
	Appreciations
	Share a sentence
8:55–9:15	Spelling activities
9:15–10:05	Reading activities
10:05–10:20	Recess and snack time
10:20–10:50	Reading continued

10:50–11:15	English/handwriting
11:15–12:00	Lunch/recess
12:00–12:10	Semisilent sustained reading
12:10–12:20	Read aloud to class
12:20–12:35	Community circle (math oriented)
	Number line
	Make the date in cents
	Add one straw each day to straw box and group into tens
	Clock work
12:35–1:05	Math (or library one day a week)
1:05–1:35	Social studies, science, or health
1:35–2:15	Art, music, physical education, or journal writing
2:15–2:25	Room cleanup
2:25	Dismissal

Figure 1.3c
A second-grade class schedule
(*Source:* Courtesy of Mary E. Gentry, second-grade teacher, Cirby Elementary School, Roseville Unified School District, Roseville, California)

8:20–9:20	Reading for morning readers (lower-level groups)
9:20–9:30	Recess (afternoon readers arrive)
9:30–9:35	Opening role, lunch count, flag salute
9:35–10:00	Language (daily oral)
10:00–10:35	Math activities
10:35–10:45	Recess
10:45–11:45	Music, spelling, or art
11:45–12:30	Lunch
12:30–12:40	Silent reading, show and tell
12:40–1:10	Science, social studies, physical education, language arts
1:10–1:30	Library
1:30–1:40	Recess (dismissal of morning readers)
1:40–2:40	Reading for afternoon readers (higher-level groups)
2:40	Dismissal of afternoon readers

Figure 1.3d
A third-grade class schedule
(*Source:* Courtesy of Gloria Morrill, third-grade teacher,
Sierra Oaks Elementary School, San Juan Unified School
District, Carmichael, California)

9:10–10:35	Classroom Business
	Math Block
	Music (Thursday 9:55–10:35)
10:35–10:45	Recess
10:45–12:10	Language Arts Block (Reading, Writing, Grammar, Speaking, Listening, Spelling)
	Physical Education (Friday 11:30–12:10)
	Computer/Library (Wed. 11:00–12:05)
12:10–12:50	Lunch
12:50–1:45	Language Arts continued (Independent reading, Teacher read-aloud, Cursive)
	Math Carousel (Friday)
1:45–2:00	Recess
2:00–3:25	Integrating Social Studies
	Science
	Art
	Physical Education (Thursday, 2:00–2:40)

Figure 1.3e
A fourth-grade class schedule
(*Source:* Courtesy of Heather Newcomb, fourth-grade teacher,
Reagan Elementary School, Dallas Public Schools, Dallas, Texas)

8:00–8:50	Language arts—Spanish (native language cognitive development)
8:50–9:15	Attendance, announcements, mad minute math drill, collect homework
9:15–9:35	ESL (M, W); community circle (T, Th, F)
9:35–10:15	Prep for teacher; art, physical education, character education for students by specialty teachers
10:15–12:25	Integrated math, science, social studies
12:25–12:30	Break
12:30–1:05	Lunch
1:05–2:00	Writer's workshop (T, Th), genre writing (M, W, F)
2:00–2:15	Journal writing
2:15–2:35	DEAR (*Drop Everything And Read*), for a sustained silent reading activity
2:35–2:45	Review homework, check off assignments completed
2:45–3:00	Cleanup; student sharing of one thing each has learned that day

Figure 1.3f
A fifth-grade schedule for a "house" of three
teachers
(*Source:* Courtesy of Stephanie Rice, Deana Romero, and Teri
Catron, fifth-grade teachers, Hugh Bish Elementary School,
Lawton, Oklahoma)*

8:45–9:00	Whole school assembly (flag salute, birthdays, announcements, songs, and sharing)
9:00–9:20	Spelling in homeroom class
9:20–10:00	Music, art, and physical education (alternating every third day)
10:00–10:10	Bathroom break, class change
10:10–11:10	Group 1–Language arts; Group 2–Math; Group 3–Science and social studies
11:10–11:15	Class change
11:15–12:15	Group 1–Math; Group 2–Science and social studies; Group 3–Language arts
12:15–12:20	Change back to homeroom class
12:20–12:45	Oral and silent reading in homeroom class
12:45–1:10	Lunch
1:10–1:30	Recess
1:30–1:35	Class change
1:35–2:35	Group 1–Science and social studies; Group 2–Language arts; Group 3–Math
2:35–3:20	Reading in homeroom class
3:20–3:25	Cleanup and dismissal

*This schedule creates a unique learning environment involving the strengths of three teachers. Each teacher has a homeroom class for spelling and reading. For science and social studies, math, and language arts, the students are divided into three groups, each of which includes one-third of the children from each teacher's assigned class. These groups are changed each quarter, thus providing children with the opportunity to work cooperatively with many different peers throughout the school year. This helps them to develop the life skill needed to work with and to adjust to new situations. The groups are created randomly, maintaining a balance of females and males. The three teachers maintain control of the scheduling of students who attend special classes for learning disabilities, speech, counseling, and tutoring. By changing the schedule every quarter, the teachers also have control of placing students with behavior problems and children with personality conflicts, thus creating a more effective learning environment for all.

THE FUNDAMENTAL CHARACTERISTIC OF EXEMPLARY ELEMENTARY SCHOOL EDUCATION

Wherever and however the students are housed, whatever the schedules, and regardless of other practices, in the end it is the dedication, commitment, and nature of the understanding of the involved adults—the teachers, administrators, bus drivers, cooks, grounds crew, security staff, custodial staff, and support personnel—that remains the incisive element. That, in our opinion, is the fundamental characteristic of exemplary elementary school education—that is, to celebrate and build upon the diverse characteristics and needs of students. That, in fact, is the essence of Chapter 2 of this edition of our resource guide.

Committed Teachers

Elementary schoolteachers represent myriad individual personalities—perhaps impossible to capture in generalizations. Let us imagine that a teaching colleague mentions that Chez Burger, in room 17, is a "fantastic teacher," "one of the best teachers in the district," "super," and "magnificent." What might be some of the characteristics you would expect to see in Chez's teaching behaviors? (Teacher responsibilities and behaviors are the topic of Chapter 3.)

We can expect Chez to (a) be understanding of and committed to the school's stated mission, (b) know the curriculum and how best to teach it, (c) be enthusiastic, motivated, and well organized, (d) show effective communication and interpersonal skills, (e) be willing to listen to the students and to risk trying their ideas, and (f) be warm, caring, accepting, and nurturing about all children.

Elementary school children need teachers who are well organized and who know how to establish and manage an active and supportive learning environment (the topic of Chapter 4), even with its multiple instructional demands. Students respond best to teachers who provide leadership and who enjoy their function as role models, advisers, mentors, and reflective decision-makers.

Decision Making

Whether a teacher of kindergarten children or of sixth graders or of children in between, during any school day you will make hundreds of nontrivial decisions, many of them instantaneously. In addition, you will have already made many decisions in preparation for the teaching day. During one school year a teacher makes literally thousands of decisions, many of which can and will affect the lives of that teacher's students for years to come. This may seem to be an awesome responsibility; indeed it is.

Initially, of course, you will make errors in judgment, but you will also learn that children can be amazingly resilient and that there are experts available who can guide you to help ensure that the children are not damaged by your mistakes. You can learn from your errors. Keep in mind that the sheer number of decisions you make each day will mean that not all will be the best decisions that could have been made had you had more time and better resources for planning.

Good Teaching Is as Much an Art as It Is a Science

Although pedagogy is based on scientific principles, good classroom teaching is as much an art as it is a science. Few rules apply to every teaching situation. In fact, decisions about the selection of content, instructional objectives and materials, teaching strategies, a teacher's response to student misbehavior, and the selection of techniques for assessment of the learning experiences are all the result of subjective judgments. While many decisions are made at a somewhat unhurried pace when you are planning for your instruction, many others will be made intuitively and *tout de suite*. Once the school day has begun, there is rarely time for making carefully thought-out judgments. At your best, you base your decisions on your teaching style, which, in turn, is based on your knowledge of school policies, pedagogical research, the curriculum, and the unique characteristics of the children in your charge. You will also base your decisions on intuition, common sense, and reflective judgment. The better your understanding and experience with schools, the curriculum, and the students, and the more time you give for thoughtful reflection, the more likely it will be that your decisions will result in the students' meeting the learning targets and educational goals. (Learning targets and educational goals are discussed in Chapter 5.) You will reflect on, conceptualize, and apply understandings from one teaching experience to the next. As your understanding about your classroom experiences accumulate, your teaching will become more routinized, predictable, and refined. The topic of reflective decision-making is presented more fully at the beginning of Chapter 3; now, to extend your awareness of the reality of elementary school teaching do Exercise 1.1.

For Your Notes

EXERCISE 1.1 CONVERSATION WITH A CLASSROOM TEACHER

Instructions: The purpose of this exercise is to interview one or more elementary schoolteachers, perhaps one who is relatively new to the classroom and one who has been teaching for 10 years or more. Use the following questions. You may duplicate blank copies of this form. Share the results with others in your class.

1. Name and location of school _____

   _____

2. Grade span of school _____

3. Date of interview _____

4. Name and grade level (and/or subject) of interviewee _____

   _____

5. In which area(s) of the school's curriculum do you work? _____

   _____

6. Why did you select teaching as a career? _____

   _____

   _____

   _____

   _____

   _____

7. Why are you teaching at this grade level? _____

   _____

   _____

   _____

   _____

   _____

8. What preparation or training did you have? _____

   _____

   _____

   _____

   _____

   _____

9. What advice about preparation can you offer? _____

   _____

   _____

EXERCISE 1.1 (continued)

_____

_____

_____

_____

10. What do you like most about teaching? _____

_____

_____

_____

_____

11. What do you like least about teaching? _____

_____

_____

_____

_____

12. What is the most important thing to know to be an effective classroom teacher? _____

_____

_____

_____

_____

13. What other specific advice do you have for those of us entering teaching at this level? _____

_____

_____

_____

_____

The Principal Can Make a Difference

As a new or visiting member of the faculty, one of your tasks is to become familiar with the administrative organization of your school and district.

One person significantly responsible for the success of any school is its principal. What are the characteristics of an effective elementary school principal? (See Figure 1.4.) Perhaps foremost are the principal's vision of what a quality school is and the drive to bring that vision to life—school improvement is the effective principal's constant theme.

Figure 1.4
Key characteristics of the exemplary elementary school principal

- Admonishes behaviors rather than personalities.
- Advocates a school of problem solvers rather than of blamers and faultfinders.
- Ensures a base of community support for the school, its students, its faculty, and its mission.
- Emphasizes the importance of making everyone feel like a winner.
- Encourages people when they have made a mistake to say "I'm sorry," rather than making them feel compelled to cover their mistakes.
- Ensures that school policies are closely and collaboratively defined and clearly communicated.
- Ensures that staff and students receive proper and timely recognition for their achievements.
- Ensures that teachers' administrative chores and classroom interruptions are limited only to those that are critically important to student learning and effective functioning of the school.
- Establishes a climate in which teachers and students share the responsibility for determining the appropriate use of time and facilities.
- Follows up promptly on recommendations, concerns, and complaints.
- Fosters professional growth and development for teachers, with opportunities for visitations, demonstrations, conferences, workshops, and projects.
- Has a vision of what an exemplary elementary school is and strives to bring that vision to life.
- Involves teachers, parents/guardians, and students in decision making and goal setting.
- Is an advocate for teachers and students.
- Is positive in outlook.
- Keeps everyone well informed of events and successes.
- Spends time each day with students.

Through personal skills in instructional leadership, the principal establishes a climate in which teachers and students share the responsibility for determining the appropriate use of time and facilities. Because exemplary elementary school educators believe in the innate potential of every child, instead of dumbing down standards and expectations, they modify the key variables of time, grouping, and instructional strategies to help each child achieve quality learning (see Chapter 8), a task nearly impossible to do without a supportive, knowledgeable, and positive and forward-thinking school principal.[19]

In addition to the school principal there sometimes is an assistant or vice-principal, especially for larger schools, a person with specific responsibilities and oversight functions, such as student activities, school discipline and security, transition programs, and curriculum and instruction. Sometimes teachers who are grade level or department chairs, or designated team leaders, may also serve administrative functions. But the principal is (or should be) the person with the final responsibility for everything that happens at the school. Where principals used to debate whether they were leaders or managers, today there is no debate—to be most effective the principal must be both.[20]

Commitment to Helping All Children Succeed in School

In any school there are students who have a high probability of dropping out. *At risk* is the term used by educators when referring to those students. Researchers have identified five categories of indicators that cause a child to be at risk: (a) Academic failure—exemplified by low marks and grades, academic failure, absences from school, low self-esteem; (b) Family instability—exemplified by moving, separation, divorce; (c) Family socioeconomic situation—exemplified by low income, negativism, lack of education; (d) Family tragedy—exemplified by parent/guardian illness or death, health problems; and (e) Personal pain—exemplified by drugs, physical and psychological abuse, suspension from school.[21] Many children, at any one time, have risk factors from more than one of these categories. Although some schools have a higher percentage of children at risk than do others, it has been estimated that by year 2020 the majority of students in the public schools in the United States will be at risk.[22]

I Pledge Allegiance to Myself

I pledge allegiance to myself
and who I want to be
I can make my dreams come true
If I believe in me.
    I pledge to stay in school and learn
    the things I need to know
    to make the world a better place
    for kids like me to grow.
        I promise to keep my dreams alive
        and be all that I can be
        I know I can, and that's because
        I pledge to stay alcohol, tobacco, and
            drug free.

    (Source unknown)

Today's movement to transform schools into caring and responsive learning environments has as its sole purpose that of helping all children, and especially those at risk, to make the transitions necessary to succeed in school and in life. The future of our nation, and indeed, our world, might rest heavily on the success of this movement.

Responsive Practices for Helping All Children Succeed in School

Because of the enormous diversity of students in the classroom, the advantage of using a combination of practices concurrently is usually greater in helping all children succeed in school than is the gain from using any singular practice by itself. The reorganization of schools (such as moving sixth graders to a middle-level school) and the restructuring of school schedules (such as YRE and extended school days), then, represent only two aspects of efforts to help all students to make successful transitions.

Other important responsive practices (including attitudes) are (a) a perception, shared by all teachers and staff, that all children can learn when they are given adequate support, although not all students need the same amount of time to learn the same thing; (b) maintaining high, although not necessarily identical, expectations for all students; (c) personalized attention, adult advocacy, and scheduling and learning plans to help students learn in a manner by which they best learn—research clearly points out that achievement increases, students learn more, and students enjoy learning and remember more of what they have learned when individual learning styles and capacities are identified and accommodated; learning style traits are known that significantly discriminate among students who are at risk of dropping out of school and students who perform well, discussed in Chapter 2; (d) engagement of parents and guardians as partners in their child's education, (e) extra time and guided attention on basic skills—such as those of thinking, writing, and reading—rather than on rote memory; (f) specialist teachers, smaller student cohorts, and smaller classes; (g) peer tutoring and cross-age coaching; and (h) attention and guidance in the development of coping skills. These responsive practices are repeated and discussed throughout this resource guide. Another responsive practice in promoting the success of all children is making connections among the home, school, and local and global communities. That is discussed next.

VEHICLES FOR SHARING INFORMATION AND RESPONSIBILITY: TELECOMMUNICATIONS NETWORKS, MEMBERS OF THE COMMUNITY, AND PARENT/GUARDIAN ORGANIZATIONS

It is well known that family involvement and support in their child's education can have a positive impact on that child's achievement at school. For example, when parents, guardians, or siblings of at-risk students get involved, the child benefits with more consistent attendance at school, more positive attitudes and actions, better grades, and higher test scores.[23] In recognition of the positive effect that parent and family involvement has on student achievement and success, the National PTA, in 1997, published *National Standards for Parent/Family Involvement Programs.*[24]

Home and School Connections

Sometimes teachers develop their own personal family-involvement programs.[25] Today many schools have adopted formal policies about home and community connections. These policies usually emphasize that parents and guardians should be included as partners in the educational program and that teachers and administrators will inform parents and guardians about their child's progress, about the school's family involvement policy, and about any programs in which family members can participate. Some schools are members of the *National Network of Partnership 2000* Schools. Efforts to foster family and community involvement are as varied as the schools and people who participate, and include (a) student-teacher-parent/guardian contracts and assignment calendars, sometimes available via the school's Web page on the Internet, (b) home visitation programs, (c) involvement of community leaders in the classroom as mentors, aides, and role models,[26] (d) newsletters, workshops,[27] and electronic hardware and software for family members to help their children, (e) homework hotlines, (f) regular phone calls[28] and personal notes home about a student's progress, and (g) involvement of students in service learning.[29] One of your tasks as a visiting or new teacher will be to discover the extent and nature of your school's efforts to involve family and community representatives in the education of the children. (Figure 11.12 of Chapter 11 presents addresses for ideas and resources for home-school partnerships.) Educators increasingly are looking at service learning as a means of helping young people connect learning with life.

Service Learning

Through service learning students learn and develop through active participation in thoughtfully organized and curriculum-connected experiences that meet community needs.[30] (See Figure 1.5 for Internet sources of additional information and descriptions of service projects.)

Community members, geographic features, buildings, monuments, historic sites, and other places in a school's geographic area constitute some of the richest instructional laboratories that can be imagined. To take advantage of this accumulated wealth of resources, as well as to build school-community partnerships, once hired by a school you are advised to begin your file of community resources. For instance, you might include files about the skills of the students' parents, guardians, or other family members, noting which ones could be resources for the study occurring in your classroom. You might also include files on various resource people who could speak to the students (see guidelines for using guest speakers in Chapter 10), on free and inexpensive materials, on sites for field trips (see guidelines for using field trips in Chapter 10), and on what other communities of teachers, students, and adult helpers have done.

Figure 1.5
Internet sources on community service learning

- *Big Dummy's Guide to Service-Learning*
  <http://www.fiu.edu/~time4chg/Library/bigdummy.html>
- *Catch the Spirit*
  <http://www.pueblo.gsa.gov/cic_text/children/spirit/spirit.htm>
- *Corporation for National Service*
  <http://www.cns.gov>
- *Links for Service-Learning*
  <http://www.bbrook.k12.nj.us/servlink.htm>
- *Learn and Serve America Exchange*
  <http://www.lsaexchange.org>
- *Learn and Serve America National Service-Learning Clearinghouse*
  <http://www.umn.edu/~serv>
- *Learning In Deed: Making a Difference Through Service-Learning*
  <http://www.LearningInDeed.org>
- *National Youth Leadership Council*
  <http://www.nylc.org>

Professional Resources File

Now is a good time to start your professional resources file and then maintain it throughout your career (see Figure 1.6). For your file, many resource ideas and sources are mentioned and listed throughout this resource guide. See, for example, Figure 10.7 in Chapter 10.

Telecommunications Networks

Teachers looking to guide their students toward becoming autonomous thinkers, effective decision makers, and lifelong learners and to make their classrooms more student-centered, collaborative, interdisciplinary, and interactive are increasingly turning to telecommunications networks and the global community. Webs of connected computers allow teachers and students from around the world to reach each other directly and gain access to quantities of information previously unimaginable. Students using networks learn and develop new inquiry and analytical skills in a stimulating environment and gain an increased appreciation of their role as world citizens. Sample Web sites

Figure 1.6
Beginning my professional resources file

A professional resources file is a project that you are advised to begin now and continue throughout your professional career. Begin your resources file either on a computer database program or on color-coded file cards that list (a) name of resource, (b) how and where to obtain the resource, (c) description of how to use the resource, and (d) evaluative comments about the resource.

Organize the file in a way that makes the most sense to you now. Cross-reference or color-code your system to accommodate the following categories of instructional aids and resources.

- Articles from print sources
- Compact disc titles
- Computer software titles
- Games
- Guest speakers and other community resources
- Internet resources
- Media catalogs
- Motivational ideas
- Photographs, pictures
- Posters, charts, graphs

- Resources to order
- Sources of free and inexpensive materials
- Student worksheets
- Test items
- Thematic units and ideas
- Unit and lesson plans and ideas
- Videocassette titles
- Videodisc titles
- Miscellaneous

and addresses are shown in Figure 1.7; others are indicated throughout this guide, such as in Figures 8.4 in Chapter 8 (especially for subject-specific sites) and Figure 10.2 in Chapter 10 (especially for sites about materials and technology). For a sample lesson plan illustrating student use of the Internet, see Figure 6.10 (Chapter 6).

THE EMERGENT OVERALL PICTURE

Certainly, no facet of education receives more attention from the media, causes more concern among parents, guardians, and teachers, or gets larger headlines than that of a decline (factual or fanciful) in students' achievement in the public schools. Reports are issued, polls taken, debates organized, and blue-ribbon commissions are formed. Community members write letters to local editors about it, news editors devote editorial space to it, television anchors comment about it, politicians use it, and documentaries and specials focus on it in full color. We read, "Students Play Catch-Up on Basic Skills," and "U.S. Students Lag Behind Other Nations," and so on. What initiated this attention that began more than a quarter-a-century ago and continues today? We are not sure, but it has never been matched in its political interest and participation, and it has affected and continues to affect both the public schools and the programs in higher education that are directly or indirectly related to teacher preparation and cer-

tification.[31] In the words of Mark Clayton, "teachers are being asked to teach more and achieve better results—all with a population that has never been more diverse or demanding."[32]

In response to the reports, educators, corporations and local businesspersons, and politicians act. Around the nation, their actions have resulted in

- Changes in standards for teacher certification.

For example, model standards describing what prospective teachers should know and be able to do to receive a teaching license were prepared and released in 1992 by the Interstate New Teacher Assessment and Support Consortium (INTASC), a project of the Council of Chief State School Officers (CCSSO), in a document entitled *Model Standards for Beginning Teacher Licensing and Development.* Representatives of at least 36 states and professional associations—including the National Education Association (NEA), the American Federation of Teachers (AFT), the American Association of Colleges for Teacher Education (AACTE), and the National Council for the Accreditation of Teacher Education (NCATE)—comprise the group. The standards are performance-based and revolve around a common core of principles of knowledge and skills that cut across disciplines. The INTASC standards were developed to be compatible with the National Board for Professional Teaching Standards (NBPTS).[33] Specifically addressing

Figure 1.7
Selected Internet sites for teachers and students

- *Artful Minds* <http://www.library.advanced.org/50072> Brain research, technology, art education resources
- *Biographical profiles of some 19th century African Americans* <http://www.brightmoments.com/blackhistory>
- *Catalog of School Reform Models* <http://www.nwrel.org/scpd/natspec/catalog>
- *Classroom Connect* <http://www.classroom.net/resource/> Resources for teachers; links to schools; lesson plan and project ideas
- *Council of the Great City Schools* <http://cgcs.org> Descriptions of programs and projects in large urban schools
- *Curriculum resources* <http://www.proteacher.com/>
- *EdIndex* <http://www.pitt.edu/~poole> Education links
- *Educational Web Design* <www.oswego.org/staff/cchamber/webdesign/edwebdesign.htm>
- *Education links* <http://www.execpc.com/~dboals/k–12.html> K–12 education links
- *Education World* <http://www.education-world.com> Electronic version of *Education Week*
- *Edsitement* <http://edsitement.neh.gov> Lesson plans and web connections for the humanities
- *ENC* <http://www.enc.org> Eisenhower National Clearinghouse for Mathematics and Science
- *E-Pals Classroom Exchange* <http://www.epals.com/index.html> Children can be matched with electronic pen pals in over 26,000 classrooms in more than 130 countries. See also *The Kidlink Network* <http://www.kidlink.org/english/general/index.html>
- *FedWorld* <http://www.fedworld.gov> Access to information from government agencies
- *GEM,* the Gateway to Educational Materials <http://www.thegateway.org/index.html> U.S. government's effort to provide access to Internet-based educational materials
- *GlobaLearn* <http://www.globalearn.org/> Students interact with remote expedition teams
- *Global Schoolnet Foundation* <http://www.gsn.org/> Global resources and links
- *GLOBE* (Global Learning and Observations to Benefit the Environment) *Program* <http://www.globe.gov> An international environmental science and education partnership
- *Go Math* <http://www.gomath.com>. Student on-line tutoring in mathematics
- *Homeschool Resources* <http://mint.net~caronfam/links.htm>
- *HomeworkCentral* <http://www.homeworkcentral.com> For lesson plans and subject research
- *Houghton Mifflin's Data Place* <http://www.eduplace.com/dataplace> Math projects for K–6. Membership necessary
- *Intercultural E-Mail Classroom Connections* <http://www.iecc.org/> A free service to help teachers and students link with classrooms from other countries and cultures.
- *Internet resources for teachers K–6* <http://www.csun.edu/~vceed009>
- *Kathy Schrock's Guide for Educators* <http://www.capecod.net/schrockguide/> Resources and information on education
- *Kwanzaa Information Center* <http://www.melanet.com/kwanzaa>
- *Latino Link* <http://www.latinolink.com/>
- *Learning Network* <http://www.learningnetwork.com> Wealth of educational resources for parents, teachers, and students
- *Library of Congress* <http://lcweb.loc.gov/homepage/lchp.html>
- *Microsoft Lesson Connection* <http://www.k12.msn.com>
- *MiddleWeb* <http://www.middleweb.com/> Middle school focus
- *National Consortium for School Networking* <http://cosn.org>
- *Novagate reference site* <http://www.novagate.com/novasurf/onlinereference.html>
- *Reading Is Fundamental* <http://www.rif.org>
- *Special Education Resources on the Internet (SERI)* <http://www.hood.edu/seri/serihome.html>
- *Study Web* <http://www.studyweb.com> Place to research topics
- *Teachers First* <http://www.teachersfirst.com> Resources for teachers
- *Teachers Helping Teachers* <http://www.pacificnet.net/~mandel/>
- *TEK Camp for Kids* <http://www.pawisland.com/mainmenu.html> Learning adventures for children to develop computer skills
- *Too Cool for Grownups* <http://www.tcfg.com/>
- *21st Century Teachers* <http://www.21ct.org> Teachers for teachers exchange
- *United Nations' CyberSchool Bus* <http://www.un.org/Pubs/CyberSchoolBus/> Curriculum units and projects, databases on United Nations member states, and global trends
- *United States Department of Education* <http://www.ed.gov/index.html>
- *Virtual Reference Desk, for Educators* <http://thorplus.lib.purdue.edu/reference/>
- *Voices of Youth* <http://www.unicef.org/voy/> Interactive for projects and information
- *Yahoo's Education Index* <http://www.yahoo.com/Education/tree.html>

standards for certification as an Early Childhood/ Generalist (ages 3–8) are the following 8 categories of standards: (a) understanding young children, (b) promoting child development and learning, (c) knowledge of integrated curriculum, (d) multiple teaching strategies for meaningful learning, (e) assessment, (f) reflective practice, (g) family partnerships, and (h) professional partnerships. For certification as a Middle Childhood/Generalist (ages 7–12) there are 11 categories of standards: (a) knowledge of students, (b) knowledge of content and curriculum, (c) learning environment, (d) respect for diversity, (e) instructional resources, (f) meaningful applications of knowledge, (g) multiple paths of knowledge, (h) assessment, (i) family involvement, (j) reflection, and (k) contributions to the profession.[34]

- Development of curriculum standards (see Chapter 5).
- Emphasis on education for cultural diversity and for ways of teaching language minority students.
- Emphasis on helping students make effective transitions from one level of schooling to the next and from school to life, with an increased focus on helping students connect what is being learned with real life as well as on making connections between subjects in the curriculum and between academics and vocations.
- Emphasis on rising test scores, reducing school dropout rates, increasing instructional time, and changing curricula.
- Formation of school-home-community connections.
- New requirements for a high school graduation.
- School restructuring to provide more meaningful curriculum options.

Key Trends and Practices Today

Key trends and practices today are listed in Figure 1.8.

Figure 1.8
Key trends and practices in today's elementary schools

- Dividing the student body and faculty into smaller cohorts, that is, the school-within-a school (SWAS) concept and using nontraditional scheduling and teaching teams.
- Facilitating students' social skills as they interact, relate to one another, solve meaningful problems, learn conflict-resolution, and develop relationships and peaceful friendships.
- Facilitating the development of students' values as related to their families, the community, and their school.
- Holding high expectations, but not necessarily the same expectations, for all students by establishing achievement targets and assessing results against those targets.
- Integrating the curriculum, especially with reading and the language arts.
- Involving parents and guardians in school decision making.
- Involving students in goal-setting and in self-assessment.
- Making multicultural education work for all students.
- Providing meaningful curriculum options with multiple pathways for academic success.
- Providing students with the time and the opportunity to think and be creative, rather than simply memorizing and repeating information.
- Redefining giftedness to include nonacademic as well as traditional academic abilities.
- Using heterogeneous grouping, cooperative learning, peer coaching, and cross-age tutoring as significant instructional strategies.
- Using the Internet in the classroom as a communication tool and learning resource.

Problems and Issues That Plague the Nation's Schools

Major problems and issues plaque our nation's schools, some of which are shown in Figure 1.9. Some of these are discussed in subsequent chap-

Figure 1.9
Problems and issues that plague the nation's
teachers and schools

- A demand for test scores and statistics that can be used to judge schools, with a concomitant controversy over the concept of grading schools and publishing the reports.
- Continuing controversy over books and their content.
- Continuing controversy over standardized norm-referenced testing.[35]
- Continuing, long-running controversy over values, morality, and sexuality education.
- Controversy created by the concept of teaching less content but teaching it better.
- Controversy over the development of a national curriculum with national assessments.[36]
- Continued controversy over traditional ability grouping or curriculum tracking.
- Controversy over the inclusion/exclusion of certain children from state mandatory testing.
- Identification and development of programs that recognize, develop, and nurture talents in all youth at all levels of education.[37]
- Low teacher salaries when compared with other college-educated workers.[38]
- Retention in grade versus social promotion.[39]
- Scarcity of teachers of color to serve as role models for minority children.[40]
- School buildings that are old and desperately in need of repair and updating.
- School security and the related problems of weapons, crime, violence, and drugs on school campuses and in school neighborhoods.[41]
- School populations that are too large.[42]
- Sexual harassment of students.[43]
- Shortage of male teachers, especially in the elementary schools.[44]
- Shortage of qualified teachers, especially in certain disciplines and in schools with high percentages of children at risk.
- Teaching and assessing for higher-order thinking skills.
- The education of teachers to work effectively with children who may be too overwhelmed by personal problems to focus on learning and to succeed in school.
- The expectation that teachers should teach more and with improved results, while with a population of students that has never been more diverse or demanding.
- The number of students at risk of dropping out of school.

ters (see index for topic locations). Perhaps you and members of your class can identify other issues and problems faced by our nation's schools.

When compared with traditional instruction, one of the characteristics of exemplary instruction today, as will be discussed throughout this resource guide, but especially in Chapter 6, is the teacher's en-

couragement of dialogue among children in the classroom as they discuss and explore their own ideas. As said in the Preface to this book, modeling the very behaviors we expect of teachers and children in the classroom is a constant theme throughout this text. For example, do Exercise 1.2 now to help start a dialogue as you begin your study of this book.

For Your Notes

EXERCISE 1.2 DIALOGUE WITH A TEACHER CANDIDATE

Instructions: The purpose of this exercise is to identify reasons other teacher candidates have selected teaching as a career goal. Select one teacher candidate, record that person's responses to the following questions, and share them with your class. (*Note to instructor:* This exercise could be used during the first week of your school term as an icebreaker.)

Date of interview _____   Name of interviewee _____

1. Why and when did you select elementary school teaching as a career? _____

_____

_____

_____

_____

_____

2. Do you look forward to being free from teaching during the summer? If so, what do you plan to

do during that time? _____

_____

_____

_____

_____

_____

3. Would you like to teach in a year-round school? Why or why not? _____

_____

_____

_____

_____

4. Are there any other teachers in your family? _____

_____

_____

_____

_____

5. Do you have a favorite grade level? a favorite subject? _____

_____

_____

_____

_____

EXERCISE 1.2 *(continued)*

6. Do you plan a lifetime career as a classroom teacher, or do you want eventually to move into a specialty or administrative position? _____

_____

_____

_____

_____

_____

7. How would you describe your current feelings about being a teacher? _____

_____

_____

_____

_____

_____

8. What specifically are you most looking forward to during this program of teacher preparation?

_____

_____

_____

_____

_____

9. What personal and professional characteristics do you feel you have that would make you an effective teacher? _____

_____

_____

_____

_____

_____

10. What else would you like to say about you and your feelings concerning the program so far? ____

_____

_____

_____

_____

_____

SUMMARY

In beginning to plan for developing your teaching competencies, you have read an overview of today's elementary schools and of the characteristics of some of the adults who work there, of trends and practices, and of problems and issues that continue to plague our nation's schools. That knowledge will be useful in your assimilation of the content explored in chapters that follow, beginning in the next chapter with the characteristics of elementary school children, how they learn, and strategies to use to effectively work with them.

Despite the many blue ribbon commissions, writers, and politicians that have and continue to vilify the failures of public school education, thousands of committed teachers, administrators, parents, and members of the community struggle daily, year after year, to provide students with a quality education.[45] Throughout the chapters of this text many exemplary schools and school programs are recognized and identified by name.

EXTENDING MY COMPETENCY: QUESTIONS FOR CLASS DISCUSSION _____

1. How would you be able to recognize an exemplary elementary school? Describe at least three characteristics you would expect to find in an exemplary elementary school. Explain why you have selected those particular characteristics.

2. Here is one elementary teacher's schedule. Read and discuss your reaction to it with your classmates.

   Rachael is a fifth-grade teacher in a low socioeconomic school within a moderately large city on the East Coast of the United States. The 34 students in her class include 10 limited-English speakers and 10 with identified learning problems. Some of the children have skills as low as those equivalent to first grade. In any given week, Rachael recycles newspapers and sells snacks to help pay for field trips because the school and the children cannot. On a typical school day recently, Rachael began her work at 7:10 a.m. with three parent conferences. The children arrived and school began at 8:15 and ran until 2:45 p.m. Rachael then tutored children until 3:30, conducted four more parent conferences, straightened her classroom and readied a few things for the next day, went home at 6:30 p.m., had dinner and then planned lessons, and read and marked papers for two hours before retiring for the night.

3. Divide your class into groups of no more than three per group. Assign each group to a particular age group (5–6, 7–8, 9–14). In a period of time, such as 15 minutes, each group is to brainstorm and list as many ways as they can that an elementary school classroom teacher could involve parents and guardians and other family members in their children's learning. Have each group share its results with the entire class.

4. From your point of view, what societal influences affect today's youth? Are crime, gangs, drugs, and images of professional athletes and musicians among those influences? Explain the effects. Research and identify what specifically, if anything, the elementary school classroom teacher should know to be able to effectively deal with the effects.

5. Have you experienced school dress codes? Some schools and districts have implemented uniform dress code policies. The theory is that a uniform dress code will reduce distractions and disruptions caused by variations in clothing; make economic disparities among children less obvious; promote student achievement by creating a more orderly learning environment; and enhance school safety and security. What is your opinion of such a program? Does a dress code policy stifle individuality? Might it erase the dangers caused by gang influence? Could it help identify people who belong on campus from those who do not? Can it stem the "one-up-manship" that pressures children? Can it be economically advantageous to parents and guardians? What happens to children if they continue to wear prohibited articles of clothing? Discuss with your classmates your thoughts and opinions about the topic.

6. As a class, identify specific techniques that elementary schools today are using in their efforts to help all children succeed in school. Divide your class into small groups (two or three students per group). Have each group assume responsibility for one or two of these techniques, finding out as much as possible about the technique, such as the extent to which it is being used, its history, successes, limitations, and so forth. Groups may wish to assume additional charges later when other strategies come to their attention as you delve deeper into this resource guide. Establish guidelines and a date for reporting results to the entire class later in the quarter or semester.

7. Explain why you believe you would or would not like to teach in an ungraded school.

8. Express your opinion on the following statement: It is not important that a child might complete elementary school education without ever having had a male or an ethnic minority teacher.

9. After reading Chapter 1, answer the following questions and share your answers with your classmates. Have your perceptions of teaching changed? What age/grade levels seem most appealing to you? Other than preparing for and obtaining your first teaching job, what is your primary short-term goal as a professional teacher? What is your primary long-term goal as a professional teacher? What kind of school setting and structure is most compatible with your goals?

10. Do you have other questions generated by the content of this chapter? If you do, list them along with ways to find the answers.

FOR FURTHER READING _____

Battista, M. T. (1999). The Mathematical Miseducation of America's Youth: Ignoring Research and Scientific Study in Education. *Phi Delta Kappan, 80*(6), 425–433.

Brandt, R. S. (Ed.). (2000). *Education in a New Era.* Alexandria, VA: Association for Supervision and Curriculum Development.

Buckley, F. J. (2000). *Team Teaching: What, Why, and How?* Thousand Oaks, CA: Sage.

Cawelti, G. (2000). Portrait of a Benchmark School. *Educational Leadership, 57*(5), 42–44.

Cooper, R. (1999). Success for All Schools, One at a Time. *Principal, 78*(3), 28–32.

Good, T. L. (1999). The Purposes of Schooling in America. Introduction. *Elementary School Journal, 99*(5), 383–389.

Goodlad, J. I. (1999). Teachers as Moral Stewards of Our Schools. *Journal for a Just and Caring Education, 5*(3), 237–241.

Manno, B. V., Finn, C. E., Jr., and Vanourek, G. (2000). Beyond the Schoolhouse Door: How Charter Schools Are Transforming U.S. Public Education. *Phi Delta Kappan, 81*(10), 736–744.

Schank, R. C. (2000). A Vision of Education for the 21st Century. *T·H·E Journal, 27*(6), 42–45.

Wahlstrom, K. L. (1999). The Prickly Politics of School Starting Times. *Phi Delta Kappan, 80*(5), 345–347.

Wang, M. C., Haertel, G. D., and Walberg, H. J. (1998). *Building Educational Resilience.* Fastback 430. Bloomington, IN: Phi Delta Kappa Educational Foundation.

NOTES _____

1. For further information on the Core Knowledge curriculum, see T. A. Mackley, *Uncommon Sense: Core Knowledge in the Classroom* (Alexandria, VA: Association for Supervision and Curriculum Development, 1999), or contact the Core Knowledge Foundation, 2012-B Morton Drive, Charlottesville, VA 22903, 800-238-3233. Visit the High Peaks Core Knowledge Elementary School at <http://bvsd.k12.co.us/schools/hp_mp/hp/information.htm#School%20Philosophy>.

2. See M. A. Dunn, Staying the Course of Open Education, *Educational Leadership, 57*(7), 20–24 (April 2000).

3. L. A. Mulholland and L. A. Bierlein, *Understanding Charter Schools,* Fastback 383 (Bloomington, IN: Phi Delta Kappa Educational Foundation, 1995), p. 7. Connect to the charter school home pages via the United States Charter School Web site at <http://www.uscharterschools.org/>. For additional information and for a copy of the *National Charter School Directory,* contact the Center for Education Reform (CER) at 800-521-2118, e-mail to cerdc@aol.com, or the Web site at <http://edreform.com/research/css9697.htm>. There are now even a few charter school districts, that is, where the entire district is comprised of charter schools. See, for example, D. H. Bowman, Nation's Largest Charter District, *Education Week, 19*(43), 3 (August 2, 2000).

4. See, for example, S. Maquire, A Community School, *Educational Leadership, 57*(6), 18–21 (March 2000); H. Raham, Full-Service Schools, *School Business Affairs, 64*(6), 24–28 (June 1998); and D. MacKenzie and V. Rogers, The Full Service School: A Management and Organizational Structure for 21st Century Schools, *Community Education Journal, 25*(3–4), 9–11 (Spring/Summer 1997).

5. Since 1997, IBO offers a Primary Years program for children ages 3 to 12, since 1992 a Middle Years program for students 11 to 16 years old, and since 1967 a Diploma program for students who are in their final two years of secondary school. See IBO's Web site at <http://www.ibo.org>.

6. See, for example, J. Zimmermann (Ed.), *The Comer School Development Program. Education Research Consumer Guide, Number 6* (Washington, DC: Office of Educational Research and Development, 1993); J. Comer, *Waiting for a Miracle* (New York: Dutton, 1997); and D. W. Woodruff, et al., Collaborating for Success: Merritt Elementary Extended School, *Journal of Education for Students Placed at Risk (JESPAR), 3*(1), 11–22 (1998).

7. National Middle School Association, *This We Believe: Developmentally Responsive Middle Schools* (Columbus, OH: Author, 1982, reissued in 1995).

8. For a book devoted exclusively to middle school teaching, see R. D. Kellough and N. G. Kellough, *Middle School Teaching: A Guide to Methods and Resources,* 3rd ed. (Upper Saddle River, NJ: Merrill/Prentice Hall, 1999).

9. K. Brooks and F. Edwards, *The Middle School in Transition: A Research Report on the Status of the Middle School Movement* (Lexington: College of Education, University of Kentucky, 1978). See, for example, the story of Oregon City High School, a ninth-grade-only school since 1990, in C. Paglin and J. Fager,

Grade Configuration: Who Goes Where? (Portland, OR: Northwest Regional Educational Laboratory, 1997), pp. 29–31, and, the Scott County Schools (Georgetown, KY) Ninth Grade Center, opened in 1996, on the Internet at <http://www.scott.k12.ky.us/9th/8thhistory.html>.

10. See, for example, D. A. Domenech, Success by Eight: A Program for 21st Century Schools, *Principal, 78*(4), 26–28, 30 (March 1999).

11. The classroom teacher to whom you are assigned during your field experience is referred to variously as the *cooperating teacher,* the *student-teaching supervising teacher,* or the *master teacher.* Throughout this resource guide, the term *cooperating teacher* is used.

12. See, for example, K. Rasmussen, Year-Round Education, *Education Update, 42*(2), 1, 3–5 (March 2000).

13. See, for example, K. Reeves, The Four-Day School Week, *School Administrator, 56*(3), 30–34 (March 1999).

14. M. H. Rosenbusch, *Guidelines for Starting an Elementary School Foreign Language Program* (Washington, DC: ERIC Clearinghouse for Assessment and Evaluation, 1995), ED 383227.

15. Sunset Elementary School is an International Studies Magnet School with language/culture programs of study in cooperation with the governments of France, Germany, and Spain. See the school's Web site at <http://cheyenne.rsmas.miami.edu/sunset/sunset.htm>.

16. To see how one state of Washington school added Spanish instruction for all its children grades K–5, see G. Ernst-Slavit and A. O. Pierce, Introducing Foreign Languages in Elementary School, *Principal, 77*(3), 31–33 (1998).

17. J. Reeves, *Elementary School Foreign Language Programs* (Washington, DC: ERIC Clearinghouse on Assessment and Evaluation, September 1989), ED 309652.

18. See, for example, D. L. Burke, *Looping: Adding Time, Strengthening Relationships* (Champaign, IL: ERIC Clearinghouse on Elementary and Early Childhood Education, 1997), ED414098; C. Forsten, J. Grant, and I. Richardson, Multiage and Looping: Borrowing from the Past, *Principal, 78*(4), 15–16, 18 (March 1999); and J. Grant, I. Richardson, and C. Forsten, In the Loop, *The School Administrator, 57*(1), 30–33 (January 2000).

19. B. J. Omotani and L. Omotani, Expect the Best, *Executive Educator, 18*(8), 27, 31 (March 1996).

20. See J. L. Doud and E. P. Keller, *The K–8 Principal in 1998: A 10-Year Study of the National Association of Elementary School Principals* (Alexandria, VA: NAESP, 1998).

21. P. L. Tiedt and I. M. Tiedt, *Multicultural Teaching: A Handbook of Activities, Information, and Resources,* 5th ed. (Boston: Allyn and Bacon, 1999), p. 35.

22. R. J. Rossi and S. C. Stringfield, What We Must Do for Students Placed at Risk, *Phi Delta Kappan, 77*(1), 73–76 (September 1995). See also the several related articles in the theme issue, The Changing Lives of Children, *Educational Leadership, 54*(7) (April 1997). Visit the home page of The National Institute on the Education of At-Risk Students at <http://www.ed.gov/offices/OERI/At-Risk/>.

23. See, for example, A. V. Shaver and R. T. Walls, Effect of Title I Parent Involvement on Student Reading and Mathematics Achievement, *Journal of Research and Development in Education, 31*(2), 90–97 (Winter 1998).

24. See P. Sullivan, The PTA's National Standards, *Educational Leadership, 55*(8), 43–44 (May 1998). For a copy of the standards contact the National PTA, 330 N. Wabash Ave., Chicago, IL 60611-3690, phone (312) 670-6782, fax (312) 670-6783.

25. See, for example, R. J. Nistler and A. Maiers, Stopping the Silence: Hearing Parents' Voices in an Urban First-Grade Family Literacy Program, *The Reading Teacher, 53*(8), 670–680 (May 2000).

26. See, for example, the Hand in Hand Web page at http://www.handinhand.org.

27. See, for example, T. Whiteford, Math for Moms and Dads, *Educational Leadership, 55*(8), 64–66 (May 1998).

28. See, for example, C. Gustafson, Phone Home, *Educational Leadership, 56*(2), 31–32 (October 1998).

29. See C. Bodinger-deUriarte, et al., *A Guide to Promising Practices in Educational Partnerships* (Washington, DC: U.S. Government Printing Office, 1996), ED392980, and the articles in the May 1998 theme issue, "engaging parents and the community in school," of *Educational Leadership,* vol. 55, no. 8.

30. See, for example, P. Sullivan, Big Help Gets Big Hand in Chicago, *Our Children, 24*(1), 21 (August/September 1998); T. M. Prosser and J. A. Levesque, Supporting Literacy Through Service Learning, *Reading Teacher, 51*(1), 32–38 (September 1997); and S. H. Billig, Research on K–12 School-Based Service Learning: The Evidence Builds, *Phi Delta Kappan, 81*(9), 658–664 (May 2000) and other related articles in the theme issue on service learning.

31. See, for example, G. I. Maeroff (Ed.), *Imaging Education: The Media and School in America* (New York: Teachers College Press, 1998), and the article by G. J. Cizek, Give Us This Day Our Daily Dread: Manufacturing Crises in Education, on the Phi Delta Kappa International Web site, <http://www.pdkintl.org/kappan/kciz9906.htm> (available December 12, 1999).

32. M. Clayton, The Goal: Great Teachers. The Plan: A Work in Progress, *The Christian Science Monitor Electronic Edition* [Online] <http://www.csmonitor.com/sections/learning/revnschools/p-1story0420.html> (available April 6, 2000).

33. For copies of the INTASC document, contact CCSSO, One Massachusetts Ave. NW, Suite 700, Washington, DC 20001, 202-408-5505, <http://www.ccsso.org.>

34. Access the standards via Internet <http://www.nbpts.org./nbpts>. You may want to compare the standards with the 22 competencies that are identified in Chapter 3 of this resource guide and with the 22 "components of professional practice" in C. Danielson,

Enhancing Professional Practice: A Framework for Teaching (Alexandria, VA: Association for Supervision and Curriculum Development, 1996).

35. See, for example, A. Kohn, Raising the Scores, Ruining the Schools, *American School Board Journal, 186*(10), 31–34 (October 1999).

36. See, for example, S. Ohanian, *One Size Fits All: The Folly of Educational Standards* (Portsmouth, NH: Heinemann, 1999), and S. Ohanian, Goals 2000: What's in a Name? *Phi Delta Kappan, 81*(5), 233–255 (January 2000).

37. See, for example, J. Fulkerson and M. Horvich, Talent Development: Two Perspectives, and J. VanTassel-Baska, The Development of Academic Talent, both in *Phi Delta Kappan, 79*(10), 756–759 and 760–763 (respectively) (June 1998).

38. See, for example, D. J. Hoff, International Report Finds U.S. Teacher Salaries Lagging, and J. Blair, Honored Teachers Want More Pay and Respect, *Education Week, 19*(36), 5 and 11 (respectively) (May 17, 2000).

39. See, for example, K. Kelly, Retention vs. Social Promotion: Schools Search for Alternatives, *The Harvard Education Letter, 15*(1), 1–3 (January/February 1999).

40. See, for example, The Need for Minority Teachers in P. R. Rettig and M. Khodavandi, *Recruiting Minority Teachers: The UTOP Program,* Fastback 436 (Bloomington, IN: Phi Delta Kappa Educational Foundation, 1998).

41. Intended to alert teachers and parents to the warning signs exhibited by troubled children is *Early Warning-Time Response: A Guide to Safe Schools.* Written by the National Association of School Psychologists and released in August 1998, the guide is available free by calling 1-877-4ED-PUBS or from the Internet at <http://www.ed.gov/offices/OSERS/OSEP/earlywrn.html>.

42. Research repeatedly indicates that small schools (less than 400 students for an elementary school) are at least equal to and often superior to large ones on most measures. See K. Cotton, School Size, School Climate, and Student Performance, *Close-Up Number, 20* (Portland, OR: Northwest Regional Educational Laboratory, 1996) [Online 2/10/00] <http://www.nwrel.org/scpd/sirs/10/c020.html>.

43. A useful document for schools is L. A. Brown, et al., *Student-Student Sexual Harassment: A Legal Guide for Schools* (Alexandria, VA: Council of School Attorneys, National School Boards Association, 1998).

44. See, for example, K. Vail, A Few Good Men, *American School Board Journal, 186*(10), 28–30 (October 1999).

45. For example, you can read many positive findings in *Do You Know the Good News About American Education?* published in 2000 by the Center on Education Policy (CEP) and the American Youth Policy Forum. The document can be downloaded from CEP's Web site at <http://www.ctredpol.org>.

2

What Do I Need to Know About Elementary School Children: The Nature of the Challenge?

The bell rings, and the children enter your classroom, a kaleidoscope of personalities, all unexampled and idiosyncratic, each a packet of energy, with different focuses, experiences, dispositions, and learning capacities, differing proficiencies in the verbal and written use of the English language; in other words, all different challenges. Indeed, what a challenge this is: to understand and to teach 30 or so unique individuals, all at once, and to do it for 6 hours a day, 5 days a week, 180 or more days a year! What a challenge it is today, to be an elementary school teacher, whether you are teaching 5-year-olds in kindergarten or 11-year-olds in the sixth grade.

To prepare yourself for this challenge, consider the information provided in this chapter

---

A Humorous Scenario Related to Idioms: A Teachable Moment

While Lina, a third-grade student, was reciting she had a little difficulty with her throat (due to a cold) and stumbled over some words. The student teacher jokingly commented, "That's okay Lina, you must have a horse in your throat." Quickly, Monique, a recent immigrant student asked, "How could she have a horse in her throat?" The teacher ignored Monique's question. Missing this teachable moment, she continued with her planned lesson.

---

about the diverse characteristics and needs of elementary school children for it is well known that for them, their academic achievement is greatly dependent on how well their other developmental needs are understood and satisfied.

CHAPTER OBJECTIVES

Specifically, upon completion of this chapter you will be able to demonstrate

1. An awareness of appropriate curriculum options and instructional practices for specific groups of children.
2. An understanding of and appreciation for the concept and importance of multicultural education.
3. An understanding of the concept of character education and ways of teaching for positive character development.
4. An understanding of the developmental characteristics of elementary school children and their implications for appropriate practice.
5. An understanding of the significance of the concepts of learning modalities, learning styles, and learning capacities, and their implications for appropriate practice.
6. An understanding of the three-phase learning cycle and types of learning activities that might occur in each phase.
7. Your developing knowledge of practical ways of attending to individual differences while working with a cohort of students.
8. Your knowledge of the characteristics of children who are abused, and your obligation as a teacher when child abuse is suspected.

DIMENSIONS OF THE CHALLENGE

At any age children differ in many ways: physical characteristics, interests, home life, intellectual ability, learning capacities, motor ability, social skills, aptitudes and talents, language skills, experience, ideals, attitudes, needs, ambitions, hopes, and dreams. Having long recognized the importance of these individual differences, educators have made many attempts to develop systematic programs of individualized and personalized instruction. In the 1920s there were the "programmed" workbooks of the Winetka Plan. The 1960s brought a multitude of plans, such as IPI (Individually Prescribed Instruction), IGE (Individually Guided Education), and PLAN (Program for Learning in Accordance with Needs). The 1970s saw the development and growth in popularity of individual learning packages and the Individualized Education Program (IEP) for students with special needs. Although some of these efforts did not survive the test of time, others met with more success; some have been refined and are still being used. Today, for example, some schools report success using personalized learning plans for all students, not only those with special needs.[1]

Furthermore, for a variety of reasons (e.g., learning styles and learning capacities, modality preferences, information-processing habits, motivational factors, and physiological factors) all persons learn in their own ways and at individual rates. Interests, background, innate and acquired abilities, and a myriad of other influences shape how and what a person will learn. From any particular learning experience no two persons ever learn exactly the same thing.

The Classroom in a Nation of Diversity

Central to the challenge is the concept of **multicultural education,** the recognition and acceptance of students from a variety of backgrounds. The goal of this concept is to provide schooling so that all children—male and female students, students with disabilities, and students who are members of diverse racial, ethnic, and cultural groups—have equal opportunity to achieve academically. In the words of James A. Banks

> Schools should be model communities that mirror the kind of democratic society we envision. In democratic schools the curriculum reflects the cultures of the diverse groups within society, the languages and dialects that students speak are respected and valued, cooperation rather than competition is fostered among students and students

from diverse racial, ethnic and social-class groups are given equal status in the school.[2]

The variety of individual differences among students requires that teachers use teaching strategies and tactics that accommodate those differences. To most effectively teach a diverse group of students, you need skills in (a) establishing a classroom climate in which all students feel welcome and they can learn and are supported in doing so (topic of Chapter 4), (b) techniques that emphasize cooperative and social-interactive learning and that deemphasize competitive learning (topic of Chapter 8), (c) building upon students' learning styles, capacities, and modalities, and (d) strategies and techniques that have proven successful for students of specific differences. The last two are topics of this chapter.

To help you meet the challenge a wealth of information is available. As a licensed teacher you are expected to know it all, or at least to know where you can find all necessary information, and to review it when needed. Certain information you have stored in memory will surface and become useful at the most unexpected times. While concerned about all students' safety and physical well-being, you will want to remain sensitive to each child's attitudes, values, social adjustment, emotional well-being, and intellectual development. You must be prepared not only to teach one or more subjects but also to do it effectively with children of different cultural backgrounds, diverse linguistic abilities, and different learning styles, as well as with students who have been identified as having special needs because of handicapping conditions. It is, indeed, a challenge! The statistics that follow make even more clear this challenge.

The traditional two-parent, two-child family now constitutes only about 6 percent of U.S. households. Approximately one-half of the children in the United States will spend some years being raised by a single parent. Many children go home after school to places devoid of any adult supervision. And, on any given day, tens of thousands of children are homeless, that is, they have no place at all to call home.

By the middle of this century, the nation's population is predicted to reach 383 million (from 2000's approximately 282 million), a population boom that will be led by Hispanics and Asian Americans. While, by then, minority youths in the school-age population throughout the United States will average close to 40 percent, a steady increase in interracial marriages and interracial babies may challenge the traditional conceptions of multiculturalism and race.[3]

The United States truly is a multilingual, multiethnic, multicultural nation. Of children ages 5–7, approximately one out of every six speaks a language other than English at home. Many of those children have only limited proficiency in the English language (i.e., conversational speaking ability only). In many large school districts, as many as one hundred languages are represented, with as many as twenty or more different primary languages found in some classrooms. An increasing ethnic, cultural, and linguistic diversity is affecting schools all across the country, not only the large urban areas but also suburbs and small rural communities.

The overall picture that emerges is a rapidly changing, diverse student population that challenges teaching skills. Teachers who traditionally have used direct instruction (see Chapter 6) as the dominant mode of instruction have done so with the assumption that their students were relatively homogeneous in terms of experience, background, knowledge, motivation, and facility with the English language. However, no such assumption can be made today. As a classroom teacher for the 21st century, you must be knowledgeable and skilled in using teaching strategies that recognize, celebrate, and build upon the cultural, ethnic, and linguistic diversity of the classroom, the community, and the nation. In a nutshell, that is your challenge.

SUPPORTING THE CHALLENGE: STYLES OF LEARNING AND IMPLICATIONS FOR TEACHING

Classroom teachers who are most effective are those who adapt their teaching styles and methods to their students, using approaches that interest the children, that are neither too easy nor too difficult, that match the students' learning styles and learning capacities, and that are relevant to the children's lives. This adaptation process is further complicated because each child is different from every other one. All do not have the same interests, abilities, backgrounds, or learning styles and capacities. As a matter of fact, not only do children differ from one another, but also each child can change to some extent from one day to the next. What appeals to a child today may not have the same appeal tomorrow. Therefore, as teacher you need to consider both the nature of children in general (for example, methods appropriate for a particular group of children in kindergarten are unlikely to be the same as those that work best for a group of sixth graders) and each child in particular. As a student of a teacher preparation program you probably have already experienced a recent course in the psychology of learning; what follows is merely a brief synopsis of knowledge about and relevant to today's teaching and learning.

Learning Modalities

Learning modality refers to *the sensory portal* (or input channel) by which a person prefers to receive sensory reception (modality preference), or the actual way a person learns best (modality adeptness). Some children prefer learning by seeing, a *visual modality;* others prefer learning through instruction from others (through talk), an *auditory modality*; while many others prefer learning by doing and being physically involved, the *kinesthetic modality,* and by touching objects, the *tactile modality.* A person's modality preference is not always that person's modality strength.

While primary modality strength can be determined by observing children, it can also be mixed and it can change as the result of experience and intellectual maturity. The way a child learned best when in the first grade, for example, is not necessarily the child's modality strength now that the same child is in the fourth grade. As one might suspect, modality integration (i.e., engaging more of the sensory input channels, using several modalities at once or staggered) has been found to contribute to better achievement in student learning. We return to this concept in Part II of this resource guide.

Because many children have neither a preference nor a strength for auditory reception, elementary schoolteachers should severely limit their use of the lecture method of instruction, that is, of placing too much reliance on formal teacher talk (discussed in Chapter 9). Furthermore, instruction that uses a singular approach, such as auditory (e.g., talking to the students), cheats students who learn better another way, kinesthetic and visual learners for example.

Finally, if a teacher's verbal communication conflicts with the teacher's nonverbal messages, children can become confused, and this too can affect their learning. And when there is a discrepancy between what the teacher says and what that teacher does, the teacher's nonverbal signal will win every time. Actions do speak louder than words![4] A teacher, for example, who has just finished a lesson on the conservation of energy and does not turn off the room lights upon leaving the classroom for lunch, has, by inappropriate modeling behavior, created cognitive disequilibrium and sabotaged the real purpose for the lesson. Or, a teacher who asks children to not interrupt others when they are on task but who repeatedly interrupts children when they are on task, is confusing children with that teacher's contradictory words and behavior. A teacher's job is not that of confusing children.

As a general rule, most elementary school children prefer and learn best by touching objects, by feeling shapes and textures, by interacting with each other, and by moving things around. In contrast, learning by sitting and listening are difficult for many of them.

Learning style traits are known that significantly discriminate between students who are underachieving and at risk of not finishing school (discussed in Chapter 1) and students who perform well. Students who are underachieving and at risk need (a) frequent opportunities for mobility, (b) options and choices, (c) a variety of instructional resources, environments, and sociological groupings, (d) to learn during late morning and afternoon, rather than in the early morning, (e) informal seating, rather than wooden, steel, or plastic chairs, (f) low illumination, and (g) tactile/visual introductory resources reinforced by kinesthetic (i.e., direct experiencing and whole-body activities)/visual resources, or introductory kinesthetic/visual resources reinforced by tactile/visual resources.[5] As an example, at one problem school, after discovering that nearly two-thirds of its students were either tactile or kinesthetic learners, teachers and administrators grouped the children according to their modality strengths and altered the reading instruction schedules every three weeks so that each group of children had opportunities to learn at the best time of day. As a result, student behavior, learning achievement, and attitudes improved considerably.[6]

Regardless of grade level and subject(s) you intend to teach, you are advised to use strategies that integrate the modalities. When well designed, thematic units (discussed in Chapters 5 and 6) and project-based learning (Chapter 8) incorporate modality integration. In conclusion, then, when teaching any group of children of mixed learning abilities, mixed modality strengths, mixed language proficiency, and mixed cultural backgrounds, for the most successful teaching the integration of learning modalities is a must.

Learning Styles

Related to learning modality is **learning style,** which can be defined as independent forms of knowing and processing information. While some elementary school children may be comfortable with beginning their learning of a new idea in the abstract (e.g., visual or verbal symbolization), most need to begin with the concrete (e.g., learning by actually doing it)—see the section, Learning

Experiences Ladder, in Chapter 6. Many students prosper while working in groups, while others do not and prefer to work alone. Some are quick in their studies, whereas others are slow and methodical and cautious and meticulous. Some can sustain attention on a single topic for a long time, becoming more absorbed in their study as time passes. Others are slower starters and more casual in their pursuits but are capable of shifting with ease from topic to topic, and from subject to subject. Some can study in the midst of music, noise, or movement, whereas others need quiet, solitude, and a desk or table. The point is this: Learners vary not only in their skills and preferences in the way knowledge is received, but also in how they mentally process that information once it has been received. The latter is a person's style of learning. Learning style is not an indicator of intelligence, but rather an indicator of how a person learns.

Classifications of Learning Styles

Although there are probably as many types of learning styles as there are individuals, two major differences in how people learn are in how they perceive situations and how they process information.[7] On the basis of perceiving and processing and earlier work by Carl Jung on psychological types,[8] Bernice McCarthy identifies four major learning styles, presented in the following paragraphs.[9]

The *imaginative learner* perceives information concretely and processes it reflectively. Imaginative learners learn well by listening and sharing with others, integrating the ideas of others with their own experiences. They often have difficulty adjusting to traditional teaching, which depends less on classroom interactions and students' sharing and connecting of their prior experiences. In a traditional classroom, the imaginative learner is likely to be an at-risk student.

The *analytic learner* perceives information abstractly and processes it reflectively. The analytic learner prefers sequential thinking, needs details, and values what experts have to offer. Analytic learners do well in traditional classrooms.

The *commonsense learner* perceives information abstractly and processes it actively. The commonsense learner is pragmatic and enjoys hands-on learning. They sometimes find school frustrating unless they can see immediate use to what is being learned. In the traditional classroom, the commonsense learner is likely to be a learner who is at risk of not completing school, of dropping out.

The *dynamic learner* perceives information concretely and processes it actively. The dynamic learner also prefers hands-on learning and is excited by anything new. They are risk takers and are frustrated by learning if they see it as being tedious and sequential. In a traditional classroom, the dynamic learner also is likely to be an at-risk student.

The Three-Phase Learning Cycle

To understand conceptual development and change, researchers in the 1960s developed a Piaget-based theory of learning where students are guided from concrete, hands-on learning experiences to the abstract formulations of concepts and their formal applications. This theory became known as the three-phase learning cycle.[10] Long a popular strategy for teaching science, the learning cycle can be useful in language arts and other disciplines as well.[11]

The three phases of the learning cycle are (a) the *exploratory hands-on phase,* where students can explore ideas and experience assimilation and disequilibrium that lead to their own questions and tentative answers, (b) the *invention* or *concept development phase,* where, under the guidance of the teacher, students invent concepts and principles that help them answer their questions and reorganize their ideas, that is, the students revise their thinking to allow the new information to fit, and (c) the *expansion* or *concept application phase,* another hands-on phase where the students try out their new ideas by applying them to situations that are relevant and meaningful to them. During application of a concept the learner may discover new information which causes a change in the learner's understanding of the concept being applied. Thus, as discussed further in Chapter 9, the process of learning is cyclical.[12]

There have been more recent interpretations or modifications of the three-phase cycle, such as McCarthy's 4MAT.[13] With the 4MAT system teachers employ a learning cycle of instructional strategies to try and reach each student's learning style. As stated by McCarthy, in the cycle learners

> sense and feel, they experience, then they watch, they reflect, then they think, they develop theories, then they try out theories, they experiment. Finally, they evaluate and synthesize what they have learned in order to apply it to their next similar experience. They get smarter. They apply experience to experiences.[14]

And, in this process they are likely to be using all four learning modalities.

The *constructivist learning theory* suggests learning is a process involving the active engagement of learners who adapt the educative event to fit and expand their individual world view (as opposed to the behaviorist pedagogical assumption that learning is something done to learners)[15] and to accentuate the importance of student self-assessment. In support of that theory, some variations of the learning cycle include a fourth phase of assessment. However, because we believe that assessment of what students know or think they know should be a continual process, permeating all three phases of the learning cycle, we reject any treatment of assessment as a self-standing phase.

Learning Capacities: The Theory of Multiple Intelligences

In contrast to learning styles, Gardner introduced what he calls *learning capacities* exhibited by individuals in differing ways.[16] Originally and sometimes still referred to as *multiple intelligences,* or *ways of knowing,* capacities thus far identified are:

- *Bodily/kinesthetic:* ability to use the physical body fluidly and skillfully
- *Interpersonal:* ability to understand people and relationships
- *Intrapersonal:* ability to assess one's emotional life as a means to understand oneself and others
- *Logical/mathematical:* ability to handle chains of reasoning and to recognize patterns and orders, to work with numbers
- *Musical:* ability to perceive sounds, tones, rhythms, pitch, and variations of these; the ability to sing or to play a musical instrument
- *Naturalist:* ability to draw on materials and features of the natural environment to solve problems or fashion products
- *Verbal/linguistic:* ability to learn and recognize distinctions among words, sounds, and language
- *Visual/spatial:* ability to perceive images and to manipulate the nature of space, such as through architecture, mime, or sculpture.

As discussed earlier, and as implied in the presentation of McCarthy's four types of learners, many educators believe that many students who are at risk of not completing school are those who may be dominant in a cognitive learning style that is not in synch with traditional teaching methods. Traditional methods are largely of McCarthy's analytic style: Information is presented in a logical, linear, sequential fashion. Traditional methods also reflect three of the Gardner types: verbal/linguistic, logical/mathematical, and intrapersonal. Consequently, to better synchronize methods of instruction with learning styles, some teachers and schools, such as Essex Modern Languages Elementary Magnet School (Akron, OH), have restructured the curriculum, instruction, and assessment around Gardner's learning capacities[17] or around Sternberg's Triarchic

Figure 2.1
Classroom vignette: Using the theory of learning capacities (multiple intelligences) and multilevel instruction

In one fourth-grade classroom, during one week of a six-week thematic unit on weather, students were concentrating on learning about the water cycle. For this study of the water cycle, with the students' help the teacher divided the class into several groups of three to five students per group. While working on six projects simultaneously to learn about the water cycle:

- One group of students designed, conducted, and repeated an experiment to discover the number of drops of water that can be held on one side of a new one-cent coin versus the number that can be held on the side of a worn one-cent coin
- Working in part with the first group, a second group designed and prepared graphs to illustrate the results of the experiments of the first group
- A third group of students created and composed the words and music of a song about the water cycle
- A fourth group incorporated their combined interests in mathematics and art to design, collect the necessary materials, and create a colorful and interactive bulletin board about the water cycle
- A fifth group read about the water cycle in materials they researched from the Internet and various libraries
- A sixth group created a puppet show about the water cycle

On Friday, after each group had finished, the groups shared their projects with the class.

Theory.[18] Sternberg identifies seven metaphors for the mind and intelligence (geographic, computational, biological, epistemological, anthropological, sociological, and systems) and proposes a theory of intelligence consisting of three elements: analytical, practical, and creative.[19]

See the sample classroom scenario shown in Figure 2.1. Internet resources on learning styles and learning capacities are shown in Figure 2.2. From the preceding information about learning styles you must realize at least two facts:

1. *Intelligence is not a fixed or static reality, but can be learned, taught, and developed.* Both you and your students must understand that intelligence is not a fixed entity, but a set of characteristics that, through a feeling of "I can" and with proper coaching, can be developed. When children understand that intelligence is incre-

Figure 2.2
Internet resources on learning styles and learning capacities

- ERIC link to multiple intelligences resources at <http://www.indiana.edu/~eric_rec/ieo/bibs/multiple.html>
- Howard Gardner's Project Zero Web site at <http://pzweb.harvard.edu/HPZpages/Whatsnew.html>
- Resources on learning styles at <http://www.d.umn.edu/student/loon/acad/strat/lrnsty.html>

mental, something that is developed through use over time, they tend to be more motivated to work at learning than when they believe intelligence is a fixed entity.[20]

2. *Not all children learn and respond to learning situations in the same way.* A child may learn differently according to the situation or according to the child's ethnicity, cultural background, or socioeconomic status.[21] A teacher who, for all students, uses only one style of teaching, or who teaches to only one or a few styles of learning, day after day, is short-changing those students who learn better another way. As emphasized by Rita Dunn, when children do not learn the way we teach them, then we must teach them the way they learn.[22]

MEETING THE CHALLENGE: RECOGNIZING AND PROVIDING FOR STUDENT DIFFERENCES

From research and practical experience have come a variety of instructional techniques that make a difference. First consider the following general guidelines, most of which are discussed in further detail in later chapters as designated.

Instructional Practices That Provide for Student Differences: General Guidelines

To provide learning experiences that are consistent with what is known about ways of learning and knowing, consider the recommendations that follow and refer to them during the preactive phase of your instruction (discussed in Chapter 3).

- As frequently as is appropriate, and especially for skills development, plan the learning activities so they follow a step-by-step sequence from concrete to abstract (see the section, The Learning Experiences Ladder, in Chapter 6).
- Collaboratively plan with students challenging and engaging classroom learning activities and assignments (see especially Chapters 5, 6, 8, and 9).

- Concentrate on using student-centered instruction by using project-centered learning, discovery and inquiry strategies, simulations, and role-play (Chapters 8 and 9).
- Establish multiple learning centers within the classroom (Chapter 8).
- Maintain high expectations, but not necessarily identical, for every student; establish high standards and teach toward them without wavering (see throughout book).
- Make learning meaningful by integrating learning with life, helping each child successfully make the transitions from one level of learning to the next, one level of schooling to the next (see throughout the book).
- Provide a structured learning environment with regular and understood procedures (Chapter 4).
- Provide ongoing and frequent monitoring of individual student learning (that is, formative assessment as discussed in Chapter 11).
- Provide variations in meaningful assignments that are based on individual student abilities and interests (Chapter 8).
- Use direct instruction to teach to the development of skills for thinking and learning (Chapters 6 and 9).
- Use reciprocal peer coaching and cross-age tutoring (Chapter 8).
- Use multilevel instruction (see Figure 2.1 and also Chapter 3 and others).
- Use interactive computer programs and multimedia (Chapter 10).
- Use small-group and cooperative learning strategies (Chapter 8).

Developmental Characteristics of Children of Particular Age Groups

After many years of experience and research, experts have come to accept certain precepts about children of particular ages, regardless of their individual genetic or cultural differences. For each of the three elementary school age groups, the characteristics are presented here in four developmental categories: physical, social, emotional, and cognitive. Before going further, begin Exercise 2.1.

For Your Notes

EXERCISE 2.1   OBTAINING PERSONAL INSIGHT REGARDING THE AGE OR GRADE LEVEL THAT I MIGHT PREFER TO TEACH

Instructions: Because of the age and developmental diversity of children in grades K–6, the purpose of this exercise is to challenge you to begin thinking about the grade or age level at which you might prefer to teach.

1. As you read the developmental characteristics (pages 41 through 44), in front of each numbered item mark a plus or a minus sign, depending on the extent to which that item matters to you (plus (+) means it matters a lot; minus (−) means it does not matter to you).

2. After reading and marking all items with either a plus or a minus, for each category identify the percentage of plus and the percentage of minus signs for the category. Complete the calculations as follows: For the category *ages 5–6* there are 35 items. Dividing the number of plus signs that you gave for these by the number 35 provides the percentage of plus signs given for that category. Subtracting that percentage number from 100 provides the percentage of minus signs for the category. Continue for each of the other two categories, *ages 7–8* with its 36 items and *ages 9–14* with 43 items. Place the percentages in the blanks:

   Ages 5–6 percentage plus signs = _____

   Ages 7–8 percentage plus signs = _____

   Ages 9–14 percentage plus signs = _____

3. The category that received your highest percentage of plus signs is ages _____ . Would you concur that you have a preference toward teaching at this level? Yes or no? (circle one) Explain why or why not.

4. Compare and discuss your results of this exercise with those of your classmates. What generalizations, if any, can be made from your individual results and collective discussion?

For Your Notes

Children in the Early Primary Years (Ages 5 and 6)[23]

Physical development.   Children of ages 5 and 6 tend to:

1. Be agile but vary greatly in height and weight.
2. Be able to hop, skip, climb, jump, run, and dance.
3. Begin participating in sports such as bicycling, skiing, swimming, skating, and gymnastics.
4. Be willing to try new things even if they stumble while doing them.
5. Be able to dress themselves, although they may still have difficulty tying their shoelaces.
6. Have developed their fine motor skills so they can write, although not necessarily always on the line or in a restricted space. Their letters are not uniform, and letter reversals are common.
7. Be able to draw a crude human figure, remember a simple story, and carry a simple melody, although the range in ability is wide.
8. Begin cutting their permanent teeth, especially by age 6.

Social development.   Children of ages 5 and 6 tend to:

1. Be outgoing, self-assured, and socially conforming.
2. Form friendships in school.
3. Be sure of themselves.
4. Want to protect younger children.
5. Move easily in and out of small groups.
6. Be cooperative and helpful.
7. Be able to assume and carry out small tasks in classroom maintenance and can become quite interested in helping with classroom chores.
8. Work together, although six-year-olds become more assertive and sometimes even bossy. Six-year-olds like to make rules and are rather dogmatic about having them obeyed. They also tend to change the rules frequently and become tattletales if the rules are not obeyed.
9. Become conscious of sex differences but work together regardless of gender. However, by the end of age 6, depending on many other factors, girls and boys may insist that certain behaviors are not appropriate for the other sex.
10. Be eager to participate in games but with a strong desire to win. They may tend to pout when losing but will quickly recover from their disappointments and go on to play some more.
11. Seek affection and applause.
12. Be proud of their possessions and accomplishments.
13. Be persistent about completing tasks.

Emotional development.   Children of ages 5 and 6 tend to:

1. Go through periods of emotional ups and downs. Five-year-olds are beginning to be able to express their feelings in socially accepted ways. But by age 6, the somewhat placid 5-year-old may have turned into a child in emotional ferment. Some 6-year-olds often have stormy relations with their parents and threaten to run away; others become more competent and more stable and have more confidence in people.
2. Enjoy humor, and giggle, whisper, and act silly at times.
3. Become aware of their emotions and are sometimes alarmed and puzzled by the conflicting feelings they have.
4. Learn to wait their turn, share, and lose in games they so desperately want to win. They are learning to control their self-centered feelings and to wait to have their needs met.
5. Be able to understand right from wrong.

Cognitive development.   Children of ages 5 and 6 tend to:

1. Ask questions and acquire many intellectual and academic skills, becoming aware, for example, that symbols have meanings and that there is a technique for figuring out these symbols.
2. Become interested in the rudimentary skills of reading and writing words that before were only spoken.
3. Have an increased vocabulary.
4. Begin to learn new concepts from the printed page, though the rate at and manner in which children learn this skill vary greatly. A few 5-year-olds can read beyond their experiential background, while others are 8 before they are comfortable with reading.
5. Like to act out favorite stories and involve themselves physically as well as mentally while reading (especially 6-year-olds). For example, many need a finger or a marker to follow a line of text. They need to say the words out loud to understand their meaning.
6. Be interested in numbers and be able to do similar concrete problems. They can and do memorize number facts, though they still need a great many concrete examples before developing more abstract numerical concepts.
7. Have difficulty with concepts of time and space, although they do have a sense of their own past and future. Six-year-olds are especially interested in their parents' past, although they might confuse it with ancient history. Children of this age tend not to be able to

connect with the concepts and sequences of historical time and large numbers.
8. Become more literal and factual but still believe in (or pretend to believe in) Santa Claus, the Easter Bunny, and the Tooth Fairy.
9. Know their colors.

Children In the Late Primary Years (Ages 7 and 8)[24]

Physical development.   Children of ages 7 and 8 tend to:

1. Vary greatly in height and weight, while their rate of growth slows.
2. Be almost always hungry.
3. Be almost always on the go, perform physical skills for game playing, and enjoy team sports and feats that require daring and courage.
4. Be willing to repeat a skill over and over to mastery, although they also can dash from one activity to another.
5. Increase their fine-motor performance.
6. Have sudden spurts of energy but leave some activities uncompleted.
7. Continue losing their first teeth while permanent teeth appear.
8. Change in physique, with their bodies becoming more proportionately developed. They become awkward and clumsy in some ways yet poised and graceful in others.

Social development.   Children of ages 7 and 8 tend to:

1. Begin to prefer their own sex, with less cross-gender interaction; they are aware of distinctions between the interests of others.
2. Become more cooperative in group work.
3. Become secure in gender identification.
4. Be self-absorbed yet need people to talk to at times.
5. Work and play independently.
6. Still be learning to be good sports when they lose.
7. Still be quarrelsome and poor losers at age 7, but begin taking turns with a sense of fairness.
8. Be conscientious, more self-reliant, and able to take responsibility for routine classroom chores.
9. Be less jealous and selfish and more able to share. They also want praise and try to please.
10. Become more realistic yet continue to enjoy and engage in fantasy play.

Emotional development.   Children of ages 7 and 8 tend to:

1. Have difficulty in starting things but once started will persist to the end. They are ready to tackle new projects.
2. Worry that school might be too difficult.
3. Begin to display empathy, to see others' viewpoint, and to improve in their manners, although they can be critical of others.
4. Like games, tricks, and "putting one over" on someone.
5. Discriminate between bad and good, although they are still immature.
6. Display a sense of possession and take care of their possessions.

Cognitive development.   Children of ages 7 and 8 tend to:

1. Be actively curious and able to display a longer attention span.
2. Be able to play and stay at a task or a project over a longer period of time. They are speedy in some responses.
3. Be interested in conclusions and logical ends.
4. Like to listen to adult conversations sometimes.
5. Be aware of their community and the world, becoming increasingly aware of money, property, possessions, and ownership.
6. Enjoy exploring the unfamiliar, being interested in the inner workings of such things as mechanisms, the human body, and so on.
7. Read with greater regard for meaning by age 7 (usually) and enjoy reading (rather than being read to) by age 8. Comic books, books with humor, fairy tales, and adventure stories are favorites.
8. Have an increasing sense of time in terms of months and years.
9. Be interested in other time periods and in trips to unfamiliar places.
10. Be conscious of others' work and their own, and enjoy bartering, swapping, and starting collections, playing games, and sending and receiving correspondence.
11. Display widening differences in abilities.
12. Be able to express themselves orally and in writing, even rather poetically, often with a sense of humor.

Young Adolescents (Ages 9 to 14)[25]
Nine to 14 is the age range of young adolescents, children of upper elementary and middle school or junior high school.

Physical development.   Young adolescents tend to:

1. Be self-conscious and concerned about their physical appearance, especially increases in acne, height, and weight.
2. Be physically at risk; major causes of death are homicide, suicide, accident, and leukemia.
3. Experience accelerated physical development marked by increases in weight, height, heart

size, lung capacity, and maturity traits (e.g., in boys a break in the voice and increased muscular strength).

4. Experience bone growth faster than muscle development; uneven muscle/bone development results in a lack of coordination and awkwardness; bones may lack the protection of covering muscles and supporting tendons.

5. Experience fluctuations in basal metabolism that can result in a lack of energy alternating with spurts of activity.

6. Face responsibility for sexual behavior before full emotional and social maturity has occurred.

7. Have ravenous appetites and peculiar tastes; may overtax their digestive systems with large quantities of rich or unsuitable foods.

8. Experience increased physical health for some, while others have poor levels of endurance, strength, and flexibility; as a group they are fatter and less healthy.

9. Mature at varying rates. Girls are often taller than boys for the first two years of early adolescence and are ordinarily more physically developed than boys. The average age of menarche is 12–13.

10. Reflect a wide range of individual differences that begin to appear in prepubertal and pubertal stages of development. Boys tend to lag behind girls at this stage, and there are marked individual differences in physical development for both boys and girls. The greatest variation in physiological development and size occurs at about age 13.

11. Show changes in body contour, including temporarily large noses, protruding ears, and long arms; have posture problems.

Social development.   Young adolescents tend to:

1. Be vain and want to show off.

2. Be self-conscious about social behaviors.

3. Want social acceptance. They can be fiercely loyal to peer group values and sometimes cruel or insensitive to those outside the peer group.

4. Be affected by the high level of mobility in society; they may become anxious and disoriented when peer group ties are broken because of family relocation.

5. Be rebellious toward parents but still strongly dependent on parental values. They want to make their own choices, but the authority of the family is a critical factor in their final decisions.

6. Be socially at risk; adult values are largely shaped conceptually during adolescence, and their negative interactions with peers, parents, and teachers may compromise their ideals and commitments. Sometimes they think their parents are unrealistic about life.

7. Challenge authority figures and test the limits of acceptable behavior.

8. Experience low-risk trust relationships with adults who show a lack of sensitivity to adolescent characteristics and needs.

9. Experience often-traumatic conflicts because of conflicting loyalties to peer group and family.

10. Refer to peers as sources for standards and models of behavior; media heroes are also singularly important in shaping both behavior and fashion.

11. Sense the negative impact of adolescent behaviors on parents and teachers, realizing the thin edge between tolerance and rejection. Feelings of adult rejection can drive the adolescent into the relatively secure social environment of the peer group.

12. Strive to define sex role characteristics and search to set up positive social relationships with members of the same and opposite sex.

13. Want to know and feel that significant adults, including their parents or guardians, and teachers, love and accept them; they need frequent affirmation.

Cognitive development.   Young adolescents tend to:

1. Be egocentric; display an increased ability to convince others; exhibit independent, critical thought.

2. Display increased imaginative powers.

3. Be interested primarily in activities outside of school.

4. Be able to reason, judge, and apply experiences.

5. Experience the phenomenon of metacognition—that is, the ability to think about one's thinking and to know what one knows and does not know.

6. Exhibit a strong willingness to learn what they consider to be useful and enjoy using skills to solve real-life problems.

7. Prefer active to passive learning experiences; favor interaction with peers during learning activities.

Emotional development.   Young adolescents tend to:

1. Sulk and show anger.

2. Fall in and out of love frequently.

3. Have fears and worries.

4. Be optimistic, hopeful, and sensitive to what others think.

5. Be psychologically at risk; at no other point in human development is an individual likely to meet so much diversity in relation to one's self and others.

6. Want to be popular and to have friends.

7. Want to be an original or unique person.

8. Be vulnerable to naive opinions and one-sided arguments.

9. Exaggerate simple occurrences and believe that their personal problems, experiences, and feelings are unique to themselves.

10. Want independence from adult control but return to caring adults for help and reassurance.

11. Have an emerging sense of humor based on increased intellectual ability to see abstract relationships; they appreciate the double entendre.

12. Have chemical and hormonal imbalances that often trigger emotions that are frightening and poorly understood. They may regress to more childish behavior patterns at this point.

Because social awareness is such an important and integral part of a child's experience, exemplary elementary school programs and much of their practices are geared toward some type of social interaction. Indeed, learning is a social enterprise among learners and their teachers. While many of today's successful instructional practices rely heavily on social learning activities and interpersonal relationships, each teacher must be aware of and sensitive to individual student differences. For working with specific learners, consider the guidelines that follow and refer back to these guidelines often during your preactive phase of instruction.

Recognizing and Working with Students with Disabilities

Students with disabilities (also referred to as *exceptional students* and *special-needs students*) include those with disabling conditions or impairments in any one or more of the following categories: mental retardation, hearing, speech or language, visual, emotional, orthopedic, autism, traumatic brain injury, other health impairment, or specific learning disabilities. To the extent possible, students with disabilities must be educated with their peers in the regular classroom. Public Law 94-142, the Education for All Handicapped Children Act (EAHCA) of 1975, mandates that all children have the right to a free and appropriate education and to nondiscriminatory assessment. (Public Law 94-142 was amended in 1986 by P. L. 99-457, in 1990 by P. L. 101-476 at which time its name was changed to Individuals with Disabilities Education Act—IDEA, and in 1997 by P. L. 105-17.) Emphasizing normalizing the educational environment for students with disabilities, this legislation requires provision of the least-restrictive environment (LRE) for these students. A LRE is an environment that is as normal as possible.

Students identified as having special needs may be placed in the regular classroom for the entire school day, called *full inclusion* (as is the trend).[26] Those students may also be in a regular classroom the greater part of the school day, called *partial inclusion,* or only for designated periods. While there is no single, universally accepted definition of the term, *inclusion* is the concept that students with special needs should be integrated into general education classrooms regardless of whether they can meet traditional academic standards.[27] (The term *inclusion* has largely replaced use of an earlier and similar term, *mainstreaming.*) As a classroom teacher you will need information and skills specific to teaching learners with special needs who are included in your classroom.

Generally speaking, teaching students who have special needs requires more care, better diagnosis, greater skill, more attention to individual needs, and an even greater understanding of the students. The challenges of teaching students with special needs in the regular classroom are great enough that to do it well you need specialized training beyond the general guidelines presented here. At some point in your teacher preparation you should take one or more courses in working with the learner with handicapping conditions who is included in the regular classroom.

When a child with special needs is placed in your classroom, your task is to deal directly with the differences between this student and other students in your classroom. To do this, you should develop an understanding of the general characteristics of different types of special-needs learners, identify the child's unique needs relative to your classroom, and design lessons that teach to different needs at the same time, called **multilevel teaching,** or **multitasking,** as exemplified in Figure 2.2.[28] Remember that just because a student has been identified as having one or more special needs does not preclude that person from being gifted or talented.

Congress stipulated in P. L. 94-142 that an Individualized Educational Program (IEP) be devised annually for each special-needs child. According to that law, an IEP is developed for each student each year by a team that includes special-education teachers, the child's parents or guardians, and the classroom teachers. The IEP contains a statement of the student's present educational levels, the educational goals for the year, specifications for the services to be provided, the extent to which the student should be expected to take part in the regular education program, and the evaluative criteria for the services to be provided. Consultation by special and skilled support personnel is essential in all IEP models. A consultant works directly with teachers or with students and parents or guardians. As a classroom teacher, you may play an active role in preparing the specifications for the special-needs students assigned to your classroom, as well as have a major responsibility for implementing the program.

Guidelines for Working with Special-Needs Children in the Regular Classroom

Although the guidelines represented by the paragraphs that follow are important for teaching all students, they are especially important for working with special-needs students.

Familiarize yourself with exactly what the special needs of each learner are. Privately ask the special-needs learner whether there is anything the student would like for you to know and that you specifically can do to facilitate the student's learning while in your classroom.

Adapt and modify materials and procedures to the special needs of each student. For example, a child who has extreme difficulty sitting still for more than a few minutes will need planned changes in learning activities. When establishing student-seating arrangements in the classroom, give consideration to students according to their special needs. Try to incorporate into lessons activities that engage all learning modalities: visual, auditory, tactile, and kinesthetic.

Provide high structure and clear expectations by defining the learning objectives in behavioral terms (discussed in Chapter 5). Teach children the correct procedures for everything (Chapter 4). Break complex learning into simpler components, moving from the most concrete to the abstract, rather than the other way around. Check frequently for student understanding of instructions and procedures and for skill development and the comprehension of content. Use computers and other self-correcting materials for drill and practice and for provision of immediate and private feedback to the student.

Develop your "withitness" (discussed in Chapter 3), steadily monitoring children for signs of restlessness, frustration, anxiety, and off-task behaviors. Be ready to reassign individual learners to different activities as the situation warrants. Established classroom learning centers (discussed in Chapter 8) can be a big help.

Have all students maintain assignments for the week or some other period of time in an assignment book or in a folder that is kept in their notebooks. Post assignments in a special place in the classroom and frequently remind students of assignments and deadlines.

Maintain consistency in your expectations and in your responses. Special-needs students, particularly, can become frustrated when they do not understand a teacher's expectations and when they cannot depend on a teacher's reactions.

Plan interesting activities to bridge learning, activities that help the children connect what is being learned with their world. Learning that connects what is being learned with the real world helps motivate students and keep them on task.

Plan questions and questioning sequences and write them into your lesson plans (discussed in Chapters 6 and 7). Plan questions that you ask special-needs students so that they are most likely to answer them with confidence. Use signals to let students know that you are likely to call on them in class (e.g., prolonged eye contact or mentioning your intention to the student before class begins). After asking a question, give the student adequate time to think and respond. Then, after the student responds, build upon the student's response to indicate that the child's contribution was accepted as being important.

Provide for and teach toward student success. Provide activities and experiences that ensure each student's success and mastery at some level. Use of student portfolios (discussed in Chapter 11) can give evidence of progress and help build student confidence and self-esteem.

Provide time in class for children to work on assignments and projects. During this time, you can monitor the work of each child while looking for misconceptions and misunderstandings, thus ensuring that students get started on the right track.

Provide help in the organization of students' learning. For example, give instruction in the organization of notes and notebooks. Have a three-hole punch available in the classroom so students can put papers into their notebooks immediately, thus avoiding disorganization and loss of papers. During class presentations use an overhead projector with transparencies; students who need more time can then copy material from the transparencies. Ask students to read their notes aloud to each other in small groups, thereby aiding their recall and understanding and encouraging them to take notes for meaning rather than for rote learning. Encourage and provide for peer support, peer tutoring or coaching, and cross-age teaching (Chapter 8). Ensure that the special-needs learner is included in all class activities to the fullest extent possible.[29]

Recognizing and Working with Students of Diversity and Differences

Quickly determine the language and nationality groups represented by the children in your classroom. A major problem for recent immigrant children, and for some ethnic groups, is learning a second (or third or fourth) language. While in many schools it is not uncommon for more than half the students to come from homes where the native language is not English, standard English is a necessity in most communities of this country if a person is to become vocationally successful and enjoy a full life. Learning to communicate reasonably well in English can take an immigrant child at least a year and probably longer; some authorities say 3 to 7 years. By default, then, an increasing number of teachers are teachers of English language learning. Helpful to the success of teaching children who have limited English proficiency (LEP) are the demonstration of respect for students' cultural backgrounds, long-term teacher-student cohorts (such as, for example, in looping), and the use of active and cooperative learning.[30]

Numerous programs are specially designed for working with English as a second language (ESL) learners.[31] Most use the acronym LEP with 5 number levels, from LEP 1 that designates non-English-speaking, although the student may understand single sentences and speak simple words or phrases in English, to LEP 5, sometimes designated FEP (fluent English proficient), for the student who is fully fluent in English, although the student's overall academic achievement may still be less than desired because of language or cultural differences.[32]

Some schools use a "pullout" approach, in which part of the child's school time is spent in special bilingual classes and the student is placed in regular classrooms the rest of the time. In some schools, LEP students are placed in academic classrooms that use a simplified or "sheltered" English approach. Regardless of the program, specific techniques recommended for teaching ESL students include:

- Allowing more time for learning activities than one normally would.
- Allowing time for translation by a classroom aide or by a classmate and allowing time for discussion to clarify meaning, thus encouraging the students to transfer into English what they already know in their native language.
- Avoiding jargon or idioms (see the boxed vignette at the start of this chapter) that might be misunderstood.

- Dividing complex or extended language discourse into smaller, more manageable units.
- Giving directions in a variety of ways.
- Giving special attention to key words that convey meaning and writing them on the board.
- Reading written directions aloud and then writing the directions on the board.
- Speaking clearly and naturally but at a slower than normal pace.
- Using a variety of examples and observable models.
- Using simplified vocabulary but without talking down to children.[33]

Additional Guidelines for Working with Language-Minority Children

While they are becoming literate in English language usage, LEP students can learn the same curriculum in the various disciplines as native English-speaking students. Although the guidelines presented in the following paragraphs are important for teaching all students, they are especially important when working with language-minority students.

Present instruction that is concrete, that includes the most direct learning experiences possible. Use the most concrete (least abstract) forms of instruction (see the section, Learning Experiences Ladder, in Chapter 6).

Build upon (or connect with) what the students already have experienced and know. Building upon what children already know, or think they know, helps them to connect their knowledge and construct their understandings.

Encourage student writing (or drawing). One way is by using student journals (see also Chapters 8 and 11). Two kinds of journals are appropriate when working with LEP students: dialogue journals and response journals. Dialogue journals are used for students to write anything that is on their minds, usually on the right page. Teachers, parents or guardians, and classmates then respond on the left page, thereby "talking with" the journal writers. Response journals are used for students to write (record) their responses to what they are reading or studying.[34]

Help children learn the vocabulary. Assist the LEP students in learning two vocabulary sets: the regular English vocabulary needed for learning and the new vocabulary introduced by the subject content. For example, while learning science a student is dealing with both the regular English language vocabulary and the special vocabulary of science.

Involve members of the child's family. Students whose primary language is not English may have other differences about which you will also need to become knowledgeable. These differences are related to culture, customs, family life, and expectations. To be most successful in working with language-minority students, you should learn as much as possible about each student. To this end it can be valuable to solicit the help of the student's parent, guardian, or even an older sibling. Parents (or guardians) of new immigrant children are usually truly concerned about the education of their children and may be very interested in cooperating with you in any way possible. In a study of eight schools recognized for their exemplary practices with language-minority students, the schools were recognized for being "parent friendly," that is, for welcoming parents and guardians in a variety of innovative ways.[35]

Plan for and use all learning modalities. As with teaching children in general, in working with language-minority students in particular you need to use multisensory approaches—learning activities that involve students in auditory, visual, tactile, and kinesthetic learning activities.

Use small-group learning. Small-group learning is particularly effective with language-minority students because it provides opportunity for students to produce language in a setting that is less threatening than is speaking before the entire class.

Use the benefits afforded by modern technology. For example, computers can provide children immediate access to dictionaries and encyclopedias and in text editing and "publishing" their classroom work. Computer networking allows students to communicate and share their work with peers from around the world.

Additional Guidelines for Working with Children of Diverse Backgrounds

To be compatible with, and be able to teach, children who come from backgrounds different from yours, you need to believe that, given adequate support, all children *can* learn, regardless of gender, social class, physical characteristics, language, and ethnic or cultural backgrounds. You also need to develop special skills that include those in the following guidelines, each of which is discussed in detail in other chapters. To work successfully and most effectively with children of diverse backgrounds, you should:

- Build the learning around students' individual learning styles. Personalize learning for each child, much like what is done by using the IEP with special-needs learners. Involve students in understanding and in making important decisions about their own learning, so that they feel

ownership (i.e., a sense of empowerment and connectedness) of that learning.
- Communicate positively with every child and with the child's parents or guardians, learning as much as you can about the child and the child's culture and encouraging family members to participate in the child's learning. Involve parents, guardians, and other members of the community in the educational program so that all have a sense of ownership and responsibility and positive feelings about the school program.
- Establish and maintain high expectations, although not necessarily the same expectations, for each student.
- Teach to individuals by using a variety of strategies to achieve an objective or by using a number of different objectives at the same time (multilevel teaching).
- Use techniques that emphasize collaborative and cooperative learning and deemphasize competitive learning.

Recognizing and Working with Students Who Are Gifted

Historically, educators have used the term *gifted* when referring to a child with identified exceptional ability in one or more academic subjects. The term *talented* typically referred to a child with exceptional ability in one or more of the visual or performing arts.[36] Today, however, the terms often are used interchangeably, which is how they are used for this resource guide.

Sometimes in the regular classroom gifted students are neglected.[37] At least part of the time, it is likely to be because no single method is accepted to identify these students. For placement in special classes or programs for the gifted and talented, school districts traditionally have used grade point averages and standard intelligence quotient (IQ) scores. On the other hand, because IQ testing measures linguistic and logical/mathematical aspects of giftedness (refer to the discussion earlier in this chapter on learning capacities), it does not account for others and thus gifted children sometimes are unrecognized. They also are sometimes among the students most at risk of dropping out of school.[38] It is estimated that between 10 and 20 percent of school dropouts are students who are in the range of being intellectually gifted.[39]

To work most effectively with gifted learners, their talents first must be identified. This can be done by using tests, rating scales, and auditions and by observations in the classroom, on the playground, and from knowledge about the student's personal life. With those information sources in mind, here is a list of indicators of superior intelligence: ability to extrapolate knowledge to different circumstances; ability to manipulate a symbol system; ability to reason by analogy; ability to take on adult roles at home, such as managing the household and supervising siblings, even at the expense of school attendance and achievement; ability to think logically; ability to use stored knowledge to solve problems; creativity and artistic ability; leadership ability and an independent mind; resiliency, such as the ability to cope with school while living in poverty with dysfunctional families; strong sense of self, pride, and worth; and, understanding of one's cultural heritage.[40]

To assist you in understanding gifted children who may or may not have yet been identified as being gifted, here are some types of gifted students and the kinds of problems to which they may be prone, that is, personal behaviors that may identify them as being gifted but academically disabled, bored, and even alienated.

- *Antisocial* children, alienated by their differences from peers, may become bored and impatient troublemakers.
- *Creative, high achieving* students often feel isolated, weird, and depressed.
- *Divergent thinking* students can develop self-esteem problems when they provide answers that are logical to them but seem unusual and off-the-wall to their peers. They may have only a few peer friends.
- *Perfectionists* may exhibit compulsive behaviors because they feel as though their value comes from their accomplishments. When their accomplishments do not live up to expectations—their own, their parents', or their teachers—anxiety and feelings of inadequacy arise. When other students do not live up to the gifted student's high standards, alienation from those students is probable.
- *Sensitive* children who also are gifted may become easily depressed because they are more aware of their surroundings and of their differences.
- *Students with handicapping conditions* may be gifted. Attention-deficit disorder, dyslexia, hyperactivity, and other learning disorders sometimes mask giftedness.
- *Underachieving* students can also be gifted but fail in their studies because they learn in ways that are seldom or never challenged by classroom teachers. Although often expected to excel in everything they do, most gifted children can be underachievers in some areas. Having high expectations of themselves, underachievers

tend to be highly critical of themselves, to develop a low self-esteem, and can become indifferent and even hostile.[41]

Meaningful Curriculum Options: Multiple Pathways to Success

Because of what we now know about learning and intelligence, the trend today is to assume that each child, to some degree and in some area of learning and doing, has the potential for giftedness, and to provide sufficient curriculum options, or multiple pathways, so each student can reach those potentials. Clearly, achievement in school increases, students learn more, enjoy learning, and remember more of what they have learned when individual learning capacities, styles, and modalities are identified and accommodated.[42]

All students, not only those who have been identified as gifted, need a challenging academic environment. Educators have devised and continue to devise and refine numerous ways of attending to student differences, of providing a challenging but supportive learning environment, and of stimulating the talents and motivation of each student. Because the advantage gained from using a combination of responsive practices concurrently is seemingly greater than is the gain from using any singular practice by itself, in many instances in a given school the practices overlap and are used simultaneously. These practices are shown in Figure 2.3, most of which are discussed in various places in this resource guide. Check index for topic locations.

Additional Guidelines for Working with Gifted Children

When working in the regular classroom with a student who has special gifts and talents, you are advised to:

- Emphasize skills in critical thinking, problem solving, and inquiry.
- Identify, nurture, and showcase the student's special gift or talent.
- Involve the student in selecting and planning activities, encouraging the development of the student's leadership skills.
- Use curriculum compacting, a process that allows a student who already knows the material to pursue enriched or accelerated study.[43] Plan and provide optional and voluntary enrichment activities. Learning centers, special projects, and computer and multimedia activities

Figure 2.3
Multiple pathways to success: productive ways of attending to student differences, of providing a more challenging learning environment, and of stimulating the talents and motivation of each learner

- Adult advocacy relationships for every student
- Allowing a student to skip a traditional grade level, thereby accelerating the time a student passes through the grades
- Cooperative learning activities
- Curriculum compacting
- Extra efforts to provide academic and personal help
- High expectations for all students
- Individualized educational plans and instruction
- Integrating modern technologies into the curriculum
- Interdisciplinary teaming and thematic instruction
- Looping
- Low (no higher than 17:1) teacher-student ratio
- Multiage grouping and mid-year promotions
- Multidiscipline student-centered project-based learning
- Peer and cross-age teaching
- Problem-centered learning
- Second opportunity recovery strategies
- Service learning
- Specialized schools and nontraditional schedules

are excellent tools for provision of enriched learning activities.

- Plan assignments and activities that challenge the students to the fullest of their abilities. This does *not* mean overloading them with homework or giving identical assignments to all students. Rather, carefully plan so that the students' time spent on assignments and activities is quality time spent on meaningful learning.
- Provide in-class seminars for students to discuss topics and problems that they are pursuing individually or as members of a learning team.
- Provide independent and dyad learning opportunities. Gifted students often prefer to work alone or with another gifted student.
- Use preassessments for reading level and subject content achievement so that you are better able to prescribe objectives and activities for each child.
- Work with individual children in some planning of their own objectives and activities for learning.

Recognizing and Working with Children Who Take More Time but Are Willing to Try

Children who are slower to learn typically fall into one of two categories: (a) those who try to learn but simply need more time to do it, and (b) those who do not try, referred to variously as underachievers, recalcitrant, or reluctant learners. Practices that work well with students of one category are often not those that work well with those of the second—making life difficult for a teacher of 30 students, half who try and half who don't. It is worse still for a teacher of a group of 30 students, some who try but need time, a couple who are academically talented, a few LEP students, and several who not only seem unwilling to try but who are also disruptive in the classroom.

Remember that just because a student is slow to learn doesn't mean that the student is less intelligent; some students just take longer, for any number of reasons. The following guidelines may be helpful when working with a slow student who has indicated willingness to try

- Adjust the instruction to the child's preferred learning style, which may be different from yours and from other children in the group.
- Be less concerned with the amount of content coverage than with the child's successful understanding of content that is covered.
- Discover something the student does exceptionally well, or a special interest, and try and build on that.
- Emphasize basic communication skills, such as speaking, listening, reading, and writing, to ensure that the child's skills in these areas are sufficient for learning the intended content.
- Help the student learn content in small sequential steps with frequent checks for comprehension.
- If necessary, help the student to improve his or her reading skills, such as pronunciation and word meanings.
- If using a single textbook, be certain that the reading level is adequate for the student; if it is not, then for that student use other more appropriate reading materials.
- Maximize the use of in-class, on-task work and cooperative learning, with close monitoring of the student's progress.
- Vary the instructional strategies, using a variety of activities to engage the visual, verbal, tactile, and kinesthetic modalities.
- When appropriate, use frequent positive reinforcement, with the intention of increasing the child's self-esteem.

Recognizing and Working with Recalcitrant Learners

For working with recalcitrant learners you can use many of the same guidelines from the preceding list, except that you should understand that the reasons for these students' behaviors may be quite different from those for the other category of slow learners. Slower-learning students who are willing to try may be slow because of their learning style or because of genetic reasons, or a combination of the two. But they can and will learn. Recalcitrant learners, on the other hand, may be generally quick and bright thinkers but reluctant even to try because of a history of failure, a history of boredom with school, a poor self-concept, severe personal problems that distract from school, or any variety and combination of reasons, many of which are psychological in nature.

Whatever the case, you need to know that a student identified as being a slow or recalcitrant learner might, in fact, be quite gifted or talented in some way, but because of personal problems, may have a history of increasingly poor school attendance, poor attention to schoolwork, poor self-confidence, or an attitude problem. Consider the following guidelines when working with recalcitrant learners

- As the school year begins, learn as much about each child as you can. Be cautious in how you do it, especially with children in grades four and higher, because many of these students will be suspicious of any genuine interest in them shown by you. Be businesslike, trusting, genuinely interested, and persistent but patient. A second caution: Although you learn as much as possible about each student, what has happened in the past is history. Use that information only as insight to help you work more productively with the student.
- Early in the school term, preferably with the help of adult volunteers (e.g., professional community members as mentors have worked well at helping change the students' attitude from rebellion to hope, challenge, and success), work out an individual education program (IEP) with each student.
- Engage the children in learning by using interactive media, such as the Internet.
- Engage children in active learning with real-world problem solving and perhaps community service projects.
- Forget about trying to cover the subject, concentrating instead on student learning of some things well. A good procedure is to use thematic teaching and divide the theme into short segments. Because school attendance for these children is sometimes sporadic, try to individualize their assignments so that they can pick up where they left off and move through the curriculum in an orderly fashion even when they have been absent excessively. Try to ensure some degree of success for each child.
- Help students develop their studying and learning skills, such as concentrating, remembering, and comprehension. Mnemonics, for example, is a device these students respond to positively. Often the students are quick to create their own (see Chapter 9).
- If using a single textbook, see if the reading level is appropriate; if it is not, then for that student discard the book and select other more appropriate reading materials.
- Make sure your classroom procedures and rules are understood at the beginning of the school term and, with the guidelines presented in Chapter 4, be consistent about enforcing them.
- Maximize the use of in-class, on-task work and cooperative learning, with close monitoring of the student's progress.
- Use reciprocal teaching. For example, you teach the student how to read; the student teaches you about his or her neighborhood, or language, or hobby.
- Use simple language in the classroom. Within professional reason, be concerned less about the words the students use and the way they use them and more about the ideas they are expressing. Let the students use their own idioms without carping too much on grammar and syntax. Always take care, though, to use proper and professional English yourself.
- When appropriate, use frequent positive reinforcement with the intention of increasing the student's sense of self-esteem.

Recognizing and Working with Abused Children

Child abuse has become a grave matter of pressing national concern. Teachers in all states are now legally mandated to report any suspicion of child abuse. It is a serious moral issue not to report such suspicion, and lawsuits for negligence have been brought against educators for not doing so. To report suspicion of child abuse, you can telephone 1-800-4-A-CHILD. Proof of abuse is not necessary. Check your own state or local school district for additional guidelines and specifics.

Although physical abuse and certain kinds of neglect, such as improper clothing and inadequate dental care, may be the easiest to spot, other types of abuse such as incest, emotional, and malnutrition can be just as serious.

General characteristics of children who are abused or neglected are lack of interest in school activities, aggressive and destructive behaviors, fear of everyone and everything, fear of going home after school, fear of their parents and other adults, frequent sickness and absence from school, frequent tiredness (often falling asleep in class), less than average height and weight, short attention span, odor of alcohol, sudden and dramatic changes in behavior, unclean, unexpected crying, unexplained lacerations and bruises, withdrawal from adult contact, and withdrawal from peer interaction.[44]

An abused or neglected child in your classroom needs to feel welcome and secure while in the classroom. For additional guidance in working with such a child, contact experts from your local school district (e.g., the school psychologist) or from the children's protective services agency.

Teaching Toward Positive Character Development

In what appears to be a cycle, arising for example in the 1930s, again in the late 1960s, and again in the 1990s and continuing today, interest is high in the development of students' values, especially those of honesty, kindness, respect, and responsibility. Today this interest is in what some refer to as *character education*. Whether defined as ethics, citizenship, moral values, or personal development, character education has long been part of public education in this country.[45] Stimulated by a perceived need to act to reduce students' antisocial behaviors and to produce more respectful and responsible citizens, many schools and districts today are developing curricula in character education with the ultimate goal of "developing mature adults capable of responsible citizenship and moral action."[46]

You can teach toward positive character development in two general ways (both of which are discussed further in Chapters 3, 4, and 5): by providing a conducive classroom atmosphere where students actively and positively share in the decision making; and, by being a model that students can proudly emulate. Acquiring knowledge and developing understanding can enhance the learning of attitudes. Nevertheless, changing an attitude can be a long and tedious process, requiring the commitment of the teacher and the school, assistance from the community, and the provision of numerous experiences that will guide students to new convictions. Here are some specific practices, most of which are, as indicated, discussed further in later chapters:

- Build a sense of community in the school and in the classroom, with shared goals, optimism, cooperative efforts, and clearly identified and practiced procedures for reaching those goals (see Chapter 4).
- Collaboratively plan with students action- and community-oriented projects that relate to curriculum themes; solicit parent and community members to assist in the projects.
- Have students research and present, by advocating a particular stance on a controversial issue[47] (see Chapter 5).
- Promote higher-order thinking about value issues through the development of skills in questioning (Chapter 7).
- Sensitize students to issues and teach skills of conflict resolution through role play, simulations, and creative drama (Chapter 9).
- Share and highlight anchor examples of class and individual cooperation in serving the classroom, school, and community (see throughout the book).
- Teach children to negotiate; practice and develop skills in conflict resolution, skills such as empathy, problem solving, impulse control, and anger management (see the Emergency Teaching Kit in Chapter 12).

Resources on character education are shown in Figure 2.4. When compared with traditional

Figure 2.4
Selected resources on character education

- Character Education Institute, 8918 Tesoro Drive, San Antonio, TX 78217 (800-284-0499)
- Character Education Partnership, 918 16th Street NW, Suite 501, Washington, DC 20006 (800-988-8081). Web site: http://www.character.org
- Character Education Resources, P. O. Box 651, Contoocook, NH 03229
- Developmental Studies Center, 111 Deerwood Place, San Ramon, CA 94583 (415-838-7633)
- Ethics Resource Center, 1120 G Street NW, Washington, DC 20005 (202-434-8465)
- Jefferson Center for Character Education, 202 S. Lake Avenue, Pasadena, CA 91101 (818-792-8130). Web site: http://www.jeffersoncenter.org
- Josephson Institute of Ethics, 310 Washington Boulevard, Marina Del Rey, CA 90292 (310-306-1868)

didactic instruction, one characteristic of exemplary elementary school instruction today is the teacher's encouragement of dialogue among children in the classroom to discuss and to explore their own ideas. Modeling the very behaviors we expect of teachers and children in the classroom is, as was emphasized in the Preface, a constant theme throughout this resource guide. One purpose of Exercise 2.2 is, in a similar fashion, to start that dialogue. Do that exercise now.

EXERCISE 2.2 REFLECTING UPON MY OWN ELEMENTARY SCHOOL EXPERIENCES

Instructions: The purpose of this exercise is to help you recall your own elementary school experiences. When you have completed the exercise, share your reflections with others in your class.

Name(s), location(s), and approximate dates of elementary school(s) attended _____

_____

_____

_____

Public or private? _____

1. What do you remember most from your elementary school years? _____

_____

_____

_____

_____

2. What do you recall about your teachers? _____

_____

_____

_____

_____

3. Do you remember any one teacher most clearly? If so, why? _____

_____

_____

_____

_____

4. What do you remember most about your time in elementary school? _____

_____

_____

_____

_____

5. Is there any one grade or class that you recall with special fondness? If so, explain why. _____

_____

_____

_____

_____

EXERCISE 2.2 *(continued)*

6. Is there any one grade or class that you particularly would like to forget? If so, explain why. _____

   _____

   _____

   _____

   _____

7. What do you recall about peer, teacher, or parental pressures during your elementary school

   years? _____

   _____

   _____

   _____

   _____

8. What do you recall about your own feelings during your elementary school years? _____

   _____

   _____

   _____

   _____

9. Can you recall being in the earliest grades (K–3)? If so, what do you remember about those years?

   _____

   _____

   _____

   _____

10. What societal influences most affected you and your fellow students? _____

   _____

   _____

   _____

   _____

11. Is there any other aspect of your life during elementary school that you wish to share? _____

   _____

   _____

   _____

   _____

SUMMARY

As a classroom teacher you must acknowledge that the students in your classroom have different ways of receiving information and different ways of processing that information—different ways of knowing and of constructing their knowledge. These differences are unique and important, and, as you will learn in Part II of this resource guide, are central considerations in curriculum development, instructional practice, and the assessment of learning.

You must try to learn as much as you can about how each student learns and processes information. But because you can never know everything about each student, the more you dialogue with members of the child's family and your colleagues, vary your teaching strategies, and assist students in integrating their learning, the more likely you are to reach more of the students more of the time. In short, to be an effective elementary school classroom teacher you should: (a) learn as much about your students and their preferred styles of learning as you can, (b) develop an eclectic style of teaching, one that is flexible and adaptable, and (c) integrate the disciplines, thereby helping children make bridges or connections between their lives and all that is being learned.

EXTENDING MY COMPETENCY: QUESTIONS FOR CLASS DISCUSSION _____

1. Explain why knowledge of learning styles, learning capacities, and teaching styles is or should be important to a classroom teacher.
2. Brian, a social studies teacher, has a class of 33 sixth graders who during his expository teaching (lecture, teacher-led discussion, and recitation lessons) are restless and inattentive, creating for Brian a problem in classroom management. At Brian's invitation, the school psychologist tests the students for learning modality and finds that of the 33 students, 29 are predominately kinesthetic learners. Of what value is this information to Brian? Describe what, if anything, Brain should try as a result of this information.
3. What concerns you most about teaching? Share those concerns with others in your class. Categorize your group's concerns. By accessing an Internet teacher bulletin board see what classroom teachers are currently seemingly concerned about. Are standardized assessments, content standards, inclusion, reading, student diversity, thematic instruction, grading, group

learning, and classroom management high in frequency of concern? Are the concerns of teachers as expressed on the Internet similar to yours? As a class, devise a plan and timeline for attempting to ameliorate your concerns.
4. Give an example of how and when you would use multilevel instruction. Of what benefit is its use to students? to teachers? What particular skills must a teacher have to effectively implement multilevel instruction?
5. Identify and describe several ways that as a classroom teacher you could attend to student differences to stimulate the talents and motivation of each child.
6. Regarding the discussion of 4MAT, how would you classify your own current learning style—an imaginative learner, analytic learner, commonsense learner, or a dynamic learner? Has your learning style changed as you have gotten older? What, if anything, has accounted for any changes? Think about the developmental characteristics of young people and about different content areas of the elementary school curriculum (i.e., mathematics, social studies, science, writing). Do you think that some ages and/or content areas are more compatible with certain learning styles? Explain why or why not.
7. It is estimated that approximately 20 percent of all children ages 6 to 11 in the United States are living in poverty. Explain any relevance that this may have for you as a classroom teacher.
8. Describe any prior concepts you held that changed as a result of your experiences with this chapter. Describe the changes.
9. From your current observations and fieldwork as related to this teacher preparation program, clearly identify one specific example of educational practice that seems contradictory to exemplary practice or theory as presented in this chapter. Present your explanation for the discrepancy.
10. Do you have other questions generated by the content of this chapter? If you do, list them along with ways answers might be found.

FOR FURTHER READING _____

Armstrong, T. (1998). *Awakening Genius in the Classroom*. Alexandria, VA: Association for Supervision and Curriculum Development.

Armstrong, T. (2000). *Multiple Intelligences in the Classroom* (2d ed.). Alexandria, VA: Association for Supervision and Curriculum Development.

Baker, J. C., and Martin, F. G. (1998). *A Neural Network Guide to Teaching*. Fastback 431. Bloomington, IN: Phi Delta Kappa Educational Foundation.

Beaumont, C. J. (1999). Dilemmas of Peer Assistance in a Bilingual Full Inclusion Classroom. *Elementary School Journal, 99*(3), 233–254.

Brandt, R. (1998). *Powerful Learning.* Alexandria, VA: Association for Supervision and Curriculum Development.

Brisk, M. E., and Harrington, M. M. (2000). *Literacy and Bilingualism: A Handbook for ALL Teachers.* Mahwah, NJ: Lawrence Erlbaum.

Choate, J. S., and Rakes, T. A. (1998). *Inclusive Instruction for Struggling Readers.* Fastback 434. Bloomington, IN: Phi Delta Kappa Educational Foundation.

Clark, G., and Zimmerman, E. (1998). Nurturing the Arts in Programs for Gifted and Talented Students. *Phi Delta Kappan, 79*(10), 747–751.

Fogarty, R. (1998). The Intelligence-Friendly Classroom. *Phi Delta Kappan, 79*(9), 655–657.

Ford, D. Y., and Harris III, J. J. (1999). *Multicultural Gifted Education.* New York: Teachers College Press.

Gibb, G. S., and Dyches, T. T. (2000). *Guide to Writing Quality Individualized Education Programs: What's Best for Students with Disabilities?* Needham Heights, MA: Allyn & Bacon.

Goldman, L. (2000). *Helping the Grieving Child in School.* Fastback 460. Bloomington, IN: Phi Delta Kappa Educational Foundation.

Gonzalez, M. L., Huerta-Macias, A., and Tinajero, J. V. (Eds.). (1998). *Educating Latino Students: A Guide to Successful Practice.* Lancaster, PA: Technomic.

Good, T. L., and Brophy, J. E. (2000). *Looking in Classrooms* (8th ed., Chap. 8). New York: Addison-Wesley Longman.

Guild, P. B., and Garger, S. (1998). *Marching to Different Drummers* (2nd ed.). Alexandria, VA: Association for Supervision and Curriculum Development.

Institute for Children and Poverty. (1998). *Ten Cities, 1997–1998: A Snapshot of Family Homelessness Across America.* New York: Homes for the Homeless.

Jensen, E. (1998). *Teaching With the Brain in Mind.* Alexandria, VA: Association for Supervision and Curriculum Development.

Kalichman, S. C. (2000). *Mandated Reporting of Suspected Child Abuse: Ethics, Law, Policy* (2nd ed.). Washington, DC: American Psychological Association.

Keller, M. M., and Decoteau, G. T. (2000). *The Military Child: Mobility and Education.* Fastback 463. Bloomington, IN: Phi Delta Kappa Educational Foundation.

Kovalik, S., and Olsen, K. D. (1998). The Physiology of Learning—Just What Does Go On in There? *Schools in the Middle, 7*(4), 32–37.

Loveless, T. (1998). *The Tracking and Ability Grouping Debate.* Washington, DC: Thomas B. Fordham Foundation.

Melton, L., Pickett, W., and Sherer, G. (1999). *Improving K–8 Reading Using Multiple Intelligences.* Fastback 448. Bloomington, IN: Phi Delta Kappa Educational Foundation.

Morgan, R. R., Ponticell, J. A., and Gordon, E. E. (2000). *Rethinking Creativity.* Fastback 458. Bloomington, IN: Phi Delta Kappa Educational Foundation.

Nelson, R. F. (2000). Which Is the Best Kindergarten? *Principal, 79*(5), 38–41.

Perkins, D. N. (2000). Schools Need to Pay More Attention to "Intelligence in the Wild." *Harvard Education Letter, 16*(3), 7–8.

Samway, K. D., and Mckeon, D. (1999). *Myths and Realities: Best Practices for Language Minority Students.* Portsmouth, NH: Heinemann.

Slocumb, P. D., and Payne, R. K. (2000). *Removing the Mask: Giftedness in Poverty.* Highlands, TX: RFT Publishing.

Smutney, J. F. (1998). *Gifted Girls.* Fastback 427. Bloomington, IN: Phi Delta Kappa Educational Foundation.

Stice, C. F., and Bertrand, J. E. (Eds.). (2000). *Teaching At-Risk Students in the K–4 Classroom.* Norwood, MA: Christopher-Gordon.

Sweet, S. S. (1998). A Lesson Learned About Multiple Intelligences. *Educational Leadership, 56*(3), 50–51.

Tomlinson, C. A. (1999). *The Differentiated Classroom: Responding to the Needs of All Learners.* Alexandria, VA: Association for Supervision and Curriculum Development.

Warburton, E. (1999). Multiple Intelligences: Past, Present, Future. *NAMTA (North American Montessori Teachers Association) Journal, 24*(1), 208–223.

Westwater, A., and Wolfe, P. (2000). The Brain-Compatible Curriculum. *Educational Leadership, 58*(3):49–52.

Woodruff, D. W., Shannon, N. R., and Efimba, M. O. (1998). Collaborating for Success: Merritt Elementary Extended School. *Journal of Education for Students Placed at Risk (JESPAR), 3*(1), 11–22.

NOTES

1. As examples, a personal learning plan for each student is a feature of Celebration School (Celebration, FL)—see the Web site at <http://www.cs.osceola.k12.fl.us>; of *Community Learning Center* (preK through adults) schools—contact Designs for Learning, 1355 Pierce Butler Route, St. Paul, MN 55104, 612-645-0200; and of *Community for Learning* (K–12) schools—see <http://www.temple.edu/LSS>.

2. J. A. Banks, Multicultural and Citizenship Education in the New Century, *School Administrator, 56*(6), 8–10 (May 1999).

3. L. Baines, Future Schlock, *Phi Delta Kappan, 78*(7), 497 (March 1997).

4. See, for example, T. L. Good and J. E. Brophy, *Looking in Classrooms,* 8th ed. (New York: Addison-Wesley Longman, 2000), p. 127.

5. R. Dunn, *Strategies for Educating Diverse Learners,* Fastback 384 (Bloomington, IN: Phi Delta Kappa Educational Foundation, 1995), p. 9.

6. P. Stone, How We Turned Around a Problem School, *Principal, 72*(2), 34–36 (November 1992). See also B. G. Barron, et al., Effects of Time of Day Instruction on Reading Achievement of Below Grade Readers, *Reading Improvement, 31*(1), 59–60 (Spring 1994).

7. D. A. Kolb, *Experiential Learning: Experience as the Source of Learning and Development* (Upper Saddle River, NJ: Prentice Hall, 1984).

8. C. G. Jung, *Psychological Types* (New York: Harcourt Brace, 1923).

9. See B. McCarthy, A Tale of Four Learners: 4MAT's Learning Styles, *Educational Leadership, 54*(6), 47–51 (March 1997).

10. See R. Karplus, *Science Curriculum Improvement Study,* Teacher's Handbook (Berkeley: University of California, 1974).

11. See, for example, A. C. Rule, *Using the Learning Cycle to Teach Acronyms, a Language Arts Lesson* (ED383000, 1995). ERIC Clearinghouse on Reading, English, and Communication. Bloomington, IN.

12. The three phases of the learning cycle are comparable to the three levels of thinking, described variously by others. For example, in Elliot Eisner's *The Educational Imagination* (New York: Macmillan, 1979), the levels are referred to as "descriptive," "interpretive," and "evaluative."

13. For information about 4MAT, contact Excel, Inc., 23385 W. Old Barrington Road, Barrington, IL 60010 (847-382-7272), or at 6322 Fenworth Court, Agoura Hills, CA 91301 (818-879-7442), or via the Internet at <http://www.excelcorp.com/4mataboutlong.html>.

14. B. McCarthy, Using the 4MAT System to Bring Learning Styles to Schools, *Educational Leadership, 48*(2), 33 (October 1990).

15. R. DeLay, Forming Knowledge: Constructivist Learning and Experiential Education, *Journal of Experiential Education, 19*(2), 76–81 (August/September 1996). See also the many articles in "The Constructivist Classroom," the November 1999 (Vol. 57, No. 3) theme issue of *Educational Leadership.*

16. For Gardner's distinction between *learning style* and *intelligences,* see H. Gardner, Multiple Intelligences: Myths and Messages, *International Schools Journal, 15*(2), 8–22 (April 1996), and the many articles in the "Teaching for Multiple Intelligences" theme issue of *Educational Leadership, 55*(1) (September 1997).

17. See Chapter 2 of L. Campbell and B. Campbell, *Multiple Intelligences and Student Achievement: Success Stories From Six Schools* (Alexandria VA: Association for Supervision and Curriculum Development, 1999), and T. R. Hoerr, *Becoming a Multiple Intelligences School* (Alexandria, VA: Association for Supervision and Curriculum Development, 2000).

18. See, for example, L. English, "Uncovering Students' Analytic, Practical, and Creative Intelligences: One School's Application of Sternberg's Triarchic Theory," *School Administrator, 55*(1), 28–29 (January 1998).

19. See R. J. Sternberg, Teaching and Assessing for Successful Intelligence, *School Administrator, 55*(1), 26–27, 30–31 (January 1998).

20. See, for example, R. J. Marzano, 20th Century Advances in Instruction, Chapter 4 (pp. 67–95) of R. S. Brandt (Ed.), *Education in a New Era* (Alexandria, VA: ASCD Yearbook, Association for Supervision and Curriculum Development, 2000), p. 76.

21. See P. Guild, The Culture/Learning Style Connection, *Educational Leadership, 51*(8), 16–21 (May 1994).

22. Dunn, *Educating Diverse Learners,* p. 30.

23. These characteristics were adapted from C. Seefeldt and N. Barbour, *Early Childhood Education,* 3rd ed. (New York: Macmillan, 1994), pp. 56–59. By permission of Prentice Hall.

24. These characteristics were adapted from Seefelt and Barbour, ibid., pp. 59–63. By permission of Prentice Hall.

25. These characteristics were adapted from *Caught in the Middle: Educational Reform for Young Adolescents in California Public Schools* (Sacramento, CA: California State Department of Education, 1987), pp. 144–148.

26. See, for example, M. L. Yell, The Legal Basis of Inclusion, *Educational Leadership, 56*(2), 70–73 (October 1998). For information about education law as related to special education students, see the Web site at <http://www.access.digex.net/~edlawinc/>.

27. E. Tiegerman-Farber and C. Radziewicz, *Collaborative Decision Making: The Pathway to Inclusion* (Upper Saddle River, NJ: Merrill/Prentice Hall, 1998), pp. 12–13.

28. For a sample lesson using multilevel instruction and a discussion of other inclusive teaching techniques, see G. M. Johnson, Inclusive Education: Fundamental Instructional Strategies and Considerations, *Preventing School Failure, 43*(2), 72–78 (Winter 1999).

29. See L. Farlow, A Quartet of Success Stories: How to Make Inclusion Work, *Educational Leadership, 53*(5), 51–55 (April 1996), and other articles in the theme issue of "Students With Special-Needs."

30. See P. Berman, et al., *School Reform and Student Diversity, Volume II: Case Studies of Exemplary Practices for LEP Students* (Berkeley, CA: National Center for Research on Cultural Diversity and Second Language Learning, 1995).

31. See, for example, F. Genesee, Teaching Linguistically Diverse Students, *Principal, 79*(5), 24–27 (May 2000).

32. D. R. Walling, *English as a Second Language: 25 Questions and Answers,* Fastback 347 (Bloomington, IN: Phi Delta Kappa Educational Foundation, 1993), pp. 12–13. By permission.

33. Ibid., p. 26. Adapted by permission of D. Walling.

34. See K. M. Johns and C. Espinoza, *Mainstreaming Language Minority Children in Reading and Writing,* Fastback 340 (Bloomington, IN: Phi Delta Kappa Educational Foundation, 1992).

35. C. Minicucci, et al., School Reform and Student Diversity, *Phi Delta Kappan, 77*(1), 77–80 (September 1995), p. 78.

36. See the discussion in G. Clark and E. Zimmerman, Nurturing the Arts in Programs for Gifted and Talented Students, *Phi Delta Kappan, 79*(10), 747–751 (June 1998).

37. See, for example, J. F. Feldhusen, Programs for the Gifted Few or Talent Development for the Many? *Phi Delta Kappan, 79*(10), 735–738 (June 1998).

38. C. Dixon, L. Mains, and M. J. Reeves, *Gifted and At Risk,* Fastback 398 (Bloomington, IN: Phi Delta Kappa Educational Foundation, 1996), p. 7. See also P. D. Slocumb and R. K. Payne, Identifying and Nurturing the Gifted Poor, *Principal, 79*(5), 28–32 (May 2000).

39. S. B. Rimm, Underachievement Syndrome: A National Epidemic, in N. Colangelo and G. A. Davis (Eds.), *Handbook of Gifted Education,* 2nd ed. (Needham Heights, MA: Allyn & Bacon, 1997), p. 416.

40. From S. Schwartz, *Strategies for Identifying the Talents of Diverse Students.* ERIC/CUE Digest, Number 122, ED 410323 (New York: ERIC Clearinghouse on Urban Education, May 1997).

41. Adapted from C. Dixon, L. Mains, and M. J. Reeves, *Gifted and At Risk,* Fastback 398 (Bloomington, IN: Phi Delta Kappa Educational Foundation, 1996), pp. 9–12. By permission of the Phi Delta Kappa Educational Foundation.

42. C. Dixon, L. Mains, and M. J. Reeves, *Gifted and At Risk,* Fastback 398 (Bloomington, IN: Phi Delta Kappa Educational Foundation, 1996), p. 21.

43. See, for example, J. J. Gallagher, Accountability for Gifted Students, *Phi Delta Kappan, 79*(10), 739–742 (June 1998).

44. D. G. Gil, *Violence Against Children: Physical Child Abuse in the United States* (Cambridge, MA: Rand McNally, 1970).

45. See K. Burrett and T. Rusnak, *Integrated Character Education,* Fastback 351 (Bloomington, IN: Phi Delta Kappa Educational Foundation, 1993).

46. Ibid., p. 15.

47. See Chapter 11 of D. W. Johnson and R. T. Johnson, *Reducing School Violence Through Conflict Resolution* (Alexandria, VA: Association for Supervision and Curriculum Development, 1995).

3

What Are the Expectations, Responsibilities, and Facilitating Behaviors of a Classroom Teacher?

The primary expectation of any teacher is to facilitate student learning. As an elementary school classroom teacher your professional responsibilities will extend well beyond the ability to work effectively with a group of children in a classroom from approximately 8:30 a.m. until mid-afternoon. In this chapter, you will learn about the many responsibilities you will assume and the competencies and behaviors necessary for fulfilling them. Four categories of responsibilities and 22 competencies are identified.

The four categories are: (a) your responsibility as a reflective decision-maker; (b) your commitment to children and to the profession; (c) your non-instructional responsibilities; and (d) your instructional responsibilities and fundamental teaching behaviors. As these competencies and categories of responsibilities are presented, you are guided through the reality of these expectations as they exist for today's elementary school classroom teacher.

CHAPTER OBJECTIVES

Specifically, as you construct your understanding of the depth and breadth of the responsibilities of being an elementary school classroom teacher, upon completion of this chapter you should be able to

1. Compare and contrast teacher *facilitating behaviors* with *instructional strategies*.
2. Compare and contrast teacher use of praise and of encouragement, and describe situations in which each is more appropriate.
3. Compare and contrast the two phrases, *hands-on* and *minds-on learning*.
4. Demonstrate an understanding of the concept of *meaningful learning*.
5. Demonstrate knowledge of safety rules and guidelines for the classroom.
6. Demonstrate your developing understanding of the concept and use of multilevel instruction.
7. Demonstrate your growing understanding of the concept of teaching style and its relevance to classroom instruction.
8. Describe the concept of locus of control and its relationship to your professional responsibilities.
9. Describe the decision-making and thought-processing phases of instruction and the types of decisions you must make during each.
10. Describe what you can and cannot do if a child while under your supervision is in need of medication or first aid.

THE TEACHER AS A REFLECTIVE DECISION MAKER

During any single school day you will make hundreds of decisions. Some decisions will have been made prior to meeting your students for instruction, others will be made during the instructional activities, and yet still others are made later as you reflect on the school day. Let's now consider further the decision-making and thought-processing phases of instruction.

Decision-Making Phases of Instruction

Instruction can be divided into four decision-making and thought-processing phases: (a) the planning or *preactive phase*, (b) the teaching or *interactive phase*, (c) the analyzing and evaluating or *reflective phase*, and (d) the application or *projective phase*.[1]

The preactive phase consists of all those intellectual functions and decisions you will make prior to actual instruction. This includes decisions about the target goals and objectives, homework assignments, what children already know and can do, ap-propriate learning activities, questions to be asked (and possible answers), and the selection and preparation of instructional materials and the classroom.

The interactive phase includes all the decisions made during the immediacy and spontaneity of the teaching act. This includes maintaining student attention, questions to be asked, types of feedback given to the children, and ongoing adjustments to the lesson plan. Decisions made by you during this phase are likely to be more intuitive, unconscious, and routine than those made during the planning phase.

The reflective phase is the time you will take to reflect on, analyze, and judge the decisions and behaviors that occurred during the interactive phase. It is during reflection that you make decisions about student learning, student grades, feedback given to parents and guardians, and adjustments on the content and instruction to follow.

As a result of this reflection, decisions are made to use what was learned in subsequent teaching actions. At this point, you are in the projective phase, abstracting from your reflection and projecting your analysis into subsequent teaching behaviors.

Reflection, Locus of Control, and Teacher Responsibility

During the reflective phase, teachers have a choice of whether to assume full responsibility for the instructional outcomes or whether to assume responsibility for only the positive outcomes of the planned instruction while placing the blame for the negative outcomes on outside forces (e.g., parents and guardians, society in general, peers, other teachers, administrators, textbooks). Where the responsibility for outcomes is placed is referred to as *locus of control*.

Teachers who are intrinsically motivated and professionally accomplished tend to assume full responsibility for the instructional outcomes, regardless of whether or not the outcomes are as intended from the planning phase.[2] Of course every teacher realizes that there are factors which the teacher cannot control, such as the negative effects on children from poverty, gangs, alcohol and drug abuse, so they must do what they can within the confines of the classroom and their time with the children to reduce negative effects of such outside factors. History is brimming with examples of how a relatively few but positive moments with a truly caring and knowledgeable teacher can drastically change for the better the life of a child who until then had a history of mostly negative experiences.

Now, further your understanding by doing Exercises 3.1 and 3.2.

EXERCISE 3.1 THE TEACHER AS A REFLECTIVE DECISION-MAKER

Instructions: The purpose of this exercise is to learn more about the nature of the decisions and the decision-making process used by teachers. To accomplish this, you are to talk with and observe one elementary (or middle) school teacher for one hour. Obtain permission from a cooperating teacher by explaining the purpose of your observations. A follow-up thank-you note would be appropriate.

Using the following format, tabulate the number of decisions the teacher makes during that period. You may first want to make your tabulations on a separate sheet of paper, and then organize and transfer them to this page. To tabulate the decisions made before and after instruction, confer with the teacher after class. Share the results with your classmates.

School, teacher, and class observed: _____

1. Decisions made before instruction (examples: objectives of lesson; amount of time to be devoted

   to particular activities; classroom management procedures) _____

   _____

   _____

   _____

   _____

   _____

   _____

   _____

2. Decisions made during instruction (examples: called on someone to answer a question; remained

   silent until students in back corner became quiet; talked with a tardy student) _____

   _____

   _____

   _____

   _____

   _____

   _____

   _____

3. Decisions made after instruction (examples: to review a particular concept tomorrow; to arrange

   a conference to talk with a student about his hostility in class; to make a revision in Friday's

   homework assignment) _____

   _____

   _____

EXERCISE 3.1 *(continued)*

_____

_____

_____

_____

_____

_____

4. What was the total number of decisions made by this teacher before instruction? _____ during instruction? _____ after instruction? _____ Compare your results with those of others in your class.

5. Did you observe any evidence that this teacher assumed full responsibility for the learning outcomes of this class session? If so, describe the evidence. _____

_____

_____

6. What percentage of all decisions by this teacher were planned? _____ spontaneous? _____

7. Did you share your results of this exercise with the cooperating teacher? What were his or her reactions? _____

_____

_____

_____

_____

_____

_____

8. What are your conclusions from this exercise? _____

_____

_____

_____

_____

_____

_____

_____

EXERCISE 3.2 THE PREACTIVE PHASE OF INSTRUCTION

Instructions: Mentally rehearsing the teacher's actions before meeting the students is absolutely essential for effective teaching and learning. The purpose of this exercise is to stress the importance of clearly and fully thinking about what you will do and say in the classroom in order to identify possible problems. Follow these steps:

1. Select a grade level.

2. Objective of lesson: Students will design a name tag for their desks during a 20-minute period.

3. Without looking ahead at step 4, write a lesson plan for this activity. (Although you have not yet learned the details of lesson planning, outline the steps you would follow and the things you would say to your students in order to accomplish the objective.) _____

_____

_____

_____

_____

_____

_____

4. To analyze the thoroughness of your preactive thinking, respond to the following questions:

_____

  a. Are materials listed in your plan? _____

  b. Are those materials readily available in your classroom? _____

  c. Will the paper or tag board need to be precut? _____

  d. How large can the name tags be? _____

  e. How and where will they be attached to each desk? _____

  f. Should they be flat or three-dimensional? _____

  _____

  _____

  g. Do you have markers or crayons, or are the students expected to have them? _____

  h. Will students need scissors? _____

  i. Do you have left-handed scissors available if needed? _____

  j. Should name tags have first name and last name or last initial? _____

  k. Can other words or designs be added? _____

  l. When and how will materials be distributed and collected? _____

  _____

  _____

EXERCISE 3.2 *(continued)*

m. What plan do you have for absent or tardy students? _____

_____

_____

5. Share the results of your steps 1–4 with members of your class. Did others come up with other questions relevant to the preplanning for this instructional period? If so, share them with the rest of the class. _____

_____

_____

_____

_____

_____

_____

_____

_____

_____

_____

_____

_____

_____

_____

_____

_____

_____

_____

_____

_____

_____

Conclusion: A teacher who practices thorough preactive planning should have planned answers for each of these questions.

TEACHING STYLE

Teaching style is the way teachers teach, which includes their distinctive mannerisms complemented by their choices of teaching behaviors and strategies. A teacher's style affects the way that teacher presents information and interacts with the students. It clearly is the manner and pattern of those interactions with students that determine a teacher's effectiveness in promoting student learning, positive attitudes about learning, and students' self-esteem.

A teacher's style is determined by the teacher's personal characteristics (especially the teacher's own learning style), experiences, and knowledge of research findings about how children learn. Teaching style can be altered, intentionally or unintentionally, as a result of changes in any of these three areas.

While there are other ways to label and to describe teaching styles, we shall consider two contrasting styles—the *traditional* and the *facilitating* styles (see Table 3.1)—to emphasize that while today's teacher must use aspects from each (that is, be eclectic in style choice), there must be a strong inclination toward the facilitating style.

Multilevel Instruction

As emphasized in Chapter 2, children in your classroom have their own independent ways of knowing and learning. It is important to try to attend to how each student best learns and to where each student is developmentally, that is, to personalize both the content and the methods of learning. In essence, although perhaps not as detailed as are the IEPs prepared for special education students, at various times during the school year you will be developing personalized educational plans for each student, perhaps in collaboration with members of your teaching team. To accomplish that, you can use *multilevel instruction* (known also as *multitasking*). As explained in Chapter 2 (see Figure 2.1), multilevel instruction is when individual students and groups of students are working at different tasks to accomplish the same objective or are working at different tasks to accomplish different objectives. For example, while some students may be working independently of the teacher—that is, within the facilitating mode—others may be receiving direct instruction—that is, more within the traditional mode.

When integrating student learning, as you will be learning in Part II of this resource guide,

Table 3.1
A contrast of two teaching styles

Characteristic	Traditional Style	Facilitating Style
Teacher is:	Autocratic	Democratic
	Curriculum-centered	Student-centered
	Direct	Indirect
	Dominative	Interactive
	Formal	Informal
	Informative	Inquiring
	Prescriptive	Reflective
Classroom is:	Teacher-centered	Student-centered
	Linear (seats facing front of room)	Grouped or circular
Instructional modes are:	Abstract learning	Concrete learning
	Teacher-centered discussion	Discussions
	Lectures	Peer and cross-age coaching
	Competitive learning	Cooperative learning
	Some problem-solving	Problem-solving
	Demonstrations by teacher from simple to complex	Student inquiries that start with complex tasks and use instructional scaffolding and dialogue
	Transmission of information from teacher to students	Reciprocal teaching using a dialogue between the teacher and a small group of students, and then just among students

multitasking is an important and useful, perhaps even obligatory, strategy. Project-based learning (discussed in Chapter 8) is an instructional method that easily allows for the provision of multilevel instruction.

The Theoretical Origins of Teaching Styles and Their Relation to Constructivism

Constructivist teaching and the integration of curriculum are not new to education. The importance of constructivism and curriculum integration approaches are found, for example, in the writings of John Dewey,[3] Arthur W. Combs,[4] Jean Piaget,[5] and Lev Vygotsky.[6]

Instructional styles are deeply rooted in certain theoretical assumptions about learners and their development, and while it is beyond the scope of this resource guide to explore deeply into those assumptions, there are, worth mentioning here, three major theoretical positions with research findings, each of which is based on certain philosophical and psychological assumptions that suggest different ways of working with children. The theoretical positions are described briefly in the next three paragraphs.

Tied to the theoretical positions of *romanticism-maturationism* is the assumption that the learner's mind is neutral-passive to good-active, and the main focus in teaching should be the addition of new ideas to a subconscious store of old ones. Key persons include Jean J. Rousseau and Sigmund Freud; key instructional strategies include classic lecturing with rote memorization.

Tied to the theoretical position of *behaviorism* is the assumption that the learner's mind is neutral-passive with innate reflexes and needs, and the main focus in teaching should be on the successive, systematic changes in the learner's environment to increase the possibilities of desired behavior responses. Key persons include John Locke, B. F. Skinner, A. H. Thorndike, Robert Gagné, and John Watson; key instructional strategies include programmed instruction and practice and reinforcement as in workbook drill activities.

Tied to the theoretical position of *cognitive-experimentalism* (including *constructivism*) is the assumption that the learner is a neutral-interactive purposive individual in simultaneous interaction with physical and biological environments. The main focus in teaching should be on facilitating the learner's gain and construction of new perceptions that lead to desired behavioral changes and ultimately to a more fully functioning individual. Key persons are John Dewey, Lev Vygotsky, Jerome Bruner, Jean Piaget, and Arthur W. Combs; key instructional strategies include discovery, inquiry, project-centered teaching, cooperative and social-interactive learning, and integrated curriculum.

It is our opinion that with a diversity of students, to be most effective an elementary school-teacher must be eclectic, but with a strong emphasis toward cognitive-experimentalism-constructivism because of its divergence in learning and the importance given to learning as a change in perceptions. An effective approach is to use at appropriate times the best of strategies and knowledgeable instructor behaviors, regardless of whether individually they can be classified within any style dichotomy, such as direct vs. indirect, formal vs. informal, or traditional vs. progressive, or didactic vs. facilitative.

Now, to further your understanding, do Exercise 3.3. After you complete the exercise, we review the category of commitment and professionalism.

EXERCISE 3.3 USING A QUESTIONNAIRE TO DEVELOP A PROFILE AND A STATEMENT ABOUT MY OWN EMERGING TEACHING STYLE

Instructions: The purpose of this exercise is to help you clarify and articulate your own assumptions about teaching and learning. You will develop a profile of your emerging teaching style and from that a statement representative of your current thinking about teaching and learning.

Step 1. Read each of the 50 statements below and rate your feelings about each as follows:

1 = strongly agree; *2* = neutral; *3* = strongly disagree.*

_____ 1. Most of what children learn, they learn on their own.

_____ 2. Children should be concerned about other students' reactions to their work in the classroom.

_____ 3. An important part of schooling is learning to work with others.

_____ 4. Children learn more by working on their own than by working with others.

_____ 5. Children should be given opportunities to participate actively in class planning and the implementation of lessons.

_____ 6. In an effective learning environment, grades are inappropriate.

_____ 7. Children enjoy working in a classroom that has clearly defined learning objectives and assessment criteria.

_____ 8. I favor teaching methods and classroom procedures that maximize student independence to learn from their own experiences.

_____ 9. Most of what children learn is learned from other children.

_____ 10. Children should be concerned with getting good grades.

_____ 11. An important part of teaching and learning should be to learn how to work independently.

_____ 12. A teacher should not be contradicted or challenged by a student.

_____ 13. Interchanges between children and a teacher can provide better ideas about content than those found in a textbook.

_____ 14. For children to get the most out of a class, they must be aware of the primary concerns and biases of the teacher.

_____ 15. Children should not be given high grades unless they are clearly earned.

_____ 16. Learning should help a child to become an independent thinker.

_____ 17. Most of what children learn is learned from their teachers.

_____ 18. A teacher who makes children do things they don't want to do is an ineffective teacher.

_____ 19. Learning takes place most effectively under conditions in which children are in competition with one another.

_____ 20. A teacher should try to convince students that particular ideas are valid and exciting.

*Adapted with permission from William H. Berquist and Steven R. Phillips, *A Handbook for Faculty Development* (Washington, DC: The Council for Independent Colleges, June 1975), pp. 25–27.

EXERCISE 3.3 *(continued)*

_____ 21. To do well in school, children must be assertive.

_____ 22. Facts in textbooks are usually accurate.

_____ 23. I favor the use of teaching methods and classroom procedures that maximize student and teacher interaction.

_____ 24. Most of what children learn is learned from books.

_____ 25. A teacher who lets children do whatever they want is incompetent.

_____ 26. Children can learn more by working with an enthusiastic teacher than by working alone.

_____ 27. I favor the use of teaching methods and classroom procedures that maximize student learning of basic subject-matter content.

_____ 28. Ideas of other children are useful in helping a child understand the content of lessons.

_____ 29. A child should study what the teacher says is important and not necessarily what is important to that child.

_____ 30. A teacher who does not motivate student interest in subject content is incompetent.

_____ 31. An important part of education is learning how to perform under testing and evaluation conditions.

_____ 32. Children can learn more by sharing their ideas than by keeping their ideas to themselves.

_____ 33. Teachers tend to give students too many trivial assignments.

_____ 34. Ideas contained in the textbook should be the primary source of the content taught.

_____ 35. Children should be given high grades as a means of motivating them and increasing their self-esteem.

_____ 36. The ideas a student brings into a class are useful for helping the child to understand subject content.

_____ 37. Students should study what is important to them and not necessarily what the teacher claims is important.

_____ 38. Learning takes place most effectively under conditions in which children are working independently of one another.

_____ 39. Teachers often give students too much freedom of choice in content, methods, and procedures.

_____ 40. Teachers should clearly explain what it is they expect from students.

_____ 41. Childrens' ideas about content are often better than the ideas found in textbooks.

_____ 42. Classroom discussions are beneficial learning experiences.

_____ 43. A student's education should help the student to become a successful and contributing member of society.

_____ 44. Learning takes place most effectively under conditions in which students are working cooperatively with one another.

_____ 45. Teachers often are too personal with their students.

_____ 46. A teacher should encourage children to disagree with or challenge that teacher in the classroom.

_____ 47. Children have to be able to work effectively with other people to do well in school.

_____ 48. For children to get the most out of school, they must assume at least part of the responsibility for their learning.

_____ 49. Students seem to enjoy discussing their ideas about learning with the teacher and other students.

_____ 50. A child's education should help the child to become a sensitive human being.

Step 2. From the above list of 50 items, write the numbers of those items with which you strongly agreed in one column and the numbers of those with which you strongly disagreed in the other column. Ignore those items to which you were neutral.

Strongly Agreed　　　　　　　　　　　　*Strongly Disagreed*

EXERCISE 3.3 *(continued)*

Step 3. In groups of three or four, discuss the lists you generated in Step 2 with your classmates. After the discussion, you may rerank any items you wish.

Step 4. You now have a finalized list of those items with which you agree and those with which you disagree. On the basis of those two lists, write a paragraph that summarizes your philosophy about teaching and learning. It should be no longer than one-half page in length. This statement is a theoretical representation of your present teaching philosophy.

_____

_____

_____

_____

_____

_____

_____

_____

_____

Step 5. Compare your philosophical statement with the three theoretical positions discussed earlier in this chapter. Can you clearly identify your position? Name it. _____

_____

_____

_____

_____

Explain your rationale. _____

_____

_____

_____

_____

_____

At the completion of this text, you may wish to revisit your philosophical statement and perhaps even to revise it. It will be useful for you to have your educational philosophy firmly in mind for your teaching interviews at a later date.

THE TEACHER'S PROFESSIONALISM AND COMMITMENT

The classroom teacher is expected to demonstrate commitment to the school's mission (discussed in Chapter 1) and to the personal as well as the intellectual development of the children (discussed in Chapter 2). Not only do the most accomplished teachers expect, demand, and receive positive results in learning from their students while in the classroom, they are also interested and involved in the activities of the children outside the classroom, willing to sacrifice personal time to give them attention and guidance.

Noninstructional Responsibilities

The aspects of the teacher as a decision-maker with professional commitments take on a very real dimension when you consider specific noninstruction-related and instruction-related responsibilities of the classroom teacher. Shown in Figure 3.1 are 13 categories of items that should alert you to the many noninstructional matters with which you should become familiar. Beginning teachers often underestimate their importance and the amount of time they require.

Student Physical Safety: Rules and Guidelines

One item on the list in Figure 3.1 (number 7) includes the responsibility of providing a safe environment, both psychological and physical. The psychological aspect is introduced later in this chapter and in Chapter 4, and the physical safety aspect is discussed here.

Teachers are responsible for preventing accidents and ensuring that the classroom is as safe as possible. Nevertheless, accidents and resulting injuries do occur to children at school. During a language-arts lesson, a student is injured by glass from a falling windowpane when the teacher attempts to open a stuck window. A student is injured when the child falls and lands on a lawn-sprinkler head on the playground during recess. While doing a science experiment, a student is burned by a candle flame. So, you need to understand what you can do as a classroom teacher to prevent accidents from happening. And, you need to know what you should and should not do when an accident does happen. See the classroom safety rules and guidelines in Figure 3.2, and use the items as a basis for discussion with your classmates. The school in which you ultimately teach will, of course, have its own separate written rules and guidelines that may be more or less extensive than those found in Figure 3.2.

Figure 3.1
Noninstructional responsibilities of the classroom teacher

1. Knowledgeable about activities of interest to the students
2. Familiarity with the school campus and community
3. Acquainted with members of the faculty and the support staff
4. Knowledgeable about school and district policies
5. Familiar with the backgrounds of the students
6. Knowledgeable about procedures for such routine matters as: planning and scheduling of before- and after-school activities, restroom regulations, distribution and collection of textbooks and other school materials, class dismissal, ordering of supplies, fire drills and severe weather, daily attendance records, school assemblies, sharing of instructional space with other teachers, and arranging for and preparing displays for common areas of the school
7. Performing classroom duties such as maintaining a cheerful, pleasant, productively efficient, and safe learning environment; obtaining materials needed for each lesson; keeping supplies orderly; supervising students who are helpers
8. Your expected role in the parent-teacher organization and other community participation meetings
9. The many conferences that will be needed, such as those between teacher and teacher, teacher and resource specialist, teacher and student, teacher and parent or guardian, teacher, student, and parent/guardian, teacher and administrator, and teacher and community representative
10. Professional meetings, such as those of the teaching team, other school and district committees, parent-teacher and community groups, and local, regional, state, and national professional organizations
11. Your role in the school's advisory or homeroom program
12. Your role in administering standardized assessments of student achievement
13. Time to relax and enjoy family and hobbies

Figure 3.2
Safety rules and guidelines for the elementary schoolteacher and classroom

1. Whenever an accident happens, notify the school office immediately by telephoning or sending a pair of student runners to the office.
2. You should give first aid *only* when necessary to save a child's life or limb. When life or limb is not at risk, then you should follow school policy by referring the student immediately to professional care. When immediate professional care is unavailable and you believe that immediate first aid is necessary, then you can take prudent action, as if you were that child's parent or legal guardian. But you must always be cautious and knowledgeable about what you are doing, so to not cause further injury.
3. Unless you are a licensed medical professional, you should *never* give medication to a child, whether prescription or over-the-counter. See school policy on this. Be alert for children who have allergies or other medical problems, and be aware of what you can and must do if a particular student is having a medical problem while in your classroom.
4. Rules for science investigations should be taught to the children, posted in a conspicuous place, and reviewed and rehearsed frequently.
5. When taking children on a field trip, solicit adult help, even when the destination is only a short distance from the school. A recommended guideline is one or more adults for every 10 children.
6. Maintain a neat classroom, with aisles kept clear and books, coats, and back packs in designated storage areas. Students should not wear coats while doing laboratory investigations. Loose-fitting clothing can too easily knock over equipment.
7. Be aware of eye safety precautions and regulations regarding eye protection.
8. Do not use flammable materials and alcohol burners. Use lighted candles and hot plates only with extreme care.
9. Maintain a well-supplied first aid kit in the classroom.
10. Know exactly what to do in case of emergencies, and have emergency procedures posted conspicuously in the classroom.
11. Have an adequately charged ABC-type fire extinguisher readily available.
12. Use proper waste disposal methods. Learn from the school district the regulations for disposing of various kinds of waste materials.
13. Maintain accurate labels on all drawers, cupboards, and containers.
14. Children should never be allowed to taste unknown substances.
15. Avoid having dangerous plants, animals, chemicals, and apparatus in the classroom. Instruct children to never handle or bring dead animals into the classroom.
16. Handle pets with care and caution. For example, birds can carry psittacosis and salmonella bacteria. People should wash their hands thoroughly after handling bird feeders. Turtles and other animals also can carry salmonella bacteria. Dogs, rabbits, and other animals may carry parasites. Some children are allergic to animal dander.
17. Do not store heavy items above the heads of the children.
18. Do not allow children to climb or to be in positions where they may fall.
19. Do not leave dangerously sharp objects or those that may shatter where children can obtain them without approval and supervision.
20. Avoid allowing students to overheat or to overexert themselves.
21. Never leave children unattended in the classroom or on the school campus for any reason.
22. Inspect electrical equipment for frayed cords and, if frayed, do not use.
23. Avoid overloading an electrical circuit.
24. Disconnect electrical appliances, especially heating appliances, when they are not being used. Make sure the switch is in the off position before disconnecting or connecting an electrical appliance.
25. Do not poke around the back of a computer, television set, or other electrical appliance when the appliance is plugged in.
26. Do not touch an electrical cord with wet hands.
27. Do not wrap or coil the cords of electrical appliances that are plugged in.
28. Keep magnets away from computers and other electronic appliances.
29. Employ caution when using any mechanical equipment with moving parts.
30. Under no circumstances should human body fluids be used for a science investigation or any other reason.

Instructional Responsibilities

The 16 items illustrated in Figure 3.3 portray the instructional responsibilities you will have as a classroom teacher. These responsibilities are the primary focus of study during the remainder of the content of this resource guide. After reviewing the lists of instructional and noninstructional responsibilities of the classroom teacher, do Exercise 3.4.

Figure 3.3
Instructional responsibilities of the classroom teacher

1. Becoming familiar with relevant curriculum standards and assessment tools
2. Planning units and lessons
3. Learning the interests of the children so the lessons and learning activities will reflect those interests
4. Incorporating the individual learning styles, capacities, and modalities of the students in lesson plans
5. Reading student papers
6. Assessing and recording student progress and achievements
7. Preparing the classroom
8. Providing classroom instruction
9. Thinking about professional growth and development, which may include attending university courses, attending workshops and other presentations offered by the school district or professional organizations, and reading professional literature
10. Developing an effective classroom management system
11. Reacquainting yourself with the developmental characteristics of children
12. Learning the background of children with special problems who might cause concerns in the classroom
13. Developing techniques and plans for using cross-age tutoring, peer coaching, cooperative learning, project work, and other instructional strategies
14. Identifying resources and sources
15. Devoting time to team planning
16. Holding conferences with individual children

EXERCISE 3.4 REVIEWING THE PROFESSIONAL RESPONSIBILITIES OF A FIRST-YEAR TEACHER

Instructions: The purpose of this exercise is to review the responsibilities of a first-year teacher. Have the class of teacher candidates divide into groups of four. Within each group, each member should play one of the following roles: (a) group facilitator; (b) recorder; (c) materials manager; and (d) reporter. The group is to choose one of these six categories of responsibilities:

1. Audiovisual/media
2. Classroom environment
3. Clerical
4. Instructional
5. Professional activities
6. Supervision

The group should then read the responsibilities for their selected category listed on the following cards and arrange them in prioritized order, beginning with the most important. The group facilitator will lead this discussion. Under the guidance of the materials manager, the group may cut the cards apart so that they can be physically manipulated as priorities are discussed. The recorder should take notes of the group's work, which can then be discussed to develop the report that will be made to the class.

After a prearranged discussion time, recall the entire class and ask each reporter to share the group's (a) prioritized order of responsibilities and (b) estimate of the amount of time that a beginning teacher might devote to these responsibilities each week.

As each group reports, all members of the class should enter its list of priorities and time estimate on the Recap Sheet.

After completion of this exercise, the class may wish to discuss the group dynamics of this model of cooperative learning (see Chapter 8). For discussion in either large or small groups, key questions might be:

1. Would you use this form of discussion in your own teaching?

2. How would you divide a class into groups of four?

Other questions may be generated by the group work.

CARDS FOR EXERCISE 3.4
AUDIOVISUAL/MEDIA RESPONSIBILITIES

Selecting, ordering, and returning cassettes, films, videodiscs, and other materials	
Preparing and operating equipment	Reviewing selected materials
Planning class introduction to the audiovisual materials	Other audiovisual responsibilities as determined

Estimated hours a beginning teacher will devote to audiovisual/media responsibilities each week = _____

CARDS FOR EXERCISE 3.4
CLASSROOM ENVIRONMENT RESPONSIBILITIES

Planning and constructing displays	Preparing bulletin boards
Reading, announcing, and posting class notices	Managing a classroom library
Opening and closing windows, arranging furniture, cleaning the writing board	Other classroom environment responsibilities as determined

Estimated hours a beginning teacher will devote to classroom environment responsibilities each week = _____

CARDS FOR EXERCISE 3.4
CLERICAL RESPONSIBILITIES

Maintaining attendance and tardy records	Entering grades, scores, or marks into a record book or onto the computer
Preparing progress and grade reports	Typing, drawing, and duplicating instructional materials
Locating resource ideas and materials to support lessons	Other clerical responsibilities as determined

Estimated hours a beginning teacher will devote to clerical responsibilities each week = _____

For Your Notes

CARDS FOR EXERCISE 3.4
INSTRUCTIONAL RESPONSIBILITIES

Giving additional instruction (e.g., to students who need one-to-one attention, those who have been absent, or small review groups)	Correcting student work
Preparing special learning materials	Preparing, reading, and scoring tests; helping students self-evaluate
Writing information on the board	Preparing long-range and daily lesson plans
Grouping for instruction	Other instructional responsibilities as determined

Estimated hours a beginning teacher will devote to clerical responsibilities each week = _____

CARDS FOR EXERCISE 3.4
PROFESSIONAL ACTIVITIES RESPONSIBILITIES

Researching and writing teacher reports	Attending teachers' and school district meetings
Planning and attending parent-teacher meetings	Attending local teachers' organization meetings
Attending state, regional, and national professional organizations; taking university classes	Other professional activities responsibilities as determined

Estimated hours a beginning teacher will devote to professional activities each week = _____

CARDS FOR EXERCISE 3.4
SUPERVISION RESPONSIBILITIES

Supervising before- or after-school activities	Supervising hallways, lunchrooms, and bathrooms
Supervising student assemblies	Supervising field trips
Supervising laboratory activities	Helping students settle dispute
Other supervision responsibilities as determined	

Estimated hours a beginning teacher will devote to supervision responsibilities each week = _____

For Your Notes

EXERCISE 3.4 RECAP SHEET

Audiovisual/Media Responsibilities

1. _____

2. _____

3. _____

4. _____

5. _____

Estimated hours = _____

Classroom Environment Responsibilities

1. _____

2. _____

3. _____

4. _____

5. _____

6. _____

Estimated hours = _____

Clerical Responsibilities

1. _____

2. _____

3. _____

4. _____

5. _____

6. _____

Estimated hours = _____

Instructional Responsibilities

1. _____

2. _____

3. _____

4. _____

5. _____

6. _____

7. _____

8. _____

Estimated hours = _____

EXERCISE 3.4 *(continued)*

Professional Activities Responsibilities

1. _____

2. _____

3. _____

4. _____

5. _____

6. _____

Estimated hours = _____

Supervision Responsibilities

1. _____

2. _____

3. _____

4. _____

5. _____

6. _____

7. _____

Estimated hours = _____

IDENTIFYING AND BUILDING YOUR INSTRUCTIONAL COMPETENCIES

The overall purpose of this resource guide is to assist you in building your instructional competencies. To do that, we need a starting place and this is it, beginning with the identification and presentation of 22 specific competencies.[7] You will continue to reflect on and to build upon these competencies through your study of the remaining chapters of this book and, indeed, throughout your professional career.

Characteristics of the Competent Classroom Teacher: An Annotated List

Before you read further we must caution you to please not feel overwhelmed by the following list; it may well be that no teacher expertly models all the characteristics that follow. The characteristics do, however, represent an ideal model to strive for.

1. *The teacher is knowledgeable about the subject matter content expected to be taught.* You should have both historical understanding and current knowledge of the structure of those subjects you are expected to teach, and of the facts, principles, concepts, and skills needed for those subjects. This doesn't mean you need to know everything about the subject, but more than you are likely to teach.

2. *The teacher is an "educational broker."* You will learn where and how to discover information about content you are expected to teach. You cannot know everything there is to know about each subject—indeed, you will not always be able to predict all that is learned—but you should become knowledgeable about where and how to best research it and how to assist your students in developing those same skills. Among other things, this means that you should be computer literate, that is, have the ability to understand and use computers for research, writing, and communicating, paralleling reading and writing in verbal literacy.

3. *The teacher is an active member of professional organizations, reads professional journals, dialogues with colleagues, and maintains currency both in methodology and about the students and the subject content the teacher is expected to teach.* While this resource guide offers valuable information about teaching and learning, it is much closer to the start of your professional career than it is to the end. As a teacher you are a learner among learners. Through workshops, advanced course work, and coaching and training; through the acquisition of further knowledge by reading and study; and through collaboration with and role modeling of significant and more experienced colleagues, from this

time on you will be in a perpetual learning mode about teaching and learning (see Chapter 12).

4. *The teacher understands the processes of learning.* You will ensure that students understand the lesson objectives, your expectations, and the classroom procedures, that they feel welcomed to your classroom and involved in the learning activities, and that they have some control over the pacing of their own learning. Furthermore, when preparing lessons, you will (a) consider the unique learning characteristics of each student; (b) see that content is presented in reasonably small doses—and in a logical and coherent sequence—while using learning activities that engage all learning modalities, with opportunities for guided practice and reinforcement, and (c) frequently check for student comprehension to ensure that the students are learning. (By *frequent checks for comprehension* we mean on average at least one check per minute.) Checks for comprehension can be accomplished in many ways, such as by the questions you and the children ask during the lesson, by your awareness and understanding of student facial expressions and body language, as well as by various kinds of checklists (see Chapters 7 and 11).

5. *The teacher uses effective modeling behaviors.* Your own behaviors must be consistent with those expected of your students. If, for example, you want your students to demonstrate regular and punctual attendance, to have their work done on time, to have their materials each day for learning, to demonstrate cooperative behavior and respect for the rights and possessions of others, to maintain an open and inquisitive mind, to demonstrate critical thinking, and to use proper communication skills, then you will do likewise, modeling those same behaviors and attitudes for the children. As a teacher, you serve as a very important role model for your students. Whether you realize it or not, your behavior sends important messages to students that complement curriculum content. You serve the children well when you practice that which you teach and when you model inclusive and collaborative approaches to learning. Specific guidelines for effective modeling are presented later in this chapter.

6. *The teacher is open to change, willing to take risks and to be held accountable.* If there were no difference between what is and what can be, then formal schooling would be of little value. A competent teacher knows not only of historical and traditional values and knowledge, but also of the value of change, and is willing to carefully plan and experiment, to move between that which is known and that which is not. In the words of Selma Wassermann, "no coward ever got the Great Teacher Award."[8] Realizing that little of value is ever achieved without a certain amount of

risk, and because of personal strength of convictions, the competent teacher stands ready to be held accountable, as the teacher undoubtedly will be, for assuming such risks.

7. *The teacher is nonprejudiced toward gender, sexual orientation, ethnicity, skin color, religion, physical handicaps, socioeconomic status, learning disabilities, or national origin.* Among other things, this means no sexual innuendoes, religious or ethnic jokes, or racial slurs. It means being cognizant of how teachers, male and female, knowingly or unknowingly, historically have mistreated female students and of how to avoid those same errors in your own teaching. (See Chapter 8 for specific guidelines.) It means learning about and attending to the needs of individual students in your classroom. It means having high expectations for every child.

8. *The teacher organizes the classroom and plans lessons carefully.* Long-range plans and daily lessons are prepared thoughtfully, reflected on, revised, and implemented with creative, motivating, and effective strategies and skill. Part II of this resource guide is devoted to assisting in your development of this competency.

9. *The teacher is a capable communicator.* The competent teacher uses thoughtfully selected words, carefully planned questions, expressive voice inflections, useful pauses, meaningful gestures, active listening, and productive and nonconfusing body language, some of which were carefully and thoughtfully planned during the preactive phase of instruction and others of which have, through practice and reflection, become second-nature skills. Throughout this book, but especially in Chapters 4 and 9, you will find useful suggestions for your development of this competency.

10. *The teacher can function effectively as a decision-maker.* The elementary school classroom is a complex place, busy with fast-paced activities. In a single day you may engage in a thousand or more interpersonal exchanges with children, to say nothing about the numerous exchanges possible with the many adults with whom you will be in contact. The competent teacher is in control of classroom events rather than controlled by them. The teacher initiates, rather than merely reacts, is proactive and in control of her or his interactions, having learned how to manage time to analyze and develop effective interpersonal behaviors.

11. *The teacher is in a perpetual learning mode, striving to further develop a repertoire of teaching strategies.* As discussed earlier (competency number 2) competent teachers are good students, continuing their own learning by reflecting on and assessing their work, attending workshops, studying the work of others, and talking with students, parents and guardians, and col-

leagues. (The topic of ongoing professional development is the essence of Chapter 12.)

12. *The teacher demonstrates concern for the safety and health of the children.* The competent teacher consistently models safety procedures (see, for example, Figure 3.2), ensuring precautions necessary to protect the health and psychological and physical safety of the students. The teacher strives to maintain a comfortable room temperature with adequate ventilation and to prevent safety hazards in the classroom. Students who are ill are encouraged to stay home and to get well. Rather than bringing germs to school, the teacher models this same expectation. If a teacher suspects that a student may be ill or may be suffering from neglect or abuse at home, the teacher appropriately and promptly acts upon that suspicion.

13. *The teacher demonstrates optimism for the learning of every child, while providing a constructive and positive environment for learning.* Both common sense and research tell us clearly that children enjoy and learn better from a teacher who is positive and optimistic, encouraging, nurturing, and happy, rather than from a teacher who is negative and pessimistic, discouraging, uninterested, and grumpy.

14. *The teacher demonstrates confidence in every child's ability to learn.* For a child, nothing at school is more satisfying than a teacher who demonstrates confidence in that child's abilities. Unfortunately, for some children, a teacher's show of confidence may be the only positive indicator that child ever receives. Each of us can recall with admiration a teacher (or other significant person) who demonstrated confidence in our ability to accomplish seemingly formidable tasks. A competent teacher demonstrates this confidence with each and every student. This doesn't mean that you must personally like every student with whom you will ever come into contact; it does mean that you accept each one as a person of dignity and who is worthy of receiving your respect and professional skills. Remember that each child is a work in progress.

15. *The teacher is skillful and fair in the employment of strategies for the assessment of student learning.* The competent teacher is knowledgeable about the importance of providing immediate intensive intervention when learning problems become apparent, implementing appropriate learning assessment tools, while avoiding the abuse of power afforded by the assessment process. Assessment of student learning is the focus of Chapter 11.

16. *The teacher is skillful in working with parents and guardians, colleagues, administrators, and the school support staff, maintaining and nurturing friendly and ethical professional relationships.* Teachers, parents and guardians, adminis-

trators, cooks, bus drivers, custodians, secretaries, and other adults of the school community all share one common purpose, and that is to serve the education of the children. It is done best when they do it collaboratively. An exemplary school and a skillful teacher work together to ensure that parents or guardians are involved in their children's learning (as discussed in Chapters 1 and 11).

17. *The teacher demonstrates continuing interest in professional responsibilities and opportunities.* Knowing that ultimately each and every school activity has an effect upon the classroom, the competent teacher assumes an active interest in the school community. The purpose of the school is to serve the education of the children, and the classroom is the primary, but not only, place where this occurs. Every committee meeting, school event, team meeting, faculty meeting, school board meeting, office, program, and any other planned function that is related to school life shares in the ultimate purpose of better serving the education of the children who attend that school.

18. *The teacher exhibits a wide range of interests.* This includes interest in the activities of the students and the many aspects of the school and its surrounding community. The competent teacher is interesting because of that teacher's interests; a teacher with varied interests more often motivates and captures the attention of more students. A teacher with no interests outside the classroom is likely for the children to be an exceedingly dull teacher.

19. *The teacher shares a healthy sense of humor.* The positive effects of appropriate humor (that is, humor that is not self-deprecating or disrespectful of others) on learning are well established: increases immune system activity and decreases stress-producing hormones; drops the pulse rate; reduces feelings of anxiety, tension, and stress; activates T-cells for the immune system, antibodies that fight against harmful microorganisms, and gamma interferon, a hormone that fights viruses and regulates cell growth; and increases blood oxygen. Because of these effects, humor is a stimulant to not only healthy living, but to creativity and higher-level thinking. As they should, students appreciate and learn more from a teacher who shares a healthy sense of humor and laughs with (not at) the children.

20. *The teacher is quick to recognize a child who may be in need of special attention.* A competent teacher is alert to recognize any student who demonstrates behaviors indicating a need for special attention. The teacher knows how and where to refer the student, doing so with minimal class disruption and without embarrassment to the child. For example, a pattern of increasingly poor attendance or of steady negative-attention seeking behaviors are two of the more obvious early signals of a troubled child, one who is potentially at-risk of dropping out of school.

21. *The teacher makes specific and frequent efforts to demonstrate how the subject content may be related to the lives of the students.* A potentially dry and dull topic is made significant and alive when taught by a competent teacher. Regardless of topic, somewhere there are accomplished teachers teaching that topic, and one of the significant characteristics of their effectiveness is that they make the topic alive and relevant to themselves and to their students, helping the students make relevant connections. Time and again studies point out what should be obvious: Children don't learn much from dull, meaningless "drill and kill" exercises and assignments. Such unmotivated teaching may be one of the principal causes of student loss of interest and motivation and subsequent estrangement from school. Obtaining ideas from professional journals, attending workshops, and communicating with colleagues either personally or via electronic bulletin boards and Web sites, and using project-based and interdisciplinary thematic instruction are ways of discovering how to make a potentially dry and boring topic interesting and alive for students (and for the teacher).

22. *The teacher is reliable.* The competent teacher can be relied on to fulfill professional responsibilities, promises, and commitments. A teacher who cannot be relied on is quick to lose credibility with the students (as well as with colleagues, administrators, and parents and guardians). And regardless of the teacher's potential for effectiveness, an unreliable teacher is an incompetent teacher. And for whatever reason, a teacher who is chronically absent from his or her teaching duties is a teacher "at-risk."

Specific teacher behaviors that facilitate student learning are discussed in the following section; guidelines and resources to assist in your development of these competencies permeate this resource guide.

TEACHER BEHAVIORS THAT FACILITATE STUDENT LEARNING

Your ability to perform your instructional responsibilities effectively is directly dependent upon your knowledge of children and how they best learn and your knowledge of and the quality of your teaching skills. As was said at the beginning of this chapter, development of your strategy repertoire along with your skills in using specific strategies should be ongoing throughout your teaching career.

To be most effective, you need a large repertoire from which to select a specific strategy for a particular goal with a distinctive group of children. In addition, you need skill in using that strategy. This section of this chapter is designed to help you begin building your specific strategies repertoire and to develop your skills in using these strategies.

There are basic teacher behaviors that create the conditions needed to enable students to think and to learn, whether the learning is a further understanding of concepts, the internalization of attitudes and values, the development of thinking processes, or the actuating of the most complex behaviors. The basic teacher behaviors are those that produce the following results: (a) students are physically and mentally engaged in the learning activities, (b) instructional time is efficiently used, and (c) classroom distractions and interruptions are minimal. The effectiveness with which a teacher carries out the basic behaviors can be measured by how well the students learn.

The basic teacher behaviors that facilitate student learning, discussed next, are: (a) structuring the learning environment; (b) accepting and sharing instructional accountability; (c) demonstrating withitness and overlapping; (d) providing a variety of motivating and challenging lessons; (e) modeling appropriate behaviors; (f) facilitating student acquisition of data; (g) creating a psychologically safe environment; (h) clarifying whenever necessary; (i) using periods of silence; and (j) questioning thoughtfully.

Facilitating Behaviors and Instructional Strategies: A Clarification

Clearly at least some of the 10 behaviors are also instructional strategies. *Questioning* is one example. The difference is that while the behaviors must be in place for the most effective teaching to occur, strategies—discussed in Part III—are more or less discretionary; that is, they are pedagogical techniques from which you may select but may not be obligated to use. For example, questioning and the use of silence are fundamental teaching behaviors, whereas lecturing and showing videos are not. Thus, you see, your task is twofold: (a) develop your awareness of and skills in using the fundamental teaching behaviors, and (b) develop your repertoire and skills in selecting and using appropriate instructional strategies.

Starting now and continuing throughout your teaching career, you will want to evaluate your developing competency for each of the 10 fundamental facilitating behaviors and improve in areas where you need help. Consider the following descriptions and examples, and discuss them in your class.

Structuring the Learning Environment

Structuring the learning environment means establishing an intellectual, psychological, and physical environment that enables all students to act and react productively. Specifically, you:

- Attend to the organization of the classroom as a learning laboratory to establish a positive, safe, and efficient environment for student learning.
- Establish and maintain clearly understood classroom procedures, definitions, instructions, and expectations. Help students to clarify the learning expectations and to establish clearly understood learning objectives.
- Help students assume tasks and responsibilities, thereby empowering them in their learning.
- Organize the students, helping them to organize their learning. Help students in the identification and their understanding of time and resource constraints. Provide instructional scaffolds, such as building bridges to student learning by helping students connect that which is being learned with what the students already know or think they know and have experienced.
- Plan and implement techniques for schema building, such as providing content and process outlines, visual diagrams, and opportunities for concept mapping.
- Plan units and lessons that have clear and concise beginnings and endings, with at least some of the planning done collaboratively with the students.
- Provide frequent summary reviews, often by using student self-assessment of what is being learned. Structure and facilitate ongoing formal and informal discussion based on a shared understanding of rules of discourse.
- Use techniques for students' metacognitive development, such as *think-pair-share,* in which each student is asked to think about an idea, share thoughts about it with a partner, and then share the pair's thoughts with the entire class; *think-write-pair-share,* in which each student writes his or her ideas about the new word and then shares in pairs before sharing with the entire class; and *jigsaw,* in which individuals or small groups of students are given responsibilities for separate tasks which lead to a bigger task or understanding, thereby putting together parts to make a whole (as done in this chapter with Exercise 3.4).

Accepting and Sharing Instructional Accountability

While holding students accountable for their learning, the teacher is willing to be held accountable for the effectiveness of the learning process and outcomes (the locus of control, as discussed at the beginning of this chapter). Specifically, you:

- Assume a responsibility for professional decision-making and in the risks associated with that responsibility. Share some responsibility for decision making and risk taking with the students. A primary goal in the education of children must be to see that they ultimately become accountable for themselves as learners and as citizens. To some degree, teachers are advised to work with their students as *partners* in their learning and development. One dimension of the partnership is sharing accountability. One effective way of doing that is by using student portfolios (discussed in Chapter 11).
- Communicate clearly to parents and guardians, administrators, and colleagues.
- Communicate to the students that accomplishment of learning goals and objectives is a responsibility they share with you.
- Plan exploratory activities that engage students in the learning.
- Provide continuous cues for desired learning behaviors and incentives contingent upon desired performance, such as grades, points, rewards, and privileges, and establish a clearly understood and continuous program of assessment that includes reflection and self-assessment.
- Provide opportunities for the students to demonstrate their learning, to refine and explore their questions, and to share their thinking and results.

Demonstrating Withitness and Overlapping

In 1936, in *School Begins at Two* (New York: New Republic), Harriet Johnson wrote of the early childhood teacher's need to be "with it," by which she was referring to the teacher's awareness of each child's emotions and needs as well as those of the entire group. In 1970, Jacob Kounin wrote of another kind of teacher withitness, an awareness of the entire group.[9] The teacher demonstrates withitness by being able to intervene and redirect potentially undesirable student behavior. In addition to being alert to everything that is going on in the classroom, there is another characteristic of a teacher who is withit, and that is the teacher's ability to attend to the right student. Specifically, you:

- Attend to the entire class while working with one student or with a small group of students, communicating this awareness with eye contact, hand gestures, body position and language, and clear but private verbal cues.
- Continually and simultaneously monitor all classroom activities to keep students at their tasks and to provide students with assistance and resources.
- Continue monitoring the class during any distraction such as when a visitor enters the classroom or while the students are on a field trip.
- Demonstrate an understanding of when comprehension checks and instructional transitions are appropriate or needed.
- Dwell on one topic only as long as necessary for the students' understandings.
- Quickly intervene and redirect potential undesirable student behavior (see Chapter 4).
- Refocus or shift activities for a student when that child's attention begins to fade.

Guidelines for Developing Withitness

Consider the follow guidelines for developing withitness.

- Avoid spending too much time with any one student or group; longer than 30 seconds may be approaching "too much time."
- Avoid turning your back to all or a portion of the students, such as when writing on the writing board.
- During direct instruction try to establish eye contact with each student about once every minute. It initially may sound impossible to do, but it is not; it is a skill that can be developed with practice.
- If two or more errant behaviors are occurring simultaneously in different locations, attend to the most serious first, while giving the other(s) a nonverbal gesture showing your awareness (such as by eye contact) and displeasure (such as by a frown).
- Involve all students in the act, not just any one student or group. Avoid concentrating on only those who appear most interested or responsive, sometimes referred to as the "chosen few."
- Keep students alert by calling on them randomly, asking questions and calling on an answerer, circulating from group to group during team learning activities, and frequently checking on the progress of individual students.
- Maintain constant visual surveillance of the entire class, even when talking to or working with

an individual or small group of students and when meeting a classroom visitor at the door.

- Move around the room. Be on top of potential misbehavior and quietly redirect student attention before the misbehavior occurs or gets out of control.

A prerequisite to being withit is the skill to attend to more than one matter simultaneously, referred to as *overlapping ability*. The teacher with this ability uses body language, body position, facial gestures, and hand signals to communicate with students. Consider the following examples of overlapping ability.

- Rather than having students bring their papers and problems to the teacher's desk, the teacher expects them to remain seated and to raise their hands as the teacher circulates in the room monitoring and attending to individual students.
- The teacher handles routine attendance matters while visually and/or verbally monitoring the students during their warmup activity.
- While attending to a messenger who has walked into the room, the teacher demonstrates verbally or with gestures, or both, that the students are expected to continue their work.
- While working in a small group, a student raises a hand to get the teacher's attention. The teacher, while continuing to work with another group of students, uses a hand signal to tell the student that she is aware that he wants her attention and will get to him quickly, which she does.
- Without missing a beat in his talk, the teacher aborts the potentially disruptive behavior of a student by gesturing, by making eye contact, or by moving closer to the student (an example of proximity control).

Providing a Variety of Motivating and Challenging Activities

The effective teacher uses a variety of activities that motivate and challenge all students to work to the utmost of their abilities and that engage and challenge the preferred learning styles and learning capacities of more of the students more of the time. Specifically, you:

- Collaboratively with the students, plan exciting and interesting learning activities, including those that engage children's natural interest in the mysterious and the novel.
- Demonstrate an unwavering expectation that each student will work to the best of the student's ability.

- Demonstrate optimism toward each student's potential for learning and doing.
- Show pride, optimism, and enthusiasm in learning, thinking, and teaching.
- View teaching and learning as an organic and reciprocal process that extends well beyond that which can be referred to as the traditional "2 by 4 by 6 curriculum"—that is, a curriculum that is bound by the 2 covers of the textbook, the 4 walls of the classroom, and the 6 hours of the school day.[10]

Modeling Appropriate Behaviors

Accomplished teachers model the very behaviors expected of their students. Specifically, you:

- Are prompt in returning student papers and offer comments that provide instructive and encouraging feedback to the children.
- Arrive promptly in the classroom and demonstrate on-task behaviors for the entire school day just as is expected of the students.
- Demonstrate respect for all students. For example, you do not interrupt when a student is showing rational thinking, even though you may disagree with or frown upon the words used or the direction of the student's thinking.
- Demonstrate that making errors is a natural event in learning and during problem solving and readily admit and correct a mistake made by yourself.
- Do not come to school when you are ill just as you expect children to remain at home when they are ill.
- Model and emphasize the skills, attitudes, and values of higher-order intellectual processes. Demonstrate rational problem-solving skills and explain to the students the processes being engaged while problem solving.[11]
- Model professionalism by spelling correctly, using proper grammar, and writing clearly and legibly.
- Practice communication that is clear, precise, and to the point. For example, use *I* when *I* is meant, *we* when *we* is meant. Rather than responding to student contributions with simply "good" or "okay," tell specifically what about the response was good or what made it okay.
- Practice moments of silence (see the section, Using Intervals of Silence, that follows), thus modeling thoughtfulness, reflectiveness, and restraint of impulsiveness.
- Realizing that students are also models for other students, you reinforce appropriate stu-

dent behaviors and intervene when behaviors are not appropriate (discussed in Chapter 4).

Facilitating Student Acquisition of Data

The teacher makes sure that data are accessible to students as input that they can process. Specifically, you:

- Ensure that sources of information are readily available to students for their use. Select books, media, and materials that facilitate student learning. Ensure that equipment and materials are readily available for students to use. Identify and use resources beyond the walls of the classroom and the boundaries of the school campus.
- Create a responsive classroom environment with direct learning experiences.
- Ensure that major ideas receive proper attention and emphasis.
- Provide clear and specific instructions.
- Provide feedback and feedback mechanisms about each child's performance and progress. Encourage students to organize and maintain devices such as learning portfolios to self-monitor their progress in learning and thinking (discussed in Chapter 11).
- Select anchoring (model) examples that help students bridge what is being learned with what they already know and have experienced.
- Serve as a resource person and use cooperative learning, thus regarding students as resources, too.

Creating a Psychologically Safe Environment

To encourage the positive development of student self-esteem, to provide a psychologically safe learning environment, and to encourage the most creative thought and behavior, the teacher provides an attractive and stimulating classroom environment and appropriate nonevaluative and nonjudgmental responses. Specifically, you:

- Avoid negative criticism. Criticism is often a negative value judgment, and "when a teacher responds to a child's ideas or actions with such negative words as 'poor,' 'incorrect,' or 'wrong,' the response tends to signal inadequacy or disapproval and ends the student's thinking about the task."[12]
- Frequently use minimal reinforcement (that is, nonjudgmental acceptance behaviors, such as nodding your head, writing a student's response

on the board, or saying "I understand"). Whereas elaborate or strong praise is generally unrelated to student achievement, minimal reinforcement, such as using words like *right, okay, good, uh-huh,* and *thank you,* does correlate with achievement.

However, be careful with a too frequent and thereby ineffective and even damaging use of the single word *good* following student contributions during a class discussion. Use the word only when the contribution was truly that—good—and better yet, say not only *good* but tell what specifically was good about the contribution. Doing that provides a more powerful reinforcement by demonstrating that you truly heard the student's contribution and thus in fact really thought it was good.

- Infrequently use elaborate or strong praise. By the time students are beyond the primary grades, teacher praise, a positive value judgment, has little or no value as a form of positive reinforcement. When praise is used for students in grades four and above, it should be mild, private, and for student accomplishment, rather than for effort, and for each student the frequency in using praise should be gradually reduced. When praise is reduced, a more diffused sociometric pattern develops, that is, more of the students become directly and productively involved in the learning. As emphasized by Good and Brophy, praise should be simple and direct and delivered in a natural voice without dramatizing.[13] Students beyond the primary grades are likely to perceive overly done theatrics as insincere.

Let us take pause to consider this point. Probably no statement in this resource guide raises more eyebrows than the statement that praise for most older children has little or no value as a form of positive reinforcement. After all, praise may well motivate some people. However, at what cost? Praise and encouragement are often confused and considered to be the same (see Figure 3.4), but they are not, and they do not have the same long-term results. This is explained as follows:

> For many years there has been a great campaign for the virtues of praise in helping children gain a positive self-concept and improve their behavior. This is another time when we must "beware of what works." Praise may inspire some children to improve their behavior. The problem is that they become pleasers and approval "junkies." These children (and later these adults) develop self-concepts that are totally dependent on the opinions of others. Other children resent and rebel against praise, either because they don't want to live up to the expectations of others or because they fear they can't

Figure 3.4
Examples of statements of praise versus encouragement

Statement of Praise	*Statement of Encouragement*
1. Your painting is excellent.	1. It is obvious that you enjoy painting.
2. I am delighted that you behaved so well on our class field trip.	2. I am so delighted that we all enjoyed the class field trip.
3. You did a good job on those word problems.	3. I can tell that you have been working and are enjoying it more.
4. Your oral report on your project was well done.	4. I can tell that you got really interested in your topic for the oral report on your project.
5. Great answer Louise!	5. Louise, your answer shows that you gave a lot of thought to the question.

compete with those who seem to get praise so easily. The alternative that considers long-range effects is encouragement. The long-range effect of encouragement is self-confidence. The long-range effect of praise is dependence on others.[14]

- Perceive your classroom as the place where you work, where children learn, and make that place of work and the tools available a place of pride—as stimulating and useful as possible.
- Plan within the lessons behaviors that show respect for the experiences and ideas of individual students.
- Provide positive individual student attention as often as possible. Write sincere reinforcing personalized comments on children's papers. Provide incentives and rewards for their accomplishments.
- Use nonverbal cues to show awareness and acceptance of individual students. Use paraphrasing and reflective listening. Use empathic acceptance of a child's expression of feelings, that is, demonstrating by words and gestures that, from the child's position, you understand.

Clarifying Whenever Necessary

Your responding behavior seeks further elaboration from a student about that student's idea or comprehension. Specifically, you:

- Help students to connect new content to that previously learned. Help students relate content of a lesson to students' other school and nonschool experiences. Help students make learning connections between disciplines.
- Politely invite a student to be more specific and to elaborate on or rephrase an idea, or to provide a concrete illustration of an idea.

- Provide frequent opportunity for summary reviews.
- Repeat or paraphrase a student's response, allowing the student to correct any other person's misinterpretation of what the student said or implied.
- Select instructional strategies that help students recognize and correct their prior notions about a topic.

Using Intervals of Silence

Use intervals of silence in the classroom. Specifically, you:

- Actively listen when a student is talking.
- Allow sufficient think-time, longer than two seconds, after asking a question or posing a problem. (See the section, Wait-Time, in Chapter 7.)
- Keep silent when children are working quietly or are attending to a visual display, and maintain classroom control by using nonverbal signals as your first-line intervention strategies.
- Pause while talking to allow for thinking and reflection.
- Use teacher silence to stimulate group discussion.

Questioning Thoughtfully

Use thoughtfully worded questions to induce learning and to stimulate thinking and the development of students' thinking skills. (Questioning is the topic of Chapter 7.) Specifically, you:

- Encourage student questioning without judging the quality or relevancy of a student's question. Attend to student questions, and respond and encourage other students to respond, often by building upon the content of a student's questions and of student responses.

- Help children develop their own questioning skills and provide opportunities for children to explore their own ideas, to obtain data, and to find answers to their own questions and to find solutions to their problems.
- Plan questioning sequences that elicit a variety of thinking skills, and that maneuver students to higher levels of thinking and doing.
- Use a variety of types of questions.
- Use questions to help children to explore their knowledge, to develop new understandings, and to discover ways of applying their new understandings.

SUMMARY

You have reviewed the realities of the responsibilities of today's elementary school classroom teacher. Becoming a competent teacher takes time, commitment, concentrated effort, and just plain hard work. Nobody truly knowledgeable about it ever said that competent teaching was easy.

You have learned that your professional responsibilities as a teacher will extend well beyond the 4 walls of the classroom, the 6 hours of the school day, the 5 days of the school week, and the 180 days of the school year. You learned of the many expectations (a) to demonstrate effective decision making; (b) to be committed to young people, to the school's mission, and to the profession; (c) to develop facilitating behaviors and to provide effective instruction; and (d) to fulfill numerous noninstructional responsibilities. As you have read and discussed these responsibilities, you should have begun to fully comprehend the challenge and reality of becoming a competent classroom teacher.

Teaching style is the way teachers teach, their distinctive mannerisms complemented by their choices of teaching behaviors and strategies. Style develops from tradition, from one's beliefs and experiences, and from one's knowledge of the best of research findings. You observed one teacher and that teacher's style for that lesson, and you began the development of your philosophy about teaching and learning, a philosophical statement that should be useful to you during later job interviews (see Chapter 11).

Exciting research findings continue to emerge from several related, areas: about learning, conceptual development, and thinking and from neurophysiology. The findings continue to support the hypothesis that an elementary school classroom teacher's best teaching style choice is eclectic with a bent toward the facilitating, at least until the day arrives when students of certain styles of thinking and learning can be practically matched to teachers with particular teaching styles. Future research will undoubtedly shed additional light on the relationships among pedagogy, pedagogical styles, and student thinking and learning.

Today, there seems to be much agreement that the essence of the learning process is a combined self-awareness, self-monitoring, and active reflection. Children learn these skills best when exposed to teachers who themselves effectively model those same behaviors. The most effective teaching and learning is an interactive process and involves not only learning, but also thinking about learning and learning how to learn.

The next and final chapter of Part I of this resource guide presents ways of establishing an effective learning environment within which to carry out your professional responsibilities.

EXTENDING MY COMPETENCY: QUESTIONS FOR CLASS DISCUSSION _____

1. Explain the meaning of each of the following two concepts and the extent and reason that you agree or disagree with each. (a) The teacher should hold high, but not necessarily identical, expectations for all students and never waver from those expectations. (b) The teacher should not be controlled by a concern to cover the content of the textbook by the end of the school term.
2. About four decades ago, a publication entitled *Six Areas of Teacher Competencies* (Burlingame, CA: California Teachers Association, 1964) identified six roles of the classroom teacher: director of learning, counselor and guidance worker, mediator of the culture, link with the community, member of the school staff, and member of the profession. When compared with that, have the roles changed for today's classroom teacher? If so, how?
3. Identify a public schoolteacher whom you consider to be competent and compare what you recall about that teacher's classroom with the characteristics of competent teachers as presented in this chapter. Share your comparison with others in the class.
4. Write your philosophy of education. The philosophy should be limited to one handwritten page and should indicate your understanding of how children learn and your responsibility as a classroom teacher. Share your philosophy with others in your class for their feedback. You may rework the statement from time to time, but save it; you will be revisiting it in Chapter 12.
5. Two teachers were asked, "What do you teach?" One teacher responded, "children." The other answered, "science." In small groups, discuss their

responses. From their responses, what tentative conclusions might be drawn about these two teachers? Share a summary of your group's discussion with the entire class.

6. In *Educating the Reflective Practitioner* (San Francisco: Jossey-Bass, 1987), author Donald Schon speaks of "reflection-on-action," "reflection-in-action," and "reflection-for-action." Read about and compare Schon's three types of reflections with the four phases of decision making and thought processing presented and discussed at the beginning of this chapter.

7. Explain how you now feel about being a classroom teacher—for example, motivated, excited, enthusiastic, befuddled, confused, depressed. Explain and discuss your current feelings with your classmates. Sort out common concerns and design avenues for dealing with any negative feelings you might have.

8. Describe any prior concepts you held that changed as a result of your experiences with this chapter. Describe the changes.

9. From your current observations and fieldwork as related to this teacher preparation program, clearly identify one specific example of educational practice that seems contradictory to exemplary practice or theory as presented in this chapter. Present your explanation for the discrepancy.

10. Do you have other questions generated by the content of this chapter? If you do, list them along with ways answers might be found.

FOR FURTHER READING

Bellanca, J. (1998). Teaching for Intelligence: In Search of Best Practices. *Phi Delta Kappan, 79*(9), 658–660.

Duffy, G. G. (1998). Teaching and the Balancing of Round Stones. *Phi Delta Kappan, 79*(10), 777–780.

Freiberg, H. J. (Ed.) (1999). *Perceiving, Behaving, Becoming: Lessons Learned.* Alexandria, VA: Association for Supervision and Curriculum Development.

Good, T. L., and Brophy, J. E. (2000). *Looking in Classrooms.* (8th ed., Chap. 10). New York: Addison-Wesley Longman.

Jensen, E. (1998). Emotions and Learning. Chapter 8 of E. Jensen, *Teaching With the Brain in Mind.* Alexandria, VA: Association for Supervision and Curriculum Development.

Kazemek, F. E. (1999). Why Was the Elephant Late in Getting on the Ark? Elephant Riddles and Other Jokes in the Classroom. *Reading Teacher, 52*(8), 896–898.

Lasley II, T. J. (1998). Paradigm Shifts in the Classroom. *Phi Delta Kappan, 80*(1), 84–86.

Palmer, P. J. (1998). *The Courage to Teach: Exploring the Inner Landscape of a Teacher's Life.* San Francisco: Jossey-Bass.

Stone, R. (1999). *Best Classroom Practices. What Award-Winning Elementary Teachers Do.* Thousand Oaks, CA: Corwin Press/Sage Publications.

Wassermann, S. (1999). Shazam! You're a Teacher. *Phi Delta Kappan, 80*(6), 464, 466–468.

Wilson-Saddler, D. (1997). Using Effective Praise to Produce Positive Results in the Classroom. *Teaching and Change, 4*(4), 338–357.

NOTES

1. See A. L. Costa, *The School as a Home for the Mind* (Palatine, IL: Skylight Publishing, 1991), pp. 97–106.

2. See, for example, P. Ashton and R. Webb, *Making a Difference: Teachers' Sense of Efficacy and Student Achievement* (New York: Longman, 1986).

3. J. Dewey, *How We Think* (Boston, MA: Heath, 1933).

4. A. W. Combs (Ed.), *Perceiving, Behaving, and Becoming: A New Focus for Education* (Arlington, VA: 1962 ASCD Yearbook, Association for Supervision and Curriculum Development, 1962). You may be interested in the revisit to the 1962 yearbook; see H. J. Freiberg (Ed.), *Perceiving, Behaving, Becoming: Lessons Learned* (Alexandria, VA: Association for Supervision and Curriculum Development, 1999).

5. J. Piaget, *Science of Education and the Psychology of the Child* (New York: Orion, 1970).

6. L. Vygotsky, *Mind in Society: The Development of Higher Psychological Processes* (Cambridge, MA: Harvard University Press, 1978).

7. You may want to compare these 22 competencies with the standards of the Interstate New Teacher Assessment and Support Consortium (INTASC) and with those of the National Board for Professional Teaching Standards (NBPTS) (see Chapter 1) and with the 22 "components of professional practice" in C. Danielson, *Enhancing Professional Practice: A Framework for Teaching* (Alexandria, VA: Association for Supervision and Curriculum Development, 1996).

8. S. Wassermann, Shazam! You're a Teacher, *Phi Delta Kappan, 80*(6), 464, 466–468 (February 1999).

9. J. S. Kounin, *Discipline and Group Management in Classrooms* (New York: Holt, Rinehart and Winston, 1970).

10. You may be interested in learning more about Expeditionary Learning Outward Bound (ELOB) schools. Visit the Web site at <http://www.elob.org>. Or visit an ELOB school Web site, such as Odyssey Elementary Charter School (Denver, CO) at <http:// www.odysseydenver.org/>, Springdale-Memphis Magnet School (Memphis, TN) at <http://www.memphis-schools.k12.tn.us/schools/ springdalemagnet. es/springdale.html>, or Vine Elementary School (Cincinnati, OH) at <http://www.sunburst.com/webwork/ohweb/Vine_Elementary>.

11. See, for example, J. W. Astington, Theory of Mind Goes to School, *Educational Leadership, 56*(3), 46–48 (November 1998).

12. Costa, *The School,* p. 54.

13. T. L. Good and J. E. Brophy, *Looking in Classrooms,* 8th ed., (New York: Longman, 2000), p. 142.

14. J. Nelsen, *Positive Discipline* (New York: Ballantine Books, 1987), p. 103. See also L. A. Froyen, *Classroom Management: The Reflective Teacher-Leader,* 2nd ed. (Upper Saddle River, NJ: Prentice Hall, 1993), pp. 294–298.

4

What Do I Need to Know to Establish and Maintain an Effective, Safe, and Supportive Classroom Learning Environment?

To become and to remain an effective teacher with a minimum of distractions in the classroom, you must (a) apply your knowledge of the characteristics and developmental needs of children with whom you work (Chapter 2), (b) practice the behaviors that facilitate student learning (Chapter 3), and (c) do so in a conducive learning environment. That third requirement is the principal focus of this final chapter of Part I of the resource guide. The establishment and maintenance of a conducive classroom learning environment derive from one's knowledge about children and how they learn and from careful thought and planning. These responsibilities should not be left for the new teacher to learn on the job in a sink-or-swim situation.

A conducive classroom learning environment is one that is psychologically safe, that helps the children to perceive the importance of what is being taught, that helps them realize they can achieve, and that is instructive and supportive in the procedures for learning. While it is important that they learn to control impulses and delay their need for gratification (see Characteristics of Intelligent Behavior in Chapter 9), children are more willing to spend time on a learning task when they perceive value or reward in doing so, when they possess some ownership in planning and carrying out the task, and when they feel they can indeed accomplish the task. Thoughtful and thorough planning of your procedures for classroom management is as important a part of your preactive phase of instruction (discussed in Chapter 3) as is the preparation of units and lessons (discussed in the two chapters that follow in Part II). Indeed, classroom management is perhaps the single most important factor influencing student learning. This chapter presents guidelines and resources that will help you to establish and manage a classroom environment that is safe for the children and favorable to their learning.

CHAPTER OBJECTIVES

Specifically, upon completion of this chapter you should be able to

1. Describe a teacher's reasonable first response to each of the following children: one who is aggressively violent; one who habitually lies; one who is defiant; one who tosses paper at the wastebasket; one who is sitting and doing nothing but staring out the window.
2. Describe by example how each of the following contributes to effective classroom control: a positive approach, well-planned lessons, a good start of the school term, establishment of classroom procedures and rules, consistency but with professional judgment in enforcing procedures and rules, correction of student misbehavior, and classroom management.
3. Describe perceptions that must be in place for the most conducive classroom learning environment and why they must be in place.
4. Describe steps you should take in preparing for the first few days of school.
5. Describe the advantages and disadvantages of studying children's school records to discover which students have a history of causing trouble in the classroom.
6. Describe the characteristics of an effective transition from one lesson activity to the next.
7. Describe the meaning and give an example of *sequenced consequences* as used for inappropriate student behavior.
8. Describe ways that you can help students develop self-control.
9. Explain how you will know if you are an effective manager of the classroom learning environment. Identify characteristics of a classroom environment that is both safe for children and favorable to their learning.
10. Explain the difference between direct and indirect intervention to refocus a student and describe situations where you would be most likely to use each, thereby demonstrating that you have begun building your repertoire of understandings of a teacher's options to specific classroom situations.
11. Prepare the first draft of your classroom management system.
12. With respect to classroom management, distinguish between the concepts of *consequences* and *punishment*.

THE IMPORTANCE OF PERCEPTIONS

Unless you believe your students can learn, they will not. Unless you believe you can teach them, you will not. Unless your students believe they can learn and until they want to learn, they will not.

We all know of or have heard of teachers who get the very best from their students, even from those students that many teachers find to be the most challenging to teach. Regardless of individual circumstances, those teachers (a) *know* that, when given adequate support and reinforcement, all children can learn, (b) *expect* the best from each student, (c) *establish* a classroom environment that motivates students to do their best, and (d) *manage* their classrooms so class time is efficiently used, that is, with the least amount of distraction to the learning process.

Regardless of how well planned you are for the instruction, certain perceptions by students must be in place to support the successful implementation of those plans. Students must perceive that (a) the classroom environment is supportive of their efforts, (b) you care about their learning and they are welcome in your classroom, (c) the expected learning is challenging but not impossible, and (d) the anticipated learning outcomes are worthy of their time and effort to try to achieve.

CLASSROOM CONTROL: ITS MEANING—PAST AND PRESENT

Classroom control frequently is of the greatest concern to beginning teachers—and they have good cause to be concerned. Even experienced teachers sometimes find control difficult, particularly with children who come to school with so much psychological baggage and have already become alienated due to negative experiences in their lives.

In one respect, being a classroom teacher is much like being a truck driver who must remain alert while going down a steep and winding grade; otherwise, the truck most assuredly will get out of control, veer off the highway, and crash. This chapter has been thoughtfully designed to help you with your concerns about control—and to help you avoid a crash.

Historical Meaning of Classroom Control

To set the stage for your comprehension, consider what the term *classroom control* has meant historically and what it means today. In the 1800s, instead of *classroom control,* educators spoke of *classroom discipline,* and that meant "punishment." Such an interpretation was consistent with the then-popular learning theory that assumed children were innately bad and that inappropriate behavior could be prevented by strictness or treated with punishment. Schools of the mid-1800s have been described as "wild and unruly places," and "full of idleness and disorder."[1]

By the early 1900s, educators were asking, "Why are the children still misbehaving?" The accepted answer was that the children were misbehaving *because* of the rigid punitive system. On this point, the era of progressive education began, providing students more freedom to decide what they would learn. The teacher's job, then, became one of providing a rich classroom of resources and materials to stimulate the student's natural curiosity. And since the system no longer would be causing misbehavior, punishment would no longer be necessary. Classes of the 1930s that were highly permissive, however, turned out to cause more anxiety than did the restrictive classes of the 1800s.

Today's Meaning of Classroom Control and the Concept of Classroom Management

Today, rather than classroom *discipline,* educators talk of classroom *control, the process of influencing student behavior in the classroom.* Classroom control is an important aspect of the broader concept of classroom management. Classroom control is part of a management plan designed to (a) prevent inappropriate student behaviors, (b) help children develop self-control, and (c) suggest procedures for dealing with inappropriate student behaviors.

Effective teaching requires a well-organized, businesslike classroom in which motivated students work diligently at their learning tasks, free from distractions and interruptions. Providing such a setting for learning requires careful thought and preparation and is called *effective classroom management.* Effective classroom management is the process of organizing and conducting a classroom so that it maximizes student learning.

A teacher's procedures for classroom control reflect that teacher's philosophy about how children learn and the teacher's interpretation and commitment to the school's stated mission. In sum, those procedures represent the teacher's concept of classroom management. Although often eclectic in their approaches, today's teachers share a concern for selecting management techniques that enhance student self-esteem and that empower the students; that is, the students learn how to assume control of their behavior and ownership of their learning.

While some schools subscribe heavily to one approach or another such as Albert's Cooperative Discipline model, or the Fredric Jones model, or Gordon's Teacher Effectiveness Training (TET) model, many others are more eclectic, having evolved from the historical works of several leading authorities. Let's consider what some authorities have said. To assist your understanding, refer to Table 4.1, which illustrates the main ideas of each authority and provides a comparison of their recommended approaches. As was said in the preceding paragraph, the guidelines and suggestions that are presented throughout this chapter represent an eclectic approach, borrowing from many of these authorities.

Classroom Management: Contributions of Some Leading Authorities

You are probably familiar with the term *behavior modification,* which describes several high-control techniques for changing behavior in an observable and predictable way; with **B. F. Skinner's** (1904–1990) ideas about how students learn and how behavior can be modified by using reinforcers (rewards); and with how his principles of behavior shaping have been extended by others.[2]

Table 4.1
Comparing Approaches to Classroom Management

Authority	To Know What is Going On	To Provide Smooth Transitions
Canter/Jones	Realize that the student has the right to choose how to behave in your class with the understanding of the consequences that will follow his or her choice.	Insist on decent, responsible behavior.
Dreikurs/Nelsen/Albert	Realize that the student wants status, recognition, and a feeling of belonging. Misbehavior is associated with mistaken goals of getting attention, seeking power, getting revenge, and wanting to be left alone.	Identify a mistaken student goal; act in ways that do not reinforce these goals.
Ginott	Communicate with the student to find out his/her feelings about a situation and about his/herself.	Invite student cooperation.
Glasser/Gordon/Rogers/Freiberg	Realize that the student is a rational being; he/she can control his or her own behavior.	Help the student make good choices; good choices produce good behavior and bad choices produce bad behavior.
Kounin	Develop *withitness,* a skill enabling you to see what is happening in all parts of the classroom at all times.	Avoid jerkiness, which consists of thrusts (giving directions before your group is ready), dangles (leaving one activity dangling in the verbal air, starting another one, and then returning to the first activity), and flip-flops (terminating one activity, beginning another one, and then returning to the first activity you terminated).
Skinner	Realize value of nonverbal interaction (i.e., smiles, pats, and handshakes) to communicate to students that you know what is going on.	Realize that smooth transitions may be part of your procedures for awarding reinforcers (i.e., points and tokens) to reward appropriate behavior.

To Maintain Group Alertness	To Involve Students	To Attend to Misbehavior
Set clear limits and consequences; follow through consistently; state what you expect, state the consequences and why the limits are needed.	Use firm tone of voice; keep eye contact; use nonverbal gestures and verbal statements; use hints, questions, and direct messages in requesting student behavior; give and receive compliments.	Follow through with your promises and the reasonable, previously stated consequences that have been established in your class.
Provide firm guidance and leadership.	Allow students to have a say in establishing rules and consequences in your class.	Make it clear that unpleasant consequences will follow inappropriate behavior.
Model the behavior you expect to see in your students.	Build student's self-esteem.	Give a message that addresses the situation and does not attack the student's character.
Understand that class rules are essential.	Realize that classroom meetings are effective means for attending to rules, behavior, and discipline.	Accept no excuses for inappropriate behavior; see that reasonable consequences always follow.
Avoid slowdowns (delays and time wasting) that can be caused by overdwelling (too much time spent on explanations) and by fragmentation (breaking down an activity into several unnecessary steps). Develop a group focus (active participation by all students in the group) through accountability (holding all students accountable for the concept of the lesson) and by attention (seeing all the students and using unison and individual responses).	Avoid boredom by providing a feeling of progress for the students, by offering challenges, by varying class activities, by changing the level of intellectual challenge, by varying lesson presentations, and by using many different learning materials and aids.	Understand that teacher correction influences behavior of other nearby students (the ripple effect).
Set rules, rewards, and consequences; emphasize that responsibility for good behavior rests with each student.	Involve students in "token economies," in contracts, and in charting behavior performance.	Provide tangibles to students who follow the class rules; represent tangibles as "points" for the whole class to use to "purchase" a special activity.

Figure 4.1

A sample ticket approach to classroom management [*Source:* Blossom S. Nissman, *Teacher-Tested Classroom Management Strategies* (Upper Saddle River, NJ: Merrill/Prentice Hall, 2000, pp. 110–111). Adapted by permission of Prentice Hall.]

You will need to design and print the tickets described below so they are ready to use when school begins. Sometime during the early days of the school term, when you are introducing your classroom management system to the children, post in the room and explain the following information.

GREEN TICKET = ISSUED BY TEACHER FOR POSITIVE BEHAVIOR
SILVER TICKET = ISSUED AFTER EARNING 10 GREEN TICKETS
GOLD TICKET = ISSUED AFTER EARNING 10 SILVER TICKETS

Upon receipt of a gold ticket, the student is recognized as student of the month in the classroom.
Other tickets in the system are:

RED TICKET = UNACCEPTABLE BEHAVIOR
BLACK TICKET = ISSUED AFTER RECEIVING 5 RED TICKETS

In addition to the above ticket system, supportive rewards are provided as follows:

1. Reward Box with things in it which student may reach in and "grab" after receipt of a silver ticket.
2. Ice Cream Ticket when the gold ticket is received (perhaps supported with donation from PTA).
3. A mystery gift when a second gold ticket is received (could be an item donated by local merchants).

Behavior modification begins with four steps: (a) identify the behavior to be modified; (b) record how often and under what conditions that behavior occurs: (c) cause a change by reinforcing a desired behavior with a positive reinforcer (a reward); (d) choose the type of positive reinforcers to award, such as:

- *Activity or privilege reinforcers,* such as choice of playing a game, running the projection equipment for the teacher, caring for a classroom pet, free reading, decorating the classroom, free art time, choice at a learning center, freed without penalty from doing an assignment or test, running an errand for the teacher
- *Social reinforcers,* such as verbal attention or praise, and nonverbal such as proximity of teacher to student, and facial (such as a wink) or bodily expressions (such as a handshake or pat on the back) of approval
- *Graphic reinforcers,* such as numerals and symbols made by rubber stamps
- *Tangible reinforcers,* such as candy and other edibles, badges, certificates, stickers, books
- *Token reinforcers,* such as points, stars, or script or tickets that can be accumulated and cashed in later for a tangible reinforcer, such as a trip to the pizza store or ice cream store with the teacher (see Figure 4.1)

Lee Canter, a child guidance specialist, and **Marlene Canter,** a specialist in teaching people with learning disabilities, developed their *assertive discipline* model. Using an approach that emphasizes both reinforcement for appropriate behaviors *and* punishment or consequences for inappropriate behaviors, their model emphasizes four major points. First, as a teacher, you have professional rights in your classroom and should expect appropriate student behavior. Second, your students have rights to choose how to behave in your classroom, and you should plan limits for inappropriate behavior. Third, an assertive discipline approach means you clearly state your expectations in a firm voice and explain the boundaries for behavior. And fourth, you should plan a system of positive consequences (e.g., positive messages home—see Exercise 4.1; awards and rewards; special privileges) for appropriate behavior and establish consequences (e.g., time out; withdrawal of privileges; parent/guardian conference) for inappropriate student misbehavior. Consistent follow-through is necessary.[3] Today, primarily because of its heavy reliance on the external control of student behavior with the use of threat and punishment, the assertive discipline model is considered to be "less helpful than more eclectically derived programs" that emphasize rationale explanations, logical or natural consequences, and the development of student self-control.[4]

With a *logical or natural consequences* approach, **Rudolf Dreikurs** (1897–1972), a psychiatrist specializing in child and family counseling, emphasized six points. First, be fair, firm, and friendly, and involve your students in developing and implementing class rules. Second, students need to clearly understand the standards of expected behavior and the logical consequences for misbehavior. For example, a logical consequence for a student who has painted graffiti on a school wall would be to clean the wall or pay for a school custodian to do it. Third, allow the students to be responsible not only for their own actions but also for influencing others to maintain appropriate behavior in your classroom. Fourth, encourage students to show respect for themselves and for others, and provide each student with a sense of belonging to the class. Fifth, recognize and encourage student goals of belonging, gaining status, and gaining recognition. And sixth, recognize but not reinforce correlated student goals of getting attention, seeking power, and taking revenge.[5]

Continuing the work of Dreikurs, **Linda Albert,** a former student of Dreikurs, has developed *cooperative discipline,* a detailed discipline system that is being used in many schools. The cooperative discipline model makes use of Dreikurs' fundamental concepts, with emphasis added on Three C's: capable, connect, and contribute.[6]

Also building upon the work of Dreikurs, psychotherapist **Jane Nelsen** provides guidelines for helping children develop positive feelings of self. Key points made by Nelsen and that are reflected throughout this resource guide are (a) use natural and logical consequences as a means to inspire a positive classroom atmosphere, (b) understand that children have goals that drive them toward misbehavior (attention, power, revenge, and assumed adequacy), (c) use kindness (student retains dignity) and firmness when administering consequences for a student's misbehavior, (d) establish a climate of mutual respect, (e) use class meetings to give students ownership in problem solving and goal setting, and (f) offer encouragement as a means of inspiring self-evaluation and focusing on the students' behaviors.[7]

Psychiatrist **William Glasser** developed his concept of *reality therapy* (i.e., the condition of the present, rather than of the past, contributes to inappropriate behavior) for the classroom. Glasser emphasizes that students have a responsibility to learn at school and to maintain appropriate behavior while there. He stresses that with the teacher's help, students can make appropriate choices about their behavior in school—that they can, in fact, learn self-control.[8] Glasser suggests holding class meetings that are devoted to establishing class rules, identifying standards for student behavior, matters of misbehavior, and the consequences of misbehavior. Since the publication of his first book in 1965, Glasser has expanded his message to include the student needs of belonging and love, control, freedom, and fun, asserting that if these needs are ignored and unattended at school, children are bound to become unmotivated and fail.[9]

Today's commitment to *quality education* is largely derived from the recent work of Glasser and the corresponding concept of the *person-centered classroom* as advanced by **Carl Rogers** and **H. Jerome Freiberg** in their 1994 book *Freedom to Learn* (Columbus, OH: Merrill). In schools committed to quality education and the person-centered classroom, students feel a sense of belonging, enjoy some degree of power of self-discipline, have fun learning, and experience a sense of freedom in the process.[10]

Psychologist **Haim G. Ginott,** (1922–1973), emphasized ways for teacher and student to communicate in his *communication model.* He advised teachers to send a clear message (or messages) about situations rather than about the children. He stressed that teachers must model the behavior they expect from students.[11] Ginott's suggested messages are those that express feelings appropriately, acknowledge students' feelings, give appropriate direction, and invite cooperation.

In his book *Discipline That Works: Promoting Self-Discipline in Children* (New York: Penguin, 1989), clinical psychologist **Thomas Gordon** emphasizes influence over control and decries use of reinforcement (i.e., rewards and punishment) as ineffective tools for achieving a positive influence over a child's behavior. Rather than using reinforcements for appropriate behavior and punishment for inappropriate behaviors, Gordon advocates encouragement and development of student self-control and self-regulated behavior. To have a positive influence and to encourage self-control the teacher (and school) should provide a rich and positive learning environment, with rich and stimulating learning activities. Specific teacher behaviors include active listening, sending I-messages (rather than you-messages), shifting from I-messages to listening when there is student resistance to an I-message, clearly identifying ownership of problems to the student when such is the case (i.e., not assuming ownership if it is a student's problem), and encouraging collaborative problem solving.

Psychologist **Fredric Jones** promotes the idea of helping students support their own self-control by way of a negative reinforcement method in which rewards follow good behavior.[12] Preferred activity time (PAT), for example, is an invention derived from the Jones Model. The Jones Model makes four recommendations. First, you should properly structure your classroom so students understand the **rules** (the expectation standards for classroom behavior) and **procedures** (the means for accomplishing routine tasks). Second, you maintain control by selecting appropriate instructional strategies. Third, you build patterns of cooperative work. Finally, you develop appropriate backup methods for dealing with inappropriate student behavior.

Jacob Kounin is well known for his identification of the *ripple effect* (i.e., the effect of a teacher's response to one student's misbehavior on students whose behavior was appropriate) and, as discussed in Chapter 3, of the teacher's *withitness* (i.e., the teacher's ability to remain alert in the classroom, to spot quickly and redirect potential student misbehavior, which is analogous to having "eyes in the back of your head").[13]

Developing My Own Effective Approach to Classroom Management

As you review these classic contributions to today's approaches to effective classroom management, the expert opinions as well as the research evidence will remind you of the importance of doing the following: (a) concentrating your attention on desirable student behaviors, (b) quickly and appropriately attending to inappropriate behavior, (c) maintaining alertness to all that is happening in your classroom, (d) providing smooth transitions, keeping the entire class on task, preventing dead time, (e) involving students by providing challenges, class meetings, ways to establish rules and consequences, opportunities to receive and return compliments, and chances to build self-control and self-esteem.

Using the criteria of your own philosophy, feelings, values, knowledge, and perceptions, you are encouraged to construct a classroom environment and management system that is positive and effective for you and your students, and then to consistently apply it. Use the guidelines shown in Figure 4.2 to begin the thinking process for developing your personal plan for classroom management, the process that begins now and continues in Exercise 4.3 and throughout your professional career.

PROVIDING A SUPPORTIVE LEARNING ENVIRONMENT

For you it is probably no surprise to hear that teachers whose classrooms are pleasant, positive, and challenging but supportive places to be, find that their students learn and behave better than do the students of teachers whose classroom atmospheres are harsh, negative, repressive, and unchallenging. What follows now are specific suggestions for making your classroom a pleasant, positive, and challenging place, that is, an environment that is conducive to the development of meaningful understandings.

Consider the Physical Layout

There is much in the arrangement of the classroom that can either contribute to or help prevent classroom management problems. There is no one best way to arrange learning stations in a classroom. The arrangement should be kept flexible so children may be deployed in the ways most suitable for accomplishing specific tasks.

The guideline is simple. Just as is true with adults, when children are seated side by side, it is perfectly natural for them to talk to each other. Therefore, if your purpose is to encourage social interaction as when using cooperative learning and small-group project work, seat children close together; if you would rather they work independently such as when taking independent achievement tests, separate them. It is unreasonable to place children in situations that encourage maximum interaction and then to admonish or berate them for whispering and talking. Sometimes, so to not disturb the learning going on in neighboring classrooms, you may need to remind the children to be "using their 6-inch voices."

You will not (or should not) be seated much of the time during the school day; therefore, it matters little where your teacher's desk is located except that it is out of the way.

Create a Positive Classroom Atmosphere

You have heard it before and now we say it again: All children should feel welcome in your classroom and accepted by you as individuals of dignity. Though these feelings and behaviors should be reciprocal, that is, expected of the children as well, they may have to begin with your frequent modeling of the behaviors expected of the students. You must help students know that any denial by you of a child's specific behavior is *not* a denial of that individual as a worthwhile person who is still welcomed to come to your class to learn as long as the student agrees to follow expected procedures. Specific things you can do to create a positive classroom environment, some of which are repeated from preceding chapters and others that are addressed in later chapters, are

- Admonish behavior, not persons.
- Ensure that no prejudice is ever displayed against any person.

Figure 4.2
Developing the personal classroom management system

MY EMERGING PLAN FOR CLASSROOM MANAGEMENT

Grade level (or range) _____   My name _____

Plans Before the First Day

1. Describe your classroom with respect to the physical room arrangement and organization, and the positive and caring classroom community that you aim to create.
2. Describe communication you will initiate with your students and their families prior to the first day of school.
3. Describe characteristics of your classroom that will signal to the children that it is a friendly and safe place to be.
4. Describe how you will get to know the children and what you will do to help the children get to know you and each other.

The First Day

5. Describe how you will greet the children when they arrive for the first day.
6. Describe the rules or procedural expectations that you will have already in place and how they will be presented to the children.
7. Describe how you will have children contribute to these rules and expectations.
8. Describe your classroom procedures for
   - absences; making up missed work and instruction
   - assigning helpers for classroom jobs such as taking care of pets, plants, the calendar, bathroom monitor, and so forth
   - being in the classroom before and after school, and at recess and lunch time
   - bringing toys, plants, and pets into the classroom
   - collecting notes, money, and forms
   - distributing and collecting papers and materials
   - eating and drinking in the classroom
   - going to the bathroom
   - late arrival and early dismissal
   - movement in the halls
   - storing personal belongings
   - taking attendance
   - using the classroom sink
   - using the pencil sharpener
   - using the teacher's desk
   - using the water fountain
   - using other materials and equipment
   - wearing hats and other articles of clothing in the classroom
   - what to do in an emergency situation
   - when a visitor comes into the classroom
9. Describe the morning opening; the day's closure.

Managing the Curriculum

10. Describe how you will help the children with their organization and assignments.
11. Describe your homework expectations. Will there be homework? How much and how often? Will parents and guardians be informed? If so, how? What is their involvement to be? Is there a school homework hotline?
12. Describe your procedure for incomplete, unacceptable, or incorrect student work? Is there a recovery option?
13. Do you plan to provide comments, feedback, or corrections on student work?
14. Will you use marks of some sort—grades, value words, figures, and so forth?
15. Will students be rewarded for their group work? How will you assess group learning? How will you assess individual learning from group work?
16. Describe the student portfolio expectation. Where will the portfolios be stored? When will students work on their portfolios?
17. Describe your plan for communication with parents/guardians.

Maintaining Classroom Relations and Personal Behavior

18. Describe how you will bring an off-task child back on task.
19. Describe how students will know what is and what is not an appropriate level of classroom noise.
20. Describe how you will signal a need for hands and when, if ever, it is okay to call out without using hands.
21. Describe how you will indicate your support for appropriate student behavior.
22. Describe how you will discourage inappropriate student behavior.
23. Describe your order of indirect and direct behavior intervention strategies.
24. Describe how you will signal your need for attention from the class from a distracted student.
25. Describe how you will respond when two errant behaviors are happening simultaneously but at opposing locations in the classroom.

When the Going Gets Tough

26. Describe your pattern of escalating consequences.
27. Describe how you will deal with disrespectful, inappropriate comments from students.
28. Describe how you will respond to remarks that are sexist or racist or that stereotype people in inappropriate and cruel ways.
29. Describe how you will respond to serious and dangerous student behaviors.
30. Identify one person you can go to for support.

- Attend to the classroom's physical appearance and comfort—it is your place of work; show pride in that fact.
- Be an interesting person and an optimistic and enthusiastic teacher.
- Encourage students to set high yet realistic goals for themselves, and then show them how to work in increments toward meeting their goal—letting each child know that you are confident in that child's ability to achieve.
- Help students develop their skills in interactive and cooperative learning.
- Involve students in every aspect of their learning, including the planning of classroom expectations, procedures, and learning activities, thereby empowering them—giving them part ownership and responsibility—in their learning.

- Make the learning enjoyable, at least to the extent possible and reasonable.
- Model the very expectations that you have for the children.
- Send positive messages (sometimes called "Happygrams") home to parents or guardians, even if you have to get help and write the message in the language used in the student's home (see Exercise 4.1). Think of the happygram as a brief note that praises a student for accomplishing a task or for doing something nice for someone.
- Recognize and reward truly positive behaviors and individual successes, no matter how meager they might seem to you to be.
- Use interesting and motivating learning activities.

EXERCISE 4.1 SENDING A POSITIVE MESSAGE HOME

Instructions: The purpose of this exercise is to practice writing a positive note to a student's home. For too many parents and guardians, the only communications ever received from their children's teachers are negative messages about a child's academic or social behavior. Communication to a parent can convey a positive message as well. (After writing a positive message, some teachers choose to phone it rather than sending it to the child's home.) First, think of a situation you might want to tell about, then practice writing a positive message. Ask another teacher candidate to read and react to your message. Does your message convey what you intend it to say?

1. Situation _____

   _____

   _____

   _____

2. Practice note to parent or guardian _____

   _____

   _____

   _____

   _____

   _____

   _____

   _____

   _____

   _____

3. Reaction comments _____

   _____

   _____

   _____

   _____

   _____

   _____

   _____

   _____

   _____

4. Review the comments. What areas do you want to focus on for class discussion? Talk about them with others in your class.

For Your Notes

Behaviors to Avoid

Two items in the preceding list are statements about giving encouragement. When using encouragement to motivate student learning, there are certain behaviors that you should avoid because they inhibit learning.

- Avoid comparing one child with another, or one group of children with another.
- Avoid encouraging competition among children.
- Avoid giving up or appearing to give up on any child.
- Avoid telling a child how much better she or he could be.
- Avoid using names of individuals during class meetings that are called for discussing issues.
- Avoid using qualifying statements, such as "I like what you did, but . . ." or "It's about time."

Get to Know the Children as People So to Build Intrinsic Motivation for Learning

For classes to move forward smoothly and efficiently, they should fit the learners' learning styles, learning capacities, developmental needs, and interests. To make the learning meaningful and longest lasting, build curriculum around student interests, capacities, perceptions, and perspectives (as you will learn to do in Part II that follows). Therefore, you need to know your students well enough to be able to provide learning experiences that they will find interesting, valuable, intrinsically motivating, challenging, and rewarding. Knowing your students is as important as knowing the content of the subjects you are expected to teach. The following paragraphs describe a number of things you can do to get to know your students as people.

Quickly Learn and Use Student Names

Like everyone else, children appreciate being recognized and addressed by name. Quickly learning and using their names is an important motivating strategy. To learn student's names quickly, one teacher takes snapshot photographs of each child on the first day of school. Later, children use the photographs as a portion of the covers of their portfolios. Another technique for learning names quickly is to use a seating chart. Laminate the seating chart onto a pretty neon-colored clipboard that you can carry in class. Many teachers prefer to assign "homebase" seating (an assigned seat for each child to be in at the start and end of each school day) and then make seating charts from which they can unobtrusively check the roll while students are doing seatwork. It is usually best to get your students into the lesson before taking roll and before doing other housekeeping chores. Ways of assigning student seating are discussed later in this chapter (see the section, The First Day).

Addressing students by name every time you speak to them helps you to quickly learn and remember their names. (Be sure to learn to pronounce their names correctly; that helps in making a good impression.) Another helpful way to learn student names is to return papers yourself by calling student names and then handing the papers to them, paying careful attention to look at each student and make mental notes that may help you to associate names with faces.

Classroom Sharing During the First Week of School

During the first week of school many teachers take time each day to have students present information about themselves and/or about the day's lesson or assignment. For instance, perhaps five or six students are selected each day to answer questions such as "What name would you like to be called by?" "Where did you attend school last year?" "Tell us about your hobbies and other interests." "What interested you about yesterday's lesson?" You might have your students share information of this sort with each other in dyads or small groups, while you visit each group in turn.

Still another approach is the "me-in-a-bag" activity, where each student brings to school a paper bag (one large grocery bag) that contains items brought from home that represent that student. The student is given time in class to share the items brought. [*Note:* Be sure that parents/guardians are aware of the assignment so nothing of value from home gets lost in the process.]

How the student answers such questions or participates in such activities can be as revealing about the student as is the information (or the lack thereof) that the student does share. From what is revealed during this sharing, you sometimes get clues about additional information you would like to obtain about the student.

Observe Students in the Classroom—Develop and Practice Your Withitness

During learning activities the effective teacher is constantly moving around the classroom and is alert to the individual behavior (nonverbal as well as verbal) of each child in the class, whether the student is on task or gazing off and perhaps thinking about other things. Be cautious, however; just because a child is gazing out the window does not mean that the child is not thinking about the learning task. During group work is a particularly good time to observe children and get to know more about each child's skills and interests. For the observation a behavior checklist (see Chapter 11) is sometimes useful.

Observations of and Conversations with Students Outside the Classroom

Another way to learn more about students is by observing them outside class, for example, at recess, during lunch, on the playground, and at other school events. Observations outside the classroom can give information about student personalities, friendships, interests, and potentialities. For instance, you may find that a student who seems phlegmatic, lackadaisical, or uninterested in your classroom is a real fireball on the soccer field.

Conferences and Interviews with Students

Conferences with students, and sometimes with family members as well, afford yet another opportunity to show that you are genuinely interested in each child as a person and as a student. Some teachers and teaching teams plan a series of conferences during the first few weeks in which, individually or in small groups, students are interviewed by the teacher or by the teaching team. Such conferences and interviews are managed by using open-ended questions. The teacher indicates by the questions, by listening, and by nonjudgmental and empathic responses (i.e., being able to "step into the shoes" of the student, thereby understanding from where the student is coming) a genuine interest in the students. Keep in mind, however, that children who feel they have been betrayed by prior adult associations may at first be distrustful of your sincerity. In such instances, don't force it. Be patient, but do not hesitate to take advantage of the opportunity afforded by talking with individual students outside of the regular classroom. Investing a few minutes of time in a positive conversation with a student, during which you indicate a genuine interest in that child, can pay real dividends when it comes to that child's learning in your classroom.

When using interviews with children consider having the children to individually write one or two questions that they would like to ask you in the interview. This ensures that the child is an active participant.

Student Writing and Questionnaires

Much can be learned about children by what they write (or draw). It is important to encourage writing in your classroom, and (with varying degrees of intensity) to read everything that students write and to ask for clarification when needed.

Useful for this are journals and portfolios discussed in Chapters 8 and 11.

Writing can especially help children feel more secure during the opening days of school. Here are two suggestions:

1. *Imaginary classmates for grades K–3.* Invite the children to meet two imaginary classmates and imagine their physical characteristics, clothing, personalities, and fears. Encourage them to share their thoughts about the imaginary classmates to the whole group. Suggest that when any student has a problem, the student can write anonymously to one of the imaginary classmates and "mail" it in a mailbag (a brown paper bag affixed to a bulletin board). If appropriate, distribute the mail to the students and ask them to take the role of the imaginary classmates by writing the advice they would give the sender. The advice letters can be displayed beneath the writing board, and the students can be invited to browse and read during independent reading time.

2. *An invisible student for grades 4–6.* Invite the students to imagine an invisible classmate in the room and contribute to the class a list of 15 questions about problems that they would ask the invisible student. Ask the students to copy the list and take a week to answer the questions as if they were the invisible student. At the end of the week, invite the students to read one of the questions and answers aloud to the class. If appropriate, they can suggest additional problems and concerns they are facing at school. Have each student select one problematic situation or concern and write a brief scenario in which the invisible student handles it in the best way possible. Ask for volunteers to read their short stories aloud to a small group.

Some teachers use open-ended interest-discovering and autobiographical questionnaires. Student responses to questionnaires can provide ideas about how to tailor assignments and learning activities for individual students. However, you must assure students that their answers are optional, that you are not invading their privacy.

In an *interest-discovering questionnaire* students are asked to answer questions such as "When you read for fun or pleasure, what do you usually read?" "What are your favorite movies, videos, games, or TV shows?" "Who are your favorite music video performers?" "Athletes?" "Describe your favorite hobby or other nonschool related activity." "What are your favorite sport activities to participate in and as a spectator?"

In an *autobiographical questionnaire* the student is asked to answer questions such as "Where were you born?" "What would you like to become?"

"Do you have chores at home or somewhere else?" "How do you like to spend your leisure time?" "Do you like to read?" "What do you like to read?" "Do you have a favorite hobby; what is it?" You might want to model the process by beginning it with reading the children your own autobiographical answers.

Cumulative Record, Discussions with Colleagues, and Experiential Backgrounds

Held in the school office is the cumulative record for each student, containing information recorded from year to year by teachers and other school professionals—information about the student's academic background and standardized test scores. However, the Family Educational Rights and Privacy Act (FERPA) of 1974, and its subsequent amendments and local policies, may forbid your reviewing the record, except perhaps in collaboration with an administrator or counselor and when you have a legitimate educational purpose for doing so. While you must use discretion before arriving at any conclusion about information contained in the cumulative record, the record may afford information for getting to know a particular student better. Remember, though, a student's past is history and should not be held against that child, but instead used as a means for understanding a child's experiences and current perceptions.

To better understand a child it is sometimes helpful to talk with the child's other teachers and administrators to learn of their perceptions and experiences with the student. One of the advantages of schools that use looping (see Chapter 1) or that are divided into smaller cohorts (sometimes called *families,* or *pods*), or both, is that teachers and students get to know each other better.

Another way of getting to know your students is to spend time in the neighborhoods in which they live. Observe and listen, finding and noting things that you can use as examples or as learning activities. Some school districts encourage home visits by teachers and even provide financial incentives to teachers who visit the homes of their students. Of course, teachers must exercise safety precautions when making home visits, perhaps traveling in teams rather than alone.

PREPARATION PROVIDES CONFIDENCE AND SUCCESS

For successful classroom management, beginning the school term well may make all the difference in the world. Remember that you have only one opportunity to make a first and lasting impression. Therefore, you should appear at the first class meeting as well prepared and as confident as possible. In schools genuinely responsive to students, the teachers and administrators hold high expectations for themselves and for one another.

Perhaps in the beginning you will feel nervous and apprehensive, but being ready and well prepared will help you at least appear to be confident. It is likely that every beginning teacher is to some degree nervous and apprehensive; the secret is to not appear to be nervous and apprehensive. Being well prepared provides the confidence necessary to cloud feelings of apprehension. A good antiperspirant and a slow under-the-breath counting to 10 at the start can help, too. Then, if you proceed in a businesslike, matter-of-fact way, the impetus of your well-prepared beginning will, most likely, cause the day, week, and year to proceed as desired. Your anxieties will lessen with each new school year.

Effective Organization and Administration of Activities and Materials

In a well-managed classroom student movement about the classroom is routinized, controlled, and purposeful to the learning activities; students know what to do, have the materials needed to do it, and remain on task while doing it. The classroom atmosphere is supportive, the assignments and procedures for doing them are clear, and the materials and tools used for instruction are current, interesting, and readily available. At all times, the teacher is in control of events, rather than controlled by them, ensuring that the students are spending their time on appropriate tasks.

Natural Interruptions and Disruptions to Routine

As you plan and prepare to implement your management system, you must also be aware of your own moods and high-stress days and anticipate that your own tolerance levels may vary some. Children, too, are susceptible to personal problems that can be the sources of high stress. As you come to know your students well, you will be able to ascertain when certain children are under an inordinate amount of stress and anxiety.

You must understand that classroom routines may be interrupted occasionally for perfectly natural reasons, especially on certain days and at certain times during the school year. Students will not have the same motivation and energy level on each and every day. Energy level also varies throughout the school day. Your anticipation of—and thoughtful and carefully planning for during the preactive phase of instruction—periods of high or low energy levels will preserve your own mental health. Depending on a number of factors, periods of high energy level might include: at the beginning of each school day, before a field trip, a holiday, or a school event (such as picture day or a school carnival), the day of a holiday such as Halloween or Valentine's Day, the day following a holiday, grade report or parent-conference day, immediately before and after lunch, immediately before and after recess, on a shortened day or the day a substitute teacher is present, toward the end of each school day, toward the end of school each Friday afternoon, and toward the end of the school semester or year.

How should you prepare for these so-called high-energy days? There are probably no specific guidelines that will work for all teachers in all situations in each instance from the list. However, these are days to which you need to pay extra attention during your planning, days that students could possibly be restless and more difficult to keep focused on the learning, and days when you might need to be especially forceful and consistent in your enforcement of procedures or even compassionate and more tolerant than usual. Plan instructional activities that might be more readily accepted by the students. In no instance is it our intent to imply that learning ceases and playtime takes over. The instructional time that is available to a teacher during a school year is too precious for that to happen.

CLASSROOM PROCEDURES AND GUIDELINES FOR ACCEPTABLE BEHAVIOR

It is impossible to overemphasize the importance of getting the school year off to a good beginning, so we begin this section by discussing how that is done.

Starting the School Year Well

There are just a few important keys to getting the school year off to a good beginning. First, be *prepared*. Preparation for the first day of school should include (a) becoming knowledgeable about relevant district and school policy and (b) from that knowledge determining your classroom procedures and basic expectations for the behavior of the children who are under your supervision. Second, the procedures and expectations must seem reasonable to your students and in enforcing them you must be fair and professional.

Often during your teacher preparation you will hear about the importance of the teacher being consistent. But the meaning of being consistent is not always clear. Let us explain. First of all, so we are not misunderstood, let us emphasize that consistency in enforcing your rules and expectations is important. We also emphasize, however, that being coldly consistent is not the same as being fair and professional. To be most effective, learning must be enjoyable for children; it cannot be enjoyable when a teacher consistently acts like a marine drill sergeant. As a teacher, you are a professional who deals in matters of human relations and who must exercise professional judgment. You are not a robot, nor are your students. Human beings differ from one another, and seemingly similar situations can vary substantially because the people involved are different. Consequently, your response, or lack of response, to each of two separate but quite similar situations may differ. If a student infracts upon a rule, rather than assuming why, or seeming to not care why, or to overreact to the infraction, find out why and consider all aspects of the situation before firmly deciding your response. Being consistent does not mean treating everyone the same. Frankly, a classroom of tattlers usually besieges teachers who automatically use specific consequences in response to rule violations. Avoid imposing inappropriate consequences, especially from a fear of being perceived by students as inconsistent and unfair. Children, and some adults, must learn that fair treatment does not necessarily mean identical treatment.

Third, in preparing your classroom management system, remember that too many rules and detailed procedures at the beginning can be a source of trouble. To avoid trouble, it is best at first to present only the minimum number of procedural expectations necessary for an orderly start to the school term. By establishing and sticking to a few explained general expectations (see discussion that follows under the heading, First Day), and to those that may be specific to a grade level, and to the discipline (such as science) or to an area of the school campus (such as the playground or lunch room), you can leave yourself some room for judgments and maneuvering.

Procedures Rather than Rules

To encourage a constructive and supportive classroom learning environment, we encourage you (and your students) to practice thinking in terms of *procedures* rather than rules, and, although not necessarily in the same breath, of *consequences* rather than *punishment*. The rationale is this: To many people, the term *rules* has a more negative connotation than does the term *procedures*. When working with a cohort of students, some rules are necessary but we believe that using the term *procedures* has a more positive ring to it. For example, a classroom rule might be that when one person is talking we do not interrupt that person until the person is finished. When that rule is broken, rather than reminding students of the *rule,* the emphasis can be changed to *procedure* simply by reminding the students by asking, "What is our procedure when someone is talking?" In this instance the consequence for the infraction is a gentle verbal reminder.

It is our contention that thinking in terms of and talking about *procedures* and *consequences* are more likely to contribute to a positive classroom atmosphere than using the terms *rules* and *punishment*. Like always, after considering what experienced others have to say, the final decision is only one of many that you as a professional must make and that will be influenced by your own thinking and unique situation.

Once you have decided your initial expectations you are ready to explain them to your students and to begin rehearsing a few of the procedures on the very first day of class. You will want to do this in a positive way. Elementary school children work best in a positive atmosphere, when teacher expectations are clear to them, when procedures are stated in positive terms, are clearly understood and agreed upon, and are rehearsed until they have become routine, and when consequences for behaviors that are inappropriate are reasonable, clearly understood, and fairly applied.

The First Day

On the first day you will want to cover certain major points of common interest to you and the children. The following paragraphs offer guidelines and suggestions for meeting your students the first time.

Greeting the Students
Welcome your students with a smile as they arrive and then the entire class with a friendly but businesslike demeanor. This means that you are not frowning, nor off in a corner of the room doing something else as students arrive. As you greet the children, direct them to their seat where they are to start on the first assignment. This initial assignment ensures that students have something to do immediately upon arriving to your classroom. That first assignment might be a questionnaire each student completes or a drawing to be made. This is a good time to instruct students on the expected standard for heading their papers. After giving instructions on how papers are to be handed in, rehearse the procedure by collecting this first assignment.

Student Seating
One option for student seating is to have student names on the first assignment paper and placed at student desks when students arrive at that first class meeting. That allows you to have a "home base" seating chart (discussed earlier in the chapter) ready on the first day, from which you can quickly check attendance and begin learning student names.

Information About the Class
After the first assignment has been completed, discussed, and collected, explain to students about the class—what they will be learning and how they will learn it. This is a time you may choose to solicit student input into the course content (discussed in Part II). Many teachers of grades three and up make a list of expectations, give each student a copy, and review it with them, specifically discussing the teacher's expectations about how books will be used; about student notebooks, journals, portfolios, and assignments; about what students need to furnish; and about the location of resources in the classroom and elsewhere.

Classroom Procedures and Endorsed Behavior
Now discuss in a positive way the expectations regarding classroom behavior, procedures, and routines (discussed next). Children work best when classroom expectations are well understood, with established and consistently followed routines. As said earlier it is important in the beginning that there be no more procedures than necessary to get

---

**Rules, Rewards, and Consequences
of a Kindergarten Classroom**

[*Courtesy* of Lynne Baker and Connie Thomas, Sierra Oaks Elementary School, Sacramento, California]

Rules	*Rewards*	*Consequences*
• Listen carefully	• Praise	• Verbal warning
• Follow directions	• Smiles	• Time out
• Raise a hand to speak	• Preferred activity time	• Notify principal and parent
• Respect self and others	• Self-respect	
	• Safe and productive classroom	

A Classroom Scenario: Rules in a community of learners[14]

Rules must be designed to equally support and value all members of the learning community, including teachers.

Some say students should not be allowed to drink or eat in the classroom because of the potential for a mess. From that concern, a common rule that often puts teachers and students at odds is that eating and drinking are not allowed in the classroom. The teacher who bans eating and drinking by students but keeps a cup of coffee handy is flagrantly violating the rules.

However, helping children learn how to clean up after themselves and how to react to spills is a worthwhile lesson that can be applied for the rest of an individual's life. For example, Mrs. Horn, a fifth-grade teacher, allows her students to drink from water bottles they bring to class. On the first day of class she tells the students that they can bring bottled water to class and then she instructs them about what to do when a water bottle spills in the classroom. When the inevitable spill does occur, Mrs. Horn does not interrupt her teaching for even one minute. While she continues to teach, her students know where to find extra paper towels and how to mop up the water. The students have been taught how to clean up after themselves, so a spill is not a problem. Her students, rather than Mrs. Horn, assume responsibility for their actions.

---

the class moving effectively for daily operation. Just a few expectations should be enough, such as:

- Appreciate and respect the rights and property of others.
- Arrive to the classroom promptly and stay on task until excused by the teacher.
- Listen attentively and do your best work.
- Stay safe.

Too many procedural expectations, especially at first, can be restricting and even confusing to children. Except perhaps for recent newcomers, older children usually already know these things so you shouldn't have to spend much time on the topic. Be patient with yourself, for finding and applying the proper level of control for a given group of students is one of the skills that you will develop from experience.

Although many schools traditionally posted in the halls and in the classrooms a list of prohibited behaviors, exemplary schools today focus on the positive, on endorsed attitudes and behaviors. Displaying a list of *do nots* is unlikely to encourage a positive school or classroom atmosphere; a list of *dos* does.

First Homework Assignment

End the first class meeting with a positive statement about being delighted to be working with them and then give the first homework assignment. The first homework assignment should perhaps be one that will not take too much student time, that each student can do well with minimal effort, and that, perhaps, involves obtaining the attention of a parent or guardian, such as with a

signature. Be sure to allow yourself sufficient time to demonstrate where assignments will regularly be posted and to make assignment instructions clearly understood by every student, including a reminder of how you expect students to head their papers and turn in their assignments.

What Students Need to Understand from the Start

As you prepare the guidelines, standards, and expectations for classroom behavior, consider some of the specifics about what students need to understand from the start. These specific points, then, should be reviewed and rehearsed with the children, sometimes several times, during the first week of school and then followed *consistently* throughout the school term. Important and specific things that students need to know from the start will vary considerably depending on whether you are working with say first graders or sixth graders, but generally each of the following paragraphs describes things that all students need to understand from the beginning.

Signaling the Teacher for Attention and Help

At least at the start of the school term, most teachers who are effective classroom managers expect students to raise their hands quietly (called "quiet hands") until the teacher acknowledges (usually by a nonverbal gesture, such as eye contact and a nod) that the student's hand has been seen. With that acknowledgment, the recommended procedure is that the student should lower his or her hand and return to work.

There are a number of important reasons for expecting students to raise their hands before speaking. Two are that it allows you to (a) control the noise and confusion level and (b) be proactive in deciding who speaks. The latter is important if you are to be in control of classroom events, rather than controlled by them, and you are to manage a classroom with equality, with equal attention to individuals regardless of their gender, ethnicity, proximity to the teacher, or any other personal characteristic. We are not talking here about students having to raise their hands before talking with their peers during group work; we are talking about disallowing students shouting across the room to get your attention and boisterously talking out freely during whole-class instruction.

Another important reason for expecting students to raise their hands and be recognized before speaking is to discourage impulsive outbursts, that is, to grow intellectually. An instructional responsibility shared by all teachers is to help students develop intelligent behaviors (see Chapter 9). Learning to control impulsivity is an intelligent behavior. Teaching children to control their impulsivity is a important responsibility that, in our opinion, is too often neglected by too many teachers (and too many parents and guardians).

To avoid dependence on the teacher and having too many children raising their hands for the teacher's attention, and to encourage positive interaction among the children, some teachers employ the *three-before-me* procedure. The procedure is this: When a student has a question or needs help, the student must quietly ask up to three peers before seeking help from the teacher. As we remind you many times throughout this resource guide, as a beginning teacher you need to try ideas and find what works best for you in your unique situation.

Entering and Leaving the Classroom

From the time that the class is scheduled to begin and until it officially ends, teachers who are effective classroom managers expect students to be in their assigned seats or at their learning stations and to be attentive to the teacher or to the learning activity until excused by the teacher. Students should be excused by teachers, not by bells or clocks.

Maintaining, Obtaining, and Using Materials for Learning and Items of Personal Use

Students need to know where, when, and how to store, retrieve, and care for items such as their coats, backpacks, books, pencils, and medicines; how to get papers and materials; and when to use the pencil sharpener and wastebasket. Classroom control is easiest to maintain when (a) items that students need for class activities and for their personal use are neatly and safely arranged (for example, backpacks stored under tables or chairs rather than in aisles) and located in places that require minimum foot traffic, (b) there are established procedures that students clearly expect and understand, (c) there is the least amount of student off-task time, and (d) students do not have to line up for anything. Therefore, you will want to plan the room arrangement, equipment and materials storage, preparation of equipment and materials, and transitions between activities to avoid needless delays, confusion, and safety hazards. Remember this well: Problems in classroom control will most certainly occur whenever some or all students have nothing to do, even if only briefly.

Leaving Class for a Personal Matter

Normally, students should be able to take care of the need to go to the bathroom between classes; however sometimes they do not, or for medical reasons or during long blocks of class time cannot. Reinforce the notion that they should do this between classes or during the scheduled times, but be flexible enough for the occasional student who has an immediate need. Whenever permitting a student to leave class for a personal reason, follow established school procedures, which may, for reasons of personal security, mean that students only leave the room in pairs and with a hall pass or when accompanied by an adult.

Reacting to a Visitor or an Intercom Announcement

Unfortunately, class interruptions do occur, and in too many schools they occur far too often and for reasons that are not as important as interrupting a teacher and students' learning would imply. For an important reason the principal or some other person from the school office may interrupt the class to see the teacher or a student or to make an announcement to the entire class. Students need to understand what behavior is expected of them during those interruptions. When there is a visitor to the classroom, the expected procedure should be for students to continue their learning task unless instructed otherwise by you.

When Late to Class or Leaving Early

You must abide by school policies on early dismissals and late arrivals. Make your own procedures routine so students clearly understand what they are to do if they must leave your class early (e.g., for a medical appointment) or when they arrive late. Procedures in your classroom,

Figure 4.3
Sample model of consequences
for inappropriate student
behavior

FIRST OFFENSE results in a direct but unobtrusive (often nonverbal)
reminder to the student.

SECOND OFFENSE results in a private but direct verbal reminder of
expected behavior and the consequences of continued inappropriate
behavior.

THIRD OFFENSE results in the student's being given a time out in a
supervised isolation area followed by a private teacher-student conference
and the student's return to class.

FOURTH OFFENSE results in a suspension from class until there is a
student-parent-teacher (and perhaps an administrator) conference.

and indeed throughout the school, should be such
that late-arriving and early-dismissal students do
not have to disturb you or other teachers or the
learning in progress.

When students are allowed to interrupt the
learning in progress because the teacher has not
established such procedures, and these interruptions happen repeatedly and regularly, then the
covert message conveyed, at least in that classroom if not by the hidden curriculum of the entire
school, is that academic instruction is relatively
low on the list of matters of importance.

Consequences for Inappropriate Behavior

Most teachers who are effective classroom managers routinize their procedures for handling inappropriate behavior and ensure that the children
understand the potential consequences for inappropriate behavior. The consequences are posted
in the classroom and may be similar to the four-step model shown in Figure 4.3. Whether offenses
subsequent to the first are those that occur on the
same day or within a designated period of time,
such as one week, is one of the many judgment decisions that must be made by a teacher or by members of a teaching team or the entire faculty.

Emergency Drills (Practice) or Real Emergencies

The children and everyone else at the school need
to clearly understand what to do, where to go, and
how to behave in emergency conditions, such as
those that might occur because of a fire, storm,
earthquake, or because of a bomb threat or a disruptive campus intruder. Students must be expected to behave well during practice drills, as
well as in real emergencies.

Time Out Procedure

When a time out is used to deal with a child's inappropriate behavior, the student should have
something to do during the time out. Time out is a
time for the student to be able to calm down, collect his or her thoughts, and reflect on the behavior that resulted in being assigned a time out.

The time-out area should be one where the
child is isolated from the rest of the students,
perhaps somewhere in the classroom or in another teacher's classroom, but still supervised by
an adult. One suggestion is that when instructed
to take a time out the student picks up a form
(see Figure 4.4) from a known place in the classroom and completes the form while in the time
out area. This procedure is valuable because it
(a) gives the student something constructive to
do during the time out, (b) causes the student to
reflect and assume ownership for the student's
behavior that resulted in the time-out consequence, and (c) provides documentation that
might be useful later in conferences with parents
and guardians, counselors, and school administrative personnel. A second time out for the same
student during the same school day might be
cause for a follow-up, such as a conference between the student and members of that student's
teaching team and school counselor. A third time
out during the same day may result in a trip to a
school administrator and a parent/guardian conference before the student is allowed back in the
classroom.

Now, to further your understanding of classroom management and to begin the development
of your own management system, do Exercises 4.2
and 4.3.

Figure 4.4
Sample time-out form

Time Out

Your behavior failed to pass our classroom and house expectations and agreements. Those expectations and agreements are:

- Attentive listening
- Mutual respect of the rights and property of others
- Right of each student to learn
- Appreciation of others with no put downs

Please reflect on your behavior today by answering the following questions:

1. Explain what you did in class that caused you to receive this time out. _____
    _____
    _____

2. What agreement(s) did you fail to honor by your behavior? _____
    _____
    _____

3. Did your behavior cause another person to feel embarrassed, angry, or hurt? _____
    _____
    _____

4. Did your behavior jeopardize the safety of yourself or others? _____
    _____

5. Did your behavior keep you or other students from their learning tasks? _____
    _____

6. Did your behavior keep another student from being heard by the teacher and class? _____
    _____

7. Did your behavior help or hinder the class work? _____
    _____

8. Did your behavior break a school rule? _____ If yes, which one? _____
    _____

9. Explain in your own words what positive behaviors your teacher and classmates will observe from you when
    you return to class. _____
    _____

When you are ready to honor our classroom and house expectations and agreements, do the following:

1. Return to the classroom, and place this completed and signed paper in the appropriate basket on my desk.
2. Return to your assigned seat without disturbing anyone.
3. Rejoin the classroom activity.

Student's signature _____ Date _____

For Your Notes

EXERCISE 4.2 TEACHERS' BEHAVIOR MANAGEMENT SYSTEMS

Instructions: The purpose of this exercise is to interview two teachers, from two different grade levels, to discover how they manage their classrooms. Use the outline format that follows, conduct your interviews, and then share the results with your classmates, perhaps in small groups.

1. Teacher interviewed:

2. Date: 4. School:

3. Grade level: 5. Subject(s):

6. Please describe your classroom management system. Specifically, I would like to know your procedures for the following:

   a. How are students to signal that they want your attention and help?

   b. How do you call on students during question and discussion sessions?

   c. How and when are students to enter and exit the classroom?

   d. How are students to obtain the materials for instruction?

   e. How are students to store their personal items?

   f. What are the procedures for students' going to the drinking fountain or bathroom?

   g. What are the procedures during class interruptions?

EXERCISE 4.2 *(continued)*

h. What are the procedures for tardies or early dismissal?

i. What are the procedures for turning in homework?

7. Describe your expectations for classroom behavior and the consequences for misbehavior.

In discussion with classmates following the interviews, consider the following.

Many modern teachers advocate the use of a highly structured classroom, and then, as appropriate over time during the school year, they share more of the responsibility with the students. Did you find this to be the case with the majority of teachers interviewed? Was it more or less the case in any particular grade level(s)? Was it more or less the case with any particular subject areas?

EXERCISE 4.3 BEGINNING THE DEVELOPMENT OF MY CLASSROOM MANAGEMENT SYSTEM

Instructions: The purpose of this exercise is to begin preparation of the management system that you will explain to your students during the first day or week of school. Answer the questions that follow and share those answers with your peers for their feedback. Then make changes as appropriate. (Upon completion of this chapter, you may want to revisit this exercise to make adjustments to your management plan, as you will from time to time throughout your professional career.)

1. My anticipated grade level and, if relevant, teaching subject:

2. Attention to procedures. Use a statement to explain your procedural expectation for each of the following:

   a. How are students to signal that they want your attention and help?

   b. How do you call on students during question and discussion sessions?

   c. How and when are students to enter and exit the classroom?

   d. How are students to obtain the materials for instruction?

   e. How are students to store their personal items?

   f. What are the procedures for students' going to the drinking fountain or bathroom?

   g. What are the procedures during class interruptions?

   h. What are the procedures for tardies or early dismissal?

EXERCISE 4.3 *(continued)*

    i. What are the procedures for turning in homework?

3. List of student behavior expectations that I will present to my class (no more than five):

Rule 1:

Rule 2:

Rule 3:

Rule 4:

Rule 5:

4. Explanation of consequences for broken rules:

5. How procedures, rules, or consequences may vary (if at all) according to the grade level taught or according to any other criteria, such as in team teaching:

USING POSITIVE REWARDS

Reinforcement theory contends that a person's gratification derived from receiving a reward strengthens the tendency for that person to continue to act in a certain way, while the lack of a reward (or the promise of a reward) weakens the tendency to act that way. For example, according to the theory, if students are promised a reward of "preferred activity time (PAT) on Friday" if they work well all week long, then the students are likely to work toward that reward, thus improving their standards of learning. Some educators argue that (a) once the extrinsic reinforcement (i.e., the reward from outside the learner) has been removed, the desired behavior tends to diminish; and that (b) rather than extrinsic sources of reinforcement, focus should be on increasing the student's internal sense of accomplishment, an *intrinsic reward*. Further, rewarding children for complying with expected/standard behavior sends the wrong message. It reinforces the mentality of, "What do I get (for doing what I am supposed to do)?" If common as a school practice, it carries over into home situations and eventually to adulthood. A principal does not reward a teacher for showing up on time, attending a faculty meeting, or having report cards prepared on time. Those are expected/standard behaviors. Perhaps, for the daily work of a teacher in a classroom of many diverse individuals, the practical reality is somewhere between. After all, the reality of classroom teaching is less than ideal, and all activities cannot be intrinsically rewarding. Further, for many children intrinsic rewards are often too remote to be effective.

The promise of extrinsic rewards is not always necessary or beneficial. Students generally will work harder to learn something because they want to learn it (i.e., it is intrinsically motivating) than they will merely to earn PAT, points, grades, candy, or some other form of reward (called *extrinsic motivator*). In addition, regarding the promise of PAT on Friday, so many children are so preoccupied with "the here and now" that for them the promise on Monday of preferred activity time on Friday probably will have little desired effect on their behavior on Monday. To them on Monday, Friday seems to be a long way off.

Activities that are interesting and intrinsically rewarding are not further served by the addition of extrinsic rewards. This is especially true when working with students who are already highly motivated to learn. Adding extrinsic incentives to learning activities that are already highly motivating tends to reduce student motivation. For most students, the use of extrinsic motivators should be minimal and is probably most useful in skills learning, where there is a lot of repetition and the potential for boredom. While we are fully aware of the resentment students might feel if other teachers gave out candy, stickers, and so on, and theirs did not, when students are working diligently on a highly motivating student-initiated project of study, extrinsic rewards are probably not necessary and could even have negative effects.[15]

MANAGING CLASS MEETINGS

The guidelines for the first meeting with your students hold true for every meeting thereafter. When it is time for the class to begin, you should start the learning activities at once, with no delay. By beginning your class meeting without delay you discourage the kind of fooling around and time wasting that might otherwise occur. To minimize problems in the classroom, you must practice this from the very first day of your teaching career.[16]

Once class has begun, the pace of activities should be lively enough to keep students alert and busy, without dead time, but not so fast as to discourage or lose some students. Teachers who are most effective run a businesslike classroom, where at no time does any student sit or stand around with nothing to do. To maintain a smooth and brisk pace and to lessen distractions and prevent dead time, consider the guidelines that follow.

Opening Activities

Although some schools do not use a bell system for the beginning and ending of instructional periods, many teachers still refer to the initial class activity as the *bell activity*. More frequently, perhaps, it is referred to as the *opener* or *warm-up activity*.

At the beginning of each class, to take attendance and to attend to other routine administrative matters, most teachers expect the students to be in their home base seats. You should greet the students warmly and start their learning quickly. (Unless you really want responses, it perhaps is best to avoid greeting students with a rhetorical question such as "How was your weekend?" See purposes for using Questioning in Chapter 7.) If you are teaching in a school where you must attend to attendance matters at the beginning of each class meeting and are not yet comfortable with your overlapping skill, an effective management procedure is to have the overhead projector on when students arrive in class, with the agenda and immediate assignment or warm-up activity clearly written on a transparency and displayed on the screen, which then is referred to after your greeting. Once administrative matters are completed (usually in a matter of a minute or two), the day's lesson should begin, which could mean that students will move to other stations within the classroom.

When there are no announcements or other administrative matters to cover, you should try to begin the lesson immediately. Then, within a few minutes after the students have begun their lesson activities, attend to attendance matters. Perhaps the best routine, one that requires your practice and overlapping skill, is to do both simultaneously—take attendance while starting a learning activity. Whichever the case, once the class period has begun, routines and lesson activities should move forward briskly and steadily until the official end of the class period, or, in the case of extended class periods or blocks, until a scheduled break.

Warm-up or opening activities include any variety of things, such as a specific topic or question each student responds to by writing in their journal or the same topic or question that pairs (dyads) of students discuss and write about in their journals (using the strategy referred to as *think-write-pair-share* that was described in Chapter 3). Other activities include a problem to be solved by each student or student pair, the discussion of a homework assignment, the completion of the write-up of a science activity, and the writing of individual or student dyad responses to textbook questions.

Now do Exercise 4.4 to learn further how experienced teachers open their class meetings or school day.

EXERCISE 4.4 OBSERVATION AND ANALYSIS OF HOW EXPERIENCED TEACHERS OPEN THEIR CLASS MEETINGS OR THE SCHOOL DAY

Instructions: The purpose of this exercise is for you to learn further how some experienced teachers open their class meetings. Select three experienced teachers, all of the same grade level and (if relevant) subject, in order to observe how they begin their class meetings (generally for grades 5–6) or school day (any grade). Observe only the first 10 minutes of the opening. After collecting these data, share, compile, and discuss the results as follows.

Grade level and subject discipline I observed: _____

1. Make a check for each of the following observations that you make and for each teacher place a number 1, 2, 3, and, for which of these things the teacher did first, second, third, and, during that initial 10 minutes from the time students begin entering the classroom until after the official clock start of class (i.e., when class is supposed to begin).

	✓	*Teacher 1*	*Teacher 2*	*Teacher 3*
Greeting the students	_____	_____	_____	_____
Warm and friendly?	_____	_____	_____	_____
Giving an assignment (i.e., a warmup activity)	_____	_____	_____	_____
Taking attendance	_____	_____	_____	_____
Talking with another adult	_____	_____	_____	_____
Talking with one or a few students	_____	_____	_____	_____
Readying teaching materials or equipment or bulletin board	_____	_____	_____	_____
Working at desk	_____	_____	_____	_____
Distributing student papers or materials	_____	_____	_____	_____
Other (specify)	_____	_____	_____	_____

2. For these three teachers, was there a common way in which they began class?

EXERCISE 4.4 *(continued)*

3. Compile your results with those of your classmates. Write the compilation results here.

4. Compare and contrast the results of observations for all subjects and grade levels.

5. What conclusions do you reach as a class about teachers of particular grade levels and disciplines with respect to how they spend the first 10 minutes with their students?

6. Optional. If previous year's data are available from your instructor, compare these results (number 5) with those from previous years.

Smooth Implementation of the Lesson

Lessons should move forward briskly and purposefully, with natural transitions from one lesson activity to the next and with each activity starting and ending conclusively, especially when using direct (teacher-centered) instruction. Transitions (discussed below), in particular, are a most troublesome time for many beginning teachers. Transitions are less troublesome when planned carefully during the preactive phase of instruction and written into the lesson plan.

When giving verbal instructions to students, do so quickly and succinctly, without talking too long and giving so much detail that students begin to get restless and bored. Children are quickly bored with long-winded verbal instructions from a teacher.

Once students are busy at their learning tasks, avoid interrupting them with additional verbal instructions, statements, or announcements that get them off task and that could as easily be written on the board or overhead transparency; also avoid interventions that could be communicated to a student privately without disturbing the rest of the class. Elementary and middle school children in particular are easily distracted; do not be the cause of their distractions. Modeling the very behaviors expected of the children is a continuing focus and theme for the classroom teacher.

With whole-class instruction, before starting a new activity be sure that most students have satisfactorily completed the present one. Students who finish early can work on an *anchor or transitional activity* (discussed next). End each activity conclusively before beginning a new activity, and with a relevant and carefully prepared transition bridge the new activity with the previous one so students understand the connection. Helping students understand connections is another continuing focus and theme for the classroom teacher.

With your developing skill in withitness, you will carefully and continuously monitor all students during the entire class period. If one or two children become inattentive and begin to behave inappropriately, quietly redirect their attention *without interrupting other students*.

To help in the prevention of dead time and management problems, especially when using multiple learning tasks and indirect instruction, you will want to establish and rehearse the students in the use of anchor or transitional activities.

Transitions: A Difficult Skill for Beginning Teachers

Transitions are the moments in lessons between activities or topics, times of change. It will probably take you a while to master the skill of smooth transitions. Planning and consistency are important to your mastering this important skill. With a dependable schedule and consistent routines, transitions usually occur efficiently and automatically, without disruption. Still, a large percentage of student behavior problems occur during times of transitions, especially when children must idly wait for the next activity. To avoid problems during transitions, eliminate wait times by thinking and planning ahead. During the preactive phase of instruction, plan your transitions and write them into your lesson plan.

Transitions in lessons are of two types, and at times both are used. The first is achieved by the teacher's connecting one activity to the next so students understand the relationship between the two activities. This is a *lesson transition*. The second type of transition occurs when some students have finished a learning activity but must wait, sometimes even while standing in line, for others to catch up before starting the next. This we call an *anchor or transitional activity*. The transitional activity is one intended to keep all students academically occupied, allowing no time where students have nothing to do but wait. A common example is when a test is given and some students finish while others have not. The effective teacher plans a transitional activity and gives instructions or reminders for that before students start the test.

Teachers who are most effective are those who, during the preactive phase of instruction, plan and rehearse nearly every move they and the students will make, thinking ahead to anticipate and avoid problems in the classroom. Transitions are planned and students are prepared for them by clearly established transition routines. While in transition and waiting for the start of the next activity students engage in these transitional activities. You can plan a variety of transitional activities relevant and appropriate to the topics being studied, while not necessarily related to the next activity of that particular day's lesson. Transitional activities may include any number of meaningful activities such as journal writing, worksheet activity, portfolio work, project work, homework, and work at a learning center.

As a beginning teacher, it will take time to develop finesse in your application of these guidelines for effective lesson management. During your student teaching experience, your cooperating teacher and college or university supervisor will understand that it takes time and will help you develop and hone your skills.

STUDENT MISBEHAVIOR

Student behavior in the classroom that is inappropriate can range from minor acts to very serious ones. Sometimes student behaviors seen by the teacher as inappropriate are simply the demonstration of behaviors that are learned and even encouraged in the child's home. Sometimes the causes of student misbehavior are the result of problems that originated from outside the classroom and spilled over into it. Others are simply misbehaviors that result from the fact that whenever a group of children are together for a period of time, mischief or fooling around will likely result. Still others are the result of something the teacher did or did not do. Read on attentively to the guidelines and hints that follow in the remaining pages of this chapter.

Types of Student Misbehavior

Described next are types or categories of student misbehavior that teachers sometimes have to contend with, in order of increasing seriousness.

Trivial Misbehaviors
This least-serious category includes these common misbehaviors: fooling around and not attending to assigned tasks, showing extraordinary excitement over the content of a lesson, brief whispering, and daydreaming. Fortunately, in most instances, this type of misbehavior is momentary and if anything, may need from you only a nonobtrusive intervention (such as a momentary and silent stare) and redirection (such as pointing to the student's work). If this doesn't work, then go to the second-level intervention by calling on the student by name and reminding the student of the correct procedure or of what the student is supposed to be doing and of the consequences for continued inappropriate behavior. Avoid asking an off-task student any question (such as, for example, a content question knowing full well that the student is not paying attention, or the question, "Billy, why are you doing that?" Billy probably doesn't know why). Avoid also making a threat such as "Billy, if you don't turn around and get to work I will send you outside." It is im-

portant you not make "mountains out of molehills," or you could cause more problems than you would resolve. Maintain students' focus on the lesson, rather than on the off-task behavior.

There is sometimes a tendency among beginning teachers especially when they have a problem with students goofing off and being disruptive to assume that the entire group of students is being unruly, when, in fact, more often it is only one or two or maybe three students. You want to avoid saying to the entire group of children anything that implies that they all are being unruly if, in fact, they are not. Such a false accusation will only serve to alienate the majority of the students who are being attentive to the learning task.

Disruptions to Learning
This category includes incessant talking out of turn, walking about the room aimlessly and without permission, clowning, and tossing objects, all of which most children know are unacceptable in the classroom. In handling such misbehaviors, it is important that you have explained their consequences to students, and then, following your stated procedures, promptly and consistently deal with the violations. Too many beginning teachers (and veteran teachers as well) tend to ignore these class disruptions (seemingly in hope that, if not recognized, they will discontinue). You must *not* ignore minor infractions of this type, for if you do, they most likely will escalate beyond your worst nightmare. Without displaying any anger (otherwise students are winning the battle for power), simply and quickly enforce your consequences and keep the focus on the lesson, not on the inappropriate behavior. In other words, maintain your control of classroom events, rather than become controlled by them.

Defiance, Cheating, Lying, and Stealing
When a student refuses to do what you say, the student's defiance may be worthy of temporary or permanent removal from the classroom. Depending upon your judgment of the seriousness of the act of defiance, you may simply give the student a timeout or you may suspend the student from class until there has been a conference about the situation, perhaps involving the teacher, school administrator, the student, and the student's parent or guardian.

Any cheating, lying, and stealing may be an isolated act, and the student may only need a one-on-one talk to find out what precipitated the incident and what might be done to prevent it from ever happening again. A student who habitually exhibits any of these behaviors may need to be referred to a specialist. Whenever you have reason to suspect immoral behavior, you should discuss your concerns with the school administrator.

Violence

In many ways, teaching is clearly different than it used to be. More and more often, today, starting as early as kindergarten, teachers are confronted with major problems of inappropriate behavior that have ramifications beyond the classroom or that begin elsewhere and spill over into the classroom. If this happens, you may need to ask for help and should not hesitate to do so. As a teacher, you must remain alert. In the words of Johnson and Johnson,

> Fifty years ago, the main disciplinary problems were running in halls, talking out of turn, and chewing gum. Today's transgressions include physical and verbal violence, incivility, and in some schools, drug abuse, robbery, assault, and murder. The result is that many teachers spend an inordinate amount of time and energy managing classroom conflicts. When students poorly manage their conflicts with each other and with faculty, aggression results. Such behavior is usually punished with detentions, suspensions, and expulsions. As violence increases, pressure for safe and orderly schools increases. Schools are struggling with what to do.[17]

Today's schools are adopting a variety of types of schoolwide and classroom instructional programs designed to reduce or eliminate violent, aggressive, student behaviors. For example, a number of schools report success in reducing these student hostile behaviors by using a combination of judicious discipline and class meetings.[18] Other schools have reported success by using the Second Step Violence Prevention program. Second Step is a PreK–8 curriculum designed to teach children violence prevention skills of empathy, recognizing and creating options, interpersonal cognitive problem solving, anger management, and impulse control. It is a companion to Talking About Touching, a personal safety curriculum that teaches children not to be victims of violence, and provides a "second step" in primary prevention by teaching children not to become victimizers.[19]

No Short-Term Solutions to Major Problems

Peer pressure and resentment of authority by some children can result in classroom management becoming a major concern of their teachers. Major problems may call for extra effort on the part of the teacher in understanding and in dealing with them. There are no short-term solutions for a teacher who is trying to resolve a conflict with a student who causes major problems. Although consequences such as time out, conferences, detention, and suspension may offer short-term relief, long-term total-school and community efforts may be called for.

Teacher Response to Student Misbehavior: Direct and Indirect Intervention

The goal in responding to student misbehavior is to intervene and redirect the student's focus, and to do so successfully with the least amount of classroom disturbance. Too often, teachers intervene with verbal commands—direct intervention—when nonverbal gesturing or signal interference as means of keeping students focused, such as eye contact, proximity, smiles or frowns and other facial gesturing, thumbs up or down, and body language—indirect intervention strategies—are less disruptive and often more effective in redirecting a misbehaving student.[20] While the offense might be identical, the teacher's intervention for one student might have to be direct, while for another student indirect intervention is enough to stop the misbehavior.

Order of Behavior Intervention Strategies

To redirect a student's attention, and as indicated in Figure 4.2, your usual *first effort* should be indirect intervention. This is usually a silent intervention (e.g., proximity, eye contact, body language, gesturing). Your *second effort* could be the simplest (that is, the most private) direct intervention (e.g., "Marie, please follow procedures"), perhaps followed by a reminder of the consequences for continued inappropriate behavior. Your *third effort,* one that in time interval closely follows the second (i.e., within the same class period), should follow your rules and procedures as outlined in your management system, which might mean a time out (as discussed earlier in this chapter) and a phone call to the student's parent or guardian (in private, of course). Normally, such a third effort is not necessary. A *fourth effort,* still rarer, is to suspend the student from class (and/or school) for some period of time until decisions about the future of that student in the school are made by school officials in consultation with the student, teacher, the parents or guardians, and sometimes other professionals such as the school psychologist.

Direct intervention should be reserved for repetitive and serious misbehavior. When using direct intervention, you should give a direct statement, either reminding the student of what the student is supposed to be doing or telling the student what to do. You should avoid asking rhetorical questions, such as "Philip, when are you going to stop that fooling around?" or "Marie, why are you doing that?" When giving students directions about what they are supposed to be doing, you may be asked by a student, "Why do we have to do this?" To that question, you may give a brief academic answer, but do not become defensive or make threats. And rather than spending an inordinate amount of time on the misbehavior, try to focus the student's attention on a desired behavior.

One reason that direct intervention should be held in reserve is because by interrupting the lesson to verbally intervene you are doing exactly what the student who is being reprimanded was doing—interrupting the lesson. Not only is that improper modeling but it can create a host of management problems beyond your wildest nightmares. Another reason for saving direct intervention is that, if used too often, direct intervention loses it effectiveness.

TEACHER-CAUSED STUDENT MISBEHAVIOR

As a classroom teacher, one of your major responsibilities is to model appropriate behavior and to *not* contribute to or be the cause of problems in the classroom. Some student misbehaviors and problems in the classroom are caused by or escalated by the teacher and could have been prevented or easily rectified had the teacher behaved or acted differently.

Scenarios for Case Study Review

You should avoid using negative methods of rule enforcement and ineffective forms of punishment, such as exemplified in the following scenarios. You and your classmates might decide to treat these scenarios as case studies for small groups to consider and then discuss before the whole class.

- *Capricious.* Because of her arbitrary and inconsistent enforcement of classroom rules, Fran Fickle has lost the respect and trust of her second-grade students as well as control of the class. Students are constantly testing Fran to see what they can get away with.

- *Extra Assignments.* When students in Margaret Malopropros's fifth-grade reading class misbehave, she habitually assigns extra reading and written work as punishment, even for the most minor offenses. This behavior has simply reinforced the view of many of her students that school is drudgery, so they no longer look forward to her classes, and behavior problems in her class have steadily increased since the beginning of the school year.

- *Embarrassment.* When fourth-grade teacher Denise Degradini was having difficulty with the behavior of one of her students, she got on the classroom phone, called the student's parent, and while the entire class of 33 students could overhear the conversation, told the parent about her child's behavior in class and how she was going to have to give the student a referral if the student's behavior did not improve. From that one act Denise lost all respect of her students. Class achievement grades plummeted for the rest of the year.

- *Group Punishment.* Because Fred Flock has not developed his withitness and overlapping skills, he has developed the unfortunate habit of punishing the entire group for every instance of misbehavior. Yesterday, for example, because some students were noisy during a video presentation, he gave the entire class an unannounced quiz on the content of the film. He has lost the respect of the students, students are hostile toward him, and his problems with students in the classroom are steadily growing worse.

- *Harsh and Humiliating Punishment.* Vince Van Pelt, a physical education teacher, has lost control of his classes and the respect of his students. His thrashing, whipping, tongue-lashing, and use of humiliation are ineffective and indicative of his loss of control. Parents have complained and one is suing him. The district has given Mr. Van Pelt official notice of the nonrenewal of his contract.

- *Loud Talk.* The noisiest person in Steve Shrill's fifth-grade class is Mr. Shrill. His constant and mistaken effort to talk over the student noise has led to his own yelling and screaming, to complaints from neighboring teachers about the noise in his class, and to a reprimand from the principal.

- *Lowered Marks.* Eunice Erudite, a third-grade teacher, has a policy of writing a student's name on the board each time the person is reprimanded for misbehavior. Then, when a student has accumulated five marks on the board, she lowers the student's academic grade by one letter. As a result of her not separating their academic and social behaviors, her students are not doing as well as they were at the start of the year. Parents, guardians, and students have complained about this policy to the school principal, arguing that the grades Ms. Erudite is giving do not reflect the students' academic progress or abilities.

- *Nagging.* Paul Peck's continual and unnecessary scolding and criticizing of students upsets the recipient students and arouses resentment from their peers. His nagging resolves nothing, and, like a snowball building in size as it rolls down the hill, causes Mr. Peck, a fifth-grade teacher, more and more problems in the classroom.

- *Negative Direct Intervention.* In kindergarten, Joshua swears more and more frequently and with graphic and startling language. Other students are beginning to behave similarly. Rather than giving Joshua alternative ways of expressing his feelings, Polly Premio, the teacher, verbally reprimands Joshua each time this happens and threatens to call his parents about it. Ms. Premio doesn't realize that by giving attention to Joshua's swearing she is rewarding, reinforcing, and causing the increase in Joshua's unacceptable behavior.

- *Negative Touch Control.* When Ezzard, the first-grade bully, pushes and shoves other students out of his way for no apparent reason other than to physically manipulate them, his teacher, Tony Trenchant, grabs Ezzard and yanks him into his seat. What "roughneck" Tony the teacher doesn't realize is that he is using the very behavior (physical force) that he is trying to stop Ezzard from using. This simply confuses students and teaches them (especially Ezzard) that the use of physical force is okay if you are bigger or older than the recipient of that force. In this situation, unfortunately, hostility begets hostility.

- *Overreact.* Randall, a fourth-grade student, was reading a magazine when his teacher, Harriet Harshmore, grabbed it from Randall's hands, called it "pornographic," tore out the offending pages and tossed them into a wastebasket. The magazine was *National Geographic,* and the pornographic article was on evolution and included drawings of unclothed humans. Harriet was later reprimanded by the school superintendent who said that although he supported her right to put a stop to what she considered a class disruption, Ms. Harshmore had crossed the line when she damaged the magazine. The magazine, apparently a rare collector's issue, had been borrowed from Randall's brother at his teacher's encouragement to bring reading material from home.

- *Physical Punishment.* Mr. Fit, a sixth-grade social studies teacher, punishes students by making them go outside and do push-ups or run when they misbehave in his class. Last week, Sebastian, a student whom he told to go out and run four laps around the periphery of the school grounds for "mouthing off in class," collapsed and died while running. Mr. Fit has been placed on paid leave and is being sued for negligence by Sebastian's parents.

- *Premature Judgments and Actions.* Because of second-grade teacher Kathy Kwik's impulsiveness, she does not think clearly before acting, and more than once she has reprimanded the wrong child. Because of her hasty and faulty judgments, students have lost respect for her. For them, her class has become pure drudgery.

- *Rule Breaker.* One of the rules in Patti Hugrite's first-grade class is "we keep our hands to ourselves." While Ms. Hugrite enforces that rule and applies consequences to children who break it, she frequently is seen hugging children and patting them on the back or shoulder. Students in her class are confused.

- *Threats and Ultimatums.* Threats and ultimatums from sixth-grade teacher Bonnie Badger are known to be empty; because she does not follow through, her credibility with the students has been lost. Like wildfire, the word has spread around—"We can do whatever we want in old Badger's class."

- *Too Much Hesitancy.* Because Tim Timideo is too hesitant and slow to intervene when students of his first-grade class get off task, his class has increasingly gotten further and further out of his control, and it is still early in the school year. As a result neighbor teachers are complaining about the noise from his classroom and Tim has been writing more and more referrals.

- *Writing Punishment.* Because they were "too noisy," sixth-grade science teacher Steve Scribe punished his class of 28 students by making each one hand-copy 10 pages from encyclopedias. When they submitted this assignment, he tore up the pages in front of the students while saying, "Now, I hope you have learned your lesson and from now on will be quiet." Upon hearing about this, all six of the school's English/language-arts teachers signed and filed a complaint with the principal about Mr. Scribe's use of writing for punishment.

Preventing a Ship from Sinking Is Much Easier than Saving a Sinking One: Common Mistakes to Avoid

During your beginning years of teaching, no one, including you, should expect you to be perfect. You should, however, be aware of common mistakes teachers make that often are the causes of student inattention and misbehavior. It is our estimation that as much as 95 percent of student behavior problems in the classroom are teacher-caused and preventable. In this section, you will find descriptions of 50 mistakes commonly made by beginning (and even veteran) teachers. To have a most successful beginning to your career, you will want to develop your skills so to avoid these mistakes. To avoid making these mistakes requires both knowledge of the potential errors and reflection upon one's own behaviors in relation to them.

1. *Inadequately attending to long-range and daily planning.* A teacher who inadequately plans ahead is heading for trouble. Inadequate long-term and sketchy daily planning is a precursor to ineffective teaching and, eventually, to teaching failure. Students are motivated best by teachers who clearly are working hard and intelligently for them.

2. *Emphasizing the negative.* Too many warnings to children for their inappropriate behavior—and too little recognition for their positive behaviors—do not help to establish the positive climate needed for the most effective learning to occur. Reminding students of procedures is more positive and will bring you quicker success than is reprimanding them when they do not follow procedures.

Too often, teachers try to control students with negative language, such as "There should be no talking," and "No gum or candy in class or else you will receive detention," and "No getting out of your seats without my permission." Teachers sometimes allow students, too, to use negative language on each other, such as "Shut up!" Negative language does not help instill a positive classroom climate. To encourage a positive atmosphere, use concise, positive, language. Tell students precisely what they are supposed to do rather than what they are not supposed to do. Disallow the use of disrespectful and negative language in your classroom.

3. *Not requiring students to raise hands and be acknowledged before responding.* While ineffective teachers often are ones who are controlled by class events, competent teachers are those who are in control of class events. You cannot be in control of events and your interactions with students if you allow students to shout out their comments, responses, and questions whenever they feel like it. The most successful beginning teachers quickly establish and maintain control of classroom events.

In addition, as we indicated earlier in this chapter, indulging their natural impulsivity is not helping children to grow intellectually. When students develop impulse control, they think before acting. Students can be taught to think before act-

ing or shouting out an answer. One of several reasons that teachers should insist on a show of student hands before a student is acknowledged to respond or question is to discourage students from the impulsive, disruptive, and irritating behavior of shouting out in class.[21]

4. *Allowing students' hands to be raised too long.* When students have their hands raised for long periods before you recognize them and attend to their questions or responses, you are providing them with time to fool around. Although you don't have to call on every student as soon as a student raises a hand, you should acknowledge the student quickly, such as with a nod or a wave of your hand, so the student can lower the hand and return to work. Then you should get to the student as quickly as possible. Procedures for this should be clearly understood by the students and consistently practiced by you.

5. *Spending too much with one student or one group and not monitoring the entire group.* Spending too much time with any one student or a small group of students is, in effect, ignoring the rest of the children. As a novice teacher you cannot afford to ignore the rest of the class, even for a moment.

6. *Beginning a new activity before gaining the students' attention.* A teacher who consistently fails to insist that students follow procedures and who does not wait until all students are in compliance before starting a new activity is destined for major problems in classroom control. You must establish and maintain classroom procedures. Starting an activity before all students are in compliance is, in effect, telling the students that they don't have to comply with expected procedures. You cannot afford the mistake of telling students one thing and then doing another.

7. *Pacing teacher talk and learning activities too fast.* Pacing the instructional activities is one of the more difficult skills for beginning teachers to master. Regardless of their age, students need time to disengage mentally and physically from one activity before engaging in the next. You must remember that this takes more time for a room of 25 or so students than it does for just one person, you. This is a reason that transitions need to be planned and written into your lesson plan (discussed further in Chapter 6).

8. *Using a voice level that is always either too loud or too soft.* A teacher's voice that is too loud day after day can become irritating to some students, just as one that cannot be heard or understood can become frustrating.

9. *Assigning a journal entry without giving the topic careful thought.* If the question or topic about which students are supposed to write is ambiguous or obviously hurriedly prepared—without your having given thought to how students will in-

terpret and respond to it—students will judge that the task is busywork (e.g., something to keep them busy while you take attendance). If they do it at all, it will be with a great deal of commotion and much less enthusiasm than were they writing on a topic that had meaning to them.

10. *Standing too long in one place.* Most of the time in the classroom, you should be mobile, schmoozing, "working the crowd."

11. *Sitting while teaching.* Unless you are physically unable to stand or you are teaching children of kindergarten or primary grades, in most situations there is no time to sit while teaching. It is difficult to monitor the class while seated.

12. *Being too serious and no fun.* No doubt, good teaching is serious business. But students are motivated by and respond best to teachers who obviously enjoy working with children and helping them learn.

13. *Falling into a rut by using the same teaching strategy or combination of strategies day after day.* A teacher in such a rut is likely to become boring to students. Because of the multitude of differences, children are motivated by and respond best to a variety of well-planned and meaningful learning activities.

14. *Inadequately using silence (wait time) after asking a content question.* When expected to think deeply about a question, students need time to do it. A teacher who consistently gives insufficient time to students to think is teaching only superficially and at the lowest cognitive level and is destined for problems in student motivation and classroom control.

15. *Poorly or inefficiently using instructional tools.* The ineffective use of teaching tools such as books, the overhead projector, writing board, bulletin board, and computer says to students that you are not a competent teacher. Would you want an auto mechanic who did not know how to use the tools of that trade to service your automobile? Would you want a brain surgeon who did not know how to use the tools of the trade to remove your tumor? Working with children in a classroom is no less important. Like a competent automobile mechanic or a competent surgeon, a competent teacher selects and effectively uses the best tools available for the job to be done.

16. *Ineffectively using facial expressions and body language.* As said earlier, your gestures and body language communicate more to children than your words do. For example, one sixth-grade language-arts teacher didn't understand why students would not respond to his repeated expression of "I need your attention." In one 15-minute segment, he used that expression eight times. Studying videotape of that class period helped him understand the problem. His dress was very casual, and he stood most of the time with his right hand in his pocket. At 5 feet, 8 inches, with a slight build, a rather deadpan facial expression, and an unexpressive voice, his was not a commanding presence in the classroom. After seeing himself on videotape, he returned to the class wearing a tie, and he began using his hands, face, and body more expressively. Rather than saying "I need your attention," while maintaining eye contact with the students, he waited in silence for the students to become attentive. It worked.

17. *Relying too much on teacher talk for classroom control.* Some teachers have a tendency to rely too much on teacher talk. Too much teacher talk can be deadly. Unable to discern between the important and the unimportant verbiage, children will quickly tune a teacher out.

Some teachers rely too much on verbal interaction and too little on nonverbal intervention techniques. Verbally reprimanding a student for the student's interruptions of class activities is reinforcing the very behavior you are trying to stop. In addition, verbally reprimanding a student in front of the student's peers can backfire on you. Instead, develop your indirect, silent intervention techniques such as eye contact, mobility, frown, silence, body stance, and proximity.

18. *Inefficiently using teacher time: trying to do everything yourself.* During the preactive phase of your instruction (the planning phase), think carefully about what you are going to be doing every minute, and then plan for the most efficient and therefore the most productive use of your time in the classroom. Consider the following example. During a sixth-grade language-arts brainstorming session a teacher is recording student contributions on a large sheet of butcher paper that has been taped to the classroom wall. She solicits student responses, acknowledges those responses, holds and manipulates the writing pen, walks to the wall, and writes on the paper. Each of those actions requires decisions and movements that consume precious instructional time and that can distract her from her students. An effective alternative should be to have a reliable student helper do the writing while the teacher handles the solicitation and acknowledgment of student contributions. That way she has fewer decisions and fewer actions to distract her. And she does not lose eye contact and proximity with the classroom of students.

Let us emphasize still further the importance and advantages of using student helpers in the daily events of the classroom, rather than your trying to do everything while your students sit doing little or nothing. In planning student involvement in the everyday jobs of the classroom you can be as sophisticated as you desire, from the minimum of simply having a teacher's assistant for the day help with some of the more common tasks to seeing that all children have jobs, that jobs are clearly delineated and appropriately named (such as: Allergy Supervisor—cleans and dusts; Bathroom Monitor; Assistant Teacher—helps the teacher; Census Taker—helps with attendance matters; Horticulturist or Zoo Keeper—cares for plants and animals; Librarian—collects and organizes reading materials; Mail Carrier—delivers messages and distributes papers; Materials or Equipment Manager—arranges, collects, distributes, and puts away materials and equipment), that jobs rotate and are applied for, and that, just as in real life, there are rewards for jobs well done and consequences for jobs poorly done.

19. *Talking to and interacting with only half the children in the classroom.* While leading a class discussion, there is a tendency among some beginning teachers to favor (by their eye contact and verbal interaction) only 40 to 65 percent of the students, sometimes completely ignoring the others. Knowing that they are being ignored, those students will, in time, become uninterested and perhaps unruly. Remember to spread your interactions and eye contact throughout the entire group of children.

20. *Collecting and returning student papers before assigning students something to do.* Students should have something to do while papers are being collected or returned; otherwise they are likely to get restless, inattentive, and unruly.

21. *Interrupting students when they are on task.* It is not easy to get an entire group of 30 or so children on task. Once they are on task, you do not want to be the distracter. Try to give all instructions before students begin their work. The detailed instructions should be written in your lesson plan; that way you are sure not to forget anything. Once on task, if there is an important point you wish to make, write it on the board. If you want to return papers while students are working, do it in a way and at a time that is least likely to interrupt them from their learning task.

22. *Using "Shhh" as a means of quieting students.* When you do that, you simply sound like a balloon with a slow leak. It's best to delete the sound from your professional vocabulary before children begin mimicking you with a chorus of "shhh."

23. *Using poor body positioning.* Develop your skill of withitness by always positioning your body so you can continue to visually monitor the entire class even while talking to and working with one student or a small group. Avoid turning your back to even a portion of the class.

24. *Settling for less when you should be trying for more—not getting the most from student re-* *sponses.* The most successful schools are those with teachers who expect and get the most from all students. Don't hurry a class discussion; "milk" student responses for all you can, especially when discussing a topic that students are obviously interested in. Ask a student for clarification or reasons for the student's response. Ask for verification. Have another student paraphrase what a student said. Pump students for deeper thought and meaning. Too often, the teacher will ask a question, get an abbreviated (often a one-word and low-cognitive-level) response from a student, and then move on to another topic. Instead, follow up a student's response to your question with a sequence of questions, prompting and cueing to elevate student thinking to higher levels.

25. *Using threats.* Avoid making threats of any kind. One teacher, for example, told the class that if they continued with their inappropriate talking they would lose their break time. The teacher should have had that consequence as part of the understood procedures and consequences and then taken away the break time for some students if warranted.

26. *Avoiding punishing the entire class of children for the misbehavior of a few.* While the rationale behind such action is clear (i.e., to get group peer pressure working for you), often the result is the opposite. Children who have been behaving well are alienated from the teacher because they feel they have been punished unfairly for the misbehavior of others. Those students expect the teacher to be able to handle the misbehaving students without punishing those who are not misbehaving, and they are right!

27. *Using global praise.* Global praise is pretty useless. An example is: "Class, your drawings were really wonderful." This is hollow and says nothing; simply another instance of useless verbiage from the teacher. Instead, be specific—tell what it was about their drawings that made them so wonderful. As another example, after a student's oral response to the class, rather than simply saying "very good," tell what about the student's response was so good.

28. *Using color meaninglessly.* The use of color on transparencies and the writing board is nice but will shortly lose its effectiveness unless the colors have meaning. If, for example, everything in the classroom is color-coded and students understand the meaning of the code, then use of color can serve as an important mnemonic to student learning.

29. *Verbally reprimanding a student from across the room.* This is yet another example of the needless interruption of all students. In addition, because of peer pressure (children tend to support one another) it increases the "you versus them"

syndrome. Reprimand when necessary, but do it quietly and as privately as possible.

30. *Interacting with only a "chosen few" students rather than spreading interactions around to all.* As a beginning teacher especially, it is easy to fall into a habit of interacting with only a few students, especially those who are vocal and who have significant contributions. Your job, however, is to teach all the students. To do that, you must be proactive, not reactive, in your interactions.

31. *Not intervening quickly enough during inappropriate student behavior.* When allowed to continue, inappropriate student behavior only gets worse, not better. It will not go away by itself. It's best to nip it in the bud quickly and resolutely. A teacher who ignores inappropriate behavior, even briefly, is, in effect, approving it. In turn, that approval reinforces the continuation and escalation of inappropriate behaviors.

32. *Not learning and using student names.* To expedite your success, you should quickly learn the names and then refer to children by their names (see earlier discussion in this chapter). A teacher who does not know or use names when addressing students is, in effect, viewed by the children as impersonal and uncaring.

33. *Reading student papers only for correct (or incorrect) answers and not for process and student thinking.* Reading student papers only for correct responses reinforces the false notion that the process of arriving at answers or solutions is unimportant and that alternative solutions or answers are impossible or unimportant. In effect, it negates the importance of the individual and the very nature and purpose of learning.

34. *Not putting time plans on the board for students.* Yelling out how much time is left for an activity interrupts student thinking, in effect, saying their thinking is unimportant. Demonstrate respect for their on-task behavior by not interrupting them. In this instance, write on the board before the activity begins how much time is allowed for it. Write the time it is to end. If during the activity a decision is made to change the end time, then write the changed time on the board.

35. *Asking global questions that nobody likely will answer.* Examples are "Does everyone understand?" and "Are there any questions?" and "How do you all feel about . . . ?" It is a brave child who in presence of peers is willing to admit ignorance. It is a waste of precious instructional time to ask such questions. If you truly want to check for student understanding or opinions, then do a spot check by asking specific questions, allow think time, and then call on individuals.

36. *Failing to do frequent comprehension checks (about once a minute during most direct instruction situations) to see if students are understanding.* Too often, teachers simply plow through a big chunk of the lesson, or the entire lesson, only assuming that students are understanding it. Or, in the worst-case scenario, teachers rush through a lesson without even caring if students are getting it. Children quickly recognize teachers who don't care.

37. *Using poorly worded, ambiguous questions.* Key questions you will ask during a lesson should be planned and written into your lesson plan. Refine and make precise the questions by asking them to yourself or a friend, and try to predict how students will respond to a particular question. (For more on questioning, see Chapter 7.)

38. *Trying to talk over student noise.* This simply tells students that their making noise while you are talking is acceptable behavior. When this happens, everyone, teacher included, usually gets increasingly louder during the class period. All that you will accomplish when trying to talk over a high student noise level is a sore throat by the end of the school day and, over a longer period of time, the potential for nodules on your vocal cords.

39. *Wanting to be liked by students.* Forget it. If you are a teacher, then teach. Respect is earned as a result of your effective teaching and role modeling. Liking you may come.

40. *Permitting students to be inattentive to an educationally useful media presentation.* This usually happens because the teacher has failed to give the students adequate instruction about what they should acquire from the program. Sometimes students need an additional focus provided by a written handout of questions or guidelines. Furthermore, a media presentation is usually appealing to the audio and visual modalities. To reinforce student learning, add the kinesthetic such as afforded by the writing aspect when a handout of questions is used. This provides minds-on and hands-on activities that enhance learning.

41. *Starting in stutters.* A stutter start is when the teacher begins an activity, is distracted, begins again, is distracted again, tries again to start, and so on. During stutter starts, children become increasingly restless and inattentive, and sometimes even amused by the teacher's futility, making the final start almost impossible for the teacher to achieve. Avoid stutter starts. Begin an activity clearly and decisively. This is best done by preparing lesson plans thoughtfully and in written detail. (Detailed lesson planning is discussed in Chapter 6.)

42. *Introducing too many topics simultaneously.* It is important to avoid overloading students' capacity to engage mentally by introducing too many topics at a time. If something is important for the children to learn, then give them

ample opportunity to do so before moving on to the next topic.

43. *Failing to give students a pleasant greeting on Monday or following a holiday or to remind them to have a pleasant weekend or holiday.* Children are likely to perceive such a teacher as uncaring or impersonal.

44. *Sounding egocentric.* Whether you are or are not egocentric, you want to avoid appearing so. Sometimes the distinction is subtle, although apparent, such as when a teacher says, "What I am going to do now is . . ." rather than "What we are going to do now is . . ." If you want to strive for group cohesiveness—a sense of "we-ness"—then teach not as if you are the leader and your students are the followers, but rather in a manner that empowers your students in their learning.

45. *Taking too much time to give verbal instructions for an activity.* Students become impatient and restless during long verbal instructions from the teacher. It is better to give brief instructions (a minute or two should do it) and get the students started on the task. For more complicated activities, teach three or four students the instructions and then have those students conduct mini-workshops with five or six students in each workshop group. This frees you to monitor the progress of each group.

46. *Taking too much time for an activity.* No matter what the activity, during your planning think carefully about how much time students can effectively attend to it. A general rule for most elementary school teaching (age level and other factors will dictate variation) is when only one or two learning modalities are involved (e.g., auditory and visual), the activity should not extend beyond about 15 minutes; when more than two modalities are engaged (e.g., add tactile or kinesthetic), then the activity might extend longer, say for 20 or 30 minutes.

47. *Being uptight and anxious.* Consciously or subconsciously, children are quick to detect a teacher who is afraid that events will not go well. And it's like a contagious disease—if you are uptight and anxious, your students will likely become the same. To prevent such emotions, at least to the extent they hinder your teaching effectiveness and your students' learning, you must prepare lessons carefully, thoughtfully, and thoroughly. Unless there is something personal going on in your life that is making you apprehensive, you are more likely to be in control and confident in the classroom when you have lessons that are well prepared. How do you know if your lesson is well prepared? You will know! It's when you develop a written lesson plan that you are truly excited about and looking forward to implementing, and then before doing so, you review it one more time.

If in your life you do have a personal problem that is distracting and making you anxious (and occasionally most of us do), you need to concentrate on ensuring that your anger, hostility, fear, or other negative emotions do not adversely affect your teaching and your interactions with students. Regardless of your personal problems your students will face you each day expecting to be taught by you.

48. *Failing to apply the best of what is known about how children learn.* Too many teachers unrealistically seem to expect success having all students doing the same thing at the same time rather than having several alternative activities simultaneously occurring in the classroom (called multilevel teaching or multitasking). For example, a student who is not responding well (i.e., being inattentive and disruptive) to a class discussion might behave better if given the choice of moving to a quiet reading center in the classroom or to a learning center to work alone. If after trying an alternative activity, the student continues to be disruptive, then you may have to try still another alternative activity. You may have to send the student to another supervised location (out of the classroom, to a place previously arranged by you) until you have time (after class or after school) to talk with the student about the problem.

49. *Overusing punishment for classroom misbehavior—jumping to the final step before trying alternatives.* Teachers sometimes mistakenly either ignore inappropriate student behavior (see number 31) or they skip steps for intervention, resorting too quickly to punishment. They immediately send the misbehaving student outside to stand in the hall (not a wise choice if the student is not supervised) or too quickly assign detention (a usually ineffective form of punishment). Being quick in the use of punishment is not a lesson we should be teaching children. In-between steps to consider include the use of alternative activities in the classroom (as in number 48). It is good to keep in mind that every child is a work in progress. When a child errors it is important that the child has opportunity to recover and to learn from the error.

50. *Being unclear and inconsistent.* Perhaps one of the most frequent causes of problems for teachers in the classroom derives from when they fail to say what they mean or to mean what they say. Teachers who give only vague instructions or who are inconsistent in their own behaviors only confuse students (e.g., do not enforce their own classroom procedural expectations). A teacher's job is to not confuse students.

Now do Exercise 4.5.

EXERCISE 4.5 SELECTING MEASURES OF CONTROL

Instructions: The purpose of this exercise is to help you in determining which measures of control you would apply in some selected situations. For each of the following situations, state the *first* thing you would do. Then share and discuss your responses with your colleagues.

1. A sixth-grade student reveals a knife and seriously threatens to cut you. _____

_____

_____

_____

_____

2. During a test, a student appears to be copying answers from a neighboring student's answer sheet.

_____

_____

_____

_____

3. Although you have asked a sixth-grade student to take his seat, he refuses. _____

_____

_____

_____

_____

4. While talking with a small group of students, you observe two students on the opposite side of

the room tossing paper airplanes. (The lesson has not been about airplanes.) _____

_____

_____

_____

_____

5. During small-group work, one fourth grader is aimlessly wandering around the room. _____

_____

_____

_____

_____

6. Although chewing gum is not permitted at the school, at the start of class you observe a student

chewing what you suspect to be gum. _____

_____

_____

EXERCISE 4.5 *(continued)*

_____

_____

_____

7. During band rehearsal, you (as band director) see a student about to stuff a scarf into another student's saxophone. _____

_____

_____

_____

_____

8. During the viewing of a video, two students on the opposite side of the room from you are quietly whispering. _____

_____

_____

_____

_____

9. At the start of the class period, when a student is about to take her seat, a boy pulls the chair from beneath her. She falls to the floor. _____

_____

_____

_____

_____

10. Suddenly, and for no clear reason, a student in your fourth-grade class gets up and leaves the room.

_____

_____

_____

_____

_____

_____

SUMMARY

In this chapter, you learned ways to cope with the daily challenges of classroom teaching, guidelines for effectively managing children in the classroom. Within that framework, your attention was then focused on specific approaches and additional guidelines for effective classroom management and control of the learning environment. You were offered advice for setting up and maintaining a classroom environment that is favorable to student learning and for establishing procedures for positively influencing student behavior and encouraging student learning. To become an accomplished classroom manager takes thoughtful and thorough planning, consistent and confident application, and reflective experience. Be patient with yourself as you accumulate the prerequisite knowledge and practice and hone the necessary skills.

This is the end of our overview of teaching and learning. You are now ready for Part II, planning for instruction.

EXTENDING MY COMPETENCY: QUESTIONS FOR CLASS DISCUSSION

1. Is it better to be strict with students at first and then relax once your control has been established, or to be relaxed at first and then tighten the reins later if students misbehave, or does it matter? Explain your answer.
2. Some educators argue that good classroom managers are not necessarily good teachers. Do you agree or disagree with that position? Why? Is the reverse true; that is, are good teachers necessarily good classroom managers? Explain why or why not.
3. Explain why it is important to try to prevent behavior problems before they occur. Describe at least five preventive steps you will take to reduce the number of management problems that you will have.
4. Explain the steps of what you would do if two errant behaviors occurred simultaneously in different locations in your classroom.
5. Explain what you would do if a student came to you and reported that fellow students were harassing him by throwing objects at him, slapping him, pulling his chair out from under him, and pretending to rape him.
6. An historical review of disciplinary practices used in the nation's classrooms shows that corporal punishment has been a consistent and conspicuous part of schooling since the beginning. Many educators are concerned about the increased violence in schools, represented by possession of weapons, harassment, bullying, intimidation, gang or cult activity, arson, and the continued use of corporal punishment of students. They argue that schools are responsible for turning a child's behavior into an opportunity to teach character and self-control. When self-disciplined adults create a problem, they apologize, accept the consequences, make restitution, and learn from their mistakes. We have a responsibility for teaching children to do the same. An important characteristic of exemplary schooling is that of maintaining respect for a child's dignity even when responding to the child's inappropriate behavior. What is your opinion about using corporal punishment at any level of schooling? Organize a class discussion or debate on the issue.
7. You have undoubtedly read and heard much about the importance of your being consistent about implementing the expected classroom procedures and the consequences for inappropriate behavior. When it comes to procedures and consequences, is there a danger in a teacher being too rigid or inflexible? Explain your answer. Describe an example of when, if ever, you might be likely to apply a different consequence for the same infraction but by different students.
8. Compare and contrast your own school experiences with what you have recently observed in schools, especially related to the exercises of the four chapters of Part I of this resource guide. Discuss your conclusions in small groups, then share your group's conclusions with those of the entire class.
9. From your current observations and fieldwork as related to this teacher preparation program, clearly identify one specific example of educational practice that seems contradictory to exemplary practice or theory as presented in this chapter. Present your explanation for the discrepancy.
10. Do you have questions generated by the content of this chapter? If you do, list them along with ways answers might be found.

FOR FURTHER READING

Bicard, D. F. (2000). Using Classroom Rules to Construct Behavior. *Middle School Journal, 31*(5), 37–45.

Bodine, R. J., and Crawford, D. K. (1998). *The Handbook of Conflict Resolution Education: A Guide to Building Quality Programs in Schools.* San Francisco: Jossey-Bass.

Brophy, J., and Alleman, J. (1998). Classroom Management in a Social Studies Learning Community. *Social Education, 62*(1), 56–58.

Charles, C. M., Senter, G. W., and Barr, K. B. (1999). *Building Classroom Discipline,* 6th ed. New York: Longman.

Clarke, J. I. (1999). *Time-In: When Time-Out Doesn't Work.* Seattle, WA: Parenting Press.

Cummings, C. (2000). *Winning Strategies for Classroom Management.* Alexandria, VA: Association for Supervision and Curriculum Development.

Curwin, R. L., and Mendler, A. N. (1999). *Discipline With Dignity.* Alexandria, VA: Association for Supervision and Curriculum Development.

DiGiulio, R. (2000). *Positive Classroom Management. A Step-by-Step Guide to Successfully Running the Show Without Destroying Student Dignity,* 2d ed. Thousand Oaks, CA: Corwin Press.

Edwards, C. D. (1999). *How To Handle a Hard-to-Handle Kid: A Parent's Guide to Understanding and Changing Problem Behaviors.* Minneapolis, MN: Free Spirit.

Foster-Harrison, E. S., and Adams-Bullock, A. (1998). *Creating an Inviting Classroom Environment,* Fastback 433. Bloomington, IN: Phi Delta Kappa Educational Foundation.

Freiberg, H. J. (Ed.) (1999). *Beyond Behaviorism: Changing the Classroom Management Paradigm.* Boston: Allyn & Bacon.

Gathercoal, F. (1997). *Judicious Discipline,* 4th ed. San Francisco: Caddo Gap Press.

Gibbs, J. L. (2000). Value-Based Discipline in a Fifth Grade Classroom. *Middle School Journal, 31*(5), 46–50.

Good, T. L., and Brophy, J. E. (2000). *Looking in Classrooms,* 8th ed., Chaps. 4 and 5. New York: Addison Wesley Longman.

Hansen, J. M., and Childs, J. (1998). Creating a School Where People Like to Be. *Educational Leadership, 56*(1), 14–17.

Hardin, C. J., and Harris, E. A. (2000). *Managing Classroom Crises,* Fastback 465. Bloomington, IN: Phi Delta Kappa Educational Foundation.

Jensen, E. (1998). How Threats and Stress Affect Learning. In E. Jensen, *Teaching With the Brain in Mind* (Chap. 6). Alexandria, VA: Association for Supervision and Curriculum Development.

Kelly, K. (1999). Retention vs. Social Promotion: Schools Search for Alternatives. *The Harvard Education Letter, 15*(1), 1–3.

Landau, B. M., and Gathercoal, P. (2000). Creating Peaceful Classrooms: Judicious Discipline and Class Meetings. *Phi Delta Kappan, 81*(6), 450–452, 454.

Marshall, M. (1998). *Fostering Social Responsibility,* Fastback 428. Bloomington, IN: Phi Delta Kappa Educational Foundation.

McEwan, B. (2000). *The Art of Classroom Management: Effective Practices for Building Equitable Learning Communities.* Upper Saddle River, NJ: Merrill/Prentice Hall.

Middlebrooks, S. (1998). *Getting to Know City Kids. Understanding Their Thinking, Imagining, and Socializing.* New York: Teachers College Press.

Morgan, R. R., Ponticell, J. A., and Gordon, E. E. (2000). *Rethinking Creativity,* Fastback 458. Bloomington, IN: Phi Delta Kappa Educational Foundation.

Nissman, B. S. (2000). *Teacher-Tested Classroom Management Strategies.* Upper Saddle River, NJ: Merrill/Prentice Hall.

Petrie, G., et al. (1998). Nonverbal Cues: The Key to Classroom Management. *Principal, 77*(3), 34–36.

Rhode, G., Jensen, W. R., and Reaves, H. K. (1998). *The Tough Kid Book: Practical Classroom Management Strategies.* Longmont, CO: Sopris West.

Sesno, A. H. (1998). *97 Savvy Secrets for Protecting Self and School: A Practical Guide for Today's Teachers and Administrators.* Thousand Oaks, CA: Corwin Press.

Skiba, R., and Peterson, R. (1999). The Dark Side of Zero Tolerance: Can Punishment Lead to Safe Schools? *Phi Delta Kappan, 80*(5), 372–376, 381–382.

Wachter, J. C. (1999). *Sweating the Small Stuff: Answers to Teachers' Big Problems.* Thousand Oaks, CA: Corwin.

Walters, L. S. (1999). What Makes a Good School Violence Prevention Program? *The Harvard Education Letter, 15*(1), 4–5.

NOTES

1. I. A. Hyman and J. D'Allessandro, Oversimplifying the Discipline Problem, *Education Week, 3*(29), 24 (April 11, 1984).

2. See, for example, B. F. Skinner, *Beyond Freedom and Dignity* (New York: Knopf, 1971).

3. See L. Canter and M. Canter, *Assertive Discipline: Positive Behavior Management for Today's Schools,* rev. ed. (Santa Monica, CA: Lee Canter & Associates, 1992).

4. T. L. Good and J. E. Brophy, *Looking in Classrooms,* 8th ed. (New York: Addison Wesley Longman, 2000), p. 201.

5. See, for example, R. Dreikurs, B. B. Grunwald, and F. C. Pepper, *Maintaining Sanity in the Classroom: Classroom Management Techniques,* 2nd ed. (New York: Harper & Row, 1982).

6. L. Albert, *A Teacher's Guide to Cooperative Discipline: How to Manage Your Classroom and Promote Self-Esteem* (Circle Pines, MN: American Guidance Service, 1989, revised 1996).

7. J. Nelsen, *Positive Discipline,* 2nd ed. (New York: Ballantine Books, 1987), and J. Nelsen, L. Lott, and H. S. Glenn, *Positive Discipline in the Classroom: How to Effectively Use Class Meetings and Other Positive Discipline Strategies* (Rocklin, CA: Prima Publishing, 1993). About class meetings, see also P. M. Landau and P. Gathercoal, Creating Peaceful Classrooms: Judicious Discipline and Class Meetings, *Phi Delta Kappan, 81*(6), 450–452, 454 (February 2000).

8. See, for example, W. Glasser, A New Look at School Failure and School Success, *Phi Delta Kappan, 78*(8), 597–602 (April 1997).

9. See W. Glasser, *Schools Without Failure* (New York: Harper & Row, 1969), *Control Theory in the Classroom* (New York: Harper & Row, 1986), *The Quality School* (New York: Harper & Row, 1990), and *The Quality School Teacher* (New York: HarperPerennial, 1993).

10. See H. J. Freiberg (Ed.), *Beyond Behaviorism: Changing the Classroom Management Paradigm* (Boston: Allyn & Bacon, 1997). See also H. J. Freiberg (Ed.), *Perceiving, Behaving, Becoming: Lessons Learned* (Alexandria, VA: Association for Supervision and Curriculum Development, 1999).

11. See H. G. Ginott, *Teacher and Child* (New York: Macmillan, 1971).

12. See, for example, F. Jones, *Positive Classroom Discipline* (New York: McGraw-Hill, 1987).

13. J. S. Kounin, *Discipline and Group Management in Classrooms* (New York: Holt, Rinehart and Winston, 1977).

14. Adapted from Barbara McEwan, *The Art of Classroom Management: Effective Practices for Building Equitable Learning Communities* (Upper Saddle River, NJ: Merrill/Prentice Hall, 2000), p. 39. By permission of Prentice Hall.

15. See, for example, R. R. Morgan, J. A. Ponticell, and E. E. Gordon, *Rethinking Creativity,* Fastback 458, (Bloomington, IN: Phi Delta Kappa Educational Foundation, 2000).

16. At the beginning of student teaching, you may need to follow the opening procedures already established by your cooperating teacher. If those procedures are largely ineffective, then without hesitation you should talk with your university supervisor about being reassigned to a different placement.

17. D. W. Johnson and R. T. Johnson, *Reducing School Violence Through Conflict Resolution* (Alexandria, VA: Association for Supervision and Curriculum Development, 1995), p. 1.

18. Landau and Gathercoal, Creating Peaceful Classrooms, 450–452, 454. See also B. McEwan, P. Gathercoal, V. Nimmo, Applications of Judicious Discipline: A Common Language for Classroom Management, in H. J. Freiberg, (Ed.), *Beyond Behaviorism: Changing the Classroom Management Paradigm* (Boston: Allyn & Bacon, 1999).

19. See the Internet, <http://www.air-dc.org/cecp/resources/success/second_step.htm>.

20. See, for example, G. Petrie, et al., Nonverbal Cues: The Key to Classroom Management, *Principal,* 77(3), 34–36 (January 1998).

21. For further reading about the relation between impulse control and intelligence, see D. Goleman, *Emotional Intelligence: Why It Can Matter More Than IQ* (New York: Bantam Books, 1995), and D. Harrington-Lueker, Emotional Intelligence, *High Strides,* 9(4), 1, 4–5 (March/April 1997).

II

Planning for Instruction

Part II responds to your needs concerning:

- Collaborative planning
- Curriculum alignment
- Curriculum integration
- Dealing with content and issues that may be controversial
- Direct and indirect instruction
- Documents that provide guidance for curriculum planning
- Domains of learning
- Empowering students with decision-making responsibility
- Goals, objectives, and learning outcomes
- Interweaving multimedia, including Internet resources, into instruction
- Levels of curriculum planning
- National goals and curriculum standards
- Relationships among the processes of planning, instruction, and assessment
- Selecting and developing appropriate learning activities
- Selecting and sequencing content for instruction
- Student textbooks and other reading materials
- Unit and lesson planning
- Using an externally developed curriculum program that is highly scripted

REFLECTIVE THOUGHTS

A classroom teacher is responsible for planning at three levels—the year, the units, and the lessons—with critical decisions to be made at each level.

Your challenge is to use performance-based criteria with a teaching style that encourages the development of intrinsic sources of student motivation, and that provides for coincidental learning, which goes beyond what might be considered predictable, immediately measurable, and having minimal expectations.

Teachers must be clear about what it is they want their students to learn, about the kind of evidence needed to verify their learning, and about communicating those things to the students so they are clearly understood.

Goals and objectives represent the targets, from general to specific statements of learning expectations, to which curriculum and instruction are designed and aimed. Goals guide the instructional methods; objectives drive student performance. Assessment of student achievement in learning should be an assessment of that performance.

Curriculum integration refers to a way of thinking, a way of teaching, and a way of planning and organizing the instructional program so the discrete disciplines of subject matter are related to one another in a design that (a) matches the developmental needs of the learners and (b) helps to connect their learning in ways that are meaningful to their current and past experiences.

An old-fashioned mental model of learning that assumes that a human brain is capable of doing only one thing at a time is invidiously erroneous.

Instruction should begin with an assessment of what the children already know, or think they know, about the topic of the ensuing study.

For all lessons, you want to strive for planning a clear and mesmerizing beginning, an involving lesson body, and a firm and meaningful closure.

5

Why Should I Plan and How Is Curriculum Content Selected?

Effective teaching does not just happen; it is produced through the thoughtful planning of each phase of the learning process. Most effective teachers begin their planning months before meeting students for the first time. Daily lessons form parts of a larger scheme, which is designed to accomplish the teacher's long-range goals for the semester or year and to mesh with the school's mission (discussed in Chapter 1) and expectation standards.

If learning is defined only as the accumulation of bits and pieces of information, then we already know everything about how to teach and how children learn. But the accumulation of pieces of information is at the lowest end of a spectrum of types of learning. Discoveries are still being made about the processes involved in higher forms of learning—that is, for meaningful understanding and the reflective application of that understanding. The results of recent research support the use of instructional strategies that help children make connections as they learn. These strategies include the literature-based approach to reading, discovery learning, inquiry, cooperative learning, and interdisciplinary thematic instruction, with a total curriculum that is integrated and connected to students' life experiences.

Like the construction of a bridge, learning that is the most meaningful is a gradual and sometimes painstakingly slow process. When compared with traditional instruction, teaching in a constructivist mode is slower, involving more discussion, debate, and the re-creation of ideas. Rather than following clearly defined and previously established steps, the curriculum evolves. Such a curriculum depends heavily on materials, and to a great extent it is the students' interests and questions that determine it. Less content is covered, fewer facts are memorized and tested for, and progress is sometimes tediously slow.[1]

The methodology uses what is referred to as *hands-on* and *minds-on* learning: The learner is learning by doing and is thinking about what she or he is learning and doing. When thoughtfully coupled, these approaches help construct, and often reconstruct, the learner's perceptions. Hands-on learning engages the learner's mind, causing questioning. Then, with the teacher's competent guidance, the children devise ways of investigating satisfactory, though sometimes only tentative, answers to their questions.

As a classroom teacher, your instructional task then is twofold: (a) to plan hands-on experiences, providing the materials and the supportive environment necessary for student's meaningful exploration and discovery, and (b) to know how to facilitate the most meaningful and longest-lasting learning possible once the learner's mind has been engaged by the hands-on learning. To accomplish this requires your knowledge about, and competence in the use of, varied and developmentally appropriate methods of instruction. Assisting you in the acquisition of that knowledge and competence is the primary purpose of this resource guide. The two chapters of this part of the resource guide address the planning aspect. As you proceed through these chapters and begin the development of your instructional plans, from time to time you will want to refer to particular topics in the chapters of Part III and also to the topic of assessment of student learning, Chapter 11. Instruction and assessment go hand in hand and

can not be as easily separated as might be implied from their placement in the organization of this resource guide. Their separation here is done not for your implementation of them, but, as explained in the Preface of the resource guide, for your understanding of them. The rationale for careful planning for instruction, the components of that planning, and the selection of content are the topics of this chapter.

CHAPTER OBJECTIVES

Specifically, upon completion of this chapter you should be able to

1. Compare and contrast the terms *curriculum* and *instruction*.
2. Compare and contrast *diagnostic assessment, formative assessment,* and *summative assessment* as related to curriculum and instruction.
3. Demonstrate ability to plan the sequence of content for instruction at a specific grade level.
4. Demonstrate an understanding of the rationale for planning for instruction, the levels of planning, and the components of a total instructional plan.
5. Demonstrate knowledge of the value of various types of documents that can be resources for instructional planning.
6. Demonstrate understanding of controversial topics and issues that may arise while teaching and what you might you do if and when they do arise.
7. Demonstrate understanding of how to help students develop depth of understanding while still scoring well on mandated, externally developed standardized tests.
8. Demonstrate understanding of the concept of integrated curriculum.
9. Demonstrate understanding of the value of and tools used for the diagnostic and formative assessment of student learning as related to planning for curriculum and instruction.
10. Describe the relationship of instructional planning to the preactive and reflective thought-processing phases of instruction.
11. Explain both the value and the limitations afforded by using instructional objectives.
12. Explain the difference and the relationship between *hands-on* and *minds-on* learning.
13. Explain the relationship between instructional objectives and the assessment of student learning.
14. Explain the teacher's role in instructional planning when using highly scripted and externally developed instructional plans.

15. Explain the value and limitations of textbooks for student learning.
16. Prepare instructional objectives for each of the three domains of learning and at various of levels within each domain.

PROVIDING SUCCESSFUL TRANSITIONS

Within the framework of exemplary school organization lie several components that form a comprehensive albeit ever-changing program. Central to the school's purpose and its organizational structure is the concerted effort to see that all children make successful *transitions* from one level to the next, from home to school, from one grade to the next, from elementary to middle school, from middle school to high school, and from high school to postsecondary education or work. Every aspect of the elementary school program is, in some way, designed to help children to make those transitions. Combining to form the program that students experience are two terms you will frequently encounter, *curriculum* and *instruction*.

Curriculum and Instruction: Clarification of Terms

Among educators the term *curriculum* has no singularly accepted definition. Some define it as the planned subject-matter content and skills to be presented to students. Others say *curriculum* is only that which students actually learn. Others hold the broad definition that the curriculum is all experiences students encounter, whether planned or unplanned, learned or unlearned.

Four programs are identified that contribute in different ways to student learning and that do, in fact, comprise the broadest definition of *curriculum:* (a) the program of studies (the subject content studied, sometimes referred to as the overt or formal curriculum), (b) the program of student activities (sports, clubs, and organizations, sometimes referred to as cocurricular activities), (c) the program of supporting services (transportation, meals, nurse station, etc.), and (d) the *hidden (or covert or informal) curriculum* (i.e., the unplanned and subtle message systems within schools, which are the school climate, the feelings and biases projected from the teacher and other adults to students and from the students to one another, not only in classrooms but before and after school, at social events, and in the halls, restrooms, playground, and other areas of the school that are not monitored quite as closely as are the individual classrooms). This working definition considers curriculum as the *entire school program*. Accepting this broad definition of curriculum, the curriculum embraces every planned aspect of a school's educational program, including the efforts that are planned specifically to advance conceptual and procedural knowledge as well as schoolwide services such as clubs and interest groups, visual and performing arts productions, student government, and athletic events and programs.

Instruction, too, has several definitions, some of which are not clearly distinguishable from *curriculum.* Whereas curriculum is usually associated with the content of the learning, instruction is associated with *methods*—that is, with ways of presenting content, conveying information, and facilitating student learning. Obviously, to have the most effective and positive effect on student learning, curriculum and instruction must be in tandem.

PLANNING FOR INSTRUCTION

As a classroom teacher, planning for instruction is a major part of your job, even if you are using a externally developed and highly scripted program. At some level of complexity you will be responsible for planning at three levels—the school year, the units, and the lessons—with critical decisions to be made at each level.

You need not do all your instructional planning from scratch, and you need not do all your planning alone. As a matter of fact, in many elementary schools today, especially for mathematics and reading, the curricula are purchased by the district and handed to the teachers. The program may be highly scripted and the teacher may be expected to follow the script closely or even exactly. However, it is our opinion that because writers of these programs do not know your students as well as you, to be most effective with a particular group of children, any scripted program will need tweaking by the teacher who is using it.

In many schools, curricula are developed or, in the case of scripted programs, are enhanced by a team of teachers. Teams of teachers collectively plan the curricula for their specific cohorts of students. Team members either plan together or split the responsibilities and then share their individual plans. A final plan is then developed collaboratively.

The heart of good planning is good decision making, and at the heart of good decision making is, as said in Chapter 4, knowledge of the children for whom the instruction is being planned. For every plan and at each of the three levels, you and your team of colleagues must make decisions about the goals and objectives to be set, the subject to be introduced, the materials and equipment to be used, the methods to be adopted, and the assessments to be made. This decision-making process is complicated because so many options are available at each level. Decisions made at all three levels result in a total plan.

Although the planning process continues year after year, the task becomes somewhat easier after the first year as you learn to recycle plans. The process is also made easier via research and communication by reviewing documents and sharing ideas and plans with other teachers.

Teacher-Student Collaborative Team Planning

Many teachers and teaching teams encourage their students to participate in the planning of some phase of their learning, anywhere from planning complete interdisciplinary thematic units to specific activities within a unit. Such collaborative planning tends to give students a proprietary interest in the activities, thereby increasing their motivation for learning. What students have contributed to the plan often seems more meaningful to them than what others have planned for them. Children like to see their own plans succeed. Thus, teacher-student collaboration in planning is usually an effective motivational tool.

Classrooms today tend to be more project-oriented and student- and group-centered than the traditional teacher-centered classroom of the past, in which the teacher served as the primary provider of information. Today's students more actively participate in their learning, in collaboration with the teacher. The teacher provides some structure and assistance, but the collaborative approach requires that students inquire and interact, generate ideas, seriously listen and talk with one another, and recognize that their thoughts and experiences are valuable and essential to meaningful learning. In such a collaborative atmosphere, children learn not only the subject matter content of the curriculum but develop important and valuable social skills.

Reasons for Planning

Planning is done for a number of reasons, perhaps foremost of which is to ensure curriculum coherence. Periodic lesson plans are an integral part of a larger plan, represented by grade-level goals and objectives and by the school- and district-wide mission and outcome standards. Students' learning experiences are thoughtfully planned in sequence and then orchestrated by teachers who understand the rationale for their respective positions in the curriculum. Of course, such plans do not preclude an occasional diversion from predetermined activities.

Another reason for planning is, as discussed in Chapter 2, to give considerations to students' experiential backgrounds, learning capacities and styles, reading levels, and special needs.

Planning is necessary to ensure efficient and effective teaching with a minimum of classroom control problems. After deciding *what* to teach, you face the important task of deciding *how* to teach it. To use precious instructional time efficiently, planning should be accomplished with two goals in mind: (a) to not waste anyone's time during the time allotted for instruction and (b) to select strategies that most effectively promote the anticipated student learning, that is, the target learning outcomes.

Planning helps ensure program continuation. The program must continue even if you are absent and a substitute teacher is needed. Planning provides a criterion for reflective practice and self-assessment. After a learning activity and at the end of a school term, you can reflect on and assess what was done and how it affected student learning. Planning provides a means to evaluate your teaching. Your plans represent a criterion recognized and evaluated by administrators. With those experienced in such matters, it is clear that inadequate planning is usually a precursor to incompetent teaching. Put simply, failing to plan is planning to fail.

Components of an Instructional Plan

A total instructional plan has six major components, described as follows.

Rationale component. This is a statement about why the content of the plan is important and about how students will learn it. The statement should be consistent with the school and district mission statements.

Goals and objectives component. The goals and objectives represent the learning targets, the knowledge, appreciations, and skills to be gained from studying the plan. The plan's stated goals and objectives should be consistent with the rationale statement.

Articulation component. The articulation component shows the plan's relationship to the learning that came before and the learning that will follow, such as from kindergarten through sixth grade and beyond. This is referred to as *vertical articulation*. The plan should also indicate its horizontal articulation, which is its connectedness with subjects and activities across grade level. "Writing across the curriculum" and "integrated curriculum" are examples of *horizontal articulation*. Vertical and horizontal articulations are usually represented in curriculum documents and textbook programs by scope and sequence charting.

Learning activities component. This is the presentation of organized and sequential units and lessons appropriate for the subject and the age and diversity of the learners.

Resources component. This is a listing of anticipated resources needed, such as books and other printed material, guest speakers, field trips, software, and media.

Assessment component. This is the appraisal of student learning and occurs (a) at the start of the instruction (a *preassessment* of what students already know or think they know about the topic), (b) during the instruction to make sure students are learning that which is intended (*formative assessment*), and (c) at the end of the instruction to determine whether and how well students did learn (*summative assessment*).

Planning the Scope of the Curriculum

When planning the scope of a curriculum, you must decide what is to be accomplished in that period of time, such as for a semester or for a school year. To help in setting your goals, you should (a) examine school and other resource documents for mandates and guidelines, (b) communicate with colleagues to learn of common expectations, and (c) probe, analyze, and translate your own convictions, knowledge, and skills into behaviors that foster the intellectual and psychological development of your students.

Documents That Provide Guidance for Content Selection

With the guidance of Exercises 5.1 through 5.3, you will now examine major types of documents that help guide you in selecting the content of your curriculum. These are: national curriculum standards, state department of education stan-

Figure 5.1
Internet resources on national and state curriculum standards and frameworks

General and multiple disciplines
- http://www.mcrel.org
- http://www.enc.org/reform/fworks/index.htm
- http://putwest.boces.org/Standards.html

State Standards
- http://www.statestandards.com

Discipline specific national standards
- Economics, http://www.ncee.org
- English/reading, http://www.ncte.org
- Mathematics, http://www.nctm.org
- Physical education, http://www.naspe.org
- Science, http://www.nsta.org
- Social studies, http://www.ari.net/online/standards/2.0.html
- Technology, http://www.iteawww.org
- Visual and performing arts, http://www.amc'music.com

dards and curriculum documents, school or district curriculum frameworks and courses of study, and school-adopted printed or nonprinted materials. Sources for your examination of these documents include sites on the Internet (see Figure 5.1), your college or university library, and cooperating teachers or administrative personnel at local schools.

Curriculum Standards

Curriculum standards are defined as what students should know (content) and be able to do (process and performance). At the national level, curriculum standards did not exist in the United States until those developed and released for mathematics education in 1989. Shortly after the release of the mathematics standards, support for national goals in education was endorsed by the National Governors Association, and the National Council on Education Standards and Testing recommended that in addition to those for mathematics, national standards for subject matter content in K–12 education be developed for the arts, civics/social studies, English/language-arts/reading, geography, history, and science. The U.S. Department of Education provided initial funding for the development of national standards. In 1994 the United States Congress passed the *Goals 2000: Educate America Act,* amended in 1996 with an Appropriations Act, encouraging states to set standards. Long before, however, as was done for mathematics by the National Council for Teachers of Mathematics, national organizations devoted to various disciplines were already defining standards.

What the National Standards Are

The national standards represent the best thinking by expert panels about what are the essential elements of a basic core of subject knowledge that all students should acquire. They serve not as national mandates but rather as voluntary guidelines to encourage curriculum development to promote higher student achievement. It is the discretion of state and local curriculum developers in deciding the extent to which the standards are used. Strongly influenced by the national standards, nearly all 50 states have completed or are presently developing state standards for the various disciplines.

National Standards by Content Area

The following paragraphs describe national standards development for content areas of the K–12 curriculum. The standards are available on the Internet (see Figure 5.1).

Arts (visual and performing). Developed jointly by the American Alliance for Theater and Education, the National Art Education Association, the National Dance Association, and the Music Educators National Conference, the National Standards for Arts Education were completed and released in 1994.

Economics. Developed by the National Council on Economic Education, standards for the study of economics were published in 1997.

English/language arts/reading. Developed jointly by the International Reading Association, the National Council of Teachers of English, and the University of Illinois Center for the Study of Reading, standards for English education were completed and released in 1996.

Foreign languages. Standards for Foreign Language Learning: Preparing for the 21st Century was completed and released by the American Council on the Teaching of Foreign Languages (ACTFL) in 1996.[2]

Geography. Developed jointly by the Association of American Geographers, the National Council for Geographic Education, and the National Geographic Society, standards for geography education were completed and released in 1994.[3]

History/civics/social studies. The Center for Civic Education and the National Center for Social Studies developed standards for civics and government, and the National Center for History in the Schools developed the standards for history, all of which were completed and released in 1994.

Health. Developed by the Joint Committee for National School Health Education Standards, *National Health Education Standards: Achieving Health Literacy* was published in 1995.[4]

Mathematics. In 1989, the National Council of Teachers of Mathematics (NCTM) published *Curriculum and Evaluation Standards for School Mathematics.* A revised edition was released in 2000.

Physical education. In 1995, the National Association of Sport and Physical Education (NASPE) published *Moving Into the Future: National Standards for Physical Education.*

Science. With input from the American Association for the Advancement of Science and the National Science Teachers Association, the National Research Council's National Committee on Science Education Standards and Assessment developed standards for science education, which were published in 1995.

Technology. Prepared by the International Technology Education Association, technology literacy standards were released in 2000.

American Indian Supplements to the national standards are available from the Bureau of Indian Affairs for civics and government, geography, health, language arts, mathematics, science, social studies, and the visual and performing arts.[5] The supplements are useful to school districts serving American Indian children in adapting state standards to be more culturally relevant to their communities. They may also be used by Indian nations as guides in their preparation of tribally specific local standards.

Now do Exercises 5.1 through 5.3.

EXERCISE 5.1 EXAMINING NATIONAL CURRICULUM STANDARDS

Instructions: The purpose of this exercise is to become familiar with the national curriculum standards for various subjects of the K–6 curriculum. Using the addresses of sources provided in the preceding section, "National Curriculum Standards," and other sources, such as professional journals, review the standards for your subject or subjects. Use the following questions as a guideline for small- or large-group class discussions. Following small subject-area group discussion, share the developments in each field with the rest of the class.

Subject area _____

1. Name of the standards document reviewed

2. Year of document publication

3. Developed by

4. Specific K–6 goals specified by the new standards

5. Are the standards specific as to subject-matter content for each grade level? Explain.

6. Do the standards offer specific strategies for instruction? Describe.

EXERCISE 5.1 *(continued)*

7. Do the standards offer suggestions for teaching children who are different and for children with special needs? Describe.

8. Do the standards offer suggestions or guidelines for dealing with controversial topics?

9. Do the standards offer suggestions for specific resources? Describe.

10. Do the standards refer to assessment? Describe.

11. In summary, compared with what has been taught and how it has been taught in this field, what is new with the standards?

12. Is there anything else about the standards you would like to discuss in your group?

EXERCISE 5.2 EXAMINING STATE CURRICULUM DOCUMENTS

Instructions: The purpose of this exercise is to become familiar with curriculum documents published by your state department of education. You must determine if that department publishes a curriculum framework for various subjects taught in elementary schools. State frameworks provide valuable information about both content and process, and teachers need to be aware of these documents. You may want to duplicate this form so you can use it to evaluate several documents. After examining documents that interest you, use the following questions as a guideline for small- or large-group class discussions.

1. Are there state curriculum documents available to elementary school teachers for your state? If so, describe them and explain how they can be obtained.

    Title of document:

    Source:

    Most recent year of publication:

    Other pertinent information:

2. Examine how closely the document follows the eight components presented in this chapter. Are any components omitted? Are there additional components? Specifically, check for these components:

	Yes	*No*
2.1 Statement of philosophy?	_____	_____
2.2 Evidence of a needs assessment?	_____	_____
2.3 Aims, goals, and objectives?	_____	_____
2.4 Schemes for vertical articulation?	_____	_____
2.5 Schemes for horizontal articulation	_____	_____
2.6 Recommended instructional procedures?	_____	_____
2.7 Recommended resources?	_____	_____
2.8 Assessment strategies?	_____	_____

    Other:

3. Are the documents specific as to subject-matter content for each grade level? Describe evidence of both vertical and horizontal articulation schemes.

4. Do the documents offer specific strategies for instruction? If yes, describe.

EXERCISE 5.2 *(continued)*

5. Do the documents offer suggestions and resources for working with students who are culturally different, for students with special needs, and for students who are intellectually gifted and talented? Describe.

6. Do the documents offer suggestions or guidelines for dealing with controversial topics? If so, describe.

7. Do the documents distinguish between what shall be taught (mandated) and what can be taught (permissible)?

8. Do the documents offer suggestions for specific resources?

9. Do the documents refer to assessment strategies? Describe.

10. Is there anything else about the documents you would like to discuss in your group?

EXERCISE 5.3 EXAMINING LOCAL CURRICULUM DOCUMENTS

Instructions: The purpose of this exercise is to become familiar with curriculum documents prepared by local school districts. A primary resource for what to teach is referred to as a *curriculum guide,* or *course of study,* which normally is developed by teachers of a school or district. Samples may be available in your university library or in a local school district resource center. Or perhaps you could borrow them from teachers you visit. Obtain samples from a variety of sources and then examine them using the format of this exercise. (You may duplicate this form for each document examined.) An analysis of several documents will give you a good picture of expectations. If possible, compare documents from several school districts and states.

Title of document:

District or school:

Date of document:

1. Examine how closely the documents follow the eight components. Does the document contain the following components?

	Yes	No
1.1 Statement of philosophy?	_____	_____
1.2 Evidence of needs assessment?	_____	_____
1.3 Aims, goals, and objectives?	_____	_____
1.4 Schemes for vertical articulation?	_____	_____
1.5 Schemes for horizontal articulation?	_____	_____
1.6 Recommended instructional procedures?	_____	_____
1.7 Recommended resources?	_____	_____
1.8 Assessment strategies?	_____	_____

2. Does the document list expected learning outcomes? If so, describe what they are.

3. Does the document contain detailed unit plans? If so, describe them by answering the following questions:

    3.1. Do they contain initiating activities (how to begin a unit)?

    3.2. Do they contain specific learning activities?

    3.3. Do they contain suggested enrichment activities (as for gifted and talented students)?

    3.4. Do they contain culminating activities (activities that bring a unit to a climax)?

    3.5. Do they contain assessment procedures (for determining student achievement)?

    3.6. Do they contain activities for learners with special needs? or for learners who are different in other respects?

EXERCISE 5.3 *(continued)*

4. Does it provide bibliographic entries for

   • The teacher?

   • The students?

5. Does it list audiovisual and other materials needed?

6. Does the document clearly help you understand what the teacher is expected to teach?

7. Are there questions not answered by your examination of this document? If so, list them for class discussion.

Student Textbooks

For several reasons—the recognition of the diversity of learning styles, learning capacities, and learning modalities of students, the cost of textbooks, and the availability of nonprinted materials—textbook appearance, content, and use has changed considerably in recent years and with advancing computer technology is likely to continue changing.

School districts periodically adopt new textbooks (usually every five to eight years). If you are a student teacher or a first-year teacher, this will most likely mean that someone will tell you, "Here are the student books you will be using."

Benefit of Student Textbooks to Student Learning

It is unlikely that anyone could rationally argue that textbooks are of no benefit to student learning. Textbooks can provide (a) an organization of basic or important content for the students, (b) a basis for deciding content emphasis, (c) previously tested activities and suggestions for learning, (d) information about other readings and resources to enhance student learning, and (e) a foundation for building higher-order thinking activities (e.g., inquiry discussions and student research) that help develop critical thinking skills. The textbook, however, should not be the "be all and end all" of the instructional experiences.

Problems with Reliance on a Single Textbook

The student textbook is only one of many teaching tools and not the ultimate word. Of the many ways in which you may use textbooks for student learning, the *least* acceptable is to show a complete dependence on a single book and require students simply to memorize material from it. This is the lowest level of learning; furthermore, it implies that you are unaware of other significant printed and nonprinted resources and have nothing more to contribute to student learning.

Another potential problem brought about by reliance upon a single textbook is that because textbook publishers prepare books for use in a larger market—that is, for national, regional, or statewide use—a state- and district-adopted book may not adequately address issues of special interest and importance to the community in which you teach.[6] That is one reason some teachers and schools provide supplementary printed and nonprinted resources.

Still another problem brought about by reliance upon a single source is that the adopted textbook may not be at the appropriate reading level for many children. In today's heterogeneous classrooms, the level of student reading can vary by as much as two-thirds of the chronological age of the children. This means that if the chronological age is 9 (typical for fourth-graders), the reading-level range would be 6 years; thus the class may have some students reading at only the first-grade level while others can read at the seventh-grade level.

Students and Textbook Reading Level

A frequent concern of teachers is that textbooks should be neither too easy nor too difficult for the students to read. To determine a textbook's reading level, you can use any of several techniques, such as the Fry[7] or Forecast[8] readability formulas. Since such formulas give only the technical reading level of a book, you have to interpret the results by subjectively estimating its conceptual reading level. To do so, you must consider your students' experience in light of the content, the number of new ideas introduced, and the level of abstraction of the ideas.

To determine how well students can read a text, many teachers use the Cloze technique, which was first described by J. Bormuth in 1968 and has since appeared in a number of versions.[9] The technique is as follows. Select from the book several typical passages of 400 to 415 words. Delete every eighth word except for those in the first and last sentences, proper names, numbers, and initial words in sentences. You will probably have deleted about 50 words. Replace the deleted words with blanks, duplicate the passages, and distribute them to the students. Ask them to fill in the blanks with the most appropriate words they can supply. Collect the papers. Score them by counting all the student-supplied words that are the same as those in the original text and dividing this number by the total number of blanks: Some educators recommend that you count only words that are exactly the same; others would allow synonyms. Perhaps you should not count synonyms or verbs of a different tense.[10]

$$\text{Score} = \frac{\text{number of same words supplied}}{\text{number of blanks}}$$

You can assume that students who score better than 50 percent can read the book quite well, that students who score between 40 and 50 percent can read the book at the level of instruction, and that students who score below 40 percent will probably find the reading difficult and frustrating.

To conduct a silent and informal reading inventory of a book, you can have students read four or five pages of the text and then give them a 10-item quiz on the content. Consider the text as too

Figure 5.2
Methods for helping
students develop their
higher-level thinking skills
and their comprehension
of expository material[12]

- **KWL:** Students recall what they already know (**K**) about a topic, determine what they want to learn (**W**), and later assess what they have learned (**L**).
- **KWLQ:** Students record what they already know about a topic (**K**), formulate questions about what they want to learn about the topic (**W**), search for answers to their questions (**L**), and ask questions for further study (**Q**).
- **PQRST: preview, question, read, state** the main idea, and **test** yourself by answering the questions you posed earlier.
- **Reciprocal reading:** students take turns asking questions, summarizing, making predictions about, and clarifying a story.
- **SQ3R: survey** the chapter, ask **questions** about what was read, **read, recite,** and **review.**
- **SQ4R: survey** the chapter, ask **questions** about what was read, **read** to answer the questions, **recite** the answers, **record** important items from the chapter into their notebooks, then **review** it all.
- **SRQ2R: survey, read, question, recite,** and **review.**

---

difficult for a student who scores less than 70 percent on the quiz. Or you can conduct an oral and informal reading inventory by having students read a 100-word passage. The text may be too difficult if the students stumble over or miss more than 5 percent of the words.[11]

Guidelines for Textbook Use

Generally speaking, students benefit by having their own copies of a textbook in the current edition. However, because of budget constraints, this may not always be possible. The book may be outdated; quantities may be limited. When the latter is the case, students may not be allowed to take the books home or perhaps may only occasionally do so. In other classrooms, there may be no textbook at all.

Progressing through a textbook from the front cover to the back in one school term is not necessarily an indicator of good teaching. The textbook is one resource; to enhance their learning, students should be encouraged to use a variety of resources. Encourage students to search additional sources to update the content of the textbook. This is especially important in certain disciplines such as science and social sciences, where the amount of new information is growing rapidly and students may have textbooks that are several years old. For both the latest and historical information on certain topics students should research the library and reliable sources on the Internet. Obtain and maintain supplementary reading materials for student use in the classroom. School and community librarians and resource specialists usually are delighted to cooperate with teachers in the selection and provision of such resources.

Personalize the learning for students of various reading abilities. Consider differentiated reading and workbook assignments in the textbook and several supplementary sources (see multireading approach, a topic that follows). Except to make life simpler for the teacher, there is no advantage in all students working out of the same book and doing the same exercises. Some students benefit from the drill, practice, and reinforcement afforded by workbooks and computer programs that accompany textbooks, but this is not true for all students, nor do all benefit from the same activity.

In fact, the traditional workbook may eventually become extinct, as it is replaced by the computer technology. Computers and other interactive media provide students with a psychologically safer learning environment in which they have greater control over the pace of the instruction, can repeat instruction if necessary, and can ask for clarification without the fear of having to do so publicly.

Several methods have been invented by teachers to help students develop their higher-level thinking skills and their comprehension of expository material. Some of these methods are shown in Figure 5.2.

Just because something is in print or on the Internet does not mean it is necessarily accurate or even true. However much time we spend teaching students how to find things on the Internet, we need to expend even more effort teaching them how to interpret what they have found.[13] Whether printed text or text on the Internet, encourage students to be alert for errors in the text, both in content and printing. You might even give them some sort of credit reward, such as points, when they bring an error to your attention. This helps students develop the skills of critical reading, critical thinking, and healthy skepticism. For example, a history book is reported to have stated that the first person to lead a group through the length of the Grand Canyon was John Wesley Powell. Critically thinking students quickly made the point that perhaps Powell was only the first white person to do this, that Native Americans had traveled the length of the Grand Canyon for centuries.[14]

Multireading Approach

Rather than a single textbook approach, some teachers use a strategy that incorporates multiple readings that vary in detail and vocabulary but that have a common focus.[15] This strategy gives children a choice in what they read. The multiple readings allow for differences in reading ability and interest level, and stimulate a sharing of what is read and being learned. The use of multiple sources can be helpful in encouraging children to evaluate written communications and to think critically. By using a teacher's guide such as the sample in Figure 5.3, all the children can be directed toward specific information and concepts, but they do not have to all read the same selections.

Now, uses Exercise 5.4 to examine student textbooks and accompanying teachers' editions.

Figure 5.3
Sample multiple readings guide and children's bibliography to assist students in multiple readings about America's revolutionary times

---

Multitext Guide: America's Revolutionary Times in 1776

- <u>Purpose:</u> To engage children in multiple readings, critical thinking, and problem solving related to America's revolutionary times in 1776.

- <u>Activities:</u>
  1. The bibliography that follows includes books suitable for a wide range of reading levels. Teachers and students can add titles to the list. The students can respond to the following questions (and to their own questions) after multitext reading:
     a. What features of the family (government, recreation, school, society, etc.) seem to have been important to the people in 1776?
     b. What occupations seemed to have been most important? What inventions (tools, machines) appear to have been most useful?
     c. What do the answers to these questions tell us about the way of life of the people who lived at this time?
  2. Have the students from each group report to the whole group on the responses to the questions. Ask the students to then dictate or write a paragraph summarizing the responses. Consider these questions during the summarizing:
     a. What is the main idea of the paragraph (page, chapter, story)? What details support the main idea? What sequence of points can be remembered?
     b. In what way can you organize what you read, and tell or write a summary to make the story about the revolution clear to others? Did you arrive at any generalizations? Did you predict any outcomes?
     c. In what way is the information you read relevant (verifiable, backed up by a qualified author, valid with supported/unsupported assumptions, opinionated or factual).
  3. The students in grades 3 and up can examine history through two or more story sources related to this event and write individual paragraphs that compare (point out similarities) or contrast (point out differences) various views and evaluate what was read. Students then can meet with partners to read their paragraphs aloud to one another and offer suggestions to one another for rewriting the paragraphs.

- <u>Bibliography</u>
  Anderson. J. *Spanish Pioneers of the Southwest.* Illustrated by G. Ancona. (New York: Dutton, 1989). A contrast of the lives of a pioneer family in a Spanish community in New Mexico in the 1700s with the lives of the colonists on the U.S. east coast. Grades 3–6.
  Banim, L. *A Spy in the King's colony.* Illustrated by T. Yuditskaya. (New York: Silver Moon Press, 1994). In Boston in 1775, 11-year-old Emily Parker, suspects Robert Babcock of being a Loyalist spy and helps deliver a coded note to General Washington about the movement of cannon from Fort Ticonderoga to Farmingham. Grades 4–5.
  Davis, B. *Black Heroes of the American Revolution.* (San Diego: Harcourt, 1976). Depicts the contributions of African Americans during America's Revolutionary War with drawings, etchings, related reading list, and index. Grades 4–6.

(continued)

Figure 5.3 *(continued)*

Gilbin, J. C. *George Washington: A Picture Book Biography.* Illustrated by M. Dooling. (New York: Scholastic, 1992). Describes Washington's life from boyhood through adulthood. Grades K–3.

Gilbin, J. C. *Thomas Jefferson: A Picture Book Biography.* Illustrated by M. Dooling. (New York: Scholastic, 1995). Gives an account of Jefferson's life from boyhood through adulthood. Grades K–3.

Gray, G. *How Far, Felipe?* (New York: HarperCollins, 1978). Felipe and his family move from Mexico to California with the expedition of Colonel Juan de Anza in 1775. Their lifestyles can be compared and contrasted with those of the colonists on America's east coast during this time period. Grades K–3.

Hansen, J. *The Captive.* (New York: Scholastic, 1994). This story is based on a journal of the 1700s about Kofi, 12-year-old son of an Ashanti chief, who is sold and sent to America after his father's murder by a family slave. Kofi eventually returns to Africa. Grades 5–8.

Hudson, J. *Dawn Rider.* (New York: Putnam, 1990). This fictional account of Kit Fox, a 16-year-old Blackfoot girl, can be contrasted with the experience of a colonial contemporary. Kit is forbidden to ride horses but she disobeys the rules when her people's camp is attacked. Grades 6 and up.

Kinsey-Warock, N. *Wilderness Cat.* Illustrated by M. Graham. (Minneapolis: Cobblehill, 1992). This fictional account of Serena's family as they move to Canada in the 1700s can be contrasted with the experiences of their contemporaries in the colonies in the eastern United States. Grades 4–6.

Kirkpatrick, K. *Redcoats and Petticoats.* Illustrated by R. Himler. (New York: Holiday House, 1999). Read historical endnotes first before reading the story to get a clear picture of what was going on: Set in 1778 in Setauket, Long Island, this is the story of Thomas Strong and his family who were a part of the Setauket Spy Ring fighting the Tories. His mother hangs clothing in patterns on a clothesline as a code to signal loyal patriots across the Long Island Sound. Map included. Grades 3–6.

Lunn, J. *Charlotte.* Illustrated by B. Deines. (Toronto: Tundra, 1998). When Charlotte visits her loyalist cousins, her rebel father forbids her to return home. Grades 2–4.

McGovern, A. *Secret Soldier: The Story of Deborah Sampson.* (New York: Scholastic, 1991). A true story of Deborah who disguised herself as a boy to join America's revolutionary army. Grades 3–7.

Millender, D. H. *Crispus Attucks: Black Leader of Colonial Patriots.* (New York: Macmillan, 1986). Biography of a colonial African American and his contribution to America's revolution. Grades 5 and up.

Rinaldi, A. *Cast Two Shadows.* (New York: Harcourt/Gulliver, 1998). Fourteen-year-old Caroline Whittaker, daughter of a household slave, feels the effects of the revolution in 1780 in Camden, South Carolina. Her brother Johnny is a loyalist and her father supports the Patriots. Grades 5–6.

Wade, M. D. *Benedict Arnold.* (New York: Franklin Watts, 1995). This tells of Arnold's life from boyhood, his service as a general in the Revolutionary War, his heroic deeds (including his leadership at the Battle of Saratoga), his later traitorous actions, and his death in London. Also includes information about his wife, Peggy Shippen. Grades 3 and up.

Walker, S. M. *The 18 Penny Goose.* Illustrated by E. Beier. (San Francisco: HarperCollins, 1998). A colonial family has to leave a pet goose behind when fleeing from British soldiers. The soldiers spare the pet. Grades 1–2.

EXERCISE 5.4 EXAMINING STUDENT TEXTBOOKS AND TEACHER'S EDITIONS

Instructions: The purpose of this exercise is to become familiar with textbooks that you may be using in your teaching. Student textbooks are usually accompanied by a teacher's edition that contains specific objectives, teaching techniques, learning activities, assessment instruments, test items, and suggested resources. Your university library, local schools, and cooperating teachers are sources for locating and borrowing these enhanced textbooks. For your subject field of interest, select a textbook that is accompanied by a teacher's edition and examine the contents of both using the following format. If there are no standard textbooks available for your teaching field (such as might be the case for art, home economics, industrial arts, music, and physical education), then select a field in which there is a possibility you might teach. Beginning teachers are often assigned to teach in more than one field—sometimes, unfortunately, in fields for which they are untrained or have only minimal training. After completion of this exercise, share the book and your analysis of it with your colleagues.

Title of book:

Author(s):

Publisher:

Date of most recent publication:

Recommended grade level:

1. Analyze the teacher's edition for the following elements.

	Yes	*No*
a. Are its goals consistent with the goals of local and state curriculum documents?	_____	_____
b. Are there specific objectives for each lesson?	_____	_____
c. Does the book have scope and sequence charts for teacher reference?	_____	_____
d. Are the units and lessons sequentially developed, with suggested time allotments?		
e. Are there any suggested provisions for individual differences?	_____	_____
for reading levels?	_____	_____
for students with special needs?	_____	_____
for students who are gifted and talented?	_____	_____
for students who have limited proficiency in English?	_____	_____
f. Does it recommend specific techniques and strategies?	_____	_____
g. Does it have listings of suggested aids, materials, and resources?	_____	_____
h. Are there suggestions for extension activities (to extend the lessons beyond the usual topic or time)?	_____	_____
i. Does the book have specific guidelines for assessment of student learning?	_____	_____

EXERCISE 5.4 *(continued)*

2. Analyze the student textbook for the following elements.

		Yes	*No*
a.	Does it treat the content with adequate depth?	_____	_____
b.	Does it treat ethnic minorities and women fairly?	_____	_____
c.	Is the format attractive?	_____	_____
d.	Does the book have good quality binding with suitable type size?	_____	_____
e.	Are illustrations and visuals attractive and useful?	_____	_____
f.	Is the reading clear and understandable for the students?	_____	_____

3. Would you like to use this textbook? Give reasons why or why not.

THINKING ABOUT THE SEQUENCING OF CONTENT

As you have reviewed the rationale and components of instructional planning, and examined state and local curriculum documents, national standards, and student reading materials, you have undoubtedly reflected on your own opinion regarding content that should be included in a subject at a particular grade level. Now it is time to obtain some practical experience in long-range planning. While some authors believe that the first step in preparing to teach is to write the learning objectives, others believe that a more logical starting point is to prepare a sequential topic outline—the next step in this chapter—from which you can then prepare the major learning objectives (Chapter 6).

The topic outlines and learning objectives and even scripted lessons may be presented to most beginning teachers with the expectation that they will teach from them. For you this may be the case, but someone had to have written those curriculum materials and that someone was one or more classroom teachers. As a teacher candidate, you must know how this is done for someday it will be your task. To experience preparing a content outline (either semester or year long) for a subject and grade level that you intend to teach, do Exercise 5.5 now.

For Your Notes

EXERCISE 5.5 PREPARING A CONTENT OUTLINE

Instructions: The purpose of this exercise is for you to organize your ideas about subject content and the sequencing of content. Unless instructed otherwise by your instructor, you should select the grade level and the discipline (e.g., mathematics, science, social studies, English/language arts) or specify the several disciplines if it is a multidisciplinary content outline.

With *three levels of headings* (see example that follows), prepare a sequential topic outline (on a separate piece of paper as space is not provided here) for a subject and grade level you intend to teach. Identify the subject by title, and clearly state the grade level. This outline is of topic content only and does *not* need to include student activities associated with the learning of that content (i.e., do not include experiments, assignments, or assessment strategies).

For example, for the study of earth science, three levels of headings might include

I. The Earth's surface

    A. Violent changes in Earth's surface

        1. Earthquakes

        2. Volcanoes

    B. Earth's land surface

        1. Rocks

etc.

If the study of earth science was just one unit for a grade level's study of the broader area of "science," then three levels of headings for that study might include

I. Earth science

    A. The Earth's surface

        1. Violent changes in Earth's surface

etc.

Share your completed outline to obtain feedback from your colleagues and university instructor. Because content outlines are never to be "carved into stone," make adjustments to your outline when and as appropriate.

EXERCISE 5.5 *(continued)*

Content Outline Assessment Checklist

For the development of your own outline, and for the assessment of outlines by others, here is a content outline assessment checklist:

• Does the outline follow a logical sequence, with each topic logically leading to the next?

Yes _____ No _____ Comment:

• Does the content assume prerequisite knowledge or skills that the students are likely to have?

Yes _____ No _____ Comment:

• Is the content inclusive, and to an appropriate depth?

Yes _____ No_____ Comment:

• Does the content consider individual student differences?

Yes _____ No _____ Comment:

• Does the content allow for interdisciplinary studies?

Yes _____ No _____ Comment:

• Is the outline complete; are there serious content omissions?

Yes _____ No _____ Comment:

• Is there content that is of questionable value for this level of instruction?

Yes _____ No _____ Comment:

Save your content outline and this completed exercise for later when you are working on Exercise 5.11 and exercises in Chapter 6.

PREPARING FOR AND DEALING WITH CONTROVERSY

Controversial content and issues abound in teaching for example, in English/language arts, over certain books in mathematics, over the extent of the use of calculators in the classroom; in science, over biological evolution; and in social studies, over values and moral issues. As a general rule, trust your intuition: If you have concern that a particular topic or activity might create controversy, it probably will. During your teaching career, you undoubtedly will have to make decisions about how you will handle such matters. When selecting content or methods that might be controversial, consider as guidelines the information in the paragraphs that follow.

Maintain a perspective with respect to your own goal, which is at the moment to obtain your teaching credential, and then a teaching job, and then perhaps tenure. Our point is that student teaching is not a good time to become swathed in controversy. If you communicate closely with your cooperating teacher and your college or university supervisor, you should be able to prevent most major problems dealing with controversial issues.

Sometimes, during normal discussion in the classroom, a controversial topic will emerge spontaneously, catching the teacher off-guard. If this happens, think before saying anything. Consider suspending further discussion on the topic until you have opportunity to review the issue with colleagues or your supervisors. Controversial topics can seem to arise from nowhere for any teacher, and this is perfectly normal.[16] Children are works in progress! They need to be allowed to develop their skill in flexible thinking (one of the characteristics of intelligent behavior discussed in Chapter 9) which they can only do as they learn to consider alternative points of view and to deal with several sources of information simultaneously. They are in process of developing their moral and value systems, and they need and want to know how adults feel about issues that are important to them, particularly those adults they hold in esteem—their teachers. For some children, unfortunately, their classroom teacher may be the only adult to whom they can hold in esteem. Students need to discuss issues that are important to society, and there is absolutely nothing wrong with dealing with those issues as long as certain guidelines are observed.

First, students should learn about all sides of an issue. Controversial issues are open-ended and should be treated as such. They do not have "right" answers or "correct" solutions. If they did, there would be no controversy. (As used in this book, an *issue* differs from a *problem* in that a problem generally has a solution, whereas an issue has many opinions and several alternative solutions.) Therefore, the focus should be on process as well as on content. A major goal is to help children learn how to deal with controversy and to mediate wise decisions on the basis of carefully considered information. Another goal is to help children learn how to disagree without being disagreeable—how to resolve conflict. To that end children need to learn the difference between conflicts that are destructive and those that can be constructive, in other words, to see that conflict (disagreement) can be healthy, that it can have value. A third goal, of course, is to help students learn about the content of an issue so, when necessary, they can make decisions based on knowledge, not on ignorance.

Second, as with all lesson plans, one dealing with a topic that could lead to controversy should be well thought out ahead of time—that is, during the preactive phase of instruction. Potential problem areas and resources must be carefully considered and prepared for in advance. As we have said before (see Chapter 3, for example), problems for the teacher are most likely to occur when insufficient attention is given to the preactive phase of instruction and decision making.

Third, at some point all persons directly involved in an issue have a right to input—students, parents and guardians, community representatives, and other faculty. This does not mean that people outside of the school have the right to censor a teacher's plan, but it does mean that parents (or guardians) and students should have the right *sans penalty* to not participate and to select an alternate activity. Most school districts have written policies that deal with challenges to instructional content or materials. As a beginning teacher, you should become aware of the policies of your school district. In addition, professional associations such as the NCTE, NCSS, NBTA, and NSTA each have published guidelines for dealing with controversial content or materials. NCTE offers an online resource about censorship: <http://www.ncte.org/censorship/>.

Fourth, there is nothing wrong with children knowing a teacher's opinion about an issue as long as it is clear that the students may disagree sans reprisal or academic penalty. However, it is probably best to give your opinion only after the children have had full opportunity to study and report on facts and opinions from other sources. Sometimes it is helpful to assist students in separating facts from opinions on a particular issue being studied by setting up a fact-opinion table on the overhead or on the writing board, with the issue stated at the

Figure 5.4
Fact-opinion table

The issue:	
Statements of fact:	Statements of opinion:

top followed by two parallel columns, one for facts, the other for related opinions (see Figure 5.4).

A characteristic that has made the United States such a great nation is the freedom for its entire people to speak out on issues. This freedom should not be excluded from public school classrooms. Teachers and students should be encouraged to express their opinions about the great is-sues of today, to study the issues, to suspend judgment while collecting data, and then to form and accept each other's reasoned opinions. As educators we must understand the difference between teaching truth, values, and morals, and teaching *about* truth, values, and morals.

As a public school teacher there are limits to your academic freedom, much greater than are the limits on a university professor. You must understand this fact. The primary difference is that the students with whom you will be working are not yet adults. As children they must be protected from dogma and allowed the freedom to learn and to develop their values and opinions, free from coercion from those who have power and control over their learning.

Now that you have read our opinion and suggested guidelines, what do you think about this topic, which should be important to you as a teacher? Use Exercise 5.6 for the development and expression of your opinion.

EXERCISE 5.6 DEALING WITH CONTROVERSIAL CONTENT AND ISSUES

Instructions: The purpose of this exercise is for you to discover controversial content and issues that you may face as a teacher and to consider what you can and will do about them. After completing this exercise, share it with members of your class.

1. After studying current periodicals and talking with colleagues in the schools you visit, list two potentially controversial topics that you are likely to encounter as a teacher. (Two examples are given for you.)

Issue   *Source*

Human cloning _____   *Time, March 1997* _____

Use of calculators in mathematics _____   *(ongoing)* _____

_____   _____

2. Take one of these issues, and identify opposing arguments and current resources.

_____

_____

_____

_____

3. Identify your own positions on this issue.

_____

_____

_____

_____

4. How well can you accept students (and parents or guardians) who assume the opposite position?

_____

_____

_____

_____

5. Share the preceding with other teacher candidates. Note comments that you find helpful or enlightening.

_____

_____

_____

_____

For Your Notes

AIMS, GOALS, AND OBJECTIVES: THE ANTICIPATED LEARNING OUTCOME

Now that you have examined content typical of the curriculum and have experienced preparing a content outline for a subject at a grade level at which you intend to teach, you are ready to write instructional objectives for that content learning. *Instructional objectives* (also called *learning objectives*) are *statements describing what the student will be able to do upon completion of the instructional experience.* Whereas some authors distinguish between *instructional objectives* (hence referring to objectives that are *not* behavior specific) and *behavioral* or *performance objectives* (objectives that *are* behavior specific), the terms are used here as if they are synonymous to emphasize the importance of writing instructional objectives in terms that are measurable. *Terminal objective* is sometimes used to distinguish between instructional objectives that are intermediate and those that are final, or terminal, to an area of learning.

As a teacher, you frequently will encounter the compound structure that reads "goals and objectives," as you likely found in the curriculum documents that you reviewed (Exercises 5.1 through 5.4). A distinction needs to be understood. The easiest way to understand the difference between the two words, *goals* and *objectives,* is to look at your *intent.*

Goals are ideals that you intend to reach, that is, ideals that you (and/or others) would like to have accomplished. Goals may be stated as teacher goals, as student goals, or, collaboratively, as team goals. Ideally, in all three, the goal is the same. If, for example, the goal is to improve students' reading skills, it could be stated as follows:

"To help students develop their reading skills"	*Teacher or course goal*
or	
"To improve my reading skills"	*Student goal*

Educational goals are general statements of intent and are prepared early in curriculum planning. (*Note:* Some writers use the phrase "general goals and objectives," but that is incorrect usage. Goals *are* general; objectives are specific.) Goals are useful when planned cooperatively with students and/or when shared with students as advance mental organizers to establish a mind-set. The students then know what to expect and will begin to prepare mentally to learn it. From the goals, objectives are prepared. Objectives are *not* intentions. They are the actual behaviors teachers intend to cause students to display. In short, objectives are what students *do.*

So, in summary, the most general educational objectives are often called *aims;* the general objectives of schools, curricula, and courses are called *goals;* the objectives of units and lessons are called *instructional* (or *learning*) objectives. Aims are more general than goals, goals are more general than objectives. Instructional objectives are quite specific. *Aims, goals, and objectives represent the targets, from general to specific statements of learning expectations, to which curriculum and instruction are designed and aimed.*

Instructional Objectives and Their Relationship to Aligned Curriculum and Authentic Assessment

As implied in the preceding paragraphs, goals guide the instructional methods; objectives drive student performance. Assessment of student achievement in learning should be an assessment of that performance. When the assessment procedure does match the instructional objectives, that is sometimes referred to as assessment that is *aligned* or *authentic* (discussed in Chapter 11). [If the term *authentic assessment* sounds rather silly to you, we agree. After all, if the objectives and assessment don't match, then that particular assessment should be discarded or modified until it does match. In other words, assessment that is not authentic is "poor assessment" and should not be used.] When objectives, instruction, and assessment match the stated goals we have what is referred to as an *aligned curriculum.* [Again, a curriculum that does not align is nonsensical and should be corrected or discarded.]

Goals are general statements, usually not even complete sentences, often beginning with the infinitive *to,* which identify what the teacher intends the students to learn. Objectives, stated in performance terms, are specific actions and should be written as complete sentences that include the verb *will* to *indicate what each student is expected to be able to do as a result of the instructional experience.* The last part of the previous sentence is emphasized because when writing instructional objectives for their unit and lesson plans, one of the most common errors made by beginning teachers is to state what *they* intend to do rather than what the anticipated student performance is. The value of stating learning objectives in terms of student performance is well documented by research.[17]

While instructional goals may not always be quantifiable (that is, readily measurable),

Figure 5.5
Examples of goals and objectives

Goals
1. To acquire knowledge about the physical geography of North America.
2. To develop an appreciation for music.
3. To develop enjoyment for reading.

Objectives
1. On a map the student will identify specific mountain ranges of North America.
2. The student will identify 10 different musical instruments by listening to a tape recording of the Boston Pops Symphony Orchestra and identify which instrument is being played at specified times as determined by the teacher.
3. The student will read two books, three short stories, and five newspaper articles at home, within a 2-month period. The student will maintain a daily written log of these activities.

instructional objectives should be measurable. Furthermore, those objectives then become the essence of what is measured for in instruments designed to assess student learning—they are the learning targets. Consider the examples shown in Figure 5.5.

Learning Targets and Goal Indicators

One purpose for writing objectives in performance terms is to be able to assess with precision whether the instruction has resulted in the desired behavior. In many schools the educational goals are established as *learning targets,* competencies that the students are expected to achieve. These goals are then divided into performance objectives, sometimes referred to as *goal indicators.* Instruction is designed to teach toward those objectives. When students perform the competencies called for by these objectives, their education is considered successful. Over recent years, this has become known variously as *criterion-referenced, competency-based, performance-based, results-driven,* or *outcome-based education.* Expecting students to achieve one set of competencies before moving on to the next set is called *mastery learning* (see Chapter 8). The success of the student achievement, teacher performance, and the school may each be assessed according to these criteria.

Overt and Covert Performance Outcomes

Assessment is not difficult to accomplish when the desired performance outcome is *overt* behavior, that is, when it can be observed directly. Each of the sample objectives of the preceding section is an example of an objective that is overt. Assessment is more difficult to accomplish when the desired behavior is *covert,* that is, when it is not directly observable. While certainly no less im-

portant, behaviors that call for "appreciation," "discovery," or "understanding," for example, are not directly observable because they occur within a person and so are covert behaviors. Since covert behavior cannot be observed directly, the only way to tell whether the objective has been achieved is to observe behavior that may be indicative of that achievement. The objective, then, is written in overt language, and evaluators can only assume or trust that the observed behavior is, in fact, reasonably close to being indicative of the expected learning outcome.

Furthermore, when assessing whether an objective has been achieved and that learning has occurred, the assessment device must be consistent with the desired learning outcome; otherwise the assessment is not aligned—it is invalid. As said earlier, when the measuring device and the learning objective are compatible, we say that the assessment is authentic. For example, a person's competency to teach literacy skills to children in the second grade is best (i.e., with highest reliability) measured by directly observing that person *doing* that very thing—teaching literacy skills to second graders. Using a standardized paper-and-pencil test of multiple-choice items to determine a person's ability to teach specific literacy skills to second-grade students is not authentic assessment.

Balance of Behaviorism and Constructivism

While behaviorists assume a definition of learning that deals only with changes in observable (overt) behavior, constructivists hold that learning entails the construction or reshaping of mental schemata and that mental processes mediate learning. Thus, people who adhere to constructivism or cognitivism are concerned with both overt and covert behaviors.[18] Does this mean that you must be one or the other, a behaviorist or a constructivist? Probably not. For now, the point is that when writing instructional objectives, you should write most or all of your basic expectations (minimal competency expectations) in overt terms (the topic of the next section). On the other hand, you can not be expected to foresee all learning that occurs nor to translate all that is learned into performance terms—most certainly not before it occurs.

Teaching Toward Multiple Objectives, Understandings, and Appreciations

Any effort to write all learning objectives in performance terms is, in effect, to neglect the individual learner for whom it purports to be concerned; such an approach does not allow for diversity among learners. Learning that is most meaningful to children is not so neatly or easily predicted or isolated. Rather than teaching one objective at a time, much of the time you will direct your teaching toward the simultaneous learning of multiple objectives, understandings, and appreciations. However, when assessing for learning, assessment is cleaner when objectives are assessed one at a time. More on this matter of objectives and their use in teaching and learning follows later in this chapter. Let's now review how instructional objectives are prepared.

PREPARING INSTRUCTIONAL OBJECTIVES

When preparing instructional objectives, you must ask yourself, "How is the student to demonstrate that the objective has been reached?" The objective must include an action that demonstrates that the objective has been achieved. Inherited from behaviorism, this portion of the objective is sometimes called the *anticipated measurable performance.*

Figure 5.6
Verbs to avoid when writing overt objectives

appreciate	enjoy	indicate	like
believe	familiarize	know	realize
comprehend	grasp	learn	understand

Four Key Components

When completely written in performance terms, an instructional objective has four key components. To aid your understanding and remembering, a useful mnemonic is to refer to these as the ABCDs of writing instructional objectives.

One component is the *audience.* This *A* of the ABCDs refers to the student for whom the objective is intended. To address this, sometimes teachers begin their objectives with the phrase "The student will be able to. . ." or, to personalize the objective, "You will be able to. . ." (*Note:* To conserve space and to eliminate useless language, in examples that follow we eliminate use of "be able to," and write simply "The student will. . ." For brevity writers of objectives sometimes use the abbreviation "TSWBAT . . ." for "The student will be able to . . .")

The second key component is the expected *behavior,* the *B* of the ABCDs. This second component represents the important learning target. The expected behavior (or performance) should be written with verbs that are measurable—that is, with action verbs—so that it is directly observable that the objective, that is, the target, has been reached. As discussed in the preceding section, some verbs are too vague, ambiguous, and not clearly measurable. When writing objectives, you should avoid verbs that are not clearly measurable, verbs that are covert, such as *appreciate, comprehend,* and *understand* (see Figure 5.6). For the three examples given earlier, for Objectives 1 and 2 the behaviors (action or overt verbs) are *will identify,* and, for Objective 3, the behaviors are *will read* and *maintain.*

Now do Exercise 5.7 to assess and to further your understanding.

EXERCISE 5.7 RECOGNIZING VERBS THAT ARE ACCEPTABLE FOR OVERT OBJECTIVES—A SELF-CHECK EXERCISE

Instructions: The purpose of this exercise is to check your recognition of verbs that are suitable for use in overt objectives. From the list of verbs below, circle those that *should not* be used in overt objectives—that is, those verbs that describe covert behaviors not directly observable and measurable. Check your answers against the answer key that follows. Discuss any problems with the exercise with your classmates and instructor.

1. apply	11. design	21. know
2. appreciate	12. diagram	22. learn
3. believe	13. enjoy	23. name
4. combine	14. explain	24. outline
5. comprehend	15. familiarize	25. predict
6. compute	16. grasp*	26. realize
7. create	17. identify	27. select
8. define	18. illustrate	28. solve
9. demonstrate	19. indicate	29. state
10. describe	20. infer	30. understand

Answer key: The following verbs should be circled: 2, 3, 5, 13, 15, 16, 21, 22, 26, 30. If you missed more than a couple, then you need to read the previous sections again and discuss your errors with your classmates and instructor.

*Note: Words in English often have more than one meaning. For example, *grasp* as listed here for use in overt objectives; for the latter it would not.

Most of the time, when writing objectives for your unit and lesson plans, you will not bother yourself with including the next two components. As you will learn, however, they are important for assessment.

The third ingredient is the *conditions,* the C of the ABCDs, the setting in which the behavior will be demonstrated by the student and observed by the teacher. Conditions are forever changing; although the learning target should be clearly recognizable long before the actual instruction occurs, the conditions may not. Thus, conditions are not often included in the objectives that teachers write. For the first sample objective, the conditions are: "on a map." For the second sample objective, the conditions are: "by listening to a tape recording of the Boston Pops Symphony Orchestra," and "specified times as determined by the teacher." For the third sample, for "the student will read . . .," the conditions are: "at home within a 2-month period."

The fourth ingredient, which again is not always included in objectives written by teachers, is the *degree* (or *level*) *of expected performance*—the D of the ABCDs. This is the ingredient that allows for the assessment of student learning. When mastery learning is expected, the level of expected performance is usually omitted (because it is understood). In teaching for mastery learning, the performance-level expectation is 100 percent. In reality, however, the performance level will most likely be between 85 and 95 percent, particularly when working with a group of students rather than with an individual student. The 5 to 15 percent difference allows for human error, as can occur when using written and oral communication. Like conditions, performance levels will vary depending on the situation and purpose and thus are not normally included in the unit and lessons that teachers prepare. Now, to reinforce your comprehension, do Exercise 5.8.

EXERCISE 5.8 RECOGNIZING THE PARTS OF CRITERION-REFERENCED INSTRUCTIONAL OBJECTIVES—A SELF-CHECK EXERCISE

Instructions: The purpose of this exercise is to practice your skill in recognizing the four components of an instructional objective. In the following two objectives, identify the parts of the objectives by underlining once the *audience,* twice the *performance (behavior),* three times the *conditions,* and four times the *performance level* (that is, the degree or standard of performance).

Check your answers against the answer key that follows, and discuss any problems with this exercise with your classmates and instructor.

1. Given a metropolitan transit bus schedule, at the end of the lesson the student will be able to read the schedule well enough to determine at what times buses are scheduled to leave randomly selected locations, with at least 90 percent accuracy.

2. Given five rectangular figures, you will correctly compute the area in square centimeters of at least four, by measuring the length and width with a ruler and computing the product using an appropriate calculation method.

Exercise Answer Key:

	Objective 1	*Objective 2*
Audience (underlined once)	The student	You
Behavior (underlined twice)	will be able to read the schedule	will compute
Conditions (underlined three times)	given a metropolitan transit bus schedule	given five rectangular figures
Performance level (underlined four times)	well enough to determine (and) with at least 90 percent accuracy	correctly compute the area in square centimeters of at least four (80 percent accuracy)

Performance level is used to assess student achievement, and sometimes it is used to evaluate the effectiveness of the teaching. Student grades might be based on performance levels; evaluation of teacher effectiveness might be based on the level of student performance.

Now, with Exercise 5.9, try your skill at recognizing student learning objectives that are measurable.

EXERCISE 5.9 RECOGNIZING OBJECTIVES THAT ARE MEASURABLE— A SELF-CHECK EXERCISE

Instructions: The purpose of this exercise is to assess your ability to recognize objectives that are measurable. Place an X before each of the following that is an overt, student-centered instructional objective, that is, a clearly measurable learning objective. Although *audience, conditions,* or *performance levels* may be absent, ask yourself, "As stated, is this a student-centered and measurable objective?" If it is, place an X in the blank. A self-checking answer key follows. After checking your answers, discuss any problems with the exercise with your classmates and instructor.

_____ 1. To develop an appreciation for literature.

_____ 2. To identify those celestial bodies that are known planets.

_____ 3. To provide meaningful experiences for the students.

_____ 4. To recognize antonym pairs.

_____ 5. To boot up the program on the computer.

_____ 6. To analyze and compare patterns of data or specific quartile maps.

_____ 7. To develop skills in inquiry.

_____ 8. To identify which of the four causes is most relevant to the major events leading up to the Civil War.

_____ 9. To use maps and graphs to identify the major areas of world petroleum production and consumption.

_____ 10. To know the causes for the diminishing ozone concentration.

Exercise Answer Key: You should have marked items 2, 4, 5, 6, 8, and 9.

Items 1, 3, 7, and 10 are inadequate because of their ambiguity. Item 3 is not even a student learning objective; it is a teacher goal. "To develop" and "to know" can have too many interpretations.

Although the conditions are not given, items 2, 4, 5, 6, 8, and 9 are clearly measurable. The teacher would have no difficulty recognizing when a learner had reached those objectives. Discuss any problem you had with this exercise with your classmates and instructor.

Classifying Instructional Objectives

When planning instructional objectives, it is useful to consider the three domains of learning objectives:

cognitive domain—involves intellectual operations from the lowest level of the simple recall of information to complex, high-level thinking processes;

affective domain—involves feelings, emotions, attitudes, and values, and ranges from the lower levels of acquisition to the highest level of internalization and action;

psychomotor domain—ranges from the simple manipulation of materials to the communication of ideas, and finally to the highest level of creative performance.

The Domains of Learning and the Developmental Needs of Children

Educators attempt to design learning experiences to meet the five areas of developmental needs of the total child: intellectual, physical, emotional/psychological, social, and moral/ethical. As a teacher, you must include objectives that address learning within each of these categories of needs. While the intellectual needs are primarily within the cognitive domain and the physical are within the psychomotor, the other needs mostly are within the affective domain.

Too frequently, teachers focus on the cognitive domain while only assuming that the psychomotor and affective will take care of themselves. Many experts argue that teachers should do just the opposite; that when the affective is directly attended to, the psychomotor and cognitive naturally develop. In any case, you should plan your teaching so your students are guided from the lowest to highest levels of operation within each of the domains, separately or simultaneously.

The three developmental hierarchies are discussed next to guide your understanding of each of the five areas of needs. Notice the illustrative verbs within each hierarchy. These verbs help you fashion objectives when you are developing unit plans and lesson plans. (To see how goals and objectives fit into one lesson plan, see Figure 6.9, Chapter 6, Multiple-Day, Project-Centered, Interdisciplinary, and Transcultural Lesson Using Worldwide Communication via the Internet.) Caution however must be urged, for there can be considerable overlap among the levels at which some actions verbs may appropriately be used. For example, the verb *identifies* is appro-

priate in each of the following objectives at different levels (identified in parentheses) within the cognitive domain:

The student will identify the correct definition of the term *magnetism*. (knowledge)

The student will identify examples of the principle of magnetic attraction. (comprehension)

The student will identify the magnetic effect when two materials, one magnetic and one nonmagnetic, are brought together. (application)

The student will identify the effect when iron filings are brought into a magnetic field. (analysis)

Cognitive Domain Hierarchy

In a widely accepted taxonomy of objectives, Bloom and his associates arranged cognitive objectives into classifications according to the complexity of the skills and abilities they embodied.[19] The result was a ladder ranging from the simplest to the most complex intellectual processes. Within each domain, prerequisite to a student's ability to function at one particular level of the hierarchy is the ability to function at the preceding level or levels. In other words, when a student is functioning at the third level of the cognitive domain, that student is automatically also functioning at the first and second levels. Rather than an orderly progression from simple to complex mental operations as illustrated by Bloom's taxonomy, other researchers prefer an organization of cognitive abilities that ranges from simple information storage and retrieval, through a higher level of discrimination and concept attainment, to the highest cognitive ability to recognize and solve problems.[20]

The six major categories (or levels) in Bloom's taxonomy of cognitive objectives are (a) *knowledge*—recognizing and recalling information; (b) *comprehension*—understanding the meaning of information; (c) *application*—using information; (d) *analysis*—dissecting information into its component parts to comprehend their relationships; (e) *synthesis*—putting components together to generate new ideas; and (f) *evaluation*—judging the worth of an idea, notion, theory, thesis, proposition, information, or opinion. In this taxonomy, the top four categories or levels—application, analysis, synthesis, and evaluation—represent what are called *higher-order cognitive thinking skills*.[21]

While space does not allow elaboration here, Bloom's taxonomy includes various subcategories within each of these six major categories. It is probably less important that an objective be absolutely classified than it is to be cognizant of hierarchies of thinking and doing and to understand the importance of attending to student intellectual behavior from lower to higher levels of operation in all three domains. Discussion of each of Bloom's six categories follows.

Knowledge

The basic element in Bloom's taxonomy concerns the acquisition of knowledge—that is, the ability to recognize and recall information. (As discussed in Chapter 8, this is similar to the *input level* of thinking and questioning.) While this is the lowest of the six categories, the information to be learned may not itself be of a low level. In fact, it may be of an extremely high level. Bloom includes here knowledge of principles, generalizations, theories, structures, and methodology, as well as knowledge of facts and ways of dealing with facts.

Action verbs appropriate for this category include *choose, complete, cite, define, describe, identify, indicate, list, locate, match, name, outline, recall, recognize, select,* and *state.*

The following are examples of objectives at the knowledge level. Note especially the verb (in italics) used in each example:

- From memory, the student *will recall* the letters in the English alphabet that are vowels.
- The student *will list* the organelles found in animal cell cytoplasm.
- The student *will identify* the major parts of speech in the sentence.

The remaining five categories of Bloom's taxonomy of the cognitive domain deal with the *use* of knowledge. They encompass the educational objectives aimed at developing cognitive skills and abilities, including comprehension, application, analysis, synthesis, and evaluation of knowledge. The last four—application, analysis, synthesis, and evaluation—are referred to as *higher-order thinking skills,* as are, too, the higher categories of the affective and psychomotor domains.

Comprehension

Comprehension includes the ability to translate, explain, or interpret knowledge and to extrapolate from it to address new situations. Action verbs appropriate for this category include *change, classify, convert, defend, describe, discuss, estimate, expand, explain, generalize, infer, interpret, paraphrase, predict, recognize, retell, summarize,* and *translate.* Examples of objectives in this category are:

- From a sentence, the student *will recognize* the letters that are vowels in the English alphabet.
- The student *will describe* each of the organelles found in animal cell cytoplasm.

- The student *will recognize* the major parts of speech in the sentence.

Application

Once learners understand information, they should be able to apply it. Action verbs in this category of operation include *apply, calculate, demonstrate, develop, discover, exhibit, modify, operate, participate, perform, plan, predict, relate, show, simulate, solve,* and *use.* Examples of objectives in this category are:

- The student *will use* in a sentence a word that contains at least two vowels.
- The student *will predict* the organelles found in plant cell cytoplasm.
- The student *will demonstrate* in a complete sentence each of the major parts of speech.

Analysis

This category includes objectives that require learners to use the skills of analysis. Action verbs appropriate for this category include *analyze, arrange, break down, categorize, classify, compare, contrast, debate, deduce, diagram, differentiate, discover, discriminate, group, identify, illustrate, infer, inquire, organize, outline, relate, separate,* and *subdivide.* Examples of objectives in this category include:

- From a list of words, the student *will differentiate* those that contain vowels from those that do not.
- Under the microscope, the student *will identify* the organelles found in animal cell cytoplasm.
- The student *will analyze* a paragraph for misuse of major parts of speech.

Synthesis

This category includes objectives that involve such skills as designing a plan, proposing a set of operations, and deriving a series of abstract relations. Action verbs appropriate for this category include *arrange, assemble, categorize, classify, combine, compile, compose, constitute, create, design, develop, devise, document, explain, formulate, generate, hypothesize, imagine, invent, modify, organize, originate, plan, predict, produce, rearrange, reconstruct, revise, rewrite, summarize, synthesize, tell, transmit,* and *write.* Examples of objectives in this category are:

- From a list of words, the student *will rearrange* them into several lists according to the vowels contained in each.
- The student *will devise* a classification scheme of the organelles found in animal cell and plant cell cytoplasm according to their functions.
- The student *will write* a paragraph that correctly uses each of the major parts of speech.

Evaluation

This, the highest category of Bloom's cognitive taxonomy, includes offering opinions and making value judgments. Action verbs appropriate for this category include *appraise, argue, assess, choose, compare, conclude, consider, contrast, criticize, decide, discriminate, estimate, evaluate, explain, interpret, judge, justify, predict, rank, rate, recommend, relate, revise, standardize, support,* and *validate.* Examples of objectives in this category are:

- The student *will listen to and evaluate* other students' identifications of vowels from sentences written on the board.
- While observing living cytoplasm under the microscope, the student *will justify* her or his interpretation that certain structures are specific organelles of a plant or animal cell.
- The student *will evaluate* a paragraph written by another student for the proper use of major parts of speech.

Affective Domain Hierarchy

Krathwohl, Bloom, and Masia developed a taxonomy of the affective domain.[22] The following are their major levels (or categories), from least internalized to most internalized: (a) *receiving*—being aware of the affective stimulus and beginning to have favorable feelings toward it; (b) *responding*—taking an interest in the stimulus and viewing it favorably; (c) *valuing*—showing a tentative belief in the value of the affective stimulus and becoming committed to it; (d) *organizing*—placing values into a system of dominant and supporting values; and, (e) *internalizing*—demonstrating consistent beliefs and behavior that have become a way of life. While there is considerable overlap from one category to another within the affective domain, these categories do give a basis by which to judge the quality of objectives and the nature of learning within this area. A discussion of each of the five categories follows.

Receiving

At this level, which is the least internalized, the learner exhibits willingness to give attention to particular phenomena or stimuli, and the teacher is able to arouse, sustain, and direct that attention. Action verbs appropriate for this category include *ask, choose, describe, differentiate, distinguish, hold, identify, locate, name, point to, recall, recognize, reply, select,* and *use.* Examples of objectives in this category are:

- The student *listens attentively* to the ideas of others.
- The student *demonstrates sensitivity* to the property, beliefs, and concerns of others.

Responding

At this level, learners respond to the stimulus they have received. They may do so because of some external pressure, or because they find the stimulus interesting, or because responding gives them satisfaction. Action verbs appropriate for this category include *answer, applaud, approve, assist, command, comply, discuss, greet, help, label, perform, play, practice, present, read, recite, report, select, spend (leisure time in), tell,* and *write.* Examples of objectives at this level are:

- The student *discusses* what others have said.
- The student *cooperates* with others during group activities.

Valuing

Objectives at the valuing level deal with the learner's beliefs, attitudes, and appreciations. The simplest objectives concern the acceptance of beliefs and values; the higher ones involve learning to prefer certain values and finally becoming committed to them. Action verbs appropriate for this level include *argue, assist, complete, describe, differentiate, explain, follow, form, initiate, invite, join, justify, propose, protest, read, report, select, share, study, support,* and *work.* Examples of objectives in this category include:

- The student *protests* against racial or ethnic discrimination.
- The student *forms* an opinion on the right-to-life issue.

Organizing

This fourth level in the affective domain concerns the building of a personal value system. Here the learner is conceptualizing and arranging values into a system that recognizes their relative importance. Action verbs appropriate for this level include *adhere, alter, arrange, balance, combine, compare, defend, define, discuss, explain, form, generalize, identify, integrate, modify, order, organize, prepare, relate,* and *synthesize.* Examples of objectives in this category are:

- The student *forms judgments* concerning proper behavior in the classroom, school, and community.
- The student *defends* the values of a particular subculture.

Internalizing

This is the last and highest category within the affective domain, at which the learner's behaviors have become consistent with the learner's beliefs. Action verbs appropriate for this level include *act, complete, display, influence, listen, modify, perform, practice, propose, qualify, question, revise, serve, solve,* and *verify.* Examples of objectives in this category are:

- The student's behavior *displays* a well defined and ethical code of conduct.
- The student *performs* independently.

Psychomotor Domain Hierarchy

Whereas identification and classification within the cognitive and affective domains are generally agreed upon, there is less agreement on the classification within the psychomotor domain. Originally, the goal of this domain was simply to develop and categorize proficiency in skills, particularly those dealing with gross and fine motor control. The classification of the domain presented here follows this lead, but includes at its highest level the most creative and inventive behaviors, thus coordinating skills and knowledge from all three domains. Consequently, the objectives are in a hierarchy ranging from simple gross locomotor control to the most creative and complex, requiring originality and fine locomotor control—for example, from simply turning on a computer to designing a software program. From Harrow we offer the following taxonomy of the psychomotor domain: (a) *moving,* (b) *manipulating,* (c) *communicating,* and (d) *creating.*[23]

Moving
This level involves gross motor coordination. Action verbs appropriate for this level include *adjust, carry, clean, grasp, jump, locate, obtain,* and *walk.* Sample objectives for this category are:

- The student *will jump* a rope 10 times without missing.

- The student *will carry* the microscope to the desk correctly.

Manipulating
This level involves fine motor coordination. Action verbs appropriate for this level include *assemble, build, calibrate, connect, play, thread,* and *turns.* Sample objectives for this category are:

- The student *will assemble* a kite.
- The student *will turn* the fine adjustment until the microscope is in focus.

Communicating
This level involves the communication of ideas and feelings. Action verbs appropriate for this level include *analyze, ask, describe, draw, explain,* and *write.* Sample objectives for this category are:

- By *asking* appropriate questions the student will demonstrate active listening skills.
- The student *will draw* what the student observes on a slide through the microscope.

Creating
Creating is the highest level of this domain and of all domains and represents the student's coordination of thinking, learning, and behaving in all three domains. Action verbs appropriate for this level include *create, design,* and *invent.* Sample objectives for this category are:

- The student *will create and perform* a dance pattern.
- The student *will invent* and build a kite pattern.

Now, using Exercise 5.10, assess your recognition of performance objectives according to which domain they belong. Then, with Exercise 5.11, begin writing your own objectives for use in your teaching. You may want to correlate your work on Exercise 5.11 with Exercises 5.5, 6.7, 6.11, and 12.2.

EXERCISE 5.10 ASSESSING RECOGNITION OF OBJECTIVES ACCORDING TO DOMAIN—A SELF-CHECK EXERCISE

Instructions: The purpose of this exercise is to assess your ability to identify objectives correctly according to their domain. For each of the following instructional objectives, identify by the appropriate letter the domain involved: (*C*) cognitive, (*A*) affective, or (*P*) psychomotor. Check your answers, and discuss the results with your classmates and instructor.

_____ 1. The student will shoot free throws until he or she can complete 80 percent of the attempts.

_____ 2. The student will identify on a map the mountain ranges of the eastern United States.

_____ 3. The student will summarize the historical development of the Democratic Party in the United States.

_____ 4. The student will demonstrate a continuing desire to learn more about using the classroom computer for word processing by volunteering to work at it during free time.

_____ 5. The student will volunteer to tidy up the storage room.

_____ 6. After listening to several recordings, the student will identify their respective composers.

_____ 7. The student will translate a favorite Cambodian poem into English.

_____ 8. The student will calculate the length of the hypotenuse.

_____ 9. The student will indicate an interest in the subject by voluntarily reading additional library books about earthquakes.

_____ 10. The student will successfully stack five blocks.

Exercise Answer Key: 2, 3, 6, 7, 8 = C; 1, 10 = P; 4, 5, 9 = A

For Your Notes

EXERCISE 5.11   PREPARING MY OWN INSTRUCTIONAL OBJECTIVES

Instructions: The purpose of this exercise is to begin writing your own behavioral objectives. For a subject and grade level of your choice, prepare 10 specific behavioral objectives. Refer to Exercises 5.5, 6.5, 6.8, and 12.2. It is not necessary to include audience, conditions, and performance level unless requested by your course instructor. Exchange completed exercises with your classmates; discuss and make changes where necessary.

Subject _____

Grade level: _____

1. Cognitive knowledge _____

   _____

   _____

   _____

   _____

   _____

2. Cognitive comprehension _____

   _____

   _____

   _____

   _____

   _____

3. Cognitive application _____

   _____

   _____

   _____

   _____

   _____

4. Cognitive analysis _____

   _____

   _____

   _____

   _____

   _____

5. Cognitive synthesis _____

   _____

   _____

EXERCISE 5.11 *(continued)*

_____

_____

_____

6. Cognitive evaluation _____

_____

_____

_____

_____

_____

7. Psychomotor (low level) _____

_____

_____

_____

_____

_____

8. Psychomotor (high level) _____

_____

_____

_____

_____

_____

9. Affective (low level) _____

_____

_____

_____

_____

_____

10. Affective (highest level) _____

_____

_____

_____

_____

_____

USING THE TAXONOMIES

Theoretically, the taxonomies are so constructed that students achieve each lower level before being ready to move to the higher levels. But, because categories and behaviors overlap, as they should, this theory does not always hold in practice. Furthermore, as explained by others, feelings and thoughts are inextricably interconnected—they cannot be neatly separated as the taxonomies would imply.[24]

The taxonomies are important in that they emphasize the various levels to which instruction must aspire. For learning to be worthwhile, you must formulate and teach to objectives from the higher levels of the taxonomies as well as from the lower ones. Student thinking and behaving must be moved from the lowest to the highest levels of thinking and doing. When all is said and done, it is, perhaps, the highest level of the psychomotor domain (creating) to which we aspire.

In using the taxonomies, remember that the point is to formulate the best objectives for the job to be done. In schools that use results-driven education models (see page 166 for synonyms), those models describe levels of mastery standards (*rubrics*) for each target outcome. The taxonomies provide the mechanism for ensuring that you do not spend a disproportionate amount of time on facts and other low-level learning and can be of tremendous help where teachers are expected to correlate learning activities to one of the school's or district's outcome standards (see Figure 5.7).

Preparing objectives is essential to the preparation of good items for the assessment of student learning. Clearly communicating your performance expectations to students and then specifically assessing student learning against those expectations makes the teaching most efficient and effective, and it makes the assessment of the learning closer to being authentic. This does not mean to imply that you will always write performance objectives for everything taught, nor will you always be able to accurately measure what students have learned. As said earlier, learning that is meaningful to students is not as easily compartmentalized as the taxonomies of educational objectives would imply.

Observing for Connected (Meaningful) Learning: Logs, Portfolios, and Journals

In learning that is most important and that has the most meaning to students, the domains are inextricably interconnected. Consequently, when assessing for student learning, both during instruc-

Figure 5.7
Sample school district-expected learning outcome standards

Results-driven education helps produce people who are life-long learners, are effective communicators, have high self-esteem, and are:

PROBLEM SOLVERS
- are able to solve problems in their academic and personal lives
- demonstrate higher level analytical thinking skills when they evaluate or make decisions
- are able to set personal and career goals
- can use knowledge, not just display it
- are innovative thinkers

SELF-DIRECTED LEARNERS
- are independent workers
- can read, comprehend, and interact with text
- have self-respect with an accurate view of themselves and their abilities

QUALITY PRODUCERS
- can communicate effectively in a variety of situations (oral, aesthetic/artistic, nonverbal)
- are able to use their knowledge to create intelligent, artistic products that reflect originality
- have high standards

COLLABORATIVE WORKERS
- are able to work interdependently
- show respect for others and their points of view
- have their own values and moral conduct
- have an appreciation of cultural diversity

COMMUNITY CONTRIBUTORS
- have an awareness of civic, individual, national, and international responsibilities
- have an understanding of basic health issues
- have an appreciation of diversity

tion and at the conclusion of the instruction, you must look for those connections.

Ways of looking for connected learning include (a) maintain a teacher's (or team's) log with daily or nearly daily entries about the progress of each student, and (b) have students maintain individual learning journals and portfolios that document students' thinking, work, and learning experiences. Dated and chronologically organized items that students place in their portfolios can include notes and communications, awards, brainstorming records, photos of bulletin board contributions and of charts, posters, displays, and models made by the student, records of peer coaching, visual maps, learning contract, and demonstrations or presentations, mnemonics created by the student, peer evaluations, reading record, other contributions made to the class or to the team, record of service work, and test and grade records. The use of portfolios and student journals is discussed further in Chapter 11.

Learning That Is Not Immediately Observable

Unlike behaviorists, constructivists do not limit the definition of learning to that which is observable behavior, nor should you. Bits and pieces of new information are stored in short-term memory, where the new information is "rehearsed" until ready to be stored in long-term memory. If the information is not rehearsed, it eventually fades from memory entirely. If it is rehearsed and made meaningful through connections with other stored knowledge, then this new knowledge is transferred to and stored in long-term memory, either by changing or adding onto existing schemata or by forming new schemata. Your responsibility as a teacher is to provide learning experiences that will result in the creation of new schemata as well as the modification of existing schemata.

To be an accomplished teacher, the challenge is to use performance-based criteria, but simultaneously with a teaching style that encourages the development of intrinsic sources of student motivation and that allows, provides, and encourages coincidental learning—learning that goes beyond what might be considered predictable, immediately measurable, and representative of minimal expectations.

It has become quite clear to many teachers that to be most effective in helping children to develop meaningful understandings, much of the learning in each discipline can be made more effective and longer lasting when that learning is integrated with the whole curriculum and made meaningful to the lives of the children, rather than when simply taught as an unrelated and separate discipline at the same time each day.

If learning is defined only as being the accumulation of bits and pieces of information, then we already know how that is learned and how to teach it. However, the accumulation of pieces of information is at the lowest end of a spectrum of types of learning. For higher levels of thinking and for learning that is most meaningful and longest lasting, the results of research support using (a) a curriculum where disciplines are integrated (discussed next), and (b) instructional techniques that involve the learners in social interactive learning, such as project-centered learning, cooperative learning, peer tutoring, and cross-age teaching (topics discussed in Chapters 8 and 9).

INTEGRATED CURRICULUM

When learning about *integrated curriculum* (IC), it is easy to be confused by the plethora of terms that are used, such as *integrated studies, thematic instruction, multidisciplinary teaching, integrated curriculum, interdisciplinary curriculum,* and *interdisciplinary thematic instruction.* In essence, regardless of which of these terms is being used, the reference is to the same thing.

Because it is not always easy to tell where the term *curriculum* leaves off and the term *instruction* begins, let's assume for now that, for the sake of better understanding the meaning of *integrated curriculum,* there is no difference between the two terms. In other words, for the intent of this discussion, whether we use the term *integrated curriculum* or the term *integrated instruction,* we will be referring to the same thing.

Definition of Integrated Curriculum

The term **integrated curriculum** (or any of its synonyms mentioned above) refers to both a way of teaching and a way of planning and organizing the instructional program so the discrete disciplines of subject matter are related to one another in a design that (a) matches the developmental needs of the learners and (b) helps to connect their learning in ways that are meaningful to their current and past experiences. In that respect, IC is the antithesis of traditional disparate subject-matter oriented teaching and curriculum designations.

Integrated Curricula: Past and Present

The reason for the various terminology is, in part, because the concept of an integrated curriculum is not new. In fact, it has had a roller-coaster ride throughout most of the history of education in this country. Over time those efforts to integrate student learning have had varying labels.

Without reviewing that history, suffice to say that prior to now, in some form or another, the most recent popularity stems from the 1960s, with some of the discovery-oriented, hands-on, student-centered elementary school projects supported by the National Science Foundation. Two of these, largely defunct now, are *Elementary School Science* (ESS), a science program for grades K–6 and *Man: A Course of Study* (MACOS), a social studies program for fifth graders.

Today's interest in curriculum integration has risen from at least four not entirely unrelated

Figure 5.8
Continuum of curriculum integration

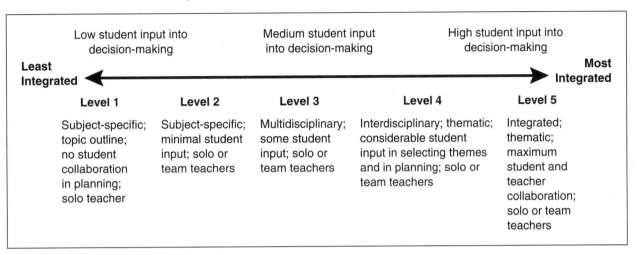

sources: (a) the success at curriculum integration that has been enjoyed by middle level schools since the beginning of the middle school movement in the 1960s, (b) the literature-based, whole-language movement in reading and language arts that began in the 1980s, (c) the diversity of children in the regular classroom coupled with growing acceptance of the philosophy that a certain percentage of school dropouts is not a viable assumption, and (d) recent research in cognitive science and neuroscience demonstrating the necessity of helping learners establish bridges between school and life, knowing and doing, content and context, with a parallel rekindled interest in constructivism as opposed to a strictly behaviorist philosophical approach to teaching and learning.

An integrated curriculum approach may not necessarily be the best approach for every school or the best for all learning for every student, nor is it necessarily the manner by which every teacher should or must always plan and teach. As evidenced by practice, the truth of this statement becomes obvious. And, as you should now be well aware, it is our belief that a teacher's best choice as an approach to instruction—and to classroom management—is one that is eclectic.

The Spectrum of Integrated Curriculum

In attempts to connect students' learning with their experiences, efforts fall at various places on a spectrum or continuum, from the least integrated instruction (level 1) to the most integrated (level 5), as illustrated in Figure 5.8. It is not our intent that this illustration be interpreted as go-ing from "worst case scenario" (far left) to "best case scenario" (far right), although some educators may interpret it in exactly that way. The fact is that there are various interpretations to curriculum integration and each teacher must personally make decisions about the use. Figure 5.8 is meant solely to show how efforts to integrate fall on a continuum of sophistication and complexity. The following is a description of each level of the continuum.

Level 1 Curriculum Integration

Level 1 is the traditional organization of curriculum and classroom instruction, where teachers plan and arrange the subject-specific scope and sequence in the format of topic outlines, much as you did for Exercise 5.5. If there is an attempt to help students connect their experiences and their learning, then it is up to individual classroom teachers to do it. An elementary school student in a school and classroom that has subject-specific instruction at varying times of the day (e.g., reading and language arts at 8:00, mathematics at 9:00, social studies at 10:30, and so on) from one or more teachers is likely learning at a level 1 instructional environment, especially when what is being learned in one subject has little or no connection with content being learned in another. The same applies for a student of the fifth or sixth grade who moves during the school day from classroom to classroom, teacher to teacher, subject to subject, and from one topic to another. A topic in science, for example, might be "earthquakes." A related topic in social studies might be "the social consequences of natural disasters." These two topics may or may not be studied by a student at the same time.

Level 2 Curriculum Integration

If the same students are learning language arts, history, mathematics, or science using a thematic approach rather than a topic outline, then they are learning at level 2. At this level, themes for one discipline are not necessarily planned and coordinated to correspond or integrate with themes of another or to be taught simultaneously. At level 2, the students may have some input into the decision-making involved in planning themes and content from various disciplines. Before going further in our presentation of the levels of curriculum integration, let's stop and consider what is a topic and what is a theme.

Integrated Thematic Unit: Topic versus Theme. The difference between what is a topic and what is a theme is not always distinct. But, for example, whereas "earthquakes" and "social consequences of natural disasters" are topics, "a survival guide to local natural disasters" could be the theme or umbrella under which these two topics could fall. In addition, themes are likely to be problem-based statements or questions, to result in a product, and are longer in duration than are topics. A *theme is the point, the message, or the idea that underlies a study.* When compared to a topic, a theme is more dynamic; the theme explains the significance of the study—it communicates to the student what the experience means. Although organized around one theme, many topics make up an ITU. Often the theme of a study becomes clearer to students when an overall guiding question is presented and discussed, such as "What could we do to improve our living environment?" or "What happens in our community after natural disasters?"[25]

Some educators say that the integrated curriculum of the 21st century will be based on broad, unchanging, and unifying concepts (that is, on conceptual themes).[26] If so, it would be a recycling of an approach of the 1960s, as supported by the writings of Jerome Bruner[27] and implemented in some of the National Science Foundation–sponsored curriculum projects of that era. In fact, there is already action in that direction. For example, forming the basis for the national curriculum standards (discussed earlier in this chapter) for social studies are 10 "thematic strands," including "people, places, and environments," and "power, authority, and governance." And, the national standards for science education are centered on unifying conceptual schemes, such as "systems, order, and organization," and "form and function."

Level 3 Curriculum Integration

When the same students are learning two or more of their core subjects (English/language arts, so-cial studies/history, mathematics, and science) around a common theme, such as the theme "natural disasters," from one or more teachers, they are then learning at level 3 integration. At this level, teachers agree on a common theme, then they *separately* deal with that theme in their individual subject areas, usually at the same time during the school year. So what the student is learning from a teacher in one class is related to and coordinated with what the student is concurrently learning in another or several others. At level 3, students may have some input into the decision-making involved in selecting and planning themes and content. Some authors may refer to levels 2 or 3 as *coordinated* or *parallel curriculum.*

Level 4 Curriculum Integration

When teachers and students collaborate on a common theme and its content and when discipline boundaries begin to disappear as teachers teach about this common theme, either solo or as an *interdisciplinary teaching team,* level 4 integration is achieved.

Level 5 Curriculum Integration

When teachers and their students have collaborated on a common theme and its content, discipline boundaries are truly blurred during instruction, and teachers of several grade levels and of various subjects teach toward student understanding of aspects of the common theme, then this is level 5, an *integrated thematic approach.*

Guidelines for integrating topics and for planning and developing an interdisciplinary thematic unit are presented in Chapter 6.

PLANNING FOR INSTRUCTION: A THREE-LEVEL AND SEVEN-STEP PROCESS

Earlier we noted that complete planning for instruction occurs at three levels: the year, the units, and the lessons. There are seven steps in the process.

1. *Course, grade level, and school goals.* Consider and understand your curriculum goals and their relationship to the mission and goals of the school. Your course is not isolated on Saturn but is an integral part of the total school curriculum organizational components described earlier in this chapter.
2. *Expectations.* Consider topics and skills that you are expected to teach, such as those found in the course of study.
3. *Academic year or semester plan.* Think about the goals you want the students to reach months

from now. Working from your tentative topic outline (Exercise 5.5) and with the school calendar in hand, you will begin by deciding the amount of time (e.g., the number of days) to be devoted to each topic (or unit), penciling those times onto the outline. (Unless you are doing your planning at a computer, you may wish to use pencil because the times are likely to be modified often.)

4. *Course schedule.* This schedule becomes a part of the information that is presented to students at the beginning of the school year and to parents and guardians at back-to-school night (see Chapter 11). However, the schedule *must* remain flexible to allow for the unexpected, such as the cancellation or interruption of a class meeting, or an extended study of a particular topic.

5. *Plans for each class meeting.* Working from the calendar plan or the course schedule, you are ready to prepare plans for each class meeting, keeping in mind the abilities and interests of your students while making decisions about appropriate strategies and learning experiences. The preparation of daily plans takes considerable time and continues throughout the year as you arrange and prepare instructional notes, demonstrations, discussion topics and questions, and classroom exercises, arrange for guest speakers, audiovisual materials and media equipment, field trips, and tools for the assessment of student learning. Because the content of each class meeting is often determined by the accomplishments of and your reflections upon the preceding one, your lessons are never "set in concrete" but need continual revisiting and assessment by you.

6. *Instructional objectives.* Once you have the finalized schedule, and as you prepare the daily plans, you will complete your preparation of the instructional objectives (begun in Exercise 5.11). Those objectives are critical for proper development of the next and final step.

7. *Assessment.* The final step is that of deciding how to assess for student achievement. Included in this component are your decisions about how you will accomplish diagnostic or preassessment (that is the assessment of what students know or think they know at the start of a new unit of study or a new topic), formative assessment (the ongoing assessment during a unit of study, that is, what the students are learning) and summative assessment (the assessment of learning at the conclusion of a unit of study, that is, what the students learned). Also included in the assessment component are your decisions about assignments (discussed in

Chapter 8) and the grading procedures (discussed in Chapter 11).

In Chapter 6, you will proceed through these seven steps as you develop your first instructional plan.

SUMMARY

In your comparison and analysis of curriculum documents and teachers' editions of student textbooks, you probably discovered that some are accompanied by sequentially designed resource units from which the teacher can select and build specific teaching units. While a resource unit is not likely to contain unit and lesson plans, it usually will contain an extensive list of objectives, a large number and variety of activities, suggested materials and their sources, and extensive bibliographies for teacher and students.

As you may have also found, some courses of study contain actual teaching units that have been prepared by teachers of the school district. Beginning teachers and student teachers often ask, "How closely must I follow the school's curriculum guide or course of study?" To obtain an answer, you must talk with teachers and administrators of the school before you begin teaching.

In conclusion, your final decisions about what content to teach are guided by (a) discussions with other teachers, (b) review of state curriculum documents, local curriculum documents, and articles in professional journals, (c) your personal convictions, knowledge, and skills, and (d) the unique characteristics of your students.

In this chapter you learned of the differences among the terms *aims, goals,* and *objectives.* Regardless of how these terms are defined, the important point is this: *Teachers must be clear about what it is they want their students to learn, must be clear about the kind of evidence needed to verify their learning, and must communicate those things to the students so they are clearly understood.*

Many teachers do not bother to write specific objectives for all the learning activities in their teaching plans. However, when teachers do prepare specific objectives (by writing them themselves or by borrowing them from textbooks and other curriculum documents), teach toward them, and assess students' progress against them, student learning is enhanced; this is called *performance-based teaching* and *criterion-referenced measurement.* It is also known as an *aligned curriculum.* In schools using results-driven education mastery learning models, those models describe levels of mastery standards or rubrics for each outcome or learning target. The taxonomies are of tremendous help in schools where teachers are expected to correlate learning activities to the school's outcome standards.

As a teacher, you will be expected to (a) plan your lessons well, (b) convey specific expectations to your students, and (c) assess their learning against that specificity. However, because it tends toward high objectivity, there is the danger that such performance-based teaching could become too objective, which can have negative consequences. If students are treated as objects, then the relationship between teacher and student becomes impersonal and counterproductive to real learning. Highly specific and impersonal teaching can be discouraging to serendipity, creativity, and the excitement of discovery, to say nothing of its possibly negative impact on the development of students' self-esteem.

Performance-based instruction works well when teaching toward mastery of basic skills, but the concept of mastery learning is inclined to imply that there is some foreseeable end to learning, an assumption that is obviously erroneous. With performance-based instruction, the source of student motivation tends to be extrinsic. Teacher expectations, marks and grades, society, and peer pressures are examples of extrinsic sources that drive student performance. To be a most effective teacher, your challenge is to use performance-based criteria together with a teaching style that encourages the development of intrinsic sources of student motivation and that allows for, provides for, and encourages coincidental learning—learning that goes beyond what might be considered as predictable, immediately measurable, and representative of minimal expectations. With a knowledge of the content of the school curriculum and the value of instructional objectives, you are now ready to prepare detailed instructional plans with sequenced lessons, the subject of the next chapter.

EXTENDING MY COMPETENCY: QUESTIONS FOR CLASS DISCUSSION

1. Can critical-thinking skills be taught while teaching mathematics? science? language arts? social studies? visual and performing arts? Explain. Pretend you are being interviewed for your first teaching job. If during a job interview the interviewer asks you to describe observable behaviors that would enable you to tell whether a child is learning to think critically, what would you tell the interviewer?

2. It is sometimes said that teaching less is better. Explain the meaning and significance of that statement. Explain why you agree or disagree with the concept.

3. Recall your own schooling. What do you really remember? Most likely you remember projects, your presentations, the lengthy research you did, and your extra effort doing artwork to accompany your presentation. Maybe you remember a compliment by a teacher or a pat on the back by peers. Most likely you do *not* remember the massive amount of factual content that was covered. Discuss this and your feelings about it with your classmates.

4. Pretend you were being interviewed for your first teaching job and were asked to describe the concept of *integrated curriculum*. What would you tell the interviewer?

5. Pretend you were being interviewed for your first teaching job and were asked to describe the concept of *outcomes-based education*. What would you tell the interviewer?

6. Some people say that it is easier to write instructional objectives after a lesson has been taught. Explain the meaning of that notion.

7. Should a teacher encourage serendipitous (coincidental) learning? If no, why not? If so, describe ways that a teacher can do it.

8. Some people believe—and some fear—that the national curriculum standards are a first step toward national assessment of student learning? Explain how you feel about this.

9. From your current observations and fieldwork as related to this teacher preparation program, clearly identify one specific example of educational practice that seems contradictory to exemplary practice or theory as presented in this chapter. Present your explanation for the discrepancy.

10. Do you have questions generated by the content of this chapter? If you do, list them along with ways answers might be found.

FOR FURTHER READING

Barton, K. C. and Smith, L. A. "Themes or Motifs? Aiming for Coherence Through Interdisciplinary Outlines." *The Reading Teacher* 54(1): 54–63 (September 2000).

Battista, M. T. (1999). The Mathematical Miseducation of America's Youth. *Phi Delta Kappan, 80*(6), 425–433.

Burns, P. C., and Roe, B. D. (1999). *Informal Reading Inventory: Preprimer to Twelfth Grade,* 5th ed. Wilmington, MA: Houghton Mifflin.

Chaney, A. L., and Burk, T. L. (1998). *Teaching Oral Communication in Grades K–8.* Boston: Allyn & Bacon.

Churma, M. (1999). *A Guide to Integrating Technology Standards Into the Curriculum.* Upper Saddle River, NJ: Merrill/Prentice Hall.

Cornett, C. E. (1999). *The Arts as Meaning Makers: Integrating Literature and the Arts Throughout the Curriculum.* Upper Saddle River, NJ: Merrill/Prentice Hall.

Cossey, R. (1999). Are California's Math Standards Up to the Challenge? *Phi Delta Kappan, 80*(6), 441–443.

Davidson, M., and Myhre, O. (2000). Measuring Reading at Grade Level. *Educational Leadership, 57*(5), 25–28.

Davison, D. M., Miller, K. W., and Metheny, D. L. (1999). *Integrating Science and Mathematics in the Elementary Curriculum,* Fastback 444. Bloomington, IN: Phi Delta Kappa Educational Foundation.

Decker, K. A. (1999). Meeting State Standards Through Integration. *Science and Children, 36*(6), 28–32, 69.

Duffy, G. G., and Hoffman, J. V. (1999). In Pursuit of an Illusion: The Flawed Search for a Perfect Method. *The Reading Teacher, 53*(1), 10–16.

Duffy-Hester, A. M. (1999). Teaching Struggling Readers in Elementary School Classrooms: A Review of Classroom Reading Programs and Principles of Instruction. *The Reading Teacher, 52*(5), 480–495.

Good, T. L., and Brophy, J. E. (2000). *Looking in Classrooms,* 8th ed., Chap. 10. New York: Addison Wesley Longman.

Jensen, E. (1998). *Teaching With the Brain in Mind.* Alexandria, VA: Association for Supervision and Curriculum Development.

Lambert, L. T. (2000). The New Physical Education. *Educational Leadership, 57*(6), 34–38.

Lerner, L. S. (1998). *State Science Standards: An Appraisal of Science Standards in 36 States.* Washington, DC: Thomas B. Fordham Foundation.

Linn, R. L., and Gronlund, N. E. (2000). *Measurement and Assessment in Teaching,* 8th ed., Chap. 3. Upper Saddle River, NJ: Merrill/Prentice Hall.

Martin, B. L., and Briggs, L. J. (1986). *The Affective and Cognitive Domains.* Englewood Cliffs, NJ: Educational Technology Publications.

National Heart Savers Association. (1999). *Health and Nutrition Curriculum. Informative and Fun for K–8!* Omaha, NE: Author.

Nuthall, G. (1999). The Way Students Learn: Acquiring Knowledge From an Integrated Science and Social Studies Unit. *Elementary School Journal, 99*(4), 303–341.

Ohanian, S. (1999). *One Size Fits Few: The Folly of Educational Standards.* Portsmouth, NH: Heinemann.

Ohanian, S. (2000). Goals 2000: What's in a Name? *Phi Delta Kappan, 81*(5), 344–355.

O'Neill, J. (2000). SMART Goals, SMART Schools. *Educational Leadership, 57*(5), 46–50.

Piazza, C. L. (1999). *Multiple Forms of Literacy: Teaching Literacy and the Arts.* Upper Saddle River, NJ: Prentice Hall.

Rubin, D. (2000). *Teaching Elementary Language Arts: A Balanced Approach,* 6th ed. Needham Heights, MA: Allyn & Bacon.

Saxe, D. W. (1998). *State History Standards: An Appraisal of History Standards in 37 States and the District of Columbia.* Washington, DC: Thomas B. Fordham Foundation.

Schmoker, M., and Marzano, R. J. (1999). Realizing the Promise of Standards-Based Education. *Educational Leadership, 56*(6), 17–21.

Stephens, E. C., and Brown, J. E. (2000). *A Handbook of Content Literacy Strategies: 75 Practical Reading and Writing Ideas.* Norwood, MA: Christopher-Gordon.

Tchudi, S., and Mitchell, D. (1999). *Exploring and Teaching the English Language Arts,* 4th ed. New York: Addison Wesley Longman.

Tomlinson, C. A. (1999). *The Differentiated Classroom,* Chap. 5. Alexandria, VA: Association for Supervision and Curriculum Development.

Victor, E., and Kellough, R. D. (2000). *Science for the Elementary and Middle School,* 9th ed. Upper Saddle River, NJ: Merrill/Prentice Hall.

Wiggins, G., and McTighe, J. (1998). *Understanding by Design.* Alexandria, VA: Association for Supervision and Curriculum Development.

Worthy, J., Moorman, M., and Turner, M. (1999). What Johnny Likes to Read Is Hard to Find in School. *Reading Research Quarterly, 34*(1), 12–27.

NOTES

1. B. Watson and R. Konicek, Teaching for Conceptual Change: Confronting Childrens' Experience, *Phi Delta Kappan, 71*(9), 680–685 (May 1990).

2. Contact ACTFL, Six Executive Plaza, Yonkers, NY 10701-6801.

3. Contact National Geographic Society, P.O. Box 1640, Washington, DC 20013-1640.

4. Contact the American Alliance for Health, Physical Education, Recreation and Dance (AAHPRD), 1900 Association Drive, Reston, VA 22091.

5. Bureau of Indian Affairs, 1849 C St, NW, Washington, DC 20240-0001. 202-208-3710; <http://www.doi.gov/bureau-indian-affairs.html>.

6. At least 24 states use statewide textbook adoption committees to review books and to then provide local districts with lists of recommended titles from which to choose.

7. See Edward Fry, A Readability Formula That Saves Time, *Journal of Reading, 11,* 587 (April 1968).

8. See Novella M. Ross, Assessing Readability of Instructional Materials, *VocEd, 54,* 10–11 (February 1979).

9. See J. Bormuth, The Cloze Readability Procedure, *Elementary English, 45,* 429–436 (April 1968).

10. See N. McKenna, Synonymic Versus Verbatim Scoring of the Cloze Procedure, *Journal of Reading, 20,* 141–143 (November 1976).

11. See M. S. Johnson and R. A. Kress, *Informal Reading Inventories* (Newark, DE: International Reading Association, 1965), and P. C. Burns and B. D. Roe, *Informal Reading Inventory: Preprimer to*

Twelfth Grade, 5th ed. (Wilmington, MA: Houghton Mifflin, 1999).

12. Source of KWL: D. M. Ogle, K-W-L: A Teaching Model That Develops Active Reading of Expository Text, *Reading Teacher, 39*(6), 564–570 (February 1986). Source of PQRST: E. B. Kelly, *Memory Enhancement for Educators,* Fastback 365 (Bloomington, IN: Phi Delta Kappa Educational Foundation, 1994), p. 18. Source of SQ3R: F. P. Robinson, *Effective Study,* rev. ed. (New York: Harper & Brothers, 1961). The original source of SQ4R is unknown. For SRQ2R, see M. L. Walker, Help for the 'Fourth-Grade Slum'—SRQ2R Plus Instruction in Text Structure or Main Idea, *Reading Horizons, 36*(1), 38–58 (1995). Source of KWLQ: P. R. Schmidt, KWLQ: Inquiry and Literacy Learning in Science, *Reading Teacher, 52*(7), 789–792 (April 1999). About reciprocal teaching, see M. M. Dermody and R. B. Speaker, Jr., Reciprocal Strategy Training in Prediction, Clarification, Question Generating and Summarization to Improve Reading Comprehension, *Reading Improvement, 36*(1), 16–23 (Spring 1999), and K. M. King and L. M. Parent Johnson, Constructing Meaning Via Reciprocal Teaching, *Reading Research and Instruction, 38*(3), 169–186 (Spring 1999).

13. A. November, *The Web—Teaching Zack to Think,* [Online] available <http://www.anovember.com/articles/zack.html>, June 25, 2000.

14. R. Reinhold, Class Struggle, *The New York Times Magazine,* September 29, 1991, p. 46.

15. See, for example, B. A. VanSledright and C. Kelly, Reading American History: The Influence of Multiple Sources on Six Fifth Graders, *Elementary School Journal, 98*(3), 239–265 (January 1998), and D. Camp, It Takes Two: Teaching With Twin Texts of Fact and Fiction, *The Reading Teacher, 53*(5), 400–408 (February 2000).

16. See, for example, H. M. Miller, Teaching and Learning About Cultural Diversity: All of Us Together Have a Story to Tell, *The Reading Teacher, 53*(8), 666–667 (May 2000).

17. See, for example, J. C. Baker and F. G. Martin, *A Neural Network Guide to Teaching,* Fastback 431 (Bloomington, IN: Phi Delta Kappa Educational Foundation, 1998), and T. L. Good and J. E. Brophy, *Looking in Classrooms,* 8th ed. (New York: Addison Wesley Longman, 2000), pp. 252–253.

18. See, for example, the articles in The Constructivist Classroom, the November 1999 (Volume 57, Number 3) theme issue of *Educational Leadership;* D. R. Geelan, Epistemological Anarchy and the Many Forms of Constructivism, *Science and Education, 6*(1–2), 15–28 (January 1997); and R. DeLay, Forming Knowledge: Constructivist Learning and Experiential Education, *Journal of Experiential Education, 19*(2), 76–81 (August/September 1996).

19. B. S. Bloom, (Ed.) *Taxonomy of Educational Objectives, Book 1, Cognitive Domain* (White Plains, NY: Longman, 1984).

20. See R. M. Gagné, L. J. Briggs, and W. W. Wager, *Principles of Instructional Design,* 4th ed. (New York: Holt, Rinehart and Winston, 1994).

21. Compare Bloom's higher-order cognitive thinking skills with R. H. Ennis's, A Taxonomy of Critical Thinking Dispositions and Abilities, and Qellmalz's Developing Reasoning Skills, both in J. B. Barron and R. J. Sternberg (Eds.), *Teaching Thinking Skills: Theory and Practice* (New York: W. H. Freeman, 1987), and with Marzano's "complex thinking strategies" in R. J. Marzano, *A Different Kind of Classroom: Teaching With Dimensions of Learning* (Alexandria, VA: Association for Supervision and Curriculum Development, 1992).

22. D. R. Krathwohl, B. S. Bloom, and B. B. Masia, *Taxonomy of Educational Goals, Book 2, Affective Domain* (New York: Longman, 1984).

23. A. J. Harrow, *Taxonomy of the Psychomotor Domain* (New York: Longman, 1977). A similar taxonomy for the psychomotor domain is that of E. J. Simpson, *The Classification of Educational Objectives in the Psychomotor Domain. The Psychomotor Domain: Volume 3* (Washington, DC: Gryphon House, 1972).

24. R. N. Caine and G. Caine, *Education on the Edge of Possibility* (Alexandria, VA: Association for Supervision and Curriculum Development, 1997), pp. 104–105.

25. For further delineation between topics and themes in integrated curriculum, see T. Shanahan, et al. (Eds.), Avoiding Some of the Pitfalls of Thematic Units, *The Reading Teacher, 48*(8), 718–719 (May 1995).

26. See, for example, E-M Lolli, Creating a Concept-Based Curriculum, *Principal, 76*(1), 26–27 (September 1996), T. L. Riley, Tools for Discovery: Conceptual Themes in the Classroom, *Gifted Child Today Magazine, 20*(1), 30–33, 50 (January/February 1997), and C. A. Tomlinson, For Integration and Differentiation Choose Concepts over Topics, *Middle School Journal, 30*(2), 3–8 (November 1998).

27. J. S. Bruner, *Process of Education* (Cambridge, MA: Harvard University Press, 1960).

6

How Do I Prepare an Instructional Plan and Daily Lessons?

The teacher's edition of the adopted curriculum program or student textbook and other resource materials may expedite your planning but should not substitute for it. As was emphasized in Chapter 5, you must know how to create a good instructional plan. In this chapter you will learn how it is done.

CHAPTER OBJECTIVES

Specifically, upon completion of this chapter you should be able to

1. Complete a unit of instruction with sequential lesson plans.

2. Demonstrate an understanding of the differences between direct and indirect instruction and the advantages and limitations of each.
3. Demonstrate understanding of self-reflection as a common thread important to the reciprocal process of teaching and learning.
4. Demonstrate understanding of the place and role of each of the four decision-making and thought-processing phases of instruction in unit planning and implementation.
5. Demonstrate understanding of the significance of the planned unit of instruction and the concept of planning curriculum and instruction as an organic process.
6. Describe the similarities and differences among the *standard unit,* the *thematic unit,* and the *interdisciplinary thematic unit.*
7. For a specified grade level, give examples of learning experiences from each of these categories, when and why you would use each one, and examples of how, why, and when they could be combined: verbal, visual, vicarious, simulated, and direct.

THE INSTRUCTIONAL UNIT

The instructional unit is a major subdivision of a course of study (for one course or a self-contained classroom there are several to many units of instruction) and is comprised of learning activities that are planned around a central theme, topic, issue, or problem. Organizing the content of the semester or year into units makes the teaching process more manageable than when no plan or only random choices are made by a teacher.

The instructional unit is not unlike a chapter in a book, an act or scene in a play, or a phase of work when undertaking a project such as building a house. Breaking down information or actions into component parts and then grouping the related parts makes sense out of learning and doing. The unit brings a sense of cohesiveness and structure to student learning and avoids the piecemeal approach that might otherwise unfold. You can learn to articulate lessons within, between, and among unit plans and focus on important elements while not ignoring tangential information of importance. Students remember "chunks" of information, especially when those chunks are related to specific units.

While the steps for developing any type of instructional unit are basically the same, units can be organized in a number of ways. For the purposes of this resource guide, we consider two basic types of units—the standard unit and the integrated thematic unit.

A *standard unit* (known also as a *conventional* or *traditional unit*) consists of a series of lessons centered on a topic, theme, major concept, or block of subject matter. Each lesson builds on the previous lesson by contributing additional subject matter, providing further illustrations, and supplying more practice or other added instruction, all of which are aimed at bringing about mastery of the knowledge and skills on which the unit is centered.

When a standard unit is centered on a central theme (theme versus topic was discussed at the end of Chapter 5), the unit may be referred to as a **thematic unit.** When, by design, the thematic unit integrates disciplines, such as combining the learning of science and mathematics, or combining social studies and English/language arts, or combining all four core (or any other) disciplines, then it is called an *integrated* (or *interdisciplinary*) *thematic unit (ITU),* or simply, an integrated unit.

Planning and Developing Any Unit of Instruction

Whether for a standard unit or an integrated thematic unit, steps in planning and developing the unit are the same and are described in the following paragraphs.

1. *Select a suitable theme, topic, issue, or problem.* These may be already laid out in your course of study or textbook or already have been agreed to by members of the teaching team. Many schools change their themes or add new ones from year to year.
2. *Select the goals of the unit and prepare the overview.* The goals are written as an overview or rationale, covering what the unit is about and what the students are to learn. In selecting the goals, you should (a) become as familiar as possible with the topic and materials used, (b) consult curriculum documents, such as courses of study, state and local frameworks and standards, and resource units for ideas, (c) decide the content and procedures (i.e., what the students should learn about the topic and how), (d) write the rationale or overview, where you summarize what you expect the students will learn about the topic, and (e) be sure your goals are congruent with those of the course or grade level program.
3. *Select suitable instructional objectives.* In doing this, you should (a) include understandings, skills, attitudes, and appreciations, (b) be specific, avoiding vagueness and generalizations, (c) write the objectives in performance terms, and (d) be as certain as possible that the objec-

tives will contribute to the major learning and target goals as presented in the overview.

4. *Detail the instructional procedures.* These procedures include the subject content and the learning activities, established as a series of lessons. Proceed with the following steps in your initial planning of the instructional procedures.

   a. By referring to curriculum documents, resource units, sources on the Internet (see, for example, Figure 1.7 in Chapter 1 and Figure 8.7 in Chapter 8), and colleagues as resources, gather ideas for learning activities that might be suitable for the unit.

   b. Check the learning activities to make sure that they will actually contribute to the learning designated in your objectives, discarding ideas that do not.

   c. Make sure that the learning activities are feasible and varied. Can you afford the time, effort, or expense? Do you have the necessary materials and equipment? If not, can they be obtained? Are the activities suited to the intellectual and maturity levels of your students? As you select activities keep in mind the needs of individual students, such as children with disabilities or who have limited English proficiency.

   d. Check resources available to be certain that they support the content and learning activities.

   e. Decide how best to introduce the unit. Provide *introductory activities* that will: arouse student interest; inform students of what the unit is about; help you learn about your students—their interests, their abilities, and their experiences and present knowledge of the topic; provide transitions that bridge this topic with what students have already learned; and that will involve the students in the planning.

   f. Plan *developmental activities* that will sustain student interest, provide for individual student differences, promote the learning as cited in the specific objectives, and promote a project.

   g. Plan *culminating activities* that will summarize what has been learned, bring together loose ends, apply what has been learned to new situations, provide all students with opportunity to demonstrate their learning, and provide transfer to the unit that follows.

5. *Plan for preassessment and assessment of student learning.* Preassess what students already know or think they know. Assessment of student progress in achievement of the learning objectives (formative evaluation) should permeate the entire unit (that is, as often as possible, assessment should be a daily component of lessons). Plan to gather information in several ways, including informal observations, checklist observations of student performance and their portfolios, and paper and pencil tests. As discussed in Chapters 5 and 11, to be meaningful, assessment must be congruent with the instructional objectives.

6. *Provide for the materials and tools of instruction.* The unit cannot function without materials. Therefore, you must plan long before the unit begins for media equipment and materials, references, reading materials, reproduced materials, and community resources. Librarians and media center personnel are usually quite willing to assist in finding appropriate materials to support a unit of instruction.

Unit Format, Inclusive Elements, and Time Duration

Follow those six steps to develop any type of unit. In addition, two general points should be made. First, while there is no single best format for a teaching unit, there are minimum inclusions. Particular formats may be best for specific disciplines or grade levels, topics, and types of activities. During your student teaching, your college or university program for teacher preparation and/or your cooperating teacher(s) may have a format that you will be expected to follow. Regardless of the format, the following seven elements should be evident in any unit plan: (a) identification of grade level, subject, topic, and time duration of the unit; (b) statement of rationale and general goals for the unit; (c) major objectives of unit; (d) materials and resources needed; (e) lesson plans; (f) assessment strategies; and (g) a statement of how the unit will attend to variations in students' reading levels, experiential backgrounds, and special needs.

Second, there is no set time duration for a unit plan, although for specific units curriculum guides will recommend certain time spans. Units may extend for a minimum of several days or, as in the case of some interdisciplinary thematic units, for several weeks to an entire school year. However, be aware that when standard units last more than 2 or 3 weeks they tend to lose the character of clearly identifiable units. For any unit of instruction, the exact time duration will be dictated by several factors, including the topic, problem, or theme, the age, interests, and maturity of the students, and the scope of the learning activities.

THEORETICAL CONSIDERATIONS FOR THE SELECTION OF INSTRUCTIONAL STRATEGIES

As you prepare to detail your instructional plan you will be narrowing in on selecting and planning the instructional activities. In Chapter 2 you learned about how children differ in learning styles and learning capacities and of the importance of varying the instructional strategies and of using multilevel instruction. In Chapter 3, you learned about specific teacher behaviors that must be in place for students to learn—structuring the learning environment; accepting and sharing instructional accountability; demonstrating withitness and overlapping; providing a variety of motivating and challenging activities; modeling appropriate behaviors; facilitating students' acquisition of data; creating a psychologically safe environment; clarifying whenever necessary; using periods of silence; and questioning thoughtfully. In the paragraphs that follow, you will learn more not only about how to implement some of those fundamental behaviors, but also about the large repertoire of other strategies, aids, media, and resources available to you (see Figure 6.1). You will learn how to select and implement from this repertoire.

Decision Making and Strategy Selection

You must make a myriad of decisions to select and implement a particular teaching strategy effectively. The selection of a strategy depends in part upon your decision whether to deliver information directly (direct, expository, or didactic teaching) or to provide students with access to information (in-

direct, or facilitative, teaching). Direct teaching tends to be teacher-centered, while indirect teaching is more student-centered. To assist in your selection of strategies it is important that you understand basic principles of learning summarized starting on page 191.

Direct and Indirect Instruction: A Clarification of Terms

You are probably well aware that professional education is rampant with its own special jargon, which can be confusing to the neophyte. Indeed, rest assured, it can even be abashing to those of us who are well-seasoned. The use of the term **direct teaching** (or its synonym, *direct instruction*), and its antonym, **direct experiences,** are examples of how confusing the jargon can be. The term *direct teaching* (or *direct instruction, expository teaching, or teacher-centered instruction*) can also have a variety of definitions, depending on who is doing the defining. [*Note:* In addition to the generic term *direct instruction,* there is the Direct Instruction Model that has evolved from an original curriculum program for beginning reading, language arts, and mathematics, developed in 1968 and published by Science Research Associates (SRA) under the name DISTAR (Direct Instruction System for Teaching and Remediation). The program for grades K–6 is comprised of highly scripted lessons that are designed around a very specific knowledge base and a well-defined set of skills.[1]] For now, you should keep this distinction in mind—do not confuse the term *direct instruction* with the term *direct experience.* The two terms indicate two separate (though not incompatible) instructional modes. The dichotomy of

Figure 6.1
A list of instructional strategies

Assignment	Group work	Panel discussion
Autotutorial	Guest speaker	Problem solving
Brainstorming	Homework	Project
Coaching	Individualized instruction	Questioning
Collaborative learning	Inquiry	Review and practice
Cooperative learning	Interactive media	Role-play
Debate	Journal writing	Self-instructional module
Demonstration	Laboratory investigation	Script writing
Diorama	Laser videodisk or compact disc	Simulation
Discovery	Learning center	Study Guide
Drama	Lecture	Symposium
Drill	Library/resource center	Telecommunication
Expository	Metacognition	Term paper
Field trip	Mock up	Textbook
Game	Multimedia	Think-pair-share

Figure 6.2
Pedagogical opposites

Delivery mode of instruction	versus	Access mode of instruction
Didactic instruction	versus	Facilitative teaching
Direct instruction	versus	Indirect instruction
Direct teaching	versus	Direct experiencing
Expository teaching	versus	Discovery learning
Teacher-centered instruction	versus	Student-centered instruction

pedagogical opposites shown in Figure 6.2 provides a useful visual distinction of the opposites. While terms in one column are similar if not synonymous, they are near or exact opposites (antonyms) of those across in the other column.

Degrees of Directness

Rather than thinking and behaving in terms of opposites as may be suggested by Figure 6.2, more likely "degrees of directness," or "degrees of indirectness" will characterize your teaching. For example, for a unit of instruction, the teacher may give directions for a culminating project in a direct or expository minilesson, followed then by a student-designed inquiry that leads to the final project.

Rather than focus your attention on the selection of a particular model of teaching, we emphasize the importance of an eclectic model—selecting the best from various models or approaches. As indicated by the example of the preceding paragraph, there will be times when you want to use a direct, teacher-centered, approach, perhaps by a minilecture or a demonstration, or both. And then there will be many more times when you will want to use an indirect, student-centered or social-interactive, approach, such as the use of cooperative learning and investigative projects. And perhaps there will be even more times when you will be doing both at the same time, for example, working with a teacher-centered approach with one small group of students, perhaps giving them direct instruction, while another group or several groups of children, in various areas of the classroom, are working on their project studies (a student-centered approach) or at learning stations. The information that follows and specific descriptions that follow in Part III will help you make decisions about when each approach is most appropriate and will provide guidelines for their use.

Principles of Classroom Instruction and Learning: A Synopsis

A child does not learn to write by learning to recognize grammatical constructions of sentences. Neither does a person learn to play soccer solely by listening to a lecture on soccer. Learning is superficial unless the instructional methods and learning activities are developmentally and intellectually appropriate—that is, unless they are (a) developmentally appropriate for the learners and (b) intellectually appropriate for the understanding, skills, and attitudes desired. Memorizing, for instance, is not the same as understanding. Yet far too often, memorization seems all that is expected of students in many classrooms. The result is low-level learning, a mere verbalism or mouthing of poorly understood words and sentences. That is not intellectually appropriate and it is not teaching, but just the orchestration of short-term memory exercises. An old-fashioned mental model of learning that assumes that a human brain is capable of doing only one thing at a time is invidiously erroneous.

When selecting the mode of instruction, bear in mind the following seven basic principles of classroom instruction and learning.

1. Although children differ in their styles of learning and in their learning capacities, all can learn.
2. To a great degree, it is the mode of instruction that determines what is learned and how well it is learned.
3. Children must be actively involved in their own learning and in the assessment of their learning.
4. You must hold high expectations for the learning of each student (but not necessarily identical expectations for every child) and not waiver from those expectations.
5. Children need constant, understandable, positive, and reliable feedback about their learning.
6. Students should be engaged in both independent study and cooperative learning and give and receive tutorial instruction.
7. No matter what else you are prepared to teach, you are primarily a teacher of literacy and of thinking, social, and learning skills.

Procedural and Conceptual Knowledge

Whereas procedural knowledge entails the recording in memory of the meanings of symbols and rules and procedures needed to accomplish tasks, conceptual knowledge refers to the understanding of relationships. Unless it is connected in meaningful ways for the formation of conceptual knowledge, the accumulation of memorized procedural knowledge is fragmented and ill-fated and will be maintained in the brain for only a brief time.

To help students establish conceptual knowledge, the learning for them must be meaningful. To help make learning meaningful for your students, you should use direct and real experiences as often as practical and possible. Vicarious experiences are sometimes necessary to provide students with otherwise unattainable knowledge; however, direct experiences that engage all the student's senses and all their learning modalities are more powerful. Students learn to write by writing and by receiving coaching and feedback about their progress in writing. They learn to play soccer by experiencing playing soccer and by receiving coaching and feedback about their developing skills and knowledge in playing the game. They learn these things best when they are actively (hands-on) and mentally (minds-on) engaged in doing them. This is real learning, learning that is meaningful; it is *authentic learning*.

Direct versus Indirect Instructional Modes: Strengths and Weaknesses of Each

Selecting an instructional strategy entails two distinct choices (modes) from which you must make a decision: Should you deliver information to students directly or should you provide students with access to information? (Refer to the comparison of pedagogical opposites in Figure 6.2.)

The *delivery mode* (known also as the *didactic, expository,* or *traditional style*) is to deliver information. Knowledge is passed on from those who know (the teachers, with the aid of textbooks or other media) to those who do not (the students). Within the delivery mode, traditional and time-honored strategies are textbook reading, the lecture, questioning, and teacher-centered or teacher-planned discussions.

With the *access mode,* instead of direct delivery of information and direct control over what is learned, the teacher provides students with access to information by working *with* the students. In collaboration with the students, experiences are designed that facilitate their building of their existing schemata and their obtaining new knowledge and skills. Within the access mode, important instructional strategies include cooperative learning, inquiry, and student-centered project-based learning, each of which most certainly will use questioning, though the questions more often will come from the students than from you or the textbook or some other source extrinsic to the student. Discussions and lectures on particular topics also may be involved. But when used in the access mode, discussions and lectures occur during or after (rather than before) direct, hands-on learning by the students. In other words, rather than preceding student inquiry, discussions and lectures *result from* student inquiry, and then may be followed by further student investigation.

You are probably more experienced with the delivery mode. To be most effective as a classroom teacher, however, you must become knowledgeable and skillful in using access strategies. For young learners, strategies within the access mode clearly facilitate their positive learning and acquisition of conceptual knowledge and help build their self-esteem.

You should appropriately select and effectively use strategies from both modes, but with a strong favor toward access strategies. Thus, from your study of the chapters that follow in Part III, you will become knowledgeable about specific techniques so you can make intelligent decisions for choosing the best strategy for particular goals and objectives for subjects you teach and the interests, needs, and maturity level of your own unique group of students.

Figures 6.3 and 6.4 provide an overview of the specific strengths and weaknesses of each mode. By comparing those figures you can see that the strengths and weaknesses of one mode are nearly mirror opposites of the other. As noted earlier, although as a teacher you should be skillful in the use of strategies from both modes, for the most developmentally appropriate teaching for most groups of elementary school children, you should concentrate more on using strategies from the access mode. Strategies within that mode are more student-centered, hands-on, and concrete; students interact with one another and are actually or closer to doing what they are learning to do—that is, the learning is likely more authentic. Learning that occurs from the use of that mode is longer lasting (fixes into long-term memory). And, as the children interact with one another and with their learning, they develop a sense of "can do," which enhances their self-esteem.

SELECTING LEARNING ACTIVITIES THAT ARE DEVELOPMENTALLY APPROPRIATE

Returning to our soccer example, can you imagine a soccer coach teaching students the skills and knowledge needed to play soccer but without ever letting them experience playing the game? Can you imagine a geography teacher teaching students

Figure 6.3
Delivery mode: its strengths and weaknesses

Delivery Mode

Strengths
- Much content can be covered within a short span of time, usually by formal teacher talk, which then may be followed by an experiential activity.
- The teacher is in control of what content is covered.
- The teacher is in control of time allotted to specific content coverage.
- Strategies within the delivery mode are consistent with competency-based instruction.
- Student achievement of specific content is predictable and manageable.

Potential Weaknesses
- The sources of student motivation are mostly extrinsic.
- Students have little control over the pacing of their learning.
- Students make few important decisions about their learning.
- There may be little opportunity for divergent or creative thinking.
- Student self-esteem may be inadequately served.

Figure 6.4
Access mode: its strengths and weaknesses

Access Mode

Strengths
- Students learn content in more depth.
- The sources of student motivation are more likely intrinsic.
- Students make important decisions about their own learning.
- Students have more control over the pacing of their learning.
- Students develop a sense of personal self-worth.

Potential Weaknesses
- Content coverage may be more limited.
- Strategies are time-consuming.
- The teacher has less control over content and time.
- The specific results of student learning are less predictable.
- The teacher may have less control over class procedures.

how to read a map without ever letting them put their eyes and hands on a real map? Can you imagine teaching children the letters of the alphabet without ever letting them put the letters together to form words? Can you imagine teaching a child to play piano without ever allowing the child to touch a real keyboard? Unfortunately, still today, too many teachers do almost those exact things—they try to teach students to do something without letting the students practice doing it.

In planning and selecting developmentally appropriate learning activities, an important rule to remember is to select activities that are as close to the real thing as possible and sensible. That is learning through direct experiencing. When students are involved in direct experiences, they are using more of their sensory input channels, their learning modalities (Chapter 2). And when all the senses are engaged, learning is more integrated, and is most effective, meaningful, and longest-lasting. This "learning by doing" is authentic learning—or, as referred to earlier, hands-on/minds-on learning.

The Learning Experiences Ladder

Figure 6.5 depicts what is called the *Learning Experiences Ladder,* a visual depiction of a range of kinds of learning experiences from which a teacher may select. Hands-on/minds-on learning just dis-

cussed is at the bottom of the ladder. At the top are abstract experiences, where the learner is exposed only to symbolization (i.e., letters and numbers) and uses only one or two senses (auditory or visual). The teacher lectures while the students sit and watch and hear. Visual and verbal symbolic experiences, while impossible to avoid when teaching, are less effective in ensuring that planned and meaningful learning occurs. This is especially so with young children, learners who have special needs, learners with ethnic and cultural differences, and LEP students. Thus, when planning learning experiences and selecting instructional materials, you are advised to select activities that engage the learners in the most direct experiences possible and that are developmentally and intellectually appropriate for your specific group of students.

As can be inferred from the Learning Experiences Ladder, when teaching about tide pools (the first example for each step), the most-effective mode is to take the students to a tide pool (direct experience), where students can see, hear, touch, smell, and perhaps even taste (if not polluted with toxins) the tide pool. The least-effective mode is for the teacher to merely talk about the tide pool (verbal experience, the most abstract and symbolic experience), engaging only one sense—auditory.

Of course, for various reasons—such as time, matters of safety, lack of resources, and geographic location of your school—you may not be able to take your students to a tide pool. You cannot always use the most direct experience, so sometimes you must select an experience higher on the ladder.

Figure 6.5
The learning
experiences ladder
Sources: Earlier versions of
this concept were Charles F.
Hoban, Sr., et al., *Visualizing
the Curriculum* (New York:
Dryden, 1937), p. 39; Jerome
S. Bruner, *Toward a Theory
of Instruction* (Cambridge,
MA: Harvard University
Press, 1966), p. 49; Edgar
Dale, *Audio-Visual Methods
in Teaching* (New York: Hold,
Rinehart & Winston, 1969),
p. 108; and Eugene C. Kim
and Richard D. Kellough, *A
Resource Guide for
Secondary School Teaching,*
2nd ed. (Englewood Cliffs,
NJ: Merrill/Prentice Hall,
1978), p. 136.

Verbal Experiences   Teacher talk, written words; engaging only one sense; using the most abstract symbolization; students physically inactive. *Examples*: (a) Listening to the teacher talk about tide pools. (b) Listening to a student report about the Grand Canyon. (c) Listening to a guest speaker talk about how the state legislature functions.

Visual Experiences   Still pictures, diagrams, charts; engaging only one sense; typically symbolic; students physically inactive. *Examples*: (a) Viewing slide photographs of tide pools. (b) Viewing drawings and photographs of the Grand Canyon. (c) Listening to a guest speaker talk about the state legislature and show slides of it in action.

Vicarious Experiences   Laser videodisc programs, computer programs, video programs; engaging more than one sense; learner indirectly "doing"; may be some limited physical activity. *Examples*: (a) Interacting with a computer program about wave action and life in tide pools. (b) Viewing and listening to a video program about the Grand Canyon. (c) Taking a field trip to observe the state legislature in action.

Simulated Experiences   Role-playing, experimenting, simulations, mock-ups, working models; all or nearly all senses engaged; activity often integrating disciplines; closest to the real thing. *Examples*: (a) Building a classroom working model of a tide pool. (b) Building a classroom working model of the Grand Canyon. (c) Designing a classroom role-play simulation patterned after the operating procedures of the state legislature.

Direct Experiences   Learner actually doing what is being learned; true inquiry; all senses engaged; usually integrates disciplines; the real thing. *Examples*: (a) Visiting and experiencing a tide pool. (b) Visiting and experiencing the Grand Canyon. (c) Designing an elected representative body to oversee the operation of the school-within-the-school program, and patterned after the state legislative assembly.

ABSTRACT ↑ ↓ CONCRETE

Self-discovery teaching is not always appropriate. Sometimes it is more appropriate to build upon what others have discovered and learned. While learners do not need to "reinvent the wheel," the most effective and longest-lasting learning is that which engages most or all of their senses. On the Learning Experiences Ladder, those are the experiences that fall within the bottom three categories—direct, simulated, and vicarious. This is true with adult learners or with kindergarten children or students of any age group in between.

Direct, Simulated, and Vicarious Experiences Help Connect Student Learning

Another value of direct, simulated, and vicarious experiences is that they tend to be interdiscipli-

nary; that is, they blur or bridge subject-content boundaries. That makes those experiences especially useful for teachers who want to help students connect the learning of one discipline with that of others and to bridge what is being learned with their own life experiences. Direct, simulated, and vicarious experiences are more like real life. That means that the learning resulting from those experiences is authentic.

PLANNING AND DEVELOPING AN INTERDISCIPLINARY THEMATIC UNIT

The six steps outlined earlier in this chapter are essential for planning any type of teaching unit, including the interdisciplinary thematic unit (ITU), which may consist of smaller subject-specific conventional units developed according to the immediately foregoing guidelines. Because developing interdisciplinary thematic units is an essential task for many of today's teachers, you should learn this process now.

The primary responsibility for the development of interdisciplinary thematic units can depend on a single teacher or upon the cooperation of several teachers. A teaching team may develop from one to several interdisciplinary thematic units a year. Over time, then, a team will have several units that are available for implementation. However, the most effective units are often those that are the most current or the most meaningful to students. This means that ever-changing global, national, and local topics provide a virtual smorgasbord from which to choose, and teachers and teaching teams must constantly update old units and develop new and exciting ones.

One teaching team's unit should not conflict with others' at the same or another grade level. If a school has two or more teams at the same grade level, for example, the teams may want to develop units on different themes and share their products. As another example, a sixth-grade team must guard against developing a unit quite similar to one that the students had in a previous grade or will have later at another grade level. Open lines of communication within, between, and among teams and schools within a school district are critical to the success of interdisciplinary thematic teaching.[2] Consider the specific steps that follow.

Steps for Developing an Interdisciplinary Thematic Unit

Ten steps to guide you in developing an ITU are:

1. *Agree on the nature or source of the unit.* Team members should view the interdisciplinary approach as a collaborative effort in which all members can participate if appropriate. Write what you want the students to receive from interdisciplinary instruction. Troubleshoot potential stumbling blocks.

2. *Discuss subject-specific curriculum frameworks, guidelines, and standards, goals and objectives, textbooks and supplemental materials, and units already in place for the school year.* Focus on what you are obligated or mandated to teach, and explain the scope and sequence of the teaching so all team members understand the constraints and limitations.

3. *Choose a theme topic and develop a timeline.* From the information provided in step 2, start listing possible theme topics that can be drawn from within the existing grade-level curriculum documents. Give-and-take is essential here, as some topics will fit certain subjects better than others. (See the section Topic Versus Theme in Chapter 5.) The chief goal is to find a topic that can be adapted without detracting from the educational plan already in place. This may require choosing and merging content from two or more other units previously planned. The theme is then drawn from the topic.

Sometimes themes are selected by the teacher or by a teaching team before meeting the students for the first time. Other times they are selected by the teachers in collaboration with students. Even when the theme is preselected, with guidance from the teacher students still should be given major responsibility for deciding the final theme title (name), topics, and corresponding learning activities. Integrated thematic instruction works best when students have ownership in the study, that is, when they have been empowered with major decision-making responsibility for their learning.

The basis for theme selection should satisfy two criteria: The theme should (a) fit within the expected scope and sequence of mandated content and (b) be of interest to the students. Regarding the first criterion, many teachers have said that when they and their students embarked on an interdisciplinary thematic study, they did so without truly knowing where the study would go or what the learning outcomes would be—and they were somewhat apprehensive about that. But when completed, their students had learned everything (or nearly everything) that the teacher would have expected them to learn were the teacher to use a more traditional content-centered approach. And, it was more fun!

When selecting a theme, consider the questions shown in Figure 6.6.

The second criterion is easy to satisfy, since the theme will most assuredly interest everyone when students are truly empowered with major decision-making responsibility for what and how they learn. So, once a general theme is selected (it satisfies the first criterion), its final title, subtopics, and corresponding procedural activities should be finalized in collaboration with the students. (See Step 7.)

4. *Establish two timelines.* The first is for the team only and is to ensure that the deadlines for specific work required in developing the unit will be met by each member. The second timeline is for both students and teachers and shows the intended length of the unit, when it will start, and, if relevant, in which classrooms it will be taught.

5. *Develop the scope and sequence for content and instruction.* To develop the unit, follow the six

Figure 6.6
Questions to ask when
selecting a theme

- Is the theme within the realm of understanding and experience of the teachers involved?
- Will the theme interest all members of the teaching team?
- Do we have sufficient materials and resources to supply information we might need?
- Does the theme lend itself to active learning experiences?
- Will this theme be of interest to students, and will it motivate them to do their best?
- Can this theme lead to a unit that is of the proper duration, not too short and not too long?
- Is the theme helpful, worthwhile, and pertinent to the instructional objectives?
- Is the theme one with which teachers are not already so familiar that they cannot share in the excitement of the learning?

steps for planning and developing a unit of instruction outlined earlier in this chapter. This should be done by each team member as well as by the group during common planning time so members can coordinate dates and activities in logical sequence and depth. This is an organic process and will generate both ideas and anxiety. Under the guidance of the team leader, members should strive to keep this anxiety at a level conducive to learning, experimenting, and arriving at group consensus.

6. *Share goals and objectives.* Each team member should have a copy of the goals and target objectives of every other team member. This helps to refine the unit and lesson plans and to prevent unnecessary overlap and confusion.

7. *Give the unit a name.* The unit has been fashioned and is held together by the theme that is chosen. Giving the theme a name and using that name informs the students that this unit of study is integrated, important, and meaningful to school and to life.

8. *Share subject-specific units, lesson plans, and printed and nonprinted materials.* Exchange the finalized unit to obtain one another's comments and suggestions. Keep a copy of each teacher's unit(s) as a resource, and see if you could present a lesson using it as your basis for the lesson (some modification may be necessary). Lesson planning is the topic that follows.

9. *Field-test the unit.* Beginning at the scheduled time and date, present the lessons. Team members may trade classes from time to time. Team teaching may take place if and when two or more classes can be combined for instruction (if a classroom space large enough is available). (*Note:* A

distinction must be made between teaching teams and team teaching; while a **teaching team** is several teachers who work together to reflect, plan, and implement a curriculum for a common cohort of children, **team teaching** refers to two or more teachers simultaneously providing instruction to students in the same classroom. Members of a teaching team may participate in team teaching.)

10. *Reflect, assess, and perhaps modify the unit.* During planning time, team members should share and discuss their successes and failures and determine what needs to be changed and how and when that should be done to make the unit successful. Adjustments can be made along the way and revisions for future use can be made after the unit.

The preceding 10 steps are not absolutes and should be viewed only as guides. Differing teaching teams and levels of teacher experience and knowledge make the strict adherence to any plan less productive than would be the use of group-generated plans. For instance, some teachers have found that the last point under step 3 could state exactly the opposite; they recommend that the topic for an interdisciplinary unit should be one that a teacher or a teaching team already knows well. And under step 7, teachers might prefer to give the unit only a tentative name or no name at all, allowing the children to decide its name. In practice, the process that works well—one that results in meaningful learning for the children and in their positive feelings about themselves, about learning, and about school—is the appropriate process.

Now do Exercises 6.1 and 6.2.

EXERCISE 6.1 GENERATING IDEAS FOR INTERDISCIPLINARY UNITS

Instructions: The purpose of this exercise is to use brainstorming to generate a list of potential topics suitable as interdisciplinary units. Divide your class into groups of three to seven. Each group is to decide the grade or age level for which their unit ideas will be generated. If the group chooses, cooperative learning can be used; group members are then assigned roles such as facilitator, recorder, reporter, monitor of thinking processes, on-task monitor, and so on. Each group is to generate as many topics as possible. One member of each group should record all ideas. Reserve discussion of ideas until no further topics are generated. Lists can be shared in the large group.

Grade-level interest of the group _____

1. Existing subject-area content units (as the group knows them to be or as they are predicted to exist)

   _____

   _____

   _____

   _____

2. Current topics of
   a. Global interest _____

   _____

   _____

   b. National interest _____

   _____

   _____

   c. Statewide interest _____

   _____

   _____

   d. Local interest _____

   _____

   _____

   e. Interest to the school _____

   _____

   _____

   f. Interest to students of this age _____

   _____

   _____

For Your Notes

EXERCISE 6.2 INTEGRATING THE TOPIC

Instructions: The purpose of this exercise is to practice weaving interdisciplinary themes into curricula. In groups of three or four, choose one idea that was generated during Exercise 6.1, and derive a list of suggestions about how that theme could be woven into the curricula of various classes, programs, and activities, as indicated below. It is possible that not all areas listed are relevant to the grade level to which your group is addressing its work. Cooperative learning can be used with appropriate roles assigned to group members. One person in the group should be the recorder. Upon completion, share your group's work (the process and product of which will be much like that of an actual interdisciplinary teaching team) with the class. Copies should be made available to those who want them.

Unit theme _____

1. In subjects of the curriculum
   a. English/Language arts _____

   _____

   _____

   b. Social studies _____

   _____

   _____

   c. Mathematics _____

   _____

   _____

   d. Science _____

   _____

   _____

   e. Reading _____

   _____

   _____

   f. Physical education _____

   _____

   _____

   g. Art _____

   _____

   _____

   h. Music _____

   _____

   _____

EXERCISE 6.2 *(continued)*

2. In cocurricular programs and activities
   a. Electives _____

   _____

   _____

   b. Clubs _____

   _____

   _____

   c. School functions _____

   _____

   _____

   d. Assemblies _____

   _____

   _____

   e. Intramurals _____

   _____

   _____

   f. Study skills _____

   _____

   _____

3. In exploratories _____

   _____

   _____

4. In homerooms _____

   _____

   _____

5. Explain how multicultural components could be incorporated into the unit.

   _____

   _____

6. As individuals and as a group, how productive was this exercise?

   _____

   _____

Developing the Learning Activities: The Heart and Spirit of the ITU

Activities that engage the students in meaningful learning constitute the heart and spirit of the ITU: The activities that start a unit into motion are called *initiating activities;* those that comprise the heart of the unit are the *ongoing developmental activities;* and those that bring the unit to a natural close are *culminating activities.* Although nearly limitless, the list in Figure 6.2 gives you an idea of the many options from which you can choose activities for any of these three categories, some of which, of course, may overlap in some regard or another and some of which might naturally fit one category better than another.

The Common Thread

Central to the selection and development of learning activities for interdisciplinary thematic instruction is a common thread of four tightly interwoven components: (a) the instruction is centered around a big and meaningful idea or theme (such as the accompanying Learning From Dinosaurs scenario) rather than on fictitious subject areas, (b) the students and the teacher share in the decision making and responsibility for learning, (c) the learning activities are selected so all students are actively engaged in their learning—that is, they are physically active (hands-on learning) and mentally active (minds-on learning)—and (d) there is steady reflection on and frequent sharing of what is being done and what is being learned.

Initiating Activities

An ITU can be initiated by a limitless variety of ways. You must decide which ways are appropriate for your educational goals and objectives, for your intended time duration, and for your own unique group of students, considering their level of maturity, interests, abilities, and skills. You might start with a current event, a community

---

Scenario: Interdisciplinary Thematic Unit: *Learning From Dinosaurs*

Once a theme is determined, instruction is planned around a sequence of activities that focus on that theme. Common to many elementary school teachers is a theme that centers on the topic of dinosaurs. Whatever its selected title might be in a given situation, a thematic unit on dinosaurs can encompass any number of multidisciplinary activities related to the topic. For example,

- *History.* Students develop a graphic time line showing the long period of time that dinosaurs were dominant on Earth; they visit a museum that features dinosaur exhibits.
- *Mathematics.* Students categorize the types of dinosaurs and create graphs illustrating the variety and proportional sizes of dinosaurs.
- *Reading, Writing, and Art.* Students create and write illustrated stories about a favorite dinosaur.
- *Science.* Students speculate both on why the dinosaurs were so successful and on the events that led to their rather quick disappearance from Earth.

In one second-grade classroom, the teacher guided her students in a thematic unit centered on dinosaurs. Learning activities integrated science and math, drawing and crafts, music and reading, and publishing original books to support the study. Connecting reading to music, the students listened to a song about each dinosaur being studied. Students read sentence strips with the words of the song. They added sound effects, sang the song several times, and added a rhythmic beat with their fingers and hands. Additionally, students prepared their own dinosaur-shape books, wrote original pages, and created illustrations. To survey favorite dinosaurs, graphing was introduced. The students built their own graph in the classroom by drawing a favorite dinosaur and contributing it to a large graph. Students used individual copies of the graph to record what was added to the large graph and marked X's with their pencils in the appropriate places. When the class graph was finished, guided by the teacher the students read it and talked about the information they had gathered.

The culminating event took place at the school's spring Open House. Each student's assignment for Open House was to bring an adult and to explain to that person what he or she had been learning at school. Confidently, the students told their visitors about dinosaurs and proudly displayed their dinosaur books, dinosaur mobiles, dinosaur body shapes made from felt, and dinosaur clay models.

problem or event, a student experience, an outdoor adventure, an artifact, a book, or something found on the Internet.

Ongoing Developmental Activities

Once the ITU has been initiated, students become occupied with a variety of ongoing activities such as those listed in Figure 6.2. In working with students in selecting and planning the ongoing learning activities, you will want to keep in mind the concept represented by the Learning Experiences Ladder (Figure 6.6) as well as the predetermined goals and target objectives (Chapter 5).

Now do Exercises 6.3, 6.4, and 6.5.

EXERCISE 6.3 INITIATING AN ITU WITH A QUESTION MAP

Instructions: The purpose of this exercise is to work with a partner or partners to write questions related to a possible theme for an ITU.

First select a topic that you know is typically taught at a grade level and in a subject area of interest to you and your partners.

Grade level: _____

With your partners taking the role of students, have your partners participate in a discussion about "what we want to know" about the topic. Write their questions on a question map on the writing board. Show the partners how you can group their related questions (main questions and subquestions) together. Ask them to think of headings for the different categories of related questions. Use the following format for recording the input:

1. Topic:

2. Main question:

3. Related subquestions:

    a.

    b.

    c.

Copy the question map from the board to this (or reverse side of) page so you can use it as a reference.

For Your Notes

EXERCISE 6.4 CONNECTING QUESTIONS AND ACTIVITIES FOR AN ITU

Instructions: The purpose of this exercise is to work to connect the questions related to your theme and to ongoing learning activities in specific detail. Learning activities should be planned around some central questions (and subquestions) about the theme. The investigative activities that are needed to inquire about the questions can provide various opportunities for you to respond to the learning styles and needs of your students.

With your partners, return to the "what we want to know" question map you completed in Exercise 6.3. Use the information to design some learning activities for the unit.

List of Learning Activities Related to the Questions and Subquestions:

1.

2.

3.

4.

5.

6.

For Your Notes

EXERCISE 6.5 PUTTING OBJECTIVES, RESOURCES, AND LEARNING ACTIVITIES TOGETHER FOR A TEACHING PLAN

Instructions: The purpose of this exercise is to write a specific teaching plan for a minimum of one day that incorporates what you have done so far: preparing goals, writing objectives, selecting resources, and selecting and planning learning activities. You may want to reference the learning activities to state frameworks, district documents, and local school curriculum. Ask a peer to read and react to your teaching plan. Does your plan convey what you intended to say? What new questions came to mind as you wrote the plan and as it was reviewed by others?

Teaching Plan

Interdisciplinary unit theme:

Main focus question:

Related subquestions:

Objectives

(What will the students learn?)

(What thinking skills, such as observing, communicating, comparing, categorizing, inferring, and applying, will the students develop?)

(What attitudes will be fostered?)

Resources

(Media, display visuals, artifacts, computer, and software)

EXERCISE 6.5 *(continued)*

Specifics of Learning Activities

Preassessment of Student Learning

(How will you determine what students know or think they know about the subject at the start of the unit?)

[Example 1: think-pair-share, where the topic/question is written on the board and students are asked in pairs to think about the topic, discuss it between themselves, and then the pairs share with the whole class what they know or think they already know about it while the teacher writes the major thoughts on the board, perhaps in the form of a concept web.]

[Example 2: using the KWL reading comprehension strategy, with the teacher directing the discussion, three columns are formed on the board or overhead projector. The left-hand column contains what students already KNOW or think they know about the topic; the middle column contains a list of what the students WANT to learn about the topic; the right-hand column is left blank and filled in at the end or during the study with what is and has been LEARNED about the topic.]

EXERCISE 6.5 *(continued)*

Formative Assessment

(Techniques used to assess student learning in progress to ensure they are on the right track)

Check ____ discipline areas drawn upon   Brief description of how

_____ 1. Sciences

_____ 2. Social sciences/history

_____ 3. Mathematics

_____ 4. Reading and language

_____ 5. Poetry and prose

_____ 6. Music and dance

_____ 7. Painting and sculpture

_____ 8. Health and physical education

_____ Other:

Feedback:

_____ 1. What was the reaction of your peer to your teaching plan?

_____ 2. In your opinion, does your plan effectively convey what you originally envisioned?

_____ 3. Does it need more detail or revision?

_____ 4. Do your selected learning activities appropriately address the varied learning styles of your students?

_____ 5. What new questions came to mind as you wrote the plan and as it was reviewed?

For Your Notes

Culminating Activity

An ITU is brought to close with a culminating activity. Such an activity often includes an exhibition or sharing of the product of the students' study. You could accept the students' suggestions for a culminating activity if it engages them in summarizing and sharing what they have learned with others. A culminating activity that brings closure to a unit can give the children an opportunity for synthesis (by assembling, constructing, creating, inventing, producing, or incorporating something) and even an opportunity to present that synthesis to an audience, such as by sharing with parents and guardians at a classroom, school, or community event or by sharing their product on the school's Web site.

With a culminating activity, you can provide opportunity for the students to move from recording information to reporting on their learning. For example, one activity might be for students to take field trips to study something related to the theme and then synthesize their learning after the trip in a way that culminates the study. On field trips, students should be given notepads similar to the ones reporters use and asked to take notes and make sketches of what they learn. They can review what questions they have on the ride to the site (see also the section, Field Trips, in Chapter 10). They can discuss what they liked and did not like on the ride back to school. After the trip, each student can choose something he or she saw and then build it to scale, so the students can have a scale model of something they saw on the trip that caught their interest. Teacher and students might devote one full afternoon, or more, to working with rulers, yardsticks, cardboard, clay, and other materials. The students could then invite other classes in to examine the scale models and listen to student reports about why an object caught their interest. Students might also present an art show of drawings about the unit's theme, with a narration that informs others about their study. You might also schedule a culminating activity that asks students to report on individual projects—the aspect each student formerly reserved for individual study.

Examples of actual culminating activities and products of an ITU are endless. Culminating activities are opportunities for students to proudly demonstrate and share their learning and in different, creative, and individual ways. Now gain further insight about bringing an ITU to closure by doing Exercise 6.6.

For Your Notes

EXERCISE 6.6 PLANNING CULMINATING ACTIVITIES

Instructions: The purpose of this exercise is to plan a closure for the unit (even though you realize that inquiry can be lifelong and has no official closure). In this exercise, you must determine what will affect the length of your unit: the interest of your students in the topic, resources available or unavailable, school holidays, the academic calendar for your school year, and any competing events, such as picture day, assemblies, athletic events, and field trips.

1. What activity/activities could you plan that would permit your students to synthesize what they have learned in the unit and then report the synthesis to a selected audience?

2. Although final decisions about culminating activities are best when made collaboratively with the students, initial thoughts by the teacher are important to be able to offer suggestions. Which of the following might you incorporate into the culmination of a unit? Explain why.

Creating new problems related to the topic and demonstrating a way to resolve them

Designing a chart, map, timeline, classroom museum of exhibits, interdisciplinary thematic fair, or classroom "main street" with booths (learning centers); reporting on the data the design represents

An oral and written presentation on an aspect of the topic; using such creative ways to present data as sketches, sculpture works, cartoons, popular songs, a comic strip format, costume props, a story board, puppets, flannel board figures, rhymes, limericks, and other forms of poetry

Creating and producing a drama

EXERCISE 6.6 *(continued)*

Writing and publishing a newsletter or brochure on the topic

Writing and publishing a book

Creating a class or student cohort Web page regarding the unit

Other

PREPARING LESSON PLANS: RATIONALE AND ASSUMPTIONS

As described at the beginning of this chapter, step 5 of the seven steps of instructional planning is the preparation of lessons for class meetings. The process of designing a lesson is important in learning to provide the most efficient use of valuable and limited instructional time and the most effective learning for the students to meet the anticipated learning outcomes.

Notice the title of this section does not refer to *daily* lesson plans, but rather simply to lesson plans. The focus is on how to prepare a lesson plan, and that plan may, in fact, be a daily plan or it may not. In some instances, a lesson plan may extend for more than one period or block of time or day, perhaps two or three. In other instances, the lesson plan is in fact a daily plan and may run for an entire class period or block of time. See The Problem of Time later in this chapter.

Accomplished elementary schoolteachers are always planning for their teaching. For the long range, they plan the scope and sequence and develop content. Within this long-range planning, they develop units, and within units, they design the activities to be used and the assessments of learning to be done. They familiarize themselves with books, materials, media, and innovations in their special fields of interest such as literacy, mathematics, science, or social studies. Yet, despite all this planning activity, the lesson plan remains pivotal to the planning process.

Consider now the rationale, description, and guidelines for writing detailed lesson plans.

Rationale for Preparing Written Lesson Plans

First, *carefully prepared and written lesson plans shows everyone—first and foremost your students, then your colleagues, your administrator, and, if you are a student teacher, your cooperating teacher and your college or university supervisor—that you are a committed professional.* Sometimes, beginning teachers are concerned with being seen by their students using a written plan in class, thinking it may suggest that the teacher has not mastered the material. On the contrary, a lesson plan is tangible evidence that you are working at your job and demonstrates respect for the students, yourself, and for the profession. A written lesson plan shows that preactive thinking and planning have taken place. There is absolutely no excuse for appearing before a classroom of children without evidence of being prepared.

Written and detailed lesson plans provide an important sense of security, which is especially useful to a beginning teacher. Like a rudder of a ship, it helps keep you on course. Without it, you are likely to drift aimlessly. Sometimes a disturbance in the classroom can distract from the lesson, causing the teacher to go off track or to forget an important part of the lesson. A written and detailed lesson plan provides a road map to guide you and help keep you on track.

Written lesson plans help you to be or become a reflective decision-maker. Without a written plan, it is difficult or impossible to analyze how something might have been planned or implemented differently after the lesson has been taught. Written lesson plans serve as resources for the next time you teach the same or a similar lesson and are useful for teacher self-assessment and for the assessment of student learning and the curriculum.

Written lesson plans help you organize material and search for loopholes, loose ends, or incomplete content. Careful and thorough planning during the preactive phase of instruction includes anticipation of how the lesson activities will develop as the lesson is being taught. During this anticipation you will actually visualize yourself in the classroom teaching the children, using that visualization to anticipate possible problems.

Written plans help other members of the teaching team understand what you are doing and how you are doing it. Written lesson plans also provide substitute teachers with a guide to follow in your absence from teaching.

Those reasons clearly express the need to write detailed lesson plans. The list is not exhaustive, however, and you may discover additional reasons why written lesson plans are crucial to effective teaching. In summary, two points are: (a) lesson planning is an important and ongoing process; and (b) teachers must take time to plan, reflect, write, test, evaluate, and rewrite their plans to reach optimal performance. In short, preparing written lesson plans is important professional work.

Assumptions About Lesson Planning

Not all teachers need elaborate written plans for every lesson. Sometimes accomplished veteran teachers need only a sketchy outline. Sometimes they may not need written plans at all. Accomplished teachers who have taught the topic many times in the past may need only the presence of a classroom of students to stimulate a pattern of presentation that has often been successful (though frequent use of old patterns may lead one into the rut of unimaginative and uninspiring teaching).

Considering the diversity among elementary schoolteachers, their instructional styles, their students, and what research has shown, certain assumptions can be made about lesson planning.

1. While not all teachers need elaborate written plans for all lessons, accomplished teachers do have clearly defined goals and objectives in mind and a planned pattern of instruction for every lesson, whether that plan is written out or not.
2. Beginning teachers need to prepare detailed written lesson plans—failing to prepare is preparing to fail.
3. Some topics and learning activities require more detailed planning than others do.
4. The depth of knowledge a teacher has about a subject or topic influences the amount of planning necessary for the lessons.
5. The skill a teacher has in remaining calm and in following a trend of thought in the presence of distraction will influence the amount of detail necessary when planning activities and writing the lesson plan.
6. A plan is more likely to be carefully and thoughtfully plotted when it is written out.
7. The diversity of children within today's public school classroom necessitates careful and thoughtful consideration about personalizing the instruction—these considerations are best exercised when they have been thoughtfully written into lesson plans.
8. While some curriculum programs—especially in reading, language arts, and mathematics—are highly scripted for the teacher, the writers of the program did not know your particular group of students. Nobody knows your group of children better than you do. Each day you will need to adjust and augment those scripted plans to personalize the learning for your own unique classroom of children.
9. There is no particular pattern or format that all teachers need to follow when writing out plans—some teacher-preparation programs have agreed on certain lesson-plan formats for their teacher candidates; you need to know if this is the case for your program.

In summary, well-written lesson plans provide many advantages: They give a teacher an agenda or outline to follow in teaching a lesson; they give a substitute teacher a basis for presenting appropriate lessons to a class, thereby retaining lesson continuity in the regular teacher's absence; they are certainly very useful when a teacher is planning to use the same lesson again in the future; they provide the teacher with something to fall back on in case of a memory lapse, an interruption, or some distraction such as a call from the office or a fire drill; using a written plan demonstrates to students that you care and are working for them; and, above all, they provide beginners security because, with a carefully prepared plan, a beginning teacher can walk into a classroom with confidence and professional pride gained from having developed a sensible framework for that day's instruction.

Thus, as a beginning teacher, you should make considerably detailed lesson plans. Naturally, this will require a great deal of work for at least the first year or two, but the reward of knowing that you have prepared and presented effective lessons will compensate for that effort.

A Continual Process

Lesson planning is a continual process even for veteran teachers, for there is always a need to keep materials and plans current and relevant. Because no two groups of children are ever exactly alike, today's lesson plan will need to be tailored to the particular needs of each group of children. Moreover, because the content of instruction and learning will change as each distinct group of children and their needs and interests give input, and as new thematic units are developed, new developments occur, or new theories are introduced, your objectives and the expected outcomes of the students, school, and teaching faculty will change.

For these reasons, lesson plans should be in a constant state of revision—never set in concrete. Once the basic framework is developed, however, the task of updating and modifying becomes minimal. If your plans are maintained on a computer, making changes from time to time is even easier.

Well Planned but Open to Last-Minute Change

The lesson plan should provide a tentative outline of the time period given for the lesson but should always remain flexible. A carefully worked-out plan may have to be set aside because of the unpredictable, serendipitous effect of a "Teachable Moment" (see accompanying vignette) or because of unforeseen circumstances, such as a delayed school bus, an impromptu school assembly program, an emergency drill, or the cancellation of school due to severe weather conditions. Student

---

Classroom Vignette: A Teachable Moment

Casey is teaching a sixth-grade humanities block, a 2-hour block course that integrates student learning in social studies, reading, and language arts. On this particular day while Casey and her students were discussing the topic of Manifest Destiny, one of the students raised his hand and when acknowledged by Casey, asked the question, "Why aren't we [referring to the United States] still adding states? [that is, adding territory to the United States]." Casey immediately replied with "There aren't any more states to add." By responding too quickly, Casey missed one of those "teachable moments," moments when the teacher has the students right where she wants them, that is, where the students are thinking and asking questions. What could Casey have done? When was Hawaii added as a state? Why hasn't Puerto Rico become a state? Guam? etc. Aren't those possibilities? Why *aren't* more states or territories being added? What are the political and social ramifications today and how do they differ from those of the 1800s?

---

teachers often are appalled at the frequency of interruptions that occur during a school day and that disrupt the planned instruction. A daily lesson planned to cover six aspects of a given topic may end with only three of the points having been considered. While far more frequent than necessary in too many schools, these disruptions are natural in a school setting and the teacher and the plans must be flexible enough to accommodate this reality.

Implementation of Today's Lesson May Necessitate Changes in Tomorrow's Plan

Although you may have your lesson plans completed for several consecutive lessons, as can be inferred by the Teachable Moment vignette at the top of this page, what actually transpires during the implementation of today's lesson is quite likely to necessitate adjustments to the lesson you have planned for tomorrow. Consequently, during student teaching in particular it is neither uncommon nor unwanted to have last-minute changes penciled in your lesson plan. If the changes are major, however, you should rewrite the plan so to avoid being confused by a messy lesson plan during its implementation.

The Problem of Time

A lesson plan should provide enough materials and activities to consume the class period or block of time allotted. When a lesson plan does not provide sufficient activity to occupy the period of time that the students are available for the lesson, that in particular is a time when teachers can expect behavior problems to begin to mount. Thus, it is best to prepare more than you likely can accomplish in a given period of time. This is not to imply that you should involve the children in meaning-

less busy work. Upper elementary grades children in particular can be very perceptive when it comes to a teacher who has finished the plan and is attempting to bluff through the minutes that remain before dismissal. And, they are not usually favorably responsive to meaningless busywork.

If you ever do get caught short—as most teachers do at one time or another—one way to avoid confusion and embarrassment is to have students work on what is known as an *anchor assignment* (or *transitional activity*). This is an ongoing assignment and students understand that whenever they have spare time in class they should be working on it. Example anchor activities include a review of material that has been covered that day or in the past several days, work on homework, journal writing, portfolio organization, work at a learning center, and long-term project work. Regardless of how you handle time remaining, it works best when you plan for it and write that aspect into your lesson plan and when the procedures for doing it are well understood by the students.

About "The Daily Planning Book"

A distinction needs to be made between lesson plans and the book for daily planning that some schools require teachers to maintain and even submit to their supervisors a week in advance. Items that a teacher writes into the boxes in a daily planning book (see Figure 6.7) most assuredly are not lesson plans; rather, the pages are a layout by which the teacher writes into the boxes to show what lessons will be taught during the day, week, month, or term. These books are useful for outlining the topics, activities, and assignments projected for the week or term, and supervisors sometimes use them to check the adequacy of teachers' course

Figure 6.7
Daily plan book

Daily Plan Book				
Grade _____ Lesson _____ Teacher _____				
Date	*Content*	*Materials*	*Procedure*	*Evaluation*
Monday				
Tuesday				
Wednesday				
Thursday				
Friday				

plans. But they are *not* lesson plans. Teachers and their supervisors who believe that the notations in the daily planning book are actual lesson plans are fooling themselves. Student teachers should not use these in place of authentic lesson plans.

CONSTRUCTING A LESSON PLAN: FORMAT, COMPONENTS, AND SAMPLES

While it is true that each teacher develops a personal system of lesson planning—the system that works best for that teacher in that teacher's unique situation—a beginning teacher needs a more substantial framework from which to work. For that, this section provides a preferred lesson plan format (Figure 6.8). Nothing is hallowed about this format, however. Review the preferred format and samples, and unless your program of teacher preparation insists otherwise, use it until you find or develop a better model.

For Guidance, Reflection, and Reference

There is good reason to question teachers who say they have no need for a written plan because they have their lessons planned "in their heads." The hours and instructional periods in a school day range from several to many, as are the numbers of children in each class. When multiplied by the number of school days in a week, a semester, or a year, the task of keeping so many things in one's head becomes mind-boggling. Few persons could

effectively do that. Until you have accumulated considerable experience, you will need to prepare and maintain detailed lesson plans for guidance, reflection, and reference. While you are student teaching and during your first few years as a beginning teacher, your lesson plans should be printed from a computer or typewritten or, if that isn't possible, written out in an intelligible style. If you have a spelling problem, do a spell check.

Basic Elements of a Lesson Plan

The written lesson plan should contain the following basic elements: (a) descriptive data, (b) goals and objectives, (c) rationale, (d) procedure, (e) assignments and assignment reminders, (f) materials and equipment, and (g) a section for assessment of student learning, reflection on the lesson, and ideas for lesson revision.

Not all seven elements and their subsections need be present in every written lesson plan, nor must they be presented in any particular order. Nor are they inclusive or exclusive. You might choose to include additional components or subsections. Figure 6.9 illustrates a format that includes the seven elements and sample subsections of those elements. Additionally, Figure 6.9 displays a completed multiple-day lesson plan that incorporates many of the developmentally appropriate learning activities discussed in this resource guide. Following are descriptions of the seven elements of the preferred format, with examples and explanations of why each is important.

Figure 6.8
Preferred lesson plan format with seven components*

---

1. Descriptive Data

Teacher _____ Class _____ Date _____ Grade level _____

Room number _____ Period _____ Unit _____ Lesson number _____ Topic _____

Anticipated noise level (high, moderate, low)

2. Goals and Objectives

Instructional goals:

Specific objectives:

[*Note:* All three domains not always present in every lesson]

Cognitive:

Affective:

Psychomotor:

3. Rationale [*Note:* Rationale not always present in every lesson]

4. Procedure [Procedure with modeling examples, planned transitions, etcetera; should usually take up most of the space of lesson plan, often a full page]

_____ minutes. Activity 1: Set (introduction)

_____ minutes. Activity 2:

(continued)

Figure 6.8 *(continued)*

_____ minutes. Activity 3: (the exact number of activities in the procedures will vary)

_____ minutes. Final Activity (Lesson Conclusion or Closure):

If time remains:

5. Assignments and Reminders of Assignments

Special notes and reminders to myself:

6. Materials and Equipment Needed

Audiovisual:

Other:

7. Assessment, Reflection, and Revision

Assessment of student learning, how it will be done:

Reflective thoughts about lesson after taught:

Suggestions for revision if used again:

*This blank lesson plan format is placed alone so, if you choose, you may remove it from the book and make copies for use in your teaching.

Figure 6.9
Lesson plan sample: multiple-day, project-centered, interdisciplinary, and transcultural lesson using worldwide communication via the Internet

---

1. Descriptive Data

Teacher _____ Class/disciplines English/Language Arts/Science Date _____ Grade Level 5–6

Unit Investigative Research & Generative Writing

Lesson Topic Writing Response and Peer Assessment via Internet

Time duration: several days

2. Goals and Objectives of Unit

Instructional Goals:

2.1. One goal for this lesson is for students to collaborate and prepare response papers to peers from around the world who have shared the results of their own experimental research findings and research paper about ozone concentrations in the atmosphere.

2.2. The ultimate goal of this unit is for students around the world to prepare and publish for worldwide dissemination a final paper about global ozone levels in the atmosphere.

Objectives:

Cognitive

a. Through cooperative group action, students will conduct experimental research to collect data about the ozone level of air in their environment. (application)

b. In cooperative groups, students will analyze the results of their experiments. (analyze)

c. Students will compile data and infer from their experimental data. (synthesis and evaluation)

d. Through collaborative writing groups, the students will prepare a final paper that summarizes their research study of local atmospheric ozone levels. (evaluation)

e. Through sharing via Internet, students will write response papers to their peers from other locations in the world. (evaluation)

f. From their own collaborative research and worldwide communications with their peers, the students will draw conclusions about global atmospheric ozone levels. (evaluation)

Affective

a. Students will respond attentively to the response papers of their peers. (attending)

b. Students will willingly cooperate with others during the group activities. (responding)

c. The students will offer opinions about the atmospheric level of ozone. (valuing)

d. The students will form judgments about local, regional, and worldwide ozone levels. (organizing)

e. The students will communicate accurately their findings and attend diligently to the work of their worldwide peers. (internalizing)

Psychomotor

a. The students will manipulate the computer so that their e-mail communications are transmitted accurately. (manipulating)

b. In a summary to the study students will describe their feelings about atmospheric ozone concentrations. (communicating)

c. The students will ultimately create a proposal for worldwide dissemination. (creating)

3. Rationale

3.1. Important to improvement in one's writing and communication skills are the processes of selecting a topic, decision making, arranging, drafting, proofing, peer review, commenting, revising, editing, rewriting, and publishing the results—processes that are focused on in the writing aspect of this unit.

3.2. Student writers need many readers to respond to their work. Through worldwide communication with peers and dissemination of their final product, this need can be satisfied.

3.3. Students learn best when they are actively pursuing a topic of interest and meaning to them. Resulting from brainstorming potential problems and arriving at their own topic, this unit provides that.

3.4. Real-world problems are interdisciplinary and transcultural; involving writing (English), science, mathematics (data collecting, graphing, etc.), and intercultural communication, this unit is an interdisciplinary transcultural unit.

(continued)

Figure 6.9 *(continued)*

4. Procedure

Content:

At the start of this unit, collaborative groups were established via Intercultural E-mail Classroom Connections (IECC) (http://www.stolaf.edu/network/iecc) with other classes from schools around the world. These groups of students conducted several scientific research experiments on the ozone level of their local atmospheric air. To obtain relative measurements of ozone concentrations in the air, students set up experiments that involved stretching rubber bands on a board, then observing the number of days until the bands broke. Students maintained daily journal logs of the temperature, barometric pressure, and wind speed/direction, and of the number of days that it took for bands to break.* After compiling their data and preparing single-page summaries of their results, via the Internet students exchanged data with other groups. From data collected worldwide students wrote a one-page summary as to what conditions may account for the difference in levels of ozone. Following the exchange of students' written responses and their subsequent revisions based on feedback from the worldwide peers, students are now preparing a final summary report about the world's atmospheric ozone level. The intention is to disseminate worldwide (to newspapers and via the Internet) this final report.

Activity 1: Introduction (_10_ minutes)
Today, in think-share-pairs, you will prepare initial responses to the e-mail responses we have received from other groups from around the world. (Teacher shares the list of places from which e-mail has been received.) Any questions before we get started?

    As we discussed earlier, here are the instructions: In your think-share-pairs (each pair is given one response received via e-mail), prepare written responses according to the following outline: (a) note points or information you would like to incorporate in the final paper to be forwarded via Internet; (b) comment on one aspect of the written response you like best; and (c) provide questions to the sender to seek clarification or elaboration. I think you should be able to finish this in about 30 minutes, so let's try for that.

Activity 2: (___30___ minutes, if needed)
Preparation of dyad responses

Activity 3: (open)
Let's now hear from each response pair.
Dyad responses are shared with whole class for discussion of inclusion in response paper to be sent via Internet.

Activity 4: (open)
Discussion, conclusion, and preparation of final drafts to be sent to each e-mail corresponder to be done by cooperative groups (the number of groups needed to be decided by the number of e-mail corresponders at this time).

Activity 5: (open)
Later, as students receive e-mail responses from other groups the responses will be printed and reviewed. The class then responds to each using the same criteria as before and returns this response to the e-mail sender.

Closure:
The process continues until all groups (from around the world) have agreed upon and prepared the final report for dissemination.

5. Assignments and Reminders
Remind students of important dates and decisions to be made

6. Materials and Equipment Needed
School computers with Internet access; printers; copies of e-mail responses

7. Assessment, Reflection, and Revision
Assessment of student learning for this lesson is formative: journals, daily checklist of student participation in groups, writing drafts
Reflective thoughts about lesson and suggestions for revision:

---

*The source of information about the science experiment is R. J. Ryder and T. Hughes, *Internet for Educators* (Upper Saddle River, NJ: Prentice Hall, 1997), p. 98.

Descriptive Data

A lesson plan's descriptive data are demographic and logistical information that identify details about the group of children. Anyone reading this information should be able to identify when and where the group meets, who is teaching it, and what is being taught. Although as the teacher you know this information, someone else may not. Members of the teaching team, administrators, mentors, and substitute teachers (and, if you are the student teacher, your university supervisor and cooperating teacher) appreciate this information, especially when asked to fill in for you, even if only for a few minutes during a class session. Most teachers discover which items of descriptive data are most beneficial in their situation and then develop their own identifiers. Remember this: The mark of a well-prepared, clearly written lesson plan is the ease with which someone else (such as another member of your teaching team or a substitute teacher) could implement it.

As shown in the sample plan of Figure 6.9 the descriptive data include:

1. *Name of course or class.* These serve as headings for the plan and facilitate orderly filing of plans.

   Language Arts / Science (integrated block course)

2. *Name of the unit.* Inclusion of this facilitates the orderly control of the hundreds of lesson plans a teacher constructs. For example:

   Unit: Investigative Research and Generative Writing

3. *Topic to be considered within the unit.* This is also useful for control and identification. For example:

   Writing Response and Peer Assessment via the Internet

Anticipated Noise Level

Although not included in the sample lesson plan, you might include in the descriptive data the category of "anticipated classroom noise level," such as "high," "moderate," or "silent or low." Its inclusion, or at least considering the idea, is useful during the planning phase of instruction in that it prompts you to think about how active and noisy the children might become during the lesson, how you might prepare for that, and whether you should advise an administrator and teachers of neighboring classrooms.

Goals and Objectives

The instructional goals are general statements of intended accomplishments from that lesson. Teachers and students need to know what the lesson is designed to accomplish. In clear, understandable language, the general goal statement provides that information. From the sample, the goals are:

- To collaborate and prepare response papers to peers from around the world who have shared the results of their own experimental research findings and research paper about ozone concentrations in the atmosphere.
- For students worldwide to prepare and publish for worldwide dissemination a final paper about worldwide ozone levels in the atmosphere.

Because the goals are also included in the unit plan, sometimes a teacher may include only the objectives in the daily lesson plan, but not the goals. As a beginning teacher, it usually is a good idea to include both.

A crucial step in the development of any lesson plan is that of setting the objectives. It is at this point that many lessons go wrong and where many beginning teachers have problems.

Learning Activity versus Learning Objective

Sometimes teachers confuse *learning activity* (*how* the students will learn it) with the *learning objective* (*what* the student will learn as a result of the learning activity). For example, teachers sometimes mistakenly list what *they* intend to do—such as "lead a discussion about the Earth's continents"—and fail to focus on just what the learning objectives in these activities truly are—that is, what the students will be able to do (performance) as a result of the instructional activity. Or, rather than specifying what the student will be able to do as a result of the learning activities, the teacher mistakenly writes what the students will do in class (the learning activity)—such as, "in pairs the students will answer the 10 questions on page 72"—as if that were the learning objective.

When you approach this step in your lesson planning, to avoid error ask yourself, "What should students learn *as a result of* the activities of this lesson?" Your answer to that question is your objective! Objectives of the lesson are included then as specific statements of performance expectations, detailing precisely what students will be able to do as a result of the instructional activities.

No Need to Include All Domains and Hierarchies in Every Lesson

Not all three domains (cognitive, affective, and psychomotor) are necessarily represented in every lesson. As a matter of fact, any given lesson plan may be directed to only one or two, or a few, specific objectives. Over the course of a unit of instruction, however, all domains, and most if not all levels within each, should be addressed.

From the sample lesson shown in Figure 6.9, sample objectives and the domain and level (in parentheses) within that domain are:

- Through cooperative group action students will conduct experimental research to collect data about the ozone level of air in their environment. (cognitive, application)
- Through the Internet students will write and share response papers to their peers from other locations in the world. (cognitive, evaluation)
- Students will form judgments about local, regional, and world ozone levels. (affective, organizing)
- Students will create a proposal for worldwide dissemination. (psychomotor, creating)

Rationale

The rationale is an explanation of why the lesson is important and why the instructional methods chosen will achieve the objectives. Parents and guardians, students, teachers, administrators, and others have the right to know why specific content is being taught and why the methods employed are being used. Prepare yourself well by always being prepared with intelligent answers to those two questions.

Teachers become reflective decision makers when they challenge themselves to think about *what* (the content) they are teaching, *how* (the learning activities) they are teaching it, and *why* (the rationale) it must be taught. Sometimes the rationale is included within the unit introduction and goals, but not in every lesson plan of the unit. Some lessons are carryovers or continuations of a lesson; we see no reason to repeat the rationale for a continuing lesson.

Procedure

The procedure consists of the instructional activities for a scheduled period of time. The substance of the lesson—the information to be presented, obtained, and learned—is the *content*. Appropriate information is selected to meet the learning objectives, the level of competence of the students, and the grade level or course requirements. To be sure your lesson actually covers what it should, you should write down exactly what minimum content you intend to cover. This material may be placed in a separate section or combined with the procedure section. It is most important to be sure that your information is written down so you can refer to it quickly and easily when you need to.

If, for instance, you intend to conduct the lesson using discussion, you should write out the key discussion questions. Or, if you are going to introduce new material using a 10-minute lecture, then you need to outline the content of that lecture. The word *outline* is not used casually—you need not have pages of notes to sift through; nor should you ever read declarative statements to your students. You should be familiar enough with the content so that an outline (in as much detail as you believe necessary) will be sufficient to carry on the lesson.

The procedure or procedures to be used, sometimes referred to as the *instructional components,* comprise the *procedure* component of the lesson plan. It is the section that outlines what you and your students will do during the lesson. Appropriate instructional activities are chosen to meet the objectives, to match the students' learning styles and individual needs, and to ensure that all students have an equal opportunity to learn. Ordinarily, you should plan this section of your lesson as an organized entity having a beginning (an introduction or set), a middle, and an end (called the *closure*) to be completed during the lesson. This structure is not always needed, because some lessons are simply parts of units or long-term plans and merely carry on activities spelled out in those long-term plans. Still, most lessons need to include in the procedure: (a) an *introduction,* the process used to prepare the students mentally for the lesson, sometimes referred to as the *set,* or *initiating activity;* (b) *lesson development,* the detailing of *activities* that occur between the beginning and the end of the lesson, including the transitions that connect activities (see discussion regarding Transitions in Chapter 4), (c) plans for *practice,* or, sometimes referred to as the follow-up—that is, ways that you intend to have students interact in the classroom, such as individual practice, in dyads, or small groups, or receive guidance or coaching from each other and from you, (d) the *lesson conclusion* (or closure), the planned process of bringing the lesson to an end, thereby providing students with a sense of completeness and, with effective teaching, accomplishment and comprehension by helping students to synthesize the information learned from the lesson, (e) a *timetable* that serves simply as a planning and implementation guide, (f) a plan for what to do if you finish the lesson and time remains, and (g) *assignments,* that is, what students are instructed to do as follow-up to the lesson, either as homework or as in-class work, providing students an opportunity to practice and enhance what is being learned. Let's now consider some of those components in detail.

Introduction to the Lesson

Like any good performance, a lesson needs an effective beginning. In many respects the introduction sets the tone for the rest of the lesson by alerting the students that the business of learning is to begin. The introduction should be an attention-getter. If it is exciting, interesting, or innovative, it can create a favorable mood for the lesson. In any case, a thoughtful introduction serves as a solid indicator that you are well prepared. While it is difficult to develop an exciting introduction to every lesson, there are always many options available by which to spice up the launching of a lesson. You might, for instance, begin the lesson by briefly reviewing the previous lesson, thereby helping students connect the learning. Another possibility is to review vocabulary words from previous lessons and to introduce new ones. Still another possibility is to use the key point of the day's lesson as an introduction and then again as the conclusion. Sometimes teachers begin a lesson by presenting strange but true scenario or by demonstrating a discrepant event (i.e., an event that is contrary to what one might expect—see Figure 7.1 in Chapter 7), or, as sometimes referred to, a "hook."[3] Yet another possibility is to begin the lesson with a writing activity on some controversial aspect of the ensuing lesson. Sample introductions are: For history, study of westward expansion:

- The teacher asks "Who has lived somewhere else other than *(name of your state)?*" After students show hands and answer, the teacher asks individuals why they moved to *(name of your state).* The teacher then asks students to recall why the first European settlers came to the United States, then moves into the next activity.

For science, study of the science process skill of predicting:

- The teacher takes a glass filled to the brim with colored water (colored so it is more visible) and asks students to discuss and predict (in dyads) how many pennies can be added to the glass before any water spills over the rim of the glass. The teacher records their predictions on the writing board.

In short, you can use the introduction of the lesson to review past learning, bridge the new lesson to the previous lesson, introduce new material, point out the objectives of the new lesson, help students connect their learning with other disciplines or with real life or, by showing what will be learned and why the learning is important, induce in students motivation and a mind-set favorable to the new lesson.

Lesson Development

The developmental activities comprise the bulk of the plan and are the specifics by which you intend to achieve your lesson objectives. They include activities that present information, demonstrate skills, provide reinforcement of previously learned material, and furnish other opportunities to develop understanding and skill. Furthermore, by actions and words, during lesson development the teacher models the behaviors expected of the children. Children need such modeling. By effective modeling, the teacher can exemplify the anticipated learning outcomes. Activities of this section of the lesson plan should be described in some detail so (a) you will know exactly what it is you plan to do and so (b) during the intensity of the class meeting, you do not forget important details and content. It is for this reason you should consider, for example, noting answers (if known) to questions you intend to ask and solutions (if known) to problems you intend to have students solve.

Lesson Conclusion

Having a concise closure to the lesson is as important as having a strong introduction. The concluding activity should summarize and secure what has ensued in the developmental stage and should reinforce the principal points of the lesson. One way to accomplish these ends is to restate the key points of the lesson. Another is to briefly outline the major points. Still another is to review the major concept. Sometimes the closure is not only a review of what was learned but also the summarizing of a question left unanswered signaling a change in your plan of activities for the next day. In other words, it becomes a transitional closure.

Timetable

To estimate the time factors in any lesson can be quite difficult, especially for a beginning teacher. A recommended procedure is during the planning to gauge the amount of time needed for each learning activity and note it alongside the activity and strategy in your plan, as shown in the preferred sample lesson plan format. Placing too much faith in your time estimate may be foolish; an estimate is more for your guidance during the preactive phase of instruction than for anything else. Another important reason for including a time plan in your lesson is to give information to students about how much time they have for a particular activity, such as a quiz or a group activity.

Assignments

When an assignment is to be given, it should be noted in the lesson plan. When to present an assignment to the students is optional—except that it should never be yelled as an afterthought as the students are leaving the classroom. Whether to be begun and completed during class time or done out of school, when giving assignments it is best to write them on the writing board, in a special place on the bulletin board, in each student's assignment log maintained in a binder, or on a handout, taking extra care to be sure that assignment specifications are clear to the students. Many teachers give assignments to their students on a weekly or other periodic basis. When given on a periodic basis, rather than daily, assignments should still be noted in your daily lesson plans to remind yourself to remind students of them.

Once assignment specifications and due dates are given, it is a good idea to not make major modifications to them, and it is especially important to not change assignment specifications several days after an assignment has been given. Last-minute changes in assignment specifications can be very frustrating to students who have already begun or completed the assignment; it shows little respect to those students. (See Learning From Assignments and Homework in Chapter 8.)

Benefits of Coached Practice

Allowing time in class for children to begin work on homework assignments and long-term projects is highly recommended; it provides opportunity for the teacher to provide individual attention to students. Being able to coach students is the reason for using in-class time to begin assignments. The benefits of *coached practice* include (a) monitoring student work so a student doesn't go too far in a wrong direction, (b) helping students to reflect on their thinking, (c) assessing the progress of individual children, (d) providing for peer tutoring, and (e) discovering or creating a "teachable moment." For the latter, for example, while observing and monitoring student practice the teacher might discover a commonly shared student misconception. The teacher then stops and discusses that and attempts to clarify the misconception or, col-

laboratively with students, plans a subsequent lesson centered on the common misconception.

Special Notes and Reminders

In their lesson plan format many teachers have a regular place for special notes and reminders. In that special section that can be referred to quickly, you can place reminders concerning such things as announcements to be made, school programs, long-term assignments, and makeup work for certain students.

Materials and Equipment to Be Used

Materials of instruction include books, media, handouts, and other supplies necessary to accomplish the lesson objectives. It is your obligation as a professional to be *certain* that the proper and necessary materials and equipment are available for the lesson; to be certain requires thoughtful planning. If a surgeon has to wait during an operation to look for surgical tools and other materials needed in order to continue the operation, not only would that surgeon and surgical team be considered incompetent, the patient's life is placed in jeopardy. Teachers who, for one reason or another, have to busy themselves during class looking for materials or equipment that should have been readied before class began are seen as being poorly prepared, incompetent, and are likely to experience classroom control problems.

Assessment, Reflection, and Revision

Details of how you will assess how well students *are* learning (formative assessment) and how well they *have learned* (summative assessment) should be included in your lesson plan. This does not mean to imply that both types of assessment will be in every daily plan, although formative assessment is likely to occur on a daily basis. Formative assessment of student learning that is taking place should be frequent, perhaps as often as on the average of once per minute during direct instruction and during individual or small group coaching. Checks for comprehension can be in the form of questions you ask and that the children ask during the lesson (in the procedural section), as well as various kinds of checklists.

For summative assessment, teachers typically use review questions at the end of a lesson (as a closure) or at the beginning of the next lesson (as a review or transfer introduction), independent

Figure 6.10
Questions for lesson self-reflection

- What is my overall feeling about today's lesson—good, fair, or bad? What made me feel this way?
- Did children seem to enjoy the lesson? What makes me think so?
- Did the objectives seem to be met? What evidence do I have?
- What aspects of the lesson went well? What makes me believe so?
- Were I to repeat the lesson, what changes might I make?
- Which students seemed to do well? Which ones should I give more attention to? Why and how?
- To what extent was this lesson personalized according to student learning styles, abilities, interests, talents, and needs? Could I do more in this regard? Why or why not?
- Did the children seem to have sufficient time to think and apply? Why or why not?
- Would I have been proud had the school superintendent been present to observe this lesson? Why or why not?

practice or summary activities at the completion of a lesson, and tests.

In most lesson plan formats, there is a section reserved for the teacher to write reflective comments about the lesson. Many student teachers seem to prefer to write their reflections at the end or on the reverse page of their lesson plans. As well as being useful to yourself, reflections about the lesson are useful for those who are supervising or mentoring you (See "Professional Development Through Mentoring" in Chapter 12). Questions you might ask yourself are shown in Figure 6.10.

Writing and later reading your reflections can provide not only ideas that may be useful if you plan to use the lesson again at some later date, but offer catharsis, easing the tension caused from teaching. To continue working effectively at a challenging task (that is, to prevent intellectual downshifting—reverting to earlier learned, lower cognitive level behaviors) requires significant amounts of reflection. Proceed now to Exercise 6.7, where you will analyze a lesson that failed; then, as instructed by your course instructor, do Exercises 6.8 and 6.9.

For Your Notes

EXERCISE 6.7 ANALYSIS OF A LESSON THAT FAILED

Instructions: The planning and structure of a lesson are often predictors of the success of its implementation. The purpose of this exercise is to read the following synopsis of the implementation of a lesson, answer the discussion questions individually, and use your responses as a basis for class discussion in small groups about the lesson.

The Setting: Sixth-grade life science class; 1:12–2:07 p.m., spring semester

Synopsis of Events

1:12	Bell rings.
1:12–1:21	Teacher directs students to read from their texts, while he or she takes attendance.
1:21–1:31	Teacher distributes a ditto to each student; students are now to label the parts of a flower shown on the handout.
1:31–1:37	Silent reading and labeling of ditto.
1:37–1:39	Teacher verbally gives instructions for working on a real flower, for example, by comparing it with the drawing on the handout. Students may use the microscopes if they want.
1:39–1:45	Teacher walks around room, giving each student a real flower.
1:45–2:05	Chaos erupts. There is much confusion, with students wandering around, throwing flower parts at each other. Teacher begins writing referrals and sends two students to the office for their misbehavior. Teacher is flustered, directs students to spend remainder of period quietly reading from their texts. Two more referrals are written.
2:05–2:07	A few students begin meandering toward the exit.
2:07	End of period (much to the delight of the teacher).

Questions for Class Discussion

1. Do you think the teacher had a lesson plan? If so, what (if any) were its good points? Its problems?

   _____

   _____

   _____

2. If you believed that the teacher had a lesson plan, do you believe that it was written and detailed? Explain your response. What is your evidence? _____

   _____

   _____

   _____

3. How might the lesson have been prepared and implemented to avoid the chaos? _____

   _____

   _____

   _____

4. Was the format of the lesson traditional? Explain. _____

   _____

   _____

EXERCISE 6.7 *(continued)*

5. Have you experienced a class such as this? Explain. _____

_____

_____

_____

6. Which teacher behaviors were probable causes of much of the chaos? (*Hint:* See Chapter 4.) _____

_____

_____

_____

7. What teacher behaviors could have prevented the chaos and made the lesson more effective? _____

_____

_____

_____

8. Within the 55-minute class period, students were expected to operate rather high on the Learning Experiences Ladder (see Figure 6.5). Consider this analysis: 9 minutes of silent reading; 10 minutes of listening; 6 minutes of silent reading and labeling; 2 minutes of listening; 6 minutes of action (the only direct experience); and an additional 22 minutes of silent reading. In all, there were approximately 49 minutes (89 percent of the class time) of abstract verbal and visual symbolization. Is this a problem? _____

_____

_____

_____

_____

_____

9. What have you learned from this exercise? _____

_____

_____

_____

_____

EXERCISE 6.8A PREPARING A LESSON PLAN

Instructions: Use the model lesson format or an alternative format that is approved by your instructor to prepare a _____-minute lesson plan (length to be decided in your class) for a grade and course of your choice. After completing your lesson plan, evaluate it yourself, modify it, and then have your modified version evaluated by at least three peers, using Exercise 6.8B for the evaluation, before turning it in for your instructor's evaluation. This exercise may be connected with Exercise 6.9.

EXERCISE 6.8B SELF- AND PEER ASSESSMENT OF MY LESSON PLAN

Instructions: You may duplicate blank copies of this form for evaluation of the lesson you developed for Exercise 6.8A. Have your lesson plan evaluated by two of your peers and yourself. For each of the items below, evaluators should check either "yes" or "no," and write instructive comments. Compare the results of your self-evaluation with the other evaluations.

	No	*Yes*	*Comments*
1. Are descriptive data adequately provided?	_____	_____	_____
2. Are the goals clearly stated?	_____	_____	_____
3. Are the objectives specific and measurable?	_____	_____	_____
4. Are objectives correctly classified?	_____	_____	_____
5. Are objectives only low-order or is higher-order thinking expected?	_____	_____	_____
6. Is the rationale clear and justifiable?	_____	_____	_____
7. Is the plan's content appropriate?	_____	_____	_____
8. Is the content likely to contribute to achievement of the objectives?	_____	_____	_____
9. Given the time frame and other logistical considerations, is the plan workable?	_____	_____	_____
10. Will the opening (set) likely engage the students?	_____	_____	_____
11. Is there a preassessment strategy?	_____	_____	_____
12. Is there a proper mix of learning activities for the time frame of the lesson?	_____	_____	_____
13. Are the activities developmentally appropriate for the intended students?	_____	_____	_____

EXERCISE 6.8B *(continued)*

	No	Yes	Comments
14. Are transitions planned?	____	____	_____
15. If relevant, are key questions written out and key ideas noted in the plan?	____	____	_____
16. Does the plan indicate how coached practice will be provided for each student?	____	____	_____
17. Is adequate closure provided in plan?	____	____	_____
18. Are materials and equipment that are needed identified and are they appropriate?	____	____	_____
19. Is there a planned formative assessment, formal or informal?	____	____	_____
20. Is there a planned summative assessment?	____	____	_____
21. Is the lesson coordinated in any way with other aspects of the curriculum?	____	____	_____
22. Is the lesson likely to provide a sense of meaning for the students by helping bridge their learning?	____	____	_____
23. Is an adequate amount of time allotted to address the information presented?	____	____	_____
24. Is a thoughtfully prepared and relevant student assignment planned?	____	____	_____
25. Could a substitute who is knowledgeable follow the plan?	____	____	_____

Additional comments:

EXERCISE 6.9 PREPARING AN INSTRUCTIONAL UNIT: BRINGING IT ALL TOGETHER

Instructions: The purpose of this exercise is threefold, to (a) give you experience in preparing an instructional unit, (b) assist you in preparing an instructional unit that you can use in your teaching, and (c) start your collection of instructional units that you may be able to use later in your teaching. This is an assignment that will take several hours to complete, and you will need to read ahead in this resource guide. Our advice, therefore, is that the assignment be started early, with a due date much later in the course. Your course instructor may have specific guidelines for your completion of this exercise; what follows is the essence of what you are to do.

First, divide your class into two teams, each with a different assignment pertaining to this exercise. The units completed by these teams are to be shared with all members of the class for feedback and possible use later.

Team 1

Members of this team, individually or in dyads, will develop standard teaching units, perhaps with different grade levels in mind. (You will need to review the content of Chapters 7–11.) Using a format that is practical, *each member or pair of this team* will develop a minimum two-week (10-day) unit for a particular grade level, subject, and topic. Regardless of format chosen, each unit plan should include the following elements:

1. Identification of (a) grade level, (b) subject, (c) topic, and (d) time duration.
2. Statement of rationale and general goals.
3. Separate listing of instructional objectives for each daily lesson. Wherever possible, the unit should include objectives from all three domains—cognitive, affective, and psychomotor.
4. List of the materials and resources needed and where they can be obtained (if you have that information). These should be listed for each daily lesson.
5. Ten consecutive daily lesson plans (see Exercise 6.8A).
6. List all items that will be used to assess student learning *during* and at *completion* of the unit of study.
7. Statement of how the unit will attend to variations in students' reading levels, socioethnic backgrounds, and special needs.

Team 2

In collaboration, members of this team will develop interdisciplinary thematic units. Depending upon the number of students in your class, Team 2 may actually comprise several teams, with each team developing an ITU. Each team should be comprised of no less than two members (e.g., a math specialist and a science specialist) and no more than four (e.g., social studies, language arts/reading, mathematics, and science).

For Your Notes

SUMMARY

You have learned of the importance of learning modalities and instructional modes. You have learned about youth, their needs, and the importance of providing an accepting and supportive learning environment, as well as about teacher behaviors that are necessary to facilitate the most meaningful student learning.

With this chapter in particular you continued building your knowledge base about why planning is important and how units with lessons are useful pedagogical tools. Developing units of instruction that integrate student learning and provide a sense of meaning for the students requires coordination throughout the curriculum. Hence, for students, learning is a process of discovering how information, knowledge, and ideas are interrelated so they can make sense out of self, of school, and of life. Preparing chunks of information into units and units into lessons helps students to process and understand knowledge. You have developed your first unit of instruction and are well on your way to becoming a competent planner of instruction.

In Part II, you have been guided through the processes necessary to prepare yourself to teach in a classroom. In Part III your attention is directed to the selection and implementation of specific strategies, aids, and resources from which you may select to facilitate student learning of particular skills and content, beginning with the use of questioning. Later, after you have studied Part III, you may choose to revisit this chapter and make revisions to your completed unit and lessons.

EXTENDING MY COMPETENCY: QUESTIONS FOR CLASS DISCUSSION _____

1. In grade level or grade range (e.g., K–2, 3–4, 5–6) interest groups, list and describe specific considerations you should give to student safety when preparing instructional plans. Share your lists with other groups.
2. Explain the importance of the notion that all teachers are teachers of literacy and of thinking, social, and learning skills. Do you agree or disagree with the notion? Why?
3. Give several reasons why both a student teacher and a first-year teacher need to prepare detailed lesson plans. Describe when, if ever, the teacher can or should divert from the written lesson plan.
4. Divide your class into grade level interest groups. Have each group devise two separate lesson plans to teach the same topic to the same group of students (identified), but where one plan uses direct instruction while the other uses indirect. Have groups share the outcomes of this activity with one another.
5. Explain why, when taught by access strategies, students learn less content but learn it more effectively. For a teacher, could this be a problem? Explain.
6. Which mode, access or delivery, do you believe better encourages student thinking? Explain. Can you find research evidence to support your conclusion? Do you believe use of either mode, access or delivery, does more to enhance the development of student self-esteem? Explain. Can you find research evidence to support your conclusion?
7. Describe observable behaviors that would enable you to tell whether a child is learning to think critically. Describe where, specifically, in a unit plan, one would expect to find these observable behaviors.
8. Describe any prior concepts you held that changed as a result of your experiences with this chapter. Describe the changes.
9. From your current observations and fieldwork as related to this teacher preparation program, clearly identify one specific example of educational practice that seems contradictory to exemplary practice or theory as presented in this chapter. Present your explanation for the discrepancy.
10. Do you have questions generated by the content of this chapter? If you do, list them along with ways answers might be found.

FOR FURTHER READING _____

Berman, S. (1999). *Performance Based Learning for the Multiple Intelligences Classroom*. Arlington Heights, IL: Skylight Professional Development.

Boucher, A. C. (1998). Critical Thinking Through Estimation. *Teaching Children Mathematics, 4*(8), 452–455.

Butzow, C. M., and Butzow, J. W. (1998). *More Science Through Children's Literature: An Integrated Approach*. Englewood, CO: Teacher Ideas Press.

Fuchs, L. (2000). *Asia and Australia: Language Arts Around the World, Volume III*. Cross Curricular Activities for Grades 4–6. Bloomington, IN: Family Learning Association.

Fuchs, L. (2000). *Central and South America: Language Arts Around the World, Volume II*. Cross Curricular Activities for Grades 4–6. Bloomington, IN: Family Learning Association.

Fuchs, L. (2000). *Europe: Language Arts Around the World, Volume I*. Cross Curricular Activities for Grades 4–6. Bloomington, IN: Family Learning Association.

Gipe, J. P. (1998). *Multiple Paths to Literacy: Corrective Reading Techniques for Classroom Teachers,* 4th ed. Upper Saddle River, NJ: Prentice Hall.

Gunning, T. G. (1998). *Assessing and Correcting Reading and Writing Difficulties.* Boston: Allyn & Bacon.

Holt, E. (1998). *Using Primary Sources in the Primary Grades,* ED419773. Bloomington, IN: Clearinghouse for Social Studies/Social Science Education.

Jensen, E. (1998). Getting the Brain's Attention. Chapter 5 of E. Jensen, *Teaching With the Brain in Mind.* Alexandria, VA: Association for Supervision and Curriculum Development.

McAllister, E. A., Hildebrand, J. M., and Ericson, J. H. (2000). *Intriguing Animals. Language Arts Theme Units, Volume IV.* Cross Curricular Activities for Primary Grades. Bloomington, IN: Family Learning Association.

McAllister, E. A., Hildebrand, J. M., and Ericson, J. H. (2000). *Our Environment. Language Arts Theme Units, Volume 1.* Cross Curricular Activities for Primary Grades. Bloomington, IN: Family Learning Association.

McAllister, E. A., Hildebrand, J. M., and Ericson, J. H. (2000). *People Around Us. Language Arts Theme Units, Volume V.* Cross Curricular Activities for Primary Grades. Bloomington, IN: Family Learning Association.

Meinbach, A. M., Fredericks, A. D., and Rothlein, L. (2000). *The Complete Guide to Thematic Units: Creating the Integrated Curriculum,* 2d ed. Norwood, MA: Christopher-Gordon.

Phillips, P., and Bickley-Green, C. (1998). Integrating Art and Mathematics. *Principal, 77*(4), 46–49.

Roberts, P. L., and Kellough, R. D. (2000). *A Guide for Developing an Interdisciplinary Thematic Unit,* 2d ed. Upper Saddle River, NJ: Merrill/Prentice Hall.

Roblyer, M. D. (1999). *Integrating Technology Across the Curriculum: A Database of Strategies and Lesson Plans.* Upper Saddle River, NJ: Merrill/Prentice Hall.

Rogers, L. K. (1999). Spelling Cheerleader. *Reading Teacher, 53*(2), 110–111.

Shanker, J. L., and Ekwall, E. E. (1998). *Locating and Correcting Reading Difficulties,* 2d ed. Upper Saddle River, NJ: Merrill/Prentice Hall.

Strickland, D. S. (1998). *Teaching Phonics Today: A Primer for Educators.* Newark, DE: International Reading Association.

Suranna, K. J. (1999–2000). Using One of the 'Standards for the English Language Arts' to Foster a Relationship Between Culture and Literacy. *Reading Teacher, 53*(4), 287–289.

NOTES

1. For additional information, see the Web site at <http://www.adihome.org> or phone 541-485-1293.
2. See G. Quinn and L. N. Restine, Interdisciplinary Teams: Concerns, Benefits, and Costs, *Journal of School Leadership, 6*(5), 494–511 (September 1996).
3. See, for example, C. Ruck, et al., Using Discrepant Events to Inspire Writing, *Science Activities, 28*(2), 27–30 (Summer 1991), and R. L. Shrigley, Discrepant Events: Why They Fascinate Students, *Science and Children, 24*(8), 24–25 (May 1987).

Strategies, Aids, Media, and Resources for Effective Instruction

Part III responds to your needs concerning:

- Academic success for each student
- Classroom discussions
- Community service learning
- Copyright guidelines
- Electronic media and the Internet for instruction
- Equality in the classroom
- Field trips
- Free and inexpensive instructional materials
- Games and simulations
- Guest speakers
- Helping children develop skills for lifelong learning
- Homework and assignments
- Ideas for motivational lessons
- Inquiry and discovery learning
- Learning centers
- Mastery learning
- Peer tutoring and cross-age teaching
- Personalizing the learning experiences
- Project-centered learning
- Questioning
- Small group and cooperative learning
- Story felt board use
- Student rights
- Student writing and journals
- Teacher talk and demonstrations
- Teaching for thinking and intelligent behavior
- The classroom writing board and bulletin board

REFLECTIVE THOUGHTS

Your teaching goals should include helping students to learn how to solve problems, to make decisions, to think creatively and critically, and to feel good about themselves and their learning. To do this, you will:

1. *Involve students in direct experiences, both hands-on and minds-on, so they use more of their sensory modalities and develop their learning capacities.*

2. *Use questioning in a way designed to guide students to higher levels of thinking and doing.*

3. *Share in the responsibility for teaching reading, writing, thinking, and study skills.*

Experiences afforded by inquiry help students understand the importance of suspending judgment and also the tentativeness of answers and solutions. With those understandings, students eventually are better able to deal with life's ambiguities.

When as a beginning teacher you are planning instruction for a distinct group of children and you have doubt about the appropriateness of a particular strategy, trust your instincts: without some modification, the strategy probably is inappropriate.

It is during extended periods of direct instruction that a beginning teacher's skills in withitness and overlapping behaviors are likely to be put to the test.

It is important that the teacher understand that what for one child may be a matter of simple recall of information, may for another require a higher-order mental activity, such as figuring something out by deduction.

As exclaimed by one teacher using interdisciplinary thematic instruction with student-centered inquiry, "I've never worked harder in my life, but I've never had this much fun, either."

The provision of recovery options for children who are works in progress seems a sensible, humanly, scholarly, and professionally responsible tactic.

Teaching all students how to access and assess Internet sites adds to their repertoire of skills for lifelong learning.

What Do I Need to Know to Effectively Use Questioning as an Instructional Tool?

A strategy that is of fundamental importance to any mode of instruction is, as introduced in Chapter 3, questioning. You will use questioning for so many purposes that you must be skilled in its use to teach effectively. Because it is so important, and because it is so frequently used and abused, this chapter is devoted to assisting you in the development of your skills in using questioning as an instructional tool.

CHAPTER OBJECTIVES

Specifically, upon completion of this chapter you should be able to

1. Compare and contrast the levels of questioning with levels of thinking.
2. Demonstrate skill in encouraging and using student questioning as a learning tool.

Classroom Scenario: Kindergarten Teacher Asks a Rhetorical Question.

At the completion of an opening reading lesson, Tara, a kindergarten teacher, asked the children, "Shall we do our math lesson now?" One of the children in the class, Mario, answered "No, I don't like math." Ignoring Mario's response Tara began the math lesson.

Could or should have Tara done anything different here? What lesson, if any, did Mario learn from the teacher's response or lack of response? What, do you believe, was the intention of Tara's question? Was there a lesson intended by Tara when she asked the question? Explain whether you believe the question was planned and written in Tara's lesson plan.

---

3. Demonstrate skill in using questioning as an instructional tool.
4. Demonstrate understanding of the types of cognitive questions.
5. Describe categories of purposes for which questioning can be used as an instructional strategy.

PURPOSES FOR USING QUESTIONING

You will adapt the type and form of each question to the purpose for which it is asked. The purposes that questions can serve can be separated into five categories, as follows.

1. *To politely give instructions.* Examples are: "Let's move on to the next problem, okay?" or, "Lupe, would you please turn out the lights so we can show the slides?" Although they probably should avoid doing so, teachers sometimes use rhetorical questions for the purpose of regaining student attention and maintaining classroom control, like, for example, "Anthony, would you please attend to your work?" Rhetorical questions can sometimes backfire on the teacher. In this case, for example, Anthony might say "No"; then the teacher would have a problem that could perhaps have been avoided had the teacher at first been more direct and simply told Anthony to attend to his work, rather than asking him if he would.

Consider the scenario at the start of this chapter, Kindergarten Teacher Asks a Rhetorical Question. It seems likely that Tara's intent was to transition from the reading lesson to the mathematics lesson. If Tara was indeed planning to ask the question, then she must be prepared to deal with and not ignore student responses to her question. An improved transition in this instance might be to simply say "It is time now for us to do our math lesson" and follow that with a transitioning question such as "Who can review for us one thing we did (or learned) yesterday in math?"

2. *To review and remind students of classroom procedures.* For example: If students continue to talk when they shouldn't, you can stop the lesson and ask, "Class, I think we need to review the procedure for listening when someone else is talking. Who can tell me, what is the procedure that we agreed upon?"

3. *To gather information.* Examples are: "How many of you have finished the assignment?" or, to find out whether a student knows something, "Briana, can you please explain to us the difference between a synonym and antonym?"

4. *To discover student knowledge, interests, or experiences.* Examples might be: "Where do you think our drinking water comes from?" or "How many of you think you know the process by which water in our city is made drinkable?" or "How many of you have visited the local water treatment plant?"

5. *To guide student thinking and learning.* It is this category of questioning that is the primary focus here. Questions in this category are used to:
   - *Develop appreciation.* For example, "Do you now understand the ecological relationship between that particular root fungus, voles, and the survival of the large conifers of the forests of the Pacific Northwest?"
   - *Develop student thinking.* For example, "What do you suppose the effects to the ecology are when standing water is sprayed with an insecticide that is designed to kill all mosquito larvae?"
   - *Diagnose learning difficulty.* For example, "What part of the problem don't you understand, Sally?"
   - *Emphasize major points.* For example, "If no one has ever been to the Sun, how do we know what it is made of?"
   - *Encourage students.* For example, "OK, so you didn't remember the formula. What really impressed me in your essay is what you did understand about photosynthesis. Do you know what part impressed me?"
   - *Establish rapport.* For example, "We have a conflict here, but I think we can resolve it if we put our heads together. What do you think ought to be our first step?"

- *Evaluate learning.* For example, "Sean, what is the effect when two rough surfaces, such as two slices of toasted bread, are rubbed together?"
- *Give practice in expression.* For example, "Yvonne, would you please share with us the examples of impressionism that you found?"
- *Help students in their metacognition (that is, their thinking about thinking).* For example, "Yes, something did go wrong in the experiment. Do you still think your original hypothesis is correct? If not, then where was the error in your thinking? Or if you still think your hypothesis is correct, then where might the error have been in the design of your experiment? How might we find out?"
- *Help students interpret materials.* For example, "Something seems to be wrong with this compass. How do you suppose we can find out what is wrong with it? For example, if the needle is marked N and S in reverse, as suggested by Hannah, how can we find out if that, in fact, is the problem?"
- *Help students organize materials.* For example, "If you really want to carry out your proposed project, then we are going to need certain information and materials. We are going to have to deal with some strategic questions here, such as, what information and materials do you think we will need, where can we find those things, who will be responsible for getting them, and how will we store and arrange them?"
- *Provide drill and practice.* For example, "Team A has prepared some questions that they would like to use as practice questions for our unit exam, and they are suggesting that we use them to play the game of Jeopardy on Friday. Is everyone okay with their idea?"
- *Provide review.* For example, "Today, in your groups, you are going to study the unit review questions I have prepared. After each group has studied and prepared its answers to these written questions, your group will choose another group and ask them your set of review questions. Each group has a different set of questions. Members of Team A are going to keep score, and the group that has the highest score from this review session will receive free pizza at tomorrow's lunch. Ready?"
- *Show agreement or disagreement.* For example, "Some people believe that stricter gun control laws would reduce acts of violence. With evidence that you have collected from recent articles from newspapers, magazines, and the Internet, do you agree with this conclusion? Explain why or why not."
- *Show relationships, such as cause and effect.* For example, "What do you suppose would be the global effect if just one inch of the entire Antarctic ice shelf were to rather suddenly melt?"
- *Build the curriculum.* It is the students' questions that provide the basis for the learning that occurs in an effective program that is inquiry based and project centered. More on this subject follows later (see Chapters 8 and 9).

Questions to Avoid Asking

Before going further, while it is important to avoid asking rhetorical questions, that is, questions for which you do not intend or even want a response, you should also avoid asking questions that call for little or no student thinking, such as those that can be answered with a simple yes or no or some other sort of alternative answer response. Unless followed up with questions calling for clarification, questions that call for simple responses such as yes or no have little or no diagnostic value; they encourage guessing and inappropriate student responses that can cause classroom control problems for the teacher.

It is even more important to avoid using questions that embarrass a student, punish a student, or in any way deny the student's dignity. Questions that embarrass or punish tend to damage the child's developing self-esteem and serve no meaningful academic or instructional purpose. While it is not always possible to predict when a student might be embarrassed by a question, a teacher should *never* deliberately ask questions for the purpose of embarrassment or punishment. In other words, avoid asking a student a content question when you know full well that the student was not paying attention and/or does not know the answer. When done deliberately to punish or embarrass, that teacher's action borders on abuse!

TYPES OF COGNITIVE QUESTIONS: A GLOSSARY

We now define, describe, and provide examples for each of the *types* of cognitive (or mental) questions that you will use in teaching. Please note that although we refer to these in the traditional fashion as cognitive questions, any question type could relate to any of the three domains of learning (cognitive, affective, or psychomotor). Further, the types of questions are not exclusive or categorically pure. For example, a question that is classed as a divergent-thinking type question might also be classed as a focus question, and vice versa. In the section that follows, your attention is focused on the levels of cognitive questions.

Clarifying Question

The clarifying question is used to gain more information from a student to help the teacher and classmates better understand a student's ideas, feelings, and thought processes. Often, asking a student to elaborate on an initial response will lead the student to think more deeply, restructure his or her thinking, and while doing so, discover a fallacy in the original response. Examples of clarifying questions are "What I hear you saying, Brandon, is that you would rather work alone than in your group. Is that correct?" "So, Molly, you think the poem is a sad one, is that right?" Research has shown a strong positive correlation between student learning and development of metacognitive skills and the teacher's use of questions that ask for clarification.[1] In addition, by seeking clarification, you are likely to be demonstrating an interest in the child as a person and in that child's thinking.

Convergent-Thinking Question

Convergent thinking questions, also called *narrow questions,* are low-order thinking questions that have a single correct answer (such as recall questions, discussed further in the next section). Examples of convergent questions are "How is the Earth classed, as a star or a planet?" "If the radius of a circle is 20 meters, what is its circumference?" "What is the name of the person who was first President of the United States?" Sometimes, like with the first example, it is good to come back with follow-up questions to move the student's thinking beyond simple recall. With this example, a follow-up question could be "Why is Earth classed as a planet?" or "What characteristics are necessary for a celestial body to be classed as a planet?"

Cueing Question

If you ask a question to which, after sufficient **wait time** (longer than 2 seconds), no students respond or to which their responses indicate they need more information, then you can ask a question that cues the answer or response you are seeking.[2] In essence, you are going backward in your ques-

tioning sequence to cue the students. For example, in the preceding example, if there is no response the teacher could ask "Who can name a characteristic that distinguishes stars and planets?"

Or, for another example, as an introduction to a lesson on the study of prefixes, a teacher asks her students, "How many legs each do crayfish, lobsters, and shrimp have?" and there is no accurate response. She might then cue the answer with the following information and question, "The class to which those animals belong is class Decapoda. Does that give you a clue about the number of legs they have?" If that clue is not enough, and after allowing sufficient time for students to think (longer than 2 seconds) then she might ask, "What is a decathlon?" or "What is the Decalogue?" or "What is the decimal system? or "What is a decimeter?" or "What is a decibel?" or "What is a decade?"

When questioning students over reading material in particular, consider using the question-answer relationship (QAR) strategy. QAR involves asking a question and, if a student is unable to respond, providing one of three types of cues. The cues are related to the level of thinking required. "Right there" is used for questions for the lowest level, that is, in which the answer can be found explicitly stated in the sentence or paragraph. "Search and think" means the answer is not directly stated and therefore must be inferred. "On your own" is used for highest-level critical thinking questions for which the answers are neither explicit nor inferred in the text.[3]

Divergent-Thinking Question

Divergent-thinking questions (also known as *broad, reflective, open-ended,* or *thought questions*) usually having no singularly correct answer. These high-order thinking questions require analysis, synthesis, or evaluation. Students must think creatively, leave the comfortable confines of the known, and reach out into the unknown. Examples of questions that require divergent thinking are, "What measures could be taken to improve safety in our community?" "What might be done to improve school spirit?" and "Who would like to tell us why they believe there are or are not any yet-undiscovered planets in our solar system?"

Evaluative Question

Whether convergent or divergent, some questions require students to place a value on something or to take a stance on some issue; these are referred to as *evaluative questions.* If the teacher and the students all agree on certain premises, then the evaluative question would also be a convergent question. If original assumptions differ, then the response to the evaluative question would be more subjective, and therefore that evaluative question would be divergent. Examples of evaluative questions are "Should the United States allow clearcutting in its national forests?" "Should school officials have the right to search student lockers?" and "Is the President of the United States or any other person above the law?"

Focus Question

This is any question that is designed to focus student thinking. For example, the first question of the preceding paragraph is a focus question when the teacher asking it is attempting to focus student attention on the economic issues involved in clear-cutting. Deliberately constructed focus questions, such as "Should every citizen have the right to own a gun?" are especially useful for stimulating student interest at the start of a unit of instruction, such as might be, in this instance, a unit on the U.S. Constitution.

Probing Question

Similar to a clarifying question, the probing question requires student thinking to go beyond superficial first-answer or single-word responses. Examples of probing questions are "Why, Sean, do you think it to be the case that every citizen has the right to have a gun?" Always be cautious, though, and not probe so far as to embarrass the student.

SOCRATIC QUESTIONING

In the fifth century B.C.E., Socrates used the art of questioning so successfully that to this day we still hear of the Socratic method.[4] What, exactly, is the Socratic method? Socrates' strategy was to ask his students a series of leading questions that gradually snarled them up to the point where they had to look carefully at their own ideas and to think rigorously for themselves. Today that strategy is referred to as the Socratic method.

Socratic discussions were informal dialogues taking place in a natural, pleasant environment. Although Socrates sometimes had to go to considerable lengths to ignite his students' intrinsic interest, their response was natural and sponta-neous. In his dialogues, Socrates tried to aid students in developing ideas. He did not impose his own notions on the students. Rather, he encouraged them to develop their own conclusions and draw their own inferences. Of course, Socrates may have had preconceived notions about what the final learning should be and carefully aimed his questions so that the students would arrive at the desired conclusions. Still, his questions were openended, causing divergent rather than convergent thinking. The students were free to go mentally wherever the facts and their thinking led them.

Throughout history, teachers have tried to adapt the methods of Socrates to the classroom. However, we must remember that Socrates used this method in the context of a one-to-one relationship between the student and himself. Some teachers have adapted it for whole-class direct instruction by asking questions first of one student and then of another, moving slowly about the class. This technique may work, but it is difficult because the essence of the Socratic method is to build question on question in a logical fashion so that each question leads the student a step further toward the understanding sought. When you spread the questions around the classroom, you may find it difficult to build up the desired sequence and to keep all the students involved in the discussion. Sometimes you may be able to use the Socratic method by directing all the questions at one student—at least for several minutes—while the other students look on and listen in. That is how Socrates did it. When the topic is interesting enough, this technique can be successful and even fun, but in the long run, the Socratic method works best when the teacher is working in one-on-one coaching situations or with small groups of children, rather than in whole-class direct instruction.

Thinking Is the Quintessential Activity

In using Socratic questioning, the focus is on the questions, not answers, and thinking is valued as the quintessential activity.[5] In essence, to conduct Socratic questioning, with the student or class identify a problem (either student- or teacher-posed) and then ask the students a series of probing questions designed to cause them to examine critically the problem and potential solutions to it. The main thrust of the questioning and the key questions must be planned in advance so that the questioning will proceed logically. To think of quality probing questions on the spur of the moment is too difficult. With guidance from your instructor, it is the Socratic method that you will be encouraged to use in a micro peer teaching exercise later in this chapter (Exercise 7.5).

LEVELS OF COGNITIVE QUESTIONS AND STUDENT THINKING

The questions you pose are cues to your students to the level of thinking expected of them, ranging from the lowest level of mental operation, requiring simple recall of knowledge (convergent thinking), to the highest, requiring divergent thought and application of that thought. It is important that you are knowledgeable about the levels of thinking, that you understand the importance of attending to student thinking from low to higher levels of operation, and that you understand that what for one child may be a matter of simple recall of information, may for another require a higher-order mental activity, such as figuring something out by deduction.

You should structure and sequence your questions (and assist students in developing their skills in structuring and sequencing questions) in a way that is designed to guide students to higher levels of thinking and to connect their understandings. For example, when children respond to your questions in complete sentences that provide supportive evidence for their ideas, it is fairly safe to assume that their thinking is connected to their knowledge and experiences and is at a higher level than were the response an imprecise and nondescriptive single-word answer.

To help your understanding, three levels of questioning and thinking are described as follows.[6] You should recognize the similarity between these three levels of questions and the six levels of thinking from Bloom's taxonomy of cognitive objectives (Chapter 5). For your daily use of questioning it is just as useful but more practical to think and behave in terms of these three levels, rather than of six.

1. *Lowest level (the data input phase): Gathering and recalling information.* At this level questions are designed to solicit from students concepts, information, feelings, or experiences that were gained in the past and stored in memory. Sample key words and desired behaviors are:

> complete, count, define, describe, identify, list, match, name, observe, recall, recite, select

Thinking involves receiving data through the sensory receptors (the senses), followed by the processing of those data. Inputting without processing is brain-dysfunctional. Information that has not been processed is stored only in short-term memory.

2. *Intermediate level (the data-processing phase): Processing information.* At this level questions are designed to draw relationships of cause and effect, to synthesize, analyze, summarize, compare, contrast, or classify data. Sample key words and desired behaviors are:

> analyze, classify, compare, contrast, distinguish, explain, group, infer, make an analogy, organize, plan, synthesize

Thinking and questioning that involve processing of information can be conscious or unconscious. When students observe the teacher thinking aloud, and when they are urged to think aloud, to think about their thinking, and to analyze it as it occurs, they are in the process of developing their intellectual skills.

At the processing level, this internal analysis of new data may challenge a learner's preconceptions (and misconceptions—also called *naïve theories*) about a phenomenon. The learner's brain will naturally resist this challenge to existing beliefs. The greater the mental challenge, the greater will be the brain's effort to draw upon data already in storage. With increasing data, the mind will gradually examine existing concepts and ultimately, as necessary, develop new mental concepts.

If there is a match between new input and existing mental concepts, no problem exists. Piaget called this process *assimilation.*[7] If, however, in processing new data there is no match with existing mental concepts, then the situation is what Piaget called *cognitive disequilibrium.* The brain is "discontented" about this disequilibrium and will drive the search for an explanation for the discrepancy. Piaget called this process *accommodation.*

While learning is enhanced by challenge, in situations that are threatening the brain is less flexible in accommodating new ideas. As discussed in Chapter 4, that is why each student must feel welcomed in the classroom and the classroom environment must be perceived by the learner as challenging but nonthreatening—what is referred to as an environment of *relaxed alertness.*[8]

Questions and experiences must be designed to elicit more than merely recall memory responses. Many teachers find it useful to use strategies that create cognitive disequilibrium, such as to demonstrate discrepant events in order to introduce lessons and concepts. Hearing about or especially seeing a discrepancy stirs the mind into processing and into higher mental activity, without which mental development does not occur. (See example in Figure 7.1.)

Figure 7.1
Example of a discrepant event demonstration

Combustible Won't Burn

Practice this first. Wrap a dollar bill (or a $20 if you are confident) around a drinking glass. While holding the bill tightly around the glass, try to ignite the bill with a match or lighter. The paper bill will not ignite because the glass conducts the heat away too rapidly, maintaining the paper below its kindling point. After removing the bill from the glass you may (if you wish and are wealthy) ignite the bill for a moment to prove to the children that it will indeed burn.

---

3. *Highest level (the data output phase): Applying and evaluating in new situations.* At the highest level of thinking questions are designed to encourage learners to think intuitively, creatively, and hypothetically, to use their imagination, to ex-pose a value system, or to make a judgment. Sample key words and desired behaviors are:

apply a principle, build a model, evaluate, extrapolate, forecast, generalize, hypothesize, imagine, judge, predict, speculate

You must use questions at the level best suited for the purpose, use questions of a variety of different levels, and structure questions in a way intended to move student thinking to higher levels. When teachers use higher-level questions, their students tend to score higher on tests of critical thinking and on standardized tests of achievement.[9]

With the use of questions as a strategy to move student thinking to higher levels, the teacher is facilitating the students' intellectual development. Developing your skill in using questioning requires attention to detail and practice. The guidelines and exercises that follow will provide that detail and some initial practice, but first, do Exercise 7.1 to check your comprehension of the levels of questions.

EXERCISE 7.1 IDENTIFYING THE COGNITIVE LEVELS OF QUESTIONS— A SELF-CHECK EXERCISE

Instructions: The purpose of this exercise is to test your understanding and recognition of the levels of questions. Mark each of the following questions with a:

1, if it is at the lowest level of mental operation, gathering and recalling data.
2, if it is at a middle level, processing data.
3, if it is at the highest level, applying or evaluating data in a new situation.

Check your answers against the key that follows. Resolve problems by discussing them with your classmates and instructor.

_____ 1. Do you recall the differences between an Asian elephant and an African elephant?

_____ 2. How are the natural habitats of the Asian and African elephants similar? How are they different?

_____ 3. Which of the elephants do you think is the more interesting?

_____ 4. For what do you think the elephant uses its tusks?

_____ 5. Do all elephants have tusks?

_____ 6. Did the trick ending make the story more interesting for you?

_____ 7. How might these evergreen needles be grouped?

_____ 8. How do these two types of pine needles differ?

_____ 9. For how many years was the Soviet Union a communist-dominated nation?

_____ 10. How many republics do you believe will be in the new Commonwealth of Independent States (the former Soviet Union) by the year 2020?

_____ 11. Why do you think the city decided to move the zoo?

_____ 12. How would the park be different today had the zoo been left there?

_____ 13. How do zoos today differ from those of the mid-19th century?

_____ 14. Should a teacher be entitled to unemployment benefits during the summer or when school is not in session?

_____ 15. If $4X + 40 = 44$, what is X?

_____ 16. What happens when I spin this egg?

_____ 17. How does this poem make you feel?

_____ 18. What will happen when we mix equal amounts of the red and yellow solutions?

_____ 19. What is the capital of West Virginia?

_____ 20. What will be the long-term global effects if the rain forests continue to be removed at the present rate?

Answer Key: 1 = 1 (recall); 2 = 2 (compare); 3 = 3 (judge); 4 = 3 (imagine); 5 = 3 (extrapolate); 6 = 3 (evaluate); 7 = 2 (classify); 8 = 2 (contrast); 9 = 1 (recall); 10 = 3 (predict); 11 = 2 (explain cause and effect); 12 = 3 (speculate); 13 = 2 (contrast); 14 = 3 (judge); 15 = 1 (recall of how to work the problem); 16 = 1 (observe); 17 = 1 (describe); 18 = 3 (hypothesize); 19 = 1 (recall); 20 = 3 (speculate or generalize)

Figure 7.2
Examples of questions that use appropriate cognitive terminology

Instead of	Say
"How else might it be done?"	"How could you *apply*. . . ?"
"Are you going to get quiet?"	"If we are going to hear what Joan has to say, what do you need to do?"
"How do you know that is so?"	"What evidence do you have?"
"What do you think might happen?"	"What do you *predict* might happen?"

GUIDELINES FOR USING QUESTIONING

As emphasized many times in several ways throughout this resource guide, the goals for instruction extend far beyond merely filling student's minds with bits and pieces of information that will likely last only a brief time in their short-term memory. You must help your students learn how to solve problems, to make intelligent decisions and value judgments, to think creatively and critically, and to feel good about themselves, their school community, and their learning. How you construct your questions and how you implement questioning is important to the realization of these goals.

Preparing Questions

When preparing questions, consider the following guidelines.

Key questions should be planned, thoughtfully worded, and written into your lesson plan. Thoughtful preparation of questions helps to ensure that they are clear and specific, not ambiguous, that the vocabulary is appropriate for the children's understanding, and that each question matches its purpose. Incorporate questions into your lessons as instructional devices, welcomed pauses, attention grabbers, and as checks for student comprehension. Thoughtful teachers even plan questions that they intend to ask specific students, targeting questions to the readiness level, interest, or learning profile of a student.

Match questions with their target purposes. Carefully planned questions allow them to be sequenced and worded to match the levels of cognition expected of students. To help students in developing their thinking skills, you need to demonstrate how to do this. To demonstrate, you must use terminology that is specific and that provides students with examples of experiences consonant with the meanings of the cognitive words. Explicitly using cognitive terms with students—terms such as apply, interpret, and predict—encourages the construction of new mental concepts.[10] See the examples in Figure 7.2.

Implementing Questioning

Careful preparation of questions is one part of the skill in questioning. Implementation is the other part. Here are guidelines for effective implementation.

Ask your well-worded question before calling on a student for a response. A common error made is when the teacher first calls on a student and then asks the question, such as "Sean, would you please tell us what you believe the author meant by the title 'We Are One'?" Although probably not intended by the teacher, as soon as the teacher called on Sean, that signaled the other students that they were released from having to think about the question. Instead, the preferred strategy is to phrase the question, allow time for all students to think, and then call on Sean and other students for their interpretations of the author's meaning by the title.

Avoid bombarding students with too much teacher talk. Sometimes teachers talk too much. This could be especially true for teachers who are nervous, as might be the case for many during initial weeks of their student teaching or when observed by their college or university supervisor or the school principal. Knowing and comprehending the guidelines presented here will help you avoid that syndrome. Remind yourself to be quiet after you ask a question that you have carefully formulated. Sometimes, due to lack of confidence and especially when a question hasn't been carefully planned, the teacher asks the question and then, with a slight change in wording, asks it again or asks several questions, one after another. That is too much verbiage. It's called "shotgun questioning" and only confuses children, allowing too little time between questions for them to think and to process the question.

After asking a question, provide students with adequate time to think. The pause after asking a question is called *wait time* (or *think time*). Knowing the subject better than the children know it and having given prior thought to the topic, too many teachers after asking a question fail to allow students sufficient time to think, especially for questions that extend beyond mere recall of information, that is, that require processing of information and higher-order thinking. In addition, children quickly learn to play the "game"— that is, they learn that when the teacher asks a question, if they remain silent long enough the teacher will probably answer the question. So, to avoid that, after asking a well-worded question you should remain quiet for awhile, allowing children time to think and to respond. If you wait long enough, they usually will. You may need to rehearse your students on this procedure.

As researchers have verified ever since the now classic studies of M. B. Rowe were published more than a quarter a century ago, increasing wait time to at least 2 seconds often leads to longer and higher-quality student responses and participation by a greater number of students.[11] After asking a question, how long should you wait before you do something? You should wait at least 3 seconds, and as long as 5 or sometimes even longer (when it appears it is needed because students are still thinking). Stop reading now and look at your watch or a clock to get a feeling for how long 3 seconds is. Then, observe how long 5 seconds is. Did 5 seconds seem a long time? Because most of us are not used to silence in the classroom, 3 seconds of silence can seem quite long, while 5 seconds may seem eternal. If, for some reason, students have not responded after a period of 3 to 5 seconds of wait time, then you can ask the question again (but don't reword an already carefully worded question unless you tell them you are rewording it, or else students are likely to think it is a new question). Pause for several seconds; then if you still haven't received a response you can call on a student, then another, if necessary, after sufficient wait time. Soon you will get a response that can be built upon. Avoid answering your own question!

Give the same minimum amount of wait time (think time) to all students. This, too, will require concentrated effort on your part, but is important to do. A teacher who waits for less time when calling on a low-achieving student or children of one gender or some other personal characteristic, is showing a prejudice or a lack of confidence in certain students, both of which are detrimental when a teacher is striving to establish for all students a positive, equal, and safe environment for classroom learning. Show confidence in all students, and never discriminate by expecting less or more from some than from others. While some students may take longer to respond, it is not necessarily because they are not thinking or have less ability. There may be cultural differences to think about, in that some cultures simply allow more wait time than others. The important point here is to individualize to allow students who need more time to have it. Variation in wait time allowed should not be used to single out some children and to lead to lower expectations but rather to allow for higher expectations.

Practice gender equity. To practice gender equity when using questions, here are four rules to follow: (a) Avoid going to a boy to bail out a girl who fails to answer a question, and (b) avoid going to a boy to improve upon a girl's answer. For the first, without seeming to badger, try to give the student clues until she can answer with success. For the second, hold and demonstrate high expectations for all students. (c) Allow equal wait time regardless of student gender. (d) Call on boys and girls equally.

Practice calling on all students. Related to the fourth rule of the preceding paragraph, you must call on not just the bright or the slow, not just the boys or the girls, not only those in the front or middle of the room, but all of them. To do these things takes concentrated effort on your part, but it is important. To ensure that students are called on equally, some teachers have in hand laminated copies of their seating charts, perhaps on bright neon-colored clipboards (gives children a visual focus), and, with a wax pencil or water soluble marker, they make a mark next to the name of the student each time he or she is called on. With the seating chart laminated and using erasable markers, the marks can be erased at the end of the day and the seating chart used over and over. Additional suggestions for practicing equity in the classroom are discussed in Chapter 8.

Require students to raise their hands and be called on. When you ask questions, instead of allowing students to randomly shout out their answers, require students to raise their hands and be called on before responding. Establish that procedure at the beginning of the school year and stick with it. This helps to ensure that you call on all students equally, fairly distributing your interactions with the students, and that girls are not interacted with less because boys tend to be more obstreperous. Even in college classrooms, male students tend to be more vocal than female students do and, when allowed by the instructor, tend to outtalk and to interrupt their female peers. Even in same-gender classrooms, some students tend to be more vocal while others are less so and, when allowed by the instructor, tend to monopolize and control the flow of the verbal interactions. Regardless of grade level, every teacher has the responsibility to guarantee a nonbiased classroom and an equal distribution of interaction time in the classroom. That is impossible to do if students are allowed to talk at will.

Another important reason for this advice is to aid children in their learning to control their impulsivity. Self-control of one's impulsivity is one of the characteristics of intelligent behavior presented and discussed in Chapter 9. One of your many instructional responsibilities is to help children to practice and develop this skill.

Actively involve as many students as possible in the questioning-answering discussion session. The traditional method of the teacher asking a question and then calling on a student to respond is essentially a one-on-one interaction. Many students, those not called on, are likely to view that as their opportunity to disengage in the lesson at hand. Even though you call on one student, you want the other students to not mentally disengage. There are many effective ways to keep all engaged. Consider the following.

To keep all students mentally engaged, call on students who are sitting quietly and have not raised their hands as well as those who have, but avoid badgering or humiliating an unwilling participant. When a student has no response, you might suggest that the student think about it and you will come back to the student to ensure that the student eventually understands or has an answer to the original question.

You can increase the number of students involved when you divide a single question into several parts. For example, "What are the causes of the Civil War? Who can give one reason?" followed then by "Who can give another?" Or, you can involve several students in answering a single question. For example, ask one student for an answer to a question, such as "What was the first battle of the Civil War?" a second to read the text aloud to verify the student's answer, and sometimes a third to explore the reason or thinking that makes it the accepted answer.

Still another very effective way to encourage maximum student participation is to arrange classroom seating in a circle rather than in rows or clusters, so that every member of the classroom, including the teacher, is seated in the circle's perimeter and is equally visible to every other member.

Carefully gauge your responses to students' responses to your questions. The way you respond to students' answers influences students' subsequent participation. For example, if when asked "What is 3×6?" the student answers "9," or when asked "What is the verb in this sentence?" the student responds "what," your cueing, prompting, and guiding the child to correct and understandable answers allows children to avoid embarrassment in front of peers when they give incorrect or misunderstood answers to your questions. Responses by the teacher that encourage student participation include probing for elaboration, discussing student answers, probing with cueing and prompting questions, requesting justification, asking how answers were arrived at, and providing positive reinforcement.

Use strong praise sparingly. A teacher's use of strong praise is sometimes okay, especially with kindergarten and early primary grade children. But for older students and when you want students to think divergently and creatively, you should be stingy with use of strong praise to student responses. Strong praise from a teacher tends to terminate divergent and creative thinking. Strong praise can also cause children to become "praise junkies," that is, to become dependent on external sources of praise. (See discussion and Figure 3.4 in Chapter 3 about praise versus encouragement.)

One of your goals is to help children discover intrinsic sources for motivation, that is, an inner drive of intent or desire that causes them to want to learn. Use of strong praise tends to build conformity, causing students to depend on outside forces—that is, the giver of praise—for their worth rather than upon themselves. An example of a strong praise response is "That's right! Very good." On the other hand, passive acceptance responses, such as "Okay, that seems to be one possibility," keep the door open for further thinking, particularly for higher-level, divergent thinking.

Another example of a passive acceptance response is one used in brainstorming sessions, when the teacher says, "After asking the question and giving you time to think about it, I will hear your ideas and record them on the board." Only after all responses have been heard and recorded does the class begin its consideration of each. That kind of nonjudgmental acceptance of all ideas in the classroom will generate a great deal of expression of high-level thought.

Now, to better understand the art of questioning, the importance of well-worded questions and well-prepared and clear instructions, and the importance of allowing students time to think, do Exercise 7.2.

EXERCISE 7.2 WAIT TIME AND THE ART OF QUESTIONING: AN IN-CLASS SIMULATION

Instructions: The purpose of this exercise is to further your understanding of the art and power of questioning, the importance of well-worded questions with well-prepared and clear instructions, and the importance of allowing students time to think.

1. Role-play simulation: From your class ask for three volunteers. One volunteer will read the lines of Estella, a second will read the one line of student, while the third volunteer uses a stop watch to direct Estella and the student to speak their lines at the designated times. The rest of your class can pretend to be students in Estella's class.

   1:00:   *Estella:* "Think of a man whom you admire, perhaps a father figure, and write a three-sentence paragraph describing that person." Students begin their writing.

   1:00:05:   *Estella:* "Only three sentences about someone you look up to. It might be your father, uncle, anyone."

   1:00:07:   *Student:* "Does it have to be about a man?"
                   Estella: "No, it can be a man or a woman, but someone you truly admire."

   1:01:   Estella works the rows, seeing that students are on task.

   1:01:10:   *Estella:* "Three sentences are all you need to write."

   1:01:15:   *Estella:* "Think of someone you really look up to, and write three sentences in a paragraph that describes that person."

   1:01:30:   *Estella:* "Someone you would like to be like."

   1:02:   Estella continues walking around helping students who are having difficulty. All students are on task.

   1:04:   *Estella:* "Now I want you to exchange papers with the person behind or beside you, read that person's description of the person they admire, and describe a setting that you see their person in. Write a paragraph that describes that setting."

   1:04–1:05: Students exchange papers; teacher walks around seeing that everyone has received another student's paper.

   1:05:   *Estella:* "Where do you see that person being? Below the paragraph I want you to write a new paragraph describing where you see this person, perhaps in an easy chair watching a ball game, on a porch, in a car, or in the kitchen cooking."

   1:05:10:   *Estella:* "Describe a scene you see this person in."

   1:05:15:   *Estella:* "After you read the description I want you to create a setting for the person described."

   1:05:18:   Students seem confused either about what they are reading (e.g., asking the writer what a word is or means) or what they are supposed to do.

   1:05:19:   *Estella:* "Anything is fine. Use your imagination to describe the setting."

   1:05:22:   *Estella:* "Describe a setting for this person."

   1:09:   *Estella:* "Now I want you to exchange papers with yet someone else, and after reading the previous two paragraphs written by two other students, write a third paragraph describing a problem you think this admired person has."

2. After the role-play simulation, hold a whole-class discussion or small-group discussions and use the following as a springboard for your discussion: Describe what you believe are the good points and weak points of this portion of Estella's lesson and her implementation of it.

QUESTIONS FROM STUDENTS: THE QUESTION-DRIVEN CLASSROOM

Student questions can and should be used as springboards for further questioning, discussions, and inquiry. Indeed, in a constructivist learning environment, student questions often drive content. Children should be encouraged to ask questions that challenge the textbook (see, for example, the history textbook example in Chapter 5), the process, the Internet source, or other persons' statements, and they should be encouraged to seek the supporting evidence behind a statement.

Being able to ask questions may be more important than having right answers. Knowledge is derived from asking questions. Being able to recognize problems and to formulate questions is a skill and the key to problem solving and critical-thinking skill development. You have a responsibility to encourage children in your classroom to formulate questions and to help them word their questions in such a way that tentative answers can be sought. That is the process necessary to build a base of knowledge that can be drawn upon whenever necessary to link, interpret, and explain new information in new situations.

Questioning: The Cornerstone of Critical Thinking, Real-World Problem Solving, and Meaningful Learning

Real-world problem solving usually offers no absolute correct answers. Rather than "correct" answers, some are better than others. The student with a problem needs to learn how to (a) recognize the problem, (b) formulate a question about the problem (e.g., Should I hang out with this person or not? Should I tell what I know or not? Shall I join the gang or not? Should I use illegal drugs or not?), (c) collect data, and (d) arrive at a temporarily acceptable answer to the problem, while realizing that at some later time, new data may dictate a review of the former conclusion. For example, if a biochemist believes she has discovered a new enzyme, there is no textbook or teacher or any other outside authoritative source to which she may refer to find out if she is correct. Rather, on the basis of her self-confidence in problem identification, asking questions, collecting sufficient data, and arriving at a tentative conclusion based on those data, she assumes that for now her conclusion is safe.

Encourage students to ask questions about content and process. Question asking often indicates that the inquirer is curious, puzzled, and uncertain;

it is a sign of being engaged in thinking about a topic. And, yet, in too many classrooms too few students ask questions.[12] Students should be encouraged to ask questions. Actually, children are naturally curious and full of questions. Their natural curiosity should never be stifled. After all, we learn in school that what is called knowledge is in reality the answers to other peoples' prior questions.

From children, there is no such thing as a "dumb" question. Sometimes in a classroom, students, like everyone else, ask questions that could just as easily have been looked up or are seemingly irrelevant or show lack of thought or sensitivity. Those questions can consume precious class time. For a teacher, they can be frustrating. A teacher's initial reaction may be to quickly and mistakenly brush off that type of question with sarcasm, while assuming that the student is too lazy to look up an answer. In such instances, you are advised to think before responding and to respond kindly and professionally, although in the busy life of a classroom teacher that may not always be so easy to remember to do. However, be assured, there is a reason for a student's question. Perhaps the student is signaling a need for recognition or simply demanding attention.

In large schools, it is sometimes easy for a child to feel alone and insignificant (though this seems less the case with schools where teachers and students work together in teams, and, as in looping, where one cadre of teachers remains with the same cohort of children for 2 or more years).[13] When a child makes an effort to interact with you, that can be a positive sign so gauge carefully your responses to those efforts. If a child's question is really off track, off the wall, out of order, and out of context with the content of the lesson, consider this as a possible response: "That is an interesting question (or comment), and I would very much like to talk with you more about it. Could we talk at lunch or recess time?"

Avoid bluffing an answer to a question for which you do not have an answer. Nothing will cause you to lose credibility with children any faster than faking an answer. There is nothing wrong with admitting that you do not know. It helps children realize that you are human. It helps them maintain an adequate self-esteem, realizing that they are okay. What *is* important is that you know where and how to find possible answers and that you help children develop that same knowledge and those same process skills.

Now, to reinforce your understanding, do Exercises 7.3 through 7.8.

For Your Notes

EXERCISE 7.3 EXAMINING COURSE MATERIALS FOR LEVELS OF QUESTIONING

Instructions: The purpose of this exercise is to discover the level of questions found in instructional materials. It is often reported that when evaluating the levels of questions found in teacher guides, student workbooks, and tests, a very high percentage of the questions are low level, or devoted to factual recall. Examine course materials for the levels of questions presented to students. For a subject and grade level you intend to teach, examine a textbook (or other instructional material) for the questions posed to students, perhaps at the ends of the chapters. Also examine workbooks, examinations, instructional packages, and any other printed or electronic material used by students. Complete the exercise that follows; then share your findings with your classmates.

1. Materials examined (include date of publication and target students): _____

   _____

   _____

   _____

   _____

2. Questions at the recall (lowest) level: _____

   _____

   _____

   _____

   _____

   _____

3. Questions at the processing (intermediate) level: _____

   _____

   _____

   _____

   _____

   _____

4. Questions at the application (highest) level: _____

   _____

   _____

   _____

   _____

   _____

5. Approximate percentages of questions at each level: _____

   a. Recall = _____%

   b. Processing = _____%

   c. Application = _____%

EXERCISE 7.3 *(continued)*

6. Did you find evidence of question-level sequencing? If so, describe it. _____

_____

_____

_____

_____

_____

_____

_____

7. After sharing and discussing your results with your classmates, what do you conclude from this

   exercise? _____

_____

_____

_____

_____

_____

_____

_____

8. When using instructional materials that you believe have a disproportionately high percentage of

   questions at the input (or recall) level, in addition to the two examples provided, what should or could

   you do? _____

   Example 1: Have students scan chapter subheadings and develop higher-level cognitive questions

   based on the subheadings, which they would then answer through their reading._____

   Example 2: Require students to defend their answers to low-level cognitive chapter review and

   end-of-chapter questions with textual information and experience._____

_____

_____

_____

_____

_____

_____

_____

EXERCISE 7.4 OBSERVING THE COGNITIVE LEVELS OF CLASSROOM VERBAL INTERACTION

Instructions: The purpose of this exercise is to develop your skill in recognizing the levels of classroom questions. Arrange to visit an elementary school classroom, and, in the spaces provided below, tally each time you hear a question (or statement) from the teacher that causes students to gather or recall information, to process information, or to apply or evaluate data. In the left-hand column you may want to write additional key words to assist your memory. After your observation, compare and discuss the results of this exercise with your colleagues.

School and class visited _____

Date of observation _____

Level	Question or Statement
Recall level Key words: *complete, count, define, describe,* and so on	
Processing level Key words: *analyze, classify, compare,* and so on	
Application and evaluation level Key words: *apply, build, evaluate,* and so on	

For Your Notes

EXERCISE 7.5 PRACTICE IN RAISING QUESTIONS TO HIGHER LEVELS

Instructions: The purpose of this exercise is to develop your skill in raising questions from one level to the next higher level. Complete the blank spaces with questions at the appropriate levels, then share and discuss your responses with your classmates.

Recall Level	Processing Level	Application and Evaluation Level
1. How many of you read a newspaper today?	Why did you read a newspaper today?	What do you think would happen if nobody ever read a newspaper again?
2. What was today's newspaper headline?	Why was that topic important enough to be a headline?	Do you think that news item will be in tomorrow's paper?
3. Who is the vice president of the United States?	How does the work he has done compare with that done by the previous vice president?	
4. Has the United States had a woman president?		
5. (Create your own questions.)		

For Your Notes

EXERCISE 7.6 PRACTICE IN CREATING COGNITIVE QUESTIONS

Instructions: The purpose of this exercise is to provide practice in writing cognitive questions. Read the following poem. Then, compose three questions about it that cause students to identify, list, and recall; three that cause students to analyze, compare, and explain; and three that cause students to predict, apply, and hypothesize. Share and evaluate the questions with your peers.

We Are One

Truth, love, peace, and beauty,
We have sought apart
    but will find within, as our
Moods—explored, shared,
    questioned, and accepted—
Together become one and all.

Through life my friends
We can travel together,
    for we now know
Each could go it alone.

To assimilate our efforts into one,
While growing in accepting,
    and trusting, and sharing the
    individuality of the other,
Is truly to enjoy our greatest gift—
Feeling—knowing love and compassion.

Throughout life my friends
We are together,
    for we must know
We are one.

—R. D. Kellough

Recall Questions

1. To identify _____

_____

_____

_____

2. To list _____

_____

_____

_____

3. To recall _____

_____

For Your Notes

EXERCISE 7.7 A COOPERATIVE LEARNING AND MICRO PEER TEACHING EXERCISE IN THE USE OF SOCRATIC QUESTIONING—MICRO PEER TEACHING I

Instructions: The purpose of this exercise is to practice preparing and asking questions that are designed to lead student thinking from the lowest level to the highest. Before class, prepare a 5-minute lesson for posing questions that will guide the learner from lowest to highest levels of thinking. Teaching will be one-on-one, in groups of four, with each member of the group assuming a particular role—teacher, student, judge, or recorder. Each of the four members of your group will assume each of those roles once for 5 minutes. (If there are only three members in a group, the roles of judge and recorder can be combined during each 5-minute lesson; or, if there are five members in the group, one member can sit out each round or two can work together as judge.) Each member of the group should have his or her own tally sheet.

Suggested Lesson Topics

- Teaching styles
- Characteristics of youngsters of a particular age
- Learning styles of students
- Evaluation of learning achievement
- A skill or hobby
- Teaching competencies
- A particular teaching strategy
- Student teaching and what it will really be like

Each of your group members should keep the following role descriptions in mind:

- *Teacher (sender).* Pose recall (input), processing, and application (output) questions related to one of the topics above or to any topic you choose.
- *Student (receiver).* Respond to the questions of the teacher.
- *Judge.* Identify the level of each question or statement used by the teacher *and* the level of the student's response.
- *Recorder.* Tally the number of each level of question or statement used by the teacher (S = sender) as indicated by the judge; also tally the level of student responses (R = receiver). Record any problems encountered by your group.

TALLY SHEET				
	Minute	**Input**	**Processing**	**Output**
Sender _____	1 S			
Receiver _____	R			
	2 S			
	R			
	3 S			
	R			
	4 S			
	R			
	5 S			
	R			

EXERCISE 7.7 *(continued)*

	Minute	Input	Processing	Output
TALLY SHEET				
Sender _____	1 S			
Receiver _____	R			
	2 S			
	R			
	3 S			
	R			
	4 S			
	R			
	5 S			
	R			

EXERCISE 7.8 PRACTICE IN IDENTIFYING TEACHING BEHAVIORS IN CLASSROOM INTERACTION—A SELF-CHECK EXERCISE*

Instructions: The purpose of this exercise is to assess your understanding of the teacher's use of certain facilitative behaviors, including the use of questioning. It is a synthesis of what you have learned not only from this chapter but from previous chapters as well. (You may want to refer to Chapter 3.) The following is a sample classroom interaction, which includes examples of various levels of questions and structuring and responsive behaviors. See if you can identify them. Your answers should be from this list: *structuring, facilitating, active acceptance, passive acceptance, clarifying, input questioning, process questioning,* and *application questioning.* (An answer key is found at the end of this exercise.) Discuss and resolve any problems with your classmates and instructor.

Interaction		**Teacher's Behavior**
Joyce:	Ms. Clarion, here's a picture that shows how a magnet works.	
Teacher:	Okay, Joyce, would you please share this with the rest of the group? Tell us what you think is happening.	1. _____
Joyce:	Well, this girl is in the garage using a magnet to pick up things, and over here it shows all the things a magnet will pick up.	
Teacher:	What kind of things are they, Joyce?	2. _____
Joyce:	Nails, paper clips, spoons, screws, screwdr—	
Molly:	It will not pick up spoons, Joyce. I've tried it.	
Joyce:	It will too. It shows right here.	
Olivia:	I picked up a spoon with a magnet that my uncle gave me.	
Joyce:	Sure it will.	
Sarah:	No it won't, 'cause—	
Teacher:	Just a minute. We'd like to hear everyone's idea, but we can't if we all talk at once. If you'll raise your hand, then I'll know who to call on next.	3. _____
Teacher:	Now, Joyce says a magnet will pick up spoons. Sarah says that a magnet can't pick it up.	4. _____
Teacher:	Yes, Sarah, what do you think?	5. _____
Sarah:	I'm not sure, but I think it has to be metal.	
Linda:	I think it depends upon the kind of spoon. Some spoons have metal, and some are plastic and other stuff.	
Teacher:	That's another possibility.	6. _____
Teacher:	How can we solve this problem as to whether a magnet will pick up the spoons?	7. _____
Molly:	We can get some spoons and try it with our magnet.	
Teacher:	All right. Anybody know where we can get some spoons?	8. _____
José:	There's a spoon in my lunch bag.	
Olivia:	There are some spoons in the lunchroom. Can we go get them?	

*Adapted and modified from A. L. Costa, *The Enabling Behaviors* (Orangevale, CA: Search Models Unlimited, 1989), pp. 75–78. By permission of Arthur L. Costa.

EXERCISE 7.8 *(continued)*

Teacher: Yes, José, would you get yours? Olivia, would you get some
from the lunchroom? Be sure you ask the cook. Joyce, would
you get the magnet?   9. _____

[*Later*]

Teacher: Now, because this is José's spoon, what do you think would be
the fair thing to do?   10. _____

David: Let him try the magnet on his own spoon.

Teacher: All right, José, what do you think will happen when we touch
the magnet to your spoon?   11. _____

José: It probably won't pick it up because it's not the right kind of
stuff for a magnet to pick up.

Teacher: What do you mean, "the right kind of stuff"?   12. _____

Sarah: He means the right kind of metal.

Teacher: José, would you try it? Let's all watch.   13. _____

Molly: See, I told you a magnet wouldn't pick up a spoon.

Raul: But it does pick up some spoons.

Joyce: I don't mean all spoons, only those made of metal. The spoon
in the book is made of metal.

Linda: Is this pin made out of steel?

Teacher: No, Linda it isn't.   14. _____

Linda: I thought it was steel or stuff like that—like a piece of car.

Teacher: I don't understand what you mean, Linda. What do you mean,
"a piece of car"?   15. _____

Linda: When Dad banged up our car, you could see the shining metal
under the paint. He said it was steel.

Sarah: I think the most powerful magnet in the world might be
able to pick it up.

David: An electromagnet, I think, is the strongest magnet that was
ever invented.

Teacher: Are you saying, David, that you think a stronger magnet
would pick up the spoon?   16. _____

David: Um-hm. I think so.

Teacher: What would you want to do to find out?   17. _____

David: We could set up our electromagnet and try it.

Teacher: Okay.   18. _____

Answer Key: 1. Structuring; 2. Input questioning (listening); 3. Structuring; 4. Active acceptance; 5. Process questioning (explaining); 6. Passive acceptance; 7. Process question (problem solving); 8. Input question (locating); 9. Data acquisition (this might also be interpreted as a structuring behavior since the teacher directs the students to perform a task); 10. Application question (evaluation); 11. Application question (predicting); 12. Clarifying; 13. Data acquisition; 14. Data acquisition; 15. Clarifying; 16. Clarifying; 17. Process question (planning); 18. Passive acceptance.

SUMMARY

This chapter presented a great deal of information about one significantly important teaching strategy, questioning, perhaps the most important one in your strategy repertoire. Questioning is the cornerstone to meaningful learning, thinking, communication, and real-world problem solving. The art of its use as an instructional device and as a learning tool is something you will continue to develop throughout your teaching career.

Next, in the two chapters that follow, your attention is directed to how teachers group children in the classroom and to the selection and implementation of specific instructional strategies to facilitate students' meaningful learning of skills and content of the curriculum.

EXTENDING MY COMPETENCY: QUESTIONS FOR CLASS DISCUSSION _____

1. Have you ever noticed that some teachers seem to anticipate a lower level response to their questions from particular students? Discuss your answer with your peers.
2. Should a teacher verbally respond to every child's verbal comment or inquiry? Explain why or why not. If not, on what basis does the teacher decide when and how to respond?
3. Describe when, if ever, and how a teacher could use strong praise. Explain the difference, if any, between strong praise and positive reinforcement.
4. Explain why it is important to wait after asking students a subject-matter content-related question? How long should you wait? What should you do if after waiting a certain amount of time there is no student response?
5. To what extent should (or can) a classroom teacher allow student questions to determine content studied? To what extent should childrens' initial interest or lack of interest in a topic determine whether the topic is addressed?
6. Explain the meaning of the following statement: We should look not for what students can reiterate but for what they can demonstrate and produce. Explain why you agree or disagree with the concept.
7. How many teachers can members of your class find during a designated period of time who actually plan and write the questions they ask children during a lesson? Discuss and discuss possible explanations for the results of your investigation.
8. Describe any prior concepts you held that changed as a result of your experiences with this chapter. Describe the changes.
9. From your current observations and fieldwork as related to this teacher preparation program, clearly identify one specific example of educational practice that seems contradictory to exemplary practice or theory as presented in this chapter. Present your explanation for the discrepancy.
10. Do you have questions generated by the content of this chapter? If you do, list them along with ways answers might be found.

FOR FURTHER READING _____

Brualdi, A. C. (1998). *Classroom Questions* (ED422407). Washington, DC: ERIC Clearinghouse on Assessment and Evaluation.

Chappell, M. F., and Thompson, D. R. (1999). Modifying Our Questions to Assess Students' Thinking. *Mathematics Teaching in the Middle School, 4*(7), 470–474.

Deal, D., and Sterling, D. (1997). Kids Ask the Best Questions. *Educational Leadership, 54*(6), 61–63.

Gibson, J. (1998). Any Questions, Any Answers? *Primary Science Review, 51,* 20–21.

Good, T. L., and Brophy, J. E. (2000). *Looking in Classrooms* (8th ed., Chap. 9). New York: Addison Wesley/Longman.

Grambo, G. (1997). Questions in Your Classroom. *Gifted Child Today Magazine, 20*(3), 42–43.

Kligman, P. S., and Aihara, K. A. (1997). Observing Student-Based Questions in a Whole Language Second-Grade Classroom. *Indiana Reading Journal, 29*(3), 17–22.

Larking, L. (1984). Re Quest Helps Children Comprehend. *Australian Journal of Reading, 7*(3), 135–139.

Latham, A. (1997). Asking Students the Right Questions. *Educational Leadership, 54* (6), 84–85.

Martinello, M. L. (1998). Learning to Question for Inquiry. *Educational Forum, 62*(2), 164–171.

Ostergard, S. A. (1997). Asking Good Questions in Mathematics Class: How Long Does It Take to Learn How? *Clearing House, 71*(1), 48–50.

Spargo, P. E., and Enderstein, L. G. (1997). What Questions Do They Ask? Ausubel Rephrased. *Science and Children, 34*(6), 43–45.

Tower, C. (2000). Questions That Matter: Preparing Elementary Students for the Inquiry Process. *The Reading Teacher, 53*(7), 550–557.

Traver, R. (1998). What Is a Good Guiding Question? *Educational Leadership, 55*(6), 70–73.

NOTES _____

1. A. L. Costa, *The School as a Home for the Mind* (Palatine, IL: Skylight Publishing, 1991), p. 63.
2. Studies in wait-time began with the classic study of M. B. Rowe, Wait Time and Reward as Instructional Variables, Their Influence on Language, Logic and Fate Control: Part I. Wait Time, *Journal of Research in Science Teaching, 11*(2), 81–94 (1974). See also M. B. Rowe, Science, Silence, and Sanctions, *Science and Children, 34*(1), 35–37 (September 1996).
3. See, for example, M. E. McIntosh and R. J. Draper, Using the Question-Answer Relationship Strategy

to Improve Students' Reading of Mathematics Texts, *Clearing House, 69*(3), 154–162.

4. Socratic questioning is a main feature of Paideia schools. For information and a current listing of Paideia schools, contact the National Paideia Center, University of North Carolina Greensboro, Greensboro, NC 27402-6171; 336-334-3729, Web site: <http://www.paideia.org>.

5. B. R. Brogan and W. A. Brogan, The Socratic Questioner: Teaching and Learning in the Dialogical Classroom, *Educational Forum, 59*(3), 288–296 (Spring 1995).

6. This three-tiered model of thinking has been described variously by others. For a comparison of thinking models, see Costa, *The School,* p. 44.

7. See, for example, J. Piaget, *The Development of Thought: Elaboration of Cognitive Structures* (New York: Viking, 1977).

8. R. N. Caine and G. Caine, *Education on the Edge of Possibility* (Alexandria, VA: Association for Supervision and Curriculum Development, 1997), p. 107.

9. See, for example, B. Newton, Theoretical Basis for Higher Cognitive Questioning—An Avenue to Critical Thinking, *Education, 98*(3), 286–290 (March–April 1978), and D. Redfield and E. Rousseau, A Meta-Analysis of Experimental Research on Teacher Questioning Behavior, *Review of Educational Research, 51*(2), 237–245 (Summer 1981).

10. J. G. Brooks and M. G. Brooks, *In Search of Understanding: The Case for Constructivist Classrooms* (Alexandria, VA: Association for Supervision and Curriculum Development, 1993), p. 105.

11. See M. B. Rowe, Wait-Time and Rewards as Instructional Variables, Their Influence on Language, Logic, and Fate Control: Part One—Wait-Time, *Journal of Research in Science Teaching, 11*(2), 81–94 (June 1974); M. B. Rowe, Wait-Time: Slowing Down May Be a Way of Speeding Up, *American Educator, 11*(1), 38–47 (spring 1987); and J. Swift, C. Gooding, and P. Swift, Questions and Wait Time, in J. Dillon (Ed.), *Questioning and Discussion: A Multidisciplinary Study* (Norwood, NJ: Ablex, 1988), pp. 192–212.

12. United States Department of Education, *Tried and True: Tested Ideas for Teaching and Learning From the Regional Educational Laboratories* (Washington, DC: Office of Educational Research and Improvement, U.S. Department of Education, 1997), p. 53.

13. Our definition of a "large elementary school" is one with a population of 400 or more children. For research information about school size, see K. Cushman, How Small Schools Increase Student Learning (and What Large Schools Can Do About It), *Principal Online* (Alexandria, VA: National Association of Elementary School Principals, 1999) [Online 1/10/00] <http://www. naesp.org/comm/ p1199b.htm>; K. Cotton, School Size, School Climate, and Student Performance, *Close-Up Number, 20* (Portland, OR: Northwest Regional Educational Laboratory, 1996) [Online 2/10/00] <http://www.nwrel.org/scpd/sirs/10/c020. html>; and M. A. Raywid, Small Schools: A Reform That Works, *Educational Leadership, 55*(4), 34–39 (December/ January 1997–1998).

What Guidelines Are Available for My Use of Grouping and Assignments to Promote Positive Interaction and Quality Learning?

Rather than diluting standards and expectations, believing in the learning potential of every student, exemplary schools and accomplished teachers are able to effectively modify the key variables of time, methodology, and grouping to help individual students achieve mastery learning of the planned curriculum. In Chapter 1 we discussed ways in which time is modified. Throughout the resource guide we talk of ways of varying the methodology. In this chapter we focus on ways of grouping children to enhance positive interaction and quality learning.

In the most effective instructional environments, during any given week or even day of school, a student will likely experience a succession of group settings. Ways of grouping children for instruction is the initial topic of this chapter, from individualized instruction to dyads, small groups, and large groups. You also will learn how to ensure equality in the classroom, how to use assignments and homework, and how to coordinate various forms of independent and small-group project-based study.

CHAPTER OBJECTIVES

Specifically, upon completion of this chapter you should be able to

1. Demonstrate a theoretical and practical understanding of how to effectively use each of these instructional strategies: assignments, homework, journal writing, written and oral reports, cooperative learning, learning centers, problem-based learning, and student-centered projects.
2. Demonstrate an understanding of the meaning and importance of classroom equity and how it can be achieved.
3. Describe today's meaning of *mastery (or quality) learning* and its implications for the elementary school classroom teacher.
4. Explain how the classroom teacher can personalize the instruction to ensure success for each student.
5. Explain the advantages and disadvantages of various ways of grouping children for quality learning.
6. Present a persuasive argument in favor or against providing recovery options for students who don't do an assignment or who don't do well on it.

MASTERY LEARNING AND PERSONALIZED INSTRUCTION

Learning is an individual or personal experience. Yet as a classroom teacher you will be expected to work effectively with children on other than an individual basis—perhaps 30 or more at a time. Much has been written of the importance of personalizing the instruction for learners. Virtually all the research concerning better instructional practice emphasizes greater individualization, or personalization, of instruction.[1] We know of the individuality of the learning experience (as discussed in Chapter 2). And we know that while some elementary school children are primarily verbal learners, many more are primarily visual, tactile, or kinesthetic learners. As the teacher, though, you find yourself in the difficult position of simultaneously "treating" many separate and individual learners with individual learning capacities, styles, and preferences.

Common sense tells us that student achievement in learning is related to both the quality of attention and the length of time given to learning tasks. In 1968, Benjamin Bloom, building upon a model developed earlier by John Carroll, developed the concept of individualized instruction called **mastery learning,** saying that students need sufficient time on task (i.e., engaged time) to master content before moving on to new content.[2] From that concept Fred Keller, in the 1970s, developed an instructional plan called the *Personalized System of Instruction* (PSI), or the *Keller Plan,* which involves the student's learning from printed modules of instruction (which, today, would likely be presented as computer software programs) that allow the student greater control over the learning pace. The instruction is mastery oriented; that is, the student demonstrates mastery of the content of one module before proceeding to the next.

Today's Emphasis: Mastery (or Quality) Learning for All Students

Emphasis today is on mastery of content, also called *quality learning,* rather than *coverage of content* or *quantity of learning.* Mastery of content means that the student demonstrates his or her use of what has been learned. Because of the emphasis and research that indicates that quality learning programs positively affect achievement, the importance of the concept of mastery learning has resurfaced. For example, in today's efforts to restructure schools, two approaches—*Results-Driven Education* (RDE), also known as *Outcome-Based Education* (OBE), and the *Coalition of Essential Schools* (CES), use a goal-driven curriculum model with instruction that focuses on the construction of individual knowledge through mastery and assessment of student learning against the anticipated outcomes.[3]

In some instances, unfortunately, attention may only be on the mastery of minimum competencies; thus, students are not encouraged to work and learn to the maximum of their talents and abilities.

Assumptions About Mastery, or Quality, Learning

Today's concept of mastery, or quality, learning is based on six assumptions:

1. Mastery learning can ensure that students experience success at each level of the instruc-

tional process. Experiencing success at each level provides incentive and motivation for further learning.

2. Mastery of content, or quality learning, is possible for all students.
3. Although all students can achieve mastery, to master a particular content, some students may require more time than others. The teacher and the school must provide for this difference in time needed to complete a task successfully.
4. For quality learning to occur, instruction must be modified and adapted, not the students. Grouping of students by ability (homogeneous grouping and tracking) does not fit with the concept of mastery learning.
5. Most learning is sequential and logical.
6. Most desired learning outcomes can be specified in terms of observable and measurable performance.[4]

Components of Any Mastery Learning Model

Any instructional model designed to teach toward mastery (quality) learning will contain the following five components: (a) clearly defined instructional objectives, (b) a preassessment of the extent of the learner's present knowledge, (c) an instructional component with choices and options for students, (d) practice, reinforcement, frequent comprehension checks (both diagnostic and formative assessment), and corrective instruction at each step of the way to keep the learner on track, and (e) a summative assessment to determine the extent of student mastery of the objectives.

Strategies for Personalizing the Instruction: Working Toward Quality Learning

You can immediately provide personalized instruction by (a) starting study of a topic from where the children are in terms of what they know (or think they know) and what they want to know about the topic ("think-pair-share," discussed later in this chapter, and K-W-L, discussed in Chapter 5, are examples of strategies for doing this), (b) providing students with choices from a rich variety of pathways and hands-on experiences to learn more about the topic, (c) providing multiple instructional approaches (that is, using multilevel instruction in a variety of settings, from learning alone to direct, whole-class instruction), and (d) empowering students with responsibility and multiple opportunities for decision making, reflection, and self-assessment.

LEARNING ALONE

Some elementary school children learn well in pairs (dyads); others learn well with their peers in groups—collaboratively, cooperatively, or competitively—or collaboratively with adults; others learn well in combinations of these patterns; and some students learn best alone. Children who learn alone often are gifted, nonconforming, able to work at their own pace successfully, and comfortable using media. Or they may be seemingly underachieving but potentially able students for whom unconventional instructional strategies, such as *contract learning packages* (agreements between the teacher and individual students to proceed with tasks appropriate to their readiness, interests, or learning profiles in a sequence and at a pace each student selects) or multisensory instructional packages, encourage academic success.[5]

LEARNING IN PAIRS

It is sometimes advantageous to pair students (dyads) for learning. Several ways of doing this are described as follows.

Peer Tutoring, Mentoring, and Cross-Age Coaching

Peer mentoring, tutoring, or peer-assisted learning (PAL) is a strategy whereby one student tutors another. It is useful, for example, when one student helps another who has limited proficiency in English or when a student skilled in math helps another who is less skilled. For many years, it has been demonstrated repeatedly that peer tutoring is a significant strategy for promoting active learning. Furthermore, peer tutoring increases academic achievement not only for those being tutored but of those students doing the tutoring.[6]

Cross-age coaching is a strategy whereby one student is coached by another from a different, usually higher, grade level. This is similar to peer tutoring, except the coach is from a different age level than the student being coached.[7] As discussed in Chapter 1 and in the final section of this chapter, many schools have service learning projects that involve older students mentoring younger children.[8]

Paired Team Learning

Paired team learning is a strategy where students study and learn in teams of two. Students identified as gifted work and learn especially well when paired. Specific uses for paired team learning include drill partners, reading buddies, book report pairs, summary pairs, homework partners, project assignment pairs, and elaborating and relating pairs.

Think-Pair-Share

Think-pair-share is a strategy where students, in pairs, examine a new concept or topic about to be studied. After the students of each dyad discuss what they already know or think they know (misconceptions) about the concept, they present their perceptions to the whole group. This is an excellent technique for this type of discovery about a topic. The think-pair-share strategy can be combined in use with the K-W-L strategy (see Chapter 5). Introducing a writing step, the modification called *think-write-pair-share* is used by a student dyad thinking and then writing ideas or conclusions before sharing with the larger group.

The Learning Center

Another significantly beneficial way of pairing students for instruction (and of individualizing the instruction and learning alone and integrating the learning) is by using the learning center (LC) or learning station. [*Note:* Whereas each learning center is distinct and unrelated to others, learning stations are sequenced or in some way linked to one another.] The LC is a special place in the classroom where one student (or two, if student interaction is necessary or preferred at the center) can quietly work, explore, and learn at his or her own pace about a particular topic or to improve specific skills. All materials needed are provided at the center, including clear instructions for operation of the center. Familiar classroom examples of learning centers are the personal computer station and the reading corner.

The value of learning centers as instructional devices undoubtedly lies in the following facts. LCs can provide instructional diversity. While working at a center, the student is giving time and quality attention to the learning task (learning toward mastery) and is likely to be engaging the student's preferred learning modality or integrating several or all modalities. To adapt instruction to students' individual needs and preferences, it is possible to design a classroom learning environment that includes several *learning centers* (or called *learning stations* if the centers are somehow linked or sequenced), each of which incorporates a different medium and modality or focuses

on a special aspect of the curriculum. Students then work at the various learning centers according to their needs and preferences.

Learning centers are of three types. In the *direct-learning center,* performance expectations for cognitive learning are quite specific and the focus is on mastery of content. In the *skill center,* as in a direct-learning center, performance expectations are quite specific but the focus is on the development of a particular skill or process. In the *open-learning center,* the goal is to provide opportunity for exploration, enrichment, motivation, and creative discovery.

In all instances the primary reason for using a learning center is to individualize—to provide collections of materials and activities adjusted to the various readiness levels, interests, and learning profiles of students. Other reasons to use an LC are to provide (a) a mechanism for learning that crosses discipline boundaries, (b) a special place for a student with special needs, (c) opportunities for creative work, enrichment experiences, and multisensory experiences, and (d) opportunity to learn from learning packages that use special equipment or media of which only one or a limited supply may be available for use in your classroom (e.g., science materials, a microscope, a computer, a videodisc player, or some combination of these).

Guidelines for Constructing a Learning Center

To construct a LC, you can be as elaborate and as creative as your time, imagination, and resources allow. Students can even help you plan and create learning centers, which will relieve some of the burden from your busy schedule. The following paragraphs present guidelines for setting up and using this valuable instructional tool.

The center should be designed to be attractive, purposeful, and uncluttered. Learning centers should be activity-oriented (i.e., dependent on the student's manipulation of materials, not just paper-and-pencil tasks). The purpose of the center should be clearly understood by the students. Centers should always be used for educational purposes, *never* for punishment.

Topics or themes for the center should be related to the instructional program—for personalized review and reinforcement, remediation, or enrichment—preferably a topic or theme that integrates the student's learning by providing activities that cross discipline boundaries. Decide the purpose of the center and give the center a name, such as "Center for the Study of Wetlands," "Center of Magnetism," "Center of Earth," "Center of Our Solar System," "Our Community," "Patterns in Nature," "The United Nations," "Our Publishing Center," "Center for Global Communication," "The

Continent of Africa," "The Place for Microscopic Discovery," or "Gold Discovery," and so on. Identify the center with an attractive sign, preferably one designed and created by students.

The center should be self-directing (i.e., instructional objectives and procedures for using the center should be clearly posted and understandable to the student user). For this purpose you can use written instructions or an audio- or videocassette, a computer program, or a classroom aide. The center should also be self-correcting: student users should be able to tell by the way they have completed the task whether or not they have done it correctly and have learned.

The center should contain a variety of activities geared to the varying abilities and interest levels of the students. A choice of two or more tiered (increasing levels of complexity) activities at a center is one way to provide for this.

Materials to be used at the center should be maintained at the center, with written or verbal descriptions for use provided to the students. Materials should be safe for student use, and the center should be easily supervised at all times by you or another adult. Some centers may become more or less permanent centers, that is, remain for the school term or longer, whereas other centers may change according to what is being studied at the time.

LEARNING IN SMALL GROUPS

Small groups are those involving three to eight students, in either a teacher- or a student-directed setting. Using small groups for instruction enhances the opportunities for students to assume greater control over their own learning, sometimes referred to as *empowerment*.

Purposes for Using Small Groups

Small groups can be formed to serve a number of purposes. They might be useful for a specific learning activity (e.g., reciprocal reading groups, see Figure 5.2 in Chapter 5). Or they might be formed to complete an activity that requires materials that are of short supply or to complete a science experiment or a project, only lasting as long as the project does. Teachers have various rationales for assigning students to temporary in-class groups. Groups can be formed by grouping children according to (a) personality type (e.g., sometimes a teacher may want to team less-assertive children together to give them the opportunity for greater management of their own learning), (b) social pattern (e.g., some-

times it may be necessary to break up a group of rowdy friends, or it may be desirable to broaden the association among students), (c) common interest, (d) learning styles (e.g., forming groups of either mixed styles or of styles in common), or (e) their abilities in a particular skill or their knowledge in a particular area. One specific and well-known type of small-group instruction is the cooperative learning group.

COOPERATIVE LEARNING

Lev Vygotsky (1896–1934) studied the importance of a learner's social interactions in learning situations. Vygotsky argued that learning is most effective when learners cooperate with one another in a supportive learning environment under the careful guidance of a teacher. Cooperative learning, group problem solving, problem-based learning, and cross-age tutoring are instructional strategies used by teachers that have grown in popularity as a result of research evolving from Vygotsky's work.

Although cooperative learning is a genre of instructional strategies for which there are several models, they all share two key components: interdependence among members of the group and individual accountability for learning.[9]

The Cooperative Learning Group (CLG)

The *cooperative learning group* is a heterogeneous group (i.e., mixed according to one or more criteria, such as ability or skill level, ethnicity, learning style, learning capacity, gender, and language proficiency) of two to six students who work together in a teacher- or student-directed setting, emphasizing support for one another. Often times, a CLG consists of three or four students of mixed ability, learning styles, gender, and ethnicity, with each member of the group assuming a particular role (see discussion of roles below). Teachers usually change the membership of each group several to many times during the year.

The Theory and Use of Cooperative Learning
The theory of cooperative learning is that when small groups of students of mixed backgrounds and capabilities work together toward a common goal, members of the group increase their friendship and respect for one another. As a consequence, each individual's self-esteem is enhanced, students are more motivated to participate in higher-order thinking, and academic achievement is accomplished.[10]

Of special interest to teachers are general methods of cooperative learning, such as: "student team achievement divisions" (STAD) where the teacher presents a lesson, students work together in teams to help each other learn the material, individuals take quizzes, and team rewards are earned based on the individual scores on the quizzes; "teams-games-tournaments" (TGT) where tournaments (rather than quizzes) are held in which students compete against others of similar academic achievements and then winners contribute toward their team's score; group investigations in which students form two- to six-member groups, select subtopics from a broader whole class unit of study, and produce group reports, followed by each group making a culminating presentation.[11] Yet the primary purpose of each is for the groups to learn—which means, of course, that individuals within a group must learn. Group achievement in learning, then, is dependent upon the learning of individuals within the group. Rather than competing for rewards for achievement, members of the group cooperate with one another by helping one another learn, so that the group reward will be a good one. This is the interdependence component of cooperative learning.

Normally, the group is rewarded on the basis of group achievement, though individual members within the group can later be rewarded for individual contributions. Because of peer pressure, when using CLGs the teacher must be cautious about using group grading.[12] For example, a student's report card grade should clearly represent that student's achievement and not be lower than it can be because of who the student works with in groups. For grading purposes, bonus points can be given to all members of a group; individuals can add to their own scores when everyone in the group has reached preset standards. The preset standards must be appropriate for all members of a group. Lower standards or improvement criteria could be set for students with lower ability so everyone feels rewarded and successful. To determine each student's term grades, that is, the grades that go on reports to the child's home, individual student achievement is measured later through individual students' results on tests and a variety of other criteria, including each student's performance in the group work.

Roles within the Cooperative Learning Group

To structure the interdependent nature of cooperative learning, it is helpful to assign roles (specific duties) to each member of the CLG. These roles should be rotated, either during the activity or from one time to the next. Though titles are discretionary, five typical roles are

- *Group facilitator*—role is to keep the group on-task.

- *Materials manager*—role is to obtain, maintain, and return materials needed for the group to function.
- *Recorder*—role is to record all group activities and processes and perhaps to periodically assess how the group is doing.
- *Reporter*—role is to report group processes and accomplishments to the teacher and/or to the entire class. When using groups of four members, the roles of recorder and reporter can easily be combined.
- *Thinking monitor*—role is to identify and record the sequence and processes of the group's thinking. This role encourages metacognition and the development of thinking skills.

It is important that students understand and perform their individual roles, and that each member of the CLG performs her or his duties as expected. This is the individual accountability component. No student should be allowed to ride on the coattails of the group. To emphasize significance to and reinforce the importance of each role and to be able to readily recognize the role any student is playing during CLG activity, one teacher made a trip to an office supplier and had permanent badges made for the various CLG roles. During CLGs, then, each student attaches the appropriate badge to her or his clothing.

What Students and the Teacher Do When Using Cooperative Learning Groups

Actually, for learning by CLGs to work, each member of the CLG must understand and assume two roles or responsibilities: the role he or she is assigned as a member of the group and that of seeing that all others in the group are performing their roles. Sometimes this requires interpersonal skills that children have yet to learn or to learn well. This is where the teacher must assume some responsibility. Simply placing children into CLGs and expecting each member and each group to function and to learn the expected outcomes may not work. In other words, skills of cooperation must be taught. These are the skills of altruism, consensus seeking, giving up an idea to work on someone else's, integrating the ideas of others, knowing how to handle disagreements, knowing how to support group efforts, listening, and sharing. If all your students have not yet learned these skills, and they probably have not, then you will have to teach them. This doesn't mean that if a group is not functioning you immediately break up the group and reassign members to new groups. Part of group learning is learning the process of how to work out conflict.

A group may require your assistance to work out a conflict. With your guidance the group should be able to discover what the problem causing the conflict is, identify some options, and mediate at least a temporary solution. If a particular skill is needed, then with your guidance students identify and learn that skill.

When to Use Cooperative Learning Groups

CLGs can be used for problem solving, inquiry, opinion surveys, experiments, review, project work, test making, or almost any other instructional purpose. Just as you would for small-group work in general, you can use CLGs for most any purpose at any time; but as with any other type of instructional strategy, it should not be overused, and in the early grades the group work should be highly structured, pleasant, and for relatively brief periods of time. As students' skills in group processing develop they can be given gradually longer and more demanding group tasks.[13]

Outcomes of Using Cooperative Learning Groups

When the process is well planned and managed, the outcomes of cooperative learning include (a) improved communication and relationships of acceptance among students of differences, (b) quality learning with fewer off-task behaviors, (c) improved ability to perform four key thinking strategies—problem solving, decision making, critical thinking, and creative thinking—and (d) increased academic achievement. In the words of Good and Brophy,

> Cooperative learning arrangements promote friendships and prosocial interaction among students who differ in achievement, gender, race, or ethnicity, and they promote the acceptance of mainstreamed handicapped students by their nonhandicapped classmates. Cooperative methods also frequently have positive effects, and rarely have negative effects, on affective outcomes such as self-esteem, academic self-confidence, liking for the class, liking and feeling liked by classmates, and various measures of empathy and social cooperation.[14]

Why Some Teachers Have Difficulty Using CLGs

For the use of CLGs to work well, advanced planning and effective management are musts. As emphasized by Tomlinson, "the nest of strategies we call cooperative learning . . . [sometimes] have fallen short of expectations not because of a deficiency in the strategies themselves but because teachers apply them shallowly."[15] Sometimes, when they think they are using CLGs, teachers have difficulty and either give up trying to use the strategy or simply tell children to divide into groups for an activity and call it cooperative learning. For the strategy to work, each student must be given training in and have acquired basic skills

Figure 8.1
Resources on the use of cooperative learning

- Center for Research on the Education of Students Placed at Risk, Johns Hopkins University, 3505 N. Charles St., Baltimore, MD 21218; 410-516-8000; <http://www.csos.jhu.edu>
- Cooperative Learning Center at the University of Minnesota, 60 Peik Hall, University of Minnesota, MN 55455; 612-624-7031; <http://www.clcrc.com>
- Kagan Publishing and Professional Development, P.O. Box 72008, San Clemente, CA 92674-9208; 800-933-2667; <http://www.kagancooplearn.com>

in interaction and group processing and must realize that individual achievement rests with that of their group. And, as true for any other strategy, the use of CLGs must not be overused—teachers must vary their strategies.[16]

Children must be instructed in the necessary skills for group learning. Each student must be assigned a responsible role within the group and be held accountable for fulfilling that responsibility. When a CLG activity is in process, groups must be continually monitored by the teacher for possible breakdown of this process within a group. In other words, while children are working in groups the teacher must exercise withitness. When a potential breakdown is noticed, the teacher quickly intervenes to reset the group back on track. See Figure 8.1 for additional resources.

LEARNING IN LARGE GROUPS

Large groups are those that involve eight or more students, usually the entire class. Most often, they are teacher-directed. Student presentations and whole-class discussions are two techniques that involve the use of large groups.

Student Presentations

Students should be encouraged to be presenters for discussion of the ideas, opinions, and knowledge obtained from their own independent and small-group study. Several techniques encourage the development of certain skills, such as studying and organizing material, discovery, discussion, rebuttal, listening, analysis, suspending judgment, and critical thinking. Possible forms of discussions

Figure 8.2
Sample scoring rubric for group presentations. (Can be adapted for individual presentations).

GROUP PRESENTATION SCORING RUBRIC

5. Presentation was excellent. Clear understanding of their project and organized in delivery.
   - Made eye contact throughout presentation
   - Spoke loud enough for all to hear
   - Spoke clearly
   - Spoke for time allotted
   - Stood straight and confidently
   - Covered at least five pieces of important information
   - Introduced project
   - All members spoke

4. Presentation was well thought out and planned.
   - Made eye contact throughout most of presentation
   - Spoke loud enough and clearly most of the time
   - Spoke nearly for time allotted
   - Covered at least four pieces of important information
   - Introduced project
   - All members spoke

3. Adequate presentation. Mostly organized.
   - Made eye contact at times
   - Some of audience could hear the presentation
   - Audience could understand most of what was said
   - Spoke for about half of time allotted
   - At least half of team spoke
   - Covered at least three pieces of important information
   - Project was vaguely introduced

2–1. Underprepared presentation. Disorganized and incomplete information.
   - No eye contact during presentation
   - Most of audience was unable to hear presentation
   - Information presented was unclear
   - Spoke for only brief time
   - Covered less than three pieces of information
   - Project was not introduced or only vaguely introduced

---

involving student presentations are described in the following paragraphs.

- *Debate.* The debate is an arrangement in which members of two opposing teams, on topics pre-assigned and researched, make formal speeches. The speeches are followed by rebuttals from each team.
- *Jury Trial.* The jury trial is a discussion approach in which the class simulates a courtroom, with class members playing various roles of judge, attorneys, jury members, bailiff, and court recorder. (See the section, "Learning by Educational Games" in Chapter 9.)
- *Panel.* The panel is a setting in which from four to six students, with one designated as the chairperson or moderator, discuss a topic about which they have studied, followed by a question-and-answer period involving the entire class. The panel usually begins with each panel member giving a brief opening statement.
- *Research Report.* One or two students or a small group of students gives a report on a topic that they investigated, followed by questions and discussion by the entire class.
- *Roundtable.* The roundtable is a small group of three to five students who sit around a table and discuss among themselves (and perhaps with the rest of the class listening and perhaps later asking questions) a problem or issue that

they have studied. One member of the panel may serve as moderator.

Just as they do when using cooperating learning, students may need coaching from you to develop skills necessary to use these techniques effectively. Individually, in small groups, or in whole-class sessions, students may need coaching on how and where to gather information; how to listen, take notes, select major points, organize material, and present a position succinctly and convincingly (see Figure 8.2); how to play roles; and how to engage in dialogue and debate with one another without creating conflict.

Whole-Class Discussion

Teacher-directed whole-class discussion is a teaching technique used frequently by most teachers. On this topic, you should consider yourself an expert. Having been a student in formal education for many years, you are undoubtedly knowledgeable about the advantages and disadvantages of whole-class discussions, at least from your personal vantage point. Explore your knowledge and share your experiences by responding to Exercise 8.1. Then do Exercise 8.2, where guidelines for using whole-class discussion will be generated.

EXERCISE 8.1 WHOLE-CLASS DISCUSSION AS A TEACHING STRATEGY: WHAT DO I ALREADY KNOW?

Instructions: The purpose of this exercise is to explore your knowledge of whole-class discussion as a teaching strategy. Answer the following questions, and then share your responses with your class, perhaps in discussion groups organized by subject field or grade level.

1. Your grade-level interest or subject field: _____

2. For what reasons would you hold a whole-class discussion? _____

   _____

   _____

   _____

   _____

3. Assuming that your classroom has movable seats, how would you arrange them? _____

   _____

   _____

   _____

4. What would you do if the seats were not movable? _____

   _____

   _____

   _____

5. What rules would you establish before starting the discussion? _____

   _____

   _____

   _____

6. Should student participation be forced? Why or why not? If so, how? _____

   _____

   _____

   _____

7. How would you discourage a few students from dominating the discussion? _____

   _____

   _____

   _____

8. What preparation should the students and teacher be expected to make before beginning the

   discussion? _____

   _____

   _____

   _____

EXERCISE 8.1 *(continued)*

9. How would you handle digression from the topic? _____

_____

_____

_____

10. Should students be discussion leaders? Why or why not? If so, what training, if any, should they

receive, and how? _____

_____

_____

_____

11. What teacher roles are options during a class discussion? _____

_____

_____

_____

_____

12. When is each of these roles most appropriate? _____

_____

_____

_____

13. When, if ever, is it appropriate to hold a class meeting for discussing class procedures, not sub-

ject matter? _____

_____

_____

_____

14. Can brainstorming be a form of whole-class discussion? Why or why not? _____

_____

_____

_____

_____

15. What follow-up activities would be appropriate after a whole-class discussion? On what basis

would you decide to use each? _____

_____

_____

_____

EXERCISE 8.1 *(continued)*

16. What sorts of activities should precede a class discussion? _____

_____

_____

_____

_____

17. Should a discussion be given a set length? Why or why not? If so, how long? How is the length
    to be decided? _____

_____

_____

_____

_____

18. Should students be graded for their participation in class discussion? Why or why not? If so,
    how? On what basis? By whom? _____

_____

_____

_____

_____

19. For effective discussions, 10 to 12 feet is the maximum recommended distance between par-
    ticipants. During a teacher-led discussion, what can a teacher do to keep within this limit?

_____

_____

_____

_____

20. Are there any pitfalls or other points of importance that a teacher should be aware of when planning
    and implementing a whole-class discussion? If so, explain them and how to guard against them.

_____

_____

_____

_____

For Your Notes

EXERCISE 8.2 WHOLE-CLASS DISCUSSION AS A TEACHING STRATEGY: BUILDING UPON WHAT I ALREADY KNOW

Instructions: The purpose of this exercise is to generate a list of guidelines for using whole-class discussion as a teaching strategy. Share your responses to Exercise 8.1 with your colleagues. Then individually answer the first two questions below. Next, as a group, use all three questions to guide you as you generate a list of five general guidelines for the use of whole-class discussion as a strategy in teaching. Share your group's guidelines with the entire class. Then, as a class, derive a final list of general guidelines.

1. How effective was your small-group discussion in sharing Exercise 8.1? _____

_____

_____

_____

_____

_____

_____

_____

_____

2. What allowed for or inhibited the effectiveness of that small-group discussion? _____

_____

_____

_____

_____

_____

_____

_____

3. How effective was this small-group discussion? Why? _____

_____

_____

_____

_____

_____

_____

_____

EXERCISE 8.2 *(continued)*

General Guidelines Generated from Small-Group Discussion

1. _____

_____

2. _____

_____

3. _____

_____

4. _____

_____

5. _____

_____

General Guidelines: Final List Derived from Whole Class

_____

_____

_____

_____

_____

_____

_____

_____

_____

_____

_____

_____

_____

_____

_____

_____

_____

_____

_____

EQUALITY IN THE CLASSROOM

Especially when using direct instruction and when conducting whole-group discussions, it is easy for a teacher to develop the habit of interacting with only "the stars," only those in the front of the classroom or on one side, or only the most vocal and assertive. You must exercise caution and avoid falling into that habit. To ensure a psychologically safe and effective environment for learning for every student in your classroom, you must attend to all students and try to involve all students equally in all class activities. You must avoid any biased expectations about certain children, and you must avoid discriminating against students according to their gender, ethnicity, or any other personal characteristic. Discrimination is not only unfair, it is illegal.

Student Rights

You probably already know that as a result of legislation that occurred three decades ago—federal law Title IX of the Education Amendments of 1972, P.L. 92-318—a teacher is prohibited from discriminating among students on the basis of their gender. In all aspects of school, male and female students must be treated the same. This means, for example, that a teacher must not pit boys against girls in a quiz game—or for any other activity or reason. Further, no teacher, student, administrator, or other school employee should make sexual advances toward a student (i.e., touching or speaking in a sexual manner). Students should be informed by their schools of their rights under Title IX, and they should be encouraged to report any suspected violations of their rights to the school principal or other designated person. Many schools provide students (or parents and guardians) with a publication of their rights as students. Each school or district should have a clearly delineated statement of steps to follow in the process of protecting students' rights. See Figure 8.3 for additional resources.

Gender Discrimination

Still, today, research identifies the unintentional tendency of teachers of *both* sexes to discriminate on the basis of gender. For example, teachers, along with the rest of society, tend to have lower expectations for girls than for boys in mathematics and science. They tend to call on and encourage boys more than girls. They often let boys interrupt girls but praise girls for being polite and waiting their turn. To avoid such discrimination may take

Figure 8.3
Resources on sexual harassment in schools

- L. A. Brown, et al., *Student-to-Student Sexual Harassment: A Legal Guide for Schools* (Alexandria, VA: Council of School Attorneys, National School Boards Association, 1998).
- D. L. Siegel, revised by M. Budhos, *Sexual Harassment: Research & Resources,* available from the National Council for Research on Women, 530 Broadway at Spring St., New York, NY 10012-3920, 1995.
- N. Stein and L. Sjostrom, *Flirting or Hurting? A Teacher's Guide on Student-to-Student Sexual Harassment in Schools—Grades 6–12* (Washington, DC: NEA Professional Library, 1994).
- *Stopping Anti-Gay Abuse of Students in Public Schools: A Legal Perspective,* available from the Lambda Legal Defense and Education Fund, 666 Broadway, Station 12, New York, NY 10012-2317. Phone 212-995-8585.
- *Title IX at 25: Report Card on Gender Equity,* available from the National Women's Law Center, 11 Dupont Circle, NW, Suite 800, Washington, DC 20036, 1997.
- D. H. Wishnietsky, *Establishing School Policies on Sexual Harassment,* Fastback 370. Bloomington, IN: Phi Delta Kappa Educational Foundation, 1994.
- E. Yaffe, "Expensive, Illegal, and Wrong: Sexual Harassment in Our Schools," *Phi Delta Kappan* 77(3):K1–K15 (November 1995).

special effort on your part, no matter how aware of the problem you may be. Some researchers believe the problem is so insidious that courses about it are needed in teacher training.[17]

Ensuring Equity

To ensure equity in interaction with students, many teachers have found it helpful to ask someone secretly to tally classroom interactions between the teacher and students during a class discussion. After an analysis of the results, the teacher arrives at decisions about his or her own attending and facilitating behaviors. Such an analysis is the purpose of Exercise 8.3. You are welcome to make blank copies and share them with your teaching colleagues.

Exercise 8.3 can be modified to include responses and their frequencies according to other teacher-student interactions, such as your calling on all students equally for responses to your questions, your calling on students equally to assist you with classroom helping jobs, or your rebuking students for their inappropriate behavior.

In addition to the advice given in Chapter 7 about using questioning, many other strategies can help ensure that children are treated fairly in the classroom, including the following:

- Encourage students to demonstrate an appreciation for one another by applauding all individual and group presentations.
- Have and maintain high expectations, although not necessarily identical expectations, for all students.
- Insist on politeness in the classroom. For example, a student can be shown appreciation with a sincere "thank you" or "I appreciate your contribution," or with a genuine smile for the student's contribution to the learning process.
- Insist on students finishing sentences, without being interrupted by others. Be certain that you model this behavior yourself.

- During whole-class instruction, insist that students raise their hands and be called on by you before they speak.
- Keep a stopwatch handy to unobtrusively control the wait time given for each student. While at first this idea may sound impractical, it works.
- Use a seating chart attached to a clipboard (see the section, "Quickly Learn and Use Student Names," in Chapter 4), and next to each student's name, make a tally for each interaction you have with a student. This also is a good way to maintain records to reward students for their contributions to class discussion. The seating chart can be laminated and then used day after day by simply erasing the marks of the previous day.

Now do Exercise 8.3, through which you will examine a teacher's behavior with students according to gender (or any other personal characteristic).

EXERCISE 8.3 TEACHER INTERACTION WITH STUDENTS ACCORDING TO STUDENT GENDER OR OTHER PERSONAL CHARACTERISTIC

Instructions: The purpose of this exercise is to provide a tool for analysis of your own interactions with students according to gender. To become accustomed to the exercise, you should do a trial run in one of your university classes, then use it during your student teaching and again during your first years of teaching. The exercise can be modified to include (a) the amount of time given for each interaction, (b) the response time given by teacher according to student gender, and (c) other student characteristics, such as ethnicity.

Prior to class, select a student (this will be you during the trial run recommended above) or an outside observer, such as a colleague, to do the tallying and calculations, as follows. Ask the person to tally secretly the interactions between you and students by placing a mark after the name of each student (or on the student's position on a seating chart) with whom you have verbal interaction. If a student does the tallying, he or she should not be counted in any of the calculations.

Exact time at start _____

Exact time at end _____

Total time in minutes _____

Calculations before Tallying

a. Total number of students _____

b. Number of female students _____

c. Number of male students _____

d. Percentage of students who are female _____ (= b divided by a)

e. Percentage of students who are male _____ (= c divided by a)

(Check: d + e should = 100%)

Calculations after Tallying

f. Total females interacting _____

g. Total males interacting _____

h. Percentage of students interacting _____ (f +g divided by a)

i. Total female tallies _____

j. Total male tallies _____

k. Total of all tallies (i + j) _____

l. Percentage interacting students who are female _____ (i divided by k)

m. Percentage interacting students who are male _____ (j divided by k)

n. Most tallies for any one male _____

o. Percentage of class interactions directed to most frequently addressed male _____ (n divided by k)

p. Most tallies for any female _____

q. Percentage of class interactions directed to most frequently addressed female _____ (p divided by k)

EXERCISE 8.3 *(continued)*

Teacher Conclusions

_____

_____

_____

_____

_____

_____

_____

_____

_____

_____

_____

_____

_____

_____

_____

_____

_____

_____

_____

_____

_____

_____

_____

_____

_____

_____

_____

_____

_____

_____

_____

_____

_____

LEARNING FROM ASSIGNMENTS AND HOMEWORK

An assignment is a statement of *what* the student is to accomplish and is tied to one or more instructional objectives. Assignments, whether completed at home or at school, can ease student learning in many ways, but when poorly planned they can discourage the student and upset an entire family. *Homework* can be defined as any out-of-class task that a student is assigned as an extension of classroom learning. Like all else that you do as a teacher, it is your professional responsibility to think about and plan carefully all homework assignments that you give to students. Before giving students any assignment, consider how you would feel were you given the assignment, how you would feel were your own child given the assignment, about how much out-of-class time you expect the assignment to take, and to what extent, if any, parents and guardians should or could be involved in assisting the child in doing the assignment.

The time a student needs to complete assignments beyond school time will vary according to grade level and school policy. There seems always to be some debate about the value of homework for the elementary grades.[18] Perhaps the issue is or should be not with the value of homework per se but with the quality of the homework that is assigned. Having said that, very generally, children in grades K–3 may be expected to spend from none to about 15 minutes each school night on homework, while children in grades 4–6 may spend 40 minutes to an hour or more.

Purposes for Homework Assignments

Purposes for giving homework assignments can be any one or more of the following: to constructively extend the time that students are engaged in learning, to help students develop personal learning, to help students develop their research skills, to help students develop their study skills, to help students organize their learning, to personalize the learning, to provide a mechanism by which students receive constructive feedback, to provide students with opportunity to review and practice what has been learned, to reinforce classroom experiences, to teach new content, and to involve parents or guardians and other family members in children's learning. See Figure 8.4 (and also Figure 11.12 in Chapter 11).

Guidelines for Using Assignments

To use assignments, consider the guidelines presented in the following paragraphs.

Plan early and thoughtfully the types of assignments you will give (e.g., daily and long-range;

Figure 8.4
Things that can be done at home with a child to reinforce the child's classroom learning

A child is likely to perform well in school when one or more members of a child's family are involved in and supportive of the child's learning. Here are just a few suggestions of activities a family member can do with a child to reinforce the child's learning.

General
- Ask questions about things the child is learning and doing and encourage lengthy answers.
- Expect the child to succeed in school. Encourage the child with praise for hard work and a job well done.
- Have a special place for studying that is quiet and free of distractions.
- Have paper, pencils, crayons, and washable markers handy. This encourages children to write.
- Keep a variety of reading material in the home. Use them yourself to show you value reading and learning, too.
- Turn a cardboard box (big enough for notebooks) into a special school box to hold all school things when the child comes home. Have the child decorate the box with pictures, words, and artwork.
- Watch television with the child and talk about the things you like and don't like about the shows. Limit the viewing time.

The Arts
- Keep simple art supplies available around the house; encourage self-expression. Pictures don't have to be something that you recognize.
- Help the child make connections between art and other subjects. Look at, and talk about, book illustrations when you are reading together.
- Display the child's art and music in the home.
- Encourage the child to sing and to sway and dance to music.
- Encourage the child to learn to play a musical instrument, homemade or otherwise.

(continued)

Figure 8.4 *(continued)*

Geography
- Where are we? Teach the child your address. Look at maps together to see where you live and where the school is. How close or far are you from the school?
- What makes a place special? List some things about where you live. What is the climate like? What kinds of plants and animals share your environment?
- What impact have people had on where you live?
- What does it mean to live in a global society? Make a chart of the things that are happening in other parts of the world that affect you.
- When you talk with the child, use words that indicate direction: "We are going north to New York to visit Grandma," or "The school is three blocks west of our apartment."

History
- Get to know the history of the town or city or place where you live.
- Read with the child about people and events that have made a difference in the world.
- Select a photo of a person in your family or someone else you admire or respect. Tell the child what the person did. Why do you admire this person? Talk about the results of the person's actions.
- Share family history with the child.
- When you celebrate holidays, explain to the child what is being celebrated and why.

Mathematics
- From the time the child is very young, count everything. When you empty a grocery bag, count the number of apples. Count the number of stairs to your home.
- Help the child do math in his or her head with lots of small numbers. Ask questions: "If I have 4 cups and I need 7, how many more do I need?" or "If I need 12 drinks for the class, how many packages of 3 drinks will I need?"
- Put things into groups. When you do laundry, separate items of clothing: all the socks in one pile, shirts in another, and pants in another. Divide the socks by color and count the number of each. Draw pictures and graphs of clothes in the laundry: 4 red socks, 10 blue socks, 12 white socks.
- Show the child that you like numbers. Play number games and think of math problems as puzzles to be solved.
- Tell the child that anyone can learn math. Point out numbers in the child's life: in terms of weight, measurements involving food preparation, temperature, and time.

Reading
- Go to the library together and check out books, especially books recommended by the teacher or the librarian.
- If the child has difficulty with a word, you can help in several ways: Have the child skip the word, read the rest of the sentence, and then ask what word would make sense in the sentence; have the child use what is known about letters and the sounds they make to "sound out" the word; or supply the word and keep reading— enjoyment is the main goal.
- Listen to your child read homework to you.
- Point to the words on the page when you read. Move your finger from left to right.
- Read aloud to your child: books, newspaper and magazine articles, the cereal box, can labels, road signs.

Science
- Ask the child questions: How do you suppose a clock works? Why does a bird make a nest and what is the nest made of? How does electricity help us every day?
- Ask the child to make predictions about the weather or how fast a plant will grow or how high a piece of paper will fly with the wind. Have the child then test to see if the predictions were correct. Remind the child that it may take several tries before obtaining an answer, and even then it may only be tentative. Keep trying; keep testing.
- Have the child start collections of shells, rocks, or bugs, so that the child can see similarities and patterns.
- Help the child look at what causes things to change. What happens when a plant doesn't have water or sunlight?
- Watch ants in an anthill or around spilled food. Explain that when an ant finds food, it runs back to its "home" to "tell" the others. As it runs, it leaves a trail that other ants in the nest can smell. The ants find the food by smelling their way along the trail.

Writing
- Encourage the young child to get ready to write, by scribbling, drawing, making designs with letters.
- Have the child interview a family member or neighbor.
- Play writing and spelling games.
- Show that you write often to make lists, take down messages, write letters, write e-mail messages.
- Write often to the child: Put a note in the lunch bag, make a birthday poster, send a postcard from work.

Source: Adapted from U.S. Department of Education 1997 publication, *Learning Partners: A Guide to Educational Activities for Families.* Available [Online] <http://www.pueblo.gsa.gov/cic_text/children/lpartner/lpartner.txt> June 25, 2000.

minor and major; in class or at home, or both; individual, paired, or group), and prepare assignment specifications. Assignments must correlate with specific instructional objectives and should *never* be given as busy work or as punishment. For each assignment, let students know the purpose, for example, whether the assignment is to prepare the student for what is to come in class, to practice what has been learned in class, or to extend the learning of class activities. While an assignment is a statement of *what* the student is to accomplish, procedures are statements of *how* to do something. Although students may need some procedural guidelines in order to do an assignment, especially with respect to your expectations, generally, you will want to avoid supplying too much detail on how to do the assignment.

Use caution in giving assignments that could be controversial or that could pose a hazard to the safety of children. Heed your intuition: If you have concern about the wisdom of a particular assignment then you probably shouldn't use it, at least not without at first talking about the assignment with colleagues or an administrator. When you have concern about any assignment, and especially if you are new to the community, before giving the assignment it is probably a good idea to talk it over with your colleagues or an administrator or both. For a particular assignment, you may need to obtain parental or guardian permission and even support for students to do it, or be prepared to give an alternate assignment for some students.

Provide differentiated, tiered, or optional assignments—assignment variations given to students or selected by them on the basis of their interests, learning styles, preferred learning modalities, and learning capacities.[19] Students can select or be assigned different activities to accomplish the same objective, such as read and discuss, or they can participate with others in a more direct learning experience. After their study, as a portion of the assignment, students share what they have learned. This is an example of using multilevel teaching.

Teachers have found it beneficial to prepare individualized study guides with questions to be answered and activities to be done by the student while reading textbook chapters as homework. One advantage of a study guide is that it can make the reading more than a visual experience. A study guide can help to organize student learning by accenting instructional objectives, emphasizing important points to be learned, providing a guide for studying for tests, and encouraging the student to read the homework assignment.

As a general rule, homework assignments should stimulate thinking by arousing a student's curiosity, raising questions for further study, and encouraging and supporting the self-discipline required for independent study and learning.

Determine the resources that students will need to complete assignments, and check the availability of these resources. Resources should be readily available to all students. This is important; students can't be expected to use that which is unavailable to them. Many children will not use that which is not readily available.

Avoid yelling out assignments as students are leaving your classroom. When giving assignments in class, they should be written and posted in a special place in the classroom, a copy given to each student, or each student required to write the assignment into his or her assignment folder, taking extra care to be sure that assignment specifications are clear to students and allowing time for students to ask questions about an assignment. It is policy in some schools that students use a daily assignment book to record homework and additional reminders. In some cases, the teachers initial the page and parents/guardians are asked to sign it daily. This policy is intended to help students become organized and responsible for their own learning. Using a daily assignment book also reduces or eliminates the "I didn't know it was due today" excuse. Whatever procedure you use for giving and collecting assignments, it's important that it is followed consistently throughout the school year.

Students should be given sufficient time to complete their assignments. As a general rule, all assignments should be given much sooner than the day before they are due. In other words, avoid announcing an assignment that is due the very next day. Try to avoid changing assignment specifications after they are given. Especially avoid changing them at the last minute. Changing specifications at the last minute can be very frustrating to students who have already completed the assignment, and it shows little respect for those students.

Allow time in class for students to begin work on homework assignments so you can give them individual attention (guided or coached practice). Your ability to coach students is *the* reason for in-class time to begin work on assignments. The benefits of this coached practice include being able to (a) monitor student work so that a child does not go too far in a wrong direction, (b) help students reflect on their thinking, (c) assess the progress of individual students, and (d) discover or create a teachable moment. For example, while monitoring students doing their work, you might discover a commonly held student misconception or lack of knowledge of how to do something. Then, taking advantage of this teachable moment, you stop and talk about it and attempt to clarify the misconception or to teach the needed skill or knowledge.

Timely, constructive, and corrective feedback from the teacher on the homework—and marking or grading homework—increases the positive contributions of homework.[20] If the assignment is important for students to do, then you must give your full and prompt attention to the product of their efforts. Students are much more willing to do homework when they believe it is useful, when it is treated as an integral part of instruction, when it is read and evaluated by the teacher, and, for students in the upper grades, when it counts as part of their grade.

Provide positive and constructive comments as feedback about each child's work. Always think about the comments that you make to be relatively certain they will convey your intended message to the student. When writing comments on student papers, consider using a color other than red, such as green or blue. While to you this may sound unimportant, to many people red carries a host of negative connotations (e.g., blood, hurt, danger, stop), and children often perceive it as punitive.

Rather than grading by giving a percentage or numerical grade, with its negative connotations, many elementary schoolteachers prefer to score assignments with constructive and reinforcing comments and symbols they have created for this purpose.

You must always give attention to the development of students' reading, listening, speaking, and writing skills. Attention to these skills must also be obvious in your assignment specifications and your assignment grading policy. Reading is crucial to the development of a child's ability to write. For example, to foster high-order thinking, students should be encouraged to write (in their journals, as discussed in Chapter 5 and later in this chapter), or draw representations of, their thoughts and feelings about the material they have read.

Opportunities for Recovery

While it is important to encourage good initial efforts by students, sometimes, for a multitude of reasons, a student's first effort is inadequate or is lacking entirely. Perhaps the student is absent unexcused from school or the student does poorly on an assignment or fails to turn in an assignment on time or at all. While accepting late work from students is extra work for the teacher, and despite that allowing the resubmission of a marked or tentative-graded paper increases the amount of paperwork, many educators report that it is worthwhile to give students opportunity for recovery

and a day or so to make corrections and resubmit an assignment for an improved score. However, out of regard for students who do well from the start the teacher should consider carefully before allowing a resubmitted paper to receive an *A* grade (unless, of course, it was an *A* paper originally).

Children sometimes have legitimate reasons for not completing an assignment by the due date. Sometimes the child may have a perfectly justifiable although officially unexcused reason for being absent from school. It is our opinion that the teacher should listen and exercise professional judgment in each instance. As others have said before, there is nothing democratic about treating unequals as equals. The provision of recovery options for children who are works in progress seems a sensible, humanly, scholarly, and professionally responsible tactic.

How to Avoid Having So Many Papers to Grade That Time for Effective Planning Is Restricted

A waterloo for some beginning teachers is that of being buried under mounds of student work to be read, marked, and graded, leaving less and less time for effective planning. To keep this from happening to you, consider the following suggestions.

While in our opinion the teacher should read everything that students write (or draw), papers can be read with varying degrees of intensity and scrutiny, depending on the purpose of the assignment. For assignments that are designed for learning, understanding, and practice, you can allow students to check them themselves using either self-checking or peer-checking (but see caution that follows). During the self- or peer-checking, you can monitor the activity and record whether a student did the assignment or not, or, after the checking, you can collect the papers and do your recording. Besides reducing the amount of paperwork for you, student self- or peer-checking provides other advantages: It allows students to see and understand their errors, it encourages productive peer dialogue, and it helps them develop self-assessment techniques and standards. If, however, the purpose of the assignment is to assess mastery competence, then the papers should be read, marked, and graded only by you, the teacher.

Peer-Checking: Use with Caution
Peer checking can be a problem. Children might spend more time watching the person checking their paper than accurately checking the one given to them. And the use of peer-checking does

not necessarily allow the student to see or understand his or her mistakes.

Of even greater concern is the matter of privacy. When student A becomes knowledgeable of the academic success or lack thereof of student B, student A, the "checker," could cause emotional or social embarrassment to student B. Peer-checking of papers should perhaps be done only for the editing of classmates' drafts of stories or research projects, making suggestions about content and grammar, but not assigning a grade or marking answers right or wrong. To protect students' rights to privacy, like the public posting of grades, the use of peers' grading each other's papers also should be avoided. Harassment and embarrassment have no place in a classroom; they do not provide a safe learning environment.

PROJECT-CENTERED LEARNING: GUIDING LEARNING FROM INDEPENDENT AND GROUP INVESTIGATIONS, PAPERS, AND ORAL REPORTS

For the most meaningful student learning to occur, independent study, individual writing, student-centered projects, and oral reports should be major features of your instruction. There will be times when the children are interested in an in-depth inquiry of a topic and will want to pursue a particular topic for study. This undertaking of a learning project can be flexible—an individual student, a team of two, a small group, or the entire class can do the investigation. The *project* is a relatively long-term investigative study from which students produce something called the *culminating presentation*. It is a way for students to apply what they are learning. The culminating presentation is a final presentation that usually include three aspects: (a) an oral report that is accompanied by (b) a hands-on item of some kind (e.g., a display, play or skit, book, song or poem, video, multimedia presentation, diorama, poster, maps, charts, and so on) and (c) a written report. The latter two are usually left for a time with the teacher for the teacher's review and assessment and perhaps for long-term display in the classroom or elsewhere in the school.

Values and Purposes of Project-Centered Learning

The values and purposes of encouraging project-centered learning are to:

- Develop student skills in cooperation and social interaction.

- Develop student skills in writing, communication, and in higher-level thinking and doing.
- Foster student engagement, independent learning, and thinking skills.
- Optimize personal meaning of the learning to each child by considering, valuing, and accommodating individual interests, learning styles, learning capacities, and life experiences.
- Provide opportunity for each child to become especially knowledgeable and experienced in one area of subject content or in one process skill, thus adding to the student's knowledge and experience base and sense of importance and self-worth.
- Provide opportunity for students to become intrinsically motivated to learn because they are working on topics of personal meaning, with outcomes and even timelines that are relatively open-ended.
- Provide opportunity for students to make decisions about their own learning and to develop their skills in managing time and materials.
- Provide opportunity for children to make a meaningful contribution.

As has been demonstrated time and again, when students work together on projects, integrating knowledge as the need arises, motivation and learning follow naturally.[21]

Guidelines for Guiding Students in Project-Centered Learning

In collaboration with the teacher, students select a topic for the project. What you can do is to stimulate ideas and provide anchor studies (that is, by showing the results of other students' projects.) For example, a group of fourth-grade students from Greenbrook School (South Brunswick, NJ) created and produced an animated video about national parks.[22] Such a culminating project as that could be shown year after year to other groups of children. You can stimulate ideas by providing lists of things students might do, by mentioning each time an idea comes up in class that this would be a good idea for an independent, small-group, or class project, by having former students tell about their projects, by showing anchor studies, by suggesting Internet resources and readings that are likely to give students ideas, and by holding class discussions to brainstorm ideas.

Sometimes a teacher will write the general problem or topic in the center of a graphic web and ask the students to brainstorm some questions. The questions will lead to ways for students to investigate, draw sketches, construct models, record findings, predict items, compare and contrast, and discuss understandings. In essence, brainstorming such as this is the technique often used by teachers in collaboration with students for the selection of an interdisciplinary thematic unit of study.

Allow students to individually choose whether they will work alone, in pairs, or in small groups. If they choose to work in groups, then help them delineate job descriptions for each member of the group. For project work, groups of four or fewer children usually work better than groups of more than four. Even if the project is one the whole class is pursuing, the project should be divided into parts with individuals or small groups of students undertaking independent study of these parts.

You can keep track of the students' progress by reviewing periodic (daily or weekly) updates of their work, perhaps as maintained in their journals (see later discussion in this chapter). Set deadlines with the groups. Meet with groups daily to discuss any questions or problems they have. Based on their investigations, the students will prepare and present their findings in culminating presentations.

Provide coaching and guidance. Work with each student or student team in topic selection, as well as in the processes of written and oral reporting. Allow students to develop their own procedures, but guide their preparation of work outlines and preliminary drafts, giving them constructive feedback and encouragement along the way. Without frequent progress reporting by the children and guidance and reinforcement from the teacher, a child can get frustrated and quickly lose interest in the project. Guide students in their identification of potential resources and in the techniques of research. Your coordination with the library and other resource locations is central to the success of project-centered teaching. Frequent drafts and progress reports from the students are a must. With each of these stages, provide students with constructive feedback and encouragement. Provide written guidelines and negotiate timelines for the outlines, drafts, and the completed project.

Promote sharing. Insist that students share both the progress and the results of their study with the rest of the class. The amount of time allowed for this sharing will, of course, depend upon any of many variables. The value of this type of instructional strategy comes not only from individual contributions but also from the learning that results from the experience and the communication of that experience with others.

Without careful planning, and unless children are given steady guidance, project-based teaching can be a frustrating experience, for both the teacher and the students, and especially for a beginning teacher who is inexperienced in such a complex instructional undertaking. Students should do projects because they want to and because the project seems meaningful. Therefore, with guidance from you the students should decide *what* project to do and *how* to do it. Your role is to advise and guide students so they experience success. If the teacher lays out a project in too much detail, that project is a procedure rather than a student-centered project. There must be a balance between structure and opportunities for student empowerment via choices and decision making.

Writing Should Be a Required Component of Project-Centered Learning

Provide options but insist that writing (or drawing) be a part of each child's work. Research examining the links among writing, thinking, and learning has helped emphasize the importance of writing. Writing is a complex intellectual behavior and process that helps the learner create and record his or her understanding—that is, to construct meaning. Insist that writing be a part of the student's work (see section that follows).

When teachers use project-centered teaching with upper elementary students, a paper and an oral presentation are usually automatically required of all students. It is recommended that you use the *I-Search paper* rather than the traditional research paper. Under your careful guidance, the children (a) list things that they would like to know and from the list select one that becomes the research topic, (b) conduct the study while maintaining a log of activities and findings, which, in fact, becomes a process journal, (c) prepare a booklet of paragraphs and visual representations that present their findings, (d) prepare a summary of the findings including the significance of the study and their personal feelings, and (e) share the project as a final oral report with the teacher and classmates.

Assess the Final Product

The final product of the project, including papers, oral reports, and presentations, should be assessed and graded. The method of determining the grade should be clear to students from the beginning, along with the weight of the project grade toward the term grade. Provide students with clear de-

Figure 8.5
Sample scoring rubric
for oral presentation
of project

Project Presentation Scoring Rubric

Score 5. Excellent presentation. Clear understanding of the project and organized in
delivery.
- Made eye contact throughout presentation
- Spoke loud enough for all to hear
- Spoke clearly and distinctly
- Spoke for time allotted
- Stood straight and confidently
- Covered at least five pieces of important information
- Introduced project

Score 4. Presentation was well thought out and planned.
- Made eye contact throughout most of presentation
- Spoke loud enough and clearly most of the time
- Spoke for most of time allotted
- Covered at least four pieces of important information
- Introduced project

Score 3. Adequate presentation. Mostly organized.
- Made eye contact at times
- Some of audience could hear the presentation
- Audience could understand most of what was said
- Spoke for about half of allotted time
- Covered at least three pieces of important information
- Project was vaguely introduced

Score 2 to 1. Underprepared presentation. Disorganized and incomplete information.
- Poor eye contact during presentation
- Most of audience was unable to hear presentation
- Information presented was unclear
- Spoke for only a brief time
- Covered less than three pieces of information
- Project not introduced or only vaguely introduced

scriptions (rubrics) of how assessment and grading will be done. The final grade for the study should be based on four criteria: (a) organization, including meeting draft and progress report deadlines; (b) the quality and quantity of both content and procedural knowledge gained from the experience; (c) the quality of the student's sharing of that learning experience with the rest of the class; and (d) the quality of the student's final written or oral report. A sample scoring rubric for the oral presentation of a project is shown in Figure 8.5. (Preparing and using rubrics is discussed in Chapter 11.[23])

WRITING ACROSS THE CURRICULUM

Because writing is a discrete representation of thinking, every teacher should consider himself or herself to be a teacher of writing.

Kinds of Writing

A student should experience a variety of kinds of writing rather than the same form, year after year. Perhaps most important is that writing should be emphasized as a process that illustrates one's thinking, rather than solely as a product completed as an assignment. Writing and thinking develop best when a student experiences during any school day various forms of writing to express their ideas, such as the following.[24]

Analysis—speculation about effects. The writer conjectures about the causes and effects of a specific event.

Autobiographical incident. The writer narrates a specific event in his or her life and states or implies the significance of the event.

Character assumption. The writer writes a story or maintains a diary of his or her reading in the first person, assuming the persona of a character in a book being read or a figure in history being studied.

Evaluation. The writer presents a judgment on the worth of an item—book, movie, artwork, consumer product—and supports this with reasons and evidence.

Eyewitness account. The writer tells about a person, group, or event that was objectively observed from the outside.

Firsthand biographical sketch. Through incident and description, the writer characterizes a person he or she knows well.

Problem solving. The writer describes and analyzes a specific problem and then proposes and argues for a solution.

Report of information. The writer collects data from observation and research and chooses material that best represents a phenomenon or concept.

Story. Using dialogue and description, the writer shows conflict between characters or between a character and the environment.

Student Journals

Many teachers have their students maintain journals in which the students keep a log of their activities, findings, and thoughts (i.e., *process journals,* as discussed above) and write their thoughts about what it is they are studying (*response journals*). Actually, commonly used are two types of response journals: dialogue journals and reading-response journals. *Dialogue journals* are used for students to write anything that is on their minds, usually on the right side of a page, while peers, teachers, and parents or guardians respond on the left side of a page, thereby "talking with" the journal writer. *Response journals* are used for students to write (and perhaps draw—a "visual learning log") their reactions to what is being studied.

Purpose and Assessment of Student Journal Writing

Normally, academic journals are *not* the personal diaries of the writer's recollection of daily events and the writer's thoughts about the events. Rather, the purpose of journal writing is to en-

Figure 8.6
Resources for writing across the curriculum

- The American Literacy Council at (212) 781-0099; Web page at <http://www.under.org/alc/welcome.htm>.
- International Reading Association, 800 Barksdale Road, Newark, DE 19711.
- National Council of Teachers of English, 1111 Kenyon Road, Urbana, IL 61801, <http://www.ncte.org>.
- National Writing Project (NWP), 5627 Tolman Hall, University of California–Berkeley, Berkeley, CA 94720; Web page at <http://wwwgse.berkeley.edu/research/nwp/nwp.html>.
- Whole Language Umbrella, Unit 6-846, Marion Street, Winnipeg, Manitoba, Canada R2JOK4.
- Writing to Learn, Council for Basic Education, 725 15th Street, NW, Washington, DC 20005.

courage students to write, to think about their writing, to record their creative thoughts about *what they are learning,* and to share their written thoughts with an audience—all of which help in the development of their thinking skills, in their learning, and in their development as writers. Students are encouraged to write about experiences, both in school and out, that are related to the topics being studied. They should be encouraged to record their feelings about what and how they are learning.

Journal writing provides practice in expression and should not be graded by the teacher. Negative comments and evaluations from the teacher will discourage creative and spontaneous expression by students. Teachers should read the journal writing and then offer constructive and positive feedback; but teachers should avoid negative comments or grading the journals. For grading purposes, most teachers simply record whether or not a student does, in fact, maintain the required journal and, perhaps, meets due dates.

The National Council of Teachers of English (NCTE) has developed guidelines for journal writing. For a copy contact NCTE directly or via the Internet. Resources on writing across the curriculum, including the NCTE, are shown in Figure 8.6. Figure 8.7 shows Internet sources for many ideas and resources for teaching. See also the readings at the end of this chapter.

Figure 8.7
Selected Internet
sites for teaching
ideas

All subjects and grade levels, lessons, units, and project ideas

- *Apple Learning Exchange Lesson Plans*
  <http://henson.austin.apple.com/edres/lessonmenu.shtml>.
- *AskERIC Lesson Plan Collection*   <http://ericir.syr.edu/Virtual/Lessons>.
- *Blu Web'n PacBell* unit and lesson plan ideas
  <http://www.kn.pacbell.com;wired/bluewebn/>.
- *Columbia Education Center Lesson Plans*   <http://www.col-ed.org/cur/>.
- *eDscape*   <http://www.edscape.edu>.
- *Gander Academy's theme-related resources*
  <http://www.stemnet.nf.ca/CITE/themes.html>.
- *Global Schoolhouse*   <http://www.gsh.org>.
- *K-12 Projects*   <http://www.eagle.ca/~matink/projects.html>.
- *The Lesson Plans Page*   <http://www.lessonplanspage.com/>.
- *New York Times Learning*
  <http://www.nytimes.com/learning/teachers/lessons/archive.html>.
  Lesson plans grades 6 and up.
- *Teachers Net Lesson Exchange*   <http://www.teachers.net/lessons>.

Art

- *Crayola Art Education*   <http://www.crayola.com/art_education>.
- *Eyes on Art*   <http://www.kn.pacbell.com/wired/art/art.html>.
- *Incredible Art Department*   <http://www.in.net/~kenroar>.
- *Kinder Art*   <http://www.bconnex.net/~jarea/lessons.htm>.
- *World Wide Arts Resources*   <http://wwar.com/>.

Environmental issues

- *Earth Day Groceries Project*   <http://www.earthdaybags.org>.
- Environmental links   http://www.nceet.snre.umich.edu/>.
- World Bank's site   http://www.worldbank.org/depweb>.
- World Resources   http://www.wri.org>.

Language, language arts, and literacy

- The Anne Frank House   <http://www.channels.n1/annefran.html>.
- *Center for the Study of Books in Spanish for Children and Adolescents*
  <http://www.csusm.edu/campus_centers/csb/english/center.htm>.
- *Charlotte's Web*   <http://www2.lhric.org/pocantico/charlotte/index>.
- *The Encyclopedia Mythica*   <http://www.pantheon.org/mythica/>.
- ESL/EFL links   <http://www.pacificnet.net/~sperling/eslcafe.html>.
- Foreign language links   <http://polyglot.lss.wisc.edu/lss/lang/langlink.html>.
- *Galaxy*   <http://galaxy.einet.net/galaxy.Humanities/Literature.html>.
- Harriet Tubman and the Underground Railroad
  <http://www2.lhric.org/pocantico/tubman/tubman.html>.
- *Language and Literacy Project*   <http://www.uis.edu/~cook/langlit/index.html>.
- *The Literacy Connection*   <http://www.reading.org/links/>.
- Literature and humanities links
  <http://galaxy.einet.net/galaxy/Humanities/Literature.html>.
- Mandel's Internet site   <http://www.pacificnet.net/~mandel/LanguageArts.html>.
- *Multicultural Book Review*
  <http://www.isomedia.com/homes/jmele/homepage.html>.
- *Pacific Children's Literature*   <http://www.uog.edu/coe/paclit/index.htm>.

Mathematics

- *Math Archives*   <http://archives.math.utk.edu/>.
- *The Math Forum*   <http://forum.swarthmore.edu/>.
- More math project ideas
  <http://www.luc.edu/schools/education/csimath/zmathed.htm>.
- Math resources   <http://www-personal.umd.umich.edu/~jobrown/math.html>.
- *MathSource*   <http://mathsource.wri.com/>.
- *PBS Mathline*   <http://www.pbs.org/learn/mathline/>.
- *Plane Math*   <http://www.planemath.com/>.
- *Schoolnet: Math Department*   <http://www.schoolnet.ca/math^sci/math/>.

(continued)

Figure 8.7 *(continued)*

Music

- *American Music Conference* <http://www.amc'music.com>.
- *Music Education Resource Links* (MERL)
  <http://www.isd77.k12.mn.us/resources/staffpages/shirk/k12.music.html>.
- *Music Educator's Home Page* <http://www.athenet.net/~wslow/>.
- *Music, The Universal Language* <http://www.jumpoint/com/bluesman/>.
- Music lesson plans and other resource links
  <http://www.csun.edu/~vceed009/music.html>.
- *Virtual Library on Music* <http://syy.oulu.fi/music>.

Science

- *Animal Diversity Web* <http://www.oit.itd.umich.edu/projects/ADW>.
- *BioRap* <http://www.biorap.org>.
- *Chemistry Teaching Resources* <http://www.anachem.umu.se/eks/pointers.htm>.
- *Cody's Science Education Zone*
  <http://www.ousd.k12.ca.us/~codypren/CSEZ_Home>.
- *Co-Vis Project* <http://www.nwu.edu/mentors/welcome.html>.
- *Cyberspace Middle School* <http://www.scri.fsu.edu/~dennisl/CMS.html>.
- *Earthshots* <http://edcwww.cr.usgs.gov/Earthshots>.
- *Electronic Zoo* <http://netvet.wustl.edu/e-zoo.html>.
- *Katerpillars & Mystery Bugs*
  <http://www.uky.edu/agriculture/entomology/ythfacts/entyouth.htm>.
- *Mandel's web site* <http://www.pacificnet.net/~mandel/Science.html>.
- *NASA Spacelink* <http://spacelink.nasa/gov/.index.html>.
- *Science and Mathematics Education Resources*
  <http://www.hpec.astro.washington.edu/scied/science.html>.
- Stanford Solar Center <http://solar-center.stanford.edu>.
- *Weather Underground* <http://groundhog.sprl.umich.edu/>.
- *Windows to the Universe Project* <http://www.windows.umich.edu>.
- *Yucky Roach World* <http://www.yucky.com/roaches>.

Social and multicultural studies

- Africa Guide
  <http://www.sas.upenn.edu/African_Studies/Home_Page/AFR_GIDE.html>.
- *Amigo! Mexico Web Center* <http://www.mexonline.com/>.
- *Chicano/Latino Net* <http://latino.sscnet.ucla.edu>.
- *Cinco de Mayo* <http://www.zianet.com/hatchelementary/cinco.htm>.
- *FedWorld* <http://www.fedworld.gov>.
- *Historical Text Archive* <http://www.msstate.edu/Archives/History/index.html>.
- *The History Net* <http://www.thehistorynet.edu>.
- History/social studies resources <http://www.execpc.com/~dboals/boals.html>.
- *Houghton Mifflin Social Studies Center* <http://www.eduplace.com/ss/>.
- Links to lesson plans, unit plans, thematic units, and resources
  <http://www.csun.edu/~hcedu013/index.html>.
- Medieval Life <http://www.pastforward.co.uk/>.
- *Multicultural Pavilion at University of Virginia*
  <http://curry.edschool.virginia.edu/go/multicultural>.
- *The National Civil Rights Museum* <http://www.midsouth.rr.com/civilrights>.
- Native American resources
  <http://hanksville.phast.umass.edu/misc/NAresources.html>.
- *NetNoir—The Black Network: Black Culture News* <http://www.netnoir.com/>.
- *Scrolls from the Dead Sea*
  <http://sunsite.unc.edu/expo/deadsea.scrolls.exhibit/intro.html>.
- *Social Sciences Research Network Online* <http://www.ssrn.com/index.html>.
- *Social Science Resources Home Page* <http://www.nde.state.ne.us/SS/ss.html>.
- *The Book: A Black History Web Site* <http://www.blackhistory.com/>.
- U.S. History, *From Revolution to Reconstruction*
  <http://grid.let.rug.nl/~welling/usa/usa.html~>.
- *Women's History* <http://frank.mtsu.edu/~kmiddlet/history/women.html~>.

SUMMARY

This chapter has continued the development of your repertoire of teaching strategies. As you know, young people can be quite peer-conscious, can have relatively short attention spans for experiences in which they are uninterested, and prefer active experiences that engage many or all of their senses. Most are intensely curious about things of interest to them. Cooperative learning, student-centered projects, and teaching strategies that emphasize shared discovery and inquiry (discussed in the next chapter) within a psychologically safe environment encourage the most positive aspects of thinking and learning. Central to your strategy selection should be those strategies that encourage children to become independent thinkers and skilled learners who can help in the planning, structuring, regulating, and assessing of their own learning and learning activities.

EXTENDING MY COMPETENCY: QUESTIONS FOR CLASS DISCUSSION _____

1. Describe research that you can find on the use of cooperation versus competition in teaching. Explain why you would or would not use cooperative learning groups.

2. Do you have concerns about using project-centered teaching but not being able to cover all the content expected or mandated? Think back to your own schooling. What do you really remember? Most likely you remember projects, yours and other students' presentations, the lengthy research you did, and your extra effort for the artwork to accompany your presentation. Maybe you remember a compliment by a teacher or a pat on the back by peers. Most likely you do not remember the massive amount of content that was covered. Discuss your feelings about this with your classmates. Share common experiences and common concerns.

3. It is an aphorism that to learn something well students need time to practice it. There is a difference, however, between solitary practice and coached practice. Describe the difference and conditions where you would use each.

4. Divide into teams of four, and have each team develop one learning center. Set up and share the LCs in your classroom.

5. Explain how a teacher can tell when he or she is truly using cooperative learning groups for instruction as opposed to traditional small-group learning.

6. When a student is said to be on-task, does that necessarily imply that the student is mentally engaged? Is it possible for a student to be mentally engaged although not on-task? Explain your answers.

7. Identify and describe instructional strategies that encourage students to become independent thinkers and skilled learners. How, specifically, can a teacher determine when a child has become an independent thinker and a skilled learner? Describe the behaviors that one looks for?

8. Describe any prior concepts you held that changed as a result of your experiences with this chapter. Describe the changes.

9. From your current observations and fieldwork as related to this teacher preparation program, clearly identify one specific example of educational practice that seems contradictory to exemplary practice or theory as presented in this chapter. Present your explanation for the discrepancy.

10. Do you have questions generated by the content of this chapter? If you do, list them along with ways answers might be found.

FOR FURTHER READING _____

Antil, L. R., Jenkins, J. R., Wayne, S. K., and Vadasy, P. F. (1998). Cooperative Learning: Prevalence, Conceptualizations, and the Relation Between Research and Practice. *American Educational Research Journal, 35*(3), 419–454.

Aronson, E., and Patnoe, S. (1997). *The Jigsaw Classroom: Building Cooperation in the Classroom* (2nd ed.). New York: Longman.

Bomer, R. (1999). Writing to Think Critically: The Seeds of Social Action. *Voices From the Middle, 6*(4), 2–8.

Bouas, M. J., Thompson, P., and Farlow, N. (1997). Self-Selected Journal Writing in the Kindergarten Classroom: Five Conditions That Foster Literacy Development. *Reading Horizons, 38*(1), 3–12.

Bower, B., and Lobdell, J. (1998). History Alive! Six Powerful Constructivist Strategies. *Social Education, 62*(1), 50–53.

Brisk, M. E., and Harrington, M. M. (2000). *Literacy and Bilingualism: A Handbook for ALL Teachers.* Mahwah, NJ: Lawrence Erlbaum.

Cohen, E. G. (1998). Making Cooperative Learning Equitable. *Educational Leadership, 56*(1), 18–21.

Cornett, C. E. (1997). Beyond Retelling the Plot: Student-Led Discussions. *Reading Teacher, 50*(6), 527–528.

Duncan, D., and Lockhart, L. (2000). *I-Search, You Search, We All Learn to Research: A How-to-Do-It Manual for Teaching Elementary School Students to Solve Information Problems.* Norwich, CT: Neal-Schuman.

Dunn, M. A. (2000). Staying the Course of Open Education. *Educational Leadership, 57*(7), 20–24.

Freeman, M. S. (1999). *Building a Writing Community: A Practical Guide* (2d ed.). Gainesville, FL: Maupin House.

Gillies, R. M., and Ashman, A. F. (1998). Behavior and Interactions of Children in Cooperative Groups in Lower and Middle Elementary Grades. *Journal of Educational Psychology, 90*(4), 746–757.

Good, T. L., and Brophy, J. E. (2000). *Looking in Classrooms* (8th ed., Chaps. 7–9). New York: Addison Wesley/Longman.

Heller, N. (1998). *Technology Connections for Grades 3–5. Research Projects and Activities.* Englewood, CO: Libraries Unlimited.

Holt, P. W. (1998). The Oregon Trail: Wyoming Students Construct a CD-ROM. *Social Education, 62*(1), 41–45.

Jacobs, G. M., Gilbert, C. C., Lopriore, L., and Goldstein, S. (1998). Cooperative Learning and Second-Language Teaching: Frequently-Asked Questions. *Mosaic, 5*(2), 13–16.

Marzano, R. J.; Pickering, D. J., Pollock, J. E. *Classroom Instruction that Works.* Chapter 7, "Cooperative Learning," pp. 84–91. Alexandria, VA: Association for Supervision and Curriculum Development, 2001.

Metzger, M. (1998). Teaching Reading: Beyond the Plot. *Phi Delta Kappan, 80*(3), 240–246, 256.

Mewborn, D. S. (1999). Creating a Gender Equitable School Environment. *International Journal of Leadership in Education, 2*(2), 103–115.

Murphey, C. E. (1998). Using the Five Themes of Geography to Explore a School Site. *Social Studies Review, 37*(2), 49–52.

Paulu, N., and Darby, L. B. (Eds.). (1998). *Helping Your Students With Homework: A Guide for Teachers.* Washington, DC: U.S. Office of Educational Research and Improvement, U.S. Government Printing Office.

Ray, K. W. (1999). *Wondrous Words: Writers and Writing in the Elementary Classroom.* Urbana, IL: National Council of Teachers of English.

Smith, J. A. (2000). Singing and Songwriting Support Early Literacy Instruction. *The Reading Teacher, 53*(8), 646–649.

Solley, B. (2000). *Writers' Workshop: Reflections of Elementary and Middle School Teachers.* Needham Heights, MA: Allyn and Bacon.

Tepper, A. B. (1999). A Journey Through Geometry: Designing a City Park. *Teaching Children Mathematics, 5*(6), 348–352.

Thomason, T., and York, C. (2000). *Write on Target: Preparing Young Writers to Succeed on State Writing Achievement Tests.* Norwood, MA: Christopher-Gordon.

Tomlinson, C. A. (1999). *The Differentiated Classroom.* Alexandria, VA: Association for Supervision and Curriculum Development.

Topping, K., and Ehly, S. (Eds.) (1998). *Peer-Assisted Learning.* Mahway, NJ: Lawrence Erlbaum.

Weinman, J., and Haag, P. (1999). Gender Equity in Cyberspace. *Educational Leadership, 56*(5), 44–49.

NOTES

1. J. M. Carroll, The Copernican Plan Evaluated, *Phi Delta Kappan, 76*(2), 105–113 (October 1994).
2. See B. Bloom, *Human Characteristics and School Learning* (New York: McGraw-Hill, 1987), and J. Carroll, A Model of School Learning, *Teachers College Record, 64*(8), 723–733 (May 1963).
3. See, for example, T. R. Guskey, Defining the Differences Between Outcome-Based Education and Mastery Learning, *School Administrator, 51*(8), 34–37 (September 1994). Information about CES, such as a directory of participating schools, can be obtained from <http://www.essentialschools.org>. See also W. Malloy, Essential Schools and Inclusion: A Responsive Partnership, *Educational Forum, 60*(3), 228–236 (Spring 1996).
4. See J. Battistini, *From Theory to Practice: Classroom Application of Outcome-Based Education* (Bloomington, IN: ERIC Clearinghouse on Reading, English, and Communication, 1995), and L. Horton, *Mastery Learning,* Fastback 154 (Bloomington, IN: Phi Delta Kappa Educational Foundation, 1981).
5. R. Dunn, *Strategies for Diverse Learners,* Fastback 384 (Bloomington, IN: Phi Delta Kappa Educational Foundation, 1995), p. 15.
6. See, for example, E. S. Foster-Harrison, *Peer Tutoring for K-12 Success,* Fastback 415 (Bloomington, IN: Phi Delta Kappa Educational Foundation, 1997); E. Kreuger and B. Braun, Books and Buddies: Peers Tutoring Peers, *Reading Teacher, 52*(4), 410–414 (December/January 1998–1999); P. G. Mathes, M. L. Grek, J. K. Howard, A. E. Babyak, and S. H. Allen, Peer-Assisted Learning Strategies for First-Grade Readers: A Tool for Preventing Early Reading Failure, *Learning Disabilities Research and Practice, 14*(1), 50–60 (Winter 1999); and P. G. Mathes, J. K. Howard, S. H. Allen, and D. Fuchs, Peer-Assisted Learning Strategies for First-Grade Readers: Responding to the Needs of Diverse Learners, *Reading Research Quarterly, 33*(1), 62–94 (January/March 1998).
7. See, for example, P. F. Vadasy, et al., The Effectiveness of One-to-One Tutoring by Community Tutors for At-Risk Beginning Readers, *Learning Disability Quarterly, 20*(2), 126–139 (Spring 1997), and R. B. Schneider and D. Barone, Cross-Age Tutoring, *Childhood Education, 73*(3), 136–143 (Spring 1997).
8. See, for example, the story of a project that involved middle school students helping kindergarten children learn Spanish, in R. A. Oleksak, ChalkBoard. Teaching Spanish as a Community Service, *Our Children, 23*(2), 38 (October 1997).
9. L. S. Walters, Putting Cooperative Learning to the Test, *Harvard Education Letter, 16*(3), 1–6 (May/June 2000).
10. See, for example, J. D. Laney, et al., The Effect of Cooperative and Mastery Learning Methods on Primary Grade Students' Learning and Retention of Economic Concepts, *Early Education and Development, 7*(3), 253–274 (July 1996), and L. Cross and D. Walker-Knight, Inclusion: Developing Collaborative and Cooperative School Communities, *Educational Forum, 61*(3), 269–277 (Spring 1997).
11. For details about these CLG strategies and others, see R. E. Slavin, *Student Team Learning: A Practical Guide for Cooperative Learning,* 3rd ed. (Washington, DC: National Education Association, 1991); E. Coelho, *Learning Together in the Multicultural*

Classroom (Portsmouth, NH: Heinemann, 1994); and Y. Sharan and S. Sharan, *Expanding Cooperative Learning Through Group Investigation* (New York: Teachers College Press, 1992).

12. See S. Kagan, Group Grades Miss the Mark, *Educational Leadership, 52*(8), 68–71 (May 1995), and D. W. Johnson and R. T. Johnson, The Role of Cooperative Learning in Assessing and Communicating Student Learning, Chapter 4 in T. R. Guskey, *Communicating Student Learning,* 1996 ASCD yearbook (Alexandria, VA: Association for Supervision and Curriculum Development, 1996).

13. T. L. Good and J. E. Brophy, *Looking in Classrooms,* 8th ed. (New York: Addison Wesley/Longman, 2000), p. 296.

14. Good and Brophy, *Looking in Classrooms,* p. 291.

15. C. A. Tomlinson, *The Differentiated Classroom* (Alexandria, VA: Association for Supervision and Curriculum Development, 1999), p. 61.

16. See, for example, V. Randall, Cooperative Learning: Abused and Overused? *Gifted Child Today Magazine, 22*(2), 14–16 (March/April 1999).

17. See, for example, S. Zaher, Gender and Curriculum in the School Room, *Education Canada, 36*(1), 26–29 (Spring 1996), and S. M. Bailey, Shortchanging Girls and Boys, *Educational Leadership, 53*(8), 75–79 (May 1996). For information on how to identify equity problems and develop programs to help schools achieve academic excellence for all students, contact EQUITY 2000, 1233 20th St. NW, Washington, DC 20056-2304; 202-822-5930.

18. See, for example, S. Black, The Truth About Homework, *American School Board Journal, 183*(10), 48–51 (October 1996).

19. See, for example, M. H. Sullivan and P. V. Sequeira, The Impact of Purposeful Homework on Learning, *Clearing House, 69*(6), 346–348 (July/August 1996).

20. H. J. Walberg, Productive Teaching and Instruction: Assessing the Knowledge Base, *Phi Delta Kappan, 71*(6), 472 (February 1990).

21. See, for example, M. Tassinari, Hands-On Projects Take Students Beyond the Book, *Social Studies Review, 34*(3), 16–20 (Spring 1996); D. K. Meyer, et al., Challenge in a Mathematics Classroom: Students' Motivation and Strategies in Project-Based Learning, *Elementary School Journal, 97*(5), 501–521 (May 1997); and L. G. Katz and S. C. Chard, *Issues in Selecting Topics for Projects,* ED42403198 (Champaign, IL: ERIC Clearinghouse on Elementary and Early Childhood Education, 1998).

22. A. Algava, Animated Learning, *Educational Leadership, 56*(5), 58–60 (February 1999).

23. See also H. G. Andrade, Using Rubrics to Promote Thinking and Learning, *Educational Leadership, 57*(5), 13–18 (February 2000).

24. Adapted from Pamela L. Tiedt and Iris M. Tiedt, *Multicultural Teaching: A Handbook of Activities, Information, and Resources,* 4th ed. (Boston: Allyn and Bacon, 1995), p. 208.

What Guidelines Are Available for My Use of Teacher Talk, Demonstrations, Thinking, Inquiry, and Games?

Perhaps no other strategy is used more by teachers than is teacher talk, so this chapter begins with a presentation of guidelines for using that vital instructional strategy. A strategy related to teacher talk is the demonstration, which is addressed later in the chapter, followed by guidelines for other important strategies, namely, for thinking, inquiry and discovery, and games.

CHAPTER OBJECTIVES

Specifically, upon your completion of this chapter you should be able to

1. Characterize the relationships among thinking, problem solving, discovery, and inquiry.
2. Compare and contrast each of seven categories of games for learning.

Teaching Vignette:
A Precious Moment in Teaching
With Advice to Beginning Teachers

We share with you this teaching vignette that we find to be both humorous and indicative of creative thinking. A teacher began a social studies lesson with the question, "What comes to mind when you hear the words 'Puritan' and 'Pilgrim'?" Without hesitation, a rather quiet student voice from near the rear of the room replied, "Cooking oil and John Wayne." To us, that represented one of those rare and precious moments in teaching, reaffirming our belief that every teacher is well-advised to maintain throughout his or her teaching career a journal in which such intrinsically rewarding moments can be recorded so to be reviewed and enjoyed again years later.

---

3. Demonstrate understanding of the relationship of time, learning modality, and strategy change for effective instruction.
4. Describe characteristics of an effective demonstration.
5. Describe characteristics of the effective use of inquiry.
6. Describe how to help students learn to think and behave intelligently.
7. Describe the value, purpose, and types of advance mental organizers used when using teacher talk as an instructional strategy.
8. Describe when and how to use teacher talk for instruction.
9. Identify and describe ways of integrating strategies for integrated learning.

TEACHER TALK: FORMAL AND INFORMAL

Teacher talk encompasses both lecturing *to* students and talking *with* students. For purposes of our presentation in this resource guide, a lecture is considered formal teacher talk whereas a discussion with students is considered informal teacher talk.

Teacher Talk: General Guidelines

Certain general guidelines are appropriate whether your talk is formal or informal. First, you should begin the talk with an advance organizer. Advance organizers are introductions that mentally prepare students for a study by helping them make connections with material already learned or experienced—a *comparative organizer*—or by providing students with a conceptual arrangement of what is to be learned—an *expository organizer*.[1] The value of using advance organizers is well documented by research.[2] An advance organizer can be a brief introduction or statement about the main idea you intend to convey and how it is related to other aspects of the students' learning (an expository organizer), or it can be a presentation of a discrepancy to arouse curiosity (a comparative organizer, in this instance causing students to compare what they have observed with what they already knew or thought they knew). Preparing an organizer helps you plan and organize the sequence of ideas, and its presentation helps students organize their own learning and become motivated about it. An advance organizer can also make their learning meaningful by providing important connections between what they already know and what is being learned.

Second, your talk should be planned so that it has a clear beginning and a distinct end, with a logical order in between. During your talk, you should reinforce your words with visuals (discussed in the specific guidelines that follow). These visuals may include writing unfamiliar terms on the board (helping students learn new vocabulary), visual organizers, and prepared graphs, charts, photographs, and various audiovisuals.

Third, pacing is important. Your talk should move briskly, but not too fast. The ability to pace the instruction is a difficult skill for many beginning teachers (the tendency among many beginning teachers is to talk too fast and too much), but one that will improve with experience. Until you have developed your skill in pacing lessons you probably will need to constantly remind yourself during lessons to slow down and provide silent pauses (allowing for think-time) and frequent checks for student comprehension. Specifically, your talk should:

- Be brisk, though not too fast, but with occasional slowdowns to change the pace and to check for student comprehension. Allow students time to think, ask questions, and make notes.
- Have a time plan. A talk planned for 10 minutes, if interesting to students, will probably take longer. If not interesting to them, it will probably take less time.
- Always be planned with careful consideration to the characteristics of the students. For example, if you have a fairly high percentage of LEP students

or students with special needs, then your talk may be less brisk, sprinkled with even more visuals and repeated statements, and even more frequent checks for student comprehension. As we said earlier (Chapter 3), by *frequent checks for comprehension* we mean, on the average, at least one check per minute. Checks for comprehension can be in the form of questions you ask and that the children ask during the lesson, as well as various kinds of checklists.

Fourth, encourage student participation. Active participation by the children enhances their learning. This encouragement can be planned as questions that you ask, as time allowed for students to comment and ask questions, or as some sort of a visual and conceptual outline or other activity children can complete during the talk.

Fifth, plan a distinct ending (closure). Be sure your talk has a distinct ending, followed by another activity (during the same or next class period) that will help reinforce and secure the learning. As for all lessons, you want to strive to plan a clear and mesmerizing beginning, an involving lesson body, and a firm and meaningful closure.

Teacher Talk: Specific Guidelines

Specific guidelines for using teacher talk are presented in the following paragraphs.

Understand the various purposes for using teacher talk. Teacher talk, formal or informal, can be useful to discuss the progress of a unit of study, explain an inquiry, introduce a unit of study, present a problem, promote student inquiry or critical thinking, provide a transition from one unit of study to the next, provide information otherwise unobtainable to students, share the teacher's experiences, share the teacher's thinking, summarize a problem, summarize a unit of study, and teach a thinking skill by modeling that skill.

Clarify the objectives of the talk. Your talk should center around one idea. The learning target objectives, which should not be too numerous for one talk, should be clearly understood by the students.

Choose between informal and formal talk. Long lectures are inappropriate for most if not all elementary school teaching; spontaneous interactive informal talks of 5 to 12 minutes are preferred. You should *never* give long lectures with no teacher-student interaction. If during your student teaching you have doubt or questions about your selection and use of a particular instructional strategy, discuss your concern with your co-

operating teacher or your university supervisor, or both. When you have doubt about the appropriateness of a particular strategy, trust your instincts: Without some modification, the strategy probably is inappropriate.

Remember also, today's youth are of the "media," or "light," generation; they are accustomed to highly stimulating video interactions and "commercial breaks." For many lessons, especially those that are teacher-centered, after about 10 minutes student attention is likely to begin to stray. For that eventuality you need elements planned to recapture student attention. These planned elements can include: temporary strategy and modality shift, such as a teacher demonstration or a student inquiry; analogies to help connect the topic to students' life experiences; verbal cues, such as voice inflections; pauses to allow information to sink in; humor; visual cues, such as the use of slides, overhead transparencies, charts, board drawings, excerpts from videodiscs, real objects (realia), or body gestures; and sensory cues, such as eye contact and proximity (as in moving around the room, or casually and gently touching a student on the shoulder without interrupting your talk).

Vary strategies and activities frequently. Perhaps most useful as a strategy for recapturing student attention is to change to an entirely different strategy or learning modality. For example, from teacher talk (a teacher-centered strategy) you would change to a student activity (a student-centered strategy). Notice that changing from a lecture (mostly teacher talk) to a teacher-led discussion (mostly more teacher talk) would not be changing to an entirely different modality. Figure 9.1 provides a comparison of different changes.

As a generalization, when using teacher-centered direct instruction, with most groups of children you will want to change the learning activities about every 10 to 12 minutes. (That is one reason that in the sample lesson plan format of Figure 6.8 in Chapter 6, you find space for at least four activities, including the introduction and closure.) Although this will vary due to many variables, such as whether you are teaching first graders or sixth graders, 15 or 30 children at a time, art or mathematics, and so on, generally this means that in a 60-minute time block you should plan from three to five sequenced learning activities, with a few activities that are teacher-centered and many others that are more student-centered. And, in a 90-minute block, plan five or six learning activities. In exemplary grades K–6 classrooms, teachers often have several activities being performed *concurrently* by children as individuals, in dyads, and in small groups—that is,

Figure 9.1
Comparison of
recapturing student
attention by changing the
instructional strategy

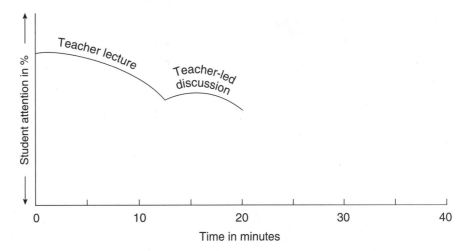

Example 1: Changing from teacher talk (lecture) to more teacher talk (e.g., teacher-led discussion).

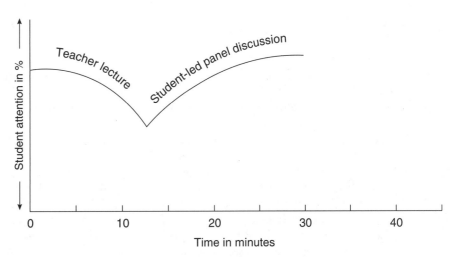

Example 2: Changing from teacher talk (teacher-centered activity) to student-led panel discussion (student-centered activity).

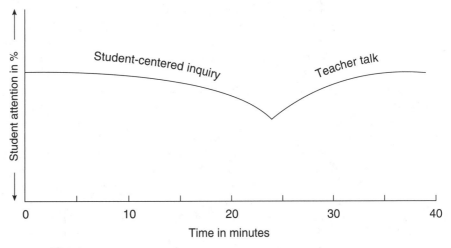

Example 3: Changing from inquiry (student-centered) to teacher-talk fueled by student questions from inquiry.

(continued)

Figure 9.1 *(continued)*

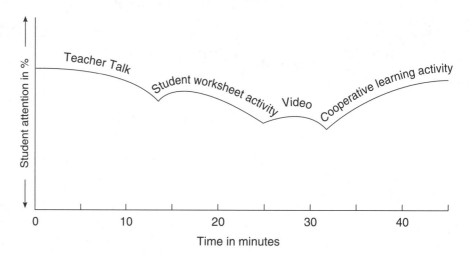

Example 4: Changing from teacher talk (teacher-centered activity) to cooperative learning activity (student-centered activity).

they are using multilevel (multitasking) instruction. Multitasking is, as we have mentioned often in this resource guide, highly recommended as a viable strategy when teaching a classroom of 15 or more children (although it is not advised when one is driving a motor vehicle). An example of multitasking is shown in Figure 2.2 of Chapter 2.

Prepare and use notes as a guide for yourself during your talk. Planning your talk and preparing notes to be used during formal and informal teacher talk is important—just as important as is implementing the talk with visuals. There is absolutely nothing wrong with using notes during your teaching. As you move around the room your notes can be carried on your attractive neon-colored clipboard. Your notes for a formal talk can first be prepared in narrative form; for class use, though, they should be reduced to an outline form. Talks to students should always be from an outline, never read from prose. The only time that a teacher's reading from prose aloud to students is appropriate is when reading a brief published article (such as from a newspaper) or portions of a story or a poem (as in reading/language arts).

In your outline, consider using color coding with abbreviated visual cues to yourself. You will eventually develop your own coding system; whatever coding system you use keep it simple lest you forget what the codes are for. Consider these examples of coding: Where transition of ideas occur and you want to allow silent moments for ideas to sink in, mark *P* for *pause,* *T* for a *transition,* and *S* for moments of *silence*; where a slide or other visual aid will be used, mark *AV* for *audiovisual*; where you intend to stop and ask a question, mark *TQ* for *teacher question,* and mark *SQ* or *?* where

you want to stop and allow time for *student questions*; where you plan to have a discussion, mark *D;* or mark *SG* where you plan *small-group work* and *L* where you plan to switch to a *laboratory* investigation; for *reviews* and *comprehension checks,* mark *R* and *CS.*

Share your note organization with the children. Teach the students how to take notes and what kinds of things they should write down. Use colored chalk or marking pens to outline and highlight your talk; have your students use colored pencils for note-taking so their notes can be color-coded to match your writing board notes.

Rehearse your talk. Rehearsing your planned talk is important. Using your lesson plan as your guide, rehearse your talk using a camcorder or while talking into a mirror or to a friend or roommate. Is the pacing proper—not too fast and not too slow? Are your choice of words, voice, and body language conveying professionalism and your thorough preparation and confidence? You may want to include a time plan for each subtopic to allow you to gauge your timing during implementation of the talk.

Avoid racing through the talk solely to complete it by a certain time. It is more important that students understand some of what you say than that you cover it all and they understand none of it. If you do not finish, continue it later.

Augment your talk with multisensory stimulation and allow for think-time. Your presentation should not overly rely on verbal communication. When using visuals, such as photographs, computer screen projections, video excerpts, or overhead transparencies, do not think that you must be constantly talking; after clearly explaining the purpose of a visual, give students sufficient time to look at it, to think about it, and to ask questions about it. The visual is new to the students, so give them time to take it in.

Carefully plan the content of your talk. The content of your talk should supplement and enhance that found in the student textbook rather than simply rehash content from the textbook. Students may never read their book if you tell them in an interesting and condensed fashion everything that they need to know from it.

Monitor your delivery. Your voice should be pleasant and interesting to listen to rather than a steady, boring monotone or a constantly shrieking, irritating, high pitch. On the other hand, it is good to show enthusiasm for what you are talking about for teaching and learning. Occasionally use dramatic voice inflections to emphasize important points and meaningful body language to give students a visual focus. So not to appear phony, practice these skills so they become second nature.

As is always the case when teaching, *avoid standing in the same spot for long periods of time.* (We consider standing for 10 minutes in the same spot to be a long time.) Even during direct instruction, you need to monitor student behavior and to use proximity (moving closer to a student) and signal interference (e.g., eye contact, body language, smile or frown, thumbs up or down) as means of keeping students focused. It is especially during extended periods of direct instruction that a beginning teacher's skills in withitness and overlapping behaviors are likely to be put to the test (see Chapter 3).

View the vocabulary of the talk as an opportunity to help students with their word morphology. The children should easily understand words you use, though you should still model professionalism and help students develop their vocabulary. During your lesson planning, predict when you are likely to use a word that is new to most students, and plan to stop to ask a student to help explain its meaning and perhaps demonstrate its derivation. Help students with word meaning. This helps students with their remembering. Remember that *all teachers are language-arts teachers.* Knowledge of word morphology is an important component of skilled reading and includes the ability to generate new words from prefixes, roots, and suffixes. For some students, nearly every subject in the curriculum is like a foreign language. That is certainly true for some LEP students, for whom teacher talk, especially formal teacher talk, should be used sparingly, if at all. Every elementary schoolteacher has the responsibility of helping children learn how to learn, and

that includes helping students develop their word comprehension skills, reading skills, thinking and memory skills, and their motivation for learning.

Give thoughtful and intelligent consideration to student diversity. During the preactive phase of planning, while preparing your talk, consider children in your classroom who are culturally and linguistically different and those who have special needs. Personalize the talk for them by choosing your vocabulary carefully and appropriately, speaking slowly and methodically, repeating often, and by planning meaningful analogies and examples and relevant audio and visual displays.

Use familiar examples and analogies to help students make relevant connections (bridges). While this sometimes takes a great deal of creative thinking as well as action during the preactive planning phase, it is important that you attempt to connect the talk with ideas and events with which the students are already familiar (such as the names of events, places, and people from their neighborhood and community). The most effective talk is one that makes frequent and meaningful connections between what students already know and what they are learning, which bridges what they are learning with what they have experienced in their lives.

Establish eye contact frequently. Your primary eye contact should be with your students—always! That important point cannot be overemphasized. Only momentarily should you look at your notes, your visuals, the projection screen, the writing board, bulletin board, and other adults or objects in the classroom. While you will probably raise your eyebrows when you read this, it is true and it is important that with practice you can learn to scan a classroom of 30 students, establishing eye contact with each student at least once a minute. To *establish* eye contact means that the student is aware that you are looking at him or her. Frequent eye contact can have two major benefits. First, as you "read" a child's body posture and facial expressions, you obtain important clues about that student's attentiveness and comprehension. Second, eye contact helps to establish rapport between you and a student. A look with a smile or a wink from the teacher to a child can say so much! Be alert, though, for children who are from cultures where eye contact is infrequent or even unwanted and could have negative consequences. In other words, don't push it!

Frequent eye contact is easier when using an overhead projector than when using the writing board. When using a writing board, you have to turn at least partially away from your audience, and you may also have to pace back and forth from the board to the students to be able to retain that important proximity to them.

While talking to the children you must remain and demonstrate your withitness, that is, you must remain aware and attentive to everything that is happening in the classroom (that is, to student behavior as well as to the content of your talk). No one ever said that good teaching is easy, or if they did they didn't know what they were talking about. But don't dismay: With the knowledge of the preceding guidelines, the cautions that follow, and with practice, experience, and intelligent reflection, you will quickly develop the skills important to being recognized as an accomplished teacher.

Cautions in Using Teacher Talk

Whether your talk is formal or informal, there are certain cautions that you need to be mindful of. Perhaps the most important is that of talking too much. If a teacher talks too much, the significance of the teacher's words may be lost because some students will tune the teacher out.

Another caution is to avoid talking too fast. Your students can hear faster than they can comprehend what they hear. It is also important to remember that your one brain is communicating with the brains of many students, each of which responds to sensory input (auditory in this instance) at different rates. Because of this, you will need to pause to let words sink in and you will need to pause during transitions from one point or activity to the next so to allow each of those many brains to make the necessary shift. It is a good idea to remind yourself to talk slowly and to check frequently for student comprehension of what you are talking about.

A third caution is to be sure you are being heard and understood. Sometimes teachers talk in too low a pitch or use words that are not understood by many of the students, or both. You should vary the pitch of your voice, and you should stop and help students with their understanding of vocabulary that may be new to them.

A fourth caution is to remember that just because students have heard something before does not necessarily mean that they understand it or that they learned it. From our earlier discussions of learning experiences (such as The Learning Experiences Ladder in Chapter 6, Figure 6.5), remember that although verbal communication is an important form of communication, because of its reliance on the use of abstract symbolization it is not always a very reliable form of communication.

Teacher talk relies on words and on skill in listening, a skill that is not mastered by many children (or for that matter, even many adults). For that and other reasons, to ensure student understanding, it is good to reinforce your teacher talk with either direct or simulated learning experiences.

A related caution is to resist believing that children have attained a skill or have mastered content that was taught previously by you or by another teacher. During any discussion, rather than assuming that your students know something, you should ensure they know it. For example, if the discussion and a student activity involve a particular thinking skill, then you will want to make sure that students know how to use that skill (thinking skills are discussed later in this chapter).

Still another problem is talking in a humdrum monotone. Children need teachers whose voices exude enthusiasm and excitement (though not to be overdone) about the subject and about teaching and learning. A voice that demonstrates enthusiasm for teaching and learning is more likely to motivate children to learn. Enthusiasm and excitement for learning are contagious.

DEMONSTRATION

Children enjoy demonstrations because the demonstrator is actively engaged in a learning activity rather than merely verbalizing about it. Demonstrations can be used in teaching at any grade level for a variety of purposes. During a social studies lesson, the teacher uses role-play to demonstrate violation of first amendment rights. A teacher demonstrates steps in solving a mathematics problem. During a language-arts lesson, the teacher demonstrates clustering to students ready for a creative writing assignment. During a science lesson, the teacher demonstrates the effect of the absence of light on a plant leaf. In physical education, the teacher demonstrates the proper way to serve in volleyball.

Purposes of Demonstrations

A demonstration can be designed to serve any of the following purposes: to establish problem recognition; to assist in recognizing a solution to an identified problem; to bring an unusual closure to a lesson or unit of study; to demonstrate a thinking skill; to model a skill used in conflict resolution; to give students opportunity for vicarious participation in active learning; to illustrate a particular point of content; to introduce a lesson or unit of study in a way that grabs the students' attention; to reduce potential safety hazards; to review; to save time and resources (as opposed to the entire class doing that which is being demonstrated); and to set up a discrepancy recognition.

Guidelines for Using Demonstrations

When planning a demonstration, you should consider the following guidelines.

Decide what is the most effective way to conduct the demonstration, for example as a verbal or a silent demonstration; by a student or by the teacher; by the teacher with a student helper; to the entire class or to small groups; or by some combination of these such as first by the teacher followed by a repeat of the demonstration by a student or a succession of students.

Be sure that the demonstration is visible to all students. Consider the use of special lighting to highlight the demonstration. For example, a slide projector can be set up and used as a spotlight. Or an overhead projector can be used when the materials of the demonstration are transparent.

Practice with the materials and procedure before demonstrating to the students. During your practice, try to prepare for anything that could go wrong during the live demonstration; if you don't, as Murphy's Law says, if anything can go wrong, it probably will. Then, if something does go wrong during the live demonstration, use that as an opportunity for a teachable moment; engage the children in working with you to try to figure out what went wrong or if that isn't feasible, go to Plan B (see Chapter 10).

Consider your pacing of the demonstration, allowing for enough student wait-see and think-time. At the start of the demonstration, explain its purpose and the learning objectives. Remember this adage: Tell them what you are going to do, show them, and then tell them what they saw. As with any lesson, plan your closure and allow time for questions and discussion. During the demonstration, as in other types of teacher talk, use frequent pauses to check for student understanding.

Be sure that the demonstration table and area are free of unnecessary objects that could distract or be in the way. If the planned demonstration will pose a safety hazard to the children or to yourself, or both, don't do it. Select a safe alternate demonstration.

TEACHING THINKING FOR INTELLIGENT BEHAVIOR

Pulling together what has been learned about learning and brain functioning, teachers are encouraged to integrate explicit thinking instruction into daily lessons, to teach children the skills necessary for intelligent behavior.

Characteristics of Intelligent Behavior

Characteristics of intelligent behavior that you should model, teach for, and observe developing in your students, as identified by Costa,[3] are described in the following paragraphs.

Persistence. Persistence is the act of sticking to an idea or a task until it is completed. Consider the following examples.

- *Thomas Edison.* Persistent in his efforts to invent the electric light bulb, Edison tried approximately three thousand filaments before finding one that worked.
- *Wilma Rudolf.* Because of childhood diseases, Rudolf, at age 10, could not walk without the aid of leg braces. Only 10 years later, at the age of 20, having won three gold medals in the 1960 World Olympics she was declared to be the fastest running woman in the world.
- *Babe Ruth.* For years Ruth owned not only the highest number of home runs in professional baseball but also the highest number of strikeouts.
- *Margaret Sanger.* Born in 1883, Sanger persevered in her belief in a woman's right to control her own fertility. Nearly single-handedly and against formidable odds she founded the birth-control movement in the United States, beginning in 1914 with her founding of the National Birth Control League. In 1953 Sanger was named the first president of the International Planned Parenthood Federation.

Decreasing impulsivity. Impulsive behavior can create or worsen conflict and can inhibit effective problem solving.[4] Persons with impulse control think before acting. Students can be taught to think before shouting out an answer, before beginning a task, and before arriving at conclusions with insufficient supporting information. As we have emphasized before in this resource guide (Chapters 4 and 7), one reason teachers should usually insist on a show of student hands before a student is acknowledged to respond or question is to help children develop control over the impulsive behavior of shouting out in class.[5]

Listening to others with understanding and empathy. Some psychologists believe that the ability to listen to others, to empathize with and to understand their point of view, is one of the highest forms of intelligent behavior. Empathic behavior is an important skill for conflict resolution. Piaget refers to this behavior as *overcoming egocentrism.* In class meetings, brainstorming sessions, think tanks, town meetings, advisory councils, board meetings, and legislative bodies, people from various walks of life convene to share their thinking, to explore their ideas, and to broaden their perspectives by listening to and considering the ideas and reactions of others.

Cooperative thinking—social intelligence. Humans are social beings. Real-world problem solving has become so complex that seldom can any person go it alone. Not all students come to school knowing how to work effectively in groups. They may exhibit competitiveness, narrow-mindedness, egocentrism, ethnocentrism, or criticism of others' values, emotions, and beliefs. Altruism, consensus seeking, giving up an idea to work on someone else's, integrating the ideas of others, knowing how to handle disagreements, knowing how to support group efforts, listening, and sharing—those are behaviors indicative of intelligent human beings, and they can be learned by children at school and in the classroom.

Flexibility in thinking. Sometimes called *lateral thinking,*[6] flexibility in thinking is the ability to approach a problem from a new angle, using a novel approach. With modeling by the teacher, children can develop this behavior as they learn to consider alternative points of view and to deal with several sources of information simultaneously.

Metacognition. Metacognition, learning to plan, monitor, assess, and reflect on one's own thinking, is another characteristic of intelligent behavior. Cooperative learning groups, journals, portfolio conferences, self-assessment, and thinking aloud in dyads are strategies that can be used to help children develop this intelligent behavior.[7] Your thinking aloud is good modeling for your students, helping them to develop their own cognitive skills of thinking, learning, and reasoning.[8]

Striving for accuracy and precision. Teachers can observe children growing in this behavior when students take time to check over their work, review the procedures, avoid drawing conclusions prematurely, and use concise and descriptive language.

Sense of humor. The positive effects of humor on the body's physiological functions are well established: a drop in the pulse rate, an increase of oxygen in the blood, the activation of antibodies that fight against harmful microorganisms, and the release of gamma interferon, a hormone that fights viruses and regulates cell growth. Humor liberates creativity and provides high-level thinking skills, such as anticipation, finding novel relationships, and visual imagery. The acquisition of a sense of humor follows a developmental sequence similar to that described by Piaget[9] and Kohlberg.[10] Initially, young children may find humor in all the wrong things—human frailty, ethnic humor, sacrilegious riddles, ribald profanities. Later, creative children thrive on finding incongruity and will demonstrate a whimsical frame of mind during problem solving. Remember, however, that to be most effective as a tool for teaching and learning, the humor used should not be self-degrading or offensive to anyone.

Questioning and problem posing. Children are usually full of questions, and, unless discouraged, they do ask them. We want students to be alert to, and recognize, discrepancies and phenomena in their environment and to freely inquire about their causes. In exemplary school programs, students are encouraged to ask questions (see Chapter 7) and then from those questions to develop a problem-solving strategy to investigate their questions.

Drawing on knowledge and applying it to new situations. A major goal of formal education is for students to apply school-learned knowledge to real-life situations. To develop skills in drawing on past knowledge and applying that knowledge to new situations, children must be given opportunity to practice doing that very thing. Project-based learning (discussed in Chapter 8), and problem recognition and problem solving (discussed next in this chapter), are ways of providing that opportunity.

Taking risks: venture forth and explore ideas beyond the usual zone of comfort. Such exploration, of course, must be done with thoughtfulness; it must not be done in ways that could put the child at risk psychologically or physically. Using the analogy of a turtle going nowhere until it sticks its neck out, teachers should model this behavior and provide opportunities for children to develop this intelligent behavior by using techniques such as brainstorming strategies, divergent-thinking questioning, think-pair-share, cooperative learning, inquiry, and project-based learning.

Using all the senses. As discussed previously in this and previous chapters (especially Chapters 2 and 6), as often as is appropriate and feasible, children should be encouraged to learn to use and develop all their sensory input channels—that is, the verbal, visual, tactile, and kinesthetic—for learning.

Ingenuity, originality, insightfulness = Creativity. All children must be encouraged to do and discouraged from saying "I can't." Students must be taught in such a way as to encourage intrinsic motivation rather than reliance on extrinsic sources. Teachers must be able to offer criticism so the student understands that the criticism is not a criticism of the student's self. In exemplary programs, children learn the value of feedback. They learn the value of their own intuition, of guessing, of risking—they learn "I can."

Wonderment, inquisitiveness, curiosity, and the enjoyment of problem solving: A sense of efficacy as a thinker. Young children express wonderment, an expression that should never be stifled. Through effective teaching, all students can recapture that sense of wonderment as an effective teacher guides them into a feeling of "I can' and an expression of "I enjoy."

We should strive to help our own students develop these characteristics of intelligent behavior. In Chapter 3 you learned of specific teacher behaviors that facilitate this development. At the end of Chapter 7, with Exercise 7.8, you reviewed some of them. Now, let's review additional research findings that offer important considerations in the facilitation of student learning and intelligent behavior.

Direct Teaching for Thinking and Intelligent Behavior

The curriculum of any school includes the development of skills that are used in thinking, skills such as *classifying, comparing, concluding, generalizing, inferring,* and others (see Figure 9.3). Because the academic achievement of children increases when they are taught thinking skills directly, many researchers and educators concur that direct instruction should be given to all children on how to think and behave intelligently.[11] Several research perspectives have influenced today's interest in the direct teaching of thinking. The *cognitive view of intelligence* asserts that intellectual ability is not fixed but can be developed. The *constructivist approach to learning* maintains that learners actively and independently construct knowledge by creating and coordinating relationships in their mental repertoire. The *social psychology view of classroom experience* focuses on the learner as an individual who is a member of various peer groups and a society. The *perspective of information processing* deals with the processes of acquiring information, remembering, and problem solving.[12]

Rather than assuming that children have developed thinking skills, teachers should devote classroom time to teaching them directly. When teaching a thinking skill directly, the subject content becomes the vehicle for thinking. For example, a social studies lesson can teach children how to distinguish fact and opinion; a language-arts lesson instructs children how to compare and analyze; a science lesson can teach children how to set up a problem for their inquiry.

Inquiry teaching and discovery learning are both useful tools for learning and for teaching thinking skills. For further insight and additional strategies, as well as for the many programs concerned with teaching thinking, see the resources in this chapter's footnotes and the list of readings at the end of the chapter.[13]

INQUIRY TEACHING AND DISCOVERY LEARNING

Intrinsic to the effectiveness of both inquiry and discovery is the assumption that students would rather actively seek knowledge than receive it through traditional expository (i.e., information delivery) methods such as lectures, demonstrations, and textbook reading. While inquiry and discovery are important teaching tools, there is sometimes confusion about exactly what inquiry teaching is and how it differs from discovery learning. The distinction should become clear as you study the following descriptions of these two important tools for teaching and learning.

Problem Solving

Perhaps a major reason why inquiry and discovery are sometimes confused is that, in both, students are actively engaged in problem solving. By *problem solving,* we mean the intellectual ability to accomplish the following: (a) recognize and define or describe a problem, (b) specify a desired or preferred outcome, (c) identify possible solutions, (d) select a procedure to resolve the problem, (e) apply the procedure, (f) evaluate outcomes, and (g) revise these steps where necessary.

Inquiry versus Discovery

Problem solving is *not* a teaching strategy but a high-order intellectual behavior that facilitates learning. What a teacher can and should do is to provide opportunities for students to identify and tentatively

Table 9.1
Levels of Inquiry

Skill	Level I	Level II	Level III
Problem identification	By teacher or textbook	By teacher or textbook	By student
Process of solving the problem	Decided by teacher or textbook	Decided by student	Decided by student
Identification of tentative solution	Resolved by student	Resolved by student	Resolved by student

Figure 9.2
The inquiry cycle

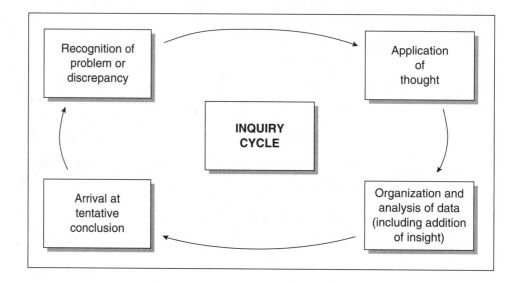

solve problems. Experiences in inquiry and discovery can provide those opportunities. With the processes involved in inquiry and discovery, teachers can help students develop the skills necessary for effective problem solving. Two major differences between discovery and inquiry are (a) who recognizes and identifies the problem and (b) the percentage of decisions that are made by the students. Table 9.1 shows three levels of inquiry, each level defined according to what the student does and decides.

It should be evident from Table 9.1 that what is called *Level I inquiry* is actually traditional, didactic, "cookbook" teaching, where both the problem and the process for resolving it are defined for the student. The student then works through the process to its inevitable resolution. If the process is well designed, the result is inevitable, because the student *discovers* what was intended by the writers of the program. This level is also called *guided inquiry* or *discovery*, because the students are carefully guided through the investigation to (the predicable) discovery.

Level I is in reality a strategy within the *delivery mode*, the advantages of which were described in Chapter 6. Because Level I inquiry is highly manageable and the learning outcome is predictable, it is probably best for teaching basic concepts and principles. Students who never experience learning

beyond Level I are missing an opportunity to engage their highest mental operations, and they seldom (or never) get to experience more motivating, real-life problem solving. Furthermore, those students may come away with the false notion that problem solving is a linear process, which it is not. As illustrated in Figure 9.2, true inquiry is cyclical rather than linear. For that reason, Level I is *not* true inquiry because it is a linear process. Real-world problem solving is a cyclical rather than a linear process. One enters the cycle whenever a discrepancy or problem is observed and recognized, and that can occur at any point in the cycle.

True Inquiry

By the time children are in the upper elementary school grades, they should be provided experiences for true inquiry, which begins with *Level II*, where students actually decide and design processes for their inquiry. True inquiry emphasizes the tentative nature of conclusions, which makes the activity more like real-life problem solving, in which decisions are always subject to revision if and when new data so prescribe.

At *Level III* inquiry students recognize and identify the problem, decide the processes, and

---

**Real-Life Scenario: Problem Solving and Decision Making in the Real World
Is an Integrated and Interdisciplinary Inquiry Activity**

On any given day or specified time period, teacher and students can look at a problem or subject of study from the point of view of many separate disciplines. Such an interdisciplinary approach, to some extent, has been adopted not only by educators but by other professionals as well. It is the mode of meaningful learning and real-life problem solving.

For example, consider the fact-finding and decision-making approach of public officials in one state when confronted with the task of making decisions about projects proposed for watersheds in their state. While gathering information, the officials brought in a state hydrologist. The hydrologist led the officials into the field to demonstrate specific ways by which efforts had helped control erosion and rehabilitate damaged streams. The officials were taken by the hydrologist to a natural creek, where they donned high waders and were led down the stream to examine various features of that complex natural stream. The hydrologist pointed out evidence of the creek's past meanders, patterns that had been incorporated into rehabilitation projects. In addition to listening to this scientist's point of view, the public officials listened to other experts to consider, for example, related economic and political issues before making final decisions about projects that had been proposed for watersheds in that state.

During interdisciplinary thematic units, students study a topic and its underlying ideas as well as related knowledge from various disciplines on an ongoing basis. The teacher, sometimes with the help of students and other teachers and adults, introduces experiences designed to illustrate ideas and skills from various disciplines, just as the hydrologist introduced information from hydrology. For instance, the teacher might stimulate communication skills through creative writing and other projects. Throughout the unit, the students are guided in exploring ideas related to different disciplines to integrate their knowledge.

---

reach a conclusion. In project-centered learning, students are usually engaged at this level of inquiry. By the time students are in middle grades, Level III inquiry should be a major strategy for instruction, which is often the case in schools that use cross-age teaching and interdisciplinary thematic instruction. But it is not easy; like most good teaching practices it is a lot of work. But also like good teaching in general, the intrinsic rewards make the effort worthwhile. As exclaimed by one teacher using interdisciplinary thematic instruction with student-centered inquiry, "I've never worked harder in my life, but I've never had this much fun, either."

The Critical Thinking Skills
of Discovery and Inquiry

In true inquiry, students generate ideas and then design ways to test those ideas. The various processes used represent the many critical thinking skills. Some of those skills are concerned with generating and organizing data; others are concerned with building and using ideas. Figure 9.3 provides four categories of these thinking processes and illustrates the place of each within the inquiry cycle.

Some processes in the cycle are discovery processes and others are inquiry processes. Inquiry

processes include the more complex mental operations, including all those in the idea-using category. Project-based learning provides an avenue for doing that, as does problem-centered teaching.

Inquiry learning is a higher-level mental operation that introduces the concept of the discrepant event, something that establishes cognitive disequilibrium (using the element of surprise to challenge prior notions) to help students develop skills in observing and being alert for discrepancies. Such a strategy provides opportunities for students to investigate their own ideas about explanations. Inquiry, like discovery, depends upon skill in problem solving; the difference between the two is in the amount of decision-making responsibility given to students. Experiences afforded by inquiry help students understand the importance of suspending judgment and also the tentativeness of answers and solutions. With those understandings, students eventually can better deal with life's ambiguities. When children are not provided these important educational experiences, their education is incomplete.

One of the most effective ways of stimulating inquiry is to use materials that provoke students' interest. These materials should be presented in a nonthreatening, noncompetitive context, so students can think laterally and

Figure 9.3
Inquiry cycle processes

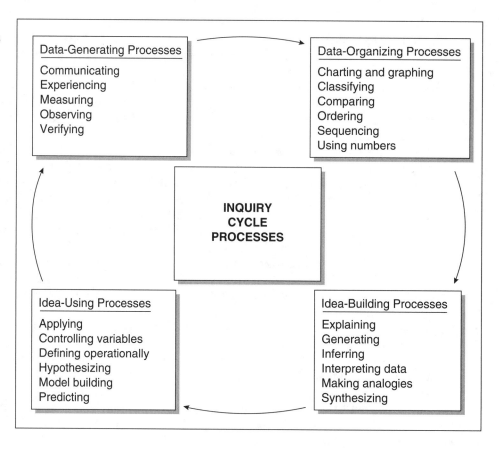

hypothesize openly and freely. The teacher's role is to encourage students to form as many hypotheses as possible and then support their hypotheses with reasons. After the students suggest several ideas, the teacher should begin to move on to higher-order, more abstract, questions that involve the development of generalizations and evaluations. True inquiry problems have a special advantage in that they can be used with almost any group of students. Members of a group approach the problem as an adventure in thinking and apply it to whatever background they can muster. Background experience may enrich a student's approach to the problem, but is not crucial to the use or understanding of the evidence presented to the student. Locating a Colony, Figure 9.4, is a Level II inquiry. As a class, follow the instructions of that inquiry now.

INTEGRATING STRATEGIES FOR INTEGRATED LEARNING

In today's exemplary elementary school classrooms, instructional strategies are combined to establish the most effective teaching-learning experience. For example, in an integrated language-

arts program, teachers are interested in their students' speaking, reading, listening, thinking, study, and writing skills. These skills (and not textbooks) form a holistic process that is the primary aspect of integrated language arts.

In the area of speaking skills, oral discourse (discussion) in the classroom has a growing research base that promotes methods of teaching and learning through oral language. These methods include cooperative learning, instructional scaffolding, and inquiry teaching.

In cooperative learning groups, students discuss and use language for learning that benefits both their content learning and skills in social interaction. Working in heterogeneous groups, students participate in their own learning and can extend their knowledge base and cultural awareness with students of different backgrounds. When students share information and ideas, they are completing difficult learning tasks, using divergent thinking and decision making, and developing their understanding of concepts. As issues are presented and responses are challenged, student thinking is clarified. Students assume the responsibility for planning within the group and for carrying out their assignments. When needed, the teacher models an activity with one group in front of the class, and when integrated with student

Figure 9.4

Locating a colony: a Level II inquiry

(*Source:* Adapted by permission from unpublished material provided by Jennifer Devine and Dennis Devine.)

Presentation of the Problem. In groups of three or four, students receive the following information.

Background. You (your group is considered as one person) are one of 120 passengers on the ship, the *Prince Charles.* You left England 12 weeks ago. You have experienced many hardships, including a stormy passage, limited rations, sickness, cold and damp weather, and hot, foul air below deck. Ten of your fellow immigrants to the New World, including three children, have died and been buried at sea. You are now anchored at an uncertain place, off the coast of the New World, which your captain believes to be somewhere north of the Virginia Grants. Seas are so rough and food so scarce that you and your fellow passengers have decided to settle here. A landing party has returned with a map they made of the area. You, as one of the elders, must decide at once where the settlement is to be located. The tradesmen want to settle along the river, which is deep, even though this seems to be the season of low water levels. Within ten months they expect deep-water ships from England with more colonists and merchants. Those within your group who are farmers say they must have fertile, workable land. The officer in charge of the landing party reported seeing a group of armed natives who fled when approached. He feels the settlement must be located so that it can be defended from the natives and from the sea.

Directions, step one: You (your group) are to select a site on the attached map which you feel is best suited for a colony. Your site must satisfy the different factions aboard the ship. A number of possible sites are already marked on the map (letters *A–G*). You may select one of these locations or use them as reference points to show the location of your colony. When your group has selected its site, list and explain the reasons for your choice. When each group has arrived at its tentative decision, these will be shared with the whole class.

Directions, step two: After each group has made its presentation and argument, a class debate is held about where the colony should be located.

Notes to teacher: For the debate, have a large map drawn on the writing board or on an overhead transparency, where each group's mark can be made for all to see and discuss. After each group has presented its argument for its location and against the others, we sug-

gest that you then mark on the large map the two, three, or more hypothetical locations (assuming that, as a class, there yet is no single favorite location). Then take a straw vote of the students, allowing each to vote on his or her own, independently rather than as members of groups. At this time you can terminate the activity by saying that if the majority of students favor one location, then that, in fact, is the solution to the problem—that is, the colony is located wherever the majority of class members believe it should be. No sooner will that statement be made by you than someone will ask, "Are we correct?" or "What is the right answer?" They will ask such questions because, as students in school, they are used to solving problems that have right answers (Level I inquiry teaching). In real-world problems, however, there are no "right" answers, though some answers may seem better than others. It is the process of problem solving that is important. You want your students to develop confidence in their ability to solve problems and understand the tentativeness of "answers" to real-life problems.

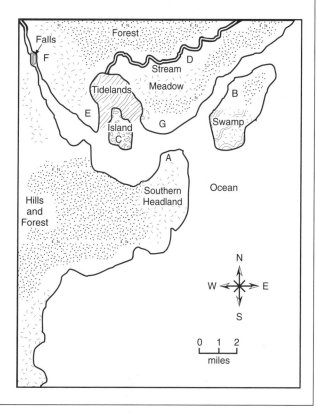

questions, the modeling can become inquiry teaching. Activities can include any from a variety of heuristics (a heuristic is a tool used in solving a problem or understanding an idea), such as the following:

Brainstorming. Members generate ideas related to a key word and record them. Clustering or chunking, mapping, and the Venn diagram (all discussed below) are variations of brainstorming.

Think-pair-share (see Chapter 8).

Chunking or clustering. Groups of students apply mental organizers by clustering information into chunks for easier manipulation and remembering.

Memory strategies. The teacher and students model the use of acronyms, mnemonics, rhymes, or clustering of information into categories to promote learning. Sometimes, such as in memorizing the social security number, one must learn by rote information that is not connected to any prior knowledge. To do that it is helpful to break the information to be learned into smaller chunks, such as dividing the nine digit social security number into smaller chunks of information (with, in this instance, each chunk separated by a hyphen). Learning by rote is also easier if one can connect that which is to be memorized to some prior knowledge. Strategies such as these are used to bridge the gap between rote learning and meaningful learning and are known as *mnemonics.*[14] Sample mnemonics are:

- The ABCDs of writing instructional objectives (Chapter 5), CASE for using classroom bulletin boards, and TOPS for using story felt boards (both in Chapter 10).

- The notes on a treble staff are *FACE* for the space notes and *Empty Garbage Before Dad Flips* (*EGBDF*) for the line notes. The notes on the bass staff are *All Cows Eat Granola Bars* or *Grizzly Bears Don't Fly Airplanes* (*GBDFA*).

- The order of the planets from the Sun are *My Very Educated Mother Just Served Us Nine Pizzas* (*M*ercury, *V*enus, *E*arth, *M*ars, *J*upiter, *S*aturn, *U*ranus, *N*eptune, and *P*luto—though, in reality, Pluto and Neptune alternate in this order because of their elliptical orbits).

- The names of the Great Lakes: *HOMES* for *H*uron, *O*ntario, *M*ichigan, *E*rie, and *S*uperior.

- To recall the order of operations when solving algebraic equations remember *P*lease (parentheses) *E*xcuse (exponents) *M*y (multiply) *D*ear (divide) *A*unt (add) *S*ally (subtract).

- Visual mnemonics are useful too, such as remembering that Italy is shaped in the form of a boot.

Comparing and contrasting. Similarities and differences among items are found and recorded.

Visual tools. A variety of terms for the visual tools useful for learning have been invented—some of which are synonymous—terms such as brainstorming web, mindmapping web, spider map, cluster, concept map,[15] cognitive map, semantic map, Venn diagram, visual scaffold, and graphic organizer. Hyerle separates these visual tools into three categories according to purpose: (a) *brainstorming tools* (such as mind mapping, webbing, and clustering) for the purpose of developing one's knowledge and creativity; (b) *task-specific organizers* (such as life cycle diagrams used in biology, decision trees used in mathematics, and text structures used in reading); and (c) *thinking process maps* (such as concept mapping) for encouraging cognitive development across disciplines.[16] It is the latter about which we are interested here.

Based on Ausubel's theory of meaningful learning,[17] thinking process mapping has been found useful for helping learners in changing prior notions—their misconceptions, sometimes referred to as *naïve views.* It can help students in their ability to organize and represent their thoughts, as well as help them connect new knowledge to their past experiences and precepts.[18] Simply put, concepts can be thought of as classifications that attempt to organize the world of objects and events into a smaller number of categories. In everyday usage, the term *concept* means idea, as when someone says, "My concept of love is not the same as yours." Concepts embody a meaning that develops in complexity with experience and learning over time. For example, the concept of love that is held by a second grader is unlikely to be as complex as that held by the child's teacher. Thinking process mapping is a graphical way of demonstrating the relationship between and among concepts.

Typically, a thinking process map refers to a visual or graphic representation of concepts with bridges (connections) that show relationships. Figure 9.5 shows a partially complete thinking process map where students have made connections of concept relationships between fruit farm-

Figure 9.5
Sample partially
complete thinking
process map

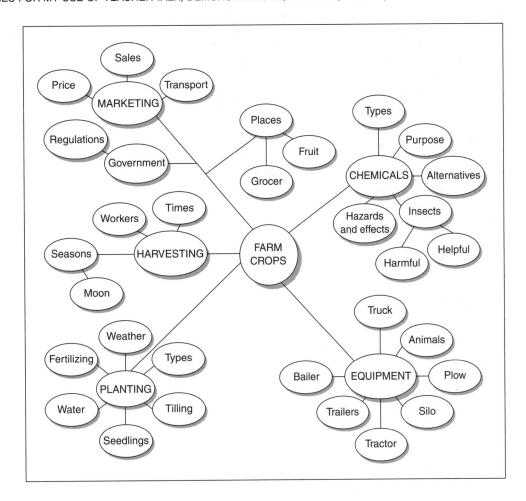

ing and marketing. The typical procedure for thinking process mapping is to have the students (a) identify important concepts in materials being studied, often by circling those concepts, (b) rank order the concepts from the most general to the most specific, and (c) arrange the concepts on a sheet of paper, connect related ideas with lines, and define the connections between the related ideas. For young children, pictures may be used in each of the circles rather than words.

Inferring. For instance, students assume the roles of people (real or fictional) and infer their motives, personalities, and thoughts.

Multiple sources. Use multiple texts to demonstrate the interpretive nature of historical events.[19]

Outlining. Each group of children completes an outline that contains some of the main ideas but with subtopics omitted.

Paraphrasing. In a brief summary, each student restates a short selection of what was read or heard.

Reciprocal teaching. In classroom dialogue, students take turns at generating questions, summarizing, clarifying, and predicting.[20]

Study strategies. Important strategies that should be taught explicitly include vocabulary expansion, reading and interpreting graphic information, locating resources, using advance organizers, adjusting one's reading rate, and skimming, scanning, and study reading.[21]

Textbook study strategies. Students use the *SQ4R* or related study strategies (see Chapter 5).

Vee mapping. This is a road map completed by students, as they learn, showing the route they follow from prior knowledge to new and future knowledge.

Venn diagramming. This is a technique for comparing two concepts or, for example, two stories, to show similarities and differences. Using stories as an example, a student is asked to draw two circles that intersect and to mark the circles *one* and *two,* and the area where they intersect *three.* In circle one, the student lists characteristics of one story, and in circle two she or he lists the characteristics of the second story. In the area of the intersection, marked three, the student lists characteristics common to both stories.

Visual learning log (VLL). This variation of the road map is completed by students showing the route they follow from prior knowledge to new and future knowledge, except that the VLL consists of pictograms (free-form drawings) that each student makes and that are maintained in a journal.

To further explore inquiry teaching and integrated learning, do Exercise 9.1.

EXERCISE 9.1 A STUDY OF INQUIRY AND STRATEGY INTEGRATION

Instructions: The purpose of this exercise is to analyze the Locating a Colony inquiry (the Level II inquiry of Figure 9.4 that you did with your classmates) and the discussion in the text about integrating strategies, and then to synthesize that information for use in your own teaching. We suggest that you first answer the questions in this exercise and then share your answers with others in your discipline (in groups of about four). Finally, share your group's collective responses with the entire class.

1. My subject field and/or grade level interest: _____

   _____

2a. How I could use the Locating a Colony inquiry (for what purpose, goals, or objectives): _____

   _____

   _____

   _____

2b. Content in my class that students might be expected to learn from doing the Locating a Colony

   inquiry: _____

   _____

   _____

   _____

3. In what way could I involve my students in cooperative learning while doing the Locating a

   Colony inquiry: _____

   _____

   _____

   _____

4. How brainstorming could be used while doing the Locating a Colony inquiry: _____

   _____

   _____

   _____

5. How clustering could be used while doing the Locating a Colony inquiry: _____

   _____

   _____

   _____

6. How thinking process mapping could be used while doing the Locating a Colony inquiry:

   _____

   _____

   _____

EXERCISE 9.1 *(continued)*

7. How comparing and contrasting could be used while doing the Locating a Colony inquiry:

_____

_____

_____

_____

8. How outlining could be used while doing the Locating a Colony inquiry: _____

_____

_____

_____

_____

9. How paraphrasing could be used while doing the Locating a Colony inquiry: _____

_____

_____

_____

_____

10. How summarizing could be used while doing the Locating a Colony inquiry: _____

_____

_____

_____

_____

11. How memory strategies could be used while doing the Locating a Colony inquiry: _____

_____

_____

_____

12. How inferring could be used while doing the Locating a Colony inquiry: _____

_____

_____

_____

13. What other skills could be taught while doing the Locating a Colony inquiry? For each, describe how.

_____

_____

_____

LEARNING BY EDUCATIONAL GAMES

Devices classified as educational games include a wide variety of learning activities, such as simulations, role play and sociodrama activities, mind games, board games, computer games, and sporting games, all of which provide valuable learning experiences for participants. These experiences tend to involve several senses and involve several learning modalities to engage higher-order thinking skills and to be quite effective as learning tools.

Of all the arts, drama involves the learner-participant most fully—intellectually, emotionally, physically, verbally, and socially. Interactive drama, which is role-playing, is a simplified form of drama, a method by which children can become involved with literature. Studies show that children's comprehension increases and they are highly motivated to read if they are involved in analyzing and actively responding to the characters, plot, and setting of the story being read.[22]

Simulations, a more complex form of drama, serve many of the developmental needs of children. They provide for interaction with peers and allow children of different backgrounds and talents to cooperatively work on a common project. They engage children in physical activity and give them opportunity to try out different roles, which help them to better understand themselves. Simulations can provide concrete experiences that help children to understand complex concepts and issues, and they provide opportunities for exploring values and developing skill in decision making.[23]

For example, to give children authentic economic experiences, more than 200 schools in at least 40 states participate in MicroSociety, a program of simulated real-world experiences for use in grades K–8. In collaboration with parents and guardians, community members, and teachers, students build a miniature community in the school, establishing a center of commerce and governance where they earn wages, pay taxes, resolve issues in court, and operate businesses. At the Johnsontown Road Elementary School (Louisville, KY), for example, students run their own simulated town, from policing the halls of the school to paying rent on their desks with play money.[24]

Educational games can play an integral role in interdisciplinary teaching and serve as valuable resources for enriching the effectiveness of students' learning. As with any other instructional strategy, the use of games should follow a clear educational purpose, have a careful plan, and be congruent with your school's instructional objectives and the stated mission.

Classification of Educational Games

What are educational games? Seven types of games fall under the general heading of *educational games*. Table 9.2 shows the seven types, with characteristics and examples of each. Certain types have greater educational value than do others. Games that do not emphasize the element of competition—that are not contests—are particularly recommended for use in the academic classroom (types 1, 3, and 5 in Table 9.2).

Purposes of Educational Games

Games can be powerful tools for teaching and learning. A game can serve one or more of the following purposes: (a) add variety and change of

Table 9.2
Classification of Educational Games

Type	Characteristics	Examples
1. Pure game*	Fun	*Ungame, New Games*
2. Pure contest	Stimulates competition; built-in inefficiency‡	Political contests, e.g., U.S. presidential race
3. Pure simulation*	Models reality	Toddler play
4. Contest/game	Stimulates competition; fun; built-in inefficiency	Golf; bowling; *Trivial Pursuit*
5. Simulation/game*	Models reality; fun	*SIMCITY; Our Town's Planning Commission Meeting*§
6. Contest/simulation	Stimulates competition; models reality; built-in inefficiency	Boxcar Derby of Akron, OH
7. Simulation/game/contest	Models reality; fun; stimulates competition; built-in inefficiency	*Monopoly, Life, Careers*

*These game types do not emphasize competition and thus are particularly recommended for use in the classroom as learning tools.
‡Rules for accomplishing the game objective make accomplishment of that objective less than efficient. For example, in golf the objective is to get the ball into the hole with the least amount of effort, but to do that, one has to take a peculiarly shaped stick (the club) and hit the ball, find it, and hit it again, continuing that sequence until the ball is in the hole. Yet, common sense tells us that the best way to get the ball into the hole with the least amount of effort would be simply to pick up the ball and place it by hand into the hole.
§See J. V. Vort, Our Town's Planning Commission Meeting, *Journal of Geography, 96*(4), 183–190 (July–August 1997).

Figure 9.6
Sample professional journals with educational games

- J. Bassett, "The Pullman Strike of 1894," *OAH Magazine of History* 11(2):34–41 (Winter 1997). Role-play simulation.
- D. Bogan and D. Wood, "Simulating Sun, Moon, and Earth Patterns," *Science Scope* 21(2):46, 48 (October 1997). Role-play for middle school.
- C. Collyer, "Winter Secrets: An Instant Lesson Plan," *Pathways: The Ontario Journal of Outdoor Education* 9(2):18–20 (April 1997). Instructions for two games about predator-prey relationships.
- P. Cunningham, "Reading Clinic. Making Decoding Fun with This Cross-Checking Game," *Instructor* 107(2):74–75 (September 1997). For teaching K–3.
- S. A. Farin, "Acting Atoms," *Science Scope* 21(3):46 (November/December 1997). Role-play for middle school.
- J. Gorman, "Strategy Games: Treasures from Ancient Times," *Mathematics Teaching in the Middle School* 3(2):110–116 (October 1997). Presents several games for integrating history and mathematics.
- S. Hightshoe, "Sifting Through the Sands of Time: A Simulated Archaeological Special Feature," *Social Studies and the Young Learner* 9(3):28–30 (January/February, 1997). For elementary and middle school.
- M. J. Howle, "Play-Party Games in the Modern Classroom," *Music Educators Journal* 83(5):24–28 (March 1997). Introduces games that were popular on the 19th-century American frontier.
- T. Levy, "The Amistad Incident: A Classroom Reenactment," *Social Education* 59(5):303–308 (September 1995).
- T. M. McCann, "A Pioneer Simulation for Writing and for the Study of Literature," *English Journal* 85(3):62–67 (March 1996).
- H. Morris, "Universal Games from A to Z," *Mathematics in School* 26(4):35–40 (September 1997). See also F. Tapson, "Mathematical Games," pp. 2–6 of same issue.
- K. D. Owens et al., "Playing to Learn: Science Games in the Classroom," *Science Scope* 20(5):31–33 (February 1997). Games for middle school that encourage abstract thinking.

Figure 9.7
Sources of educational games

- Ampersand Press, 750 Lake St., Port Townsend, WA 98368, 800-624-4263.
- Aristoplay, 450 S. Wagner Rd., Ann Arbor, MI 48103, 800-GR8-GAME.
- Carolina Biological Supply Company, 2700 York Road, Burlington, NC 27215, 800-334-5551.
- Creative Teaching Associates, P.O. Box 7766, Fresno, CA 93747, 800-767-4282.
- Dawn Publications, 14618 Tyler-Foote Rd., Nevada City, CA 95959, 800-545-7475.
- Delta Educational, 5 Hudson Park Dr., P.O. Box 915, Hudson, NH 03051, 800-258-1302.
- Harcourt Brace School Publishers, 6277 Sea Harbor Dr., Orlando, FL 32887, 800-346-8648.
- Higher-Order Thinking Company, 1733 N.E. Patterson Dr., Lee's Summit, MO 64086, 816-524-2701.
- Latz Chance Games, P.O. Box 72308, Marietta, GA 30007-2308, 888-LCH-GAME.
- Novostar Designs, 317 S. Main St., P.O. Box 1328, Burlington, NC 27216-1328, 800-659-3197.
- Optical Data School Media, 512 Means St., NW, Atlanta, GA 30318, 800-524-2481.
- Other Worlds Educational Enterprises, P.O. Box 6193, Woodland Park, CO 80866-6193, 719-687-3840.
- Summit Learning, P.O. Box 493, Fort Collins, CO 80522, 800-777-8817.
- Teacher Created Materials, 6421 Industry Way, Westminster, CA 92683, 800-662-4321.
- Young Naturalist Company, 1900 N. Main St., Newton, KS 67114, 316-283-9108.

age, (j) provide skill development in inductive thinking, (k) provide skill development in verbal communication and debate, (l) reinforce convergent thinking, (m) review and reinforce subject matter learning, (n) encourage learning through peer interaction, (o) stimulate critical thinking, (p) stimulate deductive thinking, (q) stimulate divergent and creative thinking, and, (r) teach both content and process.

Sources of Educational Games

Sources for useful educational games include professional journals (see Figure 9.6 and the readings at the end of this chapter) and the Internet. Sources of commercially available educational games for use in teaching are shown in Figure 9.7. Now do Exercise 9.2.

pace, (b) assess student learning, (c) enhance student self-esteem, (d) motivate students, (e) offer a break from the usual rigors of learning, (f) provide learning about real-life issues through simulation and role-playing, (g) provide learning through tactile and kinesthetic modalities, (h) provide problem-solving situations and experiences, (i) provide skill development and motivation through computer us-

EXERCISE 9.2 DEVELOPING A LESSON USING INQUIRY LEVEL II, THINKING SKILL DEVELOPMENT, A DEMONSTRATION, OR AN INTERACTIVE LECTURE—MICRO PEER TEACHING II

Instructions: The purpose of this exercise is to provide the opportunity for you to create a brief lesson (about 20 minutes of instructional time but to be specified by your instructor) designed for a specific grade level and subject and to try it out on your peers for their feedback in an informal (i.e., nongraded) micro peer teaching demonstration.

Divide your class into four groups. The task of members of each group is to prepare lessons (individually) that fall into one of the four categories: Level II inquiry, thinking level, demonstration, or interactive lecture. Schedule class presentations so that each class member has the opportunity to present her or his lesson and to obtain feedback from class members about it. For feedback, class members who are the "teacher's" audience can complete the assessment rubric shown after this exercise (by circling one of the three choices for each of the 10 categories) and give their completed form to the teacher for use in analysis and self-assessment. Before your class starts this exercise you may want to review the scoring rubric and make modifications to it with the class's input.

To structure your lesson plan, use one of the sample lesson plan formats presented in Chapter 6; however, each lesson should be centered around one major theme or concept and be planned for about 20 minutes of instructional time.

Group 1: Develop a Level II inquiry lesson.

Group 2: Develop a lesson designed to raise the level of student thinking.

Group 3: Develop a lesson that involves a demonstration.

Group 4: Develop a lesson that is an interactive lecture.

EXERCISE 9.2 *(continued)*

Peer and Self-Assessment Rubric for Use with Exercise 9.2

For: Group:

	1	0.5	0
1. Lesson beginning Comment:	effective	less effective	not effective
2. Sequencing Comment:	effective	less effective	rambling
3. Pacing of lesson Comment:	effective	less effective	too slow or too fast
4. Audience involvement Comment:	effective	less effective	none
5. Motivators (e.g., analogies, verbal cues, humor, visual cues, sensory cues) Comment:	effective	less effective	not apparent
6. Content of lesson Comment:	well chosen	interesting	boring or inappropriate
7. Voice of teacher Comment:	stimulating	minor problem	major problems
8. Vocabulary used Comment:	well chosen	appropriate	inappropriate
9. Eye contact Comment:	excellent	average	problems
10. Closure Comment:	effective	less effective	unclear/none

OTHER COMMENTS:

SUMMARY

Central to your selection of instructional strategies should be those strategies that encourage students to become independent thinkers and skilled learners who can help in the planning, structuring, regulating, and assessing of their own learning and learning activities.

Important to helping students construct their understandings are the cognitive tools that are available for their use. There is a large variety of useful and effective aids, media, and resources from which to draw as you plan your instructional experiences, the topic of the next and final chapter of Part III.

EXTENDING MY COMPETENCY: QUESTIONS FOR CLASS DISCUSSION

1. Many cognitive researchers agree that students should spend more time actively using knowledge to solve problems and less time reading introductory material and listening to teachers. Describe the meaning of this statement and how you feel about it with respect to your decision to become a teacher.
2. Explain why you would or would not like to teach by inquiry (Level II or III).
3. Explain the meaning of integrating strategies for integrated learning.
4. Are there any cautions that teachers need to be aware of when using games for teaching? If there are, describe them.
5. Explain some specific ways you can help children develop their skills in thinking and learning. Explain how you will determine that students have raised their skill level in thinking and learning.
6. Select one of the characteristics of intelligent behavior, and (for a grade level of your choice and time limit as decided by your class) write a lesson plan for helping students develop that behavior. Share or teach your lesson to others in your class for their analysis and suggestions.
7. Describe one teacher demonstration that is typically done by teachers of a particular grade level and subject. Describe ways that you might try to improve on the way the demonstration is typically done.
8. Describe any prior concepts you held that changed as a result of your experiences with this chapter. Describe the changes.
9. From your current observations and fieldwork as related to this teacher preparation program, clearly identify one specific example of educational practice that seems contradictory to exemplary practice or theory as presented in this chapter. Present your explanation for the discrepancy.
10. Do you have questions generated by the content of this chapter? If you do, list them along with ways answers might be found.

FOR FURTHER READING

Abdullah, M. H. (1998). *Problem-Based Learning in Language Instruction: A Constructivist Model* (Eric Digest 423550 98). Bloomington, IN: ERIC Clearinghouse on Reading, English, and Communication.

Benevino, M. M., Dengel, J., and Adams, K. (1999). Constructivist Theory in the Classroom: Internalizing Concepts Through Inquiry Learning. *Clearing House, 72*(5), 275–278.

Boston, J. A. (1998). Using Simulations. *Social Studies Review, 37* (2), 31–32.

Brisk, M. E., and Harrington, M. M. (2000). *Literacy and Bilingualism: A Handbook for ALL Teachers.* Mahwah, NJ: Lawrence Erlbaum.

Camp, D. (2000). It Takes Two: Teaching With Twin Texts of Fact and Fiction. *The Reading Teacher, 53*(5), 400–408.

Foster, S. J., and Padgett, C. S. (1999). Authentic Historical Inquiry in the Social Studies Classroom. *Clearing House, 72*(6), 357–363.

Good, T. L., and Brophy, J. E. (2000). *Looking in Classrooms* (8th ed., Chap. 9). New York: Addison Wesley/Longman.

Haroutunian-Gordon, S. (1998). A Study of Reflective Thinking: Patterns in Interpretive Discussion. *Educational Theory, 48*(1), 33–58.

Harris, B., Kohlmeier, K., and Kiel, R. D. (1999). *Crime Scene Investigation.* Englewood, CO: Teacher Ideas Press.

Heller, N. (1998). *Technology Connections for Grades 3–5. Research Projects and Activities.* Englewood, CO: Libraries Unlimited.

Hinman, L. A. (2000). What's the Buzz? A Classroom Simulation Teaches Students About Life in the Hive. *Science and Children, 37*(5), 24–27.

Jay, M. E., and Jay, H. L. (1998). *250+ Activities and Ideas for Developing Literacy Skills.* New York: Neal-Schuman.

Katz, L. G., and Chard, S. C. (1998). *Issues in Selecting Topics for Projects* (Eric Digest 424031 98). Champaign, IL: ERIC Clearinghouse on Elementary and Early Childhood Education.

Leming, J. S. (1998). Some Critical Thoughts About the Teaching of Critical Thinking. *Social Studies, 89*(2), 61–66.

Martinello, M. L. (1998). Learning to Question for Inquiry. *Educational Forum, 62*(2), 164–171.

Morgan, R. R., Ponticell, J. A., and Gordon, E. E. (2000). *Rethinking Creativity* (Fastback 458). Bloomington, IN: Phi Delta Kappa Educational Foundation.

Murphey, C. E. (1998). Using the Five Themes of Geography to Explore a School Site. *Social Studies Review, 37*(2), 49–52.

Myers, R. E. (1998). *Mind Sparklers. Fireworks for Igniting Creativity in Young Minds* (Book 1 for grades K–3). Waco, TX: Prufrock Press.

Myers, R. E. (1998). *Mind Sparklers. Fireworks for Igniting Creativity in Young Minds* (Book 2 for grades 4–8). Waco, TX: Prufrock Press.

National Research Council. (2000). *Inquiry and the National Science Education Standards: A Guide for Teaching and Learning.* Washington, DC: National Academy Press.

National Science Foundation. (2000). *Foundations, Volume 2: Inquiry—Thoughts, Views, and Strategies for the K–5 Classroom.* Alexandria, VA: Division of Elementary, Secondary, and Information Education.

Novak, J. D. (1998). *Learning, Creating, and Using Knowledge: Concept Maps™ as Facilitative Tools in Schools and Corporations.* Mahwah, NJ: Lawrence Erlbaum.

Perkins, D. N. (2000). Schools Need to Pay More Attention to "Intelligence in the Wild." *Harvard Education Letter, 16*(3), 7–8.

Pilger, M. A. (1998). *Multicultural Projects Index: Things to Make and Do to Celebrate Festivals, Cultures, and Holidays Around the World* (2nd ed.). Englewood, CO: Libraries Unlimited.

Presseisen, B. Z. (Ed.) (1999). *Teaching for Intelligence I: A Collection of Articles.* Arlington Heights, IL: Skylight Professional Development.

Raschke, D., Alper, S., and Eggers, E. (1999). Recalling Alphabet Letter Names: A Mnemonic System to Facilitate Learning. *Preventing School Failure, 43* (2), 80–83.

Ross, E. P. (1998). *Pathways to Thinking: Strategies for Developing Independent Learners K–8.* Norwood, MA: Christopher-Gordon.

Rothberg, M. (1998). Re-Enactment of the Ellis Island Experience With Sugartown Elementary School. *School Library Media Activities Monthly, 14*(5), 27–28.

Schmidt, P. R. (1999). KWLQ: Inquiry and Literacy Learning in Science. *Reading Teacher, 52*(7), 789–792.

Shanker, J. L., and Edwall, E. E. (1998). *Locating and Correcting Reading Difficulties* (7th ed.). Upper Saddle River, NJ: Merrill/Prentice Hall.

Shively, J. M., and VanFossen, P. J. (1999). Critical Thinking and the Internet: Opportunities for the Social Studies Classroom. *Social Studies, 90*(1), 42–46.

Short, K., Kaufman, G., Kaser, S., Kahn, L. H., and Crawford, K. M. (1999). "Teacher-Watching": Examining Teacher Talk in Literature Circles. *Language Arts, 76*(5), 377–385.

Sterling, D. R., and Graham, R. J. (1998). And You Were There. *Science and Children, 35*(6), 41–46.

Tower, C. (2000). Questions That Matter: Preparing Elementary Students for the Inquiry Process. *The Reading Teacher, 53*(7), 550–557.

Whittrock, C. A., and Barrow, L. H. (2000). Blow-by-Blow Inquiry. *Science and Children, 37*(5), 34–38.

NOTES

1. D. P. Ausubel, *The Psychology of Meaningful Learning* (New York: Grune & Stratton, 1963).

2. T. L. Good and J. E. Brophy, *Looking in Classrooms,* 8th ed. (New York: Addison Wesley/Longman, 2000), pp. 252–253.

3. A. L. Costa, *The School as a Home for the Mind* (Palatine, IL: Skylight Publishing, 1991), pp. 20–31. To the 14 characteristics presented here, Costa recently added *thinking interdependently* and *remaining open to continuous learning.* See A. L. Costa and B. Kallick (eds.), *Habits of Mind* (Alexandria, VA: Association for Supervision and Curriculum Development, 2000). See also 12 qualities of genius—curiosity, playfulness, imagination, creativity, wonderment, wisdom, inventiveness, vitality, sensitivity, flexibility, humor, and joy—in T. Armstrong, *Awakening Genius in the Classroom* (Alexandria, VA: Association for Supervision and Curriculum Development, 1998), pp. 2–15; and, Project Zero's 7 dispositions for good thinking—the disposition (a) to be broad and adventurous; (b) toward wondering, problem finding, and investigating; (c) to build explanations and understandings; (d) to make plans and be strategic; (e) to be intellectually careful; (f) to seek and evaluate reasons; and (g) to be metacognitive—at <http://pzweb.harvard.edu/HPZpages/PatThk.html>.

4. See, for example, M. Goos and P. Galbraith, Do It This Way! Metacognitive Strategies in Collaborative Mathematics Problem Solving, *Educational Studies in Mathematics, 30*(3), 229–260 (April 1996).

5. For further reading about the relation of impulse control to intelligence, see D. Goleman, *Emotional Intelligence: Why It Can Matter More Than IQ* (New York: Bantam Books, 1995), and D. Harrington-Lueker, Emotional Intelligence, *High Strides, 9*(4), 1, 4–5 (March/April 1997).

6. See E. de Bono, *Lateral Thinking: Creativity Step by Step* (New York: Harper & Row, 1970); B. Brodinsky, Tackling Problems Through Lateral Thinking. An Interview with Edward de Bono, *School Administrator, 42*(3), 10–13 (March 1985); or E. de Bono, Lateral Thinking: The Searching Mind, *Today's Education, 58*(8), 20–24 (November 1969).

7. Emphasizing the importance of metacognition is the following resource for teachers: N. Margulies and R. Sylwester, *Discover Your Brain: Emotion and Attention. How Our Brain Determines What's Important* (Tucson, AZ: Zephyr Press, 1998).

8. See, for example, J. W. Astington, Theory of Mind Goes to School, *Educational Leadership, 56*(3), 46–48 (November 1998).

9. J. Piaget, *The Psychology of Intelligence* (Totowa, NJ: Littlefield Adams, 1972).

10. I. Kohlberg, *The Meaning and Measurement of Moral Development* (Worcester, MA: Clark University Press, 1981).

11. See, for example, S. Haroutunian-Gordon, A Study of Reflective Thinking: Patterns in Interpretive Discussion, *Educational Theory, 48* (1), 33–58 (Winter 1998); and A. C. Boucher, Critical Thinking Through Estimation, *Teaching Children Mathematics, 4*(8), 452–455 (April 1998).

12. To learn about these and other perspectives, see M. E. Gredler, *Learning and Instruction: Theory Into Practice.* 3rd ed. (Upper Saddle River, NJ: Merrill/Prentice Hall, 1997).

13. For products for teaching thinking, contact Critical Thinking Press & Software, P.O. Box 448, Pacific Grove, CA 93950. Phone (800) 458-4849.

14. See, for example, D. Raschke, S. Alper, and E. Eggers, Recalling Alphabet Letter Names: A Mnemonic System to Facilitate Learning, *Preventing School Failure, 43*(2), 80–83 (Winter 1999).

15. See J. D. Novak, *Learning, Creating, and Using Knowledge: Concept Maps™ as Facilitative Tools in Schools and Corporations* (Mahwah, NJ: Lawrence Erlbaum, 1998).

16. D. Hyerle, *Visual Tools for Constructing Knowledge* (Alexandria, VA: Association for Supervision and Curriculum Development, 1996).

17. D. P. Ausubel, *The Psychology of Meaningful Learning* (New York: Grune & Stratton, 1963).

18. See J. D. Novak, Concept Maps and Vee Diagrams: Two Metacognitive Tools to Facilitate Meaningful Learning, *Instructional Science, 19*(1), 29–52 (1990); J. D. Novak and B. D. Gowin, *Learning How to Learn* (Cambridge, England: Cambridge University Press, 1984); and E. Plotnick, *Concept Mapping: A Graphical System for Understanding the Relationship Between Concepts,* ED407938 (Syracuse, NY: ERIC Clearinghouse on Information and Technology, 1997).

19. See, for example, R. H. Mayer, Use the Story of Anne Hutchinson to Teaching Historical Thinking, *Social Studies, 90*(3), 105–109 (May/June 1999).

20. See C. J. Carter, Why Reciprocal Teaching? *Educational Leadership, 54*(6), 64–68 (March 1997).

21. J. S. Choate and T. A. Rakes, *Inclusive Instruction for Struggling Readers,* Fastback 434 (Bloomington, IN: Phi Delta Kappa Educational Foundation, 1998).

22. R. Coney and S. Kanel, Opening the World of Literature to Children Through Interactive Drama Experiences, Paper presented at the Annual International Conference and Exhibition of the Association for Childhood Education (Portland, OR, April 9–12, 1997).

23. See, for example, T. Kaldusdal, S. Wood, and J. Truesdale, Virtualville Votes: An Interdisciplinary Project, *MultiMedia Schools, 5*(1), 30–35 (January/February 1998).

24. From Johnstontown Road Elementary School (retrieved from the World Wide Web, February 28, 1999, http://www.jefferson.k12.ky.us/Schools/Elementary/Johnston.html). For information about MicroSociety and school sites using the program, contact Micro-Society at 306 Cherry Street, Suite 200, Philadelphia, PA 19106, 215-922-4006, <http://www.microsociety.org>.

10

What Guidelines Are Available for My Use of Aids and Media Resources?

Important to helping students construct their understandings are the cognitive tools that are available for their use. You will be pleased to know that there is a large variety of useful and effective media, aids, and resources from which to draw as you plan your instructional experiences. On the other hand, you could also become overwhelmed by the sheer quantity of different materials avail-

able: textbooks, supplementary texts, pamphlets, anthologies, paperbacks, encyclopedias, tests, programmed instructional systems, dictionaries, reference books, classroom periodicals, newspapers, films, records and cassettes, computer software, transparencies, realia, games, filmstrips, audio- and videotapes, slides, globes, manipulatives, CD-ROMs, DVDs, videodiscs, and graphics. You could spend a great deal of time reviewing, sorting, selecting, and practicing with the materials and tools for your use. Although nobody can make the job easier for you, information in this chapter may expedite the process.

CHAPTER OBJECTIVES

Specifically, upon completion of this chapter you should be able to demonstrate your knowledge about:

1. Copyright guidelines for using printed and media materials.
2. Electronic media available for teaching, how they can be used, and how and where they can be obtained.
3. Guidelines for using guest speakers and field trips.
4. How to prepare for when media equipment breaks down.
5. Resources for free and inexpensive teaching materials.
6. The variety of materials and resources for use in teaching.
7. Using printed materials.
8. Using the community as a resource.
9. Using the Internet as a teaching/learning resource.
10. Using the writing board, bulletin board, and story felt board.

PRINTED MATERIALS, VISUAL DISPLAYS, AND THE INTERNET

In addition to the student textbook (see Chapter 5) and perhaps an accompanying workbook, there is a vast array of other printed materials available for use in teaching, many of which are available without cost. Printed materials include books, workbooks, pamphlets, magazines, brochures, newspapers, professional journals, periodicals, and duplicated materials including those materials copied from Internet sources.

In reviewing printed materials, factors to be alert for include (a) appropriateness of the material in both content and in reading level, (b) articles in newspapers, magazines, and periodicals, related to the content that your students will be studying or to the skills they will be learning, (c) assorted workbooks available from tradebook publishers and that emphasize thinking and problem solving rather than rote memorization [with an assortment of workbooks you can have students working

Figure 10.1
Resources for free and inexpensive printed materials

- *A Guide to Print and Nonprint Materials Available from Organizations, Industry, Governmental Agencies and Specialized Publishers.* New York: Neal Schuman.
- Educators Progress Service, Inc., 214 Center Street, Randolph, WI 53956. (414) 326-3126. *Educator's Guide to Free Materials; Educator's Guide to Free Teaching Aids.*
- *Freebies: The Magazine with Something for Nothing.* P.O. Box 5025, Carpinteria, CA 93014-5025.
- *Video Placement Worldwide (VPW).* Source of free sponsored educational materials on Internet at <http://www.vpw.com>.

on similar but different assignments depending upon their interests and abilities (an example of multilevel teaching)], (d) pamphlets, brochures, and other duplicated materials that students can read for specific information and viewpoints about particular topics, and (e) inexpensive paperback books that would provide multiple book readings for your class and that make it possible for students to read primary sources.

Sources of Free and Inexpensive Printed Materials

For free and inexpensive printed materials look for sources in your college, university, or public library, in the resource center at a local school district (sources such as those listed in Figure 10.1), and through connections on the Internet. No matter how they are obtained, free or not, when considering using materials that you have obtained you will want to ensure that the materials are appropriate for use with the age group with whom you work and that they are free of bias or an unwanted message.[1]

The Internet

Originating from a Department of Defense (DOD) project in 1969 (called ARPAnet, from the DOD's Advanced Research Projects Agency, ARPA) to establish a computer network of military researchers, its successor, the federally funded Internet, has become an enormous, steadily and rapidly expanding

Figure 10.2
Additional Internet
sites: Materials and
technology

- *Beyond the MLA Handbook: Documenting Electronic Sources on the Internet*
  <http://falcon.eku.edu/honors/beyond-mla>. See also *Citing Internet Addresses*
  <http://www.classroom.net/classroom/CitingNetResources.htm>, and J. Walker's
  MLA-Style Citations of Electronic Sources
  <http://www.cas.usf.edu/english/walker/mla.html>.
- *Big Page of School Internet Projects and Educational Technology*
  <http://www.mts.net/~jgreenco/internet.html#Index>.
- *California Instructional Technology Clearinghouse*
  <http://clearinghouse.k12.ca.us>.
- *Education Resource Organizations Directory*
  <http://oeri.edu.gov:8888/STATES/direct/SF>.
- *Education World*   <http://www.educational-world.com>.
- *Epicenter*   <http://www.epicent.com>. Information resource of software,
  textbooks, research journal articles, and professional conference listings.
- *ERIC Documents Online*   <http://ericir.syr.edu>.
- *Hewlett Packard E-mail Mentor Program*   <http://www.telementor.org>.
- *Learn the 'Net*   <http://www.learnthenet.com>.
- *Map Resources*   <http://www.gsn.org/cf/maps.html>.
- *Mathematics Archives*   <http://archives.math.utk.edu/>.
- *Middle School Home Pages Around the World*
  <http://www.deltanet.com/hewes/middle.html>.
- *National Archives and Records Administration*   <http://www.nara.gov>.
- *National Education Association (NEA)*
  <http://www.nea.org/resources/refs.html>.
- *National Endowment for the Arts Home Page*   <http://www.arts.endow.org>.
- *National Geographic Map Machine*   <http://www.nationalgeographic.com>.
- *School Match*   <http://schoolmatch.com>. Directory of U.S. schools.
- *School Page*   <http://www.eyesoftime.com/teacher/index.html>. A teacher's
  exchange.
- *Science Stuff*   <http://www.sciencestuff.com>.
- *Telementoring Young Women in Science, Engineering, and Computing*
  <http://www.edc.org/CCT/telementoring>.
- *Teachers Network*   <http://www.teachnet.org>. A teacher's exchange.
- *The 21st Century Teachers Network*   <http://www.21ct.org>. For help in using
  technology.
- *United States Copyright Office*   <http://lcweb.loc.gov/copyright>.
- *WWW4Teachers*   <http://4teachers.org>. A source about using educational
  technology.

global system of connected computer networks. Also known as the *Net,* the *Information Superhighway,* and *cyberspace,* the Internet provides literally millions of resources to explore, with thousands more added daily. You can surf the Internet and find many sources about how to use it, and you can walk into most any bookstore and find hundreds of recent titles, most of which give their authors' favorite Web sites on the Internet. (*Note: Web site* refers to a location on the World Wide Web, which is, in turn, a component or subset of the network of computers called the Internet.) However, new technologies are steadily emerging and the Internet changes every day, with some sites and resources disappearing or not kept current, others having changed their location and undergone reconstruction, and new ones appearing; it would be superfluous for us in this book, which will be around for several years, to emphasize too strongly sites that we personally have viewed and can recommend as teacher resources. Nonetheless, Figure 10.2 includes available Internet resources available that we have recently surfed and can recommend. Other sites have been mentioned in the text throughout this resource guide, and still others are listed in Figures 1.8 and 8.2 of Chapters 1 and 8, respectively. Perhaps you have found others that you can share with your classmates. To that end, complete Exercise 10.1.

EXERCISE 10.1 INTERNET SITES OF USE TO ELEMENTARY SCHOOLTEACHERS

Instructions: The purpose of this exercise is to search the Internet for sites that you find interesting and useful, or useless, for teaching and to share those sites with your classmates. Make copies of this page for each site visited; then share your results with your classmates.

Web site I investigated: http://_____

I consider the site (circle one) *highly useful, moderately useful, of no use*

Specifically for teachers of (grade level and/or subject field):

Sponsor of site:

Features of interest and usefulness:

For Your Notes

Figure 10.3
Teaching scenario:
natural disasters

Let us suppose that the students from your "house" have been working nearly all year on an interdisciplinary thematic unit entitled "surviving natural disasters" (returning to the example in Chapter 5 regarding ITU themes). As a culmination to their study they "published" a document entitled "Natural Disaster Preparation and Survival Guide for (*name of their community*)" and proudly distributed the guide to their parents and members of the community.

Long before preparing the guide, however, the students had to do research. To learn about the history of various kinds of natural disasters that had occurred or might occur locally and about the sorts of preparations a community should take for each kind of disaster, students searched sources on the Internet, such as federal documents, scientific articles, and articles from newspapers from around the world where natural disasters had occurred. They also searched in the local library and local newspaper's archives to learn of floods, tornadoes, and fires that had occurred during the past 200 years. Much to their surprise, they also learned that their community is located very near the New Madrid Fault and did, in fact, experience a serious earthquake in 1811, although none since. As a result of that earthquake, two nearby towns completely disappeared; the Mississippi River flowed in reverse, and its course changed and even caused the formation of a new lake in Tennessee.

From published and copyrighted sources, including Web sites, the students found many useful photographs, graphics, and articles, which they included in whole or in part in their "Natural Disaster Preparation and Survival Guide." They did so without obtaining permission from the original copyright holders or even citing those sources.

You and the other members of your teaching team and other people were so impressed with the student's work that students were encouraged to offer the document for publication on the school's Web site. In addition, the document was received with so much acclaim that the students decided to sell it in local stores. This would help defray the original cost of duplication and enable them to continue the supply of guides.

Cautions and Guidelines for Using the Internet

If you have yet to learn to use the Internet, we leave the mechanics of that to the many resources available to you, including the experts that can be found among your peers, on your college or university staff, and among members of any public school faculty. The remaining pages of this section address the "how" of using the Internet from an academic perspective. Let's begin with the fictitious although feasible teaching scenario illustrated in Figure 10.3.

To the scenario in Figure 10.3, there is a good aspect and there is an aspect that is not so good. The good aspect is that the children used a good technological tool (the Internet) to research a variety of sources, including many primary ones. The not-so-good aspect is that when they published their document on the Internet and when they made copies of their guide to be sold, they did so without permission from original copyright holders. They were infringing copyright law. While it would take an attorney to say for sure, with this scenario it is probable that the students, teacher, school, and the school district would be liable. As is true for other documents (such as published photos, graphics, and text), unless there is a clear statement that materials taken from the Internet are public domain, it is best to assume that they are copyrighted and should not be used without expressed permission.

Since there is such a proliferation of information today, from both printed materials and from information on the Internet, except for the obvious reliable sites such as the *New York Times* and the Library of Congress, how can a person determine the validity and currency of a particular piece of information? When searching for useful and reliable information on a particular topic, how can one be protected from wasting valuable time sifting through all the information? People need to know that just because information is found on a printed page or is published on the Internet doesn't necessarily mean that the information is accurate or current. Using a checklist, such as found on the Internet at <http://www.infopeople.org/bkmk/select.html>, and provided with examples of materials that meet and do not meet the criteria of the checklist, students can develop skill in assessing materials and information found on the Internet.

Teaching children how to access and assess Web sites adds to their repertoire of skills for lifelong

Figure 10.4
Professional journals and periodicals for teachers

The American Biology Teacher	*Mathematics Teaching in the Middle School*
American Educational Research Quarterly	*The Middle School Journal*
The American Music Teacher	*Modern Language Journal*
American Teacher	*Music Educators Journal*
The Arithmetic Teacher	*NEA Today*
The Art Teacher	*The Negro Educational Review*
Childhood Education	*The New Advocate*
The Computing Teacher	*OAH Magazine of History*
Creative Classroom	*Phi Delta Kappan*
The Earth Scientist	*Physical Education*
Educational Horizons	*Primary Voices K–6*
Educational Leadership	*The Reading Teacher*
The Elementary School Journal	*Reading Today*
English Journal	*School Arts*
English Language Teaching Journal	*School Library Journal*
The Good Apple Newspaper	*The School Musician*
The History Teacher	*School Science and Mathematics*
The Horn Book	*Science*
Instructor	*Science Activities*
Journal of Economic Education	*Science and Children*
Journal of Geography	*Science Scope*
Journal of Home Economics	*Social Education*
Journal of Learning Disabilities	*The Social Studies*
Journal of the National Association of Bilingual	*Social Studies and the Young Learner*
Educators	*Social Studies Review*
Journal of Physical Education and Recreation	*Teacher Magazine*
Journal of Reading	*Teaching K–8*
Journal of Teaching in Physical Education	*Theory and Research in Social Education*
Kappa Delta Pi Record	*TESOL Quarterly*
Language Arts	*Voices from the Middle*
Language Learning	*Writing Teacher*
Learning	*Young Children*
The Mathematics Teacher	

learning. Consider allowing each student or teams of students to become experts on specific sites during particular units of study. It might be useful to start a chronicle of student-recorded log entries about particular Web sites to provide comprehensive long-term data about those sites.

When students use information from the Internet, require that they print copies of sources of citations and materials so you can check for accuracy. These copies may be maintained in their portfolios.

Student work published on the Internet should be considered intellectual material and protected from plagiarism by others. Most school districts post a copyright notice on their home page. Someone at the school usually is assigned to supervise the school Web site to see that district and school policy and legal requirements are observed.

Professional Journals and Periodicals

Figure 10.4 lists examples of the many professional periodicals and journals that can provide useful teaching ideas and Web site information and that carry information about instructional materials and how to get them. Some of these may be in your university or college library and accessible through Internet sources. Check there for these and other titles of interest to you.

The ERIC Information Network

The Educational Resources Information Center (ERIC) system, established by the United States Office of Education, is a widely used network providing access to information and research in educa-

Figure 10.5
Selected ERIC
addresses

- *Assessment and Evaluation.* The Catholic University of America, 210 O'Boyle Hall, Washington, DC 20064-4035. <http://ericae2.educ.cua.edu>
- *Counseling and Student Services.* School of Education, 201 Ferguson Building, Univeristy of North Carolina at Greensboro, Greensboro, NC 27412-5001. <http://www.unicg.edu/~ericas2>
- *Handicapped and Gifted Children.* Council for Exceptional Children, 1920 Association Drive, Reston, VA 22191-1589. <http://www.cec.sped.org/ericed.htm>
- *Information and Technology.* Center for Science and Technology, Syracuse University, Syracuse, NY 13244-4100. <http://eric.r.syr.edu/ithame>
- *Languages and Linguistics,* Center for Applied Linguistics, 1118 22nd Street, NW, Washington, DC 20037-1214. <http://www.cal.org/ericcll/>
- *Reading, English, and Communication Skills.* Indiana University, 2805 East 10th Street, Smith Research Center, Suite 150, Bloomington, IN 47408-2698. <http://www.indiana.edu/~eric_rec>
- *Rural Education and Small Schools.* Appalachia Educational Laboratory, 1031 Quarrier Street, PO Box 1348, Charleston, WV 25325-1348. <http://aelvira.ael.org/erichp.htm>
- *Science, Mathematics, and Environmental Education.* Ohio State University, 1929 Kenny Road, Columbus, OH 43210-1080. <http://www.ericse.org.>
- *Service Learning.* Univeristy of Minnesota, College of Education and Human Development, 1954 Bufford Ave., Vo Tech Building, St. Paul, MN 55108. <http://www.nicsl.coled.um.educ>
- *Social Studies/Social Science Education,* Indiana University, Social Studies Development Center, 2805 East 10th Street, Bloomington, IN 47408-2698. <http://www.indiana.edu/~ssac/eric_chess.html>
- *Urban Education.* Teachers College, Columbia University, Institute for Urban and Minority Education, Main Hall, Rm. 303, Box 40, New York, NY 10027-6696. <http://eric_web.tc.columbia.edu>

tion. Selected clearinghouses and their addresses are shown in Figure 10.5.

Copying Printed Materials

As a teacher you must be familiar with the laws about the use of copyrighted materials, printed and nonprinted, including those obtained from sources on the Internet. Remember that just because there is no notice on a Web page that the material is copyrighted, original material is still protected by copyright law; that is just as true for the intellectual property created by a minor as it is for that of an adult.

Although space here prohibits full inclusion of U.S. legal guidelines, your local school district should be able to provide a copy of current district policies for compliance with copyright laws. District policies should include guidelines for teachers and students in publishing materials on the Internet. If no district guidelines are available, when using printed materials adhere to the guidelines shown in Figure 10.6.[2]

When preparing to make a copy you must find out whether law under the category of "permitted use" permits the copying. If not allowed under "permitted use," then you must get written permission to reproduce the material from the holder of the copyright. If the address of the source is not given on the material, addresses may be obtained from various references, such as *Literary Market Place, Audio-Visual Market Place,* and *Ulrich's International Periodical's Directory.*

The Classroom Writing Board

As is true for an auto mechanic or a brain surgeon or any other professional, a teacher needs to know when and how to use the tools of the trade. One of the tools available to most every elementary school classroom teacher is the writing board. Can you imagine an elementary school classroom without a writing board? In this section you will find guidelines for using this important tool.

Writing boards used to be, and in some schools still are, slate blackboards (slate is a type

Figure 10.6
Guidelines for copying printed materials that are copyrighted
Source: Section 107 of the 1976 Federal Omnibus Copyright Revision act.

PERMITTED USES: YOU MAY MAKE

1. Single copies of:
   - A chapter of a book
   - An article from a periodical, magazine, or newspaper
   - A short story, short essay, or short poem whether or not from a collected work
   - A chart, graph, diagram, drawing, cartoon
   - An illustration from a book, magazine, or newspaper
2. Multiple copies for classroom use (not to exceed one copy per student in a course) of:
   - A complete poem if less than 250 words
   - An excerpt from a longer poem, but not to exceed 250 words
   - A complete article, story, or essay of less than 2,500 words
   - An excerpt from a larger printed work not to exceed 10 percent of the whole or 1,000 words.
   - One chart, graph, diagram, cartoon, or picture per book or magazine issue

PROHIBITED USES: YOU MAY *NOT*

1. Copy more than one work or two excerpts from a single author during one class term (semester or year).
2. Copy more than three works from a collective work or periodical volume during one class term.
3. Reproduce more than nine sets of multiple copies for distribution to students in one class term.
4. Copy to create, replace, or substitute for anthologies or collective works.
5. Copy "consumable" works, for example, workbooks, standardized tests, or answer sheets.
6. Copy the same work year after year.

---

of metamorphic rock). In the modern classroom, however, it is more likely to be either a board that is painted plywood (chalkboard), which, like the blackboard, is also quickly becoming obsolete as is the need to be concerned about the dust created from using chalk[3]; or a white or colored (light green and light blue are common) *multipurpose dry-erase board* on which you write with special marking pens and erase with any soft cloth. In addition to providing a surface upon which you can write and draw, the multipurpose board can be used as a projection screen and as a surface to which figures cut from colored transparency film will stick. It may also have a magnetic backing.

Extending the purposes of the multipurpose board and correlated with modern technology is an *electronic whiteboard* that can transfer information that is written on it to a connected computer monitor, which in turn can save the material as a computer file. The electronic whiteboard uses dry-erase markers and special erasers that have optically encoded sleeves that enable the device to track their position on the board. The data are then converted into a display for the computer monitor, which may then be printed, cut and pasted into

other applications, sent as an e-mail or fax message, or networked to other sites.[4]

Each day, each class, and even each new idea should begin with a clean board, except for announcements that have been placed there by you or another teacher. At the end of each class, clean the board, especially if another teacher follows you in that room, as a simple professional courtesy.

Use colored chalk or marking pens to highlight your "board talk." This is especially helpful for students with learning difficulties. Beginning at the top left of the board, print or write neatly and clearly, with the writing intentionally positioned to indicate content relationships (e.g., causal, oppositional, numerical, comparative, categorical, and so on).

Use the writing board to acknowledge acceptance and to record student contributions. Print instructions for an activity on the board, in addition to giving them orally. At the top of the board frame you may find clips for hanging posters, maps, and charts.

Learn to use the board without having to turn your back entirely on students and without blocking their view of the board. When you have a lot of material to put on the board, do it before class and then cover it, or sometimes better yet, put the material on transparencies and use the overhead projector rather than the board, or use both. Be careful not to write too much information. When using the writing board to complement your lesson and teacher talk, write only key words and simple diagrams, thereby making it possible for the student's brain to process both what is seen and the elaboration provided by your words.

The Classroom Bulletin Board

Bulletin boards also are found in nearly every classroom and can be relatively inexpensively transformed into attractive and valuable instructional tools. Among other uses, the bulletin board is a convenient location for posting reminders, assignments and schedules, commercially produced materials, and to celebrate and display model student work and anchor papers. When preparing a bulletin board it is important to ensure that the board display reflects gender and ethnic equity. For effective use of the classroom bulletin board, consider the following additional suggestions.

Making a Case for Bulletin Boards

How can you effectively use a classroom bulletin board? Your classroom bulletin board will be most effective if you consider your CASE:

C: Colorful constructions and captions.

A: Attractive arrangement.

S: Simple and student prepared.

E: Enrichment and extensions of learning.

C: Colorful constructions and captions. Take time to plan the colors you select for your board, and whenever possible, include different materials for the letters and for the background of the board. For letter variety, consider patterns on bright cloth such as denim, felt, and corduroy. Search for special letters: They might be magnetic or ceramic, or precut letters of different sizes. Or make unique letters by cutting them from magazines, newspapers, posters, or stencils, or by printing the letters with rubber stamps, sponges, or vegetable prints. You may also dab colors on letter shapes with sponges, rubber stamps, or vegetable slices.

If this is sounding like a lot of extra work that you may not have the time to do, consider having students help in the preparation of your bulletin board. This will be not only a chance for them to learn and offer many creative ideas, but also an excellent way for you to get to know them better and to build rapport with them.

For the background and the borders of your board, consider using gift wrapping, wallpaper samples, shelf paper, and remnants of fabric—flowers, polka dots, plaids, solids, or checks. Corrugated cardboard makes sturdy borders: Cut out scallops, the shape of a picket fence, or jagged points for an icicle effect. Other colorful borders can be made with wide braid, rickrack, or contrasting fabric or paper. Constructions for the board may be simple ones made of yarn, ribbon, braid, cardboard pointers, maps, scrolls, banners, pennants, wheels that turn, cardboard doors that open, shuttered windows to peek through, or flaps that pull down or up for peering under or over.

If you need more bulletin board space, prepare large, lightweight screens from a cardboard carton that held a refrigerator, available from an appliance store. One creative teacher asked for, and received without charge, several empty gallon ice-cream containers from a local ice cream shop. The teacher then stacked five of them on top of one another, fastened them together with wide masking tape, painted them, and prepared her own bulletin board "totem pole" for the corner of the classroom. On that circular display space, the students placed their items about a current unit of study.

A: Attractive arrangement. Use your creative imagination to make the board attractive. Is your arrangement interesting? Does it contain an interactive component? Did you use texture? Did you consider the shapes of the items selected? Are the colors attractive? Does your caption draw student attention?

S: Simple and student prepared. The bulletin board should be simple, emphasizing one main idea, concept, topic, or theme, and the captions should be short and concise.

Are your students interested in preparing the bulletin board for your classroom? Plan a class meeting to discuss this with them. Children have great ideas.

- They can help plan. Why not let them diagram their ideas and share them with each other?
- They can discuss. Is there a more meaningful way to begin to discuss an evaluation of what they see, to discuss the internal criteria that each student brings to class, or to begin to talk about the different values that each student may have?
- They can arrange materials. Why not let them discover the concepts of balance and symmetry?
- They can construct and contribute. Will they feel they are more actively involved and are really participating if it is *their* bulletin board?
- Once the bulletin board is finished, your students can get further involved during a class

meeting at which they (a) review the board; (b) discuss the materials used, and (c) talk about the information the board is emphasizing.

Additional class projects may be planned during this meeting. For instance, do the children want a bulletin board group or committee for their class? Do they want a permanent committee or one in which the membership changes from month to month? Or do they prefer that existing cooperative learning groups assume bulletin board responsibility, with periodic rotation of that responsibility? Do they want to meet to work on the board on a regular basis? Can they work quietly and not disturb other students who may still be completing their other learning tasks? Should the committee prepare the board, or should they ask everyone to contribute ideas and items for the weekly or monthly bulletin board? Does the committee want to keep a register of students who contribute to the board? Should there be an honorary list of bulletin board illustrators? Should the authors of selected captions sign their names beneath each caption? Do they want to keep a file binder of all of the different diagrams of proposed bulletin boards? At each class meeting, should the committee discuss the proposed diagrams with the entire class? Should they ask the class to evaluate which idea would be appropriate for a particular study topic? What other records do they want to keep? Should there be a bulletin board medal or a classroom award?

E: Enrichment and extensions of learning. Illustrations on the bulletin board can accent learning topics; verbs can vitalize the captions; phrases can punctuate a student's thoughts; and alliteration can announce anything you wish. For example:

- *Animals can accent!* Pandas, panthers, and parrots can help present punctuation symbols; a giant octopus can show students eight rules to remember, eight things to do when preparing a book report, or eight activities to complete when academic work is finished early; a student can fish for anything—math facts, correctly spelled words, or the meanings of science words; a bear can help students to "bear down" on errors of any kind; a large pair of shoes can "stamp out" errors, incomplete work, forgotten school materials, or student misbehavior. Dinosaurs can begin a search for any topic, and pack rats can lead one into phrases, prose, or poetry.
- *Verbs can vitalize!* Someone or something (your choice) can "swing into" any curriculum area. Some of the verbs used often are *soar, win, buzz, rake, scurry,* and *race.*

- *Phrases point out!* Some of the short, concise phrases used as captions may include:

Pulling together for ____	Mind stretchers for ____
Bird watch for ____	Hop into ____
Peer into ____	Grow up with ____
Bone up on ____	Tune into ____
Monkey with ____	Looking good with ____
Fly high with ____	Get on track with ____

- *Alliteration announces!* Some classroom bulletin boards show Viking ships or voyages that guide a student to vocabulary words; others announce "Monsters Monitor Math Madness." Still others present "Surprises of Spring," "Fantasies of Fall," "Wonders of Winter," and "Safety in Summer," while some boards send messages about "Library Lingo," "Dictionary Dynamite," and "Thesaurus Treats."

The Story Felt Board

Interacting with figures and retelling stories on a felt (or flannel) board are excellent activities for children. This is a language experience that should be encouraged. Specialists in children's literature emphasize that felt boards provide an opportunity for children to practice telling stories more easily. Once they have seen their teacher tell a story with felt board figures, they are eager to do it themselves. In addition to its being an attention-getting strategy, another advantage in using a felt board is that the figures can be arranged in sequence to serve as cues for the story. Further, when the storyteller is finished, children can retell the story in their own words. Additionally, children *do* like to make their own figures and tell their own stories. It is important to carefully select stories that have simple settings, few characters, and fairly uncomplicated plots.

With a felt board, both adults and children can share such folktales as *The Boy Who Lived with the Bears and Other Iroquois Stories* by J. Bruchac (New York: HarperCollins, 1995), and *The Little Red Ant* and *The Great Big Crumb,* by S. Climo (New York: Clarion, 1995). Older students, grade 4 and up, may be interested in adapting some of the folktales from *Peace Tales: World Folk Tales to Talk About* by M. R. MacDonald (North Haven, CT: Linnet, 1992).

A Felt Board Is Tops

Indeed, a felt board may be considered TOPS in your classroom, since it has many uses and is a flexible teaching tool. With it, you can present lessons from any subject area or stories of any kind. Sometimes the students can follow your presentation on small, individual felt boards, and at other times they may assist you by manipulating the objects on the board. Consider the letters that spell TOPS:

T: Teacher use.

O: Object variety.

P: Planning, presenting, and plotting.

S: Student use.

T: Teacher use. For primary students, teachers may use the felt board for (a) presenting stories; (b) presenting rhymes; (c) matching rhyming pictures; (d) presenting objects; (e) listening to beginning sounds, matching them, and classifying object pictures; (f) recognizing colors and color words; (g) selecting pictures showing opposite concepts; (h) arranging objects or pictures in sequence; (i) comparing and contrasting sizes of objects; and (j) creating an individual story with unique combinations of animals, places, and objects.

There are felt cutouts of numerals for arranging in sets for math and cutouts of words, symbols, and punctuation marks for spelling, labeling, and showing quotations in conversations. Commercial bulletin board sets are easily adapted to the felt board and supply ready-made materials for such topics as traffic control symbols, insects, nutrition, the solar system, prehistoric animals, telling time, and the world of money. Primary students can plan balanced meals by selecting colorful food objects, and the life cycle of a plant or insect can be traced by intermediate-grade students; career choice can be a discussion for older students who may display people, props, and labels.

When considering story presentations, you may want to select one of the humorous stories from P. L. Roberts, *Taking Humor Seriously in Children's Literature: Literature-based Mini-Units for Children, Ages 5–12* (Lanham, Maryland: Scarecrow Press/University Press of America, 1997).

Friendship story presentations can include the following:

Grades Kindergarten through Three

Fine, E. H. *Under the Lemon Moon.* Illustrated by R. K. Moreno. (New York: Lee and Low, 1999). Rodalinda learns to be understanding and compassionate to the man who took lemons from her tree and his impoverished family who sells the fruit in the market square.

Harper, J. *Outrageous, Bodacious, Boliver Boggs.* Illustrated by J. Adinolfi. (New York: Simon and Schuster, 1996). Boliver tells tall tales (escapes rattle snakes, wrestles a bear, meets a monster) when he is late each day for school (to the amusement and entertainment of his friends).

McBratney, S. *The Caterpillar Flight.* Illustrated by J. Barton. (Cambridge, MA: Candlewick, 1996). Friendly caterpillars experience a pillow fight.

Park, F. and Park, G. *The Royal Bee.* Illustrated by C. Zhong-Yuan Zhang. (New York: Boyds Mills, 2000). Set in Korea in the late 19th century, Songho, a poor boy, is told that only privileged children may attend school. Songho listens outside the classroom door each day until he is invited in by the kind and friendly schoolmaster, answers questions, and is selected to represent the school in the Royal Bee where the best student in the land is determined.

Scruggs, A. *Jump Rope Magic.* Illustrated by David Diaz. (Chicago: Scholastic/Blue Sky, 2000). Jump rope chants of Shameka and her friends irritate grouchy Miss Minnie, a neighbor, until Shameka chants rhyme. In a fantasy scene, the two play a magical jump rope game until the neighbor is carried away into the sky.

Spellman, C. M. *When I Feel Angry.* Illustrated by N. Cote. (Niles, IL: Albert Whitman, 2000). In this animal-acting-like-a-human story, a little rabbit relates the things that make her angry (being made fun of on the playground, doing a chore in the middle of play, losing a game) and some of the ways she deals with her emotions.

Grades Four through Six

Dixon, A. *The Sleeping Lady.* Illustrated by E. Johns. (Juneau, AK: Alaska Northwest Books, 1994). A "how and why" tale that explains how friendly giants got involved with the first snowfall and how Mount Susitna was formed.

Holler, A. *Pocahontas: Powhaton Peacemaker.* Illustrated by the author. (New York: Chelsea, 1993). Life story of Pocahontas and her acts of friendship to help the English newcomers survive at Jamestown.

Your options for including the felt board in a particular lesson are quite varied: (a) you may take the total responsibility of presenting and moving the felt board objects; (b) you may encourage the students to participate and move the objects; (c) you may present the lesson while students follow the story by placing objects from their individual sets on small felt boards at their desks or tables (during a previous activity time, the students would have received ditto copies of characters, cut out the characters, and glued or pasted small bits of flannel or felt to the backs of them so to prepare their individual sets); (d) you may arrange the students into teams of two, and ask them to tell the lesson or story to one another by moving the board objects; or (e) you may assign one group to a larger board for a group presentation.

O: Object variety. The variety of objects you may use with a felt board is nearly unlimited. How can you prepare this wide collection of felt board objects?

1. *Consider pellon objects.* With *permanent* coloring pens (watercolor will come off on your hands), draw directly on white pellon. (Pellon is often used for interfacing in clothing, so white pellon is usually available in a fabric store.) Add facial features, clothing details, or other special items. One teacher adds sequins and small, glittering stars. Another adds rickrack and gold glitter. Still another adds beads and tiny buttons to a character's costume. Your art as well as that of the students show up quite well when you draw on pellon.

2. *Consider felt, flannel, and sandpaper objects.* Objects may be cut directly from these materials, or the materials may be glued to the back of any object. Students enjoy seeing sandpaper letters and bright felt or flannel cutouts of holiday items—orange pumpkins, green pine trees, red hearts, and green shamrocks.

3. *Consider objects from published material.* Save catalogs, magazines, inexpensive books, posters, greeting cards, and discarded textbooks. Cut the objects you need from these materials and back them with any of the materials that will adhere to the felt board.

4. *Consider objects from commercial felt board sets.* Visit your nearest teacher's exchange or write to a school supply company for a current catalog. Look for felt board sets or bulletin board sets that you can adapt.

5. *Consider objects with a Velcro variation.* Some teachers add a border of Velcro across the top of their felt boards so they can place real objects on the board as they tell a story or give a presentation. Other teachers place small pieces of Velcro in strategic spots on the felt board to hold, for example, Baby Bear's small chair or Mama Bear's bowl and spoon. Remember to back your realia with Velcro also.

6. *Consider objects with a magnet.* Some teachers prepare a felt board slipcover to slide over a large metal board (such as a large cookie sheet or a piece of sheet metal) to be able to use magnets. One teacher prepared a scene for the base of a green felt board to represent grass, flowers, rocks, and trees. Behind each gray felt "rock" was a circular cutout, exposing the metal sheet. This enabled the teacher to remove a felt rock at an appropriate time and place a small wooden ani-

mal, backed with a magnet, on the board to add interest and a three-dimensional quality to the presentation. Multipurpose writing boards, as discussed earlier in this chapter, usually have a metal backing so they can be used as magnet boards in much the same way. Instead of felt materials, you can use various colors of thin plastic film, which will stick to the board when smoothed into place.

7. *Consider a looped-cloth variation.* One fabric, commonly known as looped-cloth, is very useful for a slipcover for your felt board. This cloth has loops in the fabric. Put self-adhesive picture-hanging hooks on the back of the heavier objects and hang them on the loops of the cloth.

P: Planning, presenting, and plotting. Planning, presenting, and plotting are three basics crucial to your felt board story or lesson. Plan to use familiar objects if possible; present your story or lesson after preparing it thoroughly in a logical, sequential way. Plotting means that you carefully arrange your presentation. You may tell a story with a satisfying ending or share nonfiction information. The information can be facts that portray another point of view or facts about something the students might not have known before. It can be an interesting presentation of the life cycle of an insect, a review of cloud shapes, or a metamorphosis not often illustrated in student texts.

S: Student use. Get your students involved with the felt boards. Individual felt boards are quickly and easily made by pasting 8 1/2 x 11 inch pieces of felt to the outside of large manila mailing envelopes. (Students may place the objects inside the envelopes to keep them secure.) Students can brace the envelopes against a textbook at their desks. Extra bits and pieces of felt or other materials that adhere to felt can be placed inside the envelope, and additional objects may be made as needed.

What can a student do with an individual felt board?

- Place objects, along with the teacher, as the story or lesson is told; assist the teacher after the lesson by removing the objects in sequence; help to retell the story or summarize the lesson.
- Tell the story to one another in teams of two.
- Place accompanying objects on the board as an audiotape of the story or lesson is heard.
- Create original stories or presentations.
- Create original objects for the presentation of information gained from a story or a lesson.

How to Avoid Problems When Using a Felt Board

With proper planning, you can avoid the following common problems of using a felt board.

Problem: The cutouts get mixed up. You may wish to number your cutouts on their backs in order of their use in the presentation. Lay them face down on the table when you are ready to begin, and arrange them in numerical order.

Problem: The cutouts fall off the felt board. Check your board to see whether you need to add another backing of felt. Add more if needed. One teacher uses an old brush to brush up the nap on the back of the cutouts and on the board before each story. Another teacher sprays a light mist of pattern adhesive spray on the felt board before the story. (Pattern spray is available at your nearest fabric store.) Still another teacher periodically replaces the felt on the back of the cutouts. Consider backing your cutouts not with felt but with pellon. If the cutouts fall, prepare to keep your story or lesson moving smoothly by placing a short row of straight pins into the back of your board. When a cutout falls, reach back quickly, select a pin, and again attach the loose character or object. Remember not to crowd your board with too many objects at any one time. Remove objects as your presentation sequence moves along.

Problem: You lose your place in the lesson or story. Rehearse your presentation. If possible, audiotape it in advance, replay the tape, and self-evaluate. How long will the presentation take? Did you practice placing your cutouts on the board? Do you have room for them? Rehearsing with an audiotape will help your presentation flow smoothly as you develop your skill in doing more than one thing at a time. Perhaps you may want to write large, legible notes for yourself and place them on the table near the cutouts. One teacher pins large note cards on the back of the board; another prepares a low cardboard screen, about six inches high, to stand in front of the table top. This low screen, cut from three sides of a cardboard box and gaily decorated, conceals the cutouts and the teacher's notes.

THE COMMUNITY AS A RESOURCE

One of the richest resources for student learning is the local community and the people and places in it. You will want to build your own file of community resources—speakers, sources for free materials, and field trip locations. Your school or a colleague at the school may already have a community resource file available for your use. However, it may need updating. Anyway, it is better to maintain your own. A community resource file, perhaps as part of your resource file that you started in Chapter 1 (see Figure 1.6 in Chapter 1), should contain information about possible field trip locations, community resource people who could serve as guest speakers or mentors, and local agencies that can provide information and instructional materials. See Figure 10.7.

There are many ways of using community resources, and quite a variety have been demonstrated by the schools specifically mentioned throughout this resource guide (see "Schools" in index). Here, the discussion is limited to two often used, sometimes abused, instructional tools: (a) guest speakers and (b) out-of-classroom and off-campus excursions, commonly called *field trips*.

Guest Speaker

Bringing outside speakers into your classroom can be for students a valuable educational experience, but not automatically so. In essence, guest speakers can be classified across a spectrum of four types, only two of which should be considered as guest speakers for the elementary school classroom. (a) Ideally, a speaker is both informative and inspiring. (b) A speaker may be inspiring but with nothing substantive to offer, except for the possible diversion he or she might offer from the usual rigors of classroom work. (c) A speaker may be informative but boring to children. (d) At the worst end of this spectrum is the guest speaker who is both boring and uninformative. As with any other instructional experience, to make the experience most effective takes careful planning on your part. To make sure that the experience is beneficial to student learning, consider the following guidelines.

- If at all possible, meet and talk with the guest speaker in advance to inform the speaker about your students and your expectations for the presentation, and to gauge how motivational and informative the speaker might be. If you believe the speaker might be informative but boring, then perhaps you can help structure the presentation in some way to make the presentation a bit more inspiring. For example, with the speaker's cooperation, plan to stop the speaker every few minutes and involve the children in questioning and discussions of points made.
- Prepare students in advance with key points of information that you expect students to obtain.
- Prepare students with questions to ask the speaker, things the students want to find out, and information you want them to inquire about.
- Follow up the presentation with a thank you letter to the guest speaker and perhaps further questions that developed during class discussions after the speaker's presentation.

Figure 10.7
Community resources for speakers, materials, and field trips

Airport	Highway patrol station
Apiary	Historical sites and monuments
Aquarium	Industrial plant
Archeological site	Legislature session
Art gallery	Levee and water reservoir
Assembly plant	Library and archive
Bakery	Native American Indian reservation
Bird and wildlife sanctuary	Mass transit authority
Book publisher	Military installation
Bookstore	Mine
Broadcasting and TV station	Museum
Building being razed	Newspaper plant
Building under construction	Observatory
Canal lock	Oil refinery
Cemetery	Park
Chemical plant	Poetry reading
City or county planning commission	Post office and package delivery company
Courthouse	Police station
Dairy	Recycling center
Dam and flood plain	Retail store
Dock and harbor	Sanitation department
Factory	Sawmill or lumber company
Farm	Shopping mall
Fire department	Shoreline (stream, lake, wetland, ocean)
Fish hatchery	Telecommunications center
Flea market	Town meeting
Foreign embassy	Utility company
Forest and forest preserve	Universities and colleges
Freeway under construction	Warehouse
Gas company	Water reservoir and treatment plant
Geological site	Wildlife park and preserve
Health department and hospital	Weather bureau and storm center
Highway construction site	Zoo

Field Trips

What is the most memorable field trip that you were ever on as a student? What made it memorable? You may want to discuss these questions and others like them with your classmates (now) and (later) with the students in your classroom where you are a teacher.

Today's schools often have only limited funds for the transportation and liability costs for field trips. In some cases, there are no funds at all. At times, parent-teacher groups, business, and civic organizations help by providing financial resources so that students get valuable first-hand experiences that field trips so often can contribute to children's education.

To prepare for and implement a successful field trip, there are three important stages of planning—before, during, and after—and critical decisions to be made at each stage. Consider the following guidelines.

Before the Field Trip

When the field trip is your idea (and not the students), discuss the idea with members of your teaching team and with the person designated responsible for field trip authorizations, especially when transportation will be needed, *before* mentioning the idea to the children. There is no cause served by getting children excited about a trip before you know whether it is feasible.

Once the necessary, but tentative, approval from school officials has been obtained, take the trip yourself (or with team members), if possible. A previsit allows you to determine how to make the field trip most productive and what arrangements will be necessary. If a previsit is not possible, you still will need to arrange for travel directions, arrival and departure times, parking, briefing by the host, if there is one, storage of students' personal items, such as coats and lunches, provisions for eating and rest rooms, and fees, if any.

If there are fees, you need to talk with school administration about who will pay the fees. If the trip is worth taking, the school should cover the costs. If that is not possible, perhaps students can plan a fund-raising activity or financial assistance can be obtained from some other source such as the PTA or a local business partnership. If this does not work, you might consider an alternative trip or activity (such as a classroom guest speaker) that does not involve costs.

Arrange for official permission from the school administration. This usually requires a form for requesting, planning, and reporting field trips. After permission has been obtained, you can discuss the field trip with your students and arrange for permissions from parents and guardians. You need to realize that while parents or guardians sign official permission forms authorizing their children to participate in the trip, these only show that the parents or guardians are aware of what will take place and give their permission for their child to participate. Although the permission form will probably include a statement that the parent or guardian absolves the teacher and the school from liability should an accident occur, it *does not* lessen the teacher's and the school's responsibilities should there be negligence by a teacher, driver, or chaperone.

If relevant, arrange for students to be excused from their other classes while on the field trip. Using an information form prepared and signed by you and perhaps by the appropriate administrator, the students should then assume responsibility for notifying their other teachers of the planned absence from classes or other school activities and assure them that they will make up whatever work is missed. In addition, you may need to make arrangements for your own teaching duties to be covered in your absence. In some schools, teachers cooperate by filling in for those who will be gone. In other schools, substitute teachers are hired. Sometimes teachers have to hire their own substitute.

Arrange for whatever transportation is needed. Your principal, or the principal's designee, will help you with the details. In most schools, someone else handles this task. In any case, the use of private automobiles is ill advised because you and the school could be liable for the acts of the drivers.

Arrange for the collection of money that is needed for fees. If there are out-of-pocket costs to be paid by students, this information needs to be included on the permission form. No child should ever be excluded from the field trip because of lack of money. This can be a tricky issue because there may be some children who would rather steal the money for a field trip than to admit they don't have

it. Try to anticipate problems; hopefully the school has a fund or plan for such contingencies. Perhaps some agency or organization can pay for the trip so that fees need not be collected from students and potential problems of this sort are avoided.

Plan details for student safety and the monitoring of their safety from departure to return, the entire time they are your responsibility. Included should be a cell phone (many schools will provide one for use during a field trip), first-aid kit, and a system of security and student control, such as a "buddy system" where children must remain paired (and even hold hands in the case of young children) throughout the trip. The pairs sometimes are given numbers that are recorded and kept by the teacher and the chaperones, and then checked at departure time, periodically during the trip, at the time of return, and again upon return. Use adult chaperones. As a very general rule, there should be a minimum of 1 adult for every 10 children. Some districts have a policy regarding this. While on a field trip, at all times all children should be under the direct supervision of a reliable adult.

Plan the complete route and schedule, including any stops along the way. If transportation is being provided, you will need to discuss the plans with the provider.

Establish and discuss rules of behavior with your students to the extent you believe necessary. Included might be details of the trip, its purpose, directions, what they should wear and bring, academic expectations of them (consider, for example, giving each student a study guide), and follow-up activities. Also included should be information about what to do if anything should go awry, for example, if a student is late for the departure or return, loses a personal possession along the way, gets lost, is injured, becomes sick, or misbehaves. For the latter, *never* send a misbehaving student back to school alone, such as, for example, via the city's subway system or a taxi. Involve the adult chaperones in the previsit discussion. All of this information should also be included on the parental permission form.

If a field trip is supposed to promote some sort of learning, as is probably the case, then to avoid leaving the learning to happen by chance, the learning expectations need to be clearly defined and the students given an explanation of how and where they may encounter the learning experience. Before the field trip, students should be asked questions such as, "What do we already know about _____ ? What do we want to find out about _____ ? How can we find out?" and then, with their assistance, an appropriate guide can be prepared for the children to use during the field trip.

To further ensure learning and individual student responsibility for that learning, you may want to assign different roles and responsibilities to students, just as would be done in cooperative learning, ensuring that each child has a role with responsibility.

You may want to take recorders and cameras so the field trip experience can be relived and shared in class upon return. If so, roles and responsibilities for the equipment and its care and use might be assigned to students as well.

During the Field Trip

En route, while at the trip location, and on the return to school, you and the adult chaperones should monitor student behavior and learning just as you do in the classroom. If your field trip has been carefully planned according to the preceding guidelines, it should be a valuable and safe experience for all.

After the Field Trip

Plan the follow-up activities. As with any other lesson plan, the field trip lesson is complete only when there is both a proper introduction and a well-planned closure. All sorts of follow-up activities can be planned as an educational wrap-up to this educational experience. For example, a bulletin board committee can plan and prepare an attractive display summarizing the trip. Students can write about their experiences, in their journals, or as papers. Small groups can give oral reports to the class about what they did and learned. Their reports can then serve as springboards for further class discussion and perhaps further investigations. Finally, for future planning, all who were involved should contribute to a summative assessment of the experience.

MEDIA TOOLS

Your attention is now focused on teaching tools that depend upon electricity to project light and sound and to focus images on screens. Included are projectors of various sorts, computers, CD-ROMs, sound recorders, and video recorders. The intent here is *not* to provide instruction on how to operate modern equipment but to help you develop a philosophy for using it and to provide strategies for using media tools in your teaching. Consequently, to conserve space in this book, we devote no attention to traditional AV equipment, such as film, opaque, overhead, and slide projectors. There are staff members on any school faculty who gladly will assist you in locating and using those tools.

It is important to remember that the role of media tools is to aid student learning, not to teach for you. You must still select the objectives, orchestrate the instructional plan, tweak the instruction according to the needs of individual children, assess the results, and follow up the lessons, just as you have learned to do with various other instructional strategies. If you use media prudently, your teaching and students' learning will benefit. Like a competent brain surgeon or a competent auto mechanic, a competent teacher knows when and how to select and use the right tool at the right time. Would you want your child operated on by a surgeon who was unfamiliar with the tools used in surgery? The education of a child should be no less important.

When Equipment Malfunctions

When using media equipment, it is nearly always best to set up the equipment and have it ready to go before students arrive. This helps avoid problems in classroom management that can occur when there is a delay because the equipment is not ready. After all, if you were a surgeon ready to begin an operation and your tools and equipment weren't ready, your patient's life would likely be placed in extra danger. Like any other accomplished professional, a competent teacher is ready when the work is to begin.

Of course, delays may be unavoidable when equipment breaks down or if a videotape breaks or the computer screen freezes. Remember Murphy's law, which says if anything can go wrong, it will? It is particularly relevant when using media. You need to be prepared for such emergencies. Effectively planning for and responding to this eventuality is a part of your system of movement management and takes place during the preactive stage of your planning (see Chapter 3). That preparation includes consideration of a number of factors.

When equipment malfunctions, three principles should be kept in mind: (a) you want to avoid dead time in the classroom, (b) you want to avoid causing permanent damage to equipment, and (c) you want to avoid losing content continuity of a lesson. What do you do when equipment breaks down? Again, the answer is be prepared for the eventuality.

If a projector bulb goes out, quickly insert another. That means that you should have an extra bulb on hand. As simplistic as this seems, when the bulb goes, unless you have a replacement bulb, so goes an effective part of the lesson. If a tape breaks, you can do a quick temporary splice with cellophane tape. That means that tape should be readily available. If you must do a temporary splice, do it on the film or videotape that has already run through the machine rather than on the end yet to go through, so as not to mess up the machine or the film. Then, later, be sure to notify the person in charge of the tape that a temporary splice was made, so the tape can be permanently repaired before its next use. If the computer screen freezes, during direct, whole-class instruction you should probably quickly move to an alternate activity. If it is during multilevel instruction, then while maintaining your classroom withitness, you can probably take the time to treat this as a teachable moment and show the student who is working on the computer what to do, which probably would be simply how to restart the computer.

If during surgery a patient's brain artery suddenly and unexpectedly breaks, the surgeon and the surgical team is ready for that eventuality and makes the necessary repair. If while working on an automobile a part breaks, the mechanic gets a replacement part. If while teaching a fuse blows or for some other reason you lose power, and you feel that there is going to be too much dead time before the equipment is working again, that is the time to go to an alternate lesson plan. You have probably heard the expression "go to Plan B." It is a useful phrase that means without missing a beat in the lesson, to accomplish the same instructional objective or another objective, you immediately and smoothly switch to an alternate learning activity. It does not mean that you must plan two lessons for every one, but when planning a lesson that uses media equipment, you should plan in your lesson an alternative activity, just in case. Then, you move your students into the planned alternative activity quickly and smoothly.

Multimedia Program

A multimedia program is a collection of teaching/learning materials involving more than one type of medium and organized around a single theme or topic. Teaching using multiple media is sometimes referred to as "intermediality."[5] The types of media involved vary from rather simple kits—perhaps a videotape, a game, activity cards, student worksheets, and a manual of instructions for the teacher—to very sophisticated packages involving building-level site licensed computer software, student handbooks, reproducible activity worksheets, classroom wall hangings, and an online subscription to a telecommunication network. Some kits are designed for teacher's use, others by individual or small groups of students, and yet many more are designed for the collaborative use of students and teachers. Many teachers develop their own multimedia programs. Teachers sometimes incorporate multimedia programs with learning activity centers. Children can incorporate various media during their project-based learning and for their culminating presentations (see Chapter 6).[6]

Many multimedia programs are available on CD-ROM; they are designed principally as reference resources for students and teachers but include other aspects as well. One example is National Geographic's *Mammals: A Multimedia Encyclopedia,* which provides a lesson-planning guide, facts on more than 200 animals, 700 color photos, range maps, animal vocalizations, full-motion movie clips, an animal classification game, a glossary, and a printing capability. A brief selection of additional multimedia programs is shown in Table 10.1.

Television, Videos, and CD-ROMs

Everyone knows that television, videos, and CD-ROMs represent a powerful medium. Their use as aids for teaching and learning, however, may present scheduling, curriculum, and physical problems (such as restricted space, security, and old and inadequate electrical wiring) that some school districts are only beginning to be able to deal with.

Television
For purposes of professional discussion, television programming can be divided into three categories: instructional television, educational television, and general commercial television. Instructional television refers to programs specifically designed as classroom instruction. Educational television refers to programs of cable television and of public broadcasting designed to educate in general, but not aimed at classroom instruction. Commercial television programs include the entertainment and public service programs of the television networks and local stations.

Watch for announcements for special educational programs in professional journals. And, of course, television program listings can be obtained from your local commercial, educational, or cable companies or by writing directly to network stations. Some networks sponsor Internet Web sites; see <http://www.flnet.com/~tw/media/televisn.htm>.

Videos and CD-ROMs
Combined with a television monitor, the VCR (videocassette recorder) is one of the most popular and frequently used tools in today's classroom. In

Table 10.1
Selected Multimedia Programs with Sources

Title	Source (Computer: D = DOS, M = Macintosh, W = Windows)	Phone/Internet
Age of Discovery	Society for Visual Education (M,W)	(800-829-1900)
Atlas of the Ancient World	Maris Multimedia (M,W)	(415-492-2819)
Battles of the World	SoftKey Multimedia (M,W)	(510-792-2101)
Chronicle of the 20th Century	DK Multimedia (M,W)	(212-213-4800); www.dk.com
Civil War II	Entrex Software (M,W)	(800-667-0007)
Civilization II	Specturm HoloByte, Inc. (W)	(510-522-3584)
Culture & Technology	The Learning Team (M)	(800-793-8326)
Decisions, Decisions 5.0	Tom Snyder Productions (M,W)	(800-342-0236); www.teachtsp.com
Discovering America	Lawrence Productions (M,W)	(800-421-4157)
Exploring Ancient Cities	Sumeria, Inc. (M,W)	(415-904-0800)
Go West!	Steck-Vaughn (M,W)	(800-531-5015);
Greatest Moments of Our Time	E.M.M.E. Interactive (M,W)	(800-424-3663); www.steck-vaughn.com
History CD-ROMs	CLEARVUE/eav (M,W)	(800-253-2788); www.clearvue.com
Ideas That Changed the World	Integrated Communications & Entertainment	(416-868-6423)
IDIOM History	Chadwyck-Healey (W)	(800-752-0515)
Klondike Gold	DNA Multimedia (W)	(800-797-3303)
Multicultural CD	UXL (D,M)	(800-877-4253)
Oregon Trail II	Learning Company, The (M,W)	(800-685-6322)
Paths to Freedom	Encyclopedia Britannica (M)	(800-554-9862)
Robert E. Lee: Civil War General	Sierra On-Line (W)	(800-853-7788)
Social Science 2000	Decision Development Corp. (M,W)	(800-835-4332)
The American Journals CD	K–12 Micromedia Publishing (M)	(800-292-1997)
The Balkan Odyssey	Chelsea House Publishers (M,W)	(800-848-2665)
The Native Americans	Philips Media Software (M,W)	(800-883-3767)
The Voyages of the Mimi	Sunburst Communications (M,W)	(800-321-7511); www.SUNBURST.com
Time Travel to the 18th Century	Folkus Atlantic (M,W)	(800-780-8266)
Vital Links	Davidson & Associates (M,W)	(800-545-7677)
Who Built America?	Voyager (M)	(800-446-2001)
World History Interactive Library	Thynx (M,W)	(609-514-1600)
World War II	FlagTower Multimedia (W)	(617-338-8720)

addition, the VCR, combined with a video camera, makes it possible to record student activities, practice, projects, and student demonstrations and your own teaching. It gives students a marvelous opportunity to self-assess as they see and hear themselves in action.

Entire course packages, as well as supplements, are now available on videocassettes or on computer software programs. The schools where you student teach and where you eventually are employed may have a collection of such programs. Some teachers make their own.

Carefully selected programs, tapes, discs, films, and slides enhance student learning. For example, CD-ROMs offer quick and efficient accessibility of thousands of visuals, thus providing an appreciated boost to teachers of students with limited language proficiency. With the use of frame control, students can observe phenomena, and in detail, that previous students only read about.

Researchers found that students who read selections on interactive CD-ROMs scored higher on longer and more difficult comprehension passages on tests than did their peers who read the same selections in print.[7] The researchers suggest that the reason is that the CD-ROMs provide instant help for students confronting new vocabulary. Students can click on a word and hear it pronounced, defined, and used in context. Additionally, students enjoy the music, special effects, and interactive approach.

With superior sound and visual performance, just as CD-ROMs replaced videodiscs, the DVD may replace VCR tapes, and computer CD-ROMs. While in appearance it resembles the CD-ROM, the DVD can store nearly 17 gigabytes of information, provide a faster retrieval of data, and can

Figure 10.8
Resources of
information about
CD-ROM titles

- *CD-ROM Finder,* 5th ed., J. Shelton, Ed. (Medford, NJ: Learned Information, 1993).
- *CD-ROM for Librarians and Educators: A Book to Over 300 Instructional Programs,* by B. H. Sorrow and B. S. Lumpkin (Jefferson, NC: McFarland, 1993).
- *CD-ROMs in Print,* Meckler Publishing, 11 Ferry Lane West, Westport, CT 06880.
- *The Directory of Video, Computer, and Audio-Visual Products,* published annually by the International Communications Industries Association, Fairfax, VA.
- Educational Software Institute catalog, 4213 South 94th Street, Omaha, NE 68127 (800-955-5570).

be made interactive. Information about CD-ROM titles for education can be found in the sources shown in Figure 10.8.

Check school supplies catalogs and Internet resources for additional titles and sources. Generally, companies that sell computer software also sell videos and CD-ROMs. Figure 10.9 provides sample addresses from which you may obtain catalogs of information.

Computers and Computer-Based Instructional Tools

As a teacher of the 21st century, you must be computer literate—you must understand and be able to use computers as well as you can read and write. The computer can be valuable to you as a classroom teacher in several ways. For example, the computer can help you manage the instruction by obtaining information, storing and preparing test materials, maintaining attendance and grade records, and preparing programs to aid in the academic development of individual students. This category of uses of the computer is referred to as *computer-managed instruction* (CMI). The computer can also be used for instruction, *computer-assisted instruction,* by employing various instructional software programs. Additionally, the computer can be used to teach about computers and to help students develop their metacognitive skills as well as their skills in computer use.[8]

THE PLACEMENT AND USE OF COMPUTERS: THE ONLINE CLASSROOM

As we embark on this new century, teachers looking to make their classrooms more student-centered, collaborative, and interactive continue to increasingly turn to telecommunications networks. Webs of connected computers allow teachers and students from around the world to reach each other directly and gain access to quantities of information previously unimaginable. Students using networks learn new inquiry and analytical skills in a stimulating environment, and they can also gain an increased awareness of their role as world citizens.

The way you use the computer for instruction is determined by several factors, including your knowledge of and skills in its use, the number of computers that you have available for instructional use, where computers are placed in the school, the software that is available, printer availability, and the telecommunications capabilities (that is, wiring and phone lines, modems, and servers).

Schools continue to purchase or to lease computers and to upgrade their telecommunications capabilities. Regarding computer placement and equipment available, here are some possible scenarios and how classroom teachers work within each.

Scenario 1. In some schools, students go to a computer lab for a relatively brief time each week, or in some upper grades students take "computer" as an elective or as an exploratory course. Students of yours who are simultaneously enrolled in such an experience may be given special computer assignments by you that they can then share with the rest of the class.

Scenario 2. With the assistance of a computer lab and the lab technician or computer technology teacher, computers are integrated into the whole curriculum. In collaboration with members of interdisciplinary teaching teams, in a computer lab students learn to use computers, software, and sources on the Internet as tools to build their knowledge, to write stories with word processors, to illustrate diagrams with paint utilities, to create interactive reports with hypermedia, and to graph data they have gathered using spreadsheets.

Some schools, such as New York City's Mott Hall, a magnet school for gifted and talented children in grades 4 through 8, participate in a program that provides a laptop computer for every student for as long as the child is at the school.[9] The children are given training in the use of the laptop by computer technology teachers. Use of the laptop is incorporated into the

Figure 10.9
Selected resources for videotapes, computer software, CD-ROMs, and interactive multimedia

- A.D.A.M. Software, Inc., 1600 River Edge Pkwy., Station 800, Atlanta, GA 30328, 800-755-2326, ext. 3018, <http://www.adam.com>
- Agency for Instructional Technology, Box A, Bloomington, IN 47402-0120, 800-457-4509, <http://www.ait.net>
- AIMS Multimedia, 9710 DeSoto Ave., Chatsworth, CA 91311, 800-367-2467, <http//www.aims-multimedia.com>
- Broderbund Software, 500 Redwood Blvd., Novato, CA 94948, 800-474-8840, <http://www.broderbund.com>
- Central Scientific Co., P.O. Box 5229, Buffalo Grove, IL 60089, 800-626-3626, <http://www.cenconet.com>
- CLEARVUE/eav, 6465 N. Avondale Ave., Chicago, IL 60631, 800-253-2788, <http://www.CLEARVUE.com>
- Cuisenaire® Dale Seymour Publications, P.O. Box 5026, White Plains, NY 10602-5026, 800-872-1100, <http://www.aw.com/dsp/>
- D & H Distributing Co., 2525 N. 7th St., Harrisburg, PA 17110, 717-255-7841, <http://www.dandh.com>
- DK Publishing & Multimedia, 95 Madison Ave., New York, NY 10016, 212-213-4800, <http://www.dk.com>
- Educational Activities, Inc., 1937 Grand Ave., Baldwin, NY 11510, 800-645-3739, <http://www.edact.com>
- Educational Software Institute (ESI), 4213 S. 94th St., Omaha, NE 68127, 800-955-5570, http://www.edsoft.com>
- Educational Techniques & Technology, 1214C Stonehollow Drive, Kingwood, TX 77338, 800-449-9119, <http://www.ett.com>
- Environmental Media Corp., 1102 11th St., Port Royal, SC 29935, 800-368-3382, <http://www.envmedia.com>
- EME Corp., 10 Cental Pkwy., Station 312, Stuart, FL 34995, 800-848-2050, <http://www.emescience.com>
- ETA, 620 Lakeview Parkway, Vernon Hills, IL 60061-9923, 800-445-5985, <http://www.eta.universe.com>
- Harcourt School Publishers, 6277 Sea Harbor Dr., Orlando, FL 32887, 800-346-8648, <http://www.harcourt.com>
- Higher-Order Thinking Co., 1733 N.E. Patterson Dr., Lee's Summit, MO 64086, 816-524-2701.
- IBM Global Education, 4111 Northside Parkway, Atlanta, GA 30301-2150, 800-426-4968, <http://www.solutions.ibm.com/k12>
- Media Design Associates, 1093 Albion Rd., P.O. Box 3189, Boulder, CO 80307-3189, 800-228-8854, <http://www.indra.com/mediades>
- Mindscape, 88 Rowland Way, Novato, CA 94945, 800-231-3088, <http://www.mindscape.com>
- Modern School Supplies, P.O. Box 958, Hartford, CT 06143, 800-243-2329, <http://www.modernss.com>
- NASCO-Modesto, 4825 Stoddard Rd., P.O. Box 3837, Modesto, CA 95352-3827, 800-558-9595, <http://www.nascofa.com>
- Pitsco, Inc., 915 East Jefferson St., Pittsburg, KS 66762, 800-835-0686, <http://www.pitsco.com>
- Schoolmasters Science, 745 State Circle, P.O. Box 1941, Ann Arbor, MI 48106, 800-521-2832, <http://www.schoolmasters.com>
- Science Kit and Boreal Laboratories, 777 East Park Drive, Tonawanda, NY 14150, 800-828-7777, <http://www.sciencekit.com>
- Sunburst Communications, 101 Castleton St., Pleasantville, NY 10570, 800-321-7511, <http://www.sunburst.com>
- SVE & Churchill Media, 6677 N. Northwest Hwy., Chicago, IL 60631, 800-829-1900, <http://www.SVEmedia.com>
- Tom Snyder Productions, 80 Coolidge Hill Rd., Watertown, MA 02472-5003, 800-342-0236, <http://www.tomsnyder.com>
- Troll School & Library L.L.C., 100 Corporate Drive, Mahwah, NJ 07430, 800-979-8765, <http://www.troll.com>
- Videodiscovery, 1700 Westlake Ave., N., Station 600, Seattle, WA 98109-3012, 800-548-3472, <http://www.videodiscovery.com>

learning in most of their classes at school and they can take their laptop home to work on assignments.

Scenario 3. Some classrooms have a computer connected to a large-screen video monitor. The teacher or a student works the computer, and the entire class can see the monitor screen. As they view the screen, students can verbally respond to and interact with what is happening on the computer.

Scenario 4. Some classrooms are equipped with portable (battery-powered) keyboards, such as AlphaSmart, usually one for each student, and perhaps one classroom computer with printer. The AlphaSmart keyboard enables the user to type, edit, and store text, but without a more expensive computer. The stored text can later be transferred to a computer or printer.[10]

Scenario 5. You may be fortunate to have one or more computers in your classroom for all or for a part of the school year, computers with Internet connections, with CD-ROM playing capabilities, an overhead projector, and a LCD (liquid crystal display) projection system. Coupled with the overhead projector, the LCD projection system allows you to project onto your large wall screen (and TV monitor at the same time) any image from computer software. With this system, all students can see and verbally interact with the multimedia instruction.

Scenario 6. Many classrooms have at least one computer with telecommunications capability, and some have many. When this is the case in your classroom, then you most likely will have one or two students working at the computer while others are doing other learning activities (multilevel teaching). Computers can be an integral part of a learning center and an important aid in your overall effort to personalize the instruction within your classroom.

Selecting Computer Software

When selecting software programs you and your colleagues need, of course, to choose those compatible with your brand of computer(s) and with your instructional objectives.

Programs are continually being developed and enhanced to meet the technology of the new and more powerful computers being made available. For evaluating computer software programs and testing them for their compatibility with your instructional objectives, many forms are available from the local school district, the state department of education, and professional associations.

Sources of Free and Inexpensive Audiovisual Materials

For free and inexpensive audiovisual materials, check Internet sources and your college or university library for sources listed in Figure 10.10.

Using Copyrighted Video, Computer, and Multimedia Programs

You must be knowledgeable about the laws on the use of copyrighted videos and computer software materials. Although space here prohibits full in-

Figure 10.10
Resources for free and inexpensive audiovisual materials

- Best freeware and shareware at <http://wwwl.zdnet.com/pccomp/1001dl/html/1001.html>
- Professional periodicals and journals
- *Catalog of Audiovisual Materials: A Guide to Government Sources* (Ed 198 822), Arlington, VA: ERIC Documents Reproduction Service
- Educator's Progress Service, Inc., 214 Center Street, Randolph, WI 53956 (414-326-3126): *Educator's Guide to Free Audio and Video Materials; Educator's Guide to Free Films; Educator's Guide to Free Filmstrips; Guide to Free Computer Materials; Educator's Guide to Free Science Materials*
- *Video Placement Worldwide (VPW):* Source of free sponsored educational videos on Internet at <http://www.vpw.com>

clusion of United States legal guidelines, your local school district undoubtedly can provide a copy of current district policies to ensure compliance with all copyright laws. As noted earlier in the discussion about the use of printed materials that are copyrighted, when preparing to make any copy you must find out whether the copying is permitted by law under the category of "permitted use." If not allowed under "permitted use," then you must obtain written permission to reproduce the material from the holder of the copyright. Figures 10.11 and 10.12 present guidelines for the copying of videotapes and computer software.

Usually, when purchasing CD-ROMs and other multimedia software packages intended for use by schools, you are also paying for a license to modify and use its contents for instructional purposes. However, not all CD-ROMs include copyright permission, so always check the copyright notice on any disc you purchase and use. Whenever in doubt, don't use it until you have asked your district media specialists about copyrights or have obtained necessary permissions from the original source.

As yet, there are no guidelines for fair use of films, filmstrips, slides, and multimedia programs. A general rule of thumb for use of any copyrighted material is to treat the work of others as you would want your own material treated were it protected by a copyright (see Figure 10.13).

Figure 10.11
Copyright law for off-air videotaping
Source: R. Heinich, M. Molenda, J. D. Russell, and S. E. Smaldino, *Instructional Media and Technologies for Learning,* 6th ed. (Upper Saddle River, NJ: Merrill/Prentice Hall, 1999), p. 389. By permission of Prentice Hall.

PERMITTED USES

You may

1. Request your media center or audiovisual coordinator to record a program for you if you cannot or if you lack the equipment.
2. Keep a videotaped copy of a broadcast (including cable transmission) for forty-five calendar days, after which the program must be erased.
3. Use the program in class once during the first ten schools days of the forty-five calendar days, and a second time if instruction needs to be reinforced.
4. Have professional staff view the program several times for evaluation purposes during the full forty-five day period.
5. Make a few copies to meet legitimate needs, but these copies must be erased when the original videotape is erased.
6. Use only a part of the program if instructional needs warrant.
7. Enter into a licensing agreement with the copyright holder to continue use of the program.

PROHIBITED USES

You may not

1. Videotape premium cable services such as HBO without express permission.
2. Alter the original content of the program.
3. Exclude the copyright notice on the program.
4. Videorecord before a request for use is granted—the request to record must come from an instructor.
5. Keep the program, and any copies, after forty-five days.

Figure 10.12
Copyright law for use of computer software
Source: December 1980 Congressional amendment to the 1976 Copyright Act.

PERMITTED USES

You may

1. Make a single back-up or archival copy of the computer program.
2. Adapt the computer program to another language if the program is unavailable in the target language.
3. Add features to make better use of the computer program.

PROHIBITED USES

You may not

1. Make multiple copies.
2. Make replacement copies from an archival or back-up copy.
3. Make copies of copyrighted programs to be sold, leased, loaned, transmitted, or given away.

Figure 10.13
Fair use guidelines
for using multimedia
programs

1. For portions of copyrighted works used in your own multimedia production for use in teaching, follow normal copyright guidelines (e.g., the limitations on the amount of material used, whether it be motion media, text, music, illustrations, photographs, or computer software).
2. You may display your own multimedia work using copyrighted works to other teachers, such as in workshops. However, you may *not* make and distribute copies to colleagues without obtaining permission from copyright holders.
3. You may use your own multimedia production for instruction over an electronic network (e.g., distance learning) provided there are limits to access and to the number of students enrolled. You may *not* distribute such work over any electronic network (local area or wide area) without expressed permission from copyright holders.
4. You must obtain permissions from copyright holders before using any copyrighted materials in educational multimedia production for commercial reproduction and distribution or before replicating more than one copy, distributing copies to others, or for use beyond your own classroom.

SUMMARY

You have learned of the variety of tools available to supplement your instruction. When used wisely, these tools will help you to reach more of your students more of the time. As you know, teachers must meet the needs of a diversity of students—many of whom are linguistically and culturally different. The material selected and presented in this chapter should be of help in doing that. The future will undoubtedly continue bringing technological innovations that will be even more helpful—compact discs, computers, and telecommunications equipment have only marked the beginning of a revolution in teaching. As we move forward in the 21st century, new instructional delivery systems made possible by microcomputers and multimedia workstations will likely fundamentally alter what had become the traditional role of the classroom teacher during the 20th century.

You should remain alert to developing technologies for your teaching. Digital videodiscs (DVDs), CD-ROMs interfaced with computers (i.e., the use of multimedia), and telecommunications offer exciting technologies for learning. New instructional technologies are advancing at an increasingly rapid rate. You and your colleagues must maintain vigilance over new developments, constantly looking for those not only that will help make student learning meaningful and interesting and your teaching effective, but that are cost-effective as well.

EXTENDING MY COMPETENCY: QUESTIONS FOR CLASS DISCUSSION _____

1. Explain how your effective use of the writing board and bulletin board can help students see relationships among verbal concepts or information.
2. Describe what you should look for when deciding whether material that you have obtained free or inexpensively is appropriate for use in your teaching.
3. Meet with a peer and tell each other how you would respond to a parent who questioned you about the benefit of using CD-ROM material in teaching.
4. Share with others in your class your knowledge, observations, and feelings about the use of multimedia and telecommunications for teaching. From your discussion, what more would you like to know about the use of multimedia and telecommunications for teaching? How might you learn more about these things?
5. In 1922 Thomas Edison predicted that "the motion picture is destined to revolutionize our educational system and . . . in a few years it will supplant largely, if not entirely, the use of textbooks." In 1945 William Levenson of the Cleveland public schools' radio station claimed that "the time may come when a portable radio receiver will be as common in the classroom as is the blackboard." In the early 1960s B. F. Skinner believed that with the help of the new teaching machines and programmed instruction, students could learn twice as much in the same time and with the same effort as in a standard classroom. Did motion pictures, radio, programmed instruction, and television revolutionize education?

Will computers become as much a part of the classroom as writing boards? What do you predict the public school classroom of the year 2050 will be like? Will the role of a teacher be different in any way than it is today?

6. Select and identify one instructional tool that is *not* discussed in this chapter, and explain to your classmates its advantages and disadvantages for use in teaching a subject and grade level of your choice.

7. Has the purchase of new textbooks and library books become stagnated as schools increase their spending on leading-edge technology? Have any programs suffered as a result of increased expenditures on technology? How are school districts finding funds necessary for the cost of technology, such as for the cost of wiring classrooms for networking and for updated computers, and for the planning, installation, and maintenance of complex computer networks? Or are districts finding the necessary funds? In this respect, are some districts worse off or better off than others? Is this an issue? And if so, is it an issue for which every classroom teacher needs be aware?

8. Describe any prior concepts you held that changed as a result of your experiences with this chapter. Describe the changes.

9. From your current observations and fieldwork as related to this teacher preparation program, clearly identify one specific example of educational practice that seems contradictory to exemplary practice or theory as presented in this chapter. Present your explanation for the discrepancy.

10. Do you have questions generated by the content of this chapter? If you do, list them along with ways answers might be found.

FOR FURTHER READING

Barron, A. E., and Ivers, K. S. (1998). *The Internet and Instruction: Activities and Ideas* (2nd ed.). Englewood, CO: Libraries Unlimited.

Bridges, D. L., and F. L. DeVaull. (1999). Now That We Have It, What Do We Do With It? Using the Web in the Classroom. *Intervention in School and Clinic, 34*(3), 181–187.

Churma, M. (1999). *A Guide to Integrating Technology Standards into the Curriculum.* Upper Saddle River, NJ: Merrill/Prentice Hall.

Cotton, E. G. (1998). *The Online Classroom: Teaching With the Internet* (3rd ed.). Bloomington, IN: ED-INFO Press.

Curchy, C., and Kyker, K. (1998). *Educator's Survival Guide to TV Production Equipment and Setup.* Englewood, CO: Libraries Unlimited.

Dalton, B. (2000). Exploring Literacy on the Internet. *The Reading Teacher, 53*(8), 684–693.

Donlevy, J. G., and Donlevy, T. R. (1999). wNetSchool. *International Journal of Instructional Media, 26*(1), 9–10.

Ertmer, P. A.; Hruskocy, C.; and Woods, D. M. (2000). *Education on the Internet.* Upper Saddle River, NJ: Merrill/Prentice Hall.

Foshay, J. D. (1999). *Project-Based Multimedia Instruction* (Fastback 445). Bloomington, IN: Phi Delta Kappa Educational Foundation.

Harms, J. M., and Lettow, L. (1996). *Picture Books to Enhance the Curriculum.* New York: H. W. Wilson.

Harris, J. (1998). *Design Tools for the Internet-Supported Classroom.* Alexandria, VA: Association for Supervision and Curriculum Development.

Heide, A., and Stillborne, L. (1999). *The Teacher's Complete & Easy Guide to the Internet* (2nd ed.). New York: Teachers College Press.

Heller, N. (1998). *Technology Connections for Grades 3–5. Research Projects and Activities.* Englewood, CO: Libraries Unlimited.

Jarchow, E., Midkiff, R., and Pickert, S. (Eds.). (1998). *Practical Lessons to Promote a Global Perspective in Elementary Education.* Washington, DC: American Association of Colleges for Teacher Education.

Jonassen, D. H., Peck, K. L., and Wilson, B. G. (1999). *Learning With Technology: A Constructivist Perspective.* Upper Saddle River, NJ: Merrill/Prentice Hall.

Kahn, J. (1998). *Ideas and Strategies for the One-Computer Classroom.* Eugene, OR: International Society for Technology in Education.

Lapp, D., Flood, J., and Fisher, D. (1999). Intermediality: How the Use of Multiple Media Enhances Learning. *The Reading Teacher, 52*(7), 776–780.

Leu, D. J., Jr. (2000). Exploring Literacy on the Internet. *The Reading Teacher, 53*(5), 424–429.

Leu, D. J., Jr., Leu, D. D., and Leu, K. R. (1999). *Teaching With the Internet: Lessons from the Classroom.* Norwood, MA: Christopher-Gordon.

McCullen, C. (1999). The Hows and Whys of Conducting Desktop Teleconferences. *Middle Ground, 2*(3), 7–8.

Miller, E. B. (1998). *The Internet Resource Directory for K–12 Teachers and Librarians* (97/98 ed.). Englewood, CO: Libraries Unlimited.

Newby, T. J., Stepich, D. A., Lehman, J. D., and Russell, J. D. (2000). *Instructional Technology for Teaching and Learning* (2nd ed.). Upper Saddle River, NJ: Merrill/Prentice Hall.

Pinhey, L. A. (1998). *Global Education: Internet Resources* (ERIC Digest 417124). Bloomington, IN: ERIC Clearinghouse for Social Studies/Social Science Education.

Roblyer, M. D. (1999). *Integrating Technology Across the Curriculum: A Database of Strategies and Lesson Plans.* Upper Saddle River, NJ: Merrill/Prentice Hall.

Roblyer, M. D., and Edwards, J. (2000). *Integrating Educational Technology Into Teaching* (2nd ed.). Upper Saddle River, NJ: Merrill-Prentice Hall.

Schank, R. C. (2000). A Vision of Education for the 21st Century. *T·H·E Journal, 27*(6), 42–45.

Tapscott, D. (1999). Educating the Net Generation. *Educational Leadership, 56*(5), 6–11.

Teicher, J. (1999). An Action Plan for Smart Internet Use. *Educational Leadership, 56*(5), 70–74.

Wallace, R. M., Kupperman, J., Krajcik, J., and Soloway, E. (2000). Science on the Web: Students Online in a Sixth-Grade Classroom. *Journal of the Learning Sciences, 9*(1), 75–104.

Weinman, J., and Haag, P. (1999). Gender Equity in Cyberspace. *Educational Leadership, 56*(5), 44–49.

Worthy, J., Moorman, M., and Turner, M. (1999). What Johnny Likes to Read Is Hard to Find in School. *Reading Research Quarterly, 34*(1), 12–27.

Zirkel, P. A. Discipline on Field Trips. *Principal* 80(3):60–61 (January 2001).

Zirkel, P. A. Liability for Field Trips. *Principal* 80(2):60–61 (November 2000).

NOTES

1. For a copy of the National Education Association (NEA) guidelines for teachers to consider before purchasing or using commercial materials, contact NEA Communications, 1201 16th Street, NW, Washington, DC 20036; phone (202) 822-7200.

2. See also the *Copyright and Fair Use* Web site of Stanford University at <http://fairuse.stanford.edu/>.

3. See M. Mullan, Modern Classrooms See Chalkboards Left in the Dust, *Education Week, 19*(17), 6 (January 12, 2000).

4. Sources of electronic whiteboards include Micro-Touch, Tewksbury, MA (800-642-7686); Numonics, Montgomeryville, PA (215-362-2766); Smart Technologies, Calgary, AB, Canada (403-245-0333); SoftBoard, Portland, OR (888-763-8262); and TEGRITY, San Jose, CA (408-369-5150).

5. D. Lapp; J. Flood; and D. Fisher, Intermediality: How the Use of Multiple Media Enhances Learning, *Reading Teacher, 52*(7), 776–780 (April 1999).

6. For descriptions of sample multimedia projects, see J. D. Foshay, *Project-Based Multimedia Instruction,* Fastback 445 (Bloomington, IN: Phi Delta Kappa Educational Foundation, 1999), pp. 36–47.

7. R. Olson and R. Meyer, News: Survey Says CD-ROMs Boost Reading Scores, *School Library Journal, 41*(9), 108 (September 1995).

8. See, for example, X. Bornas, et al., Preventing Impulsivity in the Classroom: How Computers Can Help Teachers, *Computers in the Schools, 13*(1–2), 27–40 (1997).

9. See M. A. Zehr, Laptops for All Doesn't Mean They're Always Used, *Education Week, 19*(39), 1, 14–15 (June 7, 2000).

10. See <http://www.alphasmart.com> or contact Alpha-Smart at 20400 Stevens Creek Boulevard, Suite 300, Cupertino, CA 95014, phone 888-274-0680.

Assessment and Professional Development

Part IV discusses your needs concerning:

- Authentic assessment of student learning
- Continuing professional development
- Finding a teaching job
- Grading and reporting student achievement
- Involving students in self-assessment
- Meeting and conferencing with parents and guardians
- Performance-based assessment
- Preparing assessment items
- Preparing and administering tests
- Scoring rubrics
- Standardized and nonstandardized achievement testing
- Student teaching
- Teacher self-assessment through micro peer teaching
- The emergency teaching kit
- The role and techniques of assessment in student learning

REFLECTIVE THOUGHTS

When assessing for student achievement, it is important to use procedures that are compatible with the instructional objectives.

Performance-based assessment procedures require students to produce rather than to select responses.

That which separates the professional teacher from "anyone off the street" is the teacher's ability to go beyond mere description of a student's behavior.

For students' continued intellectual and emotional development, your comments about their work should be useful, productive, analytical, diagnostic, and prescriptive.

You must provide opportunities for students to think about what they are learning, how they are learning it, and how far they have progressed in learning it.

A teacher's concern should not be with deciding which students are better than others but to helping all of them succeed.

The primary professional task of any teacher is not to punish the learner, but to facilitate the learner's understanding (perception) of a goal, and help the learner identify acceptable behaviors positively designed to reach that goal.

Important decisions that affect an individual child's educational career should not rest on just one test score alone but on multiple sources of data.

11

How Do I Assess and Report Student Achievement?

While preceding parts of this resource guide addressed the *why* (Part I), *what* (Part II), and *how* (Part III) of teaching, Part IV focuses on the fourth and final component—the *how well,* or assessment, component. Together, as discussed in the preface of this resource guide, these four components comprise the essentials of effective instruction.

Teaching and learning are reciprocal processes that depend on and affect one another. Thus, the assessment component deals with both how well the students are learning and how well the teacher is teaching. This chapter addresses the first.

Assessment is an integral part and ongoing process in the educational arena. Curricula, buildings, materials, specific courses, teachers, specialists, administrators, equipment—all must be periodically assessed in relation to student learning, the purpose of the school. When gaps between anticipated results and student achievement exist, efforts are made to eliminate those factors that seem to be limiting the educational output or, in some other way, to improve the situation. Thus, educational progress occurs.

To learn effectively, students need to know how they are doing. Similarly, to be an effective teacher, you must be informed about what the student knows, feels, and can do so that you can help the student build on the student's skills, knowledge, and attitudes. Therefore you and your students need continuous feedback on their progress and problems to plan appropriate learning activities and to make adjustments to those already planned. If this feedback says that progress is slow, you can provide alternative activities; if it indicates that some or all of the students have already mastered the desired learning, you can eliminate unnecessary activities and practice for some or all of the students. In short, assessment provides a key for both effective teaching and learning.

The importance of continuous assessment mandates that you know various principles and techniques of assessment. This chapter explains some of those and shows you how to construct and use assessment instruments. It defines terms related to assessment, suggests procedures to use in the construction of assessment items, points out the advantages and disadvantages of different types of assessment items and procedures, and explains the construction and use of alternative assessment devices.

In addition, this chapter discusses grading (or marking) and reporting of student achievement, two responsibilities that can consume much of a teacher's time. Grading is time-consuming and frustrating for many teachers. What should be graded? Should grades or marks represent student growth, level of achievement in a group, effort, attitude, general behavior, or a combination of these? What should determine grades—homework, tests, projects, presentations, class participation and group work, or some combination of these? And, what should be their relative weights? These are just a few of the questions that plague teachers, parents and guardians, and indeed the profession; they have persisted for a century or more of education in this country.

The development of the student encompasses growth in the cognitive, affective, and psychomotor domains. Traditional objective paper-and-pencil tests provide only a portion of the data needed to indicate student progress in those do-

mains. Many experts today, as indeed they have in the past, question the traditional sources of data and encourage the search for, development of, and use of alternative means to assess more authentically the students' development of thinking and higher-level learning. While best practices in assessment continue to evolve, one point that is clear is that various techniques of assessment must be used to determine how the student works, what the student is learning, and what the student can produce as a result of that learning. As a teacher, you must develop a repertoire of means of assessing learner behavior and academic progress.

Although marks and grades have been a part of school for about 100 years, it is clear to many experts that the conventional report card with marks or grades falls short of being a developmentally appropriate procedure for reporting the academic performance or progress of children. Some schools are experimenting with other ways of reporting student achievement in learning, but letter grades for intermediate grades and higher still seem firmly entrenched.

Today's interest is (or should be) more on what the student can do (performance testing) as a result of learning than merely on what the student can recall (memory testing) from the experience. As a result of these and other concerns, a variety of systems of assessment and reporting have evolved, are still evolving, and will likely continue to evolve throughout your professional career.[1]

When teachers are aware of alternative systems, they may be able to develop assessment and reporting processes that are fair and effective for particular situations. So, after beginning with assessment, the final focus in this chapter considers today's principles and practices in grading and reporting student achievement.

CHAPTER OBJECTIVES

Specifically, upon completion of this chapter you should be able to

1. Compare and contrast a dozen types of assessment items and prepare examples of each for your own teaching.
2. Compare and contrast three avenues for assessing student learning.
3. Demonstrate an understanding of the importance and roles of assessment in teaching and learning.
4. Demonstrate knowledge of alternate assessment strategies, especially for use with affective and psychomotor domain learning.

5. Demonstrate knowledge of importance of and cautions for maintaining records of student achievement in learning.

6. Describe means by which parents and guardians can cooperate in the education of the children.

7. Describe the importance of reflection and self-assessment in teaching and learning.

8. Differentiate among diagnostic assessment, summative assessment, and formative assessment, with examples of when and how each can be used at a particular grade level or discipline.

9. Differentiate the terms *measurement, reliability,* and *validity* and their relationship to assessment.

10. Explain how and why rubrics, checklists, portfolios, and journals are used in the assessment of student learning.

11. Explain the meaning and value of using direct (also known as performance-based, criterion-referenced, or outcome-based) measurement when assessing for student achievement.

12. Explain the intended meaning of the term *authentic assessment* and demonstrate awareness of the term's synonyms.

13. Explain the meaning of *assessment* as a continuous progress.

14. Explain the value of and give an example of a performance assessment that could be used at a particular grade level or discipline.

15. Explain why criterion-referenced grading is preferred over norm-referenced grading.

PURPOSES AND PRINCIPLES OF ASSESSMENT

Assessment of achievement in student learning is designed to serve several purposes:

1. *To assist in student learning.* This is the purpose usually first thought of when speaking of assessment, and it is the principal topic of this chapter. For the classroom teacher it is (or should be) the most important purpose.

2. *To identify children's strengths and weaknesses.* Identification and assessment of children's strengths and weaknesses are necessary for two reasons: to structure and restructure the learning activities and to restructure the curriculum. Concerning the first, for example, data on student strengths and weaknesses in content and process skills are important in planning activities appropriate for both skill development and intellectual development. This is *diagnostic assessment* (known also as *preassessment* or *assessment*

of student readiness). For the second, data on student strengths and weaknesses in content and skills are useful for making appropriate modifications to the curriculum.

3. *To assess the effectiveness of a particular instructional strategy.* It is important for you to know how well a particular strategy helped accomplish a particular goal or achieve a specific objective. Skilled teachers continually reflect on and evaluate their strategy choices, using a number of sources: student achievement as measured by assessment instruments, their own intuition, informal feedback given by the students, and, sometimes, informal feedback given by colleagues, such as members of a teaching team or mentor teachers. (The topic of mentor teachers is presented in Chapter 12.)

4. *To assess and improve the effectiveness of curriculum programs.* Components of the curriculum are continually assessed by committees composed of teachers and administrators and sometimes parents, guardians, and students and other members of the school and community. The assessment is usually done both while students are learning (i.e., *formative assessment*) and after the instruction (*summative assessment*).

5. *To assess and improve teaching effectiveness.* To improve student learning, teachers are periodically evaluated on the basis of (a) their commitment to working with students at a particular level, (b) their ability to cope with students at a particular age, developmental, or grade level, and (c) their ability to show mastery of appropriate instructional techniques—techniques that are articulated throughout this resource guide.

6. *To provide data that assist in decision making about a child's future.* Assessment of student achievement is important in guiding decision making about grade level and program placement, promotion, school transfer, and eligibility for special recognition and perhaps career planning.

7. *To provide data to communicate with and involve parents and guardians in their children's learning.* Parents and guardians, communities, and school boards all share accountability for the effectiveness of students' learning. Today's schools are reaching out more than ever before and engaging parents, guardians, and the community in their children's education. All teachers play an important role in the process of communicating with, reaching out to, and involving parents, guardians, and the community.

Because the welfare and, indeed, the future of so many people depend on the outcomes of learning assessment, it is impossible to overemphasize its importance. For a learning endeavor to be successful, the learner must have answers to basic questions: Where am I going? Where am I now? How do I get where I am going? How will I know when I get there? Am I on the right track for getting there? These questions are critical to a good program of assessment. Of course, in the process of teaching and learning, the answers may be ever changing, and the teacher and students continue to assess and adjust plans as appropriate and necessary. As you have undoubtedly come to realize, the exemplary elementary school is in a mode of continuous change and progress.

Based on the preceding questions are the following principles that guide the assessment program and that are reflected in the discussions in this chapter. Although stated separately, the principles are inextricably interconnected.

- A teacher's responsibility is to facilitate student learning and to assess student progress in that learning, and for that, the teacher is, or should be, held accountable.
- Assessment is a continuous process. The selection and implementation of plans and activities require continuing monitoring and assessment to check on progress and to change or adopt strategies to promote desired behavior.
- Assessment is a reciprocal process, which includes assessment of teacher performance as well as student achievement.
- Evidence and input data for knowing how well the teacher and students are doing should come from a variety of sources and types of data-collecting devices.
- Reflection and self-assessment are important components of any successful assessment program. Reflection and self-assessment are important if children are to develop the skills necessary for them to assume increasingly greater ownership of their own learning. Reflection and self-assessment are important for a teacher's continued and developing professional competency.
- Students need to know how well they are doing.
- Teachers need to know how well they are doing.
- The program of assessment should aid teaching effectiveness and contribute to the intellectual and psychological growth of students.

TERMS USED IN ASSESSMENT

When discussing the assessment component of teaching and learning, it is easy to be confused by the plethora of terminology. The following clarification of terms is offered to aid your reading and comprehension.

Assessment and Evaluation

Although some authors distinguish between the terms **assessment** (the process of finding out what students are learning, a relatively neutral process) and **evaluation** (making sense of what was found out, a subjective process), in this text we do not. For the purposes of this resource guide, we consider the difference too slight to matter.

Measurement and Assessment

Measurement refers to quantifiable data about specific behaviors. Tests and the statistical procedures used to analyze the results are examples. Measurement is a descriptive and objective process; that is, it is relatively free from human value judgments.

Assessment includes objective data from measurement but also other types of information; some are more subjective, such as information from anecdotal records and teacher observations and ratings of student performance. In addition to the use of objective data (data from measurement), assessment also includes arriving at value judgments (the evaluation aspect of assessment) made on the basis of subjective information.

An example of the use of these terms is as follows. A teacher may share the information that Hannah Lincoln received a score in the 90th percentile on the state's fifth-grade achievement test in reading (a statement of measurement) but may add that "according to my assessment of her work in reading in my class, she has not been an outstanding student" (a statement of evaluation and assessment).

Validity and Reliability

The degree to which a measuring instrument actually measures that which it is intended to measure is the instrument's **validity.** For example, when we ask if an instrument (such as a performance assessment instrument) has validity, key questions concerning that instrument are:

- Does the instrument adequately sample the intended content?
- Does the instrument measure the cognitive, affective, and psychomotor knowledge and skills that are important to the unit of content being tested?
- Does the instrument sample all the instructional objectives of that unit?

The accuracy with which a technique consistently measures that which it does measure is its **reliability.** If, for example, you know that you weigh 118 pounds, and a scale consistently records 118 pounds when you stand on it, then that scale has reliability. However, if the same scale consistently records 110 pounds when you stand on it, we can still say the scale has reliability. By this example, then, it should be clear to you that an instrument could be reliable (it produces similar results when used again and again) although not necessarily valid. In this second instance, the scale is not measuring what it is supposed to measure, so while it is reliable, it is not valid. Although a technique might be reliable but not valid, a technique must have reliability before it can have validity. The greater the number of test items or situations for a particular content objective, the higher the reliability. The higher the reliability, the more consistency there will be in students' scores measuring their understanding of that particular objective.

Authentic Assessment: Advantages and Disadvantages

When assessing for student achievement, it is important that you use procedures that are compatible with the instructional objectives. This is referred to as **authentic assessment.** Other terms used for authentic assessment are *accurate, active, aligned, alternative,* and *direct* (see discussion in Chapter 5). Although it is sometimes used, *performance assessment* refers to the type of student response being assessed, whereas *authentic assessment* refers to the assessment situation. Although not all performance assessments are authentic, assessments that are authentic are most assuredly performance assessments.

In language arts, for example, although it may seem fairly easy to develop a criterion-referenced test, administer it, and grade it, tests often measure language skills rather than language use. It is extremely difficult to measure students' communicative competence with a test. Tests do not measure listening and talking very well, and a test on punctuation marks, for example, does not indicate students' ability to add punctuation marks to a set of sentences created by someone else or to proofread and spot punctuation errors in someone else's writing.[2] An alternative and far better approach is to examine how students use punctuation marks in their own writing. For the authentic assessment of the student's understanding of that which the student has been learning, you would use a performance-based assessment procedure.

Consider another example. "If students have been actively involved in classifying objects using multiple characteristics, it sends them a confusing message if they are then required to take a paper-and-pencil test that asks them to 'define classification' or recite a memorized list of characteristics of good classifications schemes."[3] An authentic assessment technique would be a performance item that actually involves the students in classifying objects. In other words, to obtain an accurate assessment of a student's learning, the teacher uses a performance-based assessment procedure, that is, a procedure that requires students to produce rather than to select a response.

Advantages claimed for the use of authentic assessment include (a) the direct (also known as performance-based, criterion-referenced, or outcome-based) measurement of what students should know and can do and (b) an emphasis on higher-order thinking. On the other hand, disadvantages of authentic assessment include (a) a higher cost, (b) difficulty in making results consistent and usable, and (c) problems with validity, reliability, and comparability.

Unfortunately, a teacher may never see a particular student again after a given school semester or year is over, and thus the teacher may never observe the effects he or she has had on a student's values and attitudes. In schools where groups or teams of teachers remain with the same cohort of students for longer than the traditional time—as in looping programs—those teachers often do have better opportunity to observe the positive changes in their students' values and attitudes.

ASSESSING STUDENT LEARNING: THREE AVENUES

There are three general avenues open to you for assessing a student's achievement in learning. You can assess:

1. What the student *says*—for example, the quantity and quality of a student's contributions to class discussions
2. What the student *does*—for example, a student's performance (e.g., the amount and quality of a student's participation in the learning activities and performance tests)
3. What the student *writes*—for example, as shown by items in the student's portfolio (e.g., homework assignments, checklists, project work, and written tests)

Figure 11.1
Sample form for evaluating and recording a student's verbal and nonverbal behaviors

Objective	Desired behavior	What student did, said, or wrote

Student _____ Grade/Subject _____ School _____

Observer _____ Date _____ Period/Time _____

Teacher's (observer's) comments:

Importance and Weight of Each Avenue

While your own situation and personal philosophy will dictate the levels of importance and weight you give to each avenue of assessment, you should have a strong rationale if you value and weigh the three avenues for assessment differently than one-third each.

Assessing What a Student Says and Does

When evaluating what a student says, you should (a) listen to the student's oral reports, questions, responses, and interactions with others and (b) observe the student's attentiveness, involvement in class activities, creativeness, and responses to challenges including the challenges afforded by performance testing. Notice that we say you should *listen*

and *observe*. While listening to what the student is saying, you should also be observing the student's nonverbal behaviors. For this you can use narrative observation forms (see Figure 11.1) and you can use observations with behavioral checklists and scoring rubrics (see sample checklists in Figures 11.2, 11.4, and 11.5, and sample scoring rubrics in Figures 8.2, 11.2 and 11.3), and periodic conferences with the student.

With each technique used, you must proceed from your awareness of anticipated learning outcomes (the learning target or instructional objectives), and you must assess a student's progress toward meeting those objectives. That is referred to as direct or **criterion-referenced assessment.**

Observation Form
Figure 11.1 illustrates a sample generic form for recording and evaluating teacher observations of a student's verbal and nonverbal behaviors. With

Figure 11.2
Checklist and rubric
compared

Sample rubric for assessing a student's skill in listening.

Score Point 3—Strong listener:
    Responds immediately to oral directions
    Focuses on speaker
    Maintains appropriate attention span
    Listens to what others are saying
    Is interactive
Score Point 2—Capable listener:
    Follows oral directions
    Usually attentive to speaker and to discussions
    Listens to others without interrupting
Score Point 1—Developing listener:
    Has difficulty following directions
    Relies on repetition
    Often inattentive
    Has short attention span
    Often interrupts the speaker

Sample checklist for assessing a student's skill in map work:

    Check each item if the map comes up to standard in this particular category.
    _____ 1. Accuracy
    _____ 2. Neatness
    _____ 3. Attention to details

---

modern technology, such as is afforded, for example, by the software program *Learner Profile,* a teacher can record observations electronically anywhere at any time.[4]

Checklist versus Scoring Rubric

As you can see from the sample rubric and sample checklist shown in Figure 11.2, there is little difference between what is a checklist and what is a rubric: The difference is that rubrics show the degrees for the desired characteristics while checklists usually show only the desired characteristics. The checklist could easily be made into a scoring rubric and the rubric could easily be made into a checklist.

Guidelines for Assessing What a Student Says and Does

When assessing a student's verbal and nonverbal behaviors in the classroom you should:

1. Maintain an anecdotal record book (teacher's log) or folder, with a separate section in it for your records of each student.
2. For a specific activity, list the desirable behaviors.
3. Check the list against the specific instructional objectives.
4. Record your observations as quickly as possible following your observation. Audio or video recordings, and, of course, computer software programs, can help you maintain records and check the accuracy of your memory, but if this

is inconvenient, you should spend time during school, immediately after school, or later that evening recording your observations while they are still fresh in your memory.

5. Record your professional judgment about the child's progress toward the desired behavior, but think it through before transferring it to a permanent record.
6. Write comments that are reminders to yourself, such as, "Discuss observation with the student," "Check validity of observation by further testing," and "Discuss observations with colleague."

Assessing What a Student Writes

When assessing what a student writes, you can use worksheets, written homework and assignment papers, student journal writing, student writing projects, student portfolios, and tests (all discussed later in this chapter). In many schools, portfolios, worksheets, and homework assignments are the tools usually used for the formative evaluation of each student's achievement. Tests, too, should be a part of this evaluation, but tests are also used for summative evaluation at the end of a unit and for diagnostic purposes.

Your summative evaluation of a student's achievement and any other final judgment made by you about a student can have impact upon the

Figure 11.3
Sample scoring
rubric for assessing
student writing
Source: Texas Education
Agency, *Writing Inservice
Guide for English
Language Arts and TAAS*
(Austin, TX: Author, 1993).

> *Score Point 4*—correct purpose, mode, audience; effective elaboration; consistent organization; clear sense of order and completeness; fluent
>
> *Score Point 3*—correct purpose, mode, audience; moderately well elaborated; organized but possible brief digressions; clear, effective language
>
> *Score Point 2*—correct purpose, mode, audience; some elaboration; some specific details; gaps in organization; limited language control
>
> *Score Point 1*—attempts to address audience; brief, vague, unelaborated; wanders off topic; lack of language control; little or no organization; wrong purpose and mode

emotional and intellectual development of that child. Special attention is given to this later in the section, Recording Teacher Observations and Judgments.

Guidelines for Assessing Student Writing

Use the following guidelines when assessing what a student writes.

Student writing assignments, test items, and scoring rubrics (see Figure 11.3) *should be criterion-referenced,* that is, they should correlate and be compatible with specific instructional objectives. Regardless of the avenue chosen, and their relative weights given by you, you must evaluate against the instructional objectives. Any given objective may be checked by using more than one method and more than one instrument. Subjectivity, inherent in the assessment process, may be reduced as you check for validity, comparing results of one measuring strategy against those of another.

Read everything a student writes. If it is important for the student to do the work, then it is equally important that you give your professional attention to the product of the student's efforts. Of course, as emphasized in Chapter 8, in deference to the teacher's productive and efficient use of valuable time student papers can be read with varying degrees of intensity and scrutiny, depending on the purpose of the assignment.

Provide written or verbal comments about the student's work, and be positive in those comments. Rather than just writing *good* on a student's paper, briefly state what it was about the student's work that made it good. Rather than simply saying or pointing out that the student didn't do it right, tell or show the student what is acceptable and how to achieve it. For reinforcement, use positive rewards and encouragement as frequently as possible. Remember, the child is a work in progress; if there is something that the child has yet to learn, then your job as the child's teacher is to give instruction that is necessary for the child to learn it.

Think before writing any comment on a student's paper, asking yourself how you think the student (or a parent or guardian) will interpret and react to the comment and whether that is a correct interpretation or reaction to your intended meaning.

Avoid writing evaluative comments or grades in student journals. Student journals are for encouraging students to write, to think about their thinking, and to record their creative thoughts. In journal writing, students should be encouraged to write about their experiences in and out of school and especially about their experiences and feelings related to what is being learned and how they are learning it. Writing (and drawing) in journals gives them practice in expressing themselves in written form and in connecting their learning and should provide nonthreatening freedom to do it. Avoid correcting spelling or grammar or making value statements. Comments and evaluations from teachers might discourage creative and spontaneous expression. You can write simple empathic comments such as "Thank you for sharing your thoughts," or "I think I understand why you feel that way."

When reading student journals, talk individually with students to seek clarification about their expressions but avoid pushing the child into uneasiness and sharing more than the child wants to share. Student journals are useful to the teacher in understanding the student's thought processes and writing skills and should not be graded. For grading purposes, teachers may simply record whether the student is maintaining a journal and, perhaps, a judgment about the quantity of writing in it: But no judgment should be made about the quality of the writing.

When reviewing student portfolios, discuss with children individually their learning progress as witnessed by the materials in their portfolios. As with student journals, the portfolio should not be graded or compared in any way with those of other children. Its purpose is for student self-assessment and to evidence progress in learning. For this to happen, students should maintain in their portfolios all or major samples of papers. (Student journals and portfolios are discussed further later in this chapter.)

Assessment for Affective and Psychomotor Domain Learning: Alternative Assessment Procedures

While assessment of cognitive domain learning lends itself to traditional written tests of achievement, the assessment of learning within the affective and psychomotor domains is best suited by the use of performance checklists where student behaviors can be observed in action. However, many educators today are encouraging the use of alternative assessment procedures (i.e., alternatives to traditional paper-and-pencil written testing). After all, in learning that is most important and that has the most meaning to students, the domains are inextricably interconnected. Learning that is meaningful to children is not as easily compartmentalized as the taxonomies of educational objectives would imply. Alternative assessment strategies include the use of group projects, portfolios, skits, papers, oral presentations, and performance tests.

STUDENT INVOLVEMENT IN ASSESSMENT

Students' continuous self-assessment should be planned as an important component of the assessment program. If children are to progress in their intellectual development, then they must receive instruction and guidance in how to become more responsible for their own learning. During that empowerment process they learn to think better of themselves and of their individual capabilities. To achieve this self-understanding and improved self-esteem requires the experiences afforded by successes, along with guidance in self-understanding and self-assessment.

To meet these goals, teachers provide opportunities for children to think about what they are learning, about how they are learning it, and about how far they have progressed. One procedure is for students to maintain portfolios of their work, using rating scales or checklists periodically to self-assess their progress.

Using Student Portfolios

Portfolios are used by teachers as a means of instruction and by teachers and students as one means of self-reflection and of assessing student learning. Though there is little research to support or refute the claim, educators believe that the instructional value comes from the process of the student's assembling and maintaining a personal portfolio. During that creative process the student is expected to self-reflect and to think critically about what has and is being learned, and the student is assuming some degree of responsibility for her or his own learning.[5]

Student portfolios can be grouped into four general categories. In a given situation the purpose of portfolios could transcend any combination of the four. The categories are (a) *selected works portfolio,* in which students maintain samples of their work as prompted by the teacher, (b) *showcase portfolio,* which includes selections made by each student to showcase what that student considers to be his or her best work, (c) *documentation* or *growth portfolio,* which is oriented toward outcome-driven goals and includes samples of student work from the beginning and the end of the school term (or thematic unit of study) to exemplify achievement toward those goals, and (d) *passport* or *career portfolio,* which contains samples of student work that will enable the student to transition from one school grade level to the next.

Student portfolios should be organized and, depending on the purpose (or category), should contain assignment sheets, worksheets, the results of homework, project binders, forms for student self-assessment and reflection on their work, and other class materials thought important by the students and teacher. Computer software programs are available for assisting students in electronic portfolio development and management.[6] As a model of a real-life portfolio, you can show students your career portfolio (see Chapter 12).

Portfolio Assessment: Dealing with Its Limitations

Although portfolio assessment as an alternative to traditional methods of evaluating student progress has gained momentum in recent years, establishing standards has been difficult. Research on the use of portfolios for assessment indicates that validity and reliability of teacher evaluation are often quite low.[7] And portfolio assessment is not always practical for use by every teacher. For example, if you are the sole art teacher for a school and are responsible for teaching art to all of the 375 children in the school, you are unlikely to have the time or storage capacity for 375 portfolios. For assessment of student learning, the use of checklists, rubrics, and student self-assessment may be more practical.

Before using portfolios as an alternative to traditional testing, you are advised to consider carefully and understand clearly the reasons for doing it and its practicality in your situation. Then decide carefully portfolio content, establish rubrics or expectation standards, anticipate grading problems,

Figure 11.4
Sample checklist: assessing a student's oral report

Checklist: Oral Report Assessment

Student _____   Date _____

Teacher _____   Time _____

Did the student	Yes	No	Comments
1. Speak so that everyone could hear?	_____	_____	_____
2. Finish sentences?	_____	_____	_____
3. Seem comfortable in front of the group?	_____	_____	_____
4. Give a good introduction?	_____	_____	_____
5. Seem well informed about the topic?	_____	_____	_____
6. Explain ideas clearly?	_____	_____	_____
7. Stay on the topic?	_____	_____	_____
8. Give a good conclusion?	_____	_____	_____
9. Use effective visuals to make the presentation interesting?	_____	_____	_____
10. Give good answers to questions from the audience?	_____	_____	_____

and consider and prepare for parent and guardian reactions.

While emphasizing the criteria for assessment, rating scales and checklists provide children with means of expressing their feelings and give the teacher still another source of input data for use in assessment. To provide students with reinforcement and guidance to improve their learning and development, teachers can meet with individual students to discuss their self-assessments. Such conferences should provide students with understandable and achievable short-term goals as well as help them develop and maintain an adequate self-esteem.[8]

Although almost any instrument a teacher uses for assessing student work can be used for student self-assessment, in some cases it might be better to construct specific instruments with the student's understanding of the instrument in mind. Student self-assessment and self-reflection should be done on a regular and continuing basis so comparisons can be made periodically by the student. You will need to help students learn how to analyze these comparisons. Comparisons should provide a student with information previously not recognized about his or her own progress and growth.

Using Checklists

One of the items that can be maintained by students in their portfolios is a series of checklists. Checklist items can be used easily by a student to compare with previous self-assessments. Items on the checklist will vary depending on your purpose and grade level. (See sample forms, Figures 11.4 and 11.5.) Open-ended questions allow the student to provide additional information as well as to do some expressive writing. After a student has demonstrated each of the skills satisfactorily, a check is made next to the student's name, either by the teacher alone or in conference with the student.

Guidelines for Using Portfolios for Assessment
Here are general guidelines for using student portfolios in the assessment of learning.

• Contents of the portfolio should reflect the purpose of the assignment, the school's statement of mission, and the identified educational goals and target objectives.

• Determine what materials should be kept in the portfolio and announce clearly (post schedule in

Figure 11.5
Sample checklist: student learning assessment for use with interdisciplinary thematic instruction

Checklist: Interdisciplinary Thematic Unit Learning

Student _____   Date _____

Teacher _____   Time _____

Did the student	Yes	No	Comments/Evidence
1. Identify theme, topic, main idea of the unit	_____	_____	_____
2. Identify contributions of others to the theme	_____	_____	_____
3. Identify problems related to the unit study	_____	_____	_____
4. Develop skills in:	_____	_____	_____
Applying knowledge	_____	_____	_____
Assuming responsibility	_____	_____	_____
Classifying	_____	_____	_____
Categorizing	_____	_____	_____
Decision making	_____	_____	_____
Discussing	_____	_____	_____
Gathering resources	_____	_____	_____
Impulse control	_____	_____	_____
Inquiry	_____	_____	_____
Justifying choices	_____	_____	_____
Listening to others	_____	_____	_____
Locating information	_____	_____	_____
Metacognition	_____	_____	_____
Ordering	_____	_____	_____
Organizing information	_____	_____	_____
Problem recognition/identification	_____	_____	_____
Problem solving	_____	_____	_____
Reading text	_____	_____	_____
Reading maps and globes	_____	_____	_____
Reasoning	_____	_____	_____
Reflecting	_____	_____	_____
Reporting to others	_____	_____	_____
Self-assessing	_____	_____	_____
Sharing	_____	_____	_____
Studying	_____	_____	_____
Summarizing	_____	_____	_____
Thinking	_____	_____	_____
Using resources	_____	_____	_____
Working with others	_____	_____	_____
Working independently	_____	_____	_____
(Others unique to the unit)	_____	_____	_____

Additional teacher and student comments:

room) when, how, and by what criteria portfolios will be reviewed by you.

- Ensure that the purpose of the portfolio assignment is clearly understood by yourself, the children, and their parents and guardians.
- Portfolios should be kept in the classroom.
- Responsibility for maintenance of the portfolios must be the students.
- Students should date every document that goes into their portfolios.
- The portfolio should not be graded or compared in any way with those of other students. Its overall purpose is for student self-assessment and for demonstrating progress in learning. For this to happen, students should keep in their portfolio all papers or major sample papers. For grading purposes, you can simply record whether or not the portfolio was maintained and, by checklist, whether all materials are in the portfolio that are supposed to be.

MAINTAINING RECORDS OF STUDENT ACHIEVEMENT

You must maintain well-organized and complete records of student achievement. You may do this in a written record book or on an electronic record book, whichever will be furnished by the school. At the very least, the record book should include attendance records and all records of scores on tests, homework, projects, and other assignments. The record book is a legal document that at the end of the school year must be turned in to the school office.

Daily interactions and events occur in the classroom that may provide informative data about a student's intellectual, emotional, and physical development. Maintaining a dated log of your observations of these interactions and events can provide important information that might otherwise be forgotten. At the end of a unit and again at the conclusion of a grading term, you will want to review your records. During the course of the school year, your anecdotal records (and those of other members of your teaching team) will provide important information about the intellectual, psychological, and physical development of each student and ideas for attention to be given to individual students.

Recording Teacher Observations and Judgments

You must think carefully about any written comments that you intend to make about a child. Children can be quite sensitive to what others say about them, and most particularly to comments about them made by their teachers.

Additionally, we have seen anecdotal comments in students' permanent records that said more about their teachers who made the comments than about the recipient students. Comments that have been carelessly, hurriedly, and thoughtlessly made can be detrimental to a child's welfare and progress in school. Teacher comments must be professional; that is, they must be diagnostically useful to the continued intellectual and psychological development of the child. This is true for any comment you make or write, whether on a student's paper, on the child's permanent school record, or on a message sent to the student's home.

For students' continued intellectual and psychological development, your comments should be useful, productive, analytical, diagnostic, and prescriptive. The professional teacher makes diagnoses and prepares descriptions; a professional teacher does *not* label students, such as *lazy, vulgar, slow, stupid, difficult,* or *dumb.* The professional teacher sees the behavior of a child as being goal-directed. The primary professional task of any teacher is not to punish, but to facilitate the learner's understanding (perception) of a goal and help the learner identify acceptable behaviors positively designed to reach that goal.

That which separates the professional teacher from "anyone off the street" is the teacher's ability to go beyond mere description of behavior. Keep that in mind always when you write comments that will be read by students, by their parents or guardians, and by other teachers.[9] Let us reinforce this concept by focusing your attention on Exercise 11.1.

EXERCISE 11.1 EVALUATING WRITTEN TEACHER COMMENTS— A SELF-CHECK EXERCISE

Instructions: The purpose of this exercise is to reinforce the importance of teacher comments about student behavior that go beyond that of merely describing behavior. The following comments were written by teachers on student records. Check those you consider to be professionally useful and those that are not. Then compare your responses against the key that follows. Discuss the results with your classmates and instructor.

	Yes	**No**
1. Sonja performs her writing assignments much better when done in class than when done as homework.	( )	( )
2. Lucretia was very disruptive in class during our unit on westward expansion.	( )	( )
3. Aram has a lot of difficulty staying in his seat.	( )	( )
4. Arthur seems more responsible during science experiments than during my lectures.	( )	( )
5. Razmik seems to have an excess of nervous energy, and I am concerned about his nutrition.	( )	( )
6. Su Chin did very well this year in laboratory activities but seems to have reading difficulties.	( )	( )
7. Catalina does not get along well with her peers during group learning activities.	( )	( )
8. Angela seems unable to understand my verbal instructions.	( )	( )
9. I am recommending special remediation for José, perhaps through tutoring.	( )	( )
10. I do not appreciate Dan's use of vulgarity.	( )	( )

Note: It can be argued that those comments identified as not useful, although not prescriptive, could be signals that the student might benefit from a session with the school counselor.

Exercise Answer Key: Answer Key to Exercise 11.1

1. Useful.
2. Not useful, because there are no helpful specifics. "Disruptive" is merely descriptive, not prescriptive. Also, it could cause Lucretia's future teachers to be biased against her.
3. Useful.
4. Useful.
5. Useful.
6. Useful, although additional specifics would be helpful.
7. Useful, although additional specifics would be helpful.
8. Not very useful; it may tell more about the teacher than it does about Angela.
9. Useful.
10. Not useful.

GRADING AND MARKING STUDENT ACHIEVEMENT

If conditions were ideal (which they are not), and if teachers did their job perfectly well (which many of us do not), then all students would receive top marks (the ultimate in mastery or quality learning) and there would be less of a need here to talk about grading and marking. (Believing that letter grades do not reflect the nature of the developmental progress of young children, many school districts hold off using letter grades until children are in at least the 3rd grade or even the 6th grade, and, instead, favor using developmental checklists and narratives.[10]) Mastery learning implies that some end point of learning is attainable; but there probably isn't an end point. In any case, because conditions for teaching are never ideal and we teachers are mere humans, let us continue with this topic of grading and marking that is undoubtedly of special interest to you, your students, their parents or guardians, to school counselors, administrators and members of the school board, and to many others, such as potential employers, providers of scholarships, and college admissions officers.

The term *achievement* is used frequently throughout this resource guide. What is the meaning of the term? Achievement means accomplishment, but is it accomplishment of the instructional objectives against preset standards, or is it simply accomplishment? Most teachers probably choose the former, where the teacher subjectively establishes a standard that must be met in order for a student to receive a certain grade for an assignment, project, test, quarter, semester, or course. Achievement, then, is decided by degrees of accomplishment.

Preset standards are usually expressed in percentages (degrees of accomplishment) needed for marks or *ABC* grades. If no student achieves the standard required for an *A* grade, for example, then no student receives an *A*. On the other hand, if all students meet the preset standard for the *A* grade, then all receive *A*s. Determining student grades on the basis of preset standards is referred to as *criterion-referenced grading*.

Criterion-Referenced versus Norm-Referenced Grading

While criterion-referenced grading is based on preset standards (that is, it is competency-based), norm-referenced grading measures the relative accomplishment of individuals in the group (e.g., one classroom of fourth graders) or in a larger group (e.g., all fourth graders) by comparing and ranking students and is commonly known as *grading on a curve*. Because it encourages competition and discourages cooperative learning, *norm-referenced grading is not recommended* for the determination of student grades. Norm-referenced grading is educationally dysfunctional. For your personal interest, after several years of teaching, you can produce frequency-distribution studies of grades you have given over a period of time, but *do not* give students grades that are based on a curve. It is well supported by research studies and authorities on the matter that grading and reporting should always be done in reference to learning criteria, and never "on a curve."[11] Grades for student achievement should be tied to performance levels and determined on the basis of each student's achievement toward preset standards.

In criterion-referenced grading, the aim is to communicate information about an individual student's progress in knowledge and work skills in comparison to that student's previous attainment or in the pursuit of an absolute, such as content mastery. Criterion-referenced grading is featured in continuous-progress curricula, competency-based curricula, and other programs that focus on personalized education.

Criterion-referenced grading is based on the level at which each student meets the specified objectives (standards) for the grade level or subject. The objectives must be clearly stated to represent important student learning outcomes. This approach implies that effective teaching and learning result in high grades (*A*s) or marks for most students. In fact, when a mastery concept is used, the student must accomplish the objectives before being allowed to proceed to the next learning task. The philosophy of teachers who favor criterion-referenced procedures recognizes individual potential. Such teachers accept the challenge of finding teaching strategies to help children progress from where they are to the next designated level. Instead of wondering how Juan compares with Sam, the comparison is between what Juan could do yesterday and what he can do today and how well these performances compare to the preset standard.

Most school systems use some sort of combination of both norm-referenced and criterion-referenced data usage. Sometimes both kinds of information are useful. For example, a report card for a student in the seventh grade might indicate how that student is meeting certain criteria, such as an *A* grade for addition of fractions. Another entry might show that this mastery is expected, however, in the fifth grade. Both criterion- and norm-referenced data may be communicated to the parents or guardians and the student. Appropriate procedures should be used: a criterion-referenced approach to show whether or not the student can accomplish the task, and if so, to what degree, and a norm-referenced approach to show how well that student performs compared to the larger group to which the child belongs.

Determining Grades

When determining achievement grades for student performance, you must make several important and professional decisions. While in a few schools, and for certain classes or assignments, only marks such as *E, S,* and *I* or *pass / no pass,* are used, percentages of accomplishment and letter grades are commonly used for grades 5 and up.[12]

Guidelines for Determining Grades

For determining student grades, consider the guidelines presented in the following paragraphs.

At the start of the school term, explain your marking and grading policies *first to yourself,* then to your students and to their parents or guardians at "Back-to-School night," or by a written explanation that is sent home, or both. Share sample scoring and grading rubrics with students and parents/ guardians. In fact, engaging students with you in the collaborative development of rubrics can be a potent benefit to instruction.[13]

When converting your interpretation of a student's accomplishments to a letter grade, be as objective as possible. For the selection of criteria for *ABC* grades, select a percentage standard, such as 90 percent for an *A,* 80 percent for a *B,* 70 percent for a *C,* and 60 percent for a *D.* Cutoff percentages used are your subjective decision, although the district, school, program area, or department may have established guidelines that you are expected to follow.

For the determination of students' final grades, many teachers use a point system, where things that students write, say, and do are given points (but not for journals or portfolios, except, perhaps, simply for whether the student does one or not); then the possible point total is the factor for grade determination. For example, if 90 percent is the cutoff for an *A* and 500 points are possible, then any student with 450 points or more (500 × .90) has achieved an *A.* Likewise, for a test or any other assignment, if the value is 100 points, the cutoff for an *A* is 90 (100 × .90). With a point system and preset standards, the teacher and students, at any time during the grading period, always know the current points possible and can easily calculate a student's current grade standing. Then, as far as a current grade is concerned, students always know where they stand in the course.

Build your grading policy around degrees of accomplishment rather than failure and where children proceed from one accomplishment to the next. This is **continuous promotion,** not necessarily the promotion of the student from one grade level to the next, but within the classroom. (However, some schools have eliminated grade-level designation and, in its place, use the concept of continuous promotion from the time of student entry into the school through the student's graduation or exit from it.)

Remember that *assessment* and *grading* are not synonymous. As you learned earlier, assessment implies the collection of information from a variety of sources, including measurement techniques and subjective observations. These data, then, become the basis for arriving at a final grade, which in effect is a final value judgment. Grades are one aspect of evaluation and are intended to communicate educational progress to students and to their parents or guardians. To be valid as an indicator of that progress, you must use a variety of sources of data for determination of a student's final grade.

Decide beforehand your policy about makeup work. Students will be absent and will miss assignments and tests, so it is best that your policies about late assignments and missed tests be clearly communicated to students and to their parents or guardians. For makeup work, please consider the following.

Homework Assignments. (Refer to Chapter 8 to the discussion in the section Opportunities for Recovery.)

Tests. If students are absent when tests are given, you have several options. Some teachers allow students to miss or discount one test per grading period. Another strategy is to allow each student to substitute a written homework assignment or project for one missed test. Still another option is to give the absent student the choice of either taking a makeup test or having the next test count double. When makeup tests are given, the makeup test should be taken within a week of the regular test unless there is a compelling reason (e.g., medical or family problem) why this cannot happen.

Sometimes students miss a testing period, not because of being absent from school but because of involvement in other school activities. In those instances, the student may be able to arrange to come in and take the test at another time. If a student is absent during performance testing, the logistics and possible diminished reliability of having to readminister the test for one student may necessitate giving the student an alternate paper-and-pencil test or some other option.

Quizzes. Many teachers give frequent and brief quizzes, as often as every day. As opposed to tests (see next section), quizzes are usually brief (perhaps taking only 5 minutes of class time) and intended to reinforce the importance of frequent study, checks for comprehension, and review. (However, quizzes should be prepared using the same care and precision as presented in the guidelines that follow in the sections for testing and preparation of assessment items). When quizzes are given at frequent intervals, no single quiz should count very much toward the student's final grade; therefore you will probably want to avoid having to schedule and give makeup quizzes for students who were absent during a quiz period. The following are reasonable options to administering makeup quizzes and are presented here in order of our preference. (a) Give a certain number of quizzes during a grading period, say 10, but allow a student to discount a few quiz scores, say 2 of the 10, thereby allowing the student to discount a low score or a missed quiz due to absence or both. (b) Count the next quiz double for a student who missed one due to absence. About the only problem with this option is when a student misses several quizzes. If that happens, (c) count the unit test a certain and relative percentage greater for any student who missed a quiz during that unit. By the way, we see absolutely no educational value in using "pop" or unannounced graded quizzes.

TESTING FOR ACHIEVEMENT

One source of information used for determining grades is data obtained from testing for student achievement. There are two kinds of tests, those that are standardized and those that are not.

Standardized and Nonstandardized Tests

Standardized tests are those constructed and published by commercial testing bureaus and used by states and districts to determine and compare student achievement, principally in the core subjects of reading, mathematics, and science. On usually a state or national level, norms for particular age groups of children on a test are established from its administration to large groups of children. Standardized norm-referenced tests are best for diagnostic purposes and should *not* be used by a classroom teacher for determining student grades.

As said in Chapter 1, the administration of standardized achievement tests and the use of their results have become major concerns to classroom teachers and school principals in particular. In some locales, for example, their salaries and indeed their jobs are contingent on the results of student scores on standardized achievement tests. For this resource guide, it is neither our purpose nor does space in it allow a consideration of standardized achievement testing. Rather, our focus is on nonstandardized criterion-referenced tests, ones that you design (or collaboratively design) for your own unique group of students for determination of their level of learning on particular instructional objectives. In no way do we intend to devalue the concern that you will have for standardized norm-referenced achievement testing as a classroom teacher. It simply means that our purpose and space in this resource guide does not adequately allow for in-depth attention to that particular topic (for more on this form of testing, see the recommended readings at the end of this chapter).

Competent planning, preparing, administering, and scoring of tests specifically designed for your group of students is an important professional skill. You may want to revisit the guidelines that follow while you are student teaching, and again, occasionally, during your initial years as an employed teacher.

Purposes for Testing

Tests can be designed for several purposes, and a variety of kinds of tests and alternate test items will keep your testing program interesting, useful, and reliable. As a college student, you are probably most experienced with testing for measuring achievement, but you will use tests for other reasons as well. Tests are also used to assess and aid in curriculum development; help determine teaching effectiveness; help students develop positive attitudes, appreciations, and values; help students increase their understanding and retention of facts, principles, skills, and concepts; motivate children; provide diagnostic information for planning for personalization of the instruction; provide review and drill to enhance teaching and learning; and serve as informational data for children and their parents or guardians.

Frequency of Testing

First of all, assessment for student learning should be continual; that is, it should be going on every minute of every class day. For grading or marking purposes, it is difficult to generalize about how often to formally test for student achievement, but we believe that testing should be cumulative and frequent. By *cumulative,* we mean that each assessment should assess for the child's understanding of previously learned material as well as for the current unit of study—that is, it should assess for connected learning. By *frequent,* for self-contained classes we mean as often as daily and for classes that meet for an hour or so each day we mean as often as once a week. Advantages of assessment that is cumulative include the review, reinforcement, and articulation of old material with the most recent. Advantages of frequent assessment include a reduction in student anxiety over tests and testing and an increase in the validity of the summative assessment.

Test Construction

After determining the reasons for which you are designing and administering a test, you need to identify the specific objectives the test is being designed to measure. (As you learned in Chapter 5, your written learning objectives are specific so that you can write assessment items to measure against those objectives; that is, criterion-referenced assessment.) So, the first step in test construction is identification of the purpose(s) for the test. The second step is to identify the objectives to be measured, and the third step is to prepare the test items. The best time to prepare draft items is after you have prepared your learning objectives but while the objectives are fresh in your mind, which means during the preactive phase of instruction, that is, before the lessons are taught. After a lesson is taught, during the reflective phase of instruction, you will want to rework your first draft of the test items that are related to that lesson to make any modifications to the draft items as a result of the instruction and your reflection on the instruction.

Administering Tests

For many students, test taking can be a time of high anxiety. Children demonstrate test anxiety in various ways. Just before and during testing some are quiet and thoughtful, while others are noisy and disruptive. To measure student achievement more accurately, you will want to take steps to reduce their anxiety. To control or reduce student anxieties, consider the following discussion as guidelines for administering tests.

Since children respond best to familiar routine, plan your formative assessment program so tests are given at regular intervals and administered at the same time and in the same way.

Avoid tests that are too long and that will take too much time. Sometimes beginning teachers have unreasonable expectations of elementary school children about their attention spans during testing. Frequent testing with frequent sampling of student knowledge is preferred over infrequent and long tests that attempt to cover everything.

Attend to creature comforts. Try to arrange the classroom so it is well ventilated, the temperature is comfortable, and, when giving paper-and-pencil tests individually, the seats are well spaced. If spacing is a problem, then consider space dividers (see next section) or alternate forms of the test, where students seated adjacent to one another have different forms of the same test (for example, multiple-choice answer alternatives are arranged in different order).

Before distributing the test, explain to students what they are to do when finished, such as quietly begin homework or a reading assignment, because not all of the students will finish at the same time. It is unreasonable to expect most children to just sit quietly after finishing a test; they need something to do.

When ready to test, don't drag it out. Distribute tests quickly and efficiently. Once testing has begun, avoid interrupting the students. (It is amazing to us how often we see teachers interrupt students once the students are at a task, while those same teachers resent being interrupted themselves.) Items or announcements of important information can be written on the board, or if unrelated to the test, held until all are finished with the test. Stay in the room and visually monitor the students. If the test is not going to take an instructional time period (and most shouldn't) and it's a major test, then give it at the beginning of the period, if possible, unless you are planning a test review just prior to it (though that seems rather late to conduct a meaningful review; a review just prior to giving the test is likely to only upset those children who discover they don't know the material like they thought they did). It's improbable that any teacher can effectively teach a lesson with a reasonable degree of student interest in it just prior to or immediately after a major test.

Be sure to pay special attention to children who have disabilities so they are not hampered by time, visibility, or other factors relevant to the particular test.

Controlling Cheating

Cheating on tests does occur, but there are steps you can take to discourage it or to reduce the opportunity and pressure that cause students to cheat. Consider the following.

Preventing cheating. Space students or, as mentioned before, use alternate forms of the test. Another technique used by some teachers, especially where children sit at tables rather than at individual desks, is to use space dividers. Attaching three approximately 8 × 10-inch rectangular sections of cardboard can make space dividers. The divider is placed standing in front of the student making it impossible for neighboring students to see over or around. Dividers can be made from cardboard boxes or heavy folders of various sorts. It could be a project at the beginning of the year for each student to design and make an individual space divider that is then stored in the classroom for use on test days. Students enjoy being allowed to personalize their dividers.

Frequent testing and not allowing a single test to count too much toward a term grade reduce test anxiety and the pressure that can cause cheating and increase student learning by providing important feedback to the student. Prepare test questions that are clear and not ambiguous, thereby reducing student frustration that is caused by a question or instructions that students do not understand. Avoid tests that are too long and that will take too much time. During long tests, some students get discouraged and restless, and that is a time when classroom management problems can occur.

By their sheer nature, performance tests can cause even greater pressure on children and can also provide greater opportunity for cheating. When administering performance tests to an entire class, it is best to have several monitors, such as members of your teaching team or classroom parent/guardian volunteers. When that isn't possible, some teachers test groups of children, such as cooperative learning groups, rather than individuals. Evaluation of test performance, then, would be based on group rather than individual achievement. However, we tend to agree with those who argue against the use of any kind of assessment of an individual that is based to any degree on group process and functioning. It is very difficult, if not impossible, to rationalize giving a child a grade based on a group assignment.

Consider using open-text and open-notebook tests or allowing each student to prepare a page of notes to use during the test. When students can use their books and notes, that not only reduces anxiety but it helps them with the organization of information and the retention of what has been learned.

Stopping cheating. The preceding paragraphs provide hints to prevent student cheating. If you

Table 11.1
Approximate Time to Allow for Testing as Determined by the Types of Items.*

Type of Test Item	Time Needed per Item
Matching	30 seconds per matching item
Multiple-choice	30 seconds per matching item
Completion	1 minute per item
Completion drawing	2–3 minutes
Arrangement	2–3 minutes
Identification	2–3 minutes
Short explanation	2–3 minutes
Essay and performance	10 or more minutes

*Students with disabilities or LEP students may need more time per item.

suspect cheating *is* occurring, move and stand near the suspected student. Usually that will stop it.

Dealing with cheating. When you suspect cheating *has* occurred, you are faced with a dilemma. Unless your suspicion is backed by solid proof you are advised to forget it, but keep a close watch on the student the next time. Your job is not to catch children being dishonest but to discourage dishonesty. If you have absolute proof that a student has cheated, then you are obligated to proceed with school policy on student cheating, and that may call for a session with the counselor or the student and the student's parent or guardian.

Determining the Time Needed to Take a Test

Again, avoid giving tests that are too long and that will take too much time. Preparing and administering good tests is a skill you will develop over time. Meanwhile, it is best to test frequently and to use tests that sample student achievement rather than try for a comprehensive measure of that achievement.

Some students take more time on the same test than others do. You want to avoid giving too much time, or classroom management problems will result. On the other hand, you don't want to cut short the time needed by children who can do well but need more time to think and to write. As a very general guide to time needed for different types of test items, see Table 11.1. This is only a guide for determining the approximate amount of time to allow students to complete a test. For example, for a test made up of 10 multiple-choice items, five arrangement items, and two short-explanation items, you would want to plan for about 25–30 minutes for students to complete the test.

PREPARING ASSESSMENT ITEMS

Preparing and writing good assessment items is yet another professional skill, and to become proficient at it takes study, time, practice, and reflection. Because of the importance of an assessment program, please assume this professional charge seriously and responsibly. Although poorly prepared items take no time at all to construct, they will cause you more trouble than you can ever imagine. As a professional you should take time to study different types of assessment items that can be used and how best to write them, and then practice writing them. Remember, when preparing assessment items, ensure that they match and sufficiently cover the instructional objectives. In addition, you should prepare each item carefully enough to be reasonably confident that each item will be understood by the student in the manner that you anticipate its being understood. With the diversity of children in today's public school classroom, especially with respect to their proficiency in oral and written English language and to students with disabilities, this is an especially important point. Finally, after administering a test you must take time to analyze the results and reflect on the value of each item before ever using that item again.

Classification of Assessment Items

Assessment items can be classified as verbal (oral or written words), visual (pictures and diagrams), and manipulative or performance (handling of materials and equipment, performing). Written verbal items have traditionally been most frequently used in testing. However, visual items and visual tests are useful, for example, when working with children who lack fluency with the written word or when testing students who have limited or no proficiency in English.

Performance items and tests are useful when measuring for psychomotor skill development. Common examples are performance testing of a student's ability to carry a microscope or hold a jumping rope in place (gross motor skill) or to focus a microscope or to jump rope (fine motor skill). Performance testing also can and should be a part of a wider testing program that includes testing for higher-level thinking skills and knowledge, as, for example, when a student or small group of students are given the problem of creating from discarded materials a habitat for an imaginary animal and then instructed to display, write about, and orally present their product to the rest of the class.

As noted often throughout this book, educators have rekindled their interest in this last described form of performance testing as a means of assessing learning that is closer to measuring for authentic learning. In a program for teacher preparation, micro peer teaching and the student teaching experience are examples of performance assessment, that is, assessment practices used to assess the teacher candidate's ability to teach (to perform). It seems axiomatic that assessment of student teaching is a more authentic assessment of a candidate's ability to teach than would be a written (paper-and-pencil test) or verbal (oral test) form of assessment. Although less direct and perhaps less reliable than a checklist observation and analysis of a student teacher actually teaching, an observation of a student teacher's analysis of a video recorded episode (that is, with pictures) of another teacher's performance would be another way to assess more authentically a teacher's ability to teach than would be a paper-and-pencil response item test.

Performance Testing Can Be Expensive and Time Intensive

Performance testing is usually more expensive and time-consuming than is verbal testing, which in turn is more time demanding and expensive than is written testing. However, a good program of assessment will use alternate forms of assessment and not rely solely on one form (such as written) and one type of written item (such as multiple-choice).

The type of test and items that you use depend upon your purpose and objectives. Carefully consider the alternatives within that framework. To provide validity checks and to account for the individual differences of students, a good assessment program should include items from all three types. That is what writers of articles in professional journals are referring to when they talk about **alternative assessment.** They are encouraging the use of multiple assessment items, as opposed to the traditional heavy reliance on objective items such as multiple-choice questions.

General Guidelines for Preparing for Assessment

Consider the following general guidelines when preparing for assessment. Include several kinds of items and assessment instruments (see the 12 types that follow), but keep items of the same type

Figure 11.6
Table of specifications I

CONTENT	BEHAVIORS								TOTAL
Social Studies Grade 6	*Cognitive*						Affective	Psychomotor	
Ancient Greece	Knowledge	Comprehension	Application	Analysis	Synthesis	Evaluation			
I. Vocabulary Development		2 (1, 2)	1 (2)						3
II. Concepts		2 (3, 4)	2 (4)						4
III. Applications	1 (5)	1 (5)	1 (5)	1 (5)	1 (5)	1 (5)			6
IV. Problem-solving		1 (6)		1 (6)					2
TOTAL	1	6	4	2	1	1			15

together. Ensure that content coverage is complete (i.e., that all objectives are being measured) and that each item is reliable—that is, that it measures the intended objective. One way to check item reliability is to have more than one item measuring for the same objective. Ensure that each item is clear and unambiguous to all students. Plan each item to be difficult enough for the poorly prepared student but easy enough for the student who is well prepared. The first few test items should be relatively easy, to allow some time for the children to become comfortable with the test and testing situation.

Because it is time-consuming to write good assessment items, you are advised to maintain a bank of items, with each item coded according to its matching instructional objective and its domain of learning (cognitive, affective, or psychomotor) and perhaps level within the hierarchy of a particular domain. Another code could indicate whether the item requires thinking that is recall, processing, or application. Computer software programs are available for this. Ready-made test item banks are available on computer disks and accompany many curriculum programs. If you use them, be certain that the items are well written and match your particular instructional objectives. It doesn't follow that because they were published, they are well written and match what your students were supposed to have learned. When preparing items for your test bank, use your creative thinking and best writing skills. Prepare items that match your ob-

jectives, put them aside, think about them, then work them over again and again.

Every test that you administer to your students should represent your best professional effort. It should be clean, legible, with clear instructions, and sans spelling and grammar errors. A quickly and poorly prepared test can cause you more grief than you can imagine. One that is obviously prepared hurriedly and wrought with spelling and grammar errors will quickly be frowned upon by discerning parents or guardians and by the school principal. If you are a student teacher, such sloppiness will certainly bring about an admonishment from your university supervisor and, if it continues, your speedy dismissal from the teacher preparation program.

Attaining Content Validity

To ensure that your test measures what is supposed to be measured, you can construct a table of specifications. A two-way grid indicates behavior in one dimension and content in the other (see Figures 11.6 and 11.7). In this grid, behavior relates to the three domains: cognitive, affective, and psychomotor. In Figure 11.6, the cognitive domain is divided, according to Bloom's taxonomy (Chapter 5), into six categories: knowledge or simple recall, comprehension, application, analysis, synthesis (often involving an original product in oral or written form), and evaluation. The specifi-

Figure 11.7
Table of specifications II

CONTENT	BEHAVIORS							TOTAL
	Cognitive			*Affective*		*Psychomotor*		
	Input	Processing	Application	Low	High	Low	High	
I.								
II.								
III.								
IV.								
TOTAL								

cations table of Figure 11.7 does not specify levels within the affective and psychomotor domains.

To use a table of specifications, the teacher examining objectives for the unit decides what emphasis should be given to the behavior and to the content. For instance, if vocabulary development is a concern for this sixth-grade study of ancient Greece, then probably 20% of the test on vocabulary would be appropriate, but 50% would be unsuitable. This planning enables the teacher to design a test to fit the situation rather than a haphazard test that does not correspond to the objectives either in content or behavior emphasis. Since knowledge questions are easy to write, tests often fail to go beyond that level even though the objectives state that the student will analyze and evaluate. The sample table of specifications for a sixth grade social studies unit on ancient Greece indicates a distribution of questions on a test. Since this test is to be an objective test and it is so difficult to write objective items to test affective and psychomotor behaviors, this table of specifications calls for no test items in these areas. If these categories are included in the unit objectives, other assessment devices must be used to test learning in these domains. The teacher could also show the objectives tested, as indicated within parentheses in Figure 11.6. Then, a check later on inclusion of all objectives is easy.

Preferred by some teachers is the alternative table shown in Figure 11.7. Rather than differentiating among all six of Bloom's cognitive levels, this table separates cognitive objectives into just three levels: those that require simple low-level recall of knowledge, those that require information processing, and those that require application of the new knowledge (refer to Chapter 7, Levels of Cognitive Questions and Student Thinking). In addition, the affective and psychomotor domains each are divided into low- and high-level behaviors. Another alternative, not illustrated here, is a table of specifications that shows all levels and even sublevels of each of the three domains.

TYPES OF ASSESSMENT ITEMS: DESCRIPTIONS, EXAMPLES, AND GUIDELINES FOR PREPARATION AND USAGE

This section presents descriptions, advantages and disadvantages, and guidelines for preparing and using 12 types of assessment items. When reading about the advantages and disadvantages of each, you will notice that some types are appropriate for use in performance assessment, while others are not.

Arrangement

Description: Terms or real objects are to be arranged in a specified order.

Example 1: Arrange the following lettered blocks in their order as they occur in the English alphabet.

Example 2: The assortment of balls on the table represents the planets in our solar system. (*Note:* The balls are of various sizes, such as marbles, tennis balls, basketballs, and so on, each labeled with a planetary name, with a large sphere in the center labeled the Sun.) Arrange the balls in their proper order around the Sun.

Advantages: This type of item tests for knowledge of sequence and order and is good for review, for starting discussions, and for performance assessment. Both examples are performance test items.

Disadvantages: Scoring could be difficult, so be cautious, meticulous, and open to lateral thinking (see Chapter 9) when using this type for grading purposes. For example, in question number 2 the student could rightfully place either Neptune or Pluto as the outermost planet in the solar system (because of the extreme oval shape of their orbits, Pluto and Neptune alternate in their relative positions from the Sun), or even omit Pluto (most scientists today believe that Pluto is actually the largest or nearest member of a group of icy asteroids found in the outer solar system).

Guidelines for use: To enhance reliability, you may need to give instructions to students to include the rationale for their arrangement, making it a combined arrangement and short-explanation type of assessment, allowing space for explanations on an answer sheet. Useful for individual assessment and for small heterogeneous group assessment to allow students to share and learn from their collaborative thinking and reasoning.

Completion Drawing

Description: An incomplete drawing is presented and the student is to complete it.

Example 1: Connect the following items with arrow lines to show the stages from introduction of a new bill until it becomes law (items not included here).

Example 2: In the following food web (not included here), draw arrow lines indicating which organisms are consumers and which are producers.

Advantages: This type requires less time than would a complete drawing that might be required in an essay item. Scoring is relatively easy although be advised to be alert and allow for lateral thinking.

Disadvantages: Care needs to be exercised in the instructions so students do not misinterpret the expectation.

Guidelines for use: Use occasionally for diversion, but take care in preparing. This type can be instructive when assessing for student thinking and reasoning as it can measure conceptual

knowledge. Consider making the item a combined completion-drawing, short-explanation type by having students include their rationales for the thinking behind their drawing completion. Be sure to allow space for their explanations. Useful for small heterogeneous group assessment to allow students to share and learn from their collaborative thinking and reasoning.

Completion Statement

Description: Sometimes called a "fill-in" item, an incomplete sentence is presented and the student is to complete it by filling in the blank space(s).

Example 1: A group of words that have a special meaning, such as "a skeleton in the closet," is called a(n) _____ .

Example 2: To test their hypotheses, scientists and social scientists conduct _____ .

Advantages: This type is easy to devise, take, and score.

Disadvantages: When using this type, there is a tendency to emphasize rote memory and measure procedural knowledge only. Provision of a word bank of possible answers is sometimes useful, especially with mainstreamed students, to reduce dependency on rote memory. It is difficult to write this type of item to measure for conceptual knowledge and higher levels of cognition. You must be alert for a correct response different from the expected. For example, in Example 2, although the teacher's key has *experiments* as the correct answer, a student might answer the question with *investigations* or *tests* or some other response that is equally valid.

Guidelines for use: Use occasionally for review or for preassessment of student knowledge. Avoid using this type for grading unless you can write quality items that extend student thinking beyond mere recall. In all instances, avoid copying items verbatim from the student book. As with all types, be sure to provide adequate space for students' answers and large spaces for students with motor control difficulties. Try to use only one blank per item and write so the blank is at the end of the sentence (the reason this type is called *completion*) rather than at the front or in the middle. Try also to keep the blanks equal in length. Useful for small heterogeneous group assessment to allow students to share and learn from their collaborative thinking and reasoning. Rewriting the item as a question makes the item a short-answer type which students might prefer over the completion statement type. Rewritten as short-answer questions, the two examples above would appear: (a) What do we call a group of words that have a special meaning, such as "a skeleton in the closet?" (b) What is it that scientists and social scientists conduct to test their hypotheses?

Correction

Description: This is similar to the completion type except that sentences or paragraphs are complete but with italicized or underlined words that can be changed to make the sentences correct.

Example 1: The work of the TVA was started by building *sand castles.* A *sand castle* is a wall built across a *kid* to stop its flow. The *sand castle* holds back the *football* so the *kids* do not overflow their *backpacks* and cause *tears.*

Example 2: 1, 1, 2, 3, 5, 8, *12,* 21, 34, *87,* 89

Advantages: Writing this type can be fun for the teacher for the purpose of preassessment of student knowledge or for comprehension check and review. Students may enjoy this type, especially when used only occasionally, for the tension relief afforded by the incorrect absurdities. This type can is useful for introducing words with multiple meanings.

Disadvantages: As with the completion type, the correction type tends to measure for low-level recall and rote memory (though this is not necessarily the case in Example 2; if a student is unfamiliar with the Fibonacci number series in mathematics, it would be a relatively high-level question). The underlined incorrect items could be so whimsical that they might cause more classroom disturbance than you want.

Guidelines for use: Use occasionally for diversion and discussion. Try to write items that measure for higher-level cognition. Consider making it a combined correction, short-explanation type. Be sure to allow space for student explanations.

Essay

Description: A question or problem is presented, and the student is to compose a response in the form of sustained prose, using the student's own words, phrases, and ideas, within the limits of the question or problem.

The essay item can also be considered a performance test item, perhaps the most familiar example of performance assessment.

Example 1: In the story just read does the author elaborate the setting in great detail or barely sketch it? Explain your response.

Example 2: A healthy green plant sitting in front of you has been planted in fertile soil and sealed with paraffin in a glass jar. If we place the jar on the windowsill where it will receive strong sunlight and the temperature inside the jar is maintained between 60 and 80 degrees Fahrenheit, how long do you predict the plant will live? Justify your prediction.

Advantages: This type measures conceptual knowledge and higher mental processes, such as ability to synthesize material and to express ideas in clear and precise written language. It is especially useful in integrated thematic teaching. It provides practice in written expression and can be used in performance assessment, as is the case for Example 2.

Disadvantages: Essay items require a good deal of time to read and to score. They tend to provide an unreliable sampling of achievement and are vulnerable to teacher subjectivity and unreliable scoring. Furthermore, they tend to punish the student who writes slowly and laboriously, who has limited proficiency in the written language but who may have achieved as well as a student who writes faster and is more proficient in the language. Essay items tend to favor students who have fluency with words but whose achievement may not necessarily be better. In addition, unless the students have been given instruction in the meaning of key directive verbs and in how to respond to them, the teacher should not assume that all students understand such verbs (such as *explain* in the first example and *predict* and *justify* in the second).

Guidelines for Using an Essay Item

1. When preparing an essay-only test, many questions, each requiring a relatively short prose response (see the short-explanation type, page 380), are preferable to a smaller number of questions requiring long prose responses. Briefer answers tend to be more precise, and the use of many items provides a more reliable sampling of student achievement. When preparing short prose response, be sure to avoid using words verbatim from the student textbook.

2. Allow students adequate test time for a full response.

3. Different qualities of achievement are more likely comparable when all students must answer the same questions, as opposed to providing a list of essay items from which students may select a certain number they wish to answer.

4. After preparing essay items, make a tentative scoring key, deciding the key ideas you expect students to identify and how many points will be allotted to each.

5. Students should be informed about the relative test value for each item. Point values, if different for each item, can be listed in the margin of the test next to each item.

6. Inform students of the role of spelling, grammar, and sentence structure in your scoring of their essay items.

7. When reading student essay responses, read all student papers for one item at a time in one sitting, and, while doing that, make notes to yourself; then repeat and while reading that item again, score each student's paper for that item. Repeat the process for the next item but alter the order of the pile of papers so you are not reading them in the same order by student. While scoring essay responses, keep in mind the nature of the objective being measured, which may or may not include the qualities of handwriting, grammar, spelling, punctuation, and neatness.

8. To nullify the "halo effect" that can occur when you know whose paper you are reading, have students put their name on the back of the paper or use a number code rather than having students put their names on essay papers, so that while reading the papers, you are unaware of whose paper is being read.

9. While having some understanding of a concept, many children are not yet facile with written expression, so you must remember to be patient, tolerant, positive, and prescriptive. Mark papers with positive and constructive comments, showing students how they could have explained or responded better.

10. Prior to using this type of test item, instruct students and help them practice responding to key directive verbs that will be used (see Figure 11.8).

Grouping

Description: Several items are presented, and the student is to select and group those that are in some way related.

Example 1: Separate the following words into two groups [words are not included here]; those that are nouns, place in group A and those that are not nouns, place in group B.

Example 2: Circle the figure that is least like the others [showing a wrench, screwdriver, saw, and swing].

Advantages: This type of item tests knowledge of grouping and can be used to measure conceptual knowledge, for higher levels of cognition, and to stimulate discussion. As Example 2 shows, it can be similar to a multiple-choice type item.

Disadvantages: Remain alert for the student who has an alternative but valid rationale for a different grouping.

Guidelines for use: To allow for an alternative correct response, consider making the item a combination grouping, short-explanation type, being certain to allow adequate space to encourage student explanations.

Identification

Description: Unknown "specimens" are to be identified by name or some other criterion.

Example 1: Using the 10-volume encyclopedia displayed on the table, from their covers identify the number of the volume in which you would be most likely to find information about Senegal.

Example 2: Identify each of the trees on our school grounds [the trees have been numbered] as to whether it is evergreen or deciduous.

Advantages: Verbalization (i.e., the use of abstract symbolization) is less significant, as the student is working with real materials; the teacher should be measuring for higher-level learning rather than simple recall. The item can also be written to measure for procedural understanding, such as for identification of steps in booting up a computer program. This is another useful type of test item for authentic and performance assessments.

Disadvantages: Because of a special familiarity with the material, some students may have an advantage over others; to be fair, specimens used should be equally familiar or unfamiliar to all students. This type takes more time than many of the other item types, both for the teacher to prepare and for students to do. Without help from

Figure 11.8
Meaning of key
directive verbs for
essay item responses

Compare asks for an analysis of similarity and difference, but with a greater emphasis on similarities or likenesses.

Contrast asks more for differences than for similarities.

Criticize asks for the good and bad of an idea or situation.

Define means to express clearly and concisely the meaning of a term, as from a dictionary or in the student's own words.

Diagram means to put quantities or numerical values into the form of a chart, graph, or drawing.

Discuss means to explain or argue, presenting various sides of events, ideas, or situations.

Enumerate means to name or list one after another, which is different from *explain briefly* or *tell in a few words*.

Evaluate means to express worth, value, and judgment.

Explain means to describe, with emphasis on cause and effect.

Generalize means to arrive at a valid generalization from provided specific information.

Identify means to state recognizable or identifiable characteristics.

Infer means to forecast what is likely to happen as a result of information provided.

Illustrate means to describe by means of examples, figures, pictures, or diagrams.

Interpret means to describe or explain a given fact, theory, principle, or doctrine within a specific context.

Justify means to show reasons, with an emphasis on correct, positive, and advantageous.

List means just that, to simply name items in a category or to include them in a list, without much description.

Outline means to give a short summary with headings and subheadings.

Prove means to present materials as witnesses, proof, and evidence.

Relate means to tell how specified things are connected or brought into some kind of relationship.

Summarize means to recapitulate the main points without examples or illustrations.

Trace means to follow a history or series of events, step by step, by going backward over the evidence.

other adults, classroom management could be difficult.

Guidelines for use: Whatever specimens are used, they must be familiar to all or to none of the students, and they must be clear and not confusing (e.g., fuzzy photographs or unclear photocopies, dried and incomplete plant specimens, and garbled music recordings can be confusing and frustrating to try and discern). Consider using dyad or team rather than individual testing.

Matching

Description: Students are to match related items from a list of numbered items to a list of lettered choices, or in some way to connect those items that are the same or are related. Or, to eliminate the paper-and-pencil aspect and make the item more direct, use an item such as, "Of the materials on the table, pair up those that are most alike."

Example 1: In the blank space next to each description in Column A (stem or premises column), put the letter of the correct answer from Column B (answer or response column).

A (stem column)	B (answer column)
_____ 1. $2 + 3 =$ _____	A. 0
_____ 2. $4 - 3 =$ _____	B. 1
_____ 3. $5 + 2$	C. 5
_____ 4. $3 - 3$	D. 6
	E. 7

Example 2: Match items in Column A (stem column) to those in Column B (answer column) by drawing lines connecting the matched pairs.

Column A	Column B
snake	worm
eagle	mammal
whale	reptile
praying mantis	insect
	bird

Advantages: Matching items can measure for ability to judge relationships and to differentiate among similar facts, ideas, definitions, and concepts. They are easy to score and can test a broad range of content. They reduce guessing, especially if one group (e.g., answer column) contains more items than the other, is interesting to students, and is adaptable for performance assessment.

Disadvantages: Although the matching item is adaptable for performance assessment, items are not easily adapted to measuring for higher cognition. Because all parts must be homogeneous, it is possible that clues will be given, thus reducing item validity.

Guidelines for use: The number of items in the response or answer column should exceed the number in the stem or premise column. The number of items in the stem column to be matched should not exceed 10. From 4 to 8 is the usual recommendation. Matching sets should have high homogeneity (i.e., items in both columns or groups should be of the same general category; avoid, for example, mixing dates, events, and names). Answers in the response column should be kept short, to one or two words each and should be ordered logically, such as alphabetically. If answers from the response column can be used more than once, and that is advised to avoid guessing by elimination, the directions should state this. Be prepared for the student who can legitimately defend an "incorrect" response. To eliminate the paper-and-pencil aspect and make the item more direct, use an item such as "of the materials on the table, pair up those that are most alike."

Multiple-Choice

Description: This type is similar to the completion item in that statements are presented (the stem), sometimes in incomplete form, but with several options or alternatives, requiring recognition or even higher cognitive processes rather than mere recall.

Example 1: Of four cylinders with the following dimensions, the one that would cause the highest-pitched sound would be

(a) 4 inches long and 3 inches in diameter

(b) 4 inches long and 1 inch in diameter

(c) 8 inches long and 3 inches in diameter

(d) 8 inches long and 1 inch in diameter

Example 2: Which one of the following words is spelled correctly?

(a) truely

(b) fourty

(c) arguement

(d) acquainted

Advantages: Items can be answered and scored quickly. A wide range of content and higher levels of cognition can be tested in a relatively short time. This type is excellent for all testing purposes—motivation, review, and assessment of learning.

Disadvantages: Unfortunately, because multiple-choice items are relatively easy to write, there is a tendency to write items measuring only for low levels of cognition. Multiple-choice items are excellent for major testing, but it takes care and time to write quality questions that measure higher levels of thinking and learning.

Guidelines for Using Multiple-Choice Items

1. If the item is in the form of an incomplete statement, it should be meaningful in itself and imply a direct question rather than merely lead into a collection of unrelated true and false statements.
2. Use a level of language that is easy enough for even the poorest readers and those with limited proficiency in English to understand; avoid unnecessary wordiness.

3. If there is much variation in the length of alternatives, arrange the alternatives in order from shortest to longest (i.e., first alternative is the shortest, last alternative is the longest). For single-word alternatives, consistent use of arrangement of alternatives is recommended, such as by length of answer or alphabetically.

4. Arrangement of alternatives should be uniform throughout the test and listed in vertical (column) form rather than in horizontal (paragraph) form.

5. Incorrect responses (distracters) should be plausible and related to the same concept as the correct alternative. Although an occasional humorous distracter may help relieve text anxiety, along with absurd distracters they should generally be avoided. They offer no measuring value, increase the likelihood of the student guessing the correct response, and increase the time it takes for the student to take the test.

6. It is not necessary to maintain a fixed number of alternatives for every item, but the use of less than three is not recommended. While it is not always possible to come up with four or five plausible responses, the use of four or five reduces chance responses and guessing, thereby increasing reliability for the item. (Three-choice items may be preferable for use with young children and other slower readers.) If you cannot think of enough plausible distracters, include the item on a test the first time as a completion item. As students respond, wrong answers will provide you with a number of plausible distracters that you can use the next time to make the item a multiple-choice type item.

7. Some special-needs students may work better when allowed to circle their selected response rather than writing its letter or number in a blank space.

8. Responses such as "all of the above" or "none of the above" should be used only when they will contribute more than another plausible distracter. Care must be taken that such responses answer or complete the item. "All of the above" is a poorer alternative than "none of the above" because items that use it as a correct response need to have four or five correct answers; also, if it is the right answer, knowledge of any two of the distracters will cue it.

9. Every item should be grammatically consistent. For example, if the stem is in the form of an incomplete sentence, it should be possible to complete the sentence by attaching any of the alternatives to it.

10. The stem should state a single and specific point.

11. The stem must mean the same thing to every student.

12. The item should be expressed in positive form. A negative form can present a psychological disadvantage to students. Negative items are those that ask what is *not* characteristic of something, or what is the *least* useful. Discard the item if you cannot express it in positive terminology.

13. The stem must not include clues to the correct alternative. For example, A four-sided figure whose opposite sides are parallel is called

    _____ .

    (a) an octagon
    (b) a parallelogram
    (c) a trapezoid
    (d) a triangle.

    Use of the word *parallel* clues the answer.

14. There must be only one correct or best response. However, this is easier said than done (refer to guideline 19).

15. Measuring for the understanding of definitions is better tested by furnishing the name or word and requiring choice among alternative definitions than by presenting the definition and requiring choice among alternative words.

16. Avoid using alternatives that include absolute terms such as *never* and *always.*

17. Multiple-choice items need not be entirely verbal. Consider the use of realia, charts, diagrams, videos, and other visuals. They will make the test more interesting, especially to students with low verbal abilities or to those who have limited proficiency in English, and, consequently, they will make the assessment more direct.

18. Once you have composed a series of multiple-choice items or a test comprised completely of this item type, tally the position of answers to be sure they are evenly distributed, to avoid the common psychological habit (when there are four alternatives) of having the correct alternative in the third position. In other words, when alternative choices are A, B, C, and D, or 1, 2, 3, and 4, unless the test designer is aware of and avoids it, more correct answers will be in the C or 3 position than in any other.

19. Consider providing space between test items for students to include their rationales for their responses, thus making the test a combination multiple-choice and short-explanation item type. This provides for the measurement of higher levels of cognition and encourages writing. It provides lateral thinking and provides for the student who can rationalize an alternative

that you had not considered plausible (especially possible today with the diversity of cultural experiences represented by students). For example, we recall the story of the math question on a test that asked, if a farmer saw eight crows sitting on a fence and shot three of them, how many would be left. The "correct" response on the answer key was *5*. One critical thinking student chose *none* for the response, an answer that was marked "wrong" by the teacher. However, the student was thinking that those crows that weren't shot would be frightened and would all fly away, thus the student selected *none* for the answer.

20. While scoring, on a blank copy of the test, for each item tally the incorrect responses. Analyze incorrect responses for each item to discover potential errors in your scoring key. If, for example, many students select B for an item for which your key says the correct answer is A, you may have made a mistake on your scoring key or in teaching the lesson.

21. Sometimes teachers attempt to discourage cheating by preparing several versions of the multiple-choice exam with the questions in different order. This could be giving one group of students whose order of questions is in the same sequence in which the information was originally presented and learned an unfair advantage over another group of students whose questions are in a random order. To avoid this, questions should be in random order on every version of the exam.

Performance

Description: Provided with certain conditions or materials, the student solves a problem or accomplishes some other action.

Example 1: Write a retelling of your favorite fable and create a diorama to go along with it.

Example 2: As a culminating project for a unit on sound, groups of students were challenged to design and make their own musical instruments. The performance assessment included:

1. Play your instrument for the class.
2. Show us the part of the instrument that makes the sound.
3. Describe the function of other parts of your instrument.
4. Demonstrate how you change the pitch of the sound.
5. Share with us how you made your instrument.

Figure 11.9
Procedure for setting up a performance assessment situation

1. Specify the performance objective.
2. Specify the test conditions.
3. Establish the standards or criteria (scoring rubric) for judging the quality of the process and/or product.
4. Prepare directions in writing, outlining the situation, with instructions that the students are to follow.
5. Share the procedure with a colleague for feedback before using it with students.

Advantages: Performance test item types come closer to direct measurement (authentic assessment) of certain expected outcomes than do most other types. As has been indicated in discussions of the preceding question types, other types of questions can actually be prepared as performance type items, that is, where the student actually does what he or she is being tested for.

Disadvantages: This type can be difficult and time consuming to administer to a group of students. Adequate supply of materials could be a problem. As said in our discussion of the essay type, scoring of performance items may tend to be subjective. Especially when materials are involved, it could be difficult to give makeup tests to students who were absent.

Guidelines for use: Use your creativity to design and use performance tests, since they tend to measure well the important objectives. To reduce subjectivity in scoring, prepare distinct scoring guidelines (rubrics), as was discussed in scoring essay type items and as shown, for example, in Figures 11.10 and 11.11. To set up a performance assessment situation, see instructions in Figure 11.9.

Short Explanation

Description: The short explanation question is like the essay but requires a shorter answer.

Example 1: Briefly explain in a paragraph how you would end the story. (Story not included here.)

Example 2: Briefly explain in a paragraph what is incorrect or misleading about the following drawing.

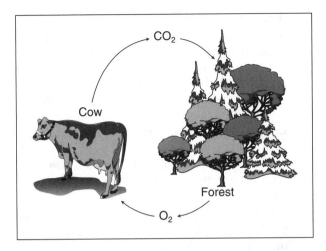

Advantages: As with the essay type item, student understanding is assessed; but this type takes less time for the teacher to read and score. In Example 2, for instance, the diagram for the cow and the forest is similar to drawings found in some science books that represent a *misconception* about our place in the natural world. The intent of the makers of such a diagram is to illustrate the interdependence of animals and plants; the lesson frequently learned, however, is that plants use carbon dioxide produced by animals and that animals use oxygen produced by plants. Following such a study, teachers and their students were interviewed and asked, "Do plants use oxygen?" The majority said no. The teachers and their students did not understand that *all* living organisms need oxygen. They held a *misconcept.* The focus in their learning had been too much on what human beings gain from interdependence, rather than on the concept of interdependence. *Artificialism* is the term used by Piaget to represent the tendency to believe that everything here on Earth is for the benefit of humans. Although it is a natural belief for children in kindergarten and the primary grades, it does represent a selfish, prejudiced, nonobjective naive theory that should be corrected. Teachers have an obligation, and an opportunity, to help children correct their misconceptions, providing that the teachers have a correct understanding of the concept. This type of test item can be useful in assessing conceptual understanding and critical thinking.

By using several questions of this type, a greater amount of content can be covered than with a lesser number of essay questions. This type of question is good practice for students to learn to express themselves succinctly in writing.

Disadvantages: Some students will have difficulty expressing themselves in a limited fashion or in writing. They need practice, coaching, and time in doing so.

Guidelines for use: This type is useful for occasional reviews and quizzes and as an alternative to other types of questions. For scoring, establish a scoring rubric and follow the same guidelines as for the essay type item.

True-False

Description: A statement is presented that students are to judge as accurate or not.

Example 1: The Emancipation Proclamation issued by President Abraham Lincoln stated that slavery was abolished in the Union. T or F?

Example 2: Christopher Columbus discovered America in 1492. T or F?

Advantages: Many items can be answered in a relatively short time, making broad content coverage possible. Scoring is quick and simple. True-false items (and other binary-choice types, such as yes/no, agree/disagree) are good as discussion starters, for review, and for diagnostic evaluation (preassessment) of what students already know or think they know.

Disadvantages: It is sometimes difficult to write true-false items that are purely true or false, without qualifying them in such a way that clues the answer. In the second sample question, for example, the student may question whether Columbus really did discover America or misunderstand the meaning of *discovered America.* Weren't there people already there when he landed? Where, in fact, did he land? What does *America* mean? Example 2 is poor also because it tests for more than one idea—*Columbus, America,* and *1492.*

Much of the content that most easily lends itself to the true-false type of test item is trivial. Students have a 50% chance of guessing the correct answer, thus giving this item type both poor validity and poor reliability. Scoring and grading give no clue about why the student missed an item. Consequently, the disadvantages of true-false items far outweigh the advantages; pure true-false items should not be used for arriving at grades. For grading purposes, you may use modified true-false items (see guideline 11 below) with space provided between items for students to write in their explanations, thus making the item a combined true-false, short-explanation type.

Guidelines for Preparing True-False Items

1. For preparing a false statement, first write a true statement, then make it false by changing a word or phrase.
2. Try to avoid using negative statements since they tend to confuse students. If a negative word is used, such as *no* or *not,* make it stand out by putting it in italics or underlining it.
3. A true-false statement should include only one idea.
4. Use close to an equal number of true and false items.
5. Try to avoid using specific determiners (e.g., *always, all,* or *none*) because they usually clue that the statement is false. Also avoid words that may clue that the statement is true (e.g., *often, probably,* and *sometimes*).
6. Avoid words that may have different meanings for different students.
7. Avoid using verbatim language from the student textbook.
8. Avoid trick items, such as a slight reversal of numbers in a date.
9. Rather than using symbols for the words *true* and *false* (sometimes teachers use symbols such as + and −) which might be confusing, or having students write the letters *T* and *F* (sometimes a student does not write the letters clearly enough for the teacher to be able to distinguish which it is), have students ei-

ther write out the words *true* and *false* or, better yet, have students simply circle *T* and *F* as indicated by the two examples above.

10. Proofread your items (or have a friend do it) to be sure that the sentences are well constructed and free from typographical errors.
11. To avoid "wrong" answers, caused by variations in thinking, and to make the item more valid and reliable, students should be encouraged to write in their rationale for selecting *true* or *false,* making the item a *modified true-false* item. For example,

When a farmer saw 8 crows sitting on the fence surrounding his cornfield, he shot 3 of them. Five were left on the fence. T or F? _____

Explanation: _____

For grading purposes, you may use modified true-false items, thus making the item a combined true-false short-explanation type, and allowing for divergent and critical thinking. Another form of modified true-false item is the *sometimes-always-never* item, where a third alternative, *sometimes,* is introduced to reduce the chance for guessing.

Now do Exercise 11.2 to start the development of your skill in writing assessment items. As you work on Exercise 11.2 you may want to correlate it with your previous work on Exercises 5.5, 6.7, and 6.11.

EXERCISE 11.2 PREPARING ASSESSMENT ITEMS

Instructions: The purpose of this exercise is to practice your skill in preparing the different types of assessment items discussed above. For use in your own teaching, select one specific instructional objective and write assessment items for it. When completed, share this exercise with your colleagues for their feedback.

Objective _____

Grade and Subject _____

  1. Arrangement item _____

     _____

     _____

     _____

     _____

  2. Completion drawing item _____

     _____

     _____

     _____

     _____

  3. Completion statement item _____

     _____

     _____

     _____

     _____

  4. Correction item _____

     _____

     _____

     _____

     _____

  5. Essay item _____

     _____

     _____

     _____

     _____

  6. Grouping item _____

     _____

EXERCISE 11.2 *(continued)*

_____

_____

_____

7. Identification item _____

_____

_____

_____

8. Matching item _____

_____

_____

_____

9. Multiple-choice item _____

_____

_____

_____

10. Performance item _____

_____

_____

_____

11. Short-explanation item _____

_____

_____

_____

12. Modified true-false item _____

_____

_____

_____

REPORTING STUDENT ACHIEVEMENT

One of your responsibilities as a classroom teacher is to report student progress in achievement to parents or guardians as well as to the school administration for record keeping. As was said at the beginning of this chapter, in some schools teachers report student progress and effort as well as achievement. As described in the discussions that follow, reporting is done in at least two, and sometimes more than two, ways.

The Grade Report

Periodically a grade report (report card) is issued (generally from four to six times a year, depending upon the school). This grade report represents an achievement grade or mark (formative evaluation). The final one of the semester is also the semester grade. In essence, the first and sometimes second reports are progress notices; the semester grade is the one that is transferred to the student's transcript of records.

In addition to the student's academic achievement in one or more subject areas, you must report the student's social behaviors (classroom conduct, social skills, work habits) while in your classroom. In some elementary schools, teachers are expected to write a descriptive narrative of each child's cognitive and social growth. In other schools, teachers indicate the child's skill level by completing a checklist. Whichever reporting form is used, you must separate your assessments of a student's social behaviors from the student's academic achievement. Academic achievement (or accomplishment) is represented by a letter (sometimes a number) grade (*A* through *E* or *F,* or *E, S,* and *U,* or *1* to *5,* and sometimes with *minuses* and *pluses*), and the social behavior by a *satisfactory* or an *unsatisfactory,* by more specific items, or supplemented by teacher-written or computer-generated comments. In most instances, for grades 1 through 6, there is a location on the reporting form for teachers to check whether basic grade-level standards have been met in the core subjects, especially in reading and mathematics.

TEACHER-PARENT/GUARDIAN COMMUNICATIONS

Study after study shows that when parents/guardians get involved in their child's school and school work, children learn better and earn better marks or grades and teachers experience more positive feelings about teaching. As a result, many schools increasingly are searching for new and improved ways to involve parents and guardians. What follows are additional suggestions and resources, specifically those involving direct communication between the classroom teacher and parents and guardians.

Contacting Parents/Guardians

While it is not always obligatory, some teachers make a point to personally contact parents or guardians, especially when a student has shown a sudden turn for either the worse or the better in academic achievement or in classroom behavior. That initiative and contact by the teacher are usually welcomed by parents and guardians and can lead to productive conferences with the teacher. An electronic conference (telephone or e-mail) can save valuable time for both the teacher and the parent/guardian.

Another way of contacting parents and guardians is by letter. Contacting a child's parent/guardian by letter gives time to think and make clear your thoughts and concerns to that parent/guardian and to invite them to respond at their convenience by letter, by phone, or by arranging to have a conference with you.

Progress Reporting to Parents/Guardians

In absence of a computer-link assignment/progress report hotline, most schools have a progress report form that, upon request by a parent or guardian, can be sent home with the child as often as weekly. It may be similar to the one shown in Figure 11.10 to show the student's progress in each of the core subjects, or perhaps like the one in Figure 11.11 that requires student self-evaluation, teacher assessment, office signature, and parental or guardian response and signature.

Meeting Parents and Guardians

You will meet some of the parents and guardians early in the school year during "Back To School" or "Meet the Teacher" night, throughout the year in individual parent/guardian conferences, and later in the year during spring open house. For the beginning teacher, these meetings with parents and guardians can be anxious times. It is also a time to celebrate your work and to solicit help from parents and guardians. The following paragraphs provide guidelines to help you with those experiences.[14]

Figure 11.10
Weekly assessment checklist: sample with teacher input only

WEEKLY ASSESSMENT CHECKLIST   For _____

	Math	Social Studies	Science	Language Arts
Number of tardies				
Number of absences				
Academic grade				
Citizenship grade				

	Usually	Sometimes	Rarely	Never
Homework turned in on time				
Class work satisfactorily completed				
Exhibits acceptable classroom behavior				
Exhibits acceptable use of time in class				
Skill level is adequate to do work				
Participates orally in class discussions				
Participates in classroom learning activities				
Assumes responsibilities for own actions				
Avoids talking excessively or out of turn				
Comes to class prepared with supplies				
Is ready to start working when class begins				
Performs well on quizzes and tests				
Is attentive and focused during class				
Shows good listening skills				
Shows good organizational skills				
Shows for assigned detentions				
Respects the property of others and of the school				
Respects the rights of others				

Other comments or concerns:

Figure 11.11
Progress Report: Subject-specific with student and parent/guardian input

---

PROGRESS REPORT: Arlington Heights School

Student: <u>Anthony von Hauser</u>   Course: <u>Introduction to Algebra grade 6</u>   Date: <u>September 14, 2001</u>

This progress report form incorporates evaluation by student, teacher, and parent. The form will be completed by the student on Wednesday and by the teacher on Thursday and reviewed by the office and returned to the student on Friday. The student will take the form home for parental review, comments, and signature.

Section I: Self-Assessment: The student is asked to evaluate progress in the course in terms of goals and how closely these goals are being achieved. Do you feel you have made progress since the last progress report?
    <u>By taking this algebra class I achieved a greater understanding of it. I feel I have made a lot of progress since I took the class in 6th grade. It is also taught much better which makes it easier.</u>

Section II: Teacher Assessment: The teacher is asked to assess the student's entry, competency, and achievement to date and make recommendations.
    <u>Anthony is doing quite well. He has had to make some adjustments from previous work habits (i.e., showing work), but he has made an excellent transition. Anthony has great skills and strong understanding of concepts.</u>

PRESENT STATUS (Rated A–F)

<u>B+</u> Class work/participation

<u>C+</u> Homework

<u>A</u>   Portfolio

<u>A</u>   Quizzes

<u>A–</u> Tests

<u>A–</u> Overall

A = Excellent

B = Above Average

C = Average

D = Below Average

F = Failing

WHAT IS NEEDED

<u>✓</u> Emphasis on homework

____ Improve class participation

____ More careful preparation for tests

<u>✓</u> Keep up the good work

____ Contact teacher

____ Improve portfolio

____ Other _____

Office Initial <u>CM</u>

Section III: Parent Evaluation and Comments: Parents are asked to respond and sign this progress report.
<u>I thank you for this timely report. I am delighted that Anthony has started off well and is liking the class. He talks at home a lot about the class and the interesting activities; a tribute to good teaching. I can tell from our conversations at home that he is feeling much better about his math capability. I thank you.</u>

                                                                        Eric von Hauser

---

Back to School or Meet the Teacher night is the evening early in the school year when parents and guardians come to the school and meet their children's teachers. The adults arrive at the student's home base and then proceed through a simulation of their child's school day; as a group, they meet each class and each teacher for a few minutes. Later, in the spring, many schools host an open house where parents and guardians may have more time to talk individually with teachers; but the major purpose of the open house is for the school and teachers to celebrate and display the work and progress of the students for that year.

Throughout the school year, there will be opportunities for you and parents or guardians to meet and to talk about their children.

At Back to School night, parents and guardians are anxious to learn as much as they can about their children's teachers. You will meet each group of adults for a brief time, perhaps about 10 minutes. During that meeting you will provide them with a copy of information about your class or course, make some straightforward remarks about yourself, talk about the class or course, its requirements, your expectations of the students, and how parents/guardians might help.

While there will be precious little time for questions from the parents and guardians, during your introduction the adults will be delighted to learn that you have your program well planned, appreciate their interest, and welcome their participation. They will be happy to hear your willingness to communicate with them.

Specifically, depending upon the grade level, parents and guardians will expect to learn about your curriculum—goals and objectives, any long-term projects, class size, schedules for tests, and marking, grading, and reporting procedures. They will want to know what you expect of them: Will there be homework, and if so, should they help their children with it? How can they contact you? Try to anticipate other questions. Your principal or colleagues can be of aid in helping you anticipate and prepare for these questions. Of course, you can never prepare for the question that comes from left field. Just remain calm and avoid being flustered (or at least appear so). The time will fly by quickly, and the children's parents and guardians will be reassured to know you are an in-control person.

Conferences

When meeting parents and guardians for conferences, you should be as specific as possible when explaining student progress in your class. And, express your appreciation for parents' or guardians' interest. Be helpful to their understanding, and don't saturate parents/guardians with more information than they need. Resist any tendency to talk too much. Allow time for the adults to ask questions. Keep your responses succinct. Never compare one child with another or with the rest of the class. If parents/guardians ask a question for which you do not have an answer, tell them you will try to find an answer and will phone them as quickly as you can. Then do it. Have students' portfolios and other work with you during the parent conference so you can show examples of what is being discussed. Also, have your grade book on hand, or a computer printout of it, but be prepared to protect from the parent/guardian the names and records of the other students.

Sometimes it is helpful to have a three-way conference, a conference with the parent or guardian, the student, and you, or a conference with the parent, the principal or counselor, and several or all of the child's teachers.[15] If, especially as a beginning teacher, you would like the presence of an administrator at a parent-teacher conference as backup, don't be hesitant to arrange that.

Some educators prefer a child-led conference, arguing that placing students in charge of the conference makes them individually accountable, encourages them to take pride in their work, and encourages student-parent or student-guardian communication about school performance.[16] But, the concept of student-led conferences also has its limitations—the most important of which perhaps is the matter of time.[17]

When a parent or guardian asks how she or he may help in the child's learning, the paragraphs that follow offer suggestions for your consideration.

Many schools have made special and successful efforts to link home and school. At some schools, through homework hotlines, parents or guardians have phone access to their children's assignment specifications and to their progress in their schoolwork, and parents or guardians with a personal computer and a modem have access to tutorial services to assist students with assignments.

Helping students become critical thinkers is one of the aims of education and one that parents and guardians can help with by reinforcing the strategies being used in the classroom. Ways to do this are to ask "what if" questions; think aloud as a model for the child's thinking development; encourage the child's own metacognition by asking questions such as, "How did you arrive at that conclusion?" or "How do you feel about your conclusion now?" and asking these questions about the child's everyday social interactions, topics that are important to the child; ask the child to elaborate on his or her ideas; accept the fact that the child may make mistakes, but encourage the child to learn from them.

Many resources are available for parents and guardians to use at home. The United States government, for example, has a variety of free or low-cost booklets available. For information contact the Consumer Information Center, Department BEST, Pueblo, CO 81009 or online at <http://www.pueblo.gsa.gov> from where many of the publications, such as *Learning Partners: A Guide to Educational Activities for Families,* may be downloaded (see also Figure 8.4 in Chapter 8). Figure 11.12 presents addresses for additional ideas and resources for home-school partnerships.

Dealing with an Angry Parent or Guardian

The paragraphs that follow offer guidelines for dealing with angry or hostile parents or guardians.

Remain calm in your discussion with the parent or guardian, allowing the parent/guardian to

Figure 11.12
Resources for developing home-school partnerships

- Alliance for Parental Involvement in Education, P.O. Box 59, East Chatham, NY 12060-0059, 518-392-6900.
- Center on Families, Communities, Schools & Children's Learning, 3505 N. Charles St., Baltimore, MD 21218, 410-516-8800.
- *Creating Partnerships With Parents: An Educator's Guide,* by D. C. Lueder, 1998. Technomic Publishing Company, 851 New Holland Ave., Box 3525, Lancaster, PA 17604, 800-233-9936.
- Family Learning Association, P. O. Box 5249, Bloomington, IN 47407.
- *Helping Your Child With Homework,* by K. J. Amundson, 1999. AASA Stock Number 236-020, American Association of School Administrators, 1801 North Moore Street, Arlington, VA 22209, Tel: 888-782-2272.
- *Helping Your Child With Science,* ERIC Digest 432447, by D. L. Haury and L. A. Milbourne, 1999. ERIC Clearinghouse for Science, Mathematics, and Environmental Education, Columbus, OH.
- *How Is My First Grader Doing in School? What to Expect and How to Help,* and *How Is My Second Grader Doing in School? What to Expect and How to Help,* both by J. R. Jacobson, 1998. Simon & Schuster, 1230 Avenue of the Americas, New York, NY 10020.
- *How to Help Your Child With Homework: Every Caring Parents' Guide to Encouraging Good Study Habits and Ending the Homework Wars (For Parents of Children Ages 6–13),* by M. C. Radencich and J. S. Schumm, 1997 edition; *The School-Savvy Parent: 365 Insider Tips to Help You Help Your Child* by R. Clark, D. Hawkins, and B. Vachon, 1999; and *What Kids Need to Succeed: Proven, Practical Ways to Raise Good Kids,* revised, expanded, updated edition, 1998, by P. L. Benson, J. Galbraith, and P. Espeland. All three by Free Spirit Publishing, 400 First Avenue North, Suite 616, Minneapolis, MN 55401-1724, 612-338-2068. See also R. Berkowitz, Helping With Homework: A Parent's Guide to Information Problem-Solving, *Emergency Librarian, 25*(4), 45–46 (March/April 1998).
- *Lifelong Learning Skills for the Preschool/Kindergarten Child: Tips for Parents. Research You Can Use. Booklet 1; Lifelong Learning Skills for the Elementary School Child: Tips for Parents. Research You Can Use. Booklet 2;* and *Lifelong Learning Skills for the Middle/Junior High School Child: Tips for Parents. Research You Can Use. Booklet 3.* All three by K. Cotton, 1998. Northwest Regional Educational Laboratory, 501 S. W. Main Street, Suite 500, Portland, OR 97204-3297, 503-275-9519.
- National Coalition for Parent Involvement in Education, Box 39, 1201 16th Street, NW, Washington, DC 20036.
- National Community Education Association, 3929 Old Lee Highway, Suite 91A, Fairfax, VA 22030-2401, 703-359-8973.
- Parents for Public Schools, P.O. Box 12807, Jackson, MS 39236-2807, 800-880-1222.
- *Working Parents Can Raise Smart Kids: The 'Time-Starved' Parent's Guide to Helping Your Child Succeed in School* by J. E. Beaulieu, A. Granzin, and D. S. Romaine, 1999. Parkland Press, 11003 "A" Street South, Tacoma, WA 98444-0646, 800-461-0070.

talk out his or her hostility while you say very little; usually, the less you say the better for the situation. What you do say must be objective and to the point of the child's work in your classroom. The parent/guardian may just need to vent frustrations that might have very little to do with you, the school, or even the child.

Do not allow yourself to be intimidated, put on the defensive, or backed into a verbal corner. If the parent/guardian tries to do so by attacking you personally, do not press your defense at this point. Perhaps the parent or guardian has made a point that you should take time to consider, and now is a good time to arrange for another conference with the parent/guardian for about a week later. In a follow-up conference, if the parent/guardian agrees, you may want to consider bringing in a mediator, such as another member of your teaching team, an administrator, or a school counselor.

You must *not* talk about other students; keep the conversation focused on this child's progress. The parent/guardian is *not* your rival or should not be. You both share a concern for the academic and emotional well-being of the child. Use your best skills in critical thinking and problem solving, trying to focus the discussion by identifying the problem, defining it, and then arriving at some decision about how mutually to go about solving it. To this end you may need to ask for help from a third party, such as the child's school counselor or an administrator. If agreed to by the parent/guardian, please take that step.

Parents and guardians do *not* need to hear about how busy you are, about your personal problems, or about how many other students you are dealing with on a daily basis, unless, of course, a parent/guardian asks. Parents/guardians expect you to be the capable professional who knows what to do and is doing it.

Now do Exercise 11.3

For Your Notes

EXERCISE 11.3 TEACHER-PARENT CONFERENCES: A ROLE-PLAYING EXERCISE

Instructions: The purpose of this exercise is to prepare your thoughts about what you might do in particular parent-teacher conference situations. Divide into teams of two and select one of the conference situations for a role-playing experience of approximately 5 minutes. Each situation includes one of the parent behaviors as its main focus. Each 5 minute role-playing can then serve as a basis for a discussion by your entire class.

Ideas for Role-Playing Teacher-Parent Conferences

1. A fourth-grade girl misses a unit test in history that you administered on Friday. You tell her that she can't make it up during class but that she can make it up after school. The next morning, the irate mother calls the principal and says that: (a) you are unfair; (b) staying late after school will cause her daughter to miss the bus; (c) there is no other transportation to the girl's home; (d) it is unsafe for a girl her age to walk that distance alone; (e) there is no money for a taxi or other transportation; and (f) there is no family car. The mother wants the test to be given at the lunch hour.

2. A sixth-grade boy is with his friends on the school bus for an environmental education outing. One boy opens his thermos and drinks the liquid. You notice the smell of wine. You take the thermos. After the students leave the bus, you check the other containers. Another thermos holds whiskey. You talk to the boys, verifying possession. Another teacher drive the two boys back to school. The parents are called, and a conference is scheduled for four o'clock that afternoon.

3. A fifth-grade girl talks incessantly during class. After several warnings, you call her parents and inform them you will have to give her a *D* in citizenship. The parents ask for a conference. At the conference, the parents suggest you do the following:
   a. Move the student away from the other students who talk.
   b. Move the student to the front of the room so she has more teacher supervision.
   c. Read the student's file. (She has a reading comprehension problem.)
   d. Consider the student's past history of grades in citizenship. (She received all marks of "outstanding" and "satisfactory" the year before.)
   e. Allow the student to bring her books home to complete work not done during class. (The student told her parents she couldn't bring her books home to complete her assignments.)
   f. Become more firm in class. (The student told her parents that the other students talked to her first and that she didn't begin the conversations in class.)

4. A parent calls to complain about the behavior of one of the third-grade students in your class. The student writes on the back of the other children's T-shirts, wipes paint from a brush onto their jeans, pushes, kicks, and tries to trip them as they walk past him in class and on the playground. This parent wants you to put a stop to this kind of behavior in your classroom and on the playground.

5. Add your own idea for a teacher-parent conference here.

_____

_____

_____

_____

_____

_____

_____

_____

_____

For Your Notes

SUMMARY

Whereas preceding parts of this resource guide addressed the *why, what,* and *how* components of teaching, this chapter has focused your attention on the fourth and final component—the *how well* component—and on the first of two aspects of that component. Assessment is an integral and ongoing factor in the teaching-learning process; consequently, this chapter has emphasized the importance of including the following in your teaching performance:

- Consider your assessment and grading procedures carefully, plan them, and explain your policies to the students and their parents and guardians.
- Involve students in the assessment process; keep students informed of their progress. Return papers promptly, review answers to all questions, and respond to inquiries about marks given.
- Maintain accurate and clear records of assessment results so that you will have an adequate supply of data on which to base your judgmental decisions about achievement.
- Make sure to explain any ambiguities that result from the terminology used, and base your assessments on the material that has been taught.
- Strive for objective and impartial assessment as you put your assessment plan into operation.
- Try to minimize arguments about grades, cheating, and teacher subjectivity by involving students in the planning, reinforcing individual student development, and providing an accepting, stimulating learning environment.
- Use a variety of instruments to collect a body of evidence to most reliably assess the learning of students that focus on their individual development.

Because teaching and learning work hand in hand and because they are reciprocal processes where one depends on and affects the other, the *how well* component deals with the assessment of both how well the students are learning and how well the teacher is teaching. This chapter has dealt with the first. In the next and final chapter of this resource guide, your attention is directed to techniques designed to help you develop your teaching skills and assess that development, a process that is now only beginning but will continue throughout your teaching career.

EXTENDING MY COMPETENCY: QUESTIONS FOR CLASS DISCUSSION _____

1. Identify a problem in grading that you personally experienced as a student in school. What was your perceived cause of the problem? How might it have been avoided? What was the resolution and how was that resolution arrived at? Was the resolution satisfactory to all concerned? Why or why not?
2. Other than a paper-and-pencil test, identify three alternative techniques for assessing student learning during or at completion of an instructional unit.
3. Investigate various ways that elementary schools are experimenting today with assessing and reporting student achievement. Share what you find with your classmates. Analyze the pros and cons of various systems of assessing and reporting.
4. When using a point system for determining student grades, is it educationally defensible to give a student a higher grade than that student's points call for? a lower grade? Give your rationale for your answers.
5. Describe any student learning activities or situations that you believe should *not* be graded but should or could be used for assessment of student learning.
6. Research the topic of student-led parent-teacher-student conferences, and report to your class what you find out about the practice.
7. Describe the roles and limitations of objectivity and subjectivity in the assessment of student learning.
8. Describe any prior concepts you held that changed as a result of your experiences with this chapter. Describe the changes.
9. From your current observations and fieldwork as related to this teacher preparation program, clearly identify one specific example of educational practice that seems contradictory to exemplary practice or theory as presented in this chapter. Present your explanation for the discrepancy.
10. Do you have questions generated by the content of this chapter? If you do, list them along with ways answers might be found.

FOR FURTHER READING _____

Allen, D. (Ed.) (1998). *Assessing Student Learning: From Grading to Understanding.* New York: Teachers College Press.

Allington, R. L., and Guice, S. (1997/1998). Learning to Read. What Research Says Parents Can Do to Help Their Children. *Our Children, 23*(4), 34–35.

Bishop, J. E., and Fransen, S. (1998). Building Community: An Alternative Assessment. *Phi Delta Kappan, 80*(1), 39–40, 57–58.

Black, P., and Dylan, W. (1998). Inside the Black Box: Raising Standards Through Classroom Assessment. *Phi Delta Kappan, 80*(2), 139–144, 146–148.

Bracey, G. W. (2000). *A Short Guide to Standardized Testing* (Fastback 459). Bloomington, IN: Phi Delta Kappa Educational Foundation.

Chase, C. I. (1999). *Contemporary Assessment for Educators.* New York: Addison Wesley/Longman.

Colby, S. A. (1999). Grading in a Standards-Based System. *Educational Leadership, 56*(6), 17–21.

Crockett, T. (1998). *The Portfolio Journey: A Creative Guide to Keeping Student-Managed Portfolios in the Classroom.* Englewood, CO: Teacher Ideas Press.

Doran, R., Chan, F., and Tamir, P. (1998). *Science Educator's Guide to Assessment.* Arlington, VA: National Science Teachers Association.

Ensign, J. (1998). Parents, Portfolios, and Personal Mathematics. *Teaching Children Mathematics, 4*(6), 346–351.

Fiderer, A. (1998). *35 Rubrics and Checklists to Assess Reading and Writing: Time-Saving Reproducible Forms for Meaningful Literacy Assessment* (grades K–2). New York: Scholastic.

Glazer, S. M. (1998). *Assessment IS Instruction: Reading, Writing, Spelling and Phonics for ALL Learners.* Norwood, MA: Christopher Gordon.

Gredler, M. E. (1999). *Classroom Assessment and Learning.* New York: Addison Wesley/Longman.

Gronlund, N. E. (1998). *Assessment of Student Achievement* (6th ed.). Needham Heights, MA: Allyn & Bacon Longman.

Gustafson, C. (1998). Phone Home. *Educational Leadership, 56*(2), 31–32.

Hoerr, T. (2000). Reporting What We Respect. *Classroom Leadership, 3*(5), 2–3.

Kelly, K. (1999). Retention vs. Social Promotion: Schools Search for Alternatives. *The Harvard Education Letter, 15*(1), 1–3.

Koch, R., and Schwartz-Petterson, J. (2000). *The Portfolio Guidebook: Implementing Quality in an Age of Standards.* Norwood, MA: Christopher-Gordon.

Linn, R. L., and Gronlund, N. E. (2000). *Measurement and Assessment in Teaching* (8th ed.). Upper Saddle River, NJ: Prentice Hall.

Marzano, R. J. *Transforming Classroom Grading.* Alexandria, VA: Association for Supervision and Curriculum Development, 2000.

McEwan, E. K. (1998). *How to Deal With Parents Who Are Angry, Troubled, Afraid, or Just Plain Crazy.* Thousand Oaks, CA: Corwin Press.

Mehrens, W. A., Popham, W. J., and Ryan, J. M. (1998). How to Prepare Students for Performance Assessments. *Educational Measurement: Issues and Practice, 17*(1), 18–22.

National Opinion Research Center. (1998). *Questions Parents Ask About Schools.* Chicago: Author.

Roe, M. F., and Vukelich, C. (1998). Literacy Portfolios: Challenges That Affect Change. *Childhood Education, 74*(3), 148–153.

Ronis, D. (2000). *Brain Compatible Assessments.* Arlington Heights, IL: Skylight.

Schurr, S. L. (1998). Teaching, Enlightening: A Guide to Student Assessment. *Schools in the Middle, 7*(3), 22–27, 30–31.

Skillings, M. J., and Ferrell, R. (2000). Student-Generated Rubrics: Bringing Students Into the Assessment Process. *The Reading Teacher, 53*(6), 452–455.

Stephens, D. and Story, J. (Eds.) (2000). *Assessment as Inquiry: Learning the Hypothesis-Test Process.* Urbana, IL: National Council of Teachers of English.

Stiggins, R. J. (2001). *Student-Involved Classroom Assessment* (3d ed.). Upper Saddle River, NJ: Merrill/Prentice Hall.

Sullivan, M. (1999). The Making of a Distinguished School. *Thrust for Educational Leadership, 28*(3), 33–35.

Taggart, G. L., Phifer, S. J., Nixon, J. A., and Wood, M. (Eds.) (1998). *Rubrics: A Handbook for Construction and Use.* Lancaster, PA: Technomic.

Trumbull, E., and Farr, B. (Eds.) (2000). *Grading and Reporting in the Age of Standards.* Norwood, MA: Christopher-Gordon.

NOTES

1. See, for example, H. Libit, Report Card Redux, *School Administrator, 56*(10), 6–10 (November 1999).

2. G. E. Tompkins and K. Hoskisson, *Language Arts: Content and Teaching Strategies* (Upper Saddle River, NJ: Prentice Hall, 1991), p. 63.

3. S. J. Rakow, Assessment: A Driving Force, *Science Scope, 15*(6), 3 (March 1992).

4. Learner Profile is available from Sunburst, 101 Castleton Street, P.O. Box 100, Pleasantville, NY 10570-0100, phone 800-321-7511.

5. See the story of the use of portfolios and teacher-student collaboration in a second-grade classroom in A. M. Courtney and T. L. Abodeeb, Diagnostic-Reflective Portfolios, *The Reading Teacher, 52*(7), 708–714 (April 1999).

6. Software packages for the development of student electronic portfolios are available, such as *Classroom Manager* from CTB Macmillan/McGraw-Hill (Monterey, CA), *Electronic Portfolio* from Learning Quest (Corvallis, OR), and *Grady Profile* from Aurbach and Associates (St. Louis, MO).

7. See, for example, K. S. Shapley and M. J. Bush, Developing a Valid and Reliable Portfolio Assessment in the Primary Grades: Building on Practical Experience, *Applied Measurement in Education, 12*(2), 11–32 (1999).

8. For a discussion of the biological importance and educational benefits of positive feedback, student

portfolios, and group learning, see R. Sylwester, The Neurobiology of Self-Esteem and Aggression, *Educational Leadership, 54*(5), 75–79 (February 1997).

9. See also A. Brualdi, *Teacher Comments on Report Cards,* ED423309 98 (Washington, DC: ERIC Clearinghouse on Assessment and Evaluation, 1998).

10. K. Lake and K. Kafka, Reporting Methods in Grades K–8, Chapter 9 in T. R. Guskey, (Ed.), *Communicating Student Learning,* 1996 Yearbook (Alexandria, VA: Association for Supervision and Curriculum Development, 1996), p. 91.

11. See, for example, T. R. Guskey (Ed.), *Communicating Student Learning,* ASCD Yearbook (Alexandria, VA: Association for Supervision and Curriculum Development, 1996), pp. 18–19, and R. J. Stiggins, *Student-Involved Classroom Assessment,* 3d ed. (Upper Saddle River, NJ: Prentice Hall, 2001), pp. 443–444.

12. For other methods being used to report student achievement, see K. Lake and K. Kafka, Reporting Methods in Grades K–8, Chapter 9 in T. R. Guskey, *Student Learning.*

13. H. G. Andrade, Using Rubrics to Promote Thinking and Learning, *Educational Leadership, 57*(5), 13–18 (February 2000).

14. For suggestions from a school administrator for "delivering powerful presentations to parents" at Back to School night, see W. B. Ribas, Tips for Reaching Parents, *Educational Leadership, 56*(1), 83–85 (September 1998).

15. See, for example, B. J. Ricci, How About Parent-Teacher-Student Conferences? *Principal, 79*(5), 53–54 (May 2000).

16. See J. Taylor, Child-Led Parent School Conferences—In Second Grade?!? *Young Children, 54*(1), 78–82 (January 1999), and J. V. Cleland, We Can Charts: Building Blocks for Student-Led Conferences, *Reading Teacher, 52*(6), 588–595 (March 1999).

17. See L. Countryman and M. Schroeder, When Students Lead Parent-Teacher Conferences, *Educational Leadership, 53*(7), 64–68 (April 1996).

How Can I Assess My Teaching Effectiveness and Continue My Professional Development?

While most of us are not born with innate teaching skills, the good news is that teaching skills can be learned and steadily improved. Teachers who wish to continue to improve their teaching can do so with help from many resources (in addition to this resource guide).

This chapter addresses the assessment of your effectiveness as a classroom teacher. It also addresses your professional development, an endeavor that will (or should) continue throughout your teaching career.

Whether you are a beginning teacher or an experienced teacher, one way to collect data and to improve your effectiveness is through periodic assessment of your teaching performance, either by an evaluation of your teaching in the real classroom or, if you are in a program of teacher preparation, by a technique called *micro peer teaching*. The latter is the focus of the final section of this chapter and is an example of a type of final performance (authentic) assessment for this resource guide.

CHAPTER OBJECTIVES

Specifically, upon completion of this chapter you should be able to demonstrate your knowledge about

1. The field components of teacher preparation, especially student teaching.
2. Finding a teaching job.
3. Remaining an alert and effective classroom teacher throughout your teaching career.

PROFESSIONAL DEVELOPMENT THROUGH STUDENT TEACHING

You are excited about the prospect of being assigned as a student teacher to your first classroom, but you are also concerned. Questions linger in your mind. Will your host (cooperating) teacher(s) like you? Will you get along? Will the children accept you? Will you be assigned to the school and grade level you prefer? What curriculum programs will you be expected to use? What will the children be like? Will there be many classroom management problems? What about mainstreamed students and students with only limited proficiency in English? Your questions will be unending.

Indeed, you *should* be excited and concerned, for this experience of student teaching is one of the most significant and important facets of your program of teacher preparation. In some programs, this practical field experience is planned as a co-experience with the college or university theory classes. In other programs, student teaching is the culminating experience. Different sequences are represented in different programs. For example, at some colleges, field teaching extends over two or three semesters. In other programs, teacher candidates first take a theory-class-first arrangement, which includes a full second semester of student teaching. Regardless of when and how your student teaching occurs, the experience is a bright and shining opportunity to hone your teaching skills in a real classroom environment. During this experience, you will be supported by an experienced college or university supervisor and by one or more carefully selected cooperating teachers, who will share with you their expertise.

Everyone concerned in the teacher preparation program—your cooperating teacher, your university instructors, school administrators, and your university supervisor—realize that this is your practicum in learning how to teach. As you practice your teaching, you will no doubt make errors, and with the understanding, wisdom, and guidance of those supervising your work, you will benefit and learn from those errors. Sometimes your fresh approach to motivation, your novel ideas for learning activities, and your energy and enthusiasm make it possible for the cooperating teacher to learn from you. After all, teaching and learning are always reciprocal processes. What is most important is that the children who are involved with you in the teaching-learning process will benefit from your role as the teacher candidate in the classroom. The following guidelines are offered to help make this practical experience beneficial to everyone involved.

Student Teaching IS the Real Thing

Because you have a classroom setting for practicing and honing your teaching skills with active, responsive, children, student teaching *is* the real thing. On the other hand, student teaching is *not* real in the sense that your cooperating teacher, not you, has the ultimate responsibility and authority for the classroom and the student's learning.

Getting Ready for Student Teaching

To prepare yourself for student teaching, you must study, plan, practice, and reflect. You should become knowledgeable about your students and their developmental backgrounds. In your theory classes, you learned a great deal about children. Review your class notes and textbooks from those courses, or select some readings suggested from chapters in Part I of this resource guide. Perhaps some of the topics will have more meaning for you now.

First Impressions

First impressions are often lasting impressions. You have heard that statement before, and now, as you get ready for this important phase of your professional preparation, you hear it again. Heed it for it is crucial to your success. Remember it as you prepare to meet your school principal and cooperating teacher for the first time; remember it as you prepare to meet your students for the first time; remember it as you prepare to meet parents and guardians for the first time; and remember it as you prepare for your university supervisor's first observation of your teaching. Remember it again as you prepare for your first teaching job interview. In each case, you have only one opportunity to make a favorable first impression.

Continuing to Get Ready for Student Teaching

In addition to the aforementioned preparations, you will need to be knowledgeable about your assigned school and the community from which its students come. Review the subject areas you will be teaching and the curriculum content and standards in those areas. Carefully discuss with your cooperating teacher (or teachers, as you may have more than one) and your university supervisor all of the responsibilities that you will be expected to assume. Since it is unlikely that you will assume all the responsibilities at once, there should be discussion of and agreement upon an approximate timeline or schedule showing dates by which you should be prepared to assume various responsibilities.

As a student teacher you may want to run through each lesson verbally, perhaps in front of a mirror, the night before teaching your lesson. Some student teachers read through each lesson, recording the lesson, playing it back, and evaluating whether the directions are clear, the instruction is mind-grabbing (or at least interesting), the sequence is logical, and the lesson closure is concise. Are your voice and body language conveying thorough preparation and confidence or are they conveying uncertainty and confusion? Still other student teachers always have a Plan B in mind (if not in hand—see Professional Development Through Preparing an Emergency Teaching Kit that follows later in this chapter) in case Plan A turns out to be inappropriate.

Student Teaching from the Cooperating Teacher's Point of View

For your consideration, information about student teaching from the viewpoint of a cooperating teacher is presented here in a question-and-answer format. You may wish to share this section with your cooperating teacher.

What is my role? As the cooperating teacher, your role is to assist when necessary: to provide guidance, to review lesson plans before they are taught, to facilitate the learning and skill development of your student teacher, and to help your student teacher become and feel like a member of the school faculty and the profession.

How can I prepare for the experience? Get to know your student teacher *before* he or she begins teaching. Develop a collegial rapport with the student teacher.

Who is my student teacher? Your student teacher is a person who is making the transition from another career or from the life of a college student to the profession of teaching. Your student teacher may be your age, or older, or younger. In any case, your student teacher may be scared to death, anxious, knowledgeable, and, when it comes to teaching philosophy, somewhere between being a romantic idealist and a pragmatic realist. Do not destroy the idealism—help the student teacher to understand and deal with the realism of everyday teaching.

It is important that you learn about the teaching experiences that your student teacher has had prior to this assignment so the student teacher and you may build from those experiences. For example, this may be your student teacher's very first teaching experience or the student teacher may have experience as a substitute teacher, teaching in another country, or student teaching at another school prior to this term.

What kind of support, criticism, and supervision should I give? Much of this you will have to decide for yourself. On the other hand, some teacher preparation programs provide training to cooperating teachers in techniques for supervising student teachers. Cooperating teachers are often selected not only because of their teaching accomplishments but also because of their skill in working with other adults. It is likely that you will be working as a member of a team that includes you (and perhaps other teachers), the student teacher, and the university supervisor. Whatever the situation, your student teacher needs support, helpful suggestions, and productive monitoring. It is unprofessional to place a student teacher into a sink-or-swim situation.

What danger signs should I be alert for? Your student teacher may be quite different from you in both appearance and style of teaching but may be potentially just as effective a teacher. Be slow and cautious in judging your student teacher's effectiveness. Offer suggestions, but do not make demands.

A student teacher that is not preparing well is likely to be heading for trouble. The saying stands: Failing to prepare is preparing to fail. Be certain to ask for and to receive lesson plans *before* they are taught, certainly in the beginning and then whenever you feel the necessity or as agreed upon by you and your student teacher.

Another danger signal is when the student teacher seems to show no real interest in the school and the students beyond the classroom. The student teacher should be prompt, should be eager to spend extra time with you, should attend faculty meetings and other school functions to whatever extent possible, and should be aware of the necessity of performing school clerical tasks. If you feel there is a lurking problem, then let the student teacher or the university supervisor (or both) know immediately. Trust your intuition. Poor communication between members of the teaching team is another danger signal.

What else should I know? Your student teacher may be employed elsewhere and have other demands on his or her time. Become aware of these other demands, but keep the educational welfare of your students paramount in your mind.

See that your student teacher is treated as a member of the faculty, is invited to faculty functions, has a personal mailbox (or is allowed to share yours, with the student teacher's name on it as well), and understands school policies, procedures, and curriculum documents and standards. See that your student teacher receives a personal copy of the school calendar with important dates marked well in advance, such as the dates for administering the state academic proficiency tests.

Once your student teacher is well grounded, the student teacher should be ready to be gradually left alone with the students for increasingly longer periods of time. For a specified time, a student teacher's goal is to work toward a competency level that enables him or her to assume increasing responsibility for everything. This means that you are nearby and on call in case of an emergency, but out of sight of the students.

Early in the program you (and other teachers who are involved) and your student teacher should work out a schedule of dates indicating when the student teacher should be prepared to assume various classroom responsibilities. This schedule should remain flexible and be reviewed by both of you almost weekly and adjusted as necessary and agreed on. Provide the university supervisor with a copy of the schedule and keep the supervisor informed of major modifications made to the schedule.

Comments from the University Supervisor

When is the supervisor coming? Is the supervisor going to be here today? Do you see a supervisor's observation of your student teaching as a pleasant experience or a painful one? Do you realize that

classroom observations of your teaching continue during your beginning years of teaching? Being observed and evaluated does not have to be a painful, nerve-racking experience for you. You don't have to become a bundle of raw nerve endings when you realize the supervisor is coming to see you. Whether you are a student teacher being observed by your university supervisor or an intern or probationary (untenured) teacher being evaluated by your principal (or by a committee of peers as is the case in some schools), some professional suggestions may help you turn an evaluating observation into a useful, professionally gratifying experience.

What to Do Before an Observation

Prepare for your evaluative visit by deciding what you do well and plan to demonstrate your best skills. Decorate your room and bulletin boards, especially by displaying student work, make sure your work area is orderly (this shows good organization), and select an academic aspect of the teaching day that demonstrates some of your best teaching skills. If your supervisor has previously targeted a weak area, plan to demonstrate growth in that area.

Many supervisors prefer that the student teacher provide them a copy of the lesson plan for the day as well as the text and any handouts and that these things be placed ahead of time at a designated place, such as in or with the student teaching binder.

Another nice thing to do in preparation for your supervisor's visit is to plan with your cooperating teacher an adult place in the classroom for the supervisor to sit. Otherwise, for example, your supervisor may be forced to stand because there is no seat available or may have extreme difficulty using a student seat, especially if in a kindergarten classroom.

What to Do During an Observation

Some supervisors choose to preannounce their visits. This is certainly true for *clinical supervision* practices. Clinical supervision is based on shared decision making between the supervisor and teacher and is focused on improving, rather than evaluating, teaching behaviors. With the use of clinical supervision, you know when the supervisor is coming, and you will probably look forward to the visit because of the rapport that has been established between members of your triad (in student teaching situations, your triad is composed of you, your cooperating teacher(s), and your university or college supervisor).

Features of effective clinical supervision include a preobservation conference, observation of teaching, and a postobservation conference. In the preobservation conference, the triad meets to discuss goals, objectives, teaching strategies, and the evaluation process. During the observation of teaching, the supervisor collects data on the classroom students' performance of objectives and on the student teacher's performance of the teaching strategies. In the postobservation conference, the student teacher, cooperating teacher, and the supervisor discuss the performances. They may compare what happened with what was expected, make inferences about students' achievement of objectives, and discuss relationships between teaching performance and student achievement. The supervisor and cooperating teacher act as educational consultants and may discuss alternative strategies for teaching at this conference or at a later one.

Sometimes your supervisor may drop in unannounced. When that happens you can take a deep breath, count to 10 (beneath your breath), and then proceed with your lesson. You will undoubtedly do just fine if you have been following the guidelines set forth in this book. Additional guidelines for a classroom observation are: Allow the observer to sit wherever he or she wishes; do not interrupt your lesson to introduce the observer, unless the observer requests it, but *do* prepare your students in advance by letting them know who may be visiting and why; do not put the observer on the spot by suddenly involving the observer in the lesson, but *do* try to discern in advance the level of participation desired by your observer.

If you have been assigned to a classroom for a student teaching experience, your college or university supervisor will meet with you and explain some of the tasks you should attend to when the supervisor visits your class. These may vary. For instance, some supervisors prefer to walk into a classroom quietly and not interrupt the learning activities. Some prefer not to be introduced to the class or to participate in the activities. Some supervisors are already well known by the students and teaching staff from prior visits to the school. Other supervisors may give you a special form to be completed before the supervisor arrives for the visit. This form often resembles a lesson plan format and includes space for your objectives, lesson procedures, motivational strategies, related activities, and method of assessing how well the students learned from the lesson. Remember, keep the line of communication open with your supervisor so you have a clear understanding of what is expected of you when the supervisor visits your classroom to observe your teaching. Without missing a beat in your lesson, you may walk over and quietly hand the observer a copy of the lesson plan and the textbook (or any other materials being used) opened to the appropriate page.

In some teacher preparation programs the student teacher is expected to maintain a student teaching binder in the classroom. (A similar expectation is common in beginning teacher mentor programs.) The binder is kept in a particular location so that the cooperating teacher may refer to it, and so that the college or university supervisor (or mentor) can pick it up upon entering the classroom and refer to it during the observation. Organized in the binder are the following: the current lesson plan, the current unit plan, previous lessons with reflections, tests and their results, assignments, classroom management plan, and a current seating chart with the students' names. The student teaching binder can, in fact, represent the start of your professional portfolio (discussed later in this chapter).

Soon after the observational visit, there should be a conference in which observations are discussed in a nonjudgmental atmosphere. It might be necessary for you to make sure that a conference is scheduled. The purposes of this postobservation conference are: for you and the observer(s) to discuss, rather than to evaluate, your teaching; and, for you to exit the conference with agreements about areas for improvement and how to accomplish those improvements. Sometimes, because of conflicting schedules, conferences may be electronic, via e-mail or phone.

What to Do During an Observation Conference

Some supervisors will arrange to have a conference with you to discuss the classroom observation and to begin to resolve any teaching problems. As a teacher or teacher candidate, you should be quite professional during the postobservation conference. For instance, one student teacher asks for additional help by requesting resources. Another takes notes and suggests developing a cooperative plan with the supervisor to improve teaching competencies. Still another discusses visiting other classrooms to observe exemplary teachers.

During other conferences, student teachers may ask for assistance in scheduling additional meetings with the supervisor. At such meetings, the teacher (or teacher candidate) views videos of selected teaching styles or methods, listens to audiotapes, conferences with another expert, or visits a nearby resource center.

Almost all supervisors conclude their conferences by leaving something in writing with the teacher or teacher candidate. This written record usually includes: a summary of teaching strengths or weaknesses, with a review of classroom management; the supervisor's recommendations; and, perhaps, steps in an overall plan for the teacher's (or student teacher's) continued professional growth and development.

What to Do After the Supervisor Leaves

In addition to observing the classes of other teachers, conferring with experts, and attending workshops and conferences, the following are ways to implement your plan for improvement. Be sure you debug your lesson plans by walking through them in advance of implementing them in the classroom. Do what you and your supervisor have agreed upon. Document your activities with a *teacher's logbook* with dated entries. If you maintain a binder for the supervisor to peruse, this documentation may be kept in the binder along with the supervisor's written comments. If you have a problem with classroom management or organization, review your written classroom management plan and procedures, comparing your plan with the guidelines presented in Chapter 4. Review your plan and procedures with your cooperating teacher, a trusted teaching colleague, or your supervisor. Obtain help when you need it. Write comments to parents or guardians about students' progress, and leave space for a return message from the parent or guardian (see, for example, Figure 11.11 of Chapter 11). Keep positive responses that you receive and share them with your supervisor at your next conference.

FINDING A TEACHING POSITION

As your successful student teaching experience draws to a close, you will embark upon finding your first paid teaching job. The guidelines that follow are provided to help you accomplish your goal.

Guidelines for Locating a Teaching Position

To prepare for finding the position you want, focus on (a) obtaining letters of recommendation from your cooperating teacher(s), your college or university supervisor, and, in some instances, the school principal, (b) your professional preparation

as evidenced by your letters of recommendation and other items in your professional portfolio (discussed next), and (c) your job interviewing skills.

First, consider the recommendations about your teaching. Most colleges and universities have a career placement center where there is probably a counselor who can advise you how to open the job placement file that will hold your professional recommendations. This enables prospective personnel directors or district personnel who are expecting to employ new teachers to review your recommendations. It is your responsibility to request letters of recommendation and, when appropriate, to supply the person writing the recommendation with the required form and an appropriately addressed stamped envelope. Sometimes the job placement files are confidential, so the recommendations will be mailed directly to the placement office. The confidentiality of recommendations may be optional, and, when possible, you may want to maintain your own copies of letters of recommendation and include them in your professional portfolio.

The letters of recommendation from educators at the school(s) where you did your student teaching should include the following information: the name of the school and district where you did your student teaching, the grade levels and subjects you taught, your proven skills in managing students of diversity in the classroom, your ability to teach the relevant subject(s), your skills in assessing student learning and in reflecting on your teaching performance and learning from that reflection, and your skills in communicating and interacting with children and adults.

Second, consider your preparation as a teacher. Teachers, as you have learned, represent a myriad of specialties. Hiring personnel will want to know how you see yourself—for example, as a primary grade teacher, as a specialist in sixth-grade core, or as an elementary school physical education or music teacher. Perhaps your interest is in teaching children at any level of elementary school or only science in grades 4 through 6. You may indicate a special interest or skill, such as competency in sign or in teaching English to second-language learners. Or, perhaps, in addition to being prepared to teach elementary school core subjects you also are musically talented or are bi- or multilingual and have had rich and varied crosscultural experiences. The hiring personnel who consider your application will be interested in your sincerity and will want to see that you are academically and socially impressive.

Last, consider your in-person interview with a district official. Sometimes, you will have several interviews or you will be interviewed simultaneously with a small group of candidates. There may be an initial screening interview by a panel of administrators and teachers from the district, followed by an interview by a school principal or by a school team composed of one or more teachers and administrators from the interested school or district. In all interviews, your verbal and nonverbal behaviors will be observed as you respond to various questions, including (a) factual questions about your student teaching, or about particular curriculum programs with which you would be expected to work, and (b) hypothetical questions, such as "What would you do if . . . ?" Often these are questions that relate to your philosophy of education (that you began writing in Chapter 3), your reasons for wanting to be a teacher, your approach to handling a particular classroom situation, and perhaps specifically your reasons for wanting to teach in this district at this particular school. Interview guidelines follow later in this section.

The Professional Career Portfolio

A way to be proactive in your job search is to create a personal professional portfolio to be shared with persons who are considering your application for employment. That is the objective of Exercise 12.1.

The professional career portfolio is organized to provide clear evidence of your teaching skills and to make you professionally desirable to hiring personnel. A professional portfolio is *not* a collection of your accomplishments randomly tossed into a folder. It *is* a deliberate, current, and organized collection of your skills, attributes, experiences, and accomplishments.

Because it would be impractical to send a complete portfolio with every application you submit, it might be advisable to have a minimum portfolio (portfolio B) that could be sent with each application, in addition to a complete portfolio (portfolio A) that you could make available upon request or that you would take with you to an interview. However it is done, the actual contents of the portfolio will vary depending on the specific job being sought; you will continually add to and delete materials from your portfolio. Exercise 12.1 suggests categories and subcategories, listed in the order that they may be best presented in portfolios A and B.[1]

EXERCISE 12.1 DEVELOPMENT OF A PROFESSIONAL PORTFOLIO

Instructions: The purpose of this exercise is to guide you in the creation of a personal professional portfolio that will be shared with persons who are considering your application for employment as a credentialed teacher.

Because it would be impractical to send a complete portfolio with every application you submit, you should consider developing a minimum portfolio (portfolio B) that could be sent with each application, in addition to a complete portfolio (portfolio A) that you could make available upon request and take with you to an interview. However it is done, the actual contents of the portfolio will vary depending on the specific job being sought; you will continually add to and delete materials from your portfolio. Suggested categories and subcategories, listed in the order that they may be best presented in portfolios A and B are as follows.

1. Table of contents of portfolio (not too lengthy)—portfolio A only.

2. Your professional résumé—both portfolios.

3. Evidence of your language and communication skills (evidence of your use of English and other languages, including American Sign)—portfolio A. (Also state this information briefly in your letter of application. See the résumé section that follows.)
   a. Your teaching philosophy (written in your own handwriting to demonstrate your handwriting). (See Exercise 3.3.)
   b. Other evidence to support this category.

4. Evidence of teaching skills—portfolio A.
   a. For planning skills, include instructional objectives and a unit plan. (See Exercises 5.11 and 6.8.)
   b. For teaching skills, include a sample lesson plan and a video of your actual teaching. (See Exercises 6.8A, 9.2, and 12.2.)
   c. For assessment skills, include a sample personal assessment and samples of student assessment. (See Exercises 9.2, 11.2, and 12.2.)

5. Letters of recommendation and other documentation to support your teaching skills—both portfolios.

6. Other (for example, personal interests related to the position for which you are applying)—portfolio A.

Resources for Locating Teaching Vacancies

Here is a variety of resources that you can consider contacting to locate teaching vacancies.

1. *Academic employment network.* A network employment page on the Internet <http://www.academploy.com/>. Contact AEN, 2665 Gray Road, Windham, ME 04062. Phone 800-890-8283. E-mail: info@academploy.com.
2. *College or university placement office.* Establishing a career placement file with your local college or university placement service is an excellent way to begin the process of locating teaching vacancies.
3. *Local school or district personnel office.* You can contact school personnel offices to obtain information about teaching vacancies and sometimes about open job interviews.
4. *County educational agency.* Local county offices of education sometimes maintain information about teaching jobs.
5. *State departments of education.* Some state departments of education maintain information about job openings statewide.
6. *Independent schools.* Contact non-public-supported schools that interest you, either directly or through educational placement services, such as:
   - European Council of Independent Schools, 21B Lavant Street, Petersfield, Hampshire, GU32 3EL, England.
   - Independent Educational Services (IES), 20 Nassau Street, Princeton, NJ 08540 (800-257-5102).
7. *Commercial placement agencies.* Teaching job listings and placement services are available from such agencies as:
   - Carney, Sandoe & Associates, 136 Boylston Street, Boston, MA 02116 (800-225-7986).
   - National Education Service Center, P.O. Box 1279, Department NS, Riverton, WY 82501-1279 (307-856-0170).
   - National Teachers Clearinghouse-SE, P.O. Box 267, Boston, MA 02118-0267 (617-267-3204).
8. *Online resources.* Job search resources available on the Internet include (see also number 10):
   - JobsinSchools.com <http://www.jobsinschools. com>
   - Teachers-Teachers.com <http://www.teachers-teachers.com>
9. *Out-of-country teaching opportunities.* Information regarding teaching positions outside the United States can be obtained from:
   - American Field Services Intercultural Programs, 313 East 43rd St., New York, NY 10017.
   - Department of Defense Dependent Schools, 4040 N. Fairfax Drive, Arlington, VA 22203-1634.
   - European Council of Independent Schools, 21B Lavant Street, Petersfield, Hampshire, GU32 3EL, England.
   - International Schools Service, P.O. Box 5910, Princeton, NJ 08543.
   - Peace Corps, Recruitment Office, 806 Connecticut Ave., NW, Washington, DC 20526.
   - Teachers Overseas Recruitment Centers, National Teacher Placement Bureaus of America, Inc., P.O. Box 09027, 4190 Pearl Rd., Cleveland, OH 44109.
   - YMCA of the USA, 101 N. Wacker Drive, Chicago, IL 60606.
10. *Professional journals and other publications.* Professional teaching journals (as found in Figure 10.3, Chapter 10) often run advertisements of teaching vacancies, as do education newspapers such as *Education Week.*[2]

State and Territorial Sources for Information About Credential Requirements

If you are interested in the credential requirements for other states and U.S. territories, check at the appropriate office of your own college or university teacher preparation program to see what information is available about requirements for states of interest to you, and whether the credential that you are about to receive has reciprocity with other states. Addresses and contact numbers for information about state credentials are available at <http://www.ed.gov/Programs/bastmp/SEA.htm>.

The Professional Résumé

Résumé preparation is the subject of how-to books, computer programs, and commercial services, but a teacher's résumé is specific. While no one can tell you exactly what type of résumé will work best for you, a few basic guidelines are especially helpful for the preparation for a teacher's résumé.

- The résumé should be no more than *two pages* in length. If it is any longer, it becomes a life history rather than a professional résumé.
- The presentation should be neat and uncluttered.
- Page size should be standard 8 1/2 × 11 inches. Oversized and undersized pages can get lost.

Figure 12.1
Sample professional résumé

Rachel Da Teacher
10 Main St, Weaverville, CA 96093
916-552-8996; e-mail Lracd@aol.com

CREDENTIAL
2002   California Preliminary Multiple Subject Credential
               CLAD (Culture and Language Academic Development) Certificate *California State University,*
               Sacramento

EDUCATION
1996   Bachelor of Arts Degree in Liberal Studies
               Saint Olaf College, Northfield, Minnesota

TEACHING EXPERIENCE
2002 (Student Teaching III)   **Wooded Oaks Elementary School (Carmichael, CA)**
               • Planned, developed, and used lessons for second- and third-grade children. Planned and
                 taught a literature unit on *The Courage of Sarah Noble* with a multicultural emphasis.
2002 (Student Teaching II)   **Harriet Lee Middle School (Woodland, CA)**
               • Planned, developed, and used lessons for a diverse group of sixth-grade students.
2001 (Student Teaching I)   **Roberson Avenue School (Rancho Cordova, CA)**
               • Observed and helped teachers of Title I children in grades K–5.
               • Prepared bilingual stories and activities; reader's theater presentations

RELATED EXPERIENCE
2001   • Developed and taught a Summer Writing Workshop for children, grades 3–10. Met with
                 students and parents and guardians to establish goals.
1997–1998   • Reader for Portola High School English department.

PHONE REFERENCES
               Dr. Guy Fontasio, Department of Teacher Education, College of Education, California State
                 University. 916-278-6155.
               Ms. Shanna Moore, Cooperating Teacher at Wooded Oaks Elementary School, Carmichael.
                 916-778-8900.

• Stationery color should be white or off-white.
• Do not give information such as your age, height, weight, marital status, number or names of your children, or a photograph of yourself, because including personal data may make it appear that you are trying to prejudice members of the hiring committee, which is simply unprofessional.
• Sentences should be clear and concise; avoid educational jargon, awkward phrases, abbreviations, or unfamiliar words.
• Organize the information carefully, in this order: your name, postal and e-mail addresses, and telephone number, followed by your education, professional experience, credential status, location of placement file, professional affiliations, and honors.
• When identifying your experiences—academic, teaching, and life—do so in *reverse chronologi-*

cal order, listing your most recent degree or your current position first. (See sample résumé in Figure 12.1.)
• Be absolutely truthful; avoid any distortions of facts about your degrees, experiences, or any other information that you provide on your résumé.
• Take time to develop your résumé, and then keep it current. Do not duplicate hundreds of copies; produce a new copy each time you apply for a job. If you maintain your résumé on a computer disc, then it is easy to make modifications and print a current copy each time one is needed.
• Prepare a cover letter to accompany your résumé written *specifically* for the position for which you are applying. Address the letter personally but formally to the personnel director. Limit the cover letter to one page, and emphasize yourself,

your teaching experiences and interests, and reasons that you are best qualified for the position. Show a familiarity with the particular school or district. Again, if you maintain a generic application letter on a computer disc, you can easily modify it to make it specific for each position.

- Have your résumé and cover letter edited by someone familiar with résumé writing and editing, perhaps an English-teaching friend. A poorly written, poorly typed, or poorly copied résumé fraught with spelling and grammar errors will guarantee that you will not be considered for the job.

- Be sure that your application reaches the personnel director by the announced deadline. If for some reason it will be late, then telephone the director, explain the circumstances, and request permission to submit your application late.

The In-Person Interview

If your application and résumé are attractive to the personnel director, you will be notified and scheduled for a personal or small-group interview, although in some instances the hiring interview may precede the request for your personal papers. Whichever the case, during the interview you should be honest, and you should be yourself. Practice an interview, perhaps with the aid of a video camera. Ask someone to role-play an interview with you and to ask you some tough questions. As you view the video, observe how you respond to questions. What is your body language conveying? Are you appearing confident?

Plan your interview wardrobe and get it ready the night before. Leave early for your interview so that you arrive in plenty of time. If possible, long before your scheduled interview, locate someone who works in the school district and discuss curriculum, classroom management policies, popular programs, and district demographics with that person. If you anticipate a professionally embarrassing question during the interview, think of diplomatic ways to respond. This means that you should think of ways to turn your weaknesses into strengths. For instance, if your cooperating teacher has mentioned that you need to continue to develop your room environment skills (meaning that you were sloppy), admit that you realize that you need to be more conscientious about keeping supplies and materials neat and tidy, but mention your concern about the students and the learning and that you realize you have a tendency to interact with students more than with objects. Assure someone that you will work on this skill, and then do it. The paragraphs that follow offer additional specific guidelines for preparing for

and handling the in-person interview. As you peruse these guidelines please know that what may seem trite and obvious to one reader is not necessarily the same to another.

You will be given a specific time, date, and place for the interview. Regardless of your other activities, accept the time, date, and location suggested, rather than trying to manipulate the interviewer around a schedule more convenient for you.

As a part of the interview you may be expected to do a formal but abbreviated (10–15 minutes) teaching demonstration. You may or may not be told in advance of this expectation. So, it is a good idea to thoughtfully develop and rehearse a model, one that you could perform on immediate request. Just in case it might be useful, some candidates carry to the interview a videotape of one of their best teaching episodes made during student teaching.

Dress for success. Regardless of what else currently you may be doing for a living, take the time necessary to make a professional and proud appearance.

Avoid coming to the interview with small children. If necessary, arrange to have them taken care of by someone.

Arrive promptly, shake your dry hands firmly with members of the committee, and initiate conversation with a friendly comment, based on your personal knowledge, about the school or district.

Be prepared to answer standard-interview questions. Sometimes school districts will send candidates the questions that will be asked during the interview; at other times, these questions are handed to the candidate upon arrival at the interview. The questions that are likely to be asked will cover the following topics:

- *Your experiences with students of the relevant age.* The committee wants to be reasonably certain that you can effectively manage and teach at this level. You should answer this question by sharing *specific* successes that demonstrate that you are a decisive and competent teacher.

- *Hobbies and travels.* The committee wants to know more about you as a person to ensure that you will be an interesting and energetic teacher to the students, as well as a congenial member of the faculty.

- *Extracurricular interests and experiences.* The committee wants to know about all the ways in which you might be helpful in the school and to know that you will promote the interests and cocurricular activities of students and the school community.

- *Classroom management techniques.* You must convince the committee that you can effectively manage a classroom of diverse learners in a manner that will help the students develop self-control and self-esteem.

- *Knowledge of the curriculum standards and the subject taught at the grade for which you are being considered.* The committee needs to be reasonably certain that you have command of the subject and its place within the developmental stages of children at this level. This is where you should show your knowledge of national standards and of state and local curriculum standards and documents.

- *Knowledge about the teaching of reading.* The committee will likely want to know your views about teaching reading, that you are knowledgeable about specific strategies for teaching reading, at any grade level.

- *Knowledge of assessment strategies relevant for use in teaching at this level.* This is your place to shine with your professional knowledge about using rubrics and performance assessment.

- *Commitment to teaching at this level.* The committee wants to be assured that you are knowledgeable about and committed to teaching and learning at this level, as opposed to just seeking this job until something better comes along.

- *Your ability to reflect on experience and to grow from that reflection.* Demonstrate that you are a reflective decision-maker and a lifelong learner.

- *Your strengths as a teacher.* The committee may ask you what you perceive as your major strength as an elementary schoolteacher. Consider your answer carefully so you can be impressive without taking an inordinate amount of time answering the question.

- *Your perceived weaknesses.* If you are asked about your weaknesses, you have an opportunity to show that you can effectively reflect and self-assess, that you can think reflectively and critically, and that you know the value of learning from your own errors and how to do it. Be prepared for this question by identifying a specific error that you have made, perhaps while student teaching and explaining how you were able to turn that error into a profitable learning experience.

Throughout the interview you should maintain eye contact with the interviewer while demonstrating interest, enthusiasm, and self-confidence. When an opportunity arises, ask one or two planned questions that demonstrate your knowledge of and interest in this position and this community and school or district.

When the interview has obviously been brought to a close by the interviewer, that is your signal to leave. Do not hang around; this might be interpreted as a sign of lacking confidence. Follow the interview with a thank-you letter addressed to the personnel director or interviewer; even if you do not get the job, you will be better remembered for future reference.[3]

Once you are employed as a teacher, your professional development continues. The sections that follow demonstrate ways in which that can happen.

PROFESSIONAL DEVELOPMENT THROUGH PREPARING AN EMERGENCY TEACHING KIT

One way to continue your professional development is to always be prepared. One way of being prepared is to have on hand your personal emergency teaching kit (ETK). What is an emergency teaching kit? It is a wide variety of teaching materials, usually which cross discipline boundaries, that a teacher collects and prepares to support a topic or a theme (such as the topic of friendships or the theme of interpersonal relationships).

Purposes of an Emergency Teaching Kit

An emergency teaching kit can be a useful strategy for teaching and learning. It can serve one to several purposes, such as to motivate children for learning, to review or reinforce content learning, to provide individual and group experiences, to emphasize intellectual processes and skills, or to provide an interdisciplinary approach if appropriate for the group.

Developing an Emergency Teaching Kit with a Multidiscipline Emphasis

To give an ETK a multidiscipline emphasis, consider the following:

- To reflect expressive arts: include a subject for creative writing; a CD, tape, or record for listenalongs or singalongs with the song's words on duplicated sheets; at activities related to the topic, stories to read aloud; poems to chant in a choral reading situation alone, as duets, or trios, alternating a line a child or as a group unison situation; riddles to solve with a partner or in a small group.

- To reflect science: plan a hands-on inquiry with all materials necessary to carry it out.

- To reflect mathematics: organize one or more activities with the necessary manipulative materials needed by children for doing it.

- To reflect social sciences: include a history activity perhaps related to the school's geographic area.

- To reflect physical education: organize games to play.
- Select relevant audiovisual and media materials.

Values of an Emergency Teaching Kit

There are many values for using an ETK. You'll understand a kit's value when you review the following:

- *Supports teacher response.* With a collection of materials for an ETK, a teacher can respond in a minute's notice and teach a one-day (or longer) unit centered around a selected theme.
- *Provides an interdisciplinary approach.* For example, one teacher prepared one master copy for each of the subject areas in a given school day, reading, spelling, writing, mathematics, and so forth. Each master reflected one aspect of the selected theme of interpersonal relationships related to the topic of friendships. During the day, the children read stories about friendships, spelled related key words, wrote about their friends and what friendship meant to them, and estimated and measured handprints and footprints of their friends in the group.
- *Allows for special features.* Additional features in the previously mentioned ETK gave the teacher an opportunity to read aloud a friendship story, to share a picture book about friends working and playing together, to read poems about friendships, and to introduce an art project. The teacher posted a brown paper bag tree (trunk formed of brown paper bags stuffed with newspaper, with leaves cut out of green art paper) on the bulletin board and introduced it as a friendship tree. The teacher told the children that they would use it to practice their friendship skills. To do this, the teacher encouraged them to participate in the following way:
  1. On the first day, the children were encouraged to compliment one another when it was appropriate. For each compliment, the teacher wrote the compliment giver's name on an index card, read the names aloud, and had the children hang the cards on the tree. The teacher said that the children could hang compliments on cards for others on the tree, too.
  2. For the second day, the teacher asked the children to report acts of kindness or friendship making by others. The names of the friendship makers were added to different colored index cards and displayed on the friendship tree.
  3. On the third day, the teacher had the children say something positive about themselves and had them write cards to tell their

own positive traits and strengths and display these on the tree.
  4. For the fourth day, the teacher led a discussion about the friendship tree and asked the children to talk about any positive changes they have noticed in one another. The children were encouraged to write and tell what they have noticed and to hang additional cards on the tree.

- *Supports thematic room environment.* Additional friendship charts and posters, collected by the teacher, also were placed on the nearby writing board rail to further set the room environment. A book display showed books about friendship and peace. Indeed, this teacher was ready for a teaching emergency with the items in this collected kit. See Figure 12.2 for more suggestions for an emergency teaching kit about multicultural friendships.

PROFESSIONAL DEVELOPMENT THROUGH REFLECTION AND SELF-ASSESSMENT

Beginning now and continuing throughout your career, you will reflect on your teaching (reflection is inevitable), and you will want to continue to grow as a professional as a result of those reflections (growth is not so inevitable unless it is self-initiated and systematically planned). The most competent professional is one who is proactive, that is, one who takes charge and initiates a continuing personal professional development. One useful way of continuing to reflect, self-assess, and to grow professionally is by maintaining a professional journal, much as your students do when they maintain journals reflecting on what they are learning. Another is by continuing to maintain the professional career portfolio that you began assembling early in your preservice program and finalized for your job search (as discussed in this chapter).

Some teachers maintain *professional logbooks*, which serve not only as documentation of their specific professional contributions and activities, but also as documentation of the breadth of their professional involvement. Some teachers maintain *research logbooks* to record questions that come up during the busy teaching day, and then establish a plan for finding answers.[4] The research logbook strategy can be of tremendous benefit to you in actively researching and improving your classroom work, but also can be of interest to colleagues. Working in teams and sharing your work with team members is still another way of continuing to reflect, self-assess, and grow as a teacher.

Figure 12.2
Emergency teaching kit: Multicultural friendships

To reflect the expressive arts

1. *Recordings for singalongs:* Select an appropriate CD, tape, or record to guide group singing and an accompanying copy master, chart, or transparency that shows the words of the songs.

Suggestions:

For All Students

Youngheart Records. *We All Live Together, Volume II*, P.O. Box 27784, Los Angeles, CA: 90027, or Cherly Melody's *Songs That Make the Heart Feel Good*, P.O. Box 251, Hopkins, MA: 01748.

2. *Stories to read or tell aloud.* Select two to four children's books to read or tell at appropriate times during the school day, such as an opening or closing, after the noon recess, or to introduce a subject area during the day.

Suggestions:

For Grades K–3

Thomas, S. M. *Somewhere Today: A Book of Peace*. Illustrated by E. Futran. Chicago: Albert Whitman, 1998. Multicultural children help one another in ways that bring peace.

For Grades 4–6

Bryant, B. *Pony Crazy*. New York: Skylark, 1995. May and Jasmine, eight-year-old neighbors, are members of the Horse Wise Pony Club. When a new family moves into the neighborhood, they make erroneous speculations. Because of their conclusions, Cory, the new girl, has her feelings hurt. After Cory is rescued from a rogue horse's attack, the three girls secure their friendship.

Kehret, P. *Don't Go Near Mrs. Tullie*. New York: Pocket Books, 1995. Rosie Saunders and her best friend, Kayo Benton, run into trouble when they decide to help an elderly neighbor find a home for her cat. This is one of the activities of their "Care Club" in their community that helps them learn from mistakes.

3. *Friendship maker stories.* Read aloud or tell a friendship story (such as Kehret's) and ask the children to identify the friendship maker in the story. Ask, "How is that animal or person a friendship maker?" Then have the children reenact the story to show how the friendship maker helped resolve the situation peacefully. Also discuss, "When a friendship dissolves, how can someone find new friends who share similar values and interests?"

Suggestions:

For Grades K–3

Chinn, K. *Sam and the Lucky Money*. Illustrated by C. Van Wright and Ying-Hwa. New York: Lee & Low, 1995. Sam receives four, bright red envelopes decorated with shiny gold emblems as part of the traditional Chinese New Year celebration, each containing a dollar. As he goes shopping with his mother, he discovers that his money won't buy as much as he had hoped. After he meets a barefoot man in the street, Sam unselfishly concludes that his four dollars would be best spent on the stranger.

For Grades 4–6

Fox, M. *Feathers and Fools*. Illustrated by N. Wilton. Boston: Harcourt, 1996. An advocate-for-peace allegory that focuses on peacocks who notice that a flock of nearby swans can both swim and fly. The peacocks wonder if the swans will use their strength aggressively against them and soon they convince themselves that they are in danger. They begin stockpiling arms—only to be used defensively, of course. Fear, tension, and war increase until they recognize one another as fellow birds, more alike than different and that they need to share the world cooperatively.

Long, C. J. *The Middle East in Search of Peace*. New Haven CT: Millbrook, 1994. An overview of the development of the present-day conflict in the Middle East and the steps that are hopefully leading to a peace. Full-color photographs, maps, and tables are included.

4. *Friendship collages.* Show the children the artists' illustrations in books about friendships as sketching models and have the children make collages that show a time when they acted as friendship makers. Have them write or dictate a sentence to explain how they behaved in that situation. Encourage volunteers to show their art work and read their writing to the whole group.

For Grades K–3

Derby, S. *My Steps*. Illustrated by A. J. Burrows. New York: Lee and Low, 1996. This is a story about a young African American girl and her friends.

Figure 12.2 *(continued)*

Gauch, P. L. *Tanya and Emily in a Dance for Two.* Illustrated by Satomi Ichikawa. New York: Phlomel, 1994. This story has the message that friends can reinforce one another's interests and skills. Tanya, a free-spirited little girl, loves to dance in an unconventional way. When a newcomer, Emily, a graceful child, joins the class, she does everything properly and their new friendship reinforces their complementary skills of free expression.

Gershator, P. *Sweet, Sweet, Fig Banana.* Illustrated by F. Millevoix. Chicago: Albert Whiteman, 1996. Set in the Caribbean, this is the story of Soto, a young boy who plants and protects a maturing green banana tree. When the bananas are ripe, Soto takes them to his friends at the market in thanks for the gifts they have given him.

Graves, B. *The Best Worst Day.* Illustrated by N. Davis. New York: Hyperion, 1996. This is a story about Lucy who wants to be best friends with Maya, a new girl in her class.

Leedy, L. *How Humans Make Friends.* Illustrated by the author. New York: Holiday, 1996. In this humorous story, Dr. Zork Tripork, from another planet, has been sent to Earth to find out how humans make friends. He reports where and how friends meet, what they do together, what they talk about and what about them makes them like one another.

Schick, E. *My Navajo Sister.* Illustrated by the author. New York: Simon & Schuster, 1996. While her family lives for a brief time on Navajo land in the Southwest, a young white girl and Genni, a Navajo girl, become friends.

Wing, N. *Jalapeno Bagels.* Illustrated by R. Casilla. New York: Atheneum, 1996. In his family owned Mexican-Jewish-American bakery, Pablo wants to take a treat to school to celebrate International Day. His father is Jewish and his mother is Mexican, so he decides to take his parents' special recipe, bagels with chopped jalapeno peppers inside. Recipes in the back of the book are from a real bakery that reflects these heritages.

For Grades 4–6

Little, M. O. *Yoshiko and the Foreigner.* Illustrated by the author. New York: Farrar, Straus & Giroux, 1996. This story is a portrayal of a cross-cultural relationship about how the narrator's Japanese mother and North American father met and fell in love. The book includes an actual wedding photograph.

Mazer, A. Editor. *American Street: A Multicultural Anthology of Stories.* New York: Persea Books, 1993. Short stories about diversity in the United States that reflect such insights as what it's like to be an African American child in a predominantly white school, to be a Jewish child put into a Christmas play, and to be a Latino trying to eat lunch with a best friend who is Jewish.

5. *Skit activities.* A teacher can include duplicated sheets of instructions for an art activity, a maze to ponder, a puzzle to solve, or patterns for making puppets which accompany a short skit or that emphasize the focus of a lesson.

Suggestions:

For all grades

Gerke, P. *Multicultural Plays for Children.* New York: Smith & Kraus, 1996. A teacher can encourage expressive art through drama with one of the scripts for 10 plays of folktales from various cultures, with titles such as *Anansi, Vasilia, The Breman Town Musicians,* and *The Little Red Hen.* Older children can rehearse a performance for younger audiences.

Mecca, J. T. *Multicultural Plays.* Nashville, TN: Incentive Publications, 1999. Easily produced multicultural plays that offer educationally sound cultural lessons.

6. *Riddles.* A teacher can read aloud riddles and point out to children that a true riddle is often a statement where the words pretend to describe one thing while actually describing another. In other words, something is described in terms of another object to suggest something else. Guessing the answers to riddles often deals with associations and comparisons.

Suggestions:

For Grades K–3

Aber, L. W. *The Big Golden Book of Riddles, Jokes, Giggles, and Rhymes.* New York: Golden/Western, 1993. This is a collection of riddles, limericks, and knock-knock jokes that children can ask one another.

Burns, D. *Here's to Ewe: Riddles about Sheep.* Illustrated by S. S. Burns. Minneapolis: Lerner, 1990. Most of these riddles have answers that are plays on words.

Eisenberg, L., and K. Hall. *Batty Riddles.* Illustrated by N. Rubet. New York: Dial, 1993. All of the questions are related to the topics of bats.

Gounaud, K. J. *A Very Mice Joke Book.* Illustrated by M. Munsinger. New York: Lothrop, Lee & Shepard, 1993. Riddles that play on the word *mice.*

Livingston, M. C. Selector. *Riddle-Me Rhymes.* Illustrated by R. Perry. New York: McElderry, 1994. Riddles from Lewis Carroll, Emily Dickinson, Mother Goose, and other sources.

Phillips, L. *Wackysaurus: Dinosaur Jokes.* Illustrated by R. Barrett. New York: Viking, 1993. These riddles have different forms, such as one-liners, two-liners, word-play, and question-answer.

For Grades 4–6

Adler, L. *Help Wanted: Riddles About Jobs.* Illustrated by S. S. Burns. Minneapolis: Lerner, 1990. This is a collection of riddles about employment, employers, and employees. Children can select their favorite future job and a related riddle to ask their friends.

Bernstein, J. E., and P. Cohen. *Why Did the Dinosaur Cross the Road?* Illustrated by C. Whiting. Niles, IL: Albert Whitman, 1990. Riddles about dinosaurs and, anachronistically, cave people.

Burns, D., and A. Burns. *Home on the Range: Ranch-Style Riddles.* Illustrated by S. S. Burke. Minneapolis: Lerner, 1994. Riddles related to the regional topic of the range.

Cole, J., and S. Calmenson. *Why Did the Chicken Cross the Road? And Other Riddles Old and New.* Illustrated by A. Tiegreen. New York: Morrow, 1994. Over 200 riddles, arranged by topic.

Maestro, M., and G. Maestro. *Riddle City, USA: A Book of Geographic Riddles.* Illustrated by G. Maestro. New York: HarperCollins, 1994. Pun-based riddles related to the 50 states.

Peterson, S. K. *Out on a Limb: Riddles About Trees and Plants.* Illustrated by S. S. Burke. Minneapolis: Lerner, 1990. Children can search for riddles about their favorite plants or trees and ask each other their questions.

7. *Poems through the day.* A teacher can read aloud poems throughout the day to integrate poetry with other areas of the curriculum. The children can be encouraged to listen to poems, put actions to the words, dramatize some poetic words, engage in choral speaking by chanting refrains, suggest music to play as background for poem recitation or suggest that the group sing "The More We Get Together" (perhaps "the More We Read a Poem, the Friendlier We'll Be"). They can recite different poetic lines, chanting high voices versus low voices in a poetic arrangement, dividing into groups with each group chiming in to make an increasing loud chant, draw or sketch the scenes a poem creates in their thoughts, and make unusual shaped poetry pages (bookmarks, greeting pop-up cards, minibooklets).

Suggestions:

For Grades K–3

Byrd, B. *The Desert Is Theirs.* Illustrated by P. Parnall. New York: Scribner, 1975. Words emphasize the friendly respect that Papago Indians give to creatures of the desert.

Morrison, L. (Ed.) *Yours Till Niagra Falls: A Book of Autograph Verses.* Illustrated by S. Wickstrom. New York: HarperCollins, 1990. After reading aloud some of these select verses, encourage children to make autograph books and collect friendship verses from all students of the class.

For Grades 4–6

Bodecker, N. M. *Hurry, Hurry, Mary Dear.* New York: Atheneum, 1976. Select the poem "Bickering" to read aloud and discuss and illustrate such phrases as "endless dickering" and "nit picker."

Cassedy, S. *Zoomrimes: Poems About Things That Go.* New York: HarperCollins, 1993. Have the students ask their friends to name a favorite "thing that goes" from ark to zeppelin and find a related poem in this collection to copy, illustrate, and read aloud to one another.

Ciardi, J. *You Read to Me and I'll Read to You.* Illustrated by E. Gorey. New York: Lippincott, 1962. Has instructions of "all the poems printed in black, you read to me" and "all poems printed in blue, I'll read to you."

Students can team with friends and read to one another.

8. *Listenalongs or readalongs.* Friendship stories can be heard with audiobooks. Sources include Recorded Books, Inc., 270 Skipjack Road, Prince Frederick, MD 20678, and Blackstone Audiobooks, P.O. Box 969, Ashland, OR 97520. If appropriate for the group, read aloud stories that have a conflict situation about friendship, and ask the children to tell what they think each conflict is about, how it got started, and how it might become resolved. Help the students relate the conflict resolution to their own experience. If desired, ask the children to write the titles of the books on slips and place on a class bulletin board to encourage others to read some of the friendship stories. Conflict-solving and friendship-building situations from stories or real life can reflect these steps for discussion:

   a. Help children decide if it is a conflict a child can handle on his or her own or one that needs an adult's assistance.

   b. Invite children to model interpersonal skills and give them a chance to practice them and then give feedback. One skill is to say "please" and "thank you" to show good manners. Another skill is to count to 10 and take time to think about what they can do, such as try again, do one small thing at a time, turn to someone else for help, and practice seeing another person's differences as being okay and interesting.

   c. Help children to think ahead to what might happen next in a given situation.

Figure 12.2 (*continued*)

9. *Additional friendship activities.*
   - Friendship Chart. Engage students in making an "It's My Friend Chart" (approximately 18″ × 24″) complete with sketched balloons labeled with pertinent information such as "My name is _____," "I was born on _____," "I am _____ years old, and my friends are _____." Display in the room.
   - "Friends" Graph. Invite students to make a "Friends" graph with the months of the year labeled down the left side of the graph. Ask them to sketch the faces or body shapes of friends, cut out the shapes, and place the shapes on the line that identifies the month in which the friends were born.
   - Friendship Crown. Ask students whose birthdays will be celebrated in the following month to each identify a friend in the class to make a birthday crown for from art paper, glitter, balloons, and so on. Students may wear their crowns on their birthdays.
   - Friendship Buttons. Students cut out circles from adhesive-backed paper. They write, "Celebrating Friendships" on the circle and add decorations by drawing and coloring with crayons. Have them remove the adhesive backing and wear the button to recognize friends.
   - Friendship Border. Students make a "Being with Friends" border for a display board in the room. Distribute art paper cut in strips (4″ × 11 1/2″), and encourage them to draw and color festive events and situations when they were enjoying a time with friends. Words denoting friendships can be added in large bold letters.
   - Friendships from History. Children create a list of historical friendships. Some personages to consider including are friendships made by George Washington Carver, Marie Curie, Louis Pasteur, Albert Einstein, Abraham Lincoln, Jackie Robinson, Sally Ride, and Sitting Bull. Then ask each child to choose a figure and read a biography about that person. Ask the children to write their reports on their selected figures. On each of the first three pages, have them summarize and illustrate events in the person's life—as a child, as a young adult, and as an older citizen. On the fourth page, focus on what makes the person a friendship maker, and on the last page, have the children respond to "what I learned about friendship making from this life story is that . . ."
   - Friendship Logo. Ask the children to illustrate sayings about friendships that they dictate, for example, "Friendship instead of fight-ship."
   - Friendship Maker of the Week. Select children as friendship maker of the week. Create a "Friend box" in which children put the names of those who have demonstrated friendship. At the end of the week, choose any or all of the names at random. Award the children with a ribbon with a friendship symbol attached and a certificate. (Perhaps you can arrange for a local fast food business to donate friendship maker coupons).
   - Friends' Bill of Rights. Challenge children to make individual posters with their own special tips for making and maintaining friendships. Tips for friendships can include "Friends are good listeners," "Friends are accepting of others—no matter how different they are," "Friends are honest," and "Friends are interested in others."
   - Friends Interview. Invite the students to interview friends about their family traditions during special celebrations—birthdays, family reunions, religious observations, and so on. For example, birthday traditions to record may include: time, place, family members attending, songs sung, food, preparers of food, table setting items, seating arrangements, and conversation remembered. Encourage students to collect anecdotes, perhaps by using recording sheets (see the example that follows). The recording sheets may have headings so that the information is gathered in a uniform manner: name of collector, name of teller, age, birthplace, type of information collected, and friends' anecdotes.

Recording Sheet: Interview of Friend

Name of collector

Name of teller   Age (optional)

Birthplace

Friend's tradition(s) or anecdote(s)

Other

- Friendship Conflict Resolution. Mention to children that they can help design a Friendship First-Aid Kit for the bulletin board in the Classroom: They can begin by realizing that everyone is different, no one is quite the same. How could they show this on the bulletin board? Tell children that the first aid kit will help eliminate fighting, teasing, and so on. The letters in *first aid* (for a classroom friendship kit) represent:

F is for: Focusing and Fairness. Finding a good time and place to talk, focus on your feelings, and focus on the problem not the person. Fairness: Talk about following the rules and also reaching a compromise with others.
I is for: Imagination. Imagine solutions and be willing to compromise.
R is for: Respect. Show care and compassion for others.
S is for: Sensitivity. Be sensitive to rights of others and their needs.
T is for Teasing. No one likes a teaser or to be teased, so make amends for teasing by doing something nice for the person being teased. Tell the teaser how you feel and if that does not work, walk away.

A is for: Angry energy and overcoming it.
I is for: Ideas and trying to make them work.
D is for: Discussion and talking about your feelings with the one who made you mad.

As one way to display a first aid kit for friendship, you can include information about friendship stories in books. What stories do the children suggest? Read aloud stories that have a conflict situation and ask the children to tell what they think each conflict is about, how it got started, and how it might be resolved. Help the children relate the conflict resolution to their own experience. Have children write the titles of the books on paper strips and place them on the bulletin board.

Additional discussion about conflict solving, from children's books or from situations suggested by the children, can include:

Step 1: Help children decide if it is a conflict a child can handle on his/her own or if it is one that needs an adult.

Step 2: Help model interpersonal skills and give children a chance to practice them and then give feedback. One skill is to say "please" and "thank you" to show good manners and to treat others the way they want to be treated; Another skill is to count to 10 and take time to think about what they can do, such as to try again, to do one small thing at a time, to turn to someone else for help, and to practice understanding another's differences as okay and interesting.

Step 3: Help children think ahead, discussing what might happen next in a selected situation.

Step 4: Teach ways a child can say "no" to pressure from others to do something they would prefer not to do or know is wrong. Have children role-play a situation where they say no and keep repeating it or tell how they feel and why they are saying no. Say "no" over and over and walk away. Ask children to decide how they would say no to one or more of the following: taking over a task someone else does not want to do; trading food at lunch; joining in doing something you know or feel is wrong.

Is telling (tattling) right or wrong in these situation? Except in situations where someone might be hurt, is it better not to tattle and to try to solve problems yourself first? Is it tattling when you help a friend in trouble?

Step 5: Help children role-play finding a friend. Situation: Keep asking others to play until you find someone who will.

Step 6: Help children role-play keeping a friend. Situation: To keep a friend, be accepting and honest and act like one yourself.

Step 7: Help children role-play a conflict situation: Get the facts, tell how you feel, and suggest ways to resolve the conflict.

Step 8: Help children demonstrate things to do instead of hitting or hurting others in some way. Things to do are: Stop and think what children can do instead of hurting someone; think of 10 things they can do to use up the energy that anger brings and to feel better; use their words to explain their feelings or describe their needs to get what they want; show how fighting can be avoided, by asking questions, listening to one another, and ending up sharing in some way; show how talking is more effective than hitting in settling a dispute; think of a way to solve the problem and if that does not work, try another idea; talk about how it is all right to get angry but that talking about angry feelings will help a child feel better; stop and think what to do to make a child feel better, for example, screaming into a pillow or marching to music; step back from what makes a child angry and think about what to do: for instance, children can write down their feelings, discuss them with the person that made them mad, dance or drum their anger out, sit back, relax, daydream, or work out angry energy by doing something positive.

Figure 12.2 *(continued)*

- Join a No-Bully Band. Related to bullying, encourage children to stand up for themselves and tell others how they feel. School officials need to know what is happening and to provide any adults needed to supervise and stop the problem from going on at school. Role-play any or all of the following:
  - a. Banding together with friends on the playground, in the cafeteria, or walking home, against a bully. Have them remember that there is strength in numbers, and the phrase, "united we stand" should carry them through the incident.
  - b. Joining another group of students when faced with bullying—what they could say or do, especially ways to hide their feelings from a bully when being teased.
  - c. Getting involved in an extracurricular activity to make friends, identify with a safe group, and establish popularity with others.
  - d. Knowing ways to alter their routine or schedule to avoid bullies.
  - e. Ways to show an air of confidence, say some one-liners, and refuse to go along with things they don't want to do, and how to share with others what is happening to them. Have children take turns in small groups practicing their appeal to others around them for fair play, to share their feelings, and to tell what is bothering them.

- Friendship Pop-Up Card. Engage children in making friendship pop-up cards, perhaps for a child who is absent due to illness. As a resource, see D. A. Carter, *The Elements of Pop-Up: A Pop-up Book for Aspiring Paper Engineers* (New York: Simon & Schuster's Children's, 1999).

A Look at My Teachalogue, with Forty Teaching Suggestions

To assist in immediate reflection and self-assessment, we provide in Figure 12.3 a "teachalogue," a summary of teaching suggestions. The teachalogue can be used as is, or it can be personalized by you, now or at any time during your career.

PROFESSIONAL DEVELOPMENT THROUGH MENTORING

Mentoring, one teacher facilitating the learning of another teacher, can aid in professional development.[5] In what is sometimes called *peer coaching,* a mentor teacher (sometimes called a *consulting teacher*) volunteers or is selected by the teacher who wishes to improve or is selected by a school administrator, formally or informally. The mentor observes and coaches the teacher to help the teacher improve. Sometimes the teacher simply wants to learn a new skill. In other instances, the teacher being coached remains with the mentor teacher for an entire school year, developing and improving old and new skills or learning how to teach with a new program. In many districts, new teachers are automatically assigned to mentor teachers for their first year, and sometimes second year, as a program of induction.

PROFESSIONAL DEVELOPMENT THROUGH INSERVICE AND GRADUATE STUDY

Inservice workshops, seminars, and programs are offered for teachers at the school level, by the district, and by other agencies such as a county office of education or a nearby college or university. Inservice seminars and workshops and programs are usually designed for specific purposes, such as to train teachers in new teaching skills, to update their knowledge in content, and to introduce them to new teaching materials or programs.[6]

University graduate study is yet another way of continuing your professional development. Some teachers pursue master's degrees in academic teaching fields, while many others pursue master's degrees in curriculum and methods of instruction or in educational administration or counseling. Some universities offer a master of arts in teaching (MAT), a program of courses in specific academic fields that are especially designed for teachers.

PROFESSIONAL DEVELOPMENT THROUGH PARTICIPATION IN PROFESSIONAL ORGANIZATIONS

There are many professional organizations, local, statewide, national, and international. Some organizations are discipline-specific, for example,

Figure 12.3
My teachalogue

Before the lesson:

1. Did you write specific objectives, and will you share them with your students?
2. Have you prepared tentative assessment strategies and items to be used to determine if objectives are being achieved?
3. Did you refer to the established course of study for your grade level and review your state and local frameworks, the teacher's manuals, and scope and sequence charts?
4. Are your motivational techniques relevant to the lesson, helping children connect their learning to real-world experiences?
5. Are you taking students' interest in a topic for granted, or does your motivational component of the lesson meet their developmental needs and interests?
6. Did you order media materials and equipment pertinent to your lesson, and did you preview these materials?
7. Did you prepare large-size demonstration materials, and will you display them so that all of the children can see them?
8. Have you planned your lesson transitions from one activity to the next or from one lesson to the next?
9. Do you have the necessary supplies and materials ready for the lesson so time is not wasted looking for them once the lesson has begun?
10. Have you mastered manuscript writing so as to provide a model for the primary grades and mastered cursive writing so as to provide a model for the intermediate and upper grades?
11. Have you established efficient, orderly routines and procedures for your class management tasks, such as collecting homework, taking roll, collecting money, sharpening pencils, distributing and collecting books, obtaining your attention, moving around in the classroom, and dismissing students for recess, for lunch, and at the end of the school day?
12. Have you planned your preassessment strategy, perhaps as an advance organizer for the lesson, to discover what the students already know, or think they know, about the concept of the lesson?
13. Have you built into your lesson plans strategies for student reflection, metacognition, and self-assessment of their learning?
14. Have you *planned* your postassessment strategies to find out whether the children have, in fact, learned that which you intend them to learn?
15. To the best of your knowledge, do your assessment strategies authentically assess the learning objectives?
16. Have you planned for frequent checks for student understanding of the material?
17. Have you considered the needs of individual children in your class, such as children who have disabilities or who have limited proficiency in the English language?
18. Do you have a contingency plan in case something goes wrong with the lesson or there is a major disruption of the learning?
19. Are you planning variation in your instructional strategies so that students not only learn subject content but also develop their thinking skills, study skills, social skills, and sense of self-worth?
20. Have you incorporated multitasking in your instruction?
21. Have you intelligently planned the physical layout of your classroom to match the nature of the instruction and learning needs of the children?

During the lesson:

22. Are you clearing the writing board before you begin a new lesson?
23. Are you remembering that sometimes material is clearer to students if they can read it as well as hear it?
24. Are you remembering to write legibly and boldly, with large letters and in an orderly manner, so all can read your writing on the writing board?
25. Are you being gracious and sympathetic to every student, showing that you have confidence in each child's abilities?
26. Are you allowing your students to participate in discussion (to talk) and be heard, and are you giving each student the individual, private, and specific reinforcement that the student deserves?
27. Are you setting the mental stage for the learning of each new idea?
28. Are you varying your class activities sufficiently to best reach each child's learning capacities and modalities?
29. Are you attempting to build on each student's ideas, questions, and contributions during the lesson?
30. Are you making clear all relationships between main ideas and details for your students, and presenting examples of abstract concepts in simple and concrete ways?
31. Are you explaining, discussing, and commenting on any media materials you use in your lesson?

Figure 12.3 *(continued)*

32. When asking questions of students, are you remembering to give them time to review the topic, to hear the frame of reference for your questions, to recognize that your questions are on their level of understanding, and to use "think time" before they respond?
33. Are you remembering to avoid answering your own questions?
34. Are you remembering to interact with and to call on the children and to give them tasks equally according to their gender and other personal characteristics?
35. Are you introducing materials (e.g., rulers, protractors, scissors, magnets, media, art supplies, felt boards) to the children *before* they are needed in your lesson?
36. Are you evincing enthusiasm in your speech and mannerisms, maintaining a moderate pace in your classroom, and insisting that all children give you their attention when you begin a lesson?
37. Are you maintaining proximity and eye contact with all the children?
38. Are you checking frequently during the lesson to see whether the children are "getting it"; that is, that they understand the content and processes being taught?

After the lesson:

39. Are you taking time to reflect on how the lesson went and on what might have been "muddy" and what was "clear," and then reteaching all or portions of it if necessary?
40. Are you making notes to yourself as follow-up to today's lesson, perhaps special attention to be given tomorrow regarding specific content or skills for particular students?

Figure 12.4
National professional associations for teachers

- American Federation of Teachers (AFT), AFL-CIO, 555 New Jersey Avenue, NW, Washington, DC 2001 <http://www.aft.org>
- Association of American Educators (AAE), 26012 Marguerite Parkway #333, Mission Viejo, CA 92692 <http://www.aaeteachers.org/info.html#board>
- National Association of Professional Educators (NAPE), Suite 300, 900 17th Street, Washington, DC 20006 <http://www.teacherspet.com/napeindx.htm>
- National Education Association (NEA), 1201 16th Street, NW, Washington, DC 20036-3290 <http://www.nea.org>

the International Reading Association, the National Council of Teachers of Mathematics, the National Council for the Social Studies, and the National Science Teachers Association (see Chapter 5). In addition, there are national teachers organizations, such as the ones shown in Figure 12.4. The NEA[7] is the oldest and the AAE and the NAPE are more recent.

Local, district, state, and national organizations have meetings that include guest speakers, workshops, and publishers' displays. Professional meetings of teachers are usually educational, enriching, and fulfilling for those who attend. In addition, many other professional associations, such as those for reading teachers, supply speakers and publish articles in their journals that are often of interest to teachers including those beyond the targeted audience.

Professional organizations publish newsletters and journals for their members, and these will likely be found in your college or university library. Sample periodicals were listed in Figure 10.3 (Chapter 10). Many professional organizations have special membership prices for teachers who are still college or university students, a courtesy that allows for an inexpensive initial affiliation with a professional association.

PROFESSIONAL DEVELOPMENT THROUGH COMMUNICATIONS WITH OTHER TEACHERS

Visiting teachers at other schools; attending inservice workshops, graduate seminars and programs; participating in teacher study groups[8] and meetings of professional organizations; participation in teacher networks[9] and sharing with teachers through video clubs,[10] teacher book clubs,[11] or by means of electronic bulletin boards are all valuable experiences, if for no other reason than talking and sharing with teachers from across the nation and around the world. These discussions include not only a sharing of "war stories" but of ideas and descriptions of programs, books, materials, and techniques that work.

As in other process skills, the teacher practices and models skill in communication, in and out of the classroom. This includes communicating with other teachers to improve one's own repertoire of strategies and knowledge about teaching as well as sharing one's experiences with others. Teaching other teachers about your own special skills and sharing your experiences are important components of the communication and professional development processes.

PROFESSIONAL DEVELOPMENT THROUGH SUMMER WORKSHOPS AND WORK EXPERIENCE

In many areas of the United States there are workshop retreats and special programs of short-term employment available to interested teachers. Often these are available especially, though not exclusively, to teachers with special interests in reading and literacy, physical education, mathematics, science, and social studies and are offered by public agencies, private industry, foundations, and research institutes. These organizations are interested in disseminating information and providing opportunities for teachers to update their skills and knowledge, with an ultimate hope that the teachers will stimulate in more students a desire to develop their physical fitness, to understand civic responsibilities, and to consider careers in science and technology. Participating industries, foundations, governments, and institutes provide on-the-job training with salaries or stipends to teachers who are selected to participate. During the program of employment and depending on the nature of that work, a variety of people (e.g., scientists, technicians, politicians, businesspersons, social workers, and sometimes university educators) meet with teachers to share experiences and discuss what is being learned and its implications for teaching and curriculum development.

Some of the programs for teachers are government-sponsored field-centered and content-specific. For example, a program may concentrate on geology, anthropology, mathematics, or reading. At another location, a program may concentrate on teaching, using a specific new or experimental curriculum. These programs, located around the country, may have university affiliation, which means that university credit may be available. Room and board, travel, and a stipend are sometimes granted to participating teachers.

Sources of information about the availability of programs include professional journals, a neighboring university or college or the local chamber of commerce, and meetings of the local or regional teacher's organization. In areas where there are no organized retreat or work experience programs for teachers, some teachers have had success in initiating their own by grant writing[12] or establishing contact with management personnel of local businesses or companies.

PROFESSIONAL DEVELOPMENT THROUGH MICRO PEER TEACHING

Micro peer teaching (MPT) is a skill-development strategy used for professional development by both preservice (prior to credentialing) and inservice (credentialed and employed) teachers. Micro peer teaching (to which you were introduced in Exercises 7.7 and 9.2) is a scaled-down teaching experience involving a:

- Limited objective
- Brief interval for teaching a lesson
- Lesson taught to a few (8–10) peers (as your students)
- Lesson that focuses on the use of one or several instructional strategies

Micro peer teaching can be a predictor of later teaching effectiveness in a regular classroom. More importantly, it can provide an opportunity to develop and improve specific teaching behaviors. A videotaped MPT allows you to see yourself in action for self-evaluation and diagnosis. Evaluation of an MPT session is based on:

- The quality of the teacher's preparation and lesson implementation
- The quality of the planned and implemented student involvement
- Whether the target objective(s) was reached
- The appropriateness of the cognitive level of the lesson

Whether a preservice or inservice teacher, you are urged to participate in one or more MPT experiences. Formatted differently from previous exercises in this resource guide, Exercise 12.2 can represent a summative performance assessment for the course for which this book is being used.

For Your Notes

EXERCISE 12.2   PULLING IT ALL TOGETHER—MICRO PEER TEACHING III

Instructions: The purpose of this exercise is to learn how to develop your own MPT experiences. You will prepare and teach a lesson that is prepared as a lesson presentation for your peers, at their level of intellectual maturity and understanding (i.e., as opposed to teaching the lesson to peers pretending that they are public school students).

This experience has two components:

1. Your preparation and implementation of a demonstration lesson
2. Your completion of an analysis of the summative peer assessment and the self-assessment, with statements of how you would change the lesson and your teaching of it were you to repeat the lesson

You should prepare and carry out a 15- to 20-minute lesson to a group of peers. The exact time limit for the lesson should be set by your group, based on the size of the group and the amount of time available. When the time limit has been set, complete the time-allowed entry (item 1) of Form A of this exercise. Some of your peers will serve as your students; others will be evaluating your teaching. (The process works best when "students" do not evaluate while being students.) Your teaching should be videotaped for self-evaluation.

For your lesson, identify one concept and develop your lesson to teach toward an understanding of that concept. Within the time allowed, your lesson should include both teacher talk and a hands-on activity for the students. Use Form A for the initial planning of your lesson. Then complete a lesson plan, selecting a lesson plan format as discussed in Chapter 6. Then present the lesson to the "students." The peers who are evaluating your presentation should use Form B of this exercise.

After your presentation, collect your peer evaluations (the Form B copies that you gave to the evaluators). Then review your presentation by viewing the videotape. After viewing the tape, prepare:

- A tabulation and statistical analysis of peer evaluations of your lesson
- A self-evaluation based on your analysis of the peer evaluations, your feelings having taught the lesson, and your thoughts after viewing the videotape
- A summary analysis that includes your selection and description of your teaching strengths and weaknesses, as indicated by this peer-teaching experience, and how you would improve were you to repeat the lesson.

Tabulation of Peer Evaluations

The procedure for tabulating the completed evaluations received from your peers is as follows:

1. *Use a blank copy of Form B for tabulating.* In the left margin of that copy, place the letters *N* (number) and σ (total) to prepare for two columns of numbers that will fall below each of those letters. In the far right margin, place the word *Score*.
2. *For each item (A through Y) on the peer evaluation form, count the number of evaluators who gave a rating (from 1 to 5) on the item.* Sometimes an evaluator may not rate a particular item, so although there may have been 10 peers evaluating your micro peer teaching, the number of evaluators giving you a rating on any one particular item could be less than 10. For each item, the number of evaluators rating that item we call *N*. Place this number in the *N* column at the far left margin on your blank copy of Form B, next to the relevant item.
3. *Using a calculator, obtain the sum of the peer ratings for each item.* For example, for item A, Lesson Preparation, you add the numbers given by each evaluator for that item. If there were 10 evaluators who gave you a number rating on that item, then your sum on that item will not be more than 50 (5×10). Because individual evaluators will make their *X* marks differently, you sometimes must estimate an individual evaluator's number rating; that is, rather than a clear rating of 3 or 3.5 on an item, you may have to estimate it as being a 3.2 or a 3.9. In the left-hand margin of your blank copy of Form B, in the σ column, place the sum for each item.
4. *Now obtain a score for each item, A through Y.* The score for each item is obtained by dividing σ by *N*. Your score for each item will range from 1 to 5. Write this dividend in the column in the right-hand margin under the word *Score* on a line parallel to the relevant item. This is the number you will use in the analysis phase.

EXERCISE 12.2 *(continued)*

Procedure for Analyzing the Tabulations

Having completed the tabulation of the peer evaluations of your teaching, you are ready to proceed with you analysis of those tabulations.

1. To proceed, you need a blank copy of Form C of this exercise, your self-analysis form.
2. On the blank copy of Form C are five items: Implementation, Personal, Voice, Materials, and Strategies.
3. In the far left margin of Form C, place the letter σ for the sum. To its right, and parallel with it, place the word *Average*. You now have arranged for two columns of five numbers each—a σ column and an *Average* column.
4. For each of the five items, get the total score for that item, as follows:
   a. *Implementation.* Add all scores (from the right-hand margin of blank Form B) for the four items a, c, x, and y. The total should be 20 or less (4×5). Place this total in the left-hand margin under σ (to the left of "1. Implementation").
   b. *Personal.* Add all scores (from the right-hand margin of blank Form B) for the nine items f, g, m, n, o, p, q, s, and t. The total should be 45 or less (9×5). Place this total in the left-hand margin under σ (to the left of "2. Personal").
   c. *Voice.* Add all scores (from the right-hand margin of blank Form B) for the three items h, i, and j. The total should be 15 or less (3×5). Place this total in the left-hand margin under σ (to the left of "3. Voice").
   d. *Materials.* Add all scores (from the right-hand margin of blank Form B) for item k. The total should be 5 or less (1×5). Place this total in the left-hand margin under σ (to the left of "4. Materials").
   e. *Strategies.* Add all scores (from the right hand margin of blank Form B) for the eight items b, d, e, l, r, u, v, and w. The total should be 40 or less (8×5). Place this total in the left-hand margin under σ (to the left of "5. Strategies").
5. Now for each of the five categories, divide the sum by the number of items in the category to get your peer evaluation average score for that category. For item 1 you will divide by 4; for item 2, by 9; for item 3, by 3; for item 4, by 1; and for item 5, by 8. For each category you should then have a final average peer evaluation score of a number between 1 and 5. If correctly done, you now have average scores for each of the five categories: Implementation, Personal, Voice, Materials, and Strategies. With those scores and evaluator's comments you can prepare your final summary analysis.

The following table includes three sample analyses of MPT lessons based *only* on the scores—that is, without reference to comments made by individual evaluators, although peer evaluator's comments are important considerations for actual analyses.

Sample Analyses of MPTs Based Only on Peer Evaluation Scores

Teacher	Category/Rating					Possible Strengths and Weaknesses
	1	2	3	4	5	
A	4.2	2.5	2.8	4.5	4.5	Good lesson, weakened by personal items and voice.
B	4.5	4.6	5.0	5.0	5.0	Excellent teaching, perhaps needing a stronger start.
C	2.5	3.0	3.5	1.0	1.5	Poor strategy choice, lack of student involvement.

EXERCISE 12.2 FORM A—MPT PREPARATION

Instructions Form A is to be used for initial preparation of your MPT lesson. (For preparation of your lesson, study Form B.) After completing Form A, proceed with the preparation of your MPT lesson using a lesson plan format as discussed in Chapter 6. A copy of the final lesson plan should be presented to the evaluators at the start of your MPT presentation.

1. Time allowed _____

2. Title or topic of lesson I will teach _____

3. Concept _____

4. Specific instructional objectives for the lesson:

   Cognitive _____

   _____

   Affective _____

   _____

   Psychomotor _____

   _____

5. Strategies to be used, including approximate time plan:

   Set introduction _____

   _____

   Transitions _____

   _____

   Closure _____

   _____

   Others _____

   _____

6. Student experiences to be provided (i.e., specify for each—visual, verbal, kinesthetic, and tactile

   experiences): _____

   _____

   _____

7. Materials, equipment, and resources needed:

   _____

   _____

   _____

For Your Notes

EXERCISE 12.2 FORM B—PEER EVALUATION

Instructions: Evaluators use Form B, making an *X* on the continuum from 5 to 1. Far left (5) is the highest rating; far right (1) is the lowest. Completed forms are collected and given to the teacher upon completion of the teacher's MPT and are reviewed by the teacher prior to reviewing his or her videotaped lesson.

To evaluators: Comments as well as marks are useful to the teacher.

To teacher: Give one copy of your lesson plan to the evaluators at the start of your MPT. (*Note:* It is best if evaluators can be together at a table at the rear of the room.)

Teacher _____ Date _____

Topic _____

Concept _____

1. Organization of Lesson	5	4	3	2	1
a. Lesson preparation evident	very		somewhat		no
b. Lesson beginning effective	yes		somewhat		poor
c. Subject-matter knowledge apparent	yes		somewhat		no
d. Strategies selection effective	yes		somewhat		poor
e. Closure effective	yes		somewhat		poor

Comments _____

_____

_____

_____

_____

_____

_____

_____

_____

_____

_____

_____

2. Lesson Implementation	5	4	3	2	1
f. Eye contact excellent	yes		somewhat		poor
g. Enthusiasm evident	yes		somewhat		no
h. Speech delivery	articulate		minor problems		poor
i. Voice inflection; cueing	effective		minor problems		poor
j. Vocabulary use	well-chosen		minor problems		poor
k. Aids, props, and materials	effective		okay		none

EXERCISE 12.2 FORM B *(continued)*

l. Use of examples and analogies	effective	need improvement	none
m. Student involvement	effective	okay	none
n. Use of overlapping skills	good	okay	poor
o. Nonverbal communication	effective	a bit confusing	distracting
p. Use of active listening	effective	okay	poor
q. Responses to students	personal and accepting	passive or indifferent	impersonal and antagonistic
r. Use of questions	effective	okay	poor
s. Use of student names	effective	okay	no
t. Use of humor	effective	okay	poor
u. Directions and refocusing	succinct	a bit vague	confusing
v. Teacher mobility	effective	okay	none
w. Use of transitions	smooth	a bit rough	unclear
x. Motivating presentation	very	somethat	not at all
y. Momentum (pacing) of lesson	smooth and brisk	okay	too slow or too fast

Comments _____

_____

_____

_____

_____

_____

_____

_____

_____

_____

_____

_____

_____

_____

_____

_____

_____

EXERCISE 12.2 FORM C—TEACHER'S SUMMATIVE PEER EVALUATION

See instructions within Exercise 12.2 for completing this form.

1. Implementation (items a, c, x, y)	5	4	3	2	1
2. Personal (items f, g, m, n, o, p, q, s, t)	5	4	3	2	1
3. Voice (items h, i, j)	5	4	3	2	1
4. Materials (item k)	5	4	3	2	1
5. Strategies (items b, d, e, l, r, u, v, w)	5	4	3	2	1

Total = _____

Comments _____

_____

_____

_____

_____

_____

_____

_____

_____

_____

_____

_____

_____

_____

_____

_____

_____

_____

_____

_____

_____

_____

_____

_____

For Your Notes

SUMMARY

Because teaching and learning go hand in hand and the effectiveness of one affects that of the other, the final two chapters of this resource guide have dealt with both aspects of the *how well* component of teacher preparation—how well the students are learning and how well the teacher is teaching.

In addition, you have been presented with guidelines about how to obtain your first teaching job and how to continue your professional development. Throughout your teaching career you will continue improving your knowledge and skills in all aspects of teaching and learning.

We wish you the very best in your new career. Be the very best teacher that you can be and for as long as you can. The nation and its youth need you.

EXTENDING MY COMPETENCY: QUESTIONS FOR CLASS DISCUSSION

1. Discover what professional teacher organizations there are in your geographical area. Share what you find with others in your class. Attend a local, regional, or national meeting of a professional teachers' association, report to your class what it was like and what you learned, and share with your class any free or inexpensive teaching materials you obtained.
2. Talk with experienced teachers and find out how they remain current in their teaching fields. Share what you find with others in your class.
3. Do you believe that any of the following—teachers' salaries, tenure, rewards, sanctions—should be tied to student achievement? Explain why or why not.
4. As a first-year teacher, which do you believe you would prefer: to be observed and evaluated by the school principal or to be observed and evaluated by a committee of peers? Explain why.
5. Explain why you would or would not take a job teaching a grade level or subject for which you have not been prepared or trained.
6. Does your state have a Web site that lists teaching vacancies? If it does, do all school districts participate? Is it possible in your state to apply electronically for teaching openings?
7. Would you be willing to have a surgical operation performed on you by an unlicensed surgeon? Would you be willing to be defended in trial by an unlicensed attorney? Would you be willing to insure your automobile by an unlicensed insurance agent? Would you be willing to leave your infant each day in the care of an unlicensed day care center? Would you be willing to leave your child each day in the care of an unlicensed teacher? Discuss your responses to these questions with your colleagues. Is the answer to any one more or less significant than the others?
8. Describe any prior concepts you held that changed as a result of your experiences with this chapter. Describe the changes.
9. From your current observations and fieldwork related to this teacher preparation program, clearly identify one specific example of educational practice that seems contradictory to exemplary practice or theory presented in this chapter. Present your explanation for the discrepancy.
10. Congratulations! You have reached the end of this resource guide, but there may be questions lingering in your mind. As before, list them and try to find answers.

FOR FURTHER READING

Backes, C. E., and Backes, L. S. (1999). Making the Best of a Learning Experience. *Techniques: Making Education and Career Connections, 74*(5), 23–24.

Cramer, G., and Hurst, B. (2000). *How to Find a Teaching Job: A Guide for Success.* Upper Saddle River, NJ: Merrill/Prentice Hall.

Good, T. L., and Brophy, J. E. (2000). *Looking in Classrooms* (8th ed., Chap. 11). New York: Addison Wesley/Longman.

Graham, P., et al. (Eds.). (1999). *Teacher/Mentor.* New York: Teachers College Press.

Hurst, C. O., and Otis, R. (2000). *Friends and Relations: Using Literature With Social Themes, Grades 3–5.* Greenfield, MA: Northeast Foundation for Children.

Kellough, R. D. (2001). *Surviving Your First Year of Teaching: Guidelines for Success* (2nd ed.). Upper Saddle River, NJ: Merrill/Prentice Hall.

Lohr, L. (1999). Assistance and Review: Teachers Get Started. *Teaching and Change, 6*(3), 295–313.

Lowenhaupt, M. A., and Stephanik, C. E. (1999). *Making Student Teaching Work: Creating a Partnership* (Fastback 447). Bloomington, IN: Phi Delta Kappa Educational Foundation.

Martin, D. B. (1999). *The Portfolio Planner: Making Professional Portfolios Work for You.* Upper Saddle River, NJ: Merrill/Prentice Hall.

Mastrilli, T. M., and Brown, D. S. (1999). Elementary Student Teachers' Cases: An Analysis of Dilemmas and Solutions. *Action in Teacher Education, 21*(1), 50–60.

Oakley, K. (1998). The Performance Assessment System: A Portfolio Assessment Model for Evaluating Beginning Teachers. *Journal of Personnel Evaluation in Education, 11*(4), 323–341.

Sullivan, S., and Glanz, J. (2000). *Supervision That Improves Teaching: Strategies and Techniques.* Thousand Oaks, CA: Corwin Press.

Wentz, P. J. *The Student Teaching Experience.* Second Edition. Upper Saddle River, NJ: Merrill/Prentice Hall, 2001.

NOTES

1. For further information, see D. B. Martin, *The Portfolio Planner: Making Professional Portfolios Work*

for You (Upper Saddle River, NJ: Merrill/Prentice Hall, 1999); G. Cramer and B. Hurst, *How to Find a Teaching Job: A Guide for Success* (Upper Saddle River, NJ: Merril/Prentice Hall, 2000); the theme issue of *Teacher Education Quarterly, 25*(1) (Winter 1998); and the Internet at <http://www.teachnet.com/>.

2. In the fall 2000, *Education Week* launched their test phase of a national online teacher job bank on which districts nationwide may post their job vacancies and on which job-seeking teachers can post their résumés. See <http://www.edweek.org>.

3. For additional suggestions for preparing for a teaching job interview, see Chapter 5 of G. Cramer and B. Hurst, *How to Find a Teaching Job,* and the Internet at <http://www.teachnet.com/>.

4. See Chapter 4, Creating a Professional Portfolio, in C. Danielson, *Enhancing Professional Practice: A Framework for Teaching* (Alexandria, VA: Association for Supervision and Curriculum Development, 1996), pp. 38–50.

5. For additional information, see The International Center for Information About New Teacher Mentoring and Induction at <http://www.teachermentors.com/MCenter%20Site/AdviceBegTchr.html>, a description of California's Beginning Teacher Support and Assessment (BSTA) Program at <http://www.ccoe.k12.ca.us/coe/curins.sbtsa/description>, and G. L. Good and J. E. Bro-phy, *Looking in Classrooms,* 8th edition. (New York: Addison Wesley/Longman, 2000), pp. 506–508.

6. See, for example, K. S. Shipiro and J. E. Clauss, Freshness in the Mountains, *Educational Leadership 57*(8), 66–68 (May 2000).

7. The NEA and AFT recently have merged in at least two states, Minnesota and Montana.

8. See, for example, G. Cramer, et al., *Teacher Study Groups for Professional Development,* Fastback 406 (Bloomington, IN: Phi Delta Kappa Educational Foundation, 1996) and G. L. Good and J. E. Brophy, *Looking in Classrooms,* pp. 482–484.

9. See, for example, A. Lieberman and M. Grolnick, Networks, Reform, and the Professional Development of Teachers, Chapter 10 (pp. 192–215) in A. Hargreaves (Ed.), *Rethinking Educational Change With Heart and Mind,* ASCD 1997 Yearbook (Alexandria, VA: Association for Supervision and Curriculum Development, 1997).

10. See, for example, M. G. Sherin, Viewing Teaching on Videotape, *Educational Leadership, 57*(8), 36–38 (May 2000).

11. See, for example, S. M. Goldberg and E. Pesko, The Teacher Book Club, *Educational Leadership, 57*(8), 39–41 (May 2000).

12. See, for example, K. Chandler, Summer Sustenance, *Educational Leadership, 57*(8), 63–65 (May 2000).

Glossary

ability grouping The assignment of students to separate classrooms or to separate activities within a classroom according to their perceived academic abilities. Homogeneous grouping is the grouping of students of similar abilities, whereas heterogeneous grouping is the grouping of students of mixed abilities.

accommodation The cognitive process of modifying a schema or creating new schemata.

accountability Reference to the concept that an individual is responsible for his or her behaviors and should be able to demonstrate publicly the worth of the activities carried out.

advance organizer Preinstructional cues that encourage a mental set, used to enhance retention of materials to be studied.

advisor-advisee A homeroom or advisory program that provides each student the opportunity to interact with peers about school and personal concerns and to develop a meaningful relationship with at least one member of the school staff.

affective domain The area of learning related to interests, attitudes, feelings, values, and personal adjustment.

aim The term sometimes used for the most general educational objectives.

alternative assessment Assessment of learning in ways that are different from traditional paper-and-pencil objective testing, such as a portfolio, project, or self-assessment. See *authentic assessment*.

American Federation of Teachers (AFT) A national professional organization of teachers founded in 1916 and currently affiliated with the American Federation of Labor and Congress of Industrial Organizations (AFL-CIO).

anticipatory set See *advance organizer*.

articulation Term used when referring to the connectedness of the various components of the formal curriculum. *Vertical articulation* is used when referring to the connectedness of the curriculum K–12; *horizontal articulation* refers to the connectedness across a grade level.

assessment The relatively neutral process of finding out what students are learning or have learned as a result of instruction. See also *evaluation*.

assignment A statement telling the student what he or she is to accomplish.

assimilation The cognitive process by which a learner integrates new information into an existing schema.

at-risk General term given to a student who shows a high potential for not completing school.

authentic assessment The use of evaluation procedures (usually portfolios and projects) that are highly compatible with the instructional objectives. Also referred to as *accurate, active, aligned, alternative, direct,* and *performance assessment*.

behavioral objective A statement of expectation describing what the learner should be able to do upon completion of the instruction and containing four components: the audience (learner), the overt behavior, the conditions, and the level or degree of performance. Also referred to as *performance* and *terminal objective*.

behaviorism A theory that equates learning with changes in observable behavior.

block scheduling The school programming procedure that provides large blocks of time (e.g., two hours) in which individual teachers or teacher teams can organize and arrange groupings of students for varied periods, thereby more effectively individualizing the instruction for students with various needs and abilities.

brainstorming An instructional strategy used to create a flow of new ideas, during which judgments of the ideas of others are forbidden.

CD-ROM (compact disc-read only memory) Digitally encoded information permanently recorded on a compact disc.

classroom control The process of influencing student behavior in the classroom.

classroom management The teacher's system of establishing a climate for learning, including techniques for preventing and handling student misbehavior.

clinical supervision A nonevaluative collegial process of facilitating teaching effectiveness by involving a triad of individuals: the student teacher, the cooperating teacher, and the university supervisor. Sometimes known as *effective supervision,* clinical supervision includes: (a) a preobservation conference between the supervisor and the student teacher to specify and agree upon the specific objectives for an observation visit; (b) a data collection observation; and (c) a postobservation conference to analyze the data collected during the observation and to set goals for a subsequent observation.

closure In a lesson, the means by which a teacher brings the lesson to an end.

coaching See *mentoring.*

cognition The process of thinking.

cognitive disequilibrium The mental state of not yet having made sense out of a perplexing (discrepant) situation.

cognitive domain The area of learning related to intellectual skills, such as retention and assimilation of knowledge.

cognitive psychology A branch of psychology devoted to the study of how individuals acquire, process, and use information.

cognitivism A theory that holds that learning entails the construction or reshaping of mental schemata and that mental processes mediate learning. Also known as *constructivism.*

common planning time A regularly scheduled time during the school day when teachers who teach the same students meet for joint planning, parent conferences, materials preparation, and student evaluation.

compact disc (CD) A 4.72-inch disc on which a laser has recorded digital information.

competency-based instruction See *performance-based instruction.*

comprehension A level of cognition that refers to the skill of understanding.

computer-assisted instruction (CAI) Instruction received by a student when interacting with lessons programmed into a computer system.

computer literacy The ability at some level on a continuum to understand and use computers.

computer-managed instruction (CMI) The use of a computer system to manage information about learner performance and learning-resources options in order to prescribe and control individual lessons.

constructivism See *cognitivism.*

continuous progress An instructional procedure that allows students to progress at their own pace through a sequenced curriculum.

convergent thinking Thinking that is directed to a preset conclusion.

cooperative learning A genre of instructional strategies that use small groups of students working together and helping one another on learning tasks, with an emphasis on support among group members rather than competition.

core curriculum Subject or discipline components of the curriculum considered absolutely necessary. Traditionally these are English/language arts, mathematics, science, and social science.

covert behavior A learner behavior that is not outwardly observable.

criterion A standard by which behavioral performance is judged.

criterion-referenced assessment Assessment in which standards are established and behaviors are judged against the preset guidelines, rather than against the behaviors of others.

critical thinking The ability to recognize and identify problems and discrepancies, to propose and to test solutions, and to arrive at tentative conclusions based on the data collected.

curriculum Originally derived from a Latin term referring to a race course for the chariots, the term still has no widely accepted definition. As used in this text, curriculum is that which is planned and encouraged for teaching and learning. This includes both school and nonschool environments, overt (formal) and hidden (informal) curriculums, and broad as well as narrow notions of content—its development, acquisition, and consequences.

deductive learning Learning that proceeds from the general to the specific. See also *expository learning.*

developmental characteristics A set of common intellectual, psychological, physical, and social characteristics that, when considered as a whole, indicate an individual's development relative to others during a particular age span.

developmental needs A set of needs unique and appropriate to the developmental characteristics of a particular age span.

diagnostic assessment See *preassessment.*

didactic teaching See *direct teaching.*

direct experience Learning by doing (applying) that which is being learned.

direct instruction Teacher-centered instruction, typically with the entire class, and where the teacher controls student attention and behaviors as opposed to permitting students greater control over their own learning and behaviors.

direct intervention Teacher use of verbal reminders or verbal commands to redirect student behavior, as opposed to nonverbal gestures or cues.

direct teaching Teacher-centered expository instruction.

discipline The process of controlling student behavior in the classroom. The term has been largely replaced by the terms *classroom control* or *classroom management*. It is also used in reference to the subject taught (e.g., language arts, science, mathematics, and so forth).

discovery learning Learning that proceeds from identification of a problem, through the development of hypotheses, the testing of the hypotheses, and the arrival at a conclusion. See also *critical thinking*.

divergent thinking Thinking that expands beyond original thought.

downshifting Reverting to earlier learned, lower cognitive level behaviors.

early adolescence The developmental stage of young people as they approach and begin to experience puberty. This stage usually occurs between 10 and 14 years of age and deals with the successful attainment of the appropriate developmental characteristics for this age span.

eclectic Using the best from a variety of sources.

effective school A school where students master basic skills, seek academic excellence in all subjects, demonstrate achievement, and display good behavior and attendance. Known also as an *exemplary school*.

elective High-interest or special-needs courses that are based on student selection from various options.

elementary school Any school that has been planned and organized especially for children of some combination of grades kindergarten through six. There are many variations, though; for example, a school might house children of preschool through seven or eight and still be called an elementary school.

empathy The ability to understand the feelings of another person.

equality Considered to be the same in status or competency level.

equilibration The mental process of moving from disequilibrium to equilibrium.

equilibrium The balance between assimilation and accommodation.

equity Fairness and justice, that is, impartiality.

evaluation Like assessment, but includes making sense out of the assessment results, usually based on criteria or a rubric. Evaluation is more subjective than is assessment.

exemplary school A school where students master basic skills, seek academic excellence in all subjects, demonstrate achievement, and display good behavior and attendance. Known also as an *effective school*.

exceptional child A child who deviates from the average in any of the following ways: mental characteristics, sensory ability, neuromotor or physical characteristics, social behavior, communication ability, or multiple handicaps. Also known as a *special-needs student* and *special education student*.

exploratory course A course designed to help students explore curriculum experiences based on their felt needs, interests, and abilities.

expository learning The traditional classroom instructional approach that proceeds as follows: presentation of information to the learners, reference to particular examples, and application of the information to the learner's experiences.

extended-year school Schools that have extended the school year calendar from the traditional 180 day to a longer period such as 210 days.

extrinsic motivators Motivation of learning by rewards outside of the learner, such as parent and teacher expectations, gifts, certificates, and grades.

facilitating behavior Teacher behavior that makes it possible for students to learn.

facilitative teaching See *indirect teaching*.

family See *school-within-a-school*.

feedback Information sent from the receiver to the originator that provides disclosure about the reception of the intended message.

flexible scheduling Organization of classes and activities in a way that allows for variation from day to day, as opposed to the traditional fixed schedule that does not vary from day to day.

formative assessment Evaluation of learning in progress.

goal, course A broad generalized statement about the expected outcomes of a course.

goal, educational A desired instructional outcome that is broad in scope.

goal, teacher A statement about what the teacher hopes to accomplish.

hands-on learning Learning by doing, or active learning.

heterogeneous grouping A grouping pattern that does not separate students into groups based on their intelligence, learning achievement, or physical characteristics.

holistic learning Learning that incorporates emotions with thinking.

homogeneous grouping A grouping pattern that separates students into groups based on their intelligence, school achievement, or physical characteristics.

house See *school-within-a-school.*

inclusion The commitment to the education of each special needs learner, to the maximum extent appropriate, in the school and classroom he or she would otherwise attend.

independent study An instructional strategy that allows a student to select a topic, set the goals, and work alone to attain them.

indirect teaching Student-centered teaching using discovery and inquiry instructional strategies.

individualized instruction See *individualized learning.*

individualized learning The self-paced process whereby individual students assume responsibility for learning through study, practice, feedback, and reinforcement with appropriately designed instructional packages or modules.

inductive learning Learning that proceeds from specifics to the general. See also *discovery learning.*

inquiry learning Like discovery learning, except here the learner designs the processes to be used in resolving the problem, thereby requiring higher levels of cognition.

inservice teacher Term used when referring to credentialed and employed teachers.

instruction Planned arrangement of experiences to help a learner develop understanding and to achieve a desirable change in behavior.

instructional module Any freestanding instructional unit that includes these components: rationale, objectives, pretest, learning activities, comprehension checks with instructive feedback, and posttest.

integrated (interdisciplinary) curriculum Curriculum organization that combines subject matter traditionally taught separately.

interdisciplinary team An organizational pattern of two or more teachers representing different subject areas. The team shares the same students, schedule, areas of the school, and the opportunity for teaching more than one subject.

interdisciplinary thematic unit (ITU) A thematic unit that crosses boundaries of two or more disciplines.

intermediate grades Term sometimes used to refer to grades 4–6. An intermediate school, for example, is an elementary school that houses children of grades 4–6.

internalization The extent to which an attitude or value becomes a part of the learner. That is, without having to think about it, the learner's behavior reflects the attitude or value.

intervention A teacher's interruption to redirect a student's behavior, either by direct intervention (e.g., by a verbal command) or by indirect intervention (e.g., by eye contact or physical proximity).

intramural program Organized activity program that features events between individuals or teams from within the school.

intrinsic motivation Motivation of learning through the student's internal sense of accomplishment.

intuition Knowing without conscious reasoning.

junior high school A school that houses grades 7–9 or 7–8 and that has a schedule and curriculum that resemble those of the senior high school (grades 9–12 or 10–12) more than they do those of the elementary school.

learning The development of understandings and the change in behavior resulting from experiences. For different interpretations of learning, see *behaviorism* and *cognitivism.*

learning center (LC) An instructional strategy that uses activities and materials located at a special place in the classroom and that is designed to allow a student to work independently at his or her own pace to learn one area of content.

learning modality The way a person receives information. Four modalities are recognized: visual, auditory, tactile (touch), and kinesthetic (movement).

learning resource center The central location in the school where instructional materials and media are stored, organized, and accessed by students and staff.

learning style The way a person learns best in a given situation.

looping An arrangement in which the cohort of students and teachers remains together as a group for several or for all the years a child is at a particular school. Also referred to as *multiyear grouping, multiyear instruction, multiyear placement,* and *teacher-student progression.*

magnet school A school that specializes in a particular academic area, such as science, mathematics and technology, the arts, or international relations. Also referred to as a *theme school.*

mainstreaming Placing an exceptional child in regular education classrooms for all (inclusion) or part (partial inclusion) of the school day.

mastery learning The concept that a student should master the content of one lesson before moving on to the content of the next.

measurement The process of collecting and interpreting data.

mentoring One-on-one coaching, tutoring, or guidance to facilitate learning.

metacognition The ability to plan, monitor, and evaluate one's own thinking.

micro peer teaching (MPT) Teaching a limited objective for a brief period to a small group of peers for the purpose of evaluation and improvement of particular teaching skills.

middle grades Grades 5–8.

middle level education Any school unit between elementary and high school.

middle school A school that has been planned and organized especially for students of ages 10–14 and that generally has grades 5–8, with grades 6–8 being the most popular grade-span organization, although many varied patterns exist. For example, a school might include only grades 7 and 8 and still be called a middle school.

minds-on learning Learning in which the learner is intellectually active, thinking about what is being learned.

misconception Faulty understanding of a major idea or concept. Also known as a *naive theory* and *conceptual misunderstanding*.

modeling The teacher's direct and indirect demonstration, by actions and by words, of the behaviors expected of students.

multicultural education A deliberate attempt to help students understand facts, generalizations, attitudes, and behaviors derived from their own ethnic roots as well as others. In this process students unlearn racism and biases and recognize the interdependent fabric of society, giving due acknowledgment for contributions made by its members.

multilevel teaching See *multitasking*.

multimedia The combined use of sound, video, and graphics for instruction.

multiple intelligences A theory of several different intelligences, as opposed to just one general intelligence; other intelligences that have been described are verbal/linguistic, musical, logical/mathematical, naturalist, visual/spatial, bodily/kinesthetic, interpersonal, and intrapersonal.

multipurpose board A writing board with a smooth plastic surface used with special marking pens rather than chalk. Sometimes called a *visual aid panel,* the board may have a steel backing and then can be used as a magnetic board as well as a screen for projecting visuals.

multitasking The simultaneous use of several levels of teaching and learning in the same classroom, with students working on different objectives or different tasks leading to the same objective. Also called *multilevel teaching*.

naïve theory See *misconception*.

National Education Association (NEA) The nation's oldest professional organization of teachers, founded in 1857 as the National Teachers Association and changed in 1879 to its present name.

norm-referenced Individual performance is judged relative to overall performance of the group (e.g., grading on a curve), as opposed to being criterion-referenced.

orientation set See *advance organizer*.

overlapping A teacher behavior where the teacher is able to attend to more than one matter at once.

overt behavior A learner behavior that is outwardly observable.

paraprofessional An adult who is not a credentialed teacher but who works with children in the classroom with and under the supervision of a credentialed person.

partial inclusion Placing special-needs children in a regular education classroom part of the day.

peer tutoring An instructional strategy that places students in a tutorial role in which one student helps another learn.

performance assessment See *authentic assessment*.

performance-based instruction Instruction designed around the instruction and assessment of student achievement against specified and predetermined objectives.

performance objective See *behavioral objective*.

portfolio assessment An alternative approach to evaluation that assembles representative samples of a student's work over time as a basis for assessment.

positive reinforcer A means of encouraging desired student behaviors by rewarding those behaviors when they occur.

preassessment Diagnostic assessment of what students know or think they know prior to the instruction.

preservice Term used when referring to teachers in training, as opposed to inservice teachers or teachers who are employed.

probationary teacher An untenured teacher. After a designated number of years in the same district, usually three, upon rehire the probationary teacher receives a tenure contract.

procedure A statement telling the student how to accomplish a task.

psychomotor domain The domain of learning that involves locomotor behaviors.

realia   Real objects used as visual props during instruction, such as political campaign buttons, plants, memorabilia, art, balls, and so forth.

reciprocal teaching   A form of collaborative teaching where the teacher and the students share the teaching responsibility and all are involved in asking questions, clarifying, predicting, and summarizing.

reflection   The conscious process of mentally replaying experiences.

reflective abstraction   See *metacognition.*

reliability   In measurement, the consistency with which an item or instrument is measured over time.

rubric   An outline of the criteria used to assess a student's work.

rules   In classroom management, rules are the standards of expectation for classroom behavior.

schema (plural: schemata)   A mental construct by which the learner organizes his or her perceptions of situations and knowledge.

school-within-a-school   Sometimes referred to as a *house, cluster, village, pod,* or *family,* it is a teaching arrangement where one team of teachers is assigned to work with the same group of about 125 students for a common block of time, for the entire school day, or, in some instances, for all the years those students are at that school.

secondary school   Traditionally, any school housing students for any combination of grades 7–12.

self-contained classroom   Commonly used in the primary grades, it is a grouping pattern where one teacher teaches all or most all subjects to one group of children.

self-paced learning   See *individualized learning.*

sequencing   Arranging ideas in logical order.

simulation   An abstraction or simplification of a real-life situation.

special-needs student   See *exceptional child.*

student teaching   A field experience component of teacher preparation, often the culminating experience, where the teacher candidate practices teaching children while under the supervision of a credentialed teacher and a university supervisor.

summative assessment   Assessment of learning after instruction is completed.

teaching   See *instruction.*

teaching style   The way teachers teach; their distinctive mannerisms complemented by their choices of teaching behaviors and strategies.

teaching team   A team of two or more teachers who work together to provide instruction to the same group of students, either alternating the instruction or team teaching simultaneously.

team teaching   Two or more teachers working together to provide instruction to a group of students.

tenured teacher   After serving a designated number of years in the same school district (usually three) as a probationary teacher, upon rehire the teacher receives a tenure contract, which means that the teacher is automatically rehired each year thereafter unless the contract is revoked by either the district or the teacher and for specific and legal reasons.

terminal behavior   That which has been learned as a direct result of instruction.

thematic unit   A unit of instruction built on a central theme or concept.

theme school   See *magnet school.*

think time   See *wait time.*

tracking   The practice of the voluntary or involuntary placement of students in different programs or courses according to their ability and prior academic performance.

traditional teaching   Teacher-centered direct instruction, typically using teacher talk, discussions, textbooks, and worksheets.

transition   In a lesson, the planned procedures that move student thinking from one idea to the next or that move their actions from one activity to the next.

validity   In measurement, the degree to which an item or instrument measures that which it is intended to measure.

village   See *school-within-a-school.*

wait time   In the use of questioning, the period of silence between the time a question is asked and the inquirer (teacher) does something, such as repeats the question, rephrases the question, calls on a particular student, answers the question him- or herself, or asks another question.

whole-language learning   A point of view with a focus on seeking or creating meaning that encourages language production, risk-taking, independence in producing language, and the use of a wide variety of print materials in authentic reading and writing situations.

withitness   The teacher's timely ability to intervene and redirect a student's inappropriate behavior.

year-round school   A school that operates as is traditional, that is, with 180 school days; but the days are spread out over 12 months rather than the more traditional 10. Most common is a 9-weeks-on, 3-weeks-off format.

young adolescent   The 9- to 14-year-old experiencing the developmental stage of early adolescence.

Index of Children's Books, Authors, and Illustrators

Name Index

Subject Index